24-4078

THE ELIZABETHAN STAGE
VOL. II

Oxford University Press, Ely House, London W. 1

GLASGOW NEW YORK TORONTO MELBOURNE WELLINGTON
CAPE TOWN SALISBURY IBADAN NAIROBI LUSAKA ADDIS ABABA
BOMBAY CALCUTTA MADRAS KARACHI LAHORE DACCA
KUALA LUMPUR HONG KONG TOKYO

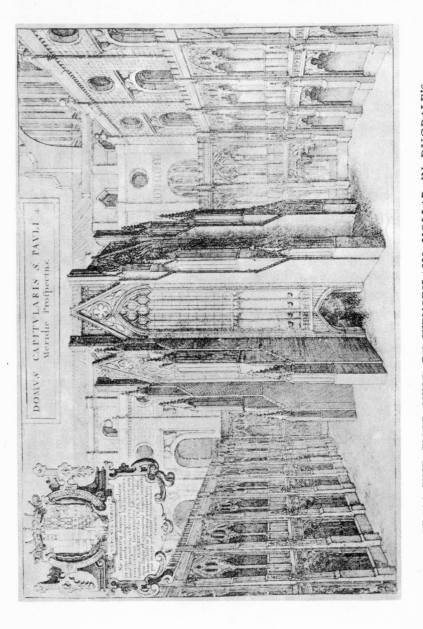

FROM THE ENGRAVING BY WENCESLAUS HOLLAR IN DUGDALE'S
St. Paul's 1658

THE ELIZABETHAN STAGE
BY E. K. CHAMBERS. VOL. II

OXFORD: AT THE CLARENDON PRESS

FIRST PUBLISHED 1923
SET IN GREAT BRITAIN
AT THE UNIVERSITY PRESS, OXFORD
AND REPRINTED LITHOGRAPHICALLY
FROM SHEETS OF THE FIRST EDITION
1945, WITH CORRECTIONS 1951, 1961, 1965, 1967

CONTENTS

VOLUME II

BOOK III. THE COMPANIES

LIST OF ILLUSTRATIONS

NOTE ON SYMBOLS

I HAVE found it convenient, especially in Appendix A, to use the symbol < following a date, to indicate an uncertain date not earlier than that named, and the symbol > followed by a date, to indicate an uncertain date not later than that named.   Thus 1903 <> 23 would indicate the composition date of any part of this book.   I have sometimes placed the date of a play in italics, where it was desirable to indicate the date of production rather than publication.

BOOK III

THE COMPANIES

'Has led the drum before the English tragedians.
All's Well that Ends Well.

XII

INTRODUCTION. THE BOY
COMPANIES

[*Bibliographical Note.*—The first systematic investigation into the history of the companies was that of F. G. Fleay, which, after tentative sketches in his *Shakespeare Manual* (1876) and *Life and Work of Shakespeare* (1886), took shape in his *Chronicle History of the Stage* (1890). Little is added by the compilations of A. Albrecht, *Das Englische Kindertheater* (1883), H. Maas, *Die Kindertruppen* (1901) and *Äussere Geschichte der Englischen Theatertruppen* (1907), and J. A. Nairn, *Boy-Actors under the Tudors and Stewarts* (*Trans. of Royal Soc. of Lit.* xxxii). W. W. Greg, *Henslowe's Diary* (1904–8), made a careful study of all the companies which had relations with Philip Henslowe, and modified or corrected many of Fleay's results. An account of the chief London companies is in A. H. Thorndike, *Shakespeare's Theater* (1916), and utilizes some new material collected in recent years. W. Creizenach, *Schauspiele der Englischen Komödianten* (1889), and E. Herz, *Englische Schauspieler und Englisches Schauspiel* (1903), have summarized the records of the travels of English actors in Germany. C. W. Wallace, besides his special work on the Chapel, has published the records of several theatrical lawsuits in *Advance Sheets from Shakespeare, the Globe, and Blackfriars* (1909), in *Nebraska University Studies*, ix (1909), 287 ; x (1910), 261 ; xiii (1913), 1, and in *The Swan Theatre and the Earl of Pembroke's Servants* (1911, *Englische Studien*, xliii. 340) ; the present writer has completed the information drawn from the *Chamber Accounts* in P. Cunningham's *Extracts from the Accounts of the Revels at Court* (1842) by articles in *M. L. R.* ii (1906), 1 ; iv (1909), 153 (cf. App. B) ; and a number of documents, new and old, including the texts of all the patents issued to companies, have been carefully edited in vol. i of the *Collections of the Malone Society* (1907–11). Finally, J. T. Murray, *English Dramatic Companies* (1910), has collected the published notices of performances in the provinces, added others from the municipal archives of Barnstaple, Bristol, Coventry, Dover, Exeter, Gloucester, Marlborough, Norwich, Plymouth, Shrewsbury, Southampton, Winchester and York, and on the basis of these constructed valuable accounts of all the London and provincial companies between 1558 and 1642. Most of the present chapter was written before Murray's book appeared, but it has been carefully revised with the aid of his new material. I have not thought it necessary to refer to my original provincial sources, where they are included in his convenient Appendix G, but in using his book it should be borne in mind that he has made a good many omissions in carrying data from this Appendix to the tables of provincial visits, which he gives for each company. For a few places I have had the advantage of sources not drawn upon by Murray, and these should be treated as the references for any facts as regards such places not discoverable in Murray's Appendix.

They are :—for Belvoir and other houses of the Earls of Rutland, *Rutland MSS.* (*Hist. MSS.*), iv. 260 ; for the house of Richard Bertie and his wife the Duchess of Suffolk at Grimsthorpe, *Ancaster MSS.* (*Hist. MSS.*), 459 ; for Wollaton, the house of Francis Willoughby, *Middleton MSS.* (*Hist. MSS.*), 446 ; for Maldon and Saffron Walden in Essex, A. Clark's extracts in *10 Notes and Queries*, vii. 181, 342, 422 ; viii. 43 ; xii. 41 ; for Newcastle-on-Tyne, G. B. Richardson, *Reprints of Rare Tracts*, vol. iii, and *10 N. Q.* xii. 222 ; for Reading, *Hist. MSS.* xi. 177 ; for Oxford, F. S. Boas in *Fortnightly Review* (Aug. 1913 ; Aug. 1918 ; May 1920) ; for Stratford, J. O. Halliwell, *Stratford-upon-Avon in the Time of the Shakespeares, illustrated by Extracts from the Council-Books* (1864) ; for Weymouth, H. J. Moule, *Weymouth and Melcombe Regis Documents* (1883), 136 ; for Dunwich, *Various Collections* (*Hist. MSS.*), vii. 82 ; for Aldeburgh, Suffolk, C. C. Stopes, *William Hunnis*, 314. References for a few other scattered items are in the foot-notes. The warning should be given that the dates assigned to some of the provincial performances are approximate, and may be in error within a year or so either way. For this there are more reasons than one. The zealous antiquaries who have made extracts from local records have not realized that precise dates might be of value, and have often named a year without indicating whether it represents the calendar year (Circumcision style) or the calendar year (Annunciation style) in which a performance fell, or the calendar year in which a regnal, mayoral, or accounting year, in which the performance fell, began or ended. When they are clearly dealing with accounting years, they do not always indicate whether these ended at Michaelmas or at some other date. They sometimes give only the year of a performance, when they might have given, precisely or approximately, the month and day of the month as well. But it is fair to add that the accounts of City Chamberlains and similar officers, from which the notices of plays are generally derived, are not always so kept as to render precise dating feasible. Some accountants specify the days, others the weeks to which their entries relate ; others put their entries in chronological order and date some of them, so that it is possible to fix the dates of the rest within limits ; others again render accounts analysed under heads, grouping all payments to players perhaps under a head of ' Gifts and Rewards ', and in such cases you cannot be sure that the companies are even entered in the order of their visits, and if months and days are not specified, cannot learn more than the year to which a visit belongs. Where, for whatever reason, I can only assign a performance to its accounting year, I generally give it under the calendar year in which the account ends. This, in the case of a London company and of a Michaelmas year (much the commonest year for municipal accounts), is pretty safe, as the touring season was roughly July to September. Some accounting years (Coventry, Marlborough, Stratford-on-Avon) end later still, but if, as at Bath, the year ends about Midsummer, it is often quite a toss-up to which of two years an entry belongs. In the case of Leicester performances before 1603, I have combined the indications of Michaelmas years in M. Bateson, *Leicester Records*, vol. iii, with those of calendar years in W. Kelly, *Notices Illustrative of the Drama* (1865), 185, and distinguished between performances before and after Michaelmas. I hope Kelly has not misled me, and that he found evidence in the entries for his dating. After 1603 he is the only source. I do not think that the amount of error which has crept into the following chapter from the various causes described is likely to be at all considerable. I have been as careful as possible and most of Murray's own extracting is excellently done. I should, however, add that the Ipswich dates, as given both here and by Murray, ii. 287,

from *Hist. MSS.* ix. 1, 248, are unreliable, because some of the rolls from
which they are taken contain membranes properly belonging to those for
other years ; cf. my notes on Leicester's (pp. 89, 91), Queen's (p 106),
Warwick's (p. 99), Derby's (p. 120), King's (p. 209).]

A. INTRODUCTION

THE present chapter contains detailed chronicles—too
often, I fear, lapsing into arid annals of performances at Court
or in the provinces—of all the companies traceable in London
during any year between 1558 and 1616. The household and
other establishments to which the companies were attached
are taken as the basis of classification. This principle is open
to criticism. Certainly it has not always the advantage of
presenting economic units. It is improbable that there was
any continuity as regards membership between the bodies of
actors successively appearing, often after long intervals,
under the names of Sussex or Hunsdon or Derby. On the
other hand, particular associations of actors can sometimes be
discerned as holding together under a change of patrons.
Thus between 1571 and 1583 Laurence and John Dutton
seem to have led a single company, which earned the nick-
name of the Chameleons, first in the service of Sir Robert
Lane and then, turn by turn, in that of the Earls of Lincoln,
Warwick, and Oxford. The real successors, again, of the
Derby's men of 1593 are less the Derby's men of 1595–1618
than the Hunsdon's men of 1594–1603, who in course of time
became the King's men without any breach of their unity
as a trading association. Nevertheless, an arrangement under
patrons is a practicable one, since companies nearly always
appear under the names of their patrons in official documents,
while an arrangement under trading associations is not.
Actors are a restless folk, and the history of the Admiral's
men, or the Queen's Revels, or the Lady Elizabeth's men,
will show how constantly their business organizations were
disturbed by the coming and going of individuals, and by the
breaking and reconstruction of the agreements on which
they were based. It is but rarely that we have any clue to
these intricacies ; and I have therefore followed the house-
holds as the best available guides, indicating breaches of
continuity and affiliations, where these appear to exist, and
adopting as far as possible an order which, without pretence
of being scientific, will bring each household under consideration roughly at the point at which its servants become of the
greatest significance to the general history of the stage. The
method may perhaps be described as that of a λαμπαδηφορία.

A study of the succession of the companies gives rise to a few general considerations. During the earlier years of Elizabeth's reign the drama is under the domination of the boy companies. This may be in part due to the long-standing humanistic tradition of the Renaissance, although the lead is in fact taken not so much by schoolboys in the stricter sense, as by the trained musical establishments of the royal chapels and still more that of the St. Paul's choir under Sebastian Westcott. More important points perhaps are, that the Gentlemen of the Chapel, who had been prominent under Henry VIII, had ceased to perform, that the royal Interluders had been allowed to decay, and that the other professional companies had not yet found a permanent economic basis in London, while their literary accomplishment was still upon a popular rather than a courtly level. Whatever the cause or causes, the fact is undeniable. Out of seventy-eight rewards for Court performances between 1558 and 1576, twenty-one went to the Paul's boys, fifteen to the royal chapels, and ten to schoolboys, making a total of forty-six, as against only thirty-two paid to adult companies. And if the first half of this period only be taken, the disproportion is still greater, for by 1567 the Paul's boys had received eleven rewards, other boys two, and the adult companies six. A complete reversal of this position coincides rather markedly with the building of the first permanent theatres in 1576. Between 1576 and 1583 the adult companies had thirty-nine rewards and the boys only seventeen. There is also a rapid growth in the number of companies. Before 1576 the Earl of Leicester's men and the Duttons were alone conspicuous. After 1576 the entertainment of a London company seems to become a regular practice with those great officers the Lord Chamberlain and the Lord Admiral, as well as with special favourites of the Queen, such as the Earl of Leicester himself or the Earl of Oxford. Stockwood in 1578 speaks of 'eighte ordinarie places' in the City as occupied by the players. A Privy Council order of the same year limits the right to perform to six companies selected to take part in the Court festivities at Christmas, namely Leicester's men, Warwick's, Sussex's, Essex's, and the Children of the Chapel and St. Paul's. Gabriel Harvey, writing to Edmund Spenser of the publication of his virelays in the following summer, says :

' Ye have preiudished my good name for ever in thrusting me thus on the stage to make tryall of my extemporall faculty, and to play Wylsons or Tarletons parte. I suppose thou wilt go nighe hande shortelye to sende my lorde of Lycesters or my lorde of Warwickes,

Vawsis, or my lord Ritches players, or sum other freshe starteupp comedanties unto me for sum newe devised interlude, or sum malt-conceivid comedye fitt for the Theater, or sum other paintid stage whereat thou and thy lively copesmates in London maye lawghe ther mouthes and bellyes full for pence or twoepence apeece.' [1]

Doubtless many of this mushroom brood of ' freshe starteupp comedanties ' never succeeded in making good their permanent footing in the metropolis. Lord Vaux's men, whom Harvey mentions, were never fortunate enough to be summoned to Court ; and the same may be said of Lord Arundel's men, Lord Berkeley's, and Lord Abergavenny's. Such men, after their cast for fortune, had to drift away into the provinces, and pad the hoof on the hard roads once more.

The next septennial period, 1583–90, witnessed the extinction, for a decade or so, of the boy companies, in spite of the new impulse given to the latter by the activity as a play-wright of John Lyly. Of forty-five Court payments made during these years, thirty apparently went to men and only fifteen to boys. This ultimate success of the professional organizations may largely have been due to their employment of such university wits as Marlowe, Peele, Greene, Lodge, and Nashe in the writing of plays, with which Lyly could be challenged on his own ground before the Court, while a sufficient supply of chronicle histories and other popular stuff could still be kept on the boards to tickle the ears of the groundlings. The undisputed pre-eminence lay during this period with the Queen's men, who made within it no less than twenty-one appearances at Court. This company enjoyed the prestige of the royal livery, transferred to it from the now defunct Interluders, which had a ready effect in the unloosing of municipal pockets. And at its foundation in 1583 it incorporated, in addition to Tarlton, whose origin is unknown, the leading members of the pre-existing companies : Wilson and Laneham from Leicester's, Adams from Sussex's, and John Dutton from Oxford's. The former fellows of these lucky ones were naturally hardly able to maintain their standing. In January 1587 Leicester's, Oxford's, and the Admiral's were still setting up their bills side by side with those of the Queen's.[2] But the first two are not heard of at Court again, and even the Admiral's were hardly able to make a show except by coalition with other companies. Thus we find the Admiral's combining with Hunsdon's in 1585, and with Strange's perhaps from 1589 onwards, and it became the destiny of this last alliance,

---

[1] E. J. L. Scott, *Letter Book of Gabriel Harvey* (Camden Soc.), 67.
[2] Cf. App. D, No. lxxviii.

under the leadership of Edward Alleyn, to dispossess the Queen's men, after the death of Tarlton in 1588, from their pride of place. The fall of the Queen's men was sudden. In 1590–1 they gave four Court plays to two by their rivals; in 1591–2 they gave one, and their rivals six. In their turn they appear to have been reduced to forming a coalition with Lord Sussex's men.

The plague-years of 1592–4 brought disaster, chaos, and change into the theatrical world. Only the briefest London seasons were possible. The necessities of travelling led to further combinations and recombinations of groups, one of which may have given rise to the ephemeral existence of Lord Pembroke's men. And, by the time the public health was restored, the Queen's had reconciled themselves to a provincial existence, and continued until 1603 to make their harvest of the royal name, as their predecessors in title had done, without returning to London at all. The combination of which Alleyn had been the centre broke up, and its component elements reconstituted themselves as the two great companies of the Chamberlain's and the Admiral's men. Between these there was a vigorous rivalry, which sometimes showed itself in awsuits, sometimes in the more legitimate form of competing plays on similar themes. Thus a popular sentiment offended by the Chamberlain's men in *I Henry IV* was at once appealed to by the Admiral's with *Sir John Oldcastle*. And when the Admiral's scored a success by their representation of forest life in *Robin Hood*, the Chamberlain's were quickly ready to counter with *As You Like It*. I think the Chamberlain's secured the better position of the two. They had their Burbadge to pit against the reputation of Alleyn ; they had their honey-tongued Shakespeare ; and they had a business organization which gave them a greater stability of membership than any company in the hands of Henslowe was likely to secure. If one may once more use the statistics of Court performances as a criterion, they are found to have appeared thirty-two times and their rivals only twenty times from 1594 to 1603. Between them the Chamberlain's and the Admiral's enjoyed for some years a practical monopoly of the London stage, which received an official recognition by the action of the Privy Council in 1597. But this state of things did not long continue. Ambitious companies, such as Pembroke's, disregarded the directions of the Council. Derby's men, Worcester's, Hertford's, one by one obtained at least a temporary footing at Court, and in 1602 the influence of the Earl of Oxford was strong enough to bring about the admission to a permanent home in London

of a third company made up of his own and Worcester's
servants. Even more dangerous, perhaps, to the monopoly
was the revival of the boy companies, Paul's in 1599 and the
Chapel in 1600. The imps not only took by their novelty
in the eyes of a younger generation of playgoers. They began
a warfare of satire, in which they 'berattled the common
stages' with a vigour and dexterity that betray the malice
of the poets against the players which had been a motive
in their rehabilitation.[1]

No material change took place at the coming of James.
The three adult companies, the Chamberlain's, the Admiral's,
Worcester's, passed respectively under the patronage of
James, Prince Henry, and Queen Anne.[2] On the death of
Prince Henry in 1612 his place was taken by the Elector
Palatine. The Children of the Chapel also received the
patronage of Queen Anne, as Children of the Queen's Revels.
The competition for popular favour continued severe. Dekker
refers to it in 1608 and the preacher Crashaw in 1610.[3]
It is to be noticed, however, that Dekker speaks only of
'a deadly war' between 'three houses', presumably regarding
the boy companies as negligible. And in fact these companies
were on the wane. By 1609 the Queen's Revels, though still in
existence, had suffered from the wearing off of novelty, from
the tendency of boys to grow older, from the plague-seasons
of 1603-4 and 1608-9, which they were less well equipped
than the better financed adults to withstand, from the
indiscretions and quarrels of their managers, and from the
loss of the Blackfriars, of which the King's men had secured
possession.[4] The Paul's boys had been bought off by the payment of a 'dead rent' or blackmail to the Master. A third
company, the King's Revels, had been started, but had failed
to establish itself.[5] The three houses were not, indeed, left

[1] Cf. ch. xi.
[2] G. Dugdale, *Time Triumphant* (1604), sig. B, 'Nay, see the beauty
of our all kinde soveraigne! not onely to the indifferent of worth, and the
worthy of honor, did he freely deale about thiese causes, but to the meane
gave grace, as taking to him the late Lord Chamberlaines servants now
the Kings acters; the Queene taking to her the Earle of Worsters servants,
that are now her acters; and the Prince, their sonne, Henry, Prince of
Wales full of hope, tooke to him the Earle of Nottingham his servants,
who are now his acters.'
[3] Cf. ch. xvi, introd., and App. C, No. lviii.
[4] Flecknoe (App. I) perhaps exaggerates the share of moral sentiment
in bringing to an end the formal connexion of the choirs with plays
(cf. p. 52).
[5] De la Boderie, in 1608 (cf. vol. i, p. 327), speaks of five companies
in London. These would be the King's, Queen's, Prince's, Revels, and
King's Revels.

with an undisputed field. Advantage was taken of the
predilection of the younger members of the royal family for
the drama, and patents were obtained, in 1610 for a Duke
of York's company, and in 1611 for a Lady Elizabeth's
company. These also had but a frail life. In 1613 the Lady
Elizabeth's, and the Queen's Revels coalesced under the
dangerous wardenship of Henslowe. In 1615 the Duke of
York's, now Prince Charles's, men joined the combination.
And finally in 1616 the Prince's men were left alone to make
up the tale of four London companies, and the Lady Elizabeth's and the Queen's Revels disappeared into the provinces. The list of men summoned before the Privy Council
in March 1615 to account for playing in Lent contains the
names of the leaders of the four companies, the King's,
the Queen's, the Palsgrave's, and the Prince's. The King's
played at the Globe and Blackfriars, the Queen's at the Red
Bull, whence they moved in 1617 to the Cockpit, the Palsgrave's at the Fortune, and the Prince's at the Hope. The
supremacy of the King's men during 1603–16 was undisputed.
Of two hundred and ninety-nine plays rewarded at Court for
that period, they gave one hundred and seventy-seven,
the Prince's men forty-seven, the Queen's men twenty-eight,
the Duke of York's men twenty, the Lady Elizabeth's men
nine, the Queen's Revels boys fifteen, and the Paul's boys
three. Their plays, moreover, were those usually selected for
performance before James himself. It is possible, however,
that the Red Bull and the Fortune were better able to hold
their own against the Globe when it came to attracting
a popular audience.

B. THE BOY COMPANIES

    i. Children of Paul's.
   ii. Children of the Chapel and Queen's Revels.
  iii. Children of Windsor.
   iv. Children of the King's Revels.
    v. Children of Bristol.
   vi. Westminster School.
  vii. Eton College.
 viii. Merchant Taylors School.
   ix. Earl of Leicester's Boys.
    x. Earl of Oxford's Boys.
   xi. Mr. Stanley's Boys.

i. THE CHILDREN OF PAUL'S

High Masters of Grammar School :—William Lily (1509–22) ; John
Ritwise (1522–32) ; Richard Jones (1532–49) ; Thomas Freeman

(1549–59) ; John Cook (1559–73) ; William Malim (1573–81) ; John Harrison (1581–96) ; Richard Mulcaster (1596–1608).

Masters of Choir School :—? Thomas Hikeman (*c.* 1521) ; John Redford (*c.* 1540) ; ? Thomas Mulliner (?) ; Sebastian Westcott (> 1557–1582) ; Thomas Giles (1584–1590 <) ; Edward Pearce (> 1600–1606 <).

[*Bibliographical Note.*—The documents bearing upon the early history of the two cathedral schools, often confused, are printed and discussed by A. F. Leach in *St. Paul's School before Colet* (*Archaeologia*, lxii. 1. 191) and in *Journal of Education* (1909), 503. M. F. J. McDonnell, *A History of St. Paul's School* (1909), carries on the narrative of the grammar school. The official chroniclers of the cathedral, perhaps owing to the loss of archives in the Great Fire, have given no connected account of the choir school ; with the material available on the dramatic side they appear to be unfamiliar. Valuable contributions are W. H. G. Flood, *Master Sebastian*, in *Musical Antiquary*, iii. 149 ; iv. 187 ; and H. N. Hillebrand, *Sebastian Westcote, Dramatist and Master of the Children of Paul's* (1915, *J. G. P.* xiv. 568). Little is added to the papers on *Plays Acted by the Children of Paul's* and *Music in St. Paul's Cathedral* in W. S. Simpson, *Gleanings from Old St. Paul's* (1889), 101, 155, by J. S. Bumpus, *The Organists and Composers of St. Paul's Cathedral* (1891), and W. M. Sinclair, *Memorials of St. Paul's Cathedral* (1909).]

Mr. Leach has succeeded in tracing the grammar school, as part of the establishment of St. Paul's Cathedral, to the beginning of the twelfth century. It was then located in the south-east corner of the churchyard, near the bell-tower, and here it remained to 1512, when it was rebuilt, endowed, and reorganized on humanist lines by Dean Colet, and thereafter to 1876, when it was transferred to Horsham in Sussex. Originally the master was one of the canons ; but by the beginning of the thirteenth century this officer had taken on the name of chancellor, and the general supervision of the actual schoolmaster, a vicar choral, was only .one of his functions. Distinct from the grammar school was the choir school, for which the responsible dignitary was not the chancellor, but the precentor, in whose hands the appoint-ment of a master of the song school rested.[1] There was, however, a third branch of the cathedral organization also concerned with the training of boys. The almonry or hospital, maintained by the chapter for the relief of the poor, seems to have been established at the end of the twelfth century,

Archaeologia, lxii. 1. 216, from statutes collected in the decanate of Ralph of Baldock (1294–1304), ' Cantoris officium est . . . pueros introducen-dos in chorum et ad cantum intitulatos examinare . . . Magistrum Scolae Cantus in ecclesia Sancti Gregorii, salva Decano et Capitulo ipsius colla-cione, preficere ' ; Dugdale, *St. Paul's* (1818), 347, from fifteenth- or early sixteenth-century manuscript of statutes, ' Magistrum Scholae Cantus constituit Cantor. Ad eum pertinet eos qui canere nequeunt instruere, pueros diligenter docere, eis non solum magistrum Cantus, sed etiam bonorum morum esse.'

and statutes of about the same date make it the duty of
a canon residentiary to assist in the maintenance of its
pueri elemosinarii, and prescribe the special services to be
rendered them at their great annual ceremony of the Boy
Bishop on Innocents' Day.[1]   In the thirteenth century the
supervision of these boys was in the hands of another subordinate official, appointed by the chapter and known as
the almoner. The number of the boys was then eight; it
was afterwards increased, apparently in 1358, to ten.[2]   The
almoner is required to provide for their literary and moral
education, and their liturgical duties are defined as consisting
of standing in pairs at the corners of the choir and carrying
candles.[3]   A later version of the statutes provides for their
musical education, and it is clear that these *pueri elemosinarii*
were in fact identical with or formed the nucleus of the boys
of the song school.[4]   During the sixteenth century the posts
of almoner and master of the song school, although technically
distinct, were in practice held together, and the holder was
ordinarily a member of the supplementary cathedral establishment known as the College of Minor Canons.[5]   To this college
had been appropriated the parish church of St. Gregory, on
the south side of St. Paul's, just west of the Chapter or
Convocation House, and here the song school was already

Archaeologia, lxii. 1. 215, from statutes collected in decanate of Ralph
de Diceto (1181–99), ' Cotidie pascat . . . duos pueros elemosinarios . . . et
secum ad Ecclesiam media nocte panem et cervisiam pro iunioribus chorum
frequentantibus defer[r]i faciat, et quolibet quarterio semel vel bis post matu-
tinas iunioribus gentaculum unum in domo sua faciat '. A thirteenth-
century statute required the *pueri de elemosinaria* to sit humbly upon the
ground when feeding in the house of a canon. Cf. *Mediaeval Stage*, i. 355,
for Diceto's statute about the Boy Bishop, with its mention of the return
of the boys ' ad Elemosinariam ', and the reforming statute of 1263.

[2] *Archaeologia*, lxii. 1. 220.

[3] Ibid. 217, 220 (*c.* 1263 ; *c.* 1310) ' Elemosinarius . . . habeat insuper
continuo secum octo pueros ad Ecclesiae ministerium ydoneos, quos
per seipsum vel alium magistrum in spectantibus ad ministerium ecclesiae
et litteratura ac bonis moribus diligenter faciat informari . . . Quociens
vero dicti pueri ad scolas vel spaciatum ire debent . . . '; Dugdale,
349 [Elemosinarius] ' octo pueros bonae indolis et honestae parentelae
habeat ; quos alat et educat in morum disciplina ; videat etiam in-
struantur in cantu et literatura, ut in omnibus apti ad ministerium Dei in
Choro esse possent '.

[4] There was a bequest to the almoner to maintain boys, apparently at
the University, after they had changed their voices, as early as 1315
(*Archaeologia*, lxii. 1. 219–22).

[5] Hennessy, 61 ; W. S. Simpson, *Charter and Statutes of the College of
Minor Canons in St. Paul's Cathedral* (*Archaeologia*, xliii. 165 ; cf. *Trans.
of London and Midd. Arch. Soc.* (1st series), iv. 231). The statutes of
c. 1521 note a dispensation of that year for Thomas Hikeman ' peticanon
and amner ' and for ' all and euery peticanon which shalbe Amneur hear-
after ' to bring a stranger to meals.

housed by the twelfth century.[1] The college had also a common hall on the north of the cathedral, near the Pardon churchyard; and hard by was the almonry in Paternoster Row.[2] The statutes left the almoner the option of either giving the boys their literary education himself, or sending them elsewhere. It naturally proved convenient to send them to the grammar school, and the almoners claimed that they had a right to admission without fees.[3] On the other side we find the grammar school boys directed by Colet to attend the Boy Bishop ceremony and make their offerings.[4] Evidently there was much give and take between song school and grammar school.

As early as 1378 the scholars of Paul's are said to have prepared a play of the History of the Old Testament for public representation at Christmas.[5] Whether they took a share in the other miracles recorded in mediaeval London, it is impossible to say. A century and a half later the boys of the grammar school, during the mastership of John Ritwise, are found contributing interludes, in the humanist fashion, to the entertainment of the Court. On 10 November 1527 they gave an anti-Lutheran play in Latin and French before the King and the ambassadors of Francis I, and in the following year the *Phormio* before Wolsey, who also saw them, if Anthony Wood can be trusted, in a *Dido* written by Ritwise

[1] Stowe, *Survey*, ii. 19; cf. the Hollar engraving in Baker, 95.

[2] Stowe, i. 327; *Archaeologia*, xliii. 171. By c. 14 of the statutes the college gates were shut at meals.

[3] Leach, *Journal of Education* (1909), 506, cites the *Registrum Elemosinariae* (ed. M. Hacket from *Harl. MS.* 1080), 'If the almoner does not keep a clerk to teach the choristers grammar, the schoolmaster of St. Paul's claims 5s. a year for teaching them, though he ought to demand nothing for them, because he keeps the school for them, as the Treasurer of St. Paul's once alleged before the Dean and Chapter is to be found in ancient deeds'. Mr. Leach adds, ' It is to be feared the Treasurer invented or misrepresented the ancient deed'. William de Tolleshunt, almoner, appears from his will of 1329 in the same register to have taught his boys himself (*Archaeologia*, lxii. 1. 220), ' Item lego pueris ecclesiae quos ego educavi senioribus in Elemosinaria existentibus cuilibet xij^d et iunioribus cuilibet vj^d '. He also left his grammar books ' et omnes quaternos sermonum de Festo Sanctorum Innocencium, quos tempore meo solebant Episcopi Puerorum pronunciare, ad remanendum in Elemosinaria praedicta imperpetuum, ad usum fructum puerorum in eadem degencium '. His logic and physic books are to be lent out ' pueris aptis ad scolatizandum, cum ab elemosinaria recesserint '.

[4] *Mediaeval Stage*, i. 356. The sermon written by Erasmus is headed *Concio . . . pronunciata . . . in nova schola Iohannis Coleti*, but Erasmus may not have known the exact procedure at St. Paul's. The earlier sermon printed by Wynkyn de Worde has ' whyche often times I radde whan I was Querester, in the Marteloge of Poulis '.

[5] *Mediaeval Stage*, ii. 380.

himself.[1] There is no evidence that Ritwise's successors followed his example by bringing their pupils to Court; and the next performances by Paul's boys, which can be definitely traced, began a quarter of a century later, and were under the control of Sebastian Westcott, master of the, song school, and were therefore presumably given by boys of that school. Westcott in 1545 was a Yeoman of the Chamber at Court.[2] He was 'scolemaister of Powles' by New Year's Day 1557, when he presented a manuscript book of ditties to Queen Mary.[3] Five years earlier, he had brought children to Hatfield, to give a play before the Princess Elizabeth; and the chances are that these were the Paul's boys.[4] With him came one Heywood, who may fairly be identified with John Heywood the dramatist; and this enables us, more conjecturally, to reduce a little further the gap in the dramatic history of the Paul's choir, for some years before, in March 1538, Heywood had already received a reward for playing an interlude with 'his children' before the Lady Mary.[5] There is nothing beyond this phrase to suggest that Heywood had a company of his own, and it is not probable that he was ever himself master of the choir school.[6] But he may very

[1] *Mediaeval Stage*, ii. 196, 215, 219. Wallace, i. 88, points out that the performers of the *Menaechmi* before Wolsey in 1527 were not the Paul's boys, but the Cardinal's gentlemen.

[2] *Chamber Accounts* (1545).

[3] Nichols, *Eliz.* i. xxxv, 'By Sebastian, scolemaister of Powles, a boke of ditties, written'.

[4] *Household Accounts of Princess Elizabeth, 1551-2 (Camden Misc.* ii), 37, 'Paid in rewarde to the Kinges Maiesties drommer and phipher, the xiij[th] of Februarye, xx[s]; M[r]. Heywoodde, xxx[s]; and to Sebastian, towardes the charge of the children with the carriage of the plaiers garmentes iiij[li], xix[s]. In thole as by warraunte appereth, vij[li], ix[s]'.

[5] F. Madden, *Expenses of Lady Mary*, 62 (March 1538), 'Item geuen to Heywood playeng an enterlude with his children bifore my lades grace, xl[s]'.

[6] Wallace, i. 77, goes against the evidence when he asserts that Heywood wrote for the Chapel. Why he asserts that Heywood 'had grown up in the Chapel under Cornish', to whom, by the way, he wantonly transfers the authorship of *The Four P. P., The Pardoner and the Frere*, and *Johan Johan*, I do not know. There is nothing to show that Heywood was a Chapel boy, and the absence of his name from the Chapel list of 1509 (cf. p. 27), when he would have been about twelve, may be taken as disposing of the notion. He is first discoverable at Court in December 1514, for which month he received wages at the rate of viij[d] a day in some undefined capacity (*Chamber Account* in *Addl. MS.* 21481, f. 178), which was shared by one John Mason, who was a Yeoman of the Crown by March 1516 (Brewer, ii. 475). By 1520 Heywood himself was a Yeoman of the Crown (Brewer, iii. 1. 499), and during 1519-21 the *Chamber Accounts* show him as also a 'singer' at £5 a quarter. Later he became player of the virginals, and has 50s. a quarter as such in the *Accounts* for 1529-31, 1538-41, and 1547-9. He was Sewer of the Chamber at the funeral of Edward in 1553. It occurs to me as just possible that Heywood's 'children' may have been neither the Chapel nor the Paul's

well have supplied them with plays, both in Westcott's time and also in that of his predecessor John Redford. Several of Heywood's verses are preserved in a manuscript, which also contains Redford's *Wyt and Science* and fragments of other interludes, not improbably intended for performance by the boys under his charge.[1] A play ' of childerne sett owte by Mr. Haywood ' at Court during the spring of 1553 may also belong to the Paul's boys.[2] Certain performances ascribed to them at Hatfield, during the Princess Elizabeth's residence there in her sister's reign, have of late fallen under suspicion of being apocryphal.[3]

From the beginning of Elizabeth's reign Westcott's theatrical enterprise stands out clearly enough. On 7 August 1559 the Queen was entertained by the Earl of Arundel at Nonsuch with ' a play of the chylderyn of Powlles and ther Master Se[bastian], Master Phelypes, and Master Haywod '.[4] If ' Master Phelypes ' was the John Philip or Phillips who wrote *Patient Grissell* (*c.* 1566), this play may also belong

boys, but the boys taken up by Philip Van Wilder for the musical establishment of the Household; cf. p. 31. But I think it is more likely that Heywood wrote for the Paul's boys throughout, as he almost certainly did in 1559. There is another hint of his connexion with them in the fact that at the coronation of Mary in 1553 he sat under a vine against the grammar school and made speeches (Holinshed (1808), iv. 6). A. W. Reed (1917, 3 *Library*, viii. 247) adds facts, and thinks the Yeoman was distinct.

[1] *Addl. MS.* 15233; cf. *Mediaeval Stage*, ii. 454. Thomas Tusser, in the *Autobiography* printed with the 1573 edition of his *Points of Good Husbandry*, is the authority for placing Redford at Paul's:

> But mark the chance, myself to 'vance,
> By friendship's lot, to Paul's I got,
> So found I grace a certain space
> Still to remain
> With Redford there, the like nowhere
> For cunning such and virtue much
> By whom some part of musicke art
> So did I gain.

From Paul's Tusser passed to Eton, before he matriculated at Cambridge in 1543. In other manuscripts compositions by Redford and Thomas Mulliner are associated, and one of these, *Addl. MS.* 30513, is inscribed ' Sum liber Thomae Mullineri, Johanne Heywoode teste '. Stafford Smith, on what authority is unknown, stated (cf. *D. N. B.*) that Mulliner was Master of St. Paul's School. If so, he may have come between Redford and Westcott. On 3 March 1564 he was admitted as organist in Corpus Christi College, Oxford (Fowler, *Hist. of C.C.C.* 426).

[2] Feuillerat, *E. and M.* 145; Wallace, i. 84. The mention of ' xij cottes for the boyes in Heywoodes play ' does not justify the assumption that the players were the Chapel. The ten established boys of the St. Paul's choir could be supplemented by probationers or the grammar school.

[3] *Mediaeval Stage*, ii. 196.

[4] Machyn, 206. 'Mr Philip' was organist of Paul's in 1557 (Nichols, *Illustrations*, iii). Fleay, 57, guesses that the play was *Nice Wanton*, which is not likely, if Heywood had a hand in it.

to the Paul's repertory. Heywood could not adapt himself again to a Protestant England, and soon left the country. Sebastian Westcott was more fortunate. In 1560 he was appointed as Head of the College of Minor Canons or Subdean.[1] Shortly afterwards, being unable to accept the religious settlement, he was sentenced to deprivation of his offices, which included that of organist, but escaped through the personal influence of Elizabeth, in spite of some searchings of the heart of Bishop Grindal as to his suitability to be an instructor of youth.[2] In fact he succeeded in remaining songmaster of Paul's for the next twenty-three years, and during that period brought his boys to Court no less than twenty-seven times, furnishing a far larger share of the royal Christmas entertainment, especially during the first decade of the reign, than any other single company. The chronicle of his plays must now be given. There was one at each of the Christmases of 1560–1 and 1561–2, one between 6 January and 9 March 1562, and one at the Christmas of 1562–3.[3] During the next winter the plague stopped London plays. At the Christmas of 1564–5 there were two by the Paul's boys, of which the second fell on 2 January, and at that of 1565–6 three, two at Court and one at the Lady Cecilia's lodging in the Savoy. There were two again at each of the Christmases of 1566–7 and 1567–8, and one on 1 January 1569. During the winter of 1569–70 the company was, exceptionally, absent from Court. They reappeared on 28 December 1570, and again at Shrovetide (25–7 February) 1571. On 28 December 1571 they gave the ‘ tragedy ’ of *Iphigenia*, which Professor Wallace identifies with the comedy called *The Bugbears*, but which might, for the matter of that, be Lady Lumley's translation from the Greek of Euripides. At the Christmas of 1572–3 they played before 7 January.

[1] Hennessy, 61.

[2] Flood cites a Vatican record of 1561 from *Catholic Record Soc.* i. 21, ‘ Sebastianus, qui organa pulsabat apud D. Paulum Londini, cum vellet eiici, tamen tum ita charus Elizabethae fuit, ut nihil schismatice agens locum suum in ea ecclesia retineat ’ ; also Grindal's letter of 1563 to Dudley in Strype, *Grindal* (ed. 1821), 113. Hillebrand adds from *Libri Vicarii Generalis (Huick 1561–74)*, iii, f. 77, that in July 1563 Westcott failed to appear before the Consistory Court and was excommunicated as ‘ contumacem ’, and from St. Paul's records (*A.* Box 77, 2059) that on 8 Nov. 1564 he gave a bond to conform or resign by the following Easter. Gee, 230, gives a list of deprived clergy from N. Sanders, *De Visibili Monarchia* (1571), 688, which includes among *Magistri Musices* ‘ Sebastianus in Cathedrali ecclesia Londinensi ’.

[3] Fleay, 15, 60, has some inaccuracies in these dates, and conjectures that among the early Paul's plays were a revival of Udall's *Ralph Roister-Doister* and Ulpian Fulwell's *Like Will to Like,* and that these contained satire of Richard Edwards and the Chapel.

On 27 December 1573 they gave *Alcmaeon*. They played on 2 February 1575, and a misfortune which befell them in the same year is recorded in a letter of 3 December from the Privy Council, which sets out that ' one of Sebastianes boyes, being one of his principall plaiers, is lately stolen and conveyed from him ', and instructs no less personages than the Master of the Rolls and Dr. Wilson, one of the Masters of Requests, to examine the persons whom he suspected and proceed according to law with them.[1] Five days later the Court of Aldermen drew up a protest against Westcott's continued Romish tendencies.[2] The next Court performance by the boys was on 6 January 1576. On 1 January 1577 they gave *Error*, and on 19 February *Titus and Gisippus*. They played on 29 December 1577, and one wonders whether it was anything amiss with that performance which led to an entry in the Acts of the Privy Council for the same day that ' Sebastian was committid to the Marshalsea '.[3] Whether this was so or not, the Paul's boys were included in the list of companies authorized to practise publicly in the City for the following Christmas. On 1 January 1579 they gave *The Marriage of Mind and Measure*, on 3 January 1580 *Scipio Africanus*, and on 6 January 1581 *Pompey*. A play on 26 December 1581 is anonymous, but may possibly be the *Cupid and Psyche* mentioned as ' plaid at Pauies ' in Gosson's *Playes Confuted* of 1582.[4]

In the course of 1582 Sebastian Westcott died, and this event led to an important development in the dramatic activities of the boys.[5] Hitherto their performances, when not

[1] Dasent, ix. 56.

[2] Hillebrand from *Repertory*, xix, f. 18, ' For asmoche as this Court ys enformed that one Sebastian that wyll not communicate with the Church of England kepe the playes and resorte of the people to great gaine and peryll of the coruptinge of the Chyldren wyth papistrie And therefore master Norton ys appoynted to goe to the Deane of Powles and to gyve him notyce of that dysorder, and to praye him to gyve suche remeadye therein, within his iurysdyccion, as he shall see meete, for Christian Relygion and good order '.

[3] Dasent, x. 127. *Cath. Record Soc.* i. 70 gives the date of Westcott's committal ' for papistry ' from *S. P. D. Eliz.* cxl. 40, as 21 Dec. 1577, and that of release as 19 March 1578. According to *S. P. D. Eliz.* cxviii. 73, Westcott was Master of the Children in 1577 and valued at £100 in goods.

[4] Gosson, *P. C.* 188.

[5] Flood (*Mus. Ant.* iv. 187) gives an abstract of his will, dated on 3 April and proved on 14 April 1582. He describes himself as almoner of St. Paul's, dwelling in the almonry and born at Chimley in Devonshire ; appoints Henry Evans overseer and Justinian Kyd executor, and leaves legacies to relatives (apparently he had no children or wife), to members of the Redford family, to ' Gyles Clothier ', to the ten choristers, to ' sometimes children of the said almenerey ', by name Bromeham, Richard Huse,

at Court, had been in their own quarters ' at Paules ', although the notice of 1578, as well as Gosson's reference, suggests that the public were not altogether excluded from their rehearsals. Probably they used their singing school, which may have been still, as in the twelfth century, the church of St. Gregory itself.[1] This privacy, even if something of a convention, had perhaps enabled them to utilize the services of the grammar school when they had occasion to make a display of erudition.[2] After Westcott's death, however, they appear to have followed the example of the Chapel, who had already

Robert Knight, Nicholas Carleton, Baylye, Nasion, and Gregory Bowringe, to ' Shepard that keepeth the door at playes ', and to Pole ' the keper of the gate '. Wallace, i. 171, cites the will from *P. C. C.* 14 and 31, Tirwhite, giving the date of confirmation as 3 July 1582. One name may be added to Westcott's list of boys from a Court Minute of Christ's Hospital on 5 March 1580 (*Musical Times*, 1 Jan. 1907), ' Mr. Sebastian, of Paulls, is appointed to have Hallawaie the younger out of this House to be one of the singing children of the Cathedral Church of Paulls in this Citie '.

[1] Gosson (1582) speaks of the plays as ' at Paules '; and Rawlidge (1628) mentions a house ' nigh Pauls ' as one of those pulled down by the City, apparently in 1596 (cf. ch. xvi). The Paul's boys, however, can hardly have been playing for some years before that date. Howes (1629) definitely specifies the singing school (cf. ch. xvi). On the other hand, Flecknoe, a late authority and in a passage dealing (inaccurately) with Jacobean rather than Elizabethan conditions, assigns the plays to ' behinde the Convocation-house in Paul's ' (App. I). This is expanded by Malone (*Variorum*, iii. 46) into ' in St. Paul's school-room, behind the Convocation-house ', and Baker, 45, suggests that they used a small yard or cloister before the doors of the Convocation House and shut off by a high wall from the main churchyard (cf. Hollar's prints in Baker, 95, 115). But I doubt if Flecknoe had anything in mind except St. Gregory's, which stood just west of the Convocation House. The hall of the College of Minor Canons is perhaps also a possibility ; but neither this nor the church is likely to have afforded a circular auditorium (cf. ch. xviii). Can they have used the Convocation House itself ?

[2] McDonnell, 27, argues for the participation of the grammar school in the plays. Obviously the phrase ' children of Paul's ', ordinarily used of the playing-boys, proves nothing one way or the other. That the plays were mainly an affair of the choir is a fair inference from the fact that they were presented at Court by the song-school masters. But there is no reason to doubt that the mediaeval give and take between the two schools continued through the sixteenth century. Hunter, *Chorus Vatum*, v. 542, quotes a manuscript life of Sir Thomas Offley, ' This Thomas Offley became a good grammarian under Mr. [William] Lillie and understood the Latin tongue perfectly ; and because he had a sweet voice he was put to learn prick-song among the choristers of St. Paul's, for that learned Mr. Lillie knew full well that knowledge in music was a help and a furtherance to all arts '. On the other hand, Dean Nowell (Churton, *Life of A. Nowell*, 190) instructed Thomas Giles in 1584 to teach the choristers catechism, writing, and music, and then to ' suffer them to resort to Paul's School that they may learn the principles of Grammar '. Some seventeenth-century performances by the grammar school, after the regular Paul's plays ceased, are upon record.

in 1576 taken a step in the direction of professionalism, by transferring their performances to Farrant's newly opened theatre at the Blackfriars. Here, if the rather difficult evidence can be trusted, the Paul's boys appear to have joined them, and to have formed part of a composite company, to which Lord Oxford's boys also contributed, and which produced the *Campaspe* and *Sapho and Phao* of the earl's follower John Lyly. Lyly took these plays to Court on 1 January and 3 March 1584, and Henry Evans, who was also associated with the enterprise, took a play called *Agamemnon and Ulysses* on 27 December. On all three occasions the official patron of the company was the Earl of Oxford. In *Agamemnon and Ulysses* it must be doubtful whether the Paul's boys had any share, for in the spring of 1584 the Blackfriars theatre ceased to be available, and the combination probably broke up.[1] This, however, was far from being the end of Lyly's connexion with the boys, for the title-pages of no less than five of his later plays acknowledge them as the presenters. They had, indeed, a four years' period of renewed activity at Court, under the mastership of Thomas Giles, who, being already almoner, became Master of the Song School on 22 May 1584, and in the following year received a royal commission to ' take up ' boys for the choir, analogous to that ordinarily granted to masters of the Chapel Children.[2] There is no specific mention of plays in

---

[1] Cf. *infra* (Chapel, Oxford's) ; ch. xvii (Blackfriars).

[2] R. Churton, *Life of Alexander Nowell*, 190, from *Reg. Nowell*, ii, f. 189 ; Nichols, *Eliz.* ii. 432 ; Collier, i. 258 ; Hazlitt, 33 ; Wallace, ii. 67, from original warrant under the Signet in *Sloane MS.* 2035[b], f. 73 :

' By the Queene,
Elizabeth.

' Whereas we haue authorysed our servaunte Thomas Gyles M[r]. of the children of the Cathedrall Churche of S[t]. Pauls within our Cittie of London to take vpp suche apte and meete Children as are most fitt to be instructed and framed in the arte and science of musicke and singinge as may be had and founde out within anie place of this our Realme of England or Wales, to be by his education and bringinge vp made meete and hable to serve vs in that behalf when our pleasure is to call for them. Wee therefore by the tenour of these presentes will and require you that ye permitt and suffer from henceforthe our saide servaunte Thomas Gyles and his deputie or deputies and every of them to take vp in anye Cathedral or Collegiate Churche or Churches and in everye other place or places of this our Realme of England and Wales, suche Childe and Children as he or they or anye of them shall finde and like of and the same Childe and Children by vertue hereof for the vse and service afouresaide, with them or anye of them to bringe awaye, withoute anye your lettes contradiccions staye or interruptions to the contrarie Charginge and commaundinge you and everie of you to be aydinge helpinge and assisting vnto the aboue named Thomas Gyles and his deputie and deputies in and aboute the due execucion of the premisses for the more spedie effectuall & bettar

the document, but its whole basis is in the service which the boys may be called upon to do the Queen in music and singing. Under Giles the company appeared at Court nine times during four winter seasons; on 26 February 1587, on 1 January and 2 February 1588, on 27 December 1588, 1 January and 12 January 1589, and on 28 December 1589, 1 January and 6 January 1590. The title-pages of Lyly's *Endymion*, *Galathea*, and *Midas* assign the representation of these plays at Court to a 2 February, a 1 January, and a 6 January respectively. *Endymion* must therefore belong to 1588 and *Midas* to 1590; for *Galathea* the most probable of the three years is 1588. *Mother Bombie* and *Love's Metamorphosis* can be less precisely dated, but doubtless belong to the period 1587–90. At some time or other, and probably before 1590, the Paul's boys performed a play of *Meleager*, of which an abstract only, without author's name, is preserved. It is not, I think, to be supposed that Lyly, although he happened to be a grandson of the first High Master of Colet's school, had any official connexion either with that establishment or with the choir school. It is true that Gabriel Harvey says of him in 1589, ' He hath not played the Vicemaster of Poules and the Foolemaster of the Theatre for naughtes '.[1] But this is merely Harvey's jesting on the old dramatic sense of the term ' vice ', and the probabilities are that Lyly's relation as dramatist to Giles as responsible manager of the company was much that which had formerly existed between John Heywood and Sebastian Westcott. Nevertheless, it was this connexion which ultimately brought the Paul's plays to a standstill. Lyly was one of the literary men employed about 1589 to answer the Martin Marprelate pamphleteers in their own vein, and to this end he availed himself of the Paul's stage, apparently with the result that, when it suited the government to disavow its instruments, that stage was incontinently suppressed.[2] The reason may

accomplisshing thereof from tyme to tyme as you and everie of you doe tendar our will and pleasure and will aunswere for doinge the contrarye at your perilles. Youen vnder our Signet at our Manour of Grenewich the 26th Day of Aprill in the 27th yere of our reign.

To all and singuler Deanes, Provostes, Maisters and Wardens of Collegies and all Ecclesiasticall persons and mynisters and to all other our officers mynisters and subiectes to whome in this case it shall apperteyne and to everye of them greetinge.'

No other commission for the Paul's choir is extant, but their rights are reserved in the commission for Windsor (q.v.) of 8 March 1560.

[1] Harvey, *Advertisement for Pap-Hatchet* (*Works*, ii. 212). Lyly was still Oxford's man but writing for Paul's, *c.* Aug. 1585 (*M. L. R.* xv. 82.).

[2] Cf. ch. ix and App. C, No. xl, especially *Pappe with an Hatchet* (Oct. 1589).

be conjectural, but the fact is undoubted. The Paul's boys disappear from the Court records after 1590. In 1591 the printer of *Endymion* writes in his preface that ' Since the Plaies in Paules were dissolved, there are certaine Commedies come to my handes by chaunce ', and the prolongation of this dissolution is witnessed to in 1596 by Thomas Nashe, who in his chaff of Gabriel Harvey's anticipated practice in the Arches says, ' Then we neede neuer wish the Playes at Powles vp againe, but if we were wearie with walking, and loth to goe too farre to seeke sport, into the Arches we might step, and heare him plead ; which would bee a merrier Comedie than euer was old Mother *Bomby* '.[1]

A last theatrical period opened for the boys with the appointment about 1600 of a new master. This was one Edward Pearce or Piers, who had become a Gentleman of the Chapel on 16 March 1589, and by 15 August 1600, when his successor was sworn in, had ' yealded up his place for the Mastership of the children of Poules '.[2] I am tempted to believe that in reviving the plays Pearce had the encouragement of Richard Mulcaster, who had become High Master of the grammar school in 1596, and during his earlier mastership of Merchant Taylors had on several occasions brought his boys to Court. Pearce is first found in the Treasurer of the Chamber's Accounts as payee for a performance on 1 January 1601, but several of the extant plays produced during this section of the company's career are of earlier date, and one of them, Marston's *1 Antonio and Mellida*, can hardly be later than 1599. A stage direction of this play apparently records the names of two of the performers as Cole and Norwood.[3] The Paul's boys, therefore, were

---

[1] *Have With You to Saffron-Walden* (*Works*, iii. 46). I do not think the reference to a twelvemonth's silence, due to envy, in the prologue to Nashe's *Summer's Last Will and Testament* (*c.* Oct. 1592) affords any justification for ascribing that play to the Paul's boys. Murray, i. 330 ; ii. 284, records a payment at Gloucester in 1590–1 ' to the children of powles '. I am sceptical about this, especially as I observe in the next year a payment for a breakfast to the Queen's men ' at Mr. Powelles '. Murray's only other municipal record for the company, at Hedon, Yorkshire, on some quite unknown date, ' Item, payd to the —— pawll plaiers ' (ii. 286), is even less satisfactory. But if the boys did travel on their suppression, they may well have gone to Croydon.

[2] Rimbault, 4. Giles must have resigned, if he was the Thomas Giles who, on 18 April 1606, was paid 100 marks a year as instructor to Henry in music (Devon, 35). He was instructor to Charles in 1613 (Reyher, 78) and figures in masks (cf. ch. vi). Fellowes, 184, 190, has two songs set by Pearce, one from *Blurt Master Constable*.

[3] *1 A. and M.* iv. i. 30, ' Enter Andrugio, Lucio, Cole, and Norwood '. Bullen thinks that the two boys played the parts named, but the action requires at least one page, who sings.

' up again ' before their rivals of the Chapel, who cannot be
shown to have begun in the Blackfriars under Henry Evans
until 1600.[1] This being so, they were probably also responsible
for Marston's revision in 1599 of *Histriomastix*, which by
giving offence to Ben Jonson, led him to satire Marston's
style in *Every Man Out of His Humour*, and so introduced
the ' war of the theatres '.[2] Before the end of 1600 they had
probably added to their repertory Chapman's *Bussy d'Ambois*,
and certainly *The Maid's Metamorphosis*, *The Wisdom of
Dr. Dodipoll*, and *Jack Drum's Entertainment*, all three of
which were entered on the Stationers' Register, and the
first two printed, during that year. *Jack Drum's Entertainment* followed in 1601 and contains the following interesting
passage of autobiography: [3]

Sir Edward Fortune. I saw the Children of *Powles* last night,
   And troth they pleas'd me prettie, prettie well :
   The Apes in time will doe it handsomely.
Planet. I faith, I like the audience that frequenteth there
   With much applause : A man shall not be chokte
   With the stench of Garlick ; nor be pasted
   To the barmie Iacket of a Beer-brewer.
Brabant Junior. 'Tis a good, gentle audience, and I hope the boies
   Will come one day into the Court of requests.
Brabant Senior. I, and they had good Plaies. But they produce
   Such mustie fopperies of antiquitie,
   And do not sute the humorous ages backs,
   With clothes in fashion.

The criticism, being a self-criticism, must not be taken too
seriously. So far as published plays are concerned, *Histriomastix* is the only one to which it applies. In Marston,
Chapman, and Middleton the company had enlisted vigorous
young playwrights, who were probably not sorry to be free
from the yoke of the professional actors, and appear to have
followed the exceptional policy of printing some at least of
their new plays as soon as they were produced.

On 11 March 1601, two months after the boys made their
first bow at Court, the Lord Mayor was ordered by the
Privy Council to suppress plays ' at Powles ' during Lent.
It is to be inferred that they were, as of old, acting in their
singing school. Confirmation is provided by a curious note
appended by William Percy to his manuscript volume of

---

[1] Wallace, ii. 153, says he has evidence of playing at Paul's in 1598,
but he does not give it. It is perhaps rash to assume that Pearce originated
the revival, as there is no proof that he came to Paul's before 1600.
[2] Cf. ch. xi.   [3] v. i. 102.

plays, presumably in sending them to be considered with a view to production by the boys. The plays bear dates in 1601–3, but it can hardly be taken for granted that they were in fact produced by the Paul's or any other company. The note runs :

A note to the Master of Children of Powles.

Memorandum, that if any of the fine and formost of these Pastorals and Comoedyes conteyned in this volume shall but overeach in length (the children not to begin before foure, after prayers, and the gates of Powles shutting at six) the tyme of supper, that then in tyme and place convenient, you do let passe some of the songs, and make the consort the shorter ; for I suppose these plaies be somewhat too long for that place. Howsoever, on your own experience, and at your best direction, be it. Farewell to you all.[1]

Both parts of Marston's *Antonio and Mellida* were entered on the Stationers' Register in the autumn of 1601 and printed in 1602. The second part may have been on the stage during 1601, and in the same year the boys probably produced John Marston's *What You Will*, and certainly played 'privately', as the Chamberlain's men did 'publicly', *Satiromastix* in which Dekker, with a hand from Marston, brought his swashing blow against the redoubtable Jonson. This also was registered in 1601 and printed in 1602. There is no sign of the boys at Court in the winter of 1601–2. In the course of 1602 their play of *Blurt Master Constable*, by Middleton, was registered and printed. They were at Court on 1 January 1603, for the last time before Elizabeth, and on 20 February 1604, for the first time before James. Either the choir school or the grammar school boys took part in the pageant speeches at the coronation triumph on 15 March 1604.[2] To the year 1604 probably belongs *Westward Ho !* which introduced to the company, in collaboration with Dekker, a new writer, John Webster. *Northward Ho !* by the same authors, followed in 1605. The company was not at Court for the winter of 1604–5, but during that of 1605–6 they gave two plays before the Princes Henry and Charles. For these the payee was not Pearce, but Edward Kirkham, who is described in the Treasurer of the Chamber's account as 'one of the Mr^es of the Childeren of Pawles'. Kirkham, who was Yeoman of the Revels, had until recently been a manager of the Children of the Revels at the Blackfriars. It may

---

[1] Collier, iii. 181. On the light thrown on the Paul's stage by these plays, cf. ch. xxi. It is conceivable that some of them may have been originally written before 1590 (cf. ch. xxiii, s.v. Percy).

[2] Cf. ch. xxiv.

have been the disgrace brought upon these by *Eastward Ho !* in the course of 1605 that led him to transfer his activities elsewhere.[1] With him he seems to have brought Marston's *The Fawn*, probably written in 1604 and ascribed in the first of the two editions of 1606 to the Queen's Revels alone, in the second to them ' and since at Poules '. The charms of partnership with Kirkham were not, however, sufficient to induce Pearce to continue his enterprise. The last traceable appearance of the Paul's boys was on 30 July 1606, when they gave *The Abuses* before James and King Christian of Denmark.[2] Probably the plays were discontinued not long afterwards. This would account for the large number of playbooks belonging to the company which reached the hands of the publishers in 1607 and 1608. The earlier policy of giving plays to the press immediately after production does not seem to have endured beyond 1602. Those now printed, in addition to *Bussy D'Ambois, What You Will, Westward Ho !* and *Northward Ho !* already mentioned, included Middleton's *Michaelmas Term, The Phoenix, A Mad World, my Masters*, and *A Trick to Catch the Old One*, together with *The Puritan*, very likely also by Middleton, and *The Woman Hater*, the first work of Francis Beaumont. *The Puritan* can be dated, from a chronological allusion, in 1606. The title-pages of *The Woman Hater, A Mad World, my Masters*, and *A Trick to Catch the Old One* specify them to have been ' lately ' acted. It is apparent from the second quarto of *A Trick to Catch the Old One* that the Children of the Blackfriars took it over and presented it at Court on 1 January 1609. This was probably part of a bargain as to which we have another record. Pearce may have had at the back of his mind a notion of reopening his theatre some day. But it is given in evidence in the lawsuit of *Keysar v. Burbadge* in 1610 that, while it was still closed, he was approached on behalf of the other ' private ' houses in London, those of the Blackfriars and the Whitefriars, and offered a ' dead rent ' of £20 a year, ' that there might be a cessation of playeinge and playes to be acted in the said howse neere St. Paules Church '.[3] This must have been in the winter of 1608–9, just as the

---

[1] Cf. *infra* (Queen's Revels).

[2] Nichols, *James*, iv. 1073, from *The King of Denmark's Welcome* (1606), ' the Youthes of Paules, commonlye cald the Children of Paules, plaide before the two Kings, a playe called *Abuses* : containing both a Comedie and a Tragedie, at which the Kinges seemed to take delight and be much pleased '. The play is lost. Fleay, ii. 80, has no justification for identifying it with *The Insatiate Countess*. *Wily Beguiled* (ch. xxiv) might be a Paul's play.

[3] C. W. Wallace, *Nebraska University Studies* (1910), x. 355 ; cf. *infra* (Queen's Revels), ch. xvii (Blackfriars).

Revels company was migrating from the Blackfriars to the Whitefriars. The agent was Philip Rosseter who, with Robert Keysar, was financially interested in the Revels company. When the King's men began to occupy the Blackfriars in the autumn of 1609, they took on responsibility for half the dead rent, but whether the arrangement survived the lawsuit of 1610 is unknown.

ii. THE CHILDREN OF THE CHAPEL AND OF THE QUEEN'S REVELS

The Children of the Chapel (1501–1603).
    Masters of the Children : William Newark (1493–1509), William Cornish (1509–23), William Crane (1523–45), Richard Bower (1545–61), Richard Edwardes (1561–6), William Hunnis (1566–97), Richard Farrant (acting, 1577–80), Nathaniel Giles (1597–1634).

The Children of the Queen's Revels (1603–5).

The Children of the Revels (1605–6).
    Masters : Henry Evans, Edward Kirkham, and others.

The Children of the Blackfriars (1606–9).

The Children of the Whitefriars (1609–10).
    Masters : Robert Keysar and others.

The Children of the Queen's Revels (1610–16).
    Masters : Philip Rosseter and others.

[*Bibliographical Note.*—Official records of the Chapel are to be found in E. F. Rimbault, *The Old Cheque Book of the Chapel Royal* (1872, *Camden Soc.*). Most of the material for the sixteenth-century part of the present section was collected before the publication of C. W. Wallace, *The Evolution of the English Drama up to Shakespeare* (1912, cited as Wallace, i), which has, however, been valuable for purposes of revision. J. M. Manly, *The Children of the Chapel Royal and their Masters* (1910, *C. H.* vi. 279), W. H. Flood, *Queen Mary's Chapel Royal* (*E. H. R.* xxxiii. 83), H. M. Hildebrand, *The Early History of the Chapel Royal* (1920, *M.P.* xviii. 233), are useful contributions. The chief published sources for the seventeenth century are three lawsuits discovered by J. Greenstreet and printed in full by F. G. Fleay, *A Chronicle History of the London Stage* (1890), 127, 210, 223. These are (a) *Clifton v. Robinson and Others* (Star Chamber, 1601), (b) *Evans v. Kirkham* (Chancery, May–June 1612), cited as *E. v. K.*, with Fleay's pages, and (c) *Kirkham v. Painton and Others* (Chancery, July–Nov. 1612), cited as *K. v. P.* Not much beyond dubious hypothesis is added by C. W. Wallace, *The Children of the Chapel at Blackfriars* (1908, cited as Wallace, ii). But Professor Wallace published an additional suit of importance, (d) *Keysar v. Burbadge and Others* (Court of Requests, Feb.–June 1610), in *Nebraska University Studies* (1910), x. 336, cited as *K. v. B.* This is apparently one of twelve suits other than Greenstreet's, which he claims (ii. 36) to have found, with other material, which may alter the story. In the meantime, I see no reason to depart from the main outlines sketched in my article on *Court Performances under James the First* (1909, *M. L. R.* iv. 153).]

The Chapel was an ancient part of the establishment of the Household, traceable far back into the twelfth century.[1] Up to the end of the fourteenth, we hear only of chaplains and clerks. These were respectively priests and laymen, and the principal chaplain came to bear the title of Dean.[2] Children of the Chapel first appear under Henry IV, who appointed a chaplain to act as Master of Grammar for them in 1401.[3] In 1420 comes the first of a series of royal commissions authorizing the impressment of boys for the Chapel service, and in 1444 the first appointment of a Master of the Children, John Plummer, by patent.[4] It is probably to the known tastes of Henry VI that the high level of musical accomplishment, which had been reached by the singers of the Chapel during the next reign was due.[5] The status and duties of the Chapel are set out with full detail in the *Liber Niger* about 1478, at which date the establishment consisted of a Dean, six Chaplains, twenty Clerks, two Yeomen or Epistolers, and eight Children. These were instructed by a Master of Song, chosen by the Dean from 'the seyd felyshipp of Chapell', and a Master of Grammar, whose services were also available for the royal Henchmen.[6] There is no further record of the Master of Grammar; but with this exception the establishment continued to exist on much the same footing, apart from

[1] *Constitutio Domus Regis* (*c.* 1135) in Hearne, *Liber Niger Scaccarii*, i. 342, ' Capellani, custos capellae et reliquiarum. Corridium duorum hominum, et quatuor servientes capellae unusquisque duplicem cibum, et duo summarii capellae unusquisque 1ᵈ in die et 1ᵈ ad ferrandum in mense '; cf. *R. O. Ld. Steward's Misc.* 298 (1279); Tout, 278, 311 (1318); *H. O.* 3, 10 (1344–8); *Life Records of Chaucer* (Chaucer Soc.), iv. 171 (1369); Nicolas, *P. C.* vi. 223 (1454).

[2] *H. O.* 10. In 1318 he was ' chief chapellain '.

[3] J. H. Wylie, *Henry IV*, iv. 208, from *Household Accounts*, ' John Bugby our chaplain retained 3 years ago pur apprendre et enformer les enfants de notre chapelle en la science de gramaire at 100/- p. a. nothing yet paid, £15 due '. A grant to John Tilbery, a boy of the King's chapel, was made on 12 Nov. 1405 (*C. P. R., Hen. IV*, iii. 96).

[4] Wallace, i. 12, 21, from *P. R.* The commission of 1420 was to John Pyamour ' uni clericorum Capellae hospicii nostri '; another of 1440 was to John Croucher, Dean. When regular Masters were instituted, the commissions seem to have been made direct to them.

[5] Wallace, i. 14, quotes laudatory accounts of the singing of the chapel by two members of the suite of Leo von Rožmital, a Bohemian who visited the English Court in 1466.

[6] *H. O.* 49. There is nothing about plays, but ' Memorandum, that the King hathe a songe before hym in his hall or chambre uppon All-hallowen day at the latter graces, by some of these clerkes and children of chappel in remembrance of Christmasse; and soe of men and children in Christmasse thorowoute. But after the songe on All-hallowen day is done, the Steward and Thesaurere of houshold shall be warned where it liketh the King to kepe his Christmasse '.

some increase of numbers, up to the seventeenth century.[1] Although subject to some general supervision from the Lord Chamberlain and to that extent part of the Chamber, it was largely a self-contained organization under its own Dean. Elizabeth, however, left the post of Dean vacant, and the responsibility of the Lord Chamberlain then became more direct.[2] It probably did not follow, at any rate in its full numbers, a progress, but moved with the Court to the larger 'standing houses', except possibly to Windsor, where there was a separate musical establishment in St. George's Chapel.[3] It does not seem, at any rate in Tudor times, to have had any relation to the collegiate chapel of St. Stephen in the old palace of Westminster.[4] The number of Children varied between eight and ten up to 1526, when it was finally fixed by Henry VIII at twelve.[5] The chaplains and clerks were collectively known in the sixteenth century

[1] At the coronation of James in 1603 (Rimbault, 127) there were a Sub-dean, 7 Ministers, the Master of the Children, an Organist, 22 ordinary Gentlemen, and a Clerk of the Check; also a Sergeant, 2 Yeomen, and a Groom of the Vestry. This agrees with the Elizabethan fee lists, which give the total number of Gentlemen as 32. The coronation list does not name Epistolers; but it is clear from the notices of appointments in Rimbault, 1, that a Gospeller and Epistoler were appointed, as next in succession to the Gentlemen's places, although it does not appear that they were necessarily ex-Children. There were also Extraordinary Gentlemen (Rimbault, 31).

[2] Cf. ch. ii.

[3] *H. O.* 160. The hall and chapel are to be kept 'at all times when his Highnesse shall lye in his castle of Windsor, his mannors of Bewlye, Richmond, Hampton Court, Greenwich, Eltham, or Woodstock'; but 'in rideing journeys and progresses', only the Master of the Children, six men, six children, and some officers of the vestry are to attend. In the seventeenth century 'all removinge weekes' were amongst the 'auntient tymes of lyberty and playinge weekes' (Rimbault, 73). But the practice may have varied. Stopes, 252, gives a Stable warrant of 1554 for a wagon 'for the necessarie conveying and cariage of the Children of our Chapel and their man from place to place, at such seasons, as they by our commandment shall remove to serve where wee shall appointe them'.

[4] A chapel of St. Stephen existed in 1205. It was rebuilt and made a free collegiate chapel in 1348, and dissolved in 1547, and the building assigned as a chamber for the House of Commons (J. T. Smith, *Antiquities of Westminster*, 72; *V. H. London*, i. 566). It may have originated as a domestic chapel, but seems to be quite distinct from the Household Chapel by the sixteenth century. Thus its St. Nicholas Bishop had an old annual reward of £1 from the Exchequer (Devon, *Issues of Exchequer*, 222; R. Henry, *Hist. of Great Britain*[3], xii. 459; Brewer, iv. 869), while the Household boys got their reward of £6 12s. 4d. from the Treasurer of the Chamber. Wallace, i. 22, notes that the Masters of the Children 'all lived' at Greenwich, which suggests that this was the Tudor head-quarters of the Chapel.

[5] Wallace, i. 22, 23, 26, 61, from patents of Masters; *Fee Lists* (*passim*).

as the Gentlemen of the Chapel, and the most important of
them, next to one who acted as subdean, was the Master of
the Children, who trained them in music and, as time went
on, also formed them into a dramatic company. The Master
generally held office under a patent during pleasure, and was
entitled in addition to his fee of 7½d. a day or £91 8s. 1½d.
a year as Gentleman and his share in the general ' rewards '
of the Chapel, to a special Exchequer annuity of 40 marks
(£26 13s. 4d.), raised in 1526 to £40, ' pro exhibicione puerorum ', which is further defined in 1510 as ' pro exhibicione
vesturarum et lectorum ' and in 1523 as ' pro sustencione et
diettes '.[1] To this, moreover, several other payments came
to be added in the course of Henry VIII's reign. Originally
the Chapel dined and supped in the royal hall; but this
proved inconvenient, and a money allowance from the
Cofferer of the Household was substituted, which was fixed
in 1544 at 1s. a day for each Gentleman and 2s. a week for
each Child.[2] The allowance for the Children was afterwards
raised to 6d. a day.[3] Long before this, however, the Masters
had succeeded in obtaining an exceptional allowance of 8d.
a week for the breakfast of each Child, which was reckoned
as making £16 a year and paid them in monthly instalments
of 26s. 8d. by the Treasurer of the Chamber. The costs of
the Masters in their journeys for the impressment of Children
were also recouped by the Treasurer of the Chamber. And
from him they also received rewards of 20s. when *Audivi
vocem* was sung on All Saints' Day, £6 13s. 4d. for the Children's
feast of St. Nicholas on 6 December, and 40s. when *Gloria
in Excelsis* was sung on Christmas and St. John's Days.
These were, of course, over and above any special rewards
received for dramatic performances.[4] In the provision of
vesturae the Masters were helped by the issue from the
Great Wardrobe of black and tawny camlet gowns, yellow
satin coats, and Milan bonnets, which presumably constituted

---

[1] R. Henry, *Hist. of Great Britain*[3], xii. 457 ; Brewer, ii. 873 ; iii. 364 ;
iv. 868 ; *Fee Lists* (*passim*) ; Wallace, i. 21, 23, 24, 26, 33, 61, from
patents and *Exchequer of Receipt, Auditor's Privy Seal Books*. The
Elizabethan fee for a Gentleman was only £30 (cf. p. 41, n. 3), but it was
increased again to £40 by James in 1604 (Rimbault, 61).

[2] *H. O.* 169, 212. The *Chamber Accounts* for Aug. 1520 include a special
payment to the Master for the diets of the boys when they accompanied
the King to Calais, at 2d. a day each.

[3] The allowance was 6d. in 1575 (Collier, i. 175 ; Nagel, 29 ; from
Harl. MS. 589, f. 220), but Hunnis's petition of 1583 (cf. p. 37) implies
that this rate was customary before Elizabeth's reign.

[4] *Chamber Accounts* (*passim*) ; cf. p. 24, n. 6. For the feast of the
Boy Bishop on St. Nicholas Day, cf. *Mediaeval Stage*, i. 336, 359, 369.

the festal and penitential arrays of the choir.[1] The boys themselves do not appear to have received any wages but, when their voices had broken, the King made provision for them at the University or otherwise, and until this could be done, the Treasurer of the Chamber sometimes paid allow-ances to the Master or some other Gentleman for their maintenance and instruction.[2]

The earlier Masters were John Plummer (1444–55), Henry Abyngdon (1455–78), Gilbert Banaster (1478–83?), probably John Melyonek (1483–5), Lawrence Squier (1486–93), and William Newark (1493–1509).[3] Some of these have left

[1] Stopes, 15, '40 surplices for the gentlemen and 16 for the children of the Chapel' (Wardrobe warrant of 7 Oct. 1533) ; 'for 10 children of the Kings Chapell, for gownes of Tawney Chamblett lined with black satin of Bruges, and Milan bonnettes for the said children, as in the same boke of apparel is declared xliiili. iiis. iiiid. For two children of the Kings Chapell, for 2 gownes of Black Chamblett, lined with black satin of Bruges 2 cotes of yellow saten of Bruges lined with Coton, and 2 Millan bonnettes, and for making and lining of said gownes and cotes as in the said boke at large it duly apperes xli xviiis . . . Item for twenty gentlemen of the King's chapell, for 20 gownes of Black Damask for the said gentlemen, cxxviili. xs. ' (Queen's Remembrancia, Wardrobe Expenses, Hen. VIII, 52/10 A).

[2] Chamber Accounts (passim). From 1510 to 1513 Robert Fairfax had 2s. a week for the diet of William Alderson and Arthur Lovekyn, the King's scholars, and £2 13s. 4d. for their teaching. In 1513 William Max, late a Child of the Chapel, had 40s. In 1514 Cornish was finding and apparelling Robert Philip and another Child of the Chapel, for £1 13s. 4d. a quarter, and in 1517 finding and teaching William Saunders, late Child of the Chapel, for the same sum, with 2d. a week for board 'when the king keepeth no household'. In 1529–30 Crane had 3d. a day wages and 20d. a week board wages for Robert Pery, and in 1530 also for William Pery. In 1531 Robert Pery was paid direct. Cunningham, xx, gives a late seventeenth-century example of a similar arrangement. In 1546 a royal letter was written for the appointment of William Bretten, late a Chapel boy, to be singing-man at Lichfield (Brewer, xxi. 1. 142). Some of the above names appear in a list of Chapel Children, William Colman, William Maxe, William Alderson, Henry Meryell, John Williams, John Graunger, Arthur Lovekyn, Henry Andrewe, Nicholas Ivy, Edward Cooke, and James Curteys, receiving liveries at the funeral of Henry VII in 1509 (Lafontaine, 3, from Ld. Ch. Records, 550, f. 131). Some amusing corre-spondence of 1518 relates to a boy Robin, whom Henry VIII wished to transfer from Wolsey's chapel to his own. It was stipulated that Cornish should treat him honestly, 'otherwise than he doth his own ', and later Cornish wrote praising the clean singing and descant of the recruit (Brewer, ii. 1246–50).

[3] J. M. Manly in C. H. vi. 279 ; C. Johnson, John Plummer (1921, Antiquaries Journal, i. 52) ; Wallace, i. 21, from patents and Exchequer payments. Wallace does not include Melyonek although (ii. 62) he gives the following commission, already printed by Collier, i. 41, and Rimbault, vii, from Harl. MS. 433, f. 189 :
' Mellenek, Ric. etc. To all and euery our subgiettes aswele spirituell as temporell thise our lettres hering or seeing greeting, We let you wite

a musical or literary reputation, and Banaster is said to have written an interlude in 1482.[1] But until the end of this period only occasional traces of dramatic performances by the Chapel can be discerned. An alleged play by the Gentlemen at the Christmas of 1485 cannot be verified.[2] The first recorded performance, therefore, is one of the disguisings at the wedding of Prince Arthur and Katharine of Spain in 1501, in which two of the children were concealed in mermaids 'singing right sweetly and with quaint hermony '.[3]

Towards the end of Henry VII's reign begins a short series of plays given at the rate of one or two a year by the Gentlemen, which lasted through 1506–12.[4] Thereafter there is no other play by the Gentlemen as such upon record until the Christmas of 1553, when they performed a morality of which

that for the confidence & trust that we haue in our trusty and welbeloued seruant John Melyonek oon of ye gentilmen of our Chapell and knowing also his expert habilitie and connyng in ye science of Musique haue licenced him and by thise presentes licence and geue him auctorite that within all places in this our realme aswele Cathedral churges coliges chappells houses of relegion and al oyer franchised & exempt places as elliswhere our colege roial at Wyndesor reserued & except may take and sease for vs and in our name al suche singing men & childre being expart in the said science of Musique as he can finde and think sufficient and able to do vs seruice. Wherfor &c Yeuen &c at Nottingham the xvj[th] day of September A[o] secundo [1484].'

Banaster did not die until 1487, but I think Melyonek must have replaced him, perhaps without a patent, under Richard III.

[1] Cf. *D. N. B.* Songs by Banaster and Newark are in *Addl. MS.* 5465 (Chambers and Sidgwick, *Early English Lyrics*, 299).

[2] Collier, i. 46 ; cf. Wallace, i. 12.   I am not sure that Collier meant 1485.

[3] Reyher, 504, from *Harl. MS.* 69, f. 34[v]. Wallace, i. 13 ; ii. 69, citing the same MS., misdates '1490', and says that eight children took part. Four singing children who had appeared in another disguising a day or two before were probably also from the Chapel.

[4] *Chamber Accounts* in Wallace, i. 28, 38 ; Bernard Andrew, *Annales Hen. VII* (Gairdner, *Memorials of Hen. VII*), 104 ; Halle, i. 25 ; Professor Wallace seems to think that the annual Christmas rewards paid by the Treasurer of the Chamber to the Gentlemen, which went on to the end of the reign, were for plays. But these were of £13 6s. 8d., whereas the reward for a play was £6 13s. 4d. They were paid on Twelfth Night, and are sometimes said to be for ' payne taking ' during Christmas. In 1510 they had an extra £6 13s. 4d. for praying for the Queen's good deliverance. The ' payne taking ' was no doubt as singers. An order of Henry VII's time (*H. O.* 121) for the wassail on Twelfth Night has, ' Item, the chappell to stand on the one side of the hall, and when the steward cometh in at the hall doore with the wassell, he must crie three tymes, Wassell, wassell, wassell ; and then the chappell to answere with a good songe '. The Gentlemen also had 40s. annually from the Treasurer of the Chamber ' to drink with their bucks ' given them for a summer feast, which was still held in the seventeenth century (Rimbault, 122).

the principal character was Genus Humanum.[1] This had been originally planned for the coronation on the previous 1 October, and as a warrant then issued states that a coronation play had customarily been given ' by the gentlemen of the chappell of our progenitoures ', it may perhaps be inferred that Edward VI's coronation play of ' the story of Orpheus ' on 22 February 1547 was also by the Gentlemen.[2] In the meantime the regular series of Chapel plays at Court had been broken after 1512, and when it was taken up again in 1517 it was not by the Gentlemen, but by the Children.[3] This is, of course, characteristic of the Renaissance.[4] But an immediate cause is probably to be found in the personality of William Cornish, a talented and energetic Master of the Children, who succeeded William Newark in the autumn of 1509, and held office until his death in 1523.[5] Cornish appears to have come of a musical family.[6] He took part

[1] Stopes, *Shakespeare's Environment*, 238 ; Feuillerat, *Ed. and Mary*, 149, 289. Professor Feuillerat says that one of the documents relating to the play refers to the ' Children of the Chapel ', and doubts whether there is a real distinction between the ' Gentlemen ' and the ' Children ' as actors.

[2] Feuillerat, *Ed. and Mary*, 3, 255. The conjecture is supported by the fact that garments belonging to the Revels were in possession of two Gentlemen of the Chapel in April 1547 (ibid., 12, 13).

[3] *Chamber Accounts* in Wallace, i. 38, 65, 70 ; Brewer, xiv. 2. 284 ; Kempe, 69 ; Collier, i. 78 ; Feuillerat, *Ed. and Mary*, 266, 288. The ' iiij Children y^t played afore ye king ' on 14 Jan. 1508 were not necessarily of the Chapel.

[4] Cf. ch. viii and *Mediaeval Stage*, ii. 192, 215.

[5] Wallace, i. 33. No patent is cited, but the privy seal for the payment to Cornish of the Exchequer annuity was dated 1 April 1510, and he was shortly afterwards paid for the Christmas and Easter quarters. Newark had died in Nov. 1509. It is therefore a little puzzling to find in a list of Exchequer fees payable during the year ended Michaelmas 1508 (R. Henry, *Hist. of Great Britain*[3], xii. 457) the item ' Willelmo Cornysshe magistro puerorum capellae regis pro excubitione eorundem puerorum 26^{ll}. 13^s. 4^d.' Probably the list was prepared retrospectively in Henry VIII's reign (cf. the analogous list in Brewer, ii. 873), and the name rather than the date is an error.

[6] The data are : (a) *Exchequer Payments* (Wallace, i. 34), Mich. 1493, ' Willelmo Cornysshe de Rege ', 100s. ; (b) *T. C. Accounts*, ' to one Cornysshe for a prophecy in rewarde ', 13s. 4d. (12 Nov. 1493) ; ' to Cornishe of the Kings Chapell ', 26s. 8d. (1 Sept. 1496) ; ' to Cornysshe for 3 pagents ' (26 Oct. 1501) ; ' m^r kyte Cornisshe and other of the Chapell y^t played affore ye king at Richemounte ', £6 13s. 4d. (25 Dec. 1508) ; (c) *Household Book of Q. Elizabeth*, 25 Dec. 1502, ' to Cornisshe for setting of a Carrall vpon Cristmas Day in reward ', 13s. 4d. ; (d) John Cornysh in list of Gent. of Chapel 23 Feb. 1504, and William Cornysh in similar lists *c.* 1509 and 22 Feb. 1511 (Lafontaine, 2, from *Ld. Ch. Records*) ; (e) Songs by ' W. Cornishe, jun.' in *Addl. MS.* 5465, by ' John Cornish ' in *Addl. MS.* 5665, by ' W. Cornish ' in *Addl. MS.* 31922 (*Early English Lyrics*, 299) ; (f) *A Treatise betweene Trouthe and Enformacon*, by

in a play given by the Gentlemen of the Chapel shortly before his appointment as Master. And although it was some years before he organized the Children into a definite company, he was the ruling spirit and chief organizer of the elaborate disguisings which glorified the youthful court of Henry VIII from the Shrovetide of 1511 to the visit of the Emperor Charles V in 1522, and hold an important place in the story, elsewhere dealt with, of the Court mask.[1] In these revels both the Gentlemen and the Children of the Chapel, as well as the King and his lords and ladies took a part, and they were often designed so as to frame an interlude, which would call for the services of skilled performers.[2]

In view of Cornish's importance in the history of the stage at Court, it is matter for regret that none of his dramatic writing has been preserved, for it is impossible to attach any value to the fantastic attributions of Professor Wallace, who credits him not only with the anonymous *Calisto and Meliboea*, *Of Gentleness and Nobility*, *The Pardoner and the Frere*, and *Johan Johan*, but also with *The Four Elements* and *The Four P. P.*, for the authorship of which by John Rastell and John Heywood respectively there is good contemporary evidence.[3]

' William Cornysshe otherwise called Nyssewhete Chapelman with . . . Henry the VIIth his raigne the xixth yere the moneth of July ' [1504], doubtless the satirical ballad on Empson referred to by Stowe, *Annales*, 816 (*B. M. Royal MS.* 18, D. 11). I think they yield an older William and a John Cornish, of whom one, probably John, arranged the three pageants at Arthur's wedding, and a William ' jun.' who must have joined the Chapel in 1503 or 1504 and became Master of the Children. The older William may be identical with the Westminster (q.v.) choir-master of 1479–80. A Christopher or ' Kit ' Cornish, referred to by Stopes, 17, and elsewhere, had no existence. This is a ghost-name, due to the juxtaposition of ' kyte ', i.e. Sir John Kite, afterwards Archbishop of Armagh, and ' Cornisshe ' in the 1508 record above.

[1] Cf. ch. v and *Mediaeval Stage*, i. 400.

[2] The *T. C. Accounts* show a reward of £200 to Cornish on 30 Nov. 1516, of which the occasion is not specified, and a payment of £18 2s. 11½d. for ' ij pagentes ' on 6 July 1517. With these possible exceptions, no expenditure on the disguisings or the interludes which formed part of them, as distinct from the independent interludes by the Children, for which Cornish received £6 13s. 4d. each, seems to have passed through these accounts. Any remuneration received by Cornish or his fellows or children for their personal services probably passed through the *Revels Accounts*.

[3] Wallace, i. 16, 50. He light-heartedly accuses my friend Mr. Pollard, me, and others of perpetuating an old mis-ascription on the strength of Bale, ' generally without consulting the *Scriptores* ', in the first edition of which (1548) Bale says that Rastell ' reliquit ', and in the second that he ' edidit ' *The Four Elements*. This Professor Wallace regards as revision by Bale of an incorrect assertion that Rastell was the author into an assertion that he was the publisher. But Bale elsewhere uses ' edidit ' to indicate authorship, as Professor Wallace might have learnt

Cornish was succeeded as Master of the Children by William Crane (1523–45) and Crane by Richard Bower, whose patent was successively renewed by Edward VI, presumably by Mary, and finally by Elizabeth on 30 April 1559.[1] His service was almost certainly continuous, and it is therefore rather puzzling to be told that a commission to take up singing children for the Chapel, similar to that of John Melyonek in 1484, was issued in February 1550 to Philip van Wilder, a Gentleman of the Privy Chamber.[2] Neither the full text nor a reference to the source for the warrant is given, and I suspect the explanation to be that it was not for the Chapel at all. Philip van Wilder was a lutenist, one of a family of musicians of whom others were in the royal service, and he may not improbably have had a commission to recruit a body of young minstrels with whom other notices suggest that he may have been connected.[3] Bower himself had a commission for the Chapel on 6 June 1552.[4] Although the Children continued to give performances at Court both under

from the notice of Heywood which he quotes on p. 80. As to *The Four P. P.* there are three early editions by three different publishers, and they all assign it to Heywood.

[1] Wallace, i. 61, 69 ; ii. 63, from patents and Exchequer payments. The Elizabethan patent is in Rymer, xv. 517.

[2] Rimbault, viii, quoting only the words ' in anie churches or chappells within England to take to the King's use, such and so many singing children and choristers, as he or his deputy should think good '. Stopes, 12, gives *Lansd. MS.* 171, and *Stowe MS.* 371, f. 31ᵛ, as references, but the commission is not in either of them.

[3] Matthew Welder appears as a lute and viol at Court in 1516 and 1517. Peter Welder was appointed in 1519 and is traceable to 1559, as a lute, viol, or flute. Henry van Wilder was a ' musician ', 1553–8. Philip Welder or van Wilder himself is first noted as a ' minstrel ' in 1526. Later he was a lute up to 1554. In 1547 he was also ' of the Privy Chamber ' and keeper of the King's musical instruments (Nagel, 6, 13, 15, 16, 18, 22, 24, 27 ; Lafontaine, 8, 9, 12 ; Brewer, i, cxi). He died 24 Jan. 1554, leaving a son, Henry, probably the one noted above (Fry, *London Inquisitions*, i. 117). The *Chamber Accounts* for 1538–41 show an allowance to him of £70 ' for six singing children ' (Stopes, 12). Several references to ' Philippe and his fellows yong mynstrels ' and to ' the children that be in the keeping of Philip and Edmund Harmon ' appear in Green Cloth documents from 30 June 1538 to 1544 (*H. O.* 166, 172, 191, 208 ; *Genealogist*, xxx. 23). Edmund Harmon was one of the royal Barbers. Finally, livery lists of 1547 show nine singing men and children under ' Mʳ. Phelips ' (Lafontaine, 7). An earlier company of ' the King's young minstrels ' than this of 1538–50 seems to have been lodged at court *c.* 1526 (Brewer, iv. 1. 865), and there were ' troyes autres nos ioesnes ministralx ' as far back as 1369 (*Life Records of Chaucer*, iv. 174). Elizabethan fee lists continue to make provision for ' six children for singing ', but there is no indication that the posts were filled up.

[4] Wallace, ii. 63, from docquet in *B. M. Royal MS.* 18, C. xxiv, f. 232. By an obvious error, the name is written by the clerk as ' Gowre '.

Crane and under Bower, it may be doubted whether they
were quite so prominent as they had been in Cornish's time.
Certainly they had to contend with the competition of the
Paul's boys. Crane himself is not known to have been
a dramatist. It has been suggested that Bower's authorship is indicated by the initials R. B. on the title-page of
Apius and Virginia (1575), but, in view of the date of the
publication, this must be regarded as very doubtful. The
chief Marian producer of plays was Nicholas Udall, but it
remains uncertain whether he wrote for the Chapel Children.
Professor Wallace has no justification whatever for his
confident assertions that John Heywood ' not only could
but did ' write plays for the Chapel, that he ' had grown up
in the Chapel under Cornish ', and that ' as dramatist and
Court-entertainer ' he ' was naturally associated with the
performances of the Chapel '.[1] There is no proof whatever
that Heywood began as a Chapel boy, and although he
certainly wrote plays for boys, they are nowhere said or
implied to have been of the Chapel company. There are scraps
of evidence which indicate that they may have been the
Paul's boys.[2] It is also conceivable that they may have
been Philip van Wilder's young minstrels.

When Elizabeth came to the throne, then, the Chapel had
already a considerable dramatic tradition behind it. But
for a decade its share in the Court revels remains somewhat
obscure. The Treasurer of the Chamber records no payments
for performances to its Masters before 1568.[3] A note in a
Revels inventory of 1560 of the employment of some white
sarcenet ' in ffurnishinge of a pley by the children of the
Chapple ' may apparently refer to any year from 1555 to
1560, and it is therefore hazardous to identify the Chapel
with the anonymous players of the interlude of 31 December
1559 which contained ' suche matter that they wher com-
mondyd to leyff off '.[4] Bower may of course have retained

---

[1] Wallace, i. 77.   [2] Cf. p. 12.

[3] It is possible that the Treasurer of the Chamber did not pay all the
rewards for plays during the earlier years of the reign ; but the suggestion
of Wallace, i. 108, that, if we had the *Books of Queen's Payments*, more
information might be available, seems to show a failure to realize the
identity of the Tudor *Books of King's Payments* with the *T. of C. Accounts*.
There might, however, be rewards in a book subsidiary to the *Privy Purse
Accounts*. I do not think that much can be made of the recital of ' playes '
as well as ' maskes ' in the preamble of the *Revels Accounts* for 1558-9,
during which the T. of C. paid no rewards, since this may be merely
' common form '.

[4] Feuillerat, *Eliz.* 34 ; cf. Appendix A. Naturally no ' reward ' would
be paid in such circumstances. Fleay, 16, 32, 60, conjectures that the
play was *Misogonus*.

Catholic sympathies, but he died on 26 July 1561, and it is difficult to suppose that the high dramatic reputation of his successor Richard Edwardes was not based upon a greater number of Court productions than actually stand to his name.[1] Edwardes had been a Gentleman of the Chapel from 1556 or earlier. His patent as Master is dated on 27 October 1561, and on the following 10 December he received a commission the terms of which served as a model for those of the next two Masterships:[2]

> Memorandum quod x° die Januarii anno infra scripto istud breve deliberatum fuit domino custodi magni Sigilli apud Westmonasterium exequendum.

Elizabeth by the grace of God Quene of England Fraunce & Ireland defender of the faythe &c. To our right welbeloued & faythfull counsaylour Sir Nicholas Bacon knight Keper of our great Seale of Englande, commaundinge you that vnder our great Seale aforsayd ye cause to be made our lettres patentes in forme followinge. To all mayours sherifs bayliefes constables & all other our officers gretinge. For that it is mete that our chappell royall should be furnysshed with well singing children from tyme to tyme we have & by these presentes do authorise our welbeloued servaunt Richard Edwardes master of our children of our sayd chappell or his deputie beinge by his bill subscribed & sealed so authorised, & havinge this our presente comyssion with hym, to take as manye well singinge children as he or his sufficient deputie shall thinke mete in all chathedrall & collegiate churches as well within libertie[s] as without within this our realme of England whatsoever they be, And also at tymes necessarie, horses, boates, barges, cartes, & carres, as he for the conveyaunce of the sayd children from any place to our sayd chappell royall [shall thinke mete] with all maner of necessaries apperteynyng to the sayd children as well by lande as water at our prices ordynarye to be redely payed when they for our service shall remove to any place or places, Provided also that if our sayd servaunt or his deputie or deputies bearers hereof in his name cannot forthwith remove the chyld or children when he by vertue of this our commyssyon hathe taken hym or them that then the sayd child or children shall remayne there vntill suche tyme as our sayd servaunt Rychard Edwardes shall send for him or them. Wherfore we will & commaunde you & everie of you to whom this our comyssion shall come to be helpinge aydinge & assistinge to the vttermost of your powers as ye

---

[1] Strype, *Survey of London* (App. i. 92), gives the date from Bower's tombstone at Greenwich, and as his death is recited in Edwardes' patent (Stopes, *Hunnis*, 146) and his will of 18 June 1561 was proved on 25 Aug. 1561 (Wallace, i. 106), it is clear that the entry of Rimbault, i, ' 1563. Rich. Bower died, M^r of the children, A° 5to ', must be an error.

[2] Wallace, *Blackfriars*, 65, from Privy Seal in P. R. O. The patent dated 10 Jan. 1562 is on *Patent Rolls, 4 Eliz.* p. 6, m. 14 *dorso*.

will answer at your vttermoste perylles. In wytnes wherof &c. Geven vnder our privie seale at our Manor of St James the fourth daye of Decembre in the fourth yere of our Raigne.

R. Jones.

At Christmas 1564–5 the boys appeared at Court in a tragedy by Edwardes, which may have been his extant *Damon and Pythias*.[1] On 2 February 1565 and 2 February 1566 they gave performances before the lawyers at the Candlemas feasts of Lincoln's Inn.[2] There is nothing to show that the Chapel had any concern with the successful play of *Palamon and Arcite*, written and produced by Edwardes for Elizabeth's visit to Oxford in September 1566. Edwardes died on the following 31 October, and on 15 November William Hunnis was appointed Master of the Children.[3] His formal patent of appointment is dated 22 April 1567, and the bill for his commission, which only differs from that of Edwardes in minor points of detail, on 18 April.[4] Hunnis had been a Gentleman at least since about 1553, with an interval of disgrace under Mary, owing to his participation in Protestant plots. He was certainly himself a dramatist, but none of his plays are known to be extant, and a contemporary eulogy speaks of his 'enterludes' as if they dated from an earlier period than that of his Mastership. It is, however, natural to suppose that he may have had a hand in some at least of the pieces which his Children produced at Court. The first of these was a tragedy at Shrovetide 1568. In the following year is said to have been published a pamphlet entitled *The Children of the Chapel Stript and Whipt*, which apparently originated in some gross offence given by the dramatic activities of the Chapel to the growing Puritan sentiment. 'Plaies', said the writer, 'will never be supprest, while her maiesties unfledged minions flaunt it in silkes and sattens. They had as well be at their Popish service, in the deuils garments.' And again, 'Even in her maiesties chappel do these pretty vpstart youthes profane the Lordes Day by the

[1] This is recorded in a Revels document, and seems a clear case of a play given by the Chapel and not paid for by the T. of C.

[2] Cf. ch. vii, p. 223.

[3] Rimbault, 2. On Hunnis, cf. ch. xxiii.

[4] Stopes, 295, translates the patent of appointment from *Auditors Patent Books*, ix, f. 144[v]; the Privy Seal is in *Privy Seals*, Series iii, 1175. Stopes also prints the patent and Wallace, ii. 66, the Signet Bill (misdescribing it as a Privy Seal) for the commission ; it is enrolled on *Patent Rolls*, 9 *Eliz.* p. 10, m. 16 *dorso*. It is varied from the model of 1562 by the inclusion of power to the Master to take up lodging for the children in transit, and to fix ' reasonable prises ' for carriage and necessaries at his discretion.

lascivious writhing of their tender limbs, and gorgeous decking
of their apparell, in feigning bawdie fables gathered from the
idolatrous heathen poets '.   I should feel more easy in drawing
inferences from this, were the book extant.[1]   But it seems to
indicate either that the controversialist of 1569 was less
careful than his successors to avoid attacks upon Elizabeth's
private ' solace ', or that the idea had already occurred to
the Master of turning his rehearsals of Court plays to profit
by giving open performances in the Chapel.   That the Court
performances themselves took place in the Chapel is possible,
but not very likely ; the usual places for them seem to have
been the Hall or the Great Chamber.[2]   But no doubt they
sometimes fell on a Sunday.

The boys played at Court on 6 January 1570 and during
Shrovetide 1571.   On 6 January 1572 they gave *Narcissus*,
and on 13 February 1575 a play with a hunt in it.[3]   On all
these occasions Hunnis was payee.   An obvious error of the
clerk of the Privy Council in entering him as ' John ' Hunnis
in connexion with the issue of a warrant for the payment of
1572 led Chalmers to infer the existence of two Masters of
the name of Hunnis.[4]   During the progress of 1575 Hunnis
contributed shows to the ' Princely Pleasures ' of Kenilworth,
and very likely utilized the services of the boys in these.[5]
And herewith his active conduct of the Chapel performances
appears to have been suspended for some years.   A play of
Mutius Scaevola, given jointly at Court by the Children of
the Chapel and the Children of Windsor on 6 January 1577,
is the first of a series for which the place of Hunnis as payee
is taken by Richard Farrant.   To this series belong unnamed
plays on 27 December 1577 and 27 December 1578, *Loyalty
and Beauty* on 2 March 1579, and *Alucius* on 27 December

---

[1] Hazlitt-Warton, iv. 217, citing f. xii of the pamphlet. I know of no
copy. One is catalogued among Bishop Tanner's books in the Bodleian,
but Stopes, 226, ' went to Oxford on purpose to see it, but found that
it had utterly vanished '.   Macray, *Annals of the Bodleian*, 211, thinks
that it may have been destroyed when Tanner's books fell into a river
during their transit from Norwich to Oxford in Dec. 1731. The pamphlet
is also cited for an example of the use of the term ' spur money ' (Bumpus,
29, with date ' 1598 ').   F. T. Hibgame (*10 N. Q.* i. 458) describes a collection of pamphlets seen by him in New York under the general title of
The Sad Decay of Discipline in our Schools (1830), which included *Some
Account of the Stripping and Whipping of the Children of the Chapel*, containing a ' realistic account of the treatment of the boys at one of the
royal chapels ', of which he thought the author might be George Colman.
[2] Cf. ch. vii.
[3] Feuillerat, *Eliz.* 244, ' Holly, Ivye, firr poles & Mosse for the Rock . . .
Hornes iij, Collers iij, Leashes iij & dogghookes iij with Bawdrickes for
the hornes in Hvnnyes playe '.
[4] *Variorum*, iii. 439.   [5] Cf. ch. xxiii (Gascoigne).

1579.[1] Farrant, who is known as a musician, had been a Gentleman of the Chapel in 1553, and had left on 24 April 1564, doubtless to take up the post of Master of the Children of Windsor, in which capacity he annually presented a play at Court from 1566–7 to 1575–6.[2] But evidently the two offices were not regarded as incompatible, for on 5 November 1570, while still holding his Mastership, he was again sworn in as Gentleman of the Chapel 'from Winsore'.[3] A recent discovery by M. Feuillerat enables us to see that his taking over of the Chapel Children from Hunnis in 1576 was part of a somewhat considerable theatrical enterprise. Stimulated perhaps by the example of Burbadge's new-built Theatre, he took a lease of some of the old Priory buildings in the Blackfriars ; and here, either for the first time, or in continuation of a similar use of the Chapel itself, which had provoked criticism, the Children appeared under his direction in performances open to the public.[4] The ambiguous relation of the Blackfriars precinct to the jurisdiction of the City Corporation probably explains the inclusion of the Chapel in the list of companies whose exercises the Privy Council instructed the City to tolerate on 24 December 1578. It is, I think, pretty clear that, although Farrant is described as Master of the Chapel Children by the Treasurer of the Chamber from 1577 to 1580, and by Hunnis himself in his petition of 1583,[5] he was never technically Master, but merely acted as deputy to Hunnis, probably even to the extent of taking all the financial risks off his hands. Farrant was paid for a comedy at Lincoln's Inn at Candlemas 1580 and is described in the entry as ' one of the Queen's chaplains '.[6] On 30 November 1580 he died and Hunnis then resumed his normal functions.[7] The Chapel played at Court on 5 February 1581, 31 December 1581, 27 February 1582, and 26 December

---

[1] W. Creizenach (*Sh.-Jahrbuch*, liv. 73) points out that the source must have been Livy, xxvi. 50.

[2] Cf. *infra* (Windsor).   [3] Rimbault, 2.

[4] Cf. ch. xvii (Blackfriars). The bare fact of this early use of the Blackfriars has, of course, long been known from the reference to comedies at the Blackfriars in Gosson, *P. C.* 188 (App. C, No. xxx), and the prologues to Lyly's *Campaspe* and *Sapho and Phao*. Fleay, 36, 39, 40, guessed that the early Blackfriars performances were at an inn, and by the Paul's boys, and that the euphuistic prose plays at the Bel Sàvage mentioned by Gosson, *S. A.* 39 (App. C, No. xxii), in 1579 were early Chapel versions of Lyly's above-named plays. But there is no evidence that either of the boy companies ever used an inn.

[5] Cf. p. 38.   [6] Cf. ch. vii, p. 223.

[7] Rimbault, 3. The Blackfriars correspondence shows that the date 1581 given in Rimbault, 56, is wrong. A warrant of 1582 for a lease in reversion to his widow Anne is in *Hatfield MSS.* ii. 539.

1582. One of these plays may have been Peele's *Arraignment of Paris*; that of 26 December 1582 was *A Game of Cards*, possibly the piece which, according to Sir John Harington, was thought ' somewhat too plaine ', and was championed at rehearsal by ' a notable wise counseller '.[1] On the first three of these occasions the Treasurer merely entered a pay-ment to the Master of the Children, without giving a name, but in the entry for the last play Hunnis is specified. It is known, moreover, that Hunnis, together with one John Newman, took a sub-lease of the Blackfriars from Farrant's widow on 20 December 1581. They do not seem to have been very successful financially, for they were irregular in their rent, and neglected their repairs. It was perhaps trepidation at the competition likely to arise from the establishment of the Queen's men in 1583, which led them to transfer their interest to one Henry Evans, a scrivener of London, from whom, when Sir William More took steps to protect himself against the breach of covenant involved in an alienation without his consent, it was handed on to the Earl of Oxford and ultimately to John Lyly.[2] In November 1583, therefore, Hunnis found himself much dissatisfied with his financial posi-tion, and drew up the following memorial, probably for sub-mission to the Board of Green Cloth of the royal household : [3]

' Maye it please your honores, William Hunnys, M^r of the Children of hir highnes Chappell, most humble beseecheth to consider of these fewe lynes. First, hir Maiestie alloweth for the dyett of xij children of hir sayd Chappell daylie vi^d a peece by the daye, and xl^li by the yeare for theyre apparell and all other furneture.

' Agayne there is no ffee allowed neyther for the m^r of the sayd children nor for his ussher, and yet neuertheless is he constrayned, over and besydes the ussher still to kepe bothe a man servant to attend vpon them and lykewyse a woman seruant to wash and kepe them cleane.

' Also there is no allowance for the lodginge of the sayd chilldren, such tyme as they attend vppon the Courte, but the m^r to his greate charge is dryuen to hyer chambers both for himself, his usher chilldren and servantes.

' Also theare is no allowaunce for ryding jornies when occasion serueth the m^r to trauell or send into sundrie partes within this realme, to take vpp and bring such children as be thought meete to be trayned for the service of hir Maiestie.

' Also there is no allowance ne other consideracion for those children whose voyces be chaunged, whoe onelye do depend vpon the charge of the sayd m^r vntill such tyme as he may preferr the same with cloath-ing and other furniture, vnto his no smalle charge.

<hr>

[1] App. C, No. xlv.
[2] Cf. ch. xvii (Blackfriars).
[3] Wallace, i. 156; Stopes, *Hunnis*, 252; from *S. P. D. Eliz.* clxiii. 88.

'And although it may be obiècted that hir Maiesties allowaunce is no whitt less then hir Maiesties ffather of famous memorie therefore allowed : yet considering the pryces of thinges present to the tyme past and what annuities the m^r then hadd out of sundrie abbies within this realme, besydes sondrie giftes from the Kinge, and dyuers perticuler ffees besydes, for the better mayntenaunce of the sayd children and office : and besides also there hath ben withdrawne from the sayd chilldren synce hir Maiesties comming to the crowne xij^d by the daye which was allowed for theyr breakefastes as may apeare by the Treasorer of the Chamber his acompt for the tyme beinge, with other allowaunces incident to the office as appeareth by the auntyent acomptes in the sayd office which I heere omytt.

'The burden heerof hath from tyme to tyme so hindred the M^rs of the Children viz. Mr Bower, Mr Edwardes, my sellf and Mr Farrant : that notwithstanding some good helpes otherwyse some of them dyed in so poore case, and so deepelie indebted that they haue not left scarcelye wherewith to burye them.

'In tender consideracion whereof, might it please your honores that the sayde allowaunce of vj^d a daye apeece for the childrens dyet might be reserued in hir Maiesties coffers during the tyme of theyre attendaunce. And in liew thereof they to be allowed meate and drinke within this honorable householde for that I am not able vppon so small allowaunce eny longer to beare so heauie a burden. Or otherwyse to be consydred as shall seeme best vnto your honorable wysdomes.

'[*Endorsed*] 1583 November. The humble peticion of the M^r of the Children of hir highnes Chappell [*and in another hand*] To haue further allowances for the finding of the children for causes within mentioned.'

The actual request made by Hunnis seems a modest one. He seems to have thought that for his boys to have the run of their teeth at the tables of Whitehall would be a better bargain than the board-wages of 6*d.* a day. Doubtless he knew their appetites. I do not think that the Green Cloth met his views, for in the next reign the 6*d.* was still being paid and was raised to 10*d.* for the benefit of Nathaniel Giles.[1] Possibly Hunnis did get back the £16 a year for breakfasts, which seems to be the fee described by him as 1*s.* a day, although that in fact works out to £18 5*s.* a year, and the £9 13*s.* 4*d.* for largess, if that also had been withdrawn, since these are included in fee lists for 1593 and 1598.[2] The 'perticuler ffees' to which he refers are presumably the allowances occasionally paid by Henry for the maintenance of boys whose voices had changed. In any case Hunnis's personal grievance must have been fully met by liberal grants

---

[1] Cf. p. 50, which suggests that the boys occasionally ate in hall at festival times.

[2] The *Chamber Accounts* show no renewal of the payments.

of Crown lands which were made him in 1585.[1] It will be
observed that he says nothing of any profits derived by him
from the dramatic activities of the Children ; whether in
the form of rewards at Court or in that of admission fees
to public performances. Plays were no part of the official
functions of the Chapel, although it is consistent with the
general policy of the reign towards the London stage to suppose
that Elizabeth and her economical ministers were well enough
content that the deficiencies of her Chapel maintenance should
be eked out, and her Christmas ' solace ' rendered possible,
out of the profits of public exercise. So far, however, as the
Chapel was concerned, this convenient arrangement was,
for the time, nearly at an end. The facts with regard to the
boy companies during 1584 are somewhat complicated.
The Treasurer of the Chamber paid the Master of the Chapel
Children, without specifying his name, for plays on 6 January
and 2 February 1584. He also paid John Lyly for plays by
the Earl of Oxford's ' servants ' on 1 January and 3 March
1584, and Henry Evans for a play by the Earl of Oxford's
' children ' on 27 December 1584. Were this all, one would
naturally assume that Oxford had brought to Court the
' lads ' who appeared under his name at Norwich in 1580,
and that these formed a company, quite distinct from the
Chapel, of which the Earl entrusted the management either
jointly or successively to Lyly and Evans. Lyly, of course,
is known to have been at one time in the Earl's service.[2]
One would then be left to speculate as to which company
played at the Blackfriars during 1584 and where the other
played. But the real puzzle begins when it is realized that
in the same year 1584 two of Lyly's plays, *Campaspe* and
Sapho and Phao, were for the first time printed, that these
have prologues ' at the Blackfriars ', that their title-pages
indicate their performance at Court, not by Oxford's company, but by the Chapel and the Paul's boys, of which latter
the Treasurer of the Chamber makes no mention, and that
the title-pages of the two issues of *Campaspe* further specify,
in the one case Twelfth Night, and in the other, which is
apparently corrected, New Year's Day, as the precise date of
performance, while that of *Sapho and Phao* similarly specifies
Shrove Tuesday. But New Year's Day and Shrove Tuesday
of 1584 are the days which the Treasurer of the Chamber
assigns not to the Chapel, but to Oxford's company ; and
even if you accept Professor Feuillerat's rather far-fetched
assumption that the days referred to in the title-pages were

---

[1] Cf. ch. xxiii (Hunnis).   [2] Cf. ch. xiii (Oxford's), ch. xxiii (Lyly).

not necessarily those falling in the year of issue, you will not find a New Year's Day, or for the matter of that a Twelfth Night, since the opening of the Blackfriars, which, if a play-day at all, is not occupied either by some Chapel or Paul's play of which the name is known, or by some other company altogether.[1] The conjecture seems inevitable that, when he found himself in financial straits and with the rivalry of the Queen's men to face in 1583, Hunnis came to an arrangement with the Paul's boys, who had recently lost Sebastian Westcott, on the one hand, and with the Earl of Oxford and his agents Lyly and Evans on the other, and put the Blackfriars at the disposal of a combination of boys from all three companies, who appeared indifferently at Court under the name of the Master or that of the Earl. In the course of 1584 Sir William More resumed possession of the Blackfriars. Henry Evans must have made some temporary arrangement to enable the company to appear at Court during the winter of 1584–5.[2] But for a year or two thereafter there were no boys acting in London until in 1586 an arrangement with Thomas Giles, Westcott's successor at St. Paul's, afforded a new opportunity for Lyly's pen.[3]

The Chapel had contributed pretty continuously to Court drama for nearly a century. They now drop out of its story for about seventeen years.[4] In addition to the two plays of Lyly, one other of their recent pieces, Peele's *Arraignment of Paris*, was printed in 1584. Two former Children, Henry Eveseed and John Bull, afterwards well known as a musician, became Gentlemen on 30 November 1585 and in January 1586 respectively.[5] Absence from Court did not entail an absolute cessation of dramatic activities. Performances by the Children are recorded at Ipswich and Norwich in 1586–7 and at Leicester before Michaelmas in 1591. There is, however, little to bear out the suggestion that the Chapel

---

[1] Feuillerat, *Eliz.* 470. *Sapho and Phao* might, however, have been the unnamed Chapel play of Shrove Tuesday (27 Feb.) 1582.

[2] Perhaps Lyly was still associated with him. F. S. Boas (*M. L. R.* vi. 92) records payments in connexion with a visit by Leicester to Christ Church, Oxford, to Mr. Lyly and his man for the loan of apparel, as well as one of £5 to one Tipslowe ' for the Revels ' (January 1585).

[3] Cf. *supra* (Paul's).

[4] I have no means of dating ' The order of the show to be done at the Turret, entring into the parke at Grenewich, the musick being within the turrett ', which is preserved in *Egerton MS.* 2877, f. 182, as ' acted before Q. Elizabeth '. A speech of forty lines beginning ' He Jove himselfe, that guides the golden sphaere ', was delivered by ' one of the biggest children of her Ma^tes Chappell ' as Goodwill, and was followed by a song beginning ' Ye Helicon muses '.

[5] Rimbault, 4. A note of Anthony Wood's (cf. *D. N. B.*) suggests that Bull joined the Chapel about 1572.

L 8-3417

furnished the boys who played at Croydon, probably in
the archbishop's palace, during the summers of 1592 and
1593, other than the fact that the author of the play produced
in 1593, *Summer's Last Will and Testament*, was Thomas
Nashe, who was also part author with Marlowe of *Dido*, one
of two plays printed as Chapel plays in 1594. The extant
text of the other play, *The Wars of Cyrus*, seems to be datable
between 1587 and 1594. Hunnis died on 6 June 1597, and on
9 June 1597 Nathaniel Giles, ' being before extraordinary ',
was sworn as a regular Gentleman of the Chapel and Master
of the Children. Giles, like Farrant, came ' from Winsore '.
Born about 1559, he was educated at Magdalen College,
Oxford, and was appointed Clerk in St. George's Chapel,
Windsor, and Master of the Children on 1 October 1595. He
earned a considerable reputation as a musician, and died
in possession of both Masterships at the age of seventy-five on
24 January 1634.[1] His patent of appointment to the Chapel
Royal is dated 14 July and his commission 15 July 1597.[2]
They closely follow in terms those granted to Hunnis.[3]

Three years later the theatrical enterprise which had been
dropped in 1584 was renewed by Giles, in co-operation with
Henry Evans, who had been associated with its final stages.
The locality chosen was again the Blackfriars, in the building
reconstructed by James Burbadge in 1596, and then inhibited,
on a petition of the inhabitants, from use as a public play-
house. Of this, being ' then or late in the tenure or occupacion
of ' Henry Evans, Richard Burbadge gave him on 2 September
1600 a lease for twenty-one years from the following Michael-

---

[1] Ashmole, *Antiquities of Berks* (ed. 1723), iii. 172, from tombstone at
St. George's, Windsor. The inscription gives him 49 years as ·Master
at Windsor, in error for 39. A second stone described as also his by
Ashmole is clearly his wife's.

[2] Wallace, ii. 59, prints both from the Privy Seals of 2 and 3 July in
the R. O. The appointment is enrolled in *Patent Rolls, 39 Eliz.* p. 12,
and the commission in *Patent Rolls, 39 Eliz.* p. 9, m. 7 *dorso.* The appointment is for life, the commission not so specified, and therefore during
pleasure only.

[3] The operative words of the appointment are ' pro nobis heredibus
et successoribus nostris damus et concedimus dilecto seruienti nostro
Nathanieli Giles officium Magistri puerorum Capellae nostrae Regiae . . .
habendum . . . durante vita sua naturali Damus etiam . . . praefato
Nathanieli Giles vada siue feoda quadraginta librarum sterling percipienda
annuatim . . . pro eruditione duodecem puerorum eiusdem Capellae nostrae
ac pro eorum conveniente exhibitione vestiturae et lectuarii . . . vnacum
omnibus et omnimodis aliis vadis feodis proficubus iurisdiccionibus auctho-
ritate priuilegiis commoditatibus regardis et aduantagiis quibuscunque
eodem officio quoquo modo debitis . . . ac . . . praedicto Nathanieli Giles
locum siue officium illud vnius generosorum nostrorum dictae Capellae
nostrae Regiae . . . vnacum feodo seu annuali redditu triginta librarum . . .

mas at a rent of £40.[1] According to Burbadge's own account
of the matter, Evans 'intended then presentlye to erect or
sett vp a companye of boyes . . . in the same ', and knowing
that the payment of the rent depended upon the possibility
of maintaining a company ' to playe playes and interludes
in the said Playhowse in such sort as before tyme had bene
there vsed ', he thought it desirable to take collateral security
in the form of a bond for £400 from Evans and his son-in-law
Alexander Hawkins.[2] Long after, the Blackfriars *Sharers
Papers* of 1635 describe the lease as being to ' one Evans
that first sett vp the boyes commonly called the Queenes
Majesties Children of the Chapell '.[3] I find nothing in this
language to bear out the contention of Professor Wallace
that Evans's occupation of the Blackfriars extended back
long before the date of his lease, and that, as already suggested
by Mr. Fleay, the Chapel plays began again, not in 1600, but
in 1597.[4] Burbadge speaks clearly of the setting up of the
company as still an intention when the lease was drawn,
and the reference to earlier plays in the house may either be
to some use of it unknown to us between 1596 and 1600,
or perhaps more probably to the performances by Evans
and others before the time of James Burbadge's reconstruction. Mr. Fleay's suggestion rested, so far as I can judge,
upon the evidence for the existence of Jonson's *Case is Altered*
as early as January 1599 and its publication as ' acted by
the children of the Blacke-friers '. But this publication was
not until 1609 and represents a revision made not long before
that date ; and as will be seen the company did not use the
name Children of the Blackfriars until about 1606. There is
no reason to suppose that they were the original producers
of the play. A confirmatory indication for 1600 as the date
of the revival may be found in the appearance of the Chapel
at Court, for the first time since 1584, on 6 January and
22 February 1601. On both occasions Nathaniel Giles was
payee. The performance of 6 January, described by the
Treasurer of the Chamber as ' a showe with musycke and
speciall songes ' was probably Jonson's *Cynthia's Revels*,

---

[1] *E. v. K.* 211 ; *K. v. P.* 224, 230, 233 (misdated 44 Eliz. for 42 Eliz.),
239. These are only short recitals in the lawsuits. Apparently the
fragmentary descriptions of the theatre in Wallace, ii. 39, 40, 41, 43, 49,
are from a fuller Latin text of the terms of the lease, possibly recited in
a common-law suit, which he has not printed in full.

[2] *K. v. P.* 230, 234.　　　　　　　　[3] Halliwell-Phillipps, i. 317.

[4] Fleay, 124, 153 ; Wallace, ii. 56 ; cf. *M. L. R.* iv. 156. An initial
date for the enterprise in 1600 fits in exactly with the seven years during
which there had been plays at the house where *K. B. P.* was produced
and the ten years' training of Keysar's company up to 1610 (cf. p. 57).

which that description well fits ; that of 22 February may have been the anonymous *Contention between Liberality and Prodigality*. Both of these were published in 1601. Jonson has preserved for us in his Folio of 1616 the list of the principal actors of *Cynthia's Revels*, who were ' Nat. Field, Sal. Pavy, Tho. Day, Ioh. Underwood, Rob. Baxter and Ioh. Frost '. The induction of the play is spoken by ' Iacke ' and two other of the Children, of whom one, impersonating a spectator, complains that ' the vmbrae, or ghosts of some three or foure playes, departed a dozen yeeres since, haue bin seene walking on your stage heere '. *Liberality and Prodigality* may be one of the old-fashioned plays here scoffed at, but it is probable that Jonson also had in mind Lyly's *Love's Metamorphosis*, which was published in 1601 as ' first playd by the Children of Paules, and now by the Children of the Chappell ', and there may have been other revivals of the same kind. The company was included in the Lenten prohibition of 11 March 1601. Later in the year they produced Jonson's *Poetaster*, containing raillery of the common stages, which stimulated a reply in Dekker's *Satiromastix*, and which, together with their growing popularity, sufficiently explains the reference to the ' aerie of children, little eyases ' in *Hamlet*.[1] The *Poetaster* was published in 1602 and the actor-list of the Folio of 1616 contains the names of ' Nat. Field, Sal Pavy, Tho. Day, Ioh. Underwood, Wil. Ostler and Tho. Marton '. The full name of Pavy, who died after acting for three years, is given as Salathiel in the epigram written to his memory by Jonson ; it appears as Salmon in a document which adds considerably to our knowledge both of the original constitution of the company and of the lines on which it was managed. This is a complaint to the Star Chamber by one Henry Clifton, Esq., of Toftrees, Norfolk, against a serious abuse of the powers of impressment entrusted under the royal commission to Nathaniel Giles.[2] Clifton alleged that Giles, in confederacy with Evans, one James Robinson and others, had set up a play-house for their own profit in the Blackfriars, and under colour of the commission had taken boys, not for the royal service in the Chapel Royal, but employment in acting interludes. He specified as so taken, ' John Chappell, a gramer schole scholler of one Mr. Spykes schole neere Criple-gate, London ; John Motteram, a gramer scholler in the free schole at Westmi[n]ster ; Nathan ffield, a scholler of a gramer

---

[1] Cf. ch. xi.

[2] Fleay, 127. Burn, 152, notes from *Bodl. Tanner MS.* 300 that among the misdemeanours punished in the Star Chamber was ' Taking up a gentle-man's son to be a stage player '.

schole in London, kepte by one Mr. Monkaster; Alvery Trussell, an apprentice to one Thomas Gyles; one Phillipp Pykman and Thomas Grymes, apprentices to Richard and Georg Chambers; Salmon Pavey, apprentice to one Peerce'. These were all children 'noe way able or fitt for singing, nor by anie the sayd confederates endevoured to be taught to singe'. Finally they had made an attempt upon Clifton's own son Thomas, a boy of thirteen, who had been seized by Robinson in Christ Church cloister on or about 13 December 1600, as he went from Clifton's house in Great St. Bartholo-mew's to the grammar school at Christ Church, and carried off to the play-house 'to exercyse the base trade of a mercynary enterlude player, to his vtter losse of tyme, ruyne and disparag-ment'. Clifton went to the Blackfriars, where his son was 'amongste a companie of lewde and dissolute mercenary players', and made a protest; but Giles, Robinson, and Evans replied that 'yf the Queene would not beare them furth in that accion, she should gett another to execute her comission for them', that 'they had aucthoritie sufficient soe to take any noble mans sonne in this land', and that 'were yt not for the benefitt they made by the sayd play howse, whoe would, should serve the Chappell with children for them'. Then they committed Thomas Clifton to the charge of Evans in his father's presence, with a threat of a whipping if he was not obedient, and 'did then and there deliuer vnto his sayd sonne, in moste scornefull disdaynfull and dispightfull manner, a scrolle of paper, conteyning parte of one of theire sayd playes or enterludes, and him, the sayd Thomas Clifton, comaunded to learne the same by harte'. Clifton appealed to Sir John Fortescue and got a warrant from him for the boy's release after a day and a night's durance. It was not, however, until a year later, on 15 Decem-ber 1601, that he made his complaint.[1] During the following Christmas Giles brought the boys to Court on 6 and 10 January and 14 February 1602, and then with the hearing of the case in the Star Chamber during Hilary Term troubles began for the syndicate. Evans was censured 'for his vnorderlie

---

[1] Wallace, ii. 84, gives the endorsed date omitted by Greenstreet and Fleay, as 'Marti decimo quinto Decembris Anno xliiij Elizabeth Regine'; the date set down for trial is indicated as 'p Octab Hillar'. This agrees with the time indication of the offence in the complaint itself as 'about one yere last past, and since your maiesties last free and generall pardon'. The pardon referred to must be that of 1597-8 (*39 Eliz.* c. 28; cf. *R. O. Statutes*, iv. 952). There was another passed by the Parliament of 1601 (*43 Eliz.* c. 19; cf. *Statutes*, iv. 1010) for all offences prior to 7 Aug. 1601, but presumably this was not yet law when the complaint was drawn. The Parliament sat to 19 December. Clifton, however, was only just in time.

carriage and behauiour in takinge vp of gentlemens childeren against theire wills and to ymploy them for players and for other misdemeanors ', and it was decreed that all assurances made to him concerning the play-house or plays should be void and should be delivered up to be cancelled.[1] Evans, however, had apparently prepared himself against this contingency by assigning his lease to his son-in-law Alexander Hawkins on 21 October 1601. This at least is one explanation of a somewhat obscure transaction. According to Evans himself, the assignment was to protect Hawkins from any risk upon the bond given to Burbadge. On the other hand, there had already been negotiations for the sale of a half interest in the undertaking to three new partners, Edward Kirkham, William Rastall, and Thomas Kendall, and it was claimed later by Kirkham that the assignment to Hawkins had been in trust to reassign a moiety to these three, in return for a contribution of capital variously stated at from £300 to £600. No such reassignment was, however, carried out.[2] But although the lease from Burbadge was certainly not cancelled as a result of the Star Chamber decree, it probably did seem prudent that the original managers of the theatre should remain in the background for a time. Nothing more is heard of James Robinson, while the partnership between Evans and Hawkins on the one side and Kirkham, Rastall, and Kendall on the other was brought into operation under articles dated on 20 April 1602. For the observance of these Evans and Hawkins gave a bond of £200.[3] Kirkham, Rastall, and Kendall in turn gave Evans a bond of £50 as security

[1] *K. v. P.* 248. The date is recited as ' in or about the three and ffortieth yeare ' of Elizabeth, i.e. 1600-1, which is not exact. The reference can hardly be to any other than the Clifton affair. No Chancery documents in the case, other than the complaint, are known. It may be presumed that censure fell on Giles and Robinson, as well as Evans, but they were not concerned in *K. v. P.* Evans, of course, was technically acting as deputy to Giles under his commission, and Wallace, ii. 71, is not justified in citing the case as evidence that ' These powers to Giles were supplemented by official concessions to Henry Evans that enabled him to rent the Blackfriars theatre and train the Queen's Children of the Chapel there, with remunerative privileges '.

[2] *K. v. P.* 224, 230, 236, 242, 244, 248, 250.

[3] *E. v. K.* 211, 216 ; *K. v. P.* 237, 240, 245. These are recitals. Wallace, ii. 91, says that he has found two copies of the original bond, but the text he prints adds nothing to *K. v. P.* 240. Clearly he is wrong in describing it as ' containing the Articles of Agreement '. That was a much more detailed document, which Evans unfortunately thought so ' long and tedious ' that he did not insert it at large in his Answer in *K. v. P.* It was doubtless analogous to the King's Revels Articles of 1608 (cf. *infra*). It provided for the rights of the partners to the use of rooms (*E. v. K.* 211) and presumably for the division of profits (*K. v. P.* 237).

for a weekly payment of 8s., 'because after the said agreements made, the complainant [Kirkham] and his said
parteners would at their directions haue the dieting and ordering of the boyes vsed about the plaies there, which before the
said complainant had, and for the which he had weekely
before that disbursed and allowed great sommes of monie'.[1]

Of the new managers, Rastall was a merchant and Kendall
a haberdasher, both of London.[2] Kirkham has generally been
assumed to be the Yeoman of the Revels, but of this there
is not, so far as I know, any definite proof. The association
did not prove an harmonious one. According to Evans,
Kirkham and his fellows made false information against him
to the Lord Chamberlain, as a result of which he was
'comaunded by his Lordship to avoyd and leave the same ',
had to quit the country, and lost nearly £300 by the charge
he was put to and the negligence of Hawkins in looking after
his profits.[3] This seems to have been in May 1602. Meanwhile the performances continued. The company did not
appear at Court during the winter of 1602-3, but *Sir Giles
Goosecap* and possibly Chapman's *Gentleman Usher* were
produced by them before the end of Elizabeth's reign ; and
on 18 September 1602 a visit was paid to the theatre by
Philipp Julius, Duke of Stettin-Pomerania, of which the
following account is preserved in the journal of Frederic
Gerschow, a member of his suite : [4]

'Von dannen sind wir auf die Kinder-comoediam gangen, welche
im Argument iudiciret eine castam viduam, war eine historia einer
königlichen Wittwe aus Engellandt. Es hat aber mit dieser Kinder-
comoedia die Gelegenheit : die Königin hält viel junger Knaben, die
sich der Singekunst mit Ernst befleissigen müssen und auf allen
Instrumenten lernen, auch dabenebenst studieren. Diese Knaben

---

[1] *K. v. P.* 244. Wallace, ii. 102, adds the actual terms of the bond.
He takes Evans's explanation to mean that hitherto Evans had maintained
the boys and the plays out of official funds supplied through Kirkham
as Yeoman of the Revels, but that now Evans's name was to be kept out
of the business, and disbursements made by his partners, who were to
pay him 8s. a week as a kind of steward. I cannot suppose that Kirkham
had been the channel of any official subvention, and, on the whole, think
it probable that the second ' compl[t] ' in the extract from the pleading
is an error for ' def[t] '. This leaves it not wholly clear why Evans should
allege his relief from great weekly disbursements as a reason for receiving
8s. a week; but if we had the Articles of Agreement, the point would
probably be clear. Possibly Evans had in the past made the equivalent
of a weekly sum of 8s. out of board-wages passed on to him by Giles.

[2] Wallace, ii. 88.

[3] *E. v. K.* 213, 217, 220.

[4] G. von Bülow and W. Powell in *R. H. S. Trans.* vi. 26 ; Wallace,
ii. 105 ; with translations.

haben ihre besondere praeceptores in allen Künsten, insonderheit sehr gute musicos.

'Damit sie nun höfliche Sitten anwenden, ist ihnen aufgelegt, wöchentlich eine comoedia zu agiren, wozu ihnen denn die Königin ein sonderlich theatrum erbauet und mit köstlichen Kleidern zum Ueberfluss versorget hat. Wer solcher Action zusehen will, muss so gut als unserer Münze acht sundische Schillinge geben, und findet sich doch stets viel Volks auch viele ehrbare Frauens, weil nutze argumenta und viele schöne Lehren, als von andern berichtet, sollen tractiret werden ; alle bey Lichte agiret, welches ein gross Ansehen macht. Eine ganze Stunde vorher höret man eine köstliche musicam instrumentalem von Orgeln, Lauten, Pandoren, Mandoren, Geigen und Pfeiffen, wie denn damahlen ein Knabe cum voce tremula in einer Basgeigen so lieblich gesungen, dass wo es die Nonnen zu Mailand ihnen nicht vorgethan, wir seines Gleichen auf der Reise nicht gehöret hatten.'

This report of a foreigner must not be pressed as if it were precise evidence upon the business organization of the Blackfriars. Yet it forms the main basis of the theory propounded by Professor Wallace that Elizabeth personally financed the Chapel plays and personally directed the limitation of the number of adult companies allowed to perform in London, as part of a deliberate scheme of reform, which her ' definite notion of what the theatre should be ' had led her to plan— a theory which, I fear, makes his *Children of the Chapel at Blackfriars* misleading, in spite of its value as a review of the available evidence, old and new, about the company.[1] Professor Wallace supposes that Edward Kirkham, acting officially as Yeoman of the Revels, was Elizabeth's agent, and that, even before he became a partner in the syndicate, he dieted the boys and supplied them with the ' köstlichen Kleidern zum Ueberfluss ' mentioned by Gerschow, accounting for the expenditure either through the Revels Accounts or through some other unspecified accounts ' yet to be discovered '.[2] Certainly no such expenditure appeared in the Revels Accounts, and no other official account with which Kirkham was concerned is known. It may be pointed out that, if we took Gerschow's account as authoritative, we should have to suppose that Elizabeth provided the theatre building, which we know she did not, and I think it may be taken for granted that her payments for the Chapel were no more than those with which we are already quite familiar, namely the Master's fee of £40 ' pro exhibicione puerorum ', the board-wages of 6d. a day for each of twelve children,

---

[1] Wallace, ii. 126, summarizes his theory ; cf. my review in *M. L. R.* v. 224. [2] Wallace, ii. 99.

possibly the breakfast allowance of £16 a year and the largess of £9 13s. 4d. for high feasts, and the occasional rewards for actual performances. None of these, of course, passed through the Revels Office, and although this office may, as in the past, have helped to furnish the actual plays at Court, the cost of exercising in public remained a speculation of the Master and his backers, who had to look for recoupment and any possible profits to the sums received from spectators. If it is true, as Gerschow seems to say, that performances were only given on Saturdays, the high entrance charge of 1s. is fully explained. The lawsuits, of course, bear full evidence to the expenditure by the members of the syndicate upon the ' setting forward ' of plays.[1] Nor is there any ground for asserting, as Professor Wallace does, that there were two distinct sets of children, one lodged in or near the palace for chapel purposes proper, and the other kept at the Blackfriars for plays.[2] It is true that Clifton charged Giles with impressing boys who could not sing, but Gerschow's account proves that there were others at the Blackfriars who could sing well enough, and it would be absurd to suppose that there was one trained choir for the stage and another for divine service. Doubtless, however, the needs of the theatre made it necessary to employ, by agree-ment or impressment, a larger number of boys than the twelve borne on the official establishment.[3] And that boys whose voices had broken were retained in the theatrical company may be inferred from the report about 1602 that the Dowager Countess of Leicester had married ' one of the playing boyes of the chappell '.[4] I cannot, finally, agree with Professor Wallace in assuming that the play attended by Elizabeth at the Blackfriars on 29 December 1601 was necessarily a public one at the theatre ; much less that it was ' only one in a series of such attendances '. She had dined with Lord Hunsdon at his house in the Blackfriars. The play may have been in his great chamber, or he may have borrowed the theatre next door for private use on an off-day. And the actors may even more probably have been his own company than the Chapel boys.[5]

The appointment of a new Lord Chamberlain by James I seems to have enabled Evans to return to England. He found

[1] E. v. K. 217 ; K. v. P. 224, 227, 229, 231, 236, 248.
[2] Wallace, ii. 73.
[3] Wallace, ii. 75, shows that the Blackfriars repertory would require twenty or twenty-five actors.   [4] Gawdy, 117.
[5] Wallace, ii. 95. Dudley Carleton wrote to John Chamberlain on 29 Dec. 1601 (S. P. D. Eliz. cclxxxii. 48), ' The Q: dined this day priuatly at my Ld Chamberlains ; I came euen now from the blackfriers where I saw her at the play with all her candidae auditrices ' ; cf. M. L. R. ii. 12.

theatrical affairs in a bad way, owing to the plague of 1603, and 'speach and treatie' arose between him and Burbadge about a possible surrender of his lease.[1] By December, however, things looked brighter. Evans did some repairs to the Blackfriars, and the enterprise continued.[2] Like the adult companies, the partners secured direct royal protection under the following patent of 4 February 1604:[3]

> De licencia speciali pro Eduardo Kirkham et aliis pro le Revell domine Regine.
>
> Iames by the grace of God &c. To all Mayors Shiriffes Iustices of Peace Baliffes Constables and to all other our officers mynisters and lovinge Subiectes to whome theis presentes shall come, greeting. Whereas the Queene our deerest wief hath for her pleasure and recreaćon when she shall thinke it fit to have any playes or shewes appoynted her servauntes Edward Kirkham Alexander Hawkyns Thomas Kendall and Robert Payne to provyde and bring vppe a convenient number of Children, whoe shalbe called children of her Revelles, knowe ye that we have appointed and authorized and by theis presentes doe authorize and appoynte the said Edward Kirkham Alexander Hawkins Thomas Kendall and Robert Payne from tyme to tyme to provide keepe and bring vppe a convenient number of Children, and them to practize and exercise in the quality of playinge by the name of Children of the Revells to the Queene within the Blackfryers in our Cytie of London, or in any other convenient place where they shall thinke fit for that purpose. Wherefore we will and commaunde [you] and everie of you to whome it shall appertayne to permytt her said Seruauntes to keepe a convenient nomber of Children by the name of Children of her Revells and them to exercise in the quality of playing according to her pleasure. Provided allwaies that noe such Playes or Shewes shalbee presented before the said Queene our wief by the said Children or by them any where publiquelie acted but by the approbacion and allowaunce of Samuell Danyell, whome her pleasure is to appoynt for that purpose. And theis our lettres Patentes shalbe your sufficient warraunte in this behalfe. In witnes whereof &c., witnes our self at Westminster the fourth day of February.
>
> per breve de priuato sigillo &c.

Apparently it was still thought better to keep the name of Evans out of the patent, and he was represented by Hawkins; of the nature of Payne's connexion with the company I know

[1] K. v. P. 235.

[2] Wallace, ii. 89, says that Evans paid £11 0s. 2d. for repairs on 8 Dec. 1603.

[3] M. S. C. i. 267, from Patent Roll, 1 Jac. I, pt. 8. Collier, i. 340, and Hazlitt, E. D. S. 40, print the signet bill, the former dating it 30 Jan. and the latter 31 Jan., and misdescribe it as a privy seal. Collier, N. F. 48, printed a forged letter from Daniel to Sir T. Egerton (cf. Ingleby, 244, 247) intended to suggest that Drayton, and perhaps also Shakespeare, had coveted his post.

nothing. The adoption of the name of Children of the Queen's Revels should perhaps be taken as indicating that, as the boy-actors grew older, the original connexion with the Chapel became looser. The use of Giles's commission as a method of obtaining recruits was probably abandoned, and there is no evidence that he had any further personal association with the theatre.[1] The commission itself was, however, renewed on 13 September 1604, with a new provision for the further education of boys whose voices had changed ;[2] and in December Giles was successful in getting the board-wages allowed for his charges raised from 6d. to 10d. a day.[3]

The Revels children started gaily on the new phase of their career, and the *Hamlet* allusion is echoed in Middleton's advice to a gallant, ' if his humour so serve him, to call in at the Blackfriars, where he should see a nest of boys able to ravish a man '.[4] They were at Court on 21 February 1604 and on 1 and 3 January 1605. Their payees were Kirkham for the first year and Evans and Daniel for the second. Evidently Daniel was taking a more active part in the management than that of a mere licenser. Their play of 1 January 1605 was Chapman's *All Fools* (1605), and to 1603–5 may also be assigned his *Monsieur d'Olive* (1606), and possibly his *Bussy d'Ambois* (1607), and Day's *Law Tricks* (1608). I venture to conjecture that the boys' companies were much more under the influence of their poets than were their adult rivals ; it is noteworthy that plays written for them got published much more rapidly than the King's or Prince's men ever permitted.[5] And it is known that one poet, who now began for the first time to work for the Blackfriars, acquired a financial interest in the undertaking. This was John Marston, to whom Evans parted, at an unspecified date, with a third of the moiety which the arrangement of 1602 had left on his hands.[6] Marston's earliest contributions were probably *The Malcontent* (1604) and *The Dutch Courtesan* (1605). From

---

[1] Wallace, ii. 80, mentions a case of the employment of a boy at the Blackfriars during James's reign under a contract with his mother.

[2] *M. S. C.* i. 359. On 7 Oct. 1605 the Wardrobe provided holland for shirts for the 12 children and ' for James Cutler, a Chappell boy gone off ' (Lafontaine, 46, from *L. C.* 804).

[3] Rimbault, 60 ; Stowe, *Annales* (ed. Howes), 1037. An order of 17 July 1604 (*H. O.* 301) continued the allowance of an increase of meat at festival times which the children had presumably enjoyed under Elizabeth.

[4] Middleton, *Father Hubburd's Tales* (*Works*, viii. 64, 77). A reference in the same book to an ant as ' this small actor in less than decimo sexto ' recalls the jest in the Induction to the *Malcontent* at the boys who played *Jeronimo* ' in decimo sexto '.

[5] Cf. ch. xi.　　　　　　　　　　　　　[6] *K. v. B.* 340.

the induction to the *Malcontent* we learn that it was appropriated by the King's men, in return for the performance by
the boys of a play on Jeronimo, perhaps the extant *1 Jeronimo*,
in which the King's claimed rights. Marston's satirical temper
did not, however, prove altogether an asset to the company;
and I fear that the deference of its directors to literary
suggestions was not compatible with that practical political
sense, which as a rule enabled the professional players to
escape conflicts with authority. The history of the next few
years is one of a series of indiscretions, which render it rather
surprising that the company should throughout have succeeded in maintaining its vitality, even with the help of constant reconstructions of management and changes of name.
The first trouble, the nature of which is unknown, appears
to have been caused by Marston's *Dutch Courtesan*. Then
came, ironically enough, the *Philotas* of the company's official
censor, Samuel Daniel. Then, in 1605, the serious affair
of *Eastward Ho!* for which Marston appears to have been
mainly responsible, although he saved himself by flight,
whereas his fellow authors, Jonson and Chapman, found themselves in prison and in imminent danger of losing their ears.[1]
I do not think that the scandal arose on the performance of the
play, but on its publication in the late autumn.[2] The company did not appear at Court during the winter of 1605–6,
but the ingenious Kirkham seems to have succeeded in transferring one of its new plays, Marston's *Fawn*, and possibly
also *Bussy D'Ambois*, to Paul's, and appeared triumphantly
before the Treasurer of the Chamber's paymaster the following spring as ' one of the Masters of the Children of Pawles '.
Meanwhile the Blackfriars company went on acting, but it
is to be inferred from the title-pages of its next group of plays,
Marston's *Sophonisba* (1606), Sharpham's *The Fleir* (1607),
and Day's *Isle of Gulls* (1606), that its misdemeanour had cost
it the direct patronage of the Queen, and that it was now only
entitled to call itself, not Children of the Queen's Revels, but
Children of the Revels.[3] Possibly the change of name also

---

[1] Cf. ch. xxiii, s.v. plays named.

[2] Kirkham and Kendall were still associated in Aug. 1605, when apparel
and properties were obtained from them for the plays at James's visit to
Oxford (*M. S. C.* i. 247). There was a performance at the Blackfriars
as late as 16 June 1605 (Wallace, ii. 125), a date connected with a dispute
in settlement of which Kirkham's bond of £50 to Evans was exchanged
for a new one to Hawkins (*K. v. P.* 244).

[3] Cf. *M. L. R.* iv. 159. The t.p. of *Sophonisba* only specifies performance
' at the Blackfriars ' ; those of *The Fleir* and *The Isle of Gulls* ' by the
Children of the Revels at the Blackfriars '. Probably the ' Children of
the Revels ' of the t.p. of Day's *Law Tricks* (1608) is also the Blackfriars

indicates that thereafter, not Daniel, but the Master of the Revels, acted as its censor. Anne herself, by the way, must have felt the snub, for it was probably at the Blackfriars that, if the French ambassador may be trusted, she had attended representations ' to enjoy the laugh against her husband '.[1] The alias, whatever it connoted, proved but an ephemeral one. By February 1606 one of the plays just named, the *Isle of Gulls*, had given a new offence. Some of those responsible for it were thrown into Bridewell, and a fresh reconstruction became imperative.[2] It was probably at this date that one Robert Keysar, a London goldsmith, came into the business. Kirkham, like Evans before him, discreetly retired from active management, and the Children, with Keysar as ' interest with them ', became ' Masters themselves ', taking the risks and paying the syndicate for the use of the hall.[3] Kirkham claims that under this arrangement the moiety of profits in which he had rights amounted to £150 a year, as against £100 a year previously earned.[4] Shortly afterwards the dissociation of the Chapel from the Blackfriars was completed by a new commission issued to Giles on 7 November 1606, to which was added the following clause :

' Prouided alwayes and wee doe straightlie charge and commaunde that none of the saide Choristers or Children of the Chappell so to be taken by force of this commission shalbe vsed or imployed as Comedians or Stage players, or to exercise or acte any Stage playes Interludes Comedies or tragedies, for that it is not fitt or decent that such as shoulde singe the praises of God Allmightie shoulde be traynèd vpp or imployed in suche lascivious and prophane exercises.' [5]

It is presumably to this pronouncement that Flecknoe refers in 1664, when he speaks of the Chapel theatre being converted to the use of the Children of the Revels, on account of the growing precision of the people and the growing licentiousness

company. No theatre is named, but the play is too early for the King's Revels, who, moreover, do not seem to be described on other t.ps. as ' Children of the Revels ' pure and simple. I take it that these t.p. descriptions follow the designations of the companies in use when the plays were last on the stage before publication, rather than those in use at the times of first production.

[1] Cf. ch. x. [2] Cf. ch. xxiii, s.v. Day.

[3] Keysar was certainly associated with Kendall by the Christmas of 1606–7, when they supplied apparel and properties for the Westminster plays ; cf. Murray, ii. 169. [4] *K. v. P.* 249.

[5] *M. S. C.* i. 362, from *P. R. O., Patent Roll, 4 James I*, p. 18, *dorso*. Collier, i. 446, long ago noted the existence of a similar clause in a Caroline commission to Giles of 1626. It was probably the choristers who assisted in a quasi-dramatic performance on 16 July 1607, when James dined with the Merchant Taylors, and Giles received the freedom of the company in reward ; cf. ch. iv.

of plays.[1] It is, however, curious to observe that the abandoned titles of the company tended to linger on in actual use. Evans in 1612 speaks of the syndicate as ' the coparteners sharers, and Masters of the Queenes Maiesties Children of the Revells (for so yt was often called) ' in 1608;[2] while the name Children of the Chapel is used in the Stationers' Register entry of *Your Five Gallants* in 1608, at Maidstone in 1610, and even in such official documents as the Revels Accounts for 1604–5 and the Chamber Accounts for 1612–13.

Under Keysar the name was Children of the Blackfriars. For a couple of years the company succeeded in keeping clear of further disaster. But on 29 March 1608 the French ambassador, M. de la Boderie, reported that all the London theatres had been closed, and were now threatened by the King with a permanent inhibition on account of two plays which had given the greatest offence.[3] Against one of these, which dealt with the domestic affairs of the French king, he had himself lodged a protest, and his description leaves no doubt that this was one of the parts of Chapman's *Conspiracy and Tragedy of Byron*, which was published, without the offending scene, later in the year, as ' acted at the Black-Friars '. The other play was a personal attack upon James himself. 'Un jour ou deux devant ', says La Boderie, ' ilz avoient dépêché leur Roi, sa mine d'Escosse, et tous ses favorits d'une estrange sorte ; car aprés luy avoir fait dépiter le ciel sur le vol d'un oyseau, et faict battre un gentilhomme pour avoir rompu ses chiens, ils le dépeignoient ivre pour le moins une fois le jour.' This piece is not extant, but I have recently come across another allusion to it in a letter of 11 March 1608 to Lord Salisbury from Sir Thomas Lake, a clerk of the signet in attendance upon the King at Thetford.[4]

' His ma^tie was well pleased with that which your lo. advertiseth concerning the committing of the players y^t have offended in ye matters of France, and commanded me to signifye to your lo. that for ye others who have offended in ye matter of ye Mynes and other lewd words, which is ye children of ye blackfriars, That though he had signified his mynde to your lo. by my lo. of Mountgommery yet I should

[1] Cf. App. I.
[2] *E. v. K.* 221 ; *K. v. P.* 246. ' The Children of the Revells ' who appeared at Leicester on 21 Aug. 1608 (Kelly, 248) might have been these boys, but might also have been the King's Revels, if the King's Revels were still in existence under that name, which is very doubtful.
[3] Cf. ch. xxiii, s.v. Chapman.
[4] *S. P. D. Jac. I*, xxxi. 73. The mine was no doubt the silver mine discovered at Hilderston near Linlithgow in 1607, and worked as a royal enterprise with little success ; cf. R. W. Cochran-Patrick, *Early Records relating to Mining in Scotland* (1878), xxxvii. 116.

repeate it again, That his G. had vowed they should never play more, but should first begg their bred and he wold have his vow performed, And therefore my lo. chamberlain by himselfe or your ll. at the table should take order to dissolve them, and to punish the maker besides.'

Sir Thomas Lake appears to have been under the impression that two companies were concerned, and that the ' matters of France ' were not played by the Children of Blackfriars. If so, we must suppose that *Byron* was originally produced elsewhere, perhaps by the King's Revels, and transferred to the Blackfriars after ' reformation ' by the Council. M. de la Boderie, however, writes as if the same company were responsible for both plays, and perhaps it is on the whole more probable that Sir Thomas Lake misunderstood the situation. I feel very little doubt that the maker of the play on the mines was once more Marston, who was certainly summoned before the Privy Council and committed to Newgate, on some offence not specified in the extant record, on 8 June 1608.[1] And this was probably the end of his stormy connexion with the stage. He disappeared from the Blackfriars and from literary life, leaving *The Insatiate Countess* unfinished, and selling the share in the syndicate which he had acquired from Evans about 1603 to Robert Keysar for £100. Before making his purchase, Keysar, who tells us that he put a value of £600 on the whole of the enterprise, got an assurance, as he thought, from the King's men that they would not come to any arrangement with Henry Evans which would prejudice his interests.[2] This the King's men afterwards denied, and as a matter of fact the negotiations, tentatively opened as far back as 1603, between Evans and Burbadge for a surrender of the lease were now coming to a head, and its actual surrender took place about August 1608.[3] On the ninth of that month Burbadge executed fresh leases of the theatre to a new syndicate representing the King's men.[4] The circumstances leading up to Evans's part in this transaction became subsequently the subject of hostile criticism by Kirkham, who asserted that the lease, which Alexander Hawkins held in trust, had been stolen from his custody by Mrs. Evans, and that the surrender was effected with the fraudulent intention of excluding Kirkham from the profits to which he was entitled under the settlement of 1602.[5] According to Evans, however, Kirkham was at least implicitly

---

[1] Cf. ch. xxiii.
[3] *E. v. K.* 222 ; *K. v. P.* 225, 231, 235, 246.
[4] Cf. ch. xvii (Blackfriars).
[2] *K. v. B.* 342.
[5] *K. v. P.* 225, 249.

a consenting party, for it was he who, after the King's inhibition had brought the profits to an end, grew weary of the
undertaking and initiated measures for winding it up. On
or about 26 July 1608 he had had the ' apparells, properties
and goods ' of the syndicate appraised and an equitable
division made. When some of the boys were committed to
prison he had ' said he would deale no more with yt, " for ",
quoth he, " yt is a base thing ", or vsed wordes to such,
or very like effect '. And he had ' delivered up their commission, which he had vnder the greate seale aucthorising
them to plaie, and discharged divers of the partners and
poetts '. In view of this, Evans claimed that he was fully
justified in coming to terms with Burbadge.[1]

After all, the King's anger proved only a flash in the pan.
Perhaps the company travelled during the summer of 1608,
if they, and not the King's Revels, were ' the Children of the
Revells ' rewarded at Leicester on 21 August.[2] But by the
following Christmas they were in London, and with Keysar
as their payee gave three plays at Court, where they had not
put in an appearance since 1604–5. Two of these were on
1 and 4 January 1609. As they still bore the name of Children
of Blackfriars, they had presumably remained on sufferance
in their old theatre, which the King's men may not
have been in a hurry to occupy during a plague-stricken
period.[3] But when a new season opened in the autumn of
1609, new quarters became necessary. These they found at
Whitefriars, which had been vacated by the failure of the
short-lived King's Revels company, and it was as the Children
of Whitefriars that Keysar brought them to Court for no less
than five plays during the winter of 1609–10. He had now
enlisted a partner in Philip Rosseter, one of the lutenists of
the royal household, who carried out a scheme, with the
co-operation of the King's men, for buying off with a ' dead
rent ' the possible competition of the Paul's boys, who had
closed their doors about 1606, but might at any moment open

---

[1] *E. v. K.* 221 ; *K. v. P.* 245. In the earlier suit Evans says that the
royal prohibition was ' vpon some misdemeanors committed in or about
the plaies there, and specially vpon the defendants [Kirkham's] acts and
doings thereabout '. Unless Kirkham was more directly concerned in the
management during 1608 than appears probable, Evans must be reflecting
upon the whole series of misdemeanours since 1604.

[2] On 9 May John Browne, ' one of the playe boyes ', was buried at
St. Anne's.

[3] *K. v. B.* 347, gives the date of surrender in 1610 as ' about the tenth
of August last past '. Probably a year's sub-tenancy under the King's
men explains the discrepancy with the ' about August in the sixt year
of his Maiesties raigne ' of *K. v. P.* 235, and the confirmatory date of the
King's men's leases.

them again.[1] More than this, through the influence of Sir Thomas Monson, Rosseter was successful in obtaining a new patent, dated on 4 January 1610, by which the Children once more became entitled to call themselves Children of the Queen's Revels.[2] It ran as follows :

De concessione Roberto Daborne & aliis.

Iames by the grace of God &c, To all Maiors Sheriffes Iustices of peace Bayliffes Constables and to all other our Officers Ministers and loving Subiects to whome theis presentes shall come Greeting. Whereas the Quene our deerest wyfe hathe for hir pleasure, and recreacion, when shee shall thinke it fitt to haue any Playes or Shewes, appoynted hir servantes Robert Daborne, Phillippe Rosseter, Iohn Tarbock, Richard Iones, and Robert Browne to prouide and bring vpp a convenient nomber of Children whoe shalbe called Children of hir Revelles, knowe ye that wee haue appoynted and authorised, and by theis presentes do authorize and appoynte the said Robert Daborne, Phillipp Rosseter, Iohn Tarbuck, Richard Iones, and Robert Browne from tyme to tyme to provide keepe and bring vpp a convenient nomber of children, and them to practice and exercise in the quality of playing, by the name of Children of the Revells to the Queene, within the white ffryers in the Suburbs of our Citty of London, or in any other convenyent place where they shall thinke fitt for that purpose. Wherfore wee will and commaund you and euery of you to whome it shall appertayne to permitt her said seruants to keepe a conuenient nomber of Children by the name of the Children of hir Revells, and them to exercise in the qualitye of playing according to hir pleasure, And theis our lettres patentes shalbe your sufficient warrant in this behaulfe. Wittnes our self at Westminster, the ffourth daye of Ianuary.

per breve de priuato sigillo.

Of the new syndicate Browne and Jones were old professional actors who had belonged to the Admiral's men a quarter of a century before, and had since been prominent, Brown in particular, as organizers of English companies for travel in Germany. Daborne was or became a playwright. Of Tarbock I know nothing ; he may have been a nominee of Keysar,

---

[1] Cf. ch. *supra* (Paul's). *K. v. B.* 355 tells us that Rosseter was in partnership with Keysar.

[2] *M. S. C.* i. 271, from *P. R.*, 7 *Jac. I*, p. 13. Ingleby, 254, gave the material part in discussing a forged draft by Collier (*N. F.* 41), in which the names of the patentees are given as ' Robert Daiborne, William Shakespeare, Nathaniel Field and Edward Kirkham '. A genuine note of the patent is in Sir Thomas Egerton's note-book (*N. F.* 40). Ingleby adds that the signet office records (cf. Phillimore, 103) show that the warrant was obtained in Dec. 1609 by the influence of Monson. He was Anne's household Chancellor and to him Rosseter and Campion dedicated their *Book of Airs* (1601) and Campion his *Third Book of Airs* (1617).

whose own name, perhaps for reasons of diplomacy, does not
appear in the patent. He may, of course, have retired, but
a lawsuit which he brought in 1610 suggests that his connexion
with the company was not altogether broken. The Whitefriars had not the tradition of the Blackfriars, and Keysar
was aggrieved at the surrender of the Blackfriars lease
by Evans over his head. On 8 February 1610 he laid a bill
in the Court of Requests against the housekeepers of the
King's men, claiming a share in their profits since the date of
surrender, which he estimated at £1,500, on the strength of
the one-sixth interest in the lease assigned by Evans to
Marston and by Marston to him.[1] He asserted that he had
kept boys two years in the hope of playing ' vpon the ceasing
of the generall sicknes ', and had spent £500 on that and on
making provision in the house, and had now, at a loss of £1,000,
had to disperse ' a companye of the moste exparte and skilful
actors within the realme of England to the number of eighteane
or twentye persons all or moste of them trayned vp in that
service, in the raigne of the late Queene Elizabeth for ten
yeares togeather and afterwardes preferred into her Maiesties
service to be the Chilldren of her Revells '.[2] Burbadge and
his fellows denied that they had made £1,500, or that they
had attempted to defraud Keysar either about the surrender
of the lease or, as he also alleged, the ' dead rent ' to Paul's,
and they pointed out that his losses were really due to the
plague. He could recover his share of the theatrical stock from
Evans. Evans had had no legal right to assign his interest
under the lease. As only the pleadings in the case and not the
depositions or the order of the court are extant, we do not
know what Evans, who was to be a witness, had to say.[3]
The fact that one of the new Blackfriars leases of 1608 was
to a Thomas Evans leaves the transaction between Henry
Evans and Burbadge not altogether free from a suspicion
of bad faith. Kirkham also found that he had been either
hasty or outwitted in 1608, and as the deaths of Rastall and
Kendall in that year had left him the sole claimant to any
interest under the arrangement of 1602, he had recourse to
litigation. In the course of 1611 and 1612 he brought a
' multiplicitie of suites ' against Evans and Hawkins, and
was finally non-suited in the King's Bench.[4] Then, in May
1612, Evans in his turn brought a Chancery action against

---

[1] *K. v. B.* 343.   [2] *K. v. B.* 343, 350.
[3] Evans, Mrs. Evans, Field, Underwood, Ostler, Baxstead, Rosseter,
Marston, and Mrs. Hawkins were to be examined for the King's men.

[4] *E. v. K.* 213. I presume that some of these are amongst the ' twelve
additional suits ' which Wallace, ii. 36, claims to have found.

Kirkham, in the hope of getting his bond of 1602 cancelled, and thus securing himself against any further persecution for petty breaches of the articles of agreement. The result of this is unknown, but in the course of it many of the incidents of 1600–8 were brought into question, and Kirkham claimed that not merely had Evans shut him out in 1604 from certain rooms in the Blackfriars which he was entitled to use, but that by the surrender of the lease in 1608 he had lost profits which he estimated at £60 a year.[1] Finally in July 1612 Kirkham brought a Chancery action against Evans, Burbadge, and John Heminges, and also against the widow of Alexander Hawkins and Edward Painton, to whom she was now married, for reinstatement in his moiety of the lease. In this suit much of the same ground was again traversed, but the Court refused to grant him any relief.

It is not altogether easy to disentangle the plays produced at the Blackfriars under Keysar from those produced immediately afterwards at the Whitefriars. The only title-page which definitely names the Children of the Blackfriars is that of Jonson's *The Case is Altered* (1609). But Chapman's *Byron* (1608) and *May Day* (1611) and Middleton's *Your Five Gallants* (n.d. ?1608) also claim to have been acted at the Blackfriars. The Q₁ of Middleton's *A Trick to Catch the Old One* (1608) assigns it to Paul's; the Q₂ both to Paul's and Blackfriars, with an indication of a Court performance on New Year's Day, which can only be that of 1 January 1609. This play, therefore, must have been taken over from Paul's, when that house closed in 1606 or 1607. As Middleton is not generally found writing for Blackfriars, *Your Five Gallants* may have been acquired in the same way. It is also extremely likely that Chapman's *Bussy d'Ambois* passed from Paul's to Blackfriars on its way to the King's men. No name of company or theatre is attached to Beaumont and Fletcher's *Knight of the Burning Pestle* (1613) or to *The Faithful Shepherdess* (c. 1609). But the *K. B. P.* was published with an epistle to Keysar as its preserver and can be securely dated in 1607–8 ; it refers to the house in which it was played as having been open for seven years, which just fits the Blackfriars. *The Faithful Shepherdess* is of 1608–9 and a boys' play ; the commendatory verses by Field, Jonson, and Chapman justify an attribution to the company with which they had to do. Chapman's *The Widow's Tears* (1612) had been staged both at Blackfriars and at Whitefriars before publication, and was probably therefore produced shortly before the

---

[1] *E. v. K.* 218. In *K. v. P.* 225, he put the total annual profits during 1608–12 at £160.

company moved house. The greatest difficulty is Jonson's *Epicoene* (S. R. 20 September 1610). No edition is known to be extant earlier than the Folio of 1616, in which Jonson ascribed the production to ' 1609 ' and to the Children of the Revels. According to the system of dating ordinarily adopted by Jonson in this Folio, ' 1609 ' should mean 1609 and not 1609–10. Yet the Children were not entitled to call themselves ' of the Revels ' during 1609. Either Jonson's chronology or his memory of the shifting nomenclature of the company has slipped. The actor-list of *Epicoene* names ' Nat. Field, Gil. Carie, Hug. Attawel, Ioh. Smith, Will. Barksted, Will. Pen, Ric. Allin, Ioh. Blaney '. Amongst these Field is the sole direct connecting link with the Chapel actor-lists of 1600 and 1601. Keysar's pleading shows us that from 1600 to 1610 the company had maintained a substantial identity throughout all its phases, as successively Children of the Chapel, Children of the Queen's Revels, Children of the Blackfriars, Children of the Whitefriars ; but part of his grievance is its dispersal, and possibly the continuity with the second Children of the Revels may not have been quite so marked. ' In process of time ', say the Burbadges in the *Blackfriars Sharers Papers* of 1635, ' the boyes growing up to bee men, which were Underwood, Field, Ostler, and were taken to strengthen the King's service '.[1] This, which is written in relation to the acquisition of the Blackfriars, is doubtless accurate as regards Ostler and Underwood, and their transfer may reasonably be placed in the winter of 1609–10. But it was not until some years later that Field joined the King's men.

The career of the second Queen's Revels, but for the temporary suppression of *Epicoene* owing to a misconstruction placed on it by Arabella Stuart, was comparatively uneventful. They are recorded at Maidstone as the Children of the Chapel about March 1610. They made no appearance at Court during the following winter, and were again travelling in the following autumn, when they came to Norwich under the leadership of one Ralph Reeve, who showed the patent of 4 January 1610, and at first claimed to be Rosseter, but afterwards admitted that he was not. As he could show no letters of deputation, he was not allowed to play, although he received a reward on the following day, which was recorded, not quite correctly, as paid to ' the master of the children of the King's Revells '. By 29 August Barksted and Carey had left the company to

---

[1] Halliwell-Phillipps, i. 317 ; cf. *Hist. Hist.* 416 (App. I), ' Some of the chapel boys, when they grew men, became actors at the Blackfriars ; such were Nathan Field and John Underwood '.

join the newly formed Lady Elizabeth's men. We may therefore place at some time before this date Barksted's completion of Marston's *Insatiate Countess*, which was published in 1613 as ' acted at Whitefriars '. The entry in the Stationer's Register of Field's *A Woman is a Weathercock* (1612) on 23 November 1611 shows that he also had begun to experiment in authorship. As this had been acted at Court, as well as by the Queen's Revels at Whitefriars, it probably dates back to the winter of 1609–10. The company returned to court on 5 January 1612 with Beaumont and Fletcher's *Cupid's Revenge*, and the Clerk of the Revels entered them as the Children of Whitefriars.[1] The travels of 1612 were under the leadership of Nicholas Long, and on 20 May another *contretemps* occurred at Norwich. The instrument of deputation was forthcoming on this occasion, but the mayor chose to interpret the patent as giving authority only to teach and instruct children, and not to perform with them ; and so once again ' the Master of the Kings Revells' got his reward of 20*s.*, but was not allowed to play. Between Michaelmas and Christmas ' the queens maiesties revellers ' were at Bristol, and at some time during 1612–13 ' two of the company of the childeren of Revells ' received a reward at Coventry. Conceivably the provincial company of Reeve and Long was a distinct organization from that in London. Rosseter was payee for four performances at Court during the winter of 1612–13. On the first occasion, in the course of November, the play was Beaumont and Fletcher's *Coxcomb* ; on 1 January and again on 9 January it was *Cupid's Revenge* ; and on 27 February it was *The Widow's Tears*. In one version of the *Chamber Accounts* the company appears this year as the Children of the Queen's Revels, but in another under the obsolete designation of Children of the Chapel. In addition to the plays already named, Chapman's *Revenge of Bussy* had been on the Whitefriars stage before it was published in 1613 ; and it is conceivable that Chapman's *Chabot* and Beaumont and Fletcher's *Monsieur Thomas* and *The Nightwalker* may be Queen's Revels plays of 1610–13. They may also, indeed, be Lady Elizabeth's plays of 1613–16, but during this period the Lady Elizabeth and the Queen's Revels appear to have been practically amalgamated, under an arrangement made between Henslowe and Rosseter in March 1613 and then modified, first in 1614, and again on the addition of Prince Charles's men to the ' combine ' in 1615. Yet in some way

[1] The *Chamber Accounts* record no payment to the company (cf. App. B, introd.).

the Children of the Revels maintained a separate individuality, at least in theory, during these years, as may be seen from the patent of 3 June 1615, which licensed Rosseter and Reeve, together with Robert Jones and Philip Kingman, to build a new Blackfriars theatre in the house known as Porter's Hall.[1] The main purpose of this undertaking was expressed to be the provision of a new house for the Children of the Queen's Revels instead of the Whitefriars, where Rosseter's lease was now expired, although it was also contemplated that use might be made of it by the Prince's and the Lady Elizabeth's players. Porter's Hall only stood for a short time before civic hostility procured its demolition, and the single play, which we can be fairly confident that the Children of the Revels gave in it, is Beaumont and Fletcher's *Scornful Lady*. This presumably fell after the amalgamation under Henslowe broke up about the time of his death early in 1616. Field appears to have joined the King's men about 1615. The Queen's Revels dropped out of London theatrical life. Their provincial travels under Nicholas Long had apparently terminated in 1612, as in 1614 he is found using the patent of the Lady Elizabeth's men (q. v.) in the provinces. But some members of the company seem to have gone travelling during the period of troubled relations with Henslowe, and are traceable at Coventry on 7 October 1615, and at Nottingham in February 1616 and again later in 1616–17. On 31 October 1617 a new Queen's Revel's company was formed by Rosseter, in association with Nicholas Long, Robert Lee of the Queen's men, and William Perry of the King's Revels.[2]

iii. THE CHILDREN OF WINDSOR

Masters of the Children :—Richard Farrant (1564–80), Nathaniel Giles (1595–1634).

The Chapel Royal at Windsor was served by an ecclesiastical college, which had been in existence as far back as the reign of Henry I, and had subsequently been resettled as St. George's Chapel in connexion with the establishment of the Order of the Garter by Edward III, finally incorporated under Edward IV, and exempted from dissolution at the Reformation. Edward III had provided for a warden, who afterwards came to be called dean, 12 canons, 13 priest vicars, 4 clerks, 6 boy choristers, and 26 ' poor knights '. The boys were to be ' endued with clear and tuneable voices ', and to succeed the clerks as their voices changed. Their number was

[1] Cf. ch. xvi.   [2] Murray, i. 361.

altered from time to time ; during the greater part of Elizabeth's reign it stood at 10. Each had an annual fee of £3 6s. 8d. They were lodged within the Castle, in a chamber north of the chapel, and next to a building founded by James Denton in 1520, known as the ' New Commons '. This is now merged in the canons' houses, but a doorway is inscribed ' Edes pro Sacellaenorum et Choristarum conviviis extructae A. D. 1519 '. There were also an epistoler and a gospeller.[1] The music was ' useyd after ye order and maner of ye quenes chappell '.[2] One of the clerks, whose position corresponded to that of the Gentlemen of the household Chapel Royal, was appointed by the Chapter of the College to act as Organist and Master of the Children. The College was privileged, like the Chapel Royal itself, to recruit its choir by impressment. A commission for this purpose, issued on 8 March 1560, merely repeats the terms of one granted by Mary, which itself had confirmed earlier grants by Henry VIII and Edward VI.[3]

The Master at Elizabeth's accession was one Preston.[4] But he was deprived, as unwilling to accept the new ecclesiastical settlement; and the first Master under whom the choristers appear to have acted at Court was Richard Farrant. He had been a Gentleman of the Chapel Royal from about 1553, but was replaced on 24 April 1564, doubtless on his appointment as Master at Windsor.[5] On the following 30 September the

[1] E. Ashmole, *Institution of the Garter* (1672), 127 ; R. R. Tighe and J. E. Davis, *Annals of Windsor*, i. 426, 477 ; *Report of Cathedrals Commission* (1854), App. 467 ; *V. H. Berks*, ii. 106 ; *H. M. C. Various MSS.* vii. 10.

[2] Tighe-Davis, ii. 45, from Stowe's account ' of the Castell of Wyndsore ' (*Harl. MS.* 367, f. 13).

[3] Nichols, i. 81, and Collier, i. 170, print a copy in *Ashm. MS.* 1113, f. 252, from the Elizabethan commission preserved at Windsor, as follows : ' Elizabeth R.

Whereas our castle of Windsor hath of old been well furnished with singing men and children, We, willing it should not be of less reputation in our days, but rather augmented and increased, declare, that no singing men or boys be taken out of the said chapel by virtue of any commission, not even for our household chapel : and we give power to the bearer of this to take any singing men and boys from any chapel, our own household and St. Paul's only excepted. Given at Westminster, this 8th of March in the second year of our reign.'

A further copy from *Ashm. MS.* 1113 is in *Addl. MS.* 4847, f. 117. Copies or notes of the three earlier commissions are in this MS. and in *Ashm. MS.* 1124. In *Ashm. MS.* 1132, f. 169, is a letter of 18 April 1599 from the Chapter to Sir R. Cecil defending their conduct in taking a singing man from Westminster.

[4] Gee, 230, in a list of deprived clergy from N. Sanders, *De Visibili Monarchia* (1571), 688, ' *Magistri Musices* . . . Prestonus in oppido Vindelisoriensi '. Can this Preston be the playwright (cf. ch. xxiii) ?

[5] Rimbault, 1 ; Stopes, *Shakespeare's Environment*, 243.

Chapter assigned a chantry to the teacher of the choristers for an increase of his maintenance.[1] On 5 November 1570, Farrant was reappointed a Gentleman of the Chapel Royal, but evidently did not resign his Mastership.[2] On 11 February 1567 he began a series of plays with the ' Children of Windsor ' at Court, which was continued at Shrovetide 1568, on 22 February and 27 December 1569, at Shrovetide 1571, on 1 January 1572, when he gave *Ajax and Ulysses*, on 1 January 1573, on 6 January 1574, when he gave *Quintus Fabius*, on 6 January 1575, when he gave *King Xerxes*, and on 27 December 1575. With the winter of 1576–7 the entries of his name in the accounts of the Treasurer take a new form; he is no longer ' M[r] of the children of the Chappell at Wyndsore ' but ' M[r] of the children of the Chappell '. The Revels Accounts for the same season record that on 6 January 1577 *Mutius Scaevola* was played at Court by ' the Children of Windsore and the Chappell ', and it is a fair inference that Farrant, in addition to exercising his own office, was now also acting as deputy to William Hunnis, the Master by patent of the Children of the Chapel Royal, and had made up a combined company from both choirs for the Christmas delectation of the Queen.[3] This interpretation of the facts was confirmed when Professor Feuillerat was able to show from the Loseley archives that in 1576 Farrant had taken a lease of rooms in the Blackfriars from Sir William More and had converted them into the first Blackfriars theatre.[4] Whether boys from Windsor continued to take a share in the performances by the Chapel during 1577–8, 1578–9, and 1579–80, for all of which Farrant was payee, we do not know ; there is no further mention of them as actors in the Court accounts, although they accompanied the singing men from Windsor to Reading during the progress of 1576.[5] Farrant died on 30 November 1580, leaving a widow Anne, who in 1582 obtained the reversion of a small lease from the Crown, and was involved in controversies with Sir William More over the Blackfriars tenement at least up to 1587.[6] He had acquired some reputation as a musician, and amongst his surviving compositions are a few which may have been intended for use in plays.[7] Farrant was succeeded at Windsor

[1] *Ashm. MS.* 1132, f. 165[a].   [2] Rimbault, 2.
[3] *M. L. R.* (1906), ii. 6.   [4] Cf. ch. xvii (Blackfriars).
[5] Cf. App. B.   [6] Rimbault, 3 ; *H. M. C., Hatfield MSS.* ii. 539.
[7] Rimbault, 182 ; *Musical Antiquary*, i. 30 ; *10 N. Q.* v. 341. A Christ Church, Oxford, MS., dated 1581, assigns to Farrant (cf. ch. xxiii) a possibly dramatic lament of Panthea for the death of Abradates, beginning ' Ah, ah, alas ye salt sea Gods '. This is assigned to Robert Parsons by *Addl. MSS.* 17786–91, which assign to Farrant a song which may come from

by Nathaniel Giles, but only after an interval of either five or fifteen years. Ashmole reports Giles's monument as crediting him with forty-nine years' service as Master of St. George's before his death in 1634.[1] There must be an inaccuracy, either here or in the date of 1 October ' 37 Eliz.' (1595) upon a copy of his indenture of appointment by the Windsor chapter, which is amongst Ashmole's papers.[2] This recites that the chapter ' are now destitute of an experte and cunnynge man ', and that Giles ' is well contented to come and serve ' them. He is granted from the previous Michaelmas to the end of his life ' the Roome and place of a Clerk within the said ffree Chappell and to be one of the Players on the Organes there, and also the office of Instructor and Master of the ten Children or Choristers of the same ffree Chappell, And the office of tutor, creansor, or governor of the same tenn Children or Coristers '. He is to have an annuity of £81 6s. 8d. and ' tholde comons howse ', wherein John Mundie lately dwelt, which he is to hold on the same terms as ' one Richarde ffarrante enioyed the same ' at a rent of £1 6s. 8d. His fee is to be ' over and besides all such giftes, rewardes or benevolences as from time to time during the naturall lief of him the said Nathanaell Gyles shall be given bestowed or ymployed to or vpon the Choristers for singinge of Balattes, playes or for the like respects whatsoever '. He is to maintain the children and to supply vacancies, ' her Maiesties comission for the taking of Children which her highnes hath alredie graunted to the said Dean and Canons being allowed vnto him the said Nathanaell Gyles for that purpose '. Evidently the door was left open for a resumption of theatrical activities, such as was afterwards brought about at the London Chapel Royal during the Mastership of Giles there; but there is no proof that such a resumption ever took place at Windsor. It is perhaps a fanciful conjecture that the boys may have helped with *The Merry Wives of Windsor* about 1600.[3]

iv. CHILDREN OF THE KING'S REVELS

Masters :—Martin Slater and others.

[*Bibliographical Note.*—The chief source of information is J. Greenstreet, *The Whitefriars Theatre in the Time of Shakspere* (*N. S. S. Trans. 1887–92*, 269), which gives the text of the bill and answer in *Androwes v. Slater* (1609, Chancery).]

a play in which Altages is a character. The writer in the *Musical Antiquary* thinks that a lament for Guichardo (not from either of the known Gismund texts) in the *Ch. Ch. MS.* is much in Farrant's style.

[1] Ashmole, *Antiquities of Berks* (ed. 1723), iii. 172 ; cf. p. 41.
[2] *Ashm. MS.* 1125, f. 41ᵛ.   [3] Cf. ch. xiii (Chamberlain's).

The accident of litigation brings into light a company of boys, who appear to have acted for a brief and troubled period, which probably ended in 1608 or early in 1609. The story is told by one George Androwes a silk-weaver of London, and begins in February 1608. At that date a part of the dissolved Whitefriars monastery was held, in contemplation of a lease from Lord Buckhurst, by Michael Drayton and Thomas Woodford. The lease was actually executed about the following March, and was for six years, eight months, and twenty days, at a rent of £50. Woodford had assigned his interest to one Lording Barry; and Barry in turn persuaded Androwes to take over a third of it, and to join a syndicate, of which the active manager was Martin Slater, who is described as a citizen and ironmonger of London, but is, of course, well known as an actor in the Admiral's and other companies. The bill incorporates the terms of Articles of Agreement entered into on 10 March 1608 by Slater on the one hand and Barry, Androwes, and Drayton, together with William Trevell, William Cooke, Edward Sibthorpe, and John Mason, all of London, gentlemen, on the other. They throw a good deal of light upon the business organization of a theatrical enterprise. Slater is to have a sixth part of the net profits of ' any playes, showes, interludes, musique, or such like exercises ' in the White-friars playhouse or elsewhere, together with lodging for himself and his family on the premises, and any profits that can be made in the house ' either by wine, beere, ale, tobacco, wood, coales, or any such commoditie '. When the ' pattent for playinge ' shall be renewed, Slater's name is to be joined in it with Drayton's, because ' if any restrainte of their playing shall happen by reason of the plague or other wise, it shalbe for more creditt of the whole company that the said Martyn shall travel with the children, and acquainte the magistrates with their busines '. During any such travel his allowance is to be increased to a share and a half, no apparel, books, or other property of the company is to be removed without the consent of the sharers, and none of them is to print any of the play-books, ' except the booke of Torrismount, and that playe not to be printed by any before twelve monthes be fully expired '. In order to avoid debt, a sixth part is to be taken up each day of the ' chardges of the howse ' for the week, including ' the gatherers, the wages, the childrens bourd, musique, booke keeper, tyre-man, tyrewoman, lights, the Maister of the revells' duties, and all other things needefull and necessary '. The children are to be ' bound ' for three years to Slater, who undertakes

not to part with ' the said younge men or ladds ' during their
apprenticeship except on the consent of his fellow sharers.

The theatrical experience of the syndicate presumably
rested with Slater and Drayton. Of Trevell, Cooke, and Sibthorpe I know nothing, except that Trevell, like Woodford,
seems still to have had an interest in the lease of the Whitefriars (cf. ch. xvii) in 1621. But Mason and Barry were the
authors respectively of *The Turk* (1610, S. R. 10 March 1609),
and *Ram Alley* (1611, S. R. 9 November 1610), the title-
pages of which ascribe them to the children of the King's
Revels, and thereby enable us to give a more definite title
to the boys, who are only described in the Chancery pleadings
as ' the Children of the revells there beinge ', that is to say,
at the Whitefriars. And we can trace the King's Revels
a little farther back than February 1608 with the aid of the
earliest of similar entries on the title-pages of other plays,
which are, in the chronological order of publication, Sharpham's *Cupid's Whirligig* (1607, S. R. 29 June 1607), Middleton's *Family of Love* (1608, S. R. 12 October 1607), Day's
Humour Out Of Breath (1608, S. R. 12 April 1608), Markham's
(and Machin's) *The Dumb Knight* (1608, S. R. 6 October 1608),
and Armin's *Two Maids of More-clack* (1609). If Lewis
Machin was the author of the anonymous *Every Woman In
Her Humour* (1609), it is possible that this ought to be added
to the list. Clearly the boys were playing at least as early
as the first half of 1607 and the agreement of 1608 must
represent a reconstruction of the original business organization. I do not find anything in the plays to prove an earlier
date than 1607, but it is quite conceivable that the King's
Revels may have come into existence as early as 1606,
perhaps with the idea of replacing the Queen's Revels after
their disgrace over *The Isle of Gulls*. But if so, the Queen's
Revels managed to hold together under another name, and
in fact proved more enduring than their rivals. Mr. Fleay,
however, suggests that the King's Revels were a continuation
of the Paul's boys, and played at the singing-school, and
apparently also that they were themselves continued as the
Duke of York's men (*H. of S.* 152, 188, 202, 206). He did not,
I think, know of *Androwes v. Slater*, but *Androwes v. Slater*
does not indicate that the King's Revels were at Whitefriars
before 1608; rather the contrary.[1] The dates render Mr. Fleay's
conjectures tempting, although it must be admitted that
there is not much evidence. But *The Family of Love* was
played in a round theatre and the Paul's house was round.

---

[1] Presumably, however, the ' Gerry ' buried out of the Whitefriars play-
house (q.v.) on 29 Sept. 1607 was of the company.

The curious description of the Duke of York's men at Leicester in 1608 as ' of the White Chapple, London ', might conceivably be a mistake for ' of the Whitefriars ', but more probably indicates that they came from the Boar's Head (cf. ch. xvi). ' The Children of the Revells' followed them at Leicester on 21 August 1608, but these may have been the Black-friars children under a not quite official name. A complete search through the Patent Rolls for 1606–8 might disinter the patent for the King's Revels, which is referred to in the Articles of Agreements ; I find no obvious clue to it in the printed index of signet bills. It seems possible that William Barksted (cf. ch. xv) may have belonged to the King's Revels.

The syndicate did not hold together long. It will be noticed that, in spite of the attempt in the articles to bar the printing of plays, these had begun to reach the stationers again as early as April 1608. The inhibition of 1608 hardly gave the company a chance, and then came the plague. They were probably broken before the end of 1608, and although Mason and Barry had at least the consolation that they had got their own plays staged, other members of the syndicate could only reflect that they had lost their money. And when dissensions broke out, and Slater sued Androwes on a bond of £200 given by the sharers for observance of the articles, and this for defaults which Androwes himself had not committed, it is not surprising that Androwes drew the conclusion that he had been a gull. He took Slater to Chancery, and alleged that he had been asked £90 and paid £70 for his share in the expectation of a profit of £100 a year, and on the understanding that the apparel was worth £400 when it was not worth £5, that he had been led into building and other expenses to the tune of £300, that the lease had been forfeited for non-payment of rent before any assignation had been made to him, and that he had been clearly told by Slater that his obligation was not to extend beyond any breaches of covenant that he might himself commit. Slater denied any responsibility for Androwes's misunderstandings, and pointed out that he had himself been the principal sufferer by the breakdown of the enterprise, since he and his family of ten had been illegally turned out of the rooms to which they were entitled under the articles of agreement, and were now driven to beg their bread. The view taken by the court is not upon record.

The company which was described as the King's Revels at Norwich in 1611 and 1612 was travelling under the Queen's Revels patent of 1610, and was therefore clearly misnamed. But a second King's Revels company did in fact come into existence through a licence given to William Hovell, William Perry, and Nathan May under the royal signet on 27 February 1615. It performed only in the provinces, and is traceable at Norwich, Coventry, and Leicester. Its warrant was condemned and withdrawn by an order of the Lord Chamberlain on 16 July 1616 (Murray, ii. 343), and in the following year the company seems to have amalgamated with the provincial relics of the Queen's Revels.

v. CHILDREN OF BRISTOL

Masters :—John Daniel (1615–17) ; Martin Slater, John Edmonds, Nathaniel Clay (1618).

A signet bill for a patent for a company of Children of Bristol under the patronage of Queen Anne was passed in June 1615, perhaps as a result of her visit to that city in 1613.[1] On 10 July Sir George Buck wrote to John Packer, the Earl of Somerset's secretary, to say that the grant had been made through the Queen's influence on behalf of Samuel Daniel, and that he was prepared to assent to it, without prejudice to his rights as Master of the Revels.[2] The actual patent, dated 13 July, is made out to Daniel's brother John.[3]

De concessione re- Iames by the grace of God &c. To all Iustices
gardante   Iohannem of peace, Mayors, Sheriffes, Bayliffes, Con-
Daniell.   stables, headboroughes and other our lovinge
subjectes and Officers greetinge. Knowe yee that wee at the mocion of our most deerelie loved consort the Queene have licenced and authorised, And by theise presentes do licence and authorise, our wel-beloved subjectes Iohn Daniell and his Assignes to entertaine and bringe vp a company of children and youthes vnder the name and title of the children of her Maiesties royall Chamber of Bristoll, to vse and exercise the arte and qualitie of playinge Comedies, histories, Enter-ludes, Moralles, Pastoralles, Stageplayes, and such other like, as they have alreadie studied or hereafter shall studie or vse, aswell for the solace and delight of our most derely loved Consort the Queene when-soever they shalbe called, as for the recreacion of our loving Subiectes, And the said Enterludes or other to shewe and exercise publiquely to their best commoditie, aswell in and about our said Citie of Bristoll in such vsuall houses as themselues shall provide, as other convenient places within the liberties and freedomes of any other Cittie, vni-versitie, Towne, or Burrowe whatsoever within our Realmes and Dominions, willing and commaundinge you and euery of you, as you tender our pleasures, not onelie to permitt and suffer them herein without any your lettes, hinderances, molestacions, and disturbances

---

[1] Phillimore, 140 ; cf. App. A.   [2] *S. P. D. Jac. I*, lxxxi. 12.
[3] *M. S. C.* i. 279, from *P. R. 13 Jac. I*, pt. 20.

during our said pleasure, but alsoe to be aydinge and assistinge vnto them, yf any wronge be done vnto them or to them offred, and to allowe them such further curtesies as have bene given to other of the like qualitie, And alsoe what further grace and favour you shall show vnto them for our sakes wee shall take kindly at your handes. Provided alwaies and our will and pleasure is, all authoritie, power, priviledge, and profitt whatsoever belonginge and properlie apperteyninge to the Maister of the Revelles in respect of his office shall remayne and abide entire and in full force, effect, and vertue, and in as ample sort as if this our Commission had never byn made. In witnes whereof &c, witnes our selfe at Westminster the seaventeenth day of Iuly.

per breve de priuato sigillo &c.

The company is not traceable in London, but Daniel brought it to Norwich in 1616–17. By April 1618 he had assigned his privilege to Martin Slater, John Edmonds and Nathaniel Clay, who obtained, presumably from the Privy Council, supplementary letters of assistance in which they are described as ' her Maiesties servants ', and are authorized to play as ' her Maiesties servants of her Royall Chamber of Bristoll '.[1] From a complaint sent in the following June by the Mayor of Exeter to Sir Thomas Lake, it emerges that, although the patent was for children, the company consisted of five youths and several grown men.[2] Slater and Edmonds still held their *status* as Queen's men (q.v.) in 1619.

vi. WESTMINSTER SCHOOL

Head Masters :—John Adams (1540) ; Alexander Nowell (1543–53) ; Nicholas Udall (1555–6) ; John Passey (1557–8, with Richard Spencer as usher) ; John Randall (1563) ; Thomas Browne (1564–9) ; Francis Howlyn (1570–1) ; Edward Graunte (1572–92) ; William Camden (1593–8, Undermaster 1575–93) ; Richard Ireland (1599–1610) ; John Wilson (1610–22).

Choir Masters (?) :—William Cornish (1480) ; John Taylor (1561-7) ; John Billingsley (1572) ; William Elderton (1574).

[*Bibliographical Note.*—The best sources of information are : R. Widmore, *History of Westminster Abbey* (1751) ; J. Welch [—C. B. Phillimore], *Alumni Westmonasterienses*, ed. 2 (1852) ; *Appendix to First Report of the Cathedral Commissioners* (1854) ; F. H. Forshall, *Westminster School, Past and Present* (1884) ; J. Sargeaunt, *Annals of Westminster School* (1898) ; A. F. Leach, *The Origin of Westminster School* in *Journal of Education*, n. s. xxvii (1905), 79. Some valuable records have been printed by

[1] *Variorum*, iii. 426 ; Collier, i. 394 ; Hazlitt, *E. D. S.* 49 ; from *S. P. D. Jac. I*, xcvii. 140.
[2] Collier, i. 396, not, as he says, from the *P. C. Register*, but from *S. P. D. Jac. I*, xcvii. 140.

E. J. L. Scott in the *Athenaeum,* and extracts from others are given in the *Observer* for 7 Dec. 1919. A. F. Leach has fixed the dates of Udall's life in *Encycl. Brit.* s.v.]

There is no trace of any grammar school in the abbey of Westminster until the fourteenth century. The *Customary* of 1259–83 (ed. E. M. Thompson for *Henry Bradshaw Soc.*) only contemplates education for the novices, and in the earliest almoner's accounts, which begin with 1282, entries of 1317 ' in maintaining Nigel at school for the love of God ' (Leach, 80) and 1339–40, ' pro scholaribus inueniendis ad scolas ' (E. H. Pearce, *The Monks of Westminster Abbey,* 79), need only refer to the support of scholars at a University. But from 1354–5 there were almonry boys (*pueri Elemosinariae*) under the charge of the Sub-Almoner, and these are traceable up to the dissolution. To them we may assign the *ludus* of the Boy Bishop on St. Nicholas' day, mentions of which have been noted in 1369, 1388, 1413, and 1540 (*Mediaeval Stage,* i. 360; Leach, 80). They had a school house near ' le Millebank ', and from 1367 the Almoner paid a *Magister Puerorum.* From 1387 he is often called *Magister Scolarum* and in the fifteenth century *Magister Scolarium.* From 1510 the boys under the *Magister* become *pueri grammatici,* and may be distinct from certain *pueri cantantes* for whom since 1479–80 the Almoner had paid a separate teacher of singing. The first of these song-masters was William Cornish, doubtless of the family so closely connected with the Chapel Royal (q.v.). In 1540 the *pueri grammatici* were re-organized as the still existing College of St. Peter, Westminster, which is therefore generally regarded as owing its origin to Henry VIII, who on the surrender of the abbey in 1540 turned it into a college of secular canons, and provided for a school of forty scholars. This endured in some form through the reactionary reign of Mary, whose favourite dramatist Nicholas Udall became its Head Master, although the date of his appointment on 16 December 1555 (A. F. Leach in *Encycl. Brit.,* s.v. Udall) makes it probable that, if he wrote his *Ralph Roister Doister* for a school at all, it was for Eton (q.v.) rather than Westminster. His predecessor Alexander Nowell is said by Strype to have ' brought in the reading of Terence for the better learning the pure Roman style ', and, as the Sub-Almoner paid ' xvi*d.* for wryting of a play for the chyldren ' as early as 1521 (*Observer*), the performance of Latin comedies by the boys may have been pre-Elizabethan. It is provided for in the statutes drafted by Dean Bill (*c.* 1560) after the restoration of her father's foundation by Elizabeth. These statutes also contemplate a good deal of interrelation between the choir school and the grammar school. They are printed in the *Report of the Cathedral Commission* (App. I, 80). The personnel of the foundation was to include (a) '*clerici duodecim*', of whom '*unus sit choristarum doctor*', (b) '*decem pueri symphoniaci sive choristae*', presumably in continuation of the former singing boys, (c) '*praeceptores duo ad erudiendam iuventutem*', (d) '*discipuli grammatici quadraginta*'. The '*praeceptores*' are distinguished later in the document as '*archididascalus*' and '*hypodidascalus*', and the former is also called '*ludimagister*'. By c. 5 the choristers are to have a preference in elections to the grammar school. The following section '*De Choristis et Choristarum Magistro*' forms part of c. 9:

'Statuimus et ordinamus ut in ecclesia nostra praedicta sint decem choristae, pueri tenerae aetatis et vocibus sonoris ad cantandum, et ad artem musicam discendam, et etiam ad musica instrumenta pulsanda apti, qui choro inserviant, ministrent, et cantent. Ad hos praeclare instituendos, unus eligatur qui sit honestae famae, vitae probae, religionis sincerae, artis musicae peritus, et ad cantandum et musica instrumenta pulsanda exercitatus, qui pueris in praedictis scientiis et exercitiis docendis aliisque muniis [? muneribus] in choro obeundis studiose vacabit. Hunc magistrum choristarum appellari volumus. Cui muneri doctores et baccalaureos musices aliis praeferendos censemus. Volumus etiam quoties eum ab ecclesia nostra abesse contingat, alterum substituat a decano vel eo absente prodecano approbandum. Prospiciat item puerorum saluti, quorum et in literis (donec ut in scholam nostram admittantur apti censebuntur) et in morum modestia et in convictu educationem et liberalem institutionem illius fidei et industriae committimus. Quod si negligens et in docendo desidiosus, aut in salute puerorum et recta eorum educatione minime providus et circumspectus, et ideo non tolerandus inveniatur, post trinam admonitionem (si se non emendaverit) ab officio deponatur. Qui quidem choristarum magister ad officium suum per se fideliter obeundum iuramento etiam adigetur. Choristae postquam octo orationis partes memoriter didicerint et scribere mediocriter noverint, ad scholam nostram ut melius in grammatica proficiant singulis diebus profestis accedant, ibique duabus minimum horis maneant, et a praeceptoribus instituantur.'

The following section '*De Comoediis et Ludis in Natali Domini exhibendis*' comes in c. 10:

'Quo iuventus maiore cum fructu tempus Natalis Christi terat, et tum actioni tum pronunciationi decenti melius se assuescat : statuimus ut singulis annis intra 12^m post festum Natalis Christi dies [? diem], vel postea arbitrio decani, ludimagister et praeceptor simul Latine unam, magister choristarum Anglice alteram comoediam aut tragoediam a discipulis et choristis suis in aula privatim vel publice agendam, curent. Quod si non prestiterint singuli quorum negligentia omittuntur decem solidis mulctentur.'

The statutes appear never to have been confirmed by the Crown, and their practical adoption was subject to certain exceptions. Thus, it is stated in the report of the Public Schools Commission in 1864 (i. 159) that there is no reason to believe that the provision giving a preference to choristers in elections for the grammar school was ever attended to.

Of plays and the like, however, there are various records. The first since 1521 is at the Lord Mayor's Day of 1561, when the Merchant Taylors' expenses for their pageant included items ' to John Tayllour, master of the Children of the late monastere of Westminster, for his children that sung and played in the pageant ', and ' to John Holt momer in reward for attendance given of the children in the pageant '. Similar payments were made to Taylor as ' M^r of the quirysters ' for the services of the children on the Ironmongers' pageant of 1566.[1] In 1562 the choristers of Westminster Abbey performed a goodly play before the Society of Parish Clerks after their annual dinner.[2] In 1564–5 comes the first of a series of Court performances, which received assistance from the Revels office. To this occasion belongs a memorandum of Thexpenses of twoo playes viz. Heautontimoroumenos Terentii and Miles Gloriosus Plauti plaied by the children of the grammer schoole in the colledge of Westminster and before the Quenes maiestie anno 1564 '.[3] The items include, ' At ye rehersing before Sir Thomas Benger for pinnes and suger candee vj$d$ ', ' For a lynke to bring thapparell from the reuells iiij$d$.', ' At the playing of Miles Glor: in M^r. Deanes howse for pinnes half a thousand vj$d$.', ' Geuen to M^r. Holte yeoman of the reuells xs.', ' To M^r. Taylor his man ', ' For one Plautus geven to ye Queenes maiestie and fowre other vnto the nobilitie xj$s$.' It is not quite clear whether the *Heautontimorumenus*, as well as the *Miles Gloriosus*, was given before the Queen, but I think not. In 1565–6 Elizabeth was again present at the play of *Sapientia Solomonis*, and there were payments ' For drawing the city and temple of Jerusalem and paynting towers ', ' To a woman that brawght her childe to the stadge and there attended uppon it ', and for a copy of the play bound ' in vellum with the Queenes Matie hir armes and sylke ribben strings ', almost certainly that still extant as *Addl. MS.* 20061 (cf.

[1] Clode, ii. 269 ; Nicholl, *Ironmongers*, 84 ; cf. ch. iv.
[2] Warton, iii. 313 ; Stowe, *Survey*, ed. Strype, v. 231.
[3] E. J. L. Scott in *Athenaeum* (1903), i. 220, from *S. P. D. Eliz.* xxxvi. 22 ; Murray, ii. 168.

App. K), which shows that Elizabeth was accompanied by Cecilia of Sweden.[1] Whether these plays were at the school or at Court is not quite clear. I should, on the whole, infer the latter, but no rewards were paid for them by the Treasurer of the Chamber. John Taylor was, however, paid for plays by the Children of Westminster during the Shrovetide of 1566-7 and the Christmas of 1567-8; John Billingesley for their *Paris and Vienna* on 19 February 1572; and William Elderton for their *Truth, Faithfulness, and Mercy* on 1 January 1574. In 1567 also the boys are recorded (*Observer*) to have played at Putney before Bishop Grindal. I suppose that Billingesley and Elderton succeeded Taylor as *Magistri Choristarum*. Taylor himself is probably the same who on 8 September 1557 was Master of the singing children at the hospital of St. Mary Woolnoth. Elderton is presumably the same who brought the Eton boys to Court in 1573. Whether he is also the bibulous balladist of the pamphleteers (cf. ch. xv) is more doubtful. The absence of a payment for *Miles Gloriosus* may suggest that this was given by the grammar school who, like the Inns of Court, did not expect a reward, and that the English plays were given by the choristers, who were on the same footing as the choristers of Paul's. I am not sure, however, that the wording of the statutes quite implies such a sharp distinction between the two sets of boys, and it will be noticed that Taylor, or his man, was in some way concerned with the Latin play. Very possibly grammar boys and choristers acted together. With 1574 the Court performances end, but expenses of plays are traceable in the college accounts in 1604-5, 1605-6, 1606-7, and 1609-10, and up to about 1640, when they stop for sixty-four years.[2]

vii. ETON COLLEGE

Head Masters:—William Malim (*c.* 1555-73); William Smyth (*c.* 1563); Reuben Sherwood (*c.* 1571); Thomas Ridley (1579); John Hammond (1583); Richard Langley (1594); Richard Wright (1611); Matthew Bust (1611-30).

[*Bibliographical Note.*—The best sources of information are J. Heywood and T. Wright, *Ancient Laws of King's College and Eton College* (1850); *Report of Public Schools Commission* (1864); W. L. Collins, *Etoniana*

---

[1] *Observer*. Other payments in this or another year were for ' a haddocke occupied in the plaie ', ' a thondre barrell ', ' drawing the tytle of the comedee '.
[2] E. J. L. Scott in *Athenaeum* (1896), i. 95; (1903) ii. 220; Murray, ii. 168 ; *Observer*.

1865) ; H. Maxwell-Lyte, *History of Eton* (1875, 4th ed. 1911) ; W. Sterry, *Annals of Eton College* (1898).]

The King's College of Our Lady of Eton beside Windsor was founded by Henry VI in 1441. The Statutes of 1444 provide for a Boy Bishop (*Mediaeval Stage*, i. 365), but the custom was discontinued before 1559–61, when William Malim prepared a *Consuetudinarium* for a Royal Commission appointed to visit the college. By this time, however, Christmas plays by the boys had become the practice, and Malim writes : [1]

' Circiter festum D. Andreae [Nov. 30] ludimagister eligere solet pro suo arbitrio scaenicas fabulas optimas et quam accommodatissimas, quas pueri feriis natalitiis subsequentibus non sine ludorum elegantia, populo spectante, publice aliquando peragant. Histrionum levis ars est, ad actionem tamen oratorum, et gestum motumque corporis decentem tantopere facit, ut nihil magis. Interdum etiam exhibet Anglico sermone contextas fabulas, quae habeant acumen et leporem.'

There are ' numerous ' entries of expenditure on these plays in the Audit Books from 1525–6 to 1572–3, of which a few only have been printed.[2] There is also an inventory, apparently undated, of articles in ' M^r. Scholemasters chamber ', which includes ' a great cheste bound about with yron to keepe the players coats in ', and a list of the apparel, beards, and properties. The Eton boys played under Udall before Cromwell in 1538 (*Mediaeval Stage*, ii. 196, 451), and it is possible that *Ralph Roister Doister* may belong to his Eton mastership.[3] The only Court performance by Eton boys on record was one on 6 January 1573, for which the payee was Elderton, presumably the William Elderton who was payee for the Westminster boys in the following year.

[1] Heywood-Wright, 632 ; Hazlitt-Warton, iii. 308.

[2] Collins, 215 (1566), ' Mr Scholemaster towards his charges about the playes laste Christmas, 20/- ' ; Maxwell-Lyte,[4] 154 (1566–7) ' To Mr Scholemaster for his charge setting furthe ij playes 19° Martii, iii^l, xiij^s, viij^d ', (1568–9) ' For ij dossen of links at iij^d the linke for the childrens showes at Christmass, vj^s ', (1572–3) ' For vj poundes of candles at the playes in the Halle, ix^d '.

[3] J. W. Hales in *Englische Studien*, xviii. 408 (cf. *Mediaeval Stage*, ii. 452), made the date of 1553–4 seem plausible, but his conjecture that the play was written for the Westminster boys is disposed of by A. F. Leach, who gives Udall's appointment to Westminster from the Chapter Act Book as 16 Dec. 1555 (*Encycl. Brit.* s.v. Udall). It might be a Court play of 1553–4, but the parody of the *Requiem* would have been an indiscretion on Udall's part at that date.

viii. MERCHANT TAYLORS SCHOOL

Head Masters :—Richard Mulcaster (1561–86) ; Henry Wilkinson (1586–92) ; Edmund Smith (1592–9) ; William Hayne (1599–1625).

The London school of the Merchant Taylors was founded in 1561, and its first master was Richard Mulcaster, or Moncaster, as his name is spelt in some of the earlier records.[1] He was a student of King's, Cambridge and Christ Church, Oxford, who had been teaching in London since 1559. The first performances by his boys, of which record remains, were in 1572–3. In that and the following year they played before the Merchant Taylors Company at the Common Hall.[2] Unfortunately the audience, who had paid for their seats, and very likely Mulcaster himself, paid more attention to the plays than to the dignitaries in whose hall they were given. The plays were therefore stopped, and the following pleasing example of civic pomposity inserted in the archives of the Company on 16 March 1574 :[3]

' Whereas at our comon playes and suche lyke exercises whiche be comonly exposed to be seene for money, everye lewd persone thinketh himself (for his penny) worthye of the chiefe and most comodious place withoute respecte of any other either for age or estimacion in the comon weale, whiche bringeth the youthe to such an impudente famyliaritie with theire betters that often tymes greite contempte of maisters, parents, and magistrats foloweth thereof, as experience of late in this our comon hall hath sufficyently declared, where by reasone of the tumultuous disordered persones repayringe hither to see suche playes as by our schollers were here lately played, the Maisters of this Worshipful Companie and their deare ffrends could not have entertaynmente and convenyente place as they ought to have had, by no provision beinge made, notwithstandinge the spoyle of this howse, the charges of this Mystery, and theire juste authoritie which did reasonably require the contrary. Therefore and ffor the causes ffirst above saide, yt is ordeyned and decreed by the authoritie of this presente Courte, with the assente and consente of all the worshipfull persones aforesaide, that henceforthe theire shall be no more plays suffered to be played in this our Comon Hall, any use or custome heretofore to the contrary in anywise notwithstandinge.'

Mulcaster, however, found more tolerant critics than his own employers. His first appearance at Court was on

[1] G. C. Moore Smith (*M. L. R.* viii. 368) has an ingenious identification of him with the Wrenock of Spenser's *Shepheards Kalendar*, xii. 41.

[2] Clode, *Hist. of Merchant Taylors Company*, i. 235, from Master's *Accounts.* Before they opened their own school the Company had plays by the Westminster boys (q.v.).

[3] Clode, i. 234.

3 February 1573.[1] On 2 February 1574 he presented *Timoclia at the Siege of Thebes* and on 23 February *Percius and Anthomiris*; at Shrovetide 1575 and on 6 March 1576 plays unnamed; and on 12 February 1583 *Ariodante and Geneuora.* A reminiscence of these performances has been left us by the seventeenth-century judge, Sir James Whitelocke, who entered the school in 1575 and left for St. John's, Oxford, in 1588 :

' I was brought up at school under M[r] Mulcaster, in the famous school of the Merchantaylors in London. . . . Yeerly he presented sum playes to the court, in which his scholers wear only actors, and I on among them, and by that meanes taughte them good behaviour and audacitye.' [2]

In 1586 Mulcaster quarrelled with the Merchant Taylors and resigned. In 1596 he became High Master of St. Paul's grammar school, but it is only conjecture that his influence counted for anything in the revival of plays by the choir master, Edward Pearce. Regular plays at Merchant Taylors probably ceased on his withdrawal. When Sir Robert Lee, one of the Company, became Lord Mayor in 1602, a payment was made to Mr. Haines, the Schoolmaster, for a wagon and the apparel of ten scholars, who represented Apollo and the Muses in Cheapside. But when James came to dine at the hall on 16 July 1607, it was thought best to apply for help to Heminges of the King's men and Nathaniel Giles of the Chapel, on the ground that the Schoolmaster and children were not familiar with such entertainments.[3]

ix. THE EARL OF LEICESTER'S BOYS

Vide ch. xiii (Earl of Leicester's men).

x. THE EARL OF OXFORD'S BOYS

Vide ch. xiii (Earl of Oxford's men).

xi. MR. STANLEY'S BOYS

Vide ch. xiii (Earl of Derby's men).

---

[1] The subject may have been Perseus and Andromeda, as the Revels prepared a picture of Andromeda this year. If so, it was probably the same play as that of 23 Feb. 1574.

[2] Whitelocke, *Liber Famelicus* (Camden Soc.), 12.

[3] Clode, i. 264, 280, 390.

XIII

THE ADULT COMPANIES

i. THE COURT INTERLUDERS

Henry VII (22 Aug. 1485—21 Apr. 1509); Henry VIII (22 Apr. 1509—28 Jan. 1547); Edward VI (28 Jan. 1547—6 July 1553); Mary (19 July 1553—24 July 1554); Philip and Mary (25 July 1554—17 Nov. 1558); Elizabeth (17 Nov. 1558—24 Mar. 1603).

THE *doyen* of the Court companies, when Elizabeth came to the throne, was the royal company of Players of Interludes. This had already half a century of history behind it. Its beginnings are probably traceable in the reign of Henry VII. Richard III had entertained a company, as Duke of Gloucester, in 1482; but nothing is known of it during his short reign from 1583 to 1585.[1] Nor is a royal company discoverable

---

[1] *Mediaeval Stage*, ii. 186, 256.

amongst the earlier records of Henry VII himself.[1] But from 1493 onwards Exchequer documents testify to the continuous existence of a body of men under the style of *Lusores Regis*, or in the vulgar tongue, Players of the King's Interludes. In 1494 there were four of them, John English, Edward May, Richard Gibson, and John Hammond, and each had an annual fee, payable out of the Exchequer, of £3 6s. 8d. In 1503 there were five, William Rutter and John Scott taking the place of Hammond, but the total Exchequer payment to the company of £13 6s. 8d. a year, seems to have remained unaltered to the end of the reign.[2] They received, however, additional sums from time to time, as ' rewards ' for performances, which were charged to the separate account of the Chamber.[3] In 1503, under the leadership of John English, they attended the Princess Margaret to Edinburgh, for her wedding with James IV of Scotland. Here they ' did their devoir ', both on the day of the wedding, 8 August, and on the following days. On 11 August they played after supper, and on 13 August they played ' a Moralite ' after dinner.[4]

[1] The documents in W. Campbell, *Materials for a History of the Reign of Henry VII*, are full for the period 1485–90. There is nothing of King's players, but certain ' stuffures ' paid for by a warrant of 25 Nov. 1485 (Campbell, i. 178) included goods delivered to John English, apparently a royal tailor or valet, ' servant unto my said sovereign '.

[2] Collier, i. 44, from a book of Exchequer payments, beginning Michaelmas 1493, in the Chapter-house (probably *Misc. Books of the Treasury of the Receipt of the Exchequer*, 131), ' xvij Die Maij [1494] John Englissh, Edwardo Maye, Rico Gibbeson, & John Hammond, Lusoribus Regis, alias, in lingua Anglicana, *les* pleyars of the kyngs enterluds, de feodis suis V mrc. p Ann: le home, per lre Regis de privato Sigillo dormant de termino Michaelis alt: pte rec: denar: separatim p manus proprias, x mrc.'. The payment was continued half-yearly. Collier adds that Mr. Ouvry owned an original receipt signed by May and English for the salaries of the same four men. It is now *Egerton MS.* 2623 (3), f. 1, and appears to be a slip cut from some Exchequer record. F. Devon, *Issues of the Exchequer*, 516, gives similar payments for Michaelmas 1494 and Michaelmas 1503 ; it is in the latter that the names of William Rutter and John Scott appear. An Exchequer declaration of 1505–6 in *Lansd. MS.* 156, f. 135, has ' To Richard Gibson, and other the kings plaiers, for their annuity for one yere, £13 6s. 8d.'. Henry, *History of Britain*, xii. 456, gives from an Exchequer annuity list of 1507–8, ' Ricardo Gybson et aliis lusoribus dom. reg. £13 6s. 8d.'.

[3] Collier, i. 49, quotes : (a) *Account* of Robert Fowler (1501–2), ' Oct. 26 [1501], Itm to John Englishe for his pagent, £6 13s. 4d. . . . Jan. 1 [1502] Itm, to the Kinges players, over 40ˢ paid by Thomas Trollop, 20ˢ ' ; (b) *Household Book of Henry VII* (1492–1505, more correctly from *Addl. MS.* 7099 in Bentley, *Excerpta Historica*, 85), ' Jan. 6 [1494] To the Kings Pleyers for a rewarde, £2 13s. 4d. . . . Jan. 7 [1502] To John Englishe the Pleyer, 10s.' ; (c) *The Kings Boke of Payments* (1506–9, apparently *Misc. Books of the Treasury of the Receipt of the Exchequer*, 214), ' Jan. 7 [1509] To the kings players in rewarde, £2 '. Both (b) and (c) are *Chamber Accounts*. [4] Leland, *Collectanea* (ed. Hearne), iv. 265.

The royal company continued under Henry VIII, who appears to have increased its numbers, and doubled the charge upon the Exchequer.[1] The financial records are, however, a little complicated. The Exchequer officials presumably continued to regard the establishment as consisting of four members drawing fees of ten instead of five marks each.[2] But the individual members were in fact paid on different scales. John English, the leader, got £6 13s. 4d. Others got £3 6s. 8d. as before, and others again only two-thirds of this amount, £2 4s. 5d. By this arrangement, it was possible to maintain an actual establishment of from eight to ten within the limits of the Exchequer allowance. It seems also to have been found convenient to transfer the responsibility for some at least of the payments from the Exchequer to the Treasurer of the Chamber.[3] The same distinction between players of different grades is also reflected in the annual rewards paid by the Treasurer of the Chamber for Christmas performances. These were increased in amount, and for a time the general reward to the players as a whole was supplemented by an additional sum to the ' old ' players. Ultimately an amalgamated sum of £6 13s. 4d. became the customary reward for the company.[4] Details of a performance of Henry Medwall's *Finding of Truth* on 6 January 1514 are related by Collier from a document which cannot be

[1] *Lansd. MS.* 171, cited by Collier, i. 72, is in fact an Elizabethan document, but a list of fees and annuities (1516) in Brewer, ii. 874 has, amongst those granted by Henry VII, ' John Englisshe and other players £13 6s. 8d.', and amongst those recently granted, ' John Englisshe and other players, in addition to the old annuity, £13 6s. 8d '.

[2] Collier, i. 97, 115, gives an Exchequer payment of 1525-6, ' Rico Hole et Georgio Mayler, et aliis lusoribus Dom. Regis, de foedis suis inter se ad x marcos per ann. sibi debit: pro festo Michaelis, anno xvij Regis nunc Henrici VIII recept. denar. per manus proprias, per litt. curr. 66s. 8d.', and was informed by Mr. Devon of a similar payment of £3 6s. 8d. in 1530, in which John Roll, Richard Hole, and Thomas Sudbury are named. A household list of c. 1526 (Brewer, iv. 869) gives as on yearly wages ' Ric. Hole and other players, £6 13s. 4d.'. One later than March 1544 (Collier, i. 133) gives 8 players at £3 6s. 8d. each.

[3] *Chamber Accounts* (Brewer, v. 303 ; xiii. 2. 524 ; xiv. 2. 303 ; xvi. 178, 698 ; xvii. 474 ; xx. 2. 515 ; Nicolas, xxviii ; Collier, i. 79, 96, 113, 116, 117 ; *Trevelyan Papers*, i. 149, 157, 170, 177, 195, 203) give John English (1521-31) at half-yearly ' fee ' or ' wages ' of £3 6s. 8d., John Slye or Slee (1539-40) at £1 13s. 4d. half-yearly, and Richard Parrowe or Parlowe (1540-5, appointed Christmas 1538), George Birch (1538-45), Robert Hinstock (1538-45), and George Maylour (1538-40), at 16s. 8d. or 11s. 1d. quarterly.

[4] *Chamber Accounts* (Brewer, ii. 1441 ; iii. 1533, &c. ; Nicolas, xxviii ; Collier, i. 76, 116). The reward for 1509-10 was £2 13s. 4d. ; during 1510-13, £3 6s. 8d. ; during 1513-21, £3 6s. 8d. to the ' players ' and £4 ' to the ' olde players ' ; and during 1529-41, £6 13s. 4d.

regarded as free from suspicion.[1] The name of Richard Gibson now disappears from the notices of the company. He may, likely enough, have given up playing on his appointment to be Porter and Yeoman Tailor of the Great Wardrobe.[2] But in his capacity of officer in charge of the Revels he must have maintained close relations with his former fellows, and his Account for 1510 records the delivery to John English of a 'red satin ladies garment, powdered, with tassels of silver of Kolen'.[3] English remained at the head of the company, and is traceable in the *Chamber Accounts* up to 1531. John Scott died in 1528–9, in singular circumstances which are detailed by a contemporary chronicler.[4] Other names which come in succession before us are those of Richard Hole, George Maylor, George Birch, John Roll or Roo (*d.* 1539), Thomas Sudbury or Sudborough (*d.* 1546), Robert Hinstock, Richard Parrowe, John Slye, and John Young.[5] Some interesting information is disclosed by two lawsuits, in both of which George Maylor figured. The first of these was a dispute between John Rastell and Henry Walton as to the dilapidations of certain playing garments, during which

---

[1] Collier, i. 69, from a 'paper, folded up in the roll [of the *Revels Account* for 1513–14] and in a different handwriting', 'Inglyshe, and the oothers of the Kynges pleyers, after pleyed an Interluyt, whiche was wryten by Mayster Midwell, but yt was so long yt was not lykyd : yt was of the fyndyng of Troth, who was caryed away by ygnoraunce and ypocresy. The foolys part was the best, but the kyng departyd before the end to hys chambre.' According to Collier, the paper is signed by William Cornish and also contains a description of a Chapel interlude. But Brewer, who calendars the *Revels Account* fully, does not notice it, and according to A. W. Reed in *T. L. S.* (3 April 1919) it cannot be traced at the R. O.

[2] Cf. ch. iii ; *Tudor Revels*, 6.

[3] Brewer, ii. 1493. In 1546–7 they had 5s. for the loan of garments to the Revels (Kempe, 71).

[4] *Grey Friars Chronicle* (C. S.), 34, 'Also this same yere John Scotte, that was one of the kynges playeres, was put in Newgate for rebukynge of the shreffes, and was there a sennet, and at the last was ledde betwene two of the offecers from Newgate thorrow London and soe to Newgat agayne, and then was delyveryd home to hys howse ; but he toke such a thowte that he dyde, for he went in hys shurte '.

[5] John Slye and John Yonge, mercer, had been players to Queen Jane before her death in 1537, and were concerned about 1538 in a Chancery suit about a horse hired "to beare there playing garmentes ' (Stopes, *Shakespeare's Environment*, 235). Perhaps this explains the annuity of £1 10s. 5d. (1d. a day) which Young drew from the Chamber during 1540–2. But he obtained a patent as King's player, with an annual fee of £3 6s. 8d., on the death of Roo in 1539 (Brewer, xiv. 1. 423), and an 'annuity' of £3 6s. 8d. on the death of Sudbury in 1546 (Brewer, xxi. 2. 156). Collier, i. 134, cites a description of him in a fee list amongst the *Fairfax MSS.* as 'Maker of Interludes, Comedies, and Playes '.

George Mayler, merchant tailor, aged 40, and George Birch, coriar, aged 32, were called to give evidence as to the value of the garments and their use for a royal banquet at Greenwich in 1527.[1] In the second Mayler was himself a party. He is here described as a glazier, and an agreement of November 1528 is recited between him and one Thomas Arthur, tailor, whom he took as an apprentice for a year, promising to teach him to play and to obtain him admission into the King's company and the right to the privileges (*libertatem*) thereof and 'the Kinges bage'. According to Mayler, he found Arthur meat and drink and 4*d.* a day, but after seven weeks Arthur left him, beguiling away three of his covenant servants upon a playing tour in the provinces, out of which they made a profit of £30. He was, adds Mayler, 'right harde and dull too taike any lernynge, whereby he was nothinge meate or apte too bee in service with the Kinges grace too maike any plaiez or interludes before his highnes'. Arthur, on the other hand, alleged that it was Mayler who had broken the indentures, and sued him before the sheriffs of London for £26 damages. Owing to the accident of Mayler's being in Ludgate prison and unable to defend himself, the jury found against him for £4, and he appealed to Chancery to remove the action to that court.[2] The King's men, even apart from their other occupations as Household servants or tradesmen, were not wholly dependent on the royal bounty. The reward at Christmas was supplemented by minor gifts from the Princess Mary, or from lords and ladies of the Court, such as the Duke of Rutland and the Countess of Devon;[3] and the glamour of the King's badge doubtless added to the liberality of the company's reception in many a monastery, country mansion, and town hall. They are found during the reign at the priories of Thetford, Dunmow (1531–2), and Durham (1532–3), at the house of the Lestranges at Hunstanton (23 October 1530), at New Romney (1526–7), Shrewsbury (1527, 1533, 1540), Leicester (1531), Norwich (1533), Bristol (1535, 1536, 1537, 1541), Cambridge (1537–8), Beverley (1540–1), and Maldon (1546–7).[4] A private performance by the King's men forms an episode in the Elizabethan play of *Sir Thomas More*, although the Mason there named cannot be traced amongst their number.

No important change in the status of the company is to

---

[1] Cf. *Mediaeval Stage*, ii. 183.
[2] G. H. Overend in *N. S. S. Trans.* (1877–9), 425.
[3] Collier, i. 93; Madden, *Privy Purse Expenses of the Princess Mary*, 104, 140; *Rutland MSS.* iv. 270; Brewer, iv. 340.
[4] Cf. Murray, *passim*, and *Mediaeval Stage*, App. E.

be observed under Edward VI. Some of the existing members seem to have retired, and four new ones, Richard Coke, John Birch, Henry Heryot, and John Smyth, were appointed.[1] The first three of these, together with two others, Richard Skinner and Thomas Southey, received a warrant to the Master of the Great Wardrobe on 15 February 1548, for the usual livery assigned to yeomen officers of the household, which consisted of three yards of red cloth, with an allowance of 3s. 4d. for the embroidering thereon of the royal initials.[2] The fees of these five, and of George Birch and Robert Hinstock, who were survivors from Henry VIII's time, are traceable, as well as the annual reward of £6 13s. 4d., in the Chamber Accounts.[3] Each now got £3 6s. 8d. a year, under a warrant of 24 December 1548. The same names appear in a list of 30 September 1552, with the exception of Robert Hinstock, whose place had probably been taken by John Browne, appointed as from the previous Christmas by a warrant of 9 June 1552, which introduced the innovation of granting him a livery allowance of £1 3s. 4d. a year instead of the actual livery.[4] If we suppose that John Smith and John Young continued to be borne on the Exchequer pay-roll, the total number of eight interlude-players provided for in fee-lists of Edward's reign is made up.[5] John Smith is probably to be identified with the 'disard' or jester of that name who took part in George Ferrers's Christmas gambols of 1552-3.[6] John Young may be the 'right worshipful esquire John Yung' to whom William Baldwin dedicated his *Beware the Cat* in 1553. He certainly survived into Elizabeth's reign and was still drawing an annuity of £3 6s. 8d. as 'agitator comediarum' in 1569-70.[7] I have not noticed any provincial performances by the company during 1547-53, except at

[1] *Royal MS.* 7, C. xvi, f. 97 (cited Collier, i. 137). The names are in a list of servants 'nuely in ordinary of the Chamber', and some illegible names of players are in an accompanying list of 'Offycers in ordynary of the Chamber of the late Kynges Majestie now discharged'.

[2] *Lord Chamberlain's Records, Misc.* v. 127, f. 23 (also with the error 'E. and P.' in Sullivan, 249), 'three broade yerdes of redd wollen clothe for a liuery coate of suche prices as the yeomen officers of oure howseholde are accustomed to haue and iijˢ and iiijᵈ vnto euery of them for the Enbrauderinge of theire saide coates withe the lettres E and R on the backe and on the breste'.

[3] *Chamber Accounts* in *Trevelyan Papers*, i. 195-205; ii. 17-31, and Collier, i. 136, 138, 148.

[4] *S. P. D. Edw. VI*, xiv.

[5] *Stowe MS.* 571, f. 27ᵛ; *Harl. MS.* 240, f. 13.

[6] Feuillerat, *Edw. and Mary*, 89, 90, 97, 98, 119; cf. *Mediaeval Stage*, i. 406, where I think I was in error in taking John Smith as a name assumed by Will Somers.

[7] *Hist. MSS.* iii. 230, from book of annuities at Penshurst.

Maldon in 1549–50, but they are referred to more than once in the archives of the Revels. The Revels Office made them an oven and weapons of wood at Shrovetide 1548 and a seven-headed dragon at Shrovetide 1549. At Christmas 1551–2 the Privy Council gave them a warrant to borrow ' apparell and other fornyture' from the Master, and Lord Darcy gave John Birch and John Browne another for garments to serve in an interlude before the King on 6 January 1552.[1] William Baldwin, in his *Beware the Cat*, relates that during the Christmas of 1552–3, they were learning ' a play of Esop's Crowe, wherin the moste part of the actors were birds'.[2] Their only other play of which the name is known is that of *Self Love*, for which Sir Thomas Chaloner gave them 20s. on a Shrove Monday in 1551–3.[3]

The company no doubt took their share in Court revels during the earlier part of Mary's reign. But when the eclipse of gaiety came upon her later years they travelled. They are noted as the King and Queen's men in 1555–6 at Ipswich and Gloucester, in 1557 at Bristol, and in 1558 at Barnstaple, and as the Queen's men in 1555 at Leicester, in 1555–6 at Beverley, in 1556–7 at Beverley, Oxford, Norwich and Exeter, and in 1557–8 at Beverley, Leicester, Maldon, Dover, Lyme Regis, and Barnstaple. The nominal establishment continued to be eight.[4] But Heriot disappears after 1552 and John Birch, Coke, and Southey after 1556, and their vacancies do not seem to have been filled.[5]

Under Elizabeth the interlude players were certainly a moribund folk. They were reappointed ' during pleasure' under a warrant of 25 December 1559, and apparently Edmund Strowdewike and William Reading took the place of George Birch and Skinner.[6] They drew their fees of £3 6s. 8d. and livery allowances of £1 3s. 4d. from the Treasurer of the Chamber. The eight posts figure on the fee-lists long after there were no holders left.[7] The last ' reward' to the

---

[1] Feuillerat, *Edw. and Mary*, 31, 39, 57, 86.

[2] Collier, i. 149. The reference to Ferrers' ' divine' and ' astronomer' (cf. *Mediaeval Stage*, i. 407) fixes the date.

[3] *Mediaeval Stage*, ii. 201, from *Lansd. MS.* 824, f. 24.

[4] Fee-list in collection of Soc. of Antiquaries, cited by Collier, i. 161.

[5] *Chamber Accounts* in Collier, i. 161 ; *Declared Accounts* (*Pipe Office*), 541, m. 2ᵛ.

[6] Reading was a London player in 1550 (App. D, No. v). The Chamber Accounts for the first few years of Elizabeth show an annuity to a George Birch under a warrant of 7 Jan. 1560.

[7] Eight players of interludes at £3 6s. 8d. each are in the fee-lists (cf. vol. i, p. 29), *Stowe MS.* 571, f. 148 (*c.* 1575–80), *Sloane MS.* 3194, f. 38 (1585), *Stowe MS.* 571, f. 168 (*c.* 1587–90), *Lansd. MS.* 171, f. 250 (*c.* 1587–91), *S. P. D. Eliz.* ccxxi, f. 16 (*c.* 1588–93), *H. O.* 256 (*c.* 1598),

company, not improbably for the anti-papal farce of 6 January
1559, is to be found in the Chamber Account for 1558–60.
It may be inferred that they never again played at Court.
They were allowed to dwindle away. Browne and Reading
died in 1563, Strowdewike on 3 June 1568, and Smith survived
in solitary dignity until 1580.[1] Up to about 1573 he kept
up some sort of provincial organization, doubtless with the
aid of unofficial associates, and the Queen's players are
therefore traceable in many municipal Account-books. In
October 1559 they were at Bristol and before Christmas at
Leicester, in 1559–60 at Gloucester, in 1560–1 at Barnstaple,
in 1561 at Faversham,[2] in October–December 1561 at Leicester,
in 1561–2 at Gloucester, Maldon, and Beverley, in July 1562
at Grimsthorpe, and on 4 October at Ipswich, in August 1563
at Bristol, in 1563–4 at Maldon, on 12 and 20 March 1564 at
Ipswich again, and on 2 August at Leicester, in 1564–5 at
Abingdon, Maldon, and Gloucester, in 1565–6 at Maldon,
Oxford, and Shrewsbury, in July 1566 at Bristol, before
29 September at Leicester, and on 9 October at Ipswich,
in July 1567 at Bristol, in 1567–8 at Oxford and Gloucester,
in 1568–9 at Abingdon, Ipswich, and Stratford-upon-Avon,

and with the error of £3 6s. in *Hargreave MS.* 215, f. 21^v (*c.* 1592–5),
Lord Chamberlain's Records, v. 33, f. 19^v (1593), *Stowe MS.* 572, f. 35^v
(*c.* 1592–6), *Harl. MS.* 2078, f. 18^v (*c.* 1592–6). The inaccurate *Cott. MS.
Titus*, B. iii, f. 176 (*c.* 1585–93) gives two 'Plaiers on Interludes' at
£3 6s. The normal entry recurs in the Jacobean *Lansd. MS.* 272, f. 27
(1614) and *Stowe MS.* 575, f. 24 (1616), but a group of the early part
of the reign (*Addl. MS.* 35848, f. 19 ; *Addl. MS.* 38008, f. 58^v ; *Soc. Antiq.
MSS.* 74, 75) have ' Plaiers on the In lute ' or ' on in Lutes ', at £3 6s. 8d.
or £3 6s., which looks like an attempt to rationalize the *Cotton MS.*
entry. And *Stowe MS.* 574, f. 16^v, has ' Players on Lute ' at £3 6s. 8d.,
which some one has corrected by inserting the normal entry. All this
suggests that many copyists of fee-lists in the seventeenth century confused the post of interlude player with that of a lute player, and the
former was therefore probably obsolete, and its fee no longer paid to the
royal players of the day (cf. ch. x). I cannot agree with E. Law, *Shakespeare a Groom of the Chamber*, 26, 64, that the interlude players survived
under James as ' mummers, who, perhaps, sang in a sort of recitative
at masques and anti-masques '.

[1] *Chamber Declared Accounts (Pipe Office)*, 541, *passim*, 542, m. 3 ;
Collier, i. 236 ; Cunningham, xxvii. I do not know how long John Young
continued to draw his Exchequer ' annuity ', but presumably he had
retired on it.

[2] Fleay, 43, says, ' There was no specific company called the Queen's
players till 1583 ; it was a generic title applied to any company who
prepared plays for the Queen's amusement. In 1561 the players probably
were the Earl of Leicester's servants.' I need hardly say that I do not
accept this, which would not explain the disappearance of the ' Queen's '
from provincial records between 1573 and 1583. For another use of the
same improvised theory by Mr. Fleay, cf. App. D, No. lxxv.

in August 1569 at Bristol, and on 7 December at Oxford, in 1569–70 at Gloucester and Maldon, before 29 September 1570 at Leicester, in 1570–1 at Winchester, and during October–December 1571 at Leicester, in 1571–2 at Oxford, on 23 May 1572 at Nottingham, and on 20 November at Maldon, in 1572–3 at Ipswich, on 7 January 1573 at Beverley, and in 1573 at Winchester. This list is not exhaustive.[1] A reward to 'the Queens Majesty's men' in the Doncaster accounts for 1575 can hardly be assumed to refer to actors.

ii. THE EARL OF LEICESTER'S MEN

Robert Dudley; 5th s. of John, 1st Duke of Northumberland, *nat.* 24 June 1532 or 1533; m. (1) Amy, d. of Sir John Robsart, 4 June 1550, (2) Douglas Lady Sheffield, d. of William, 1st Lord Howard of Effingham, May 1573, (3) Lettice Countess of Essex, d. of Sir Francis Knollys, 1578; Master of the Horse, 11 Jan. 1559; High Steward of Cambridge, 1562; Earl of Leicester, 29 Sept. 1564; Chancellor of Oxford, 31 Dec. 1564; Lord Steward, 1584–8; Absolute Governor of United Provinces, 25 Jan. 1586–12 Apr. 1588; *ob.* 4 Sept. 1588.

The earliest mention of Lord Robert Dudley's players is in a letter which he wrote in June 1559 to the Earl of Shrews-bury, Lord President of the North, as Lord Lieutenant of Yorkshire, asking licence for them to perform in that county, in accordance with the proclamation of 16 May 1559.[2] The terms of the letter suggest that the company may already have played in London, but it is probable, as nothing is said of a hearing by the Queen, that they had not been at Court. They were there at each Christmas from 1560–1 to 1562–3, and then not for a decade. They were in 1558–9 at Norwich, in 1559–60 at Oxford, Saffron Walden, and Plymouth, in July 1560 at Bristol, in October 1561 at Grimsthorpe, in 1561–2 at Oxford, Maldon, and Ipswich, in September 1562 at Bristol, where they are called 'Lord Dudley's' players, on 12 November 1563 at Leicester, and on 17 November at Ipswich, in 1563–4 at Maldon, on 2 January 1564 at Ipswich, and on 1 July at Leicester. They are also found, as the Earl of Leicester's, in 1564–5 at Maldon, on 6 April 1565 at York, on 11 August 1569 at Nottingham, in January 1570 at Bristol, on 4 May 1570 at Oxford, and in October–December at Leicester, in 1570–1 at Abingdon, Barnstaple, and Glouces-ter, on 9 August 1571 at Saffron Walden,[3] in October–

---

[1] Murray, i. 19, adds records from other towns, and A. Clark (*10 N. Q.* xi. 41) for Saffron Walden.

[2] App. D, No. xi.

[3] Nichols, *Eliz.* i. 280, ' To my L. of Leyester's men for a reward, 2*s.* 6*d.*'. Fleay, 18, says that the amount is too small to favour the

December at Leicester, in the same year at Beverley, on 15 July 1572 at Ipswich, and on 20 August at Nottingham. The gap in my records between 1565 and 1569 is bridged in the fuller list covering other towns given by Mr. Murray.[1] Information as to the company in 1572 is derived from the signatures to a letter asking for appointment by Leicester, not merely as liveried retainers but as household servants, in order to meet the terms of the proclamation of 3 January in that year.[2]

To the right honorable Earle of Lecester, their good lord and master.

Maye yt please your honour to understande that forasmuche as there is a certayne Procalmation out for the revivinge of a Statute as touchinge retayners, as youre Lordshippe knoweth better than we can enforme you thereof : We therfore, your humble Servaunts and daylye Oratours your players, for avoydinge all inconvenients that maye growe by reason of the saide Statute, are bold to trouble your Lordshippe with this our Suite, humblie desiringe your honor that (as you have bene alwayes our good Lord and Master) you will now vouchsaffe to reteyne us at this present as your houshold Servaunts and daylie wayters, not that we meane to crave any further stipend or benefite at your Lordshippes hands but our lyveries as we have had, and also your honors License to certifye that we are your houshold Servaunts when we shall have occasion to travayle amongst our frendes as we do usuallye once a yere, and as other noble-mens Players do and have done in tyme past, Wherebie we maye enjoye our facultie in your Lordshippes name as we have done hertofore. Thus beyinge bound and readie to be alwayes at your Lordshippes commandmente we committ your honor to the tuition of the Almightie.

> Long may your Lordshippe live in peace,
> A pere of noblest peres :
> In helth welth and prosperitie
> Redoubling Nestor's yeres.

Your Lordshippes Servaunts most bounden

> Iames Burbage.
> Iohn Perkinne.
> Iohn Laneham.
> William Iohnson.
> Roberte Wilson.
> Thomas Clarke.

supposition that these were players. But Elizabeth was at Saffron Walden at the time, and a present was made to the Master of the Revels of a podd of oysters costing no more than 3s. 6d. Probably Saffron Walden was an economical place, or the payment was only for some speech.

[1] Murray, i. 41.

[2] Printed in *M. S. C.* i. 348, from *MS.* F. 10 (213) in the Marquis of Bath's collection at Longleat ; also in *3 N. Q.* xi. 350. The letter is undated but followed *Procl.* 663, on which cf. ch. viii and **App. D, No. xix.**

Several of these men were to achieve distinction in their 'quality'; of none of them is there any earlier record, unless John Perkin is to be identified with the Parkins who had been in 1552-3 one of the train of the Lord of Misrule.[1] By 6 December 1571 the company were in London.[2] Three years later they obtained a very singular favour in the patent of 10 May 1574, the general bearings of which have already been discussed.[3]

pro Iacobo Burbage & aliis de licencia speciali

Elizabeth by the grace of God quene of England, &c. To all Iustices, Mayors, Sheriffes, Baylyffes, head Constables, vnder Constables, and all other our officers and mynisters gretinge. Knowe ye that we of oure especiall grace, certen knowledge, and mere mocion haue licenced and auctorised, and by these presentes do licence and auctorise, oure lovinge Subiectes, Iames Burbage, Iohn Perkyn, Iohn Lanham, William Iohnson, and Roberte Wilson, seruauntes to oure trustie and welbeloued Cosen and Counseyllor the Earle of Leycester, to vse, exercise, and occupie the arte and facultye of playenge Commedies, Tragedies, Enterludes, stage playes, and such other like as they haue alredie vsed and studied, or hereafter shall vse and studie, aswell for the recreacion of oure loving subiectes, as for oure solace and pleasure when we shall thincke good to see them, as also to vse and occupie all such Instrumentes as they haue alredie practised, or hereafter shall practise, for and during our pleasure. And the said Commedies, Tragedies, Enterludes, and stage playes, to gether with their musicke, to shewe, publishe, exercise, and occupie to their best commoditie during all the terme aforesaide, aswell within oure Citie of London and liberties of the same, as also within the liberties and fredomes of anye oure Cities, townes, Bouroughes &c whatsoeuer as

[1] *Mediaeval Stage*, i. 406; Kempe, 47. The garments provided for Ferrers by the Revels included fools' coats for 'Children, John Smyth, Ayer apparent . . . Seame 2, Parkins 3, Elderton 4'.

[2] App. D, No. xviii.

[3] Cf. ch. ix. The patent is printed from the Patent Roll in *M. S. C.* i. 262; also from a copy of the entry on the Patent Roll preserved amongst Rymer's papers in *Sloane MS.* 4625 by Steevens, *Shakespeare* (1773), ii. 156, and therefrom in *Variorum*, iii. 47. This text omits the words ' oure Citie of London and liberties of the same as also within '. Collier, i. 203, and Hazlitt, *E. D. S.* 25, printed the Signet Bill, erroneously describing it as the Privy Seal, from the State Paper Office. This has the omitted words, and Collier correctly explains the omission in Steevens's text as due to an inaccurate copyist, pointing in proof to the words ' in oure *said* Cityte of London '. This did not, however, prevent Fleay, 45, from asserting that in the Patent ' an alteration had been made from the Privy Seal ', on the ground that its terms ' infringed on the powers of the City authorities '. Such an alteration not merely did not take place, but would have been a diplomatic impossibility, as the Patent Roll was made up, not from the Letters Patent, but from the Privy Seals on which these were based.

without the same, thoroughte oure Realme of England. Willynge and commaundinge yow and everie of yowe, as ye tender our pleasure, to permytte and suffer them herein withoute anye yowre lettes, hynderaunce, or molestacion duringe the terme aforesaid, anye acte, statute, proclamacion, or commaundement heretofore made, or hereafter to be made, to the contrarie notwithstandinge. Prouyded that the said Commedies, Tragedies, enterludes, and stage playes be by the master of oure Revells for the tyme beynge before sene & allowed, and that the same be not published or shewen in the tyme of common prayer, or in the tyme of greate and common plague in oure said Citye of London. In wytnes whereof &c. wytnes oure selfe at Westminster the xth daye of Maye.   per breve de priuato sigillo

The names in this patent only differ from those in the letter of 1572 by the omission of Thomas Clarke. By the time of its issue Leicester's men were again a Court company. They had made their reappearance at the Christmas of 1572–3 with three plays, all given before the end of December. They continued to appear in every subsequent year until the formation of the Queen's men in 1583. The building of the Theatre by James Burbadge in 1576 gave them a valuable head-quarters in London[1]; but they are still found from time to time about the provinces. Their detailed adventures are as follows. In 1572–3 they were at Stratford-on-Avon, on 8 August 1573 at Beverley, on 1 September at Nottingham, and in October at Bristol. On 26 December they played *Predor and Lucia* at Court, on 28 December *Mamillia*, and on 21 February 1574 *Philemon and Philecia*. In 1573–4 they were at Oxford and Leicester, on 13 June 1574 at Maldon, on 3 December at Canterbury. In 1574 they were also at Doncaster, where they played in the church. For the Court they rehearsed *Panecia*, and this was probably either their play of 26 December in which ' my Lord of Lesters boyes ' appeared, or that of 1 January 1575, in which there were chimney-sweepers. From 9 to 27 July 1575 Elizabeth paid her historic visit to Kenilworth, and there is no proof, but much probability, that the company were called upon to take their part in her entertainment. Its chronicler, Robert Laneham, may well have been a kinsman of the player. I have not come across them elsewhere this year, except at Southampton. They played at Court on 28 December 1575 and 4 March 1576, and are described in the account for their payment as ' Burbag

---

[1] Probably they occupied the Theatre, at any rate in summer, until 1583. A letter of Gabriel Harvey's in the summer of 1579 mentions ' Lycesters ', the ' Theater ', and ' Wylson ', but in no very definite connexion with each other (cf. p. 4). The Privy Council letter of 23 Dec. 1579, for their toleration at the Blackfriars, printed by Collier, *New Facts*, 9, is a forgery (cf. ch. xvii).

and his company '. A record of them at Ipswich in 1575–6 as ' my Lorde Robertes ' men is probably misdated. On 30 December 1576 they acted *The Collier* at Court. In 1576–7 they were at Stratford-on-Avon, in September 1577 at Newcastle, and between 13 and 19 October at Bristol, where they gave *Myngo*.[1] In 1577–8 they were also at Bath. They were at Court on 26 December 1577 and were to have performed again on 11 February 1578, but were displaced for Lady Essex's men. They may have been at Wanstead in May 1578 when Leicester entertained Elizabeth with Sidney's *The May Lady*. On 1 September they were at Maldon, on 9 September at Ipswich, and on 3 November at Lord North's at Kirtling. They played *A Greek Maid* at Court on 4 January 1579.[2] Their play on 28 December 1579 fell through because Elizabeth could not be present, but they played on 6 January 1580. In 1579–80 they were at Ipswich and Durham, and from 15 to 17 May 1580 at Kirtling. Vice-Chancellor Hatcher's letter of 21 January 1580 to Burghley about Oxford's men (*vide infra*) shows that Leicester's had then recently been refused leave to play at Cambridge. They played *Delight* at Court on 26 December and appeared again on 7 February 1581. That Wilson was still a member of the company in 1581 is shown by the reference to him in the curious Latin letter written by one of Lord Shrewsbury's players on 25 April of that year.[3] In the following winter they did not come to Court, but on 10 February 1583 they returned with *Telomo*.[4]

The best of Leicester's men, including Laneham, Wilson, and Johnson, appear to have joined the Queen's company on its formation in March 1583. Probably the Queen's also took over the Theatre. James Burbadge himself may have given up acting. Nothing more is heard of Leicester's men until 1584–5, when players under his name visited Coventry, Leicester, Gloucester, and Norwich. They were at Dover in June 1585, and at Bath as late as August. These may have been either the relics of the old company, or a new one formed to attend the Earl in his expedition to aid the States-General in the Low Countries. He was appointed to the command of the English forces on 28 August, and reached Flushing on

---

[1] I should think the ' Myngs ' of Murray, ii. 214, and Collier, *Northbrooke*, viii, more likely to be palaeographically accurate than the ' Myngo ' of J. Latimer in 9 *N. Q.* xi. 444 and his *Sixteenth Century Bristol*. But a song of ' Monsieur Mingo ' exists in a setting by Orlando de Lassus (cf *E. H. R.* xxxiii. 83), and is quoted in 2 *Hen. IV*, v. iii. 78, and *Summer's Last Will and Testament*, 968.

[2] Cf. App. D, No. xl.

[3] Cf. ch. xv, s.v. Baylye.

[4] Murray, i. 41, gives additional provincial records for 1576–82.

10 December. The pageants in his honour at Utrecht, Leyden, and the Hague were remarkable. Stowe records festivities at Utrecht on St. George's Day, 23 April 1586. These included an after-dinner show of 'dauncing, vauting, and tumbling, with the forces of Hercules, which gave great delight to the strangers, for they had not seene it before '.[1] It is a reasonable inference that the performers in *The Forces of Hercules* were English.[2]   And on 24 March 1586 Sir Philip Sidney, writing to Walsingham from Utrecht, says :

'I wrote to yow a letter by Will, my lord of Lester's jesting plaier, enclosed in a letter to my wife, and I never had answer thereof . . . I since find that the knave deliverd the letters to my ladi of Lester.'[3]

That the ' jesting plaier ' was William Shakespeare is on the whole less likely than that he was the famous comic actor, William Kempe ; and this theory is confirmed by a mention in an earlier letter of 12 November 1585 from Thomas Doyley at Calais to Leicester himself of ' Mr. Kemp, called Don Gulihelmo ', as amongst those remaining at Dunkirk.[4]   Leicester returned to England in November 1586. ' Wilhelm Kempe, instrumentist ' and his lad ' Daniell Jonns ' were at the Danish Court at Helsingör in August and September of the same year ; and so, from 17 July to 18 September, were five ' instrumentister och springere ' whose names may evidently be anglicized as Thomas Stevens, George Bryan, Thomas King, Thomas Pope, and Robert Percy (cf. ch. xiv). Some or all of these men are evidently the company of English comedians referred to by Thomas Heywood as commended by the Earl of Leicester to Frederick II of Denmark. Stevens and his fellows, but not apparently

---

[1] Stowe, *Annales*, 717, from a description by William Segar.

[2] The show itself was perhaps of Italian origin, for on 17 June 1572 the Earl of Lincoln was entertained at Paris by the Duke of Anjou (2 Ellis, iii. 12, from *Cott. MS. Vesp.* F. vi, f. 93) with ' an Italian comedie, which eandid, vaulting with notable supersaltes and through hoopes, and last of all the Antiques, of carying of men one uppon an other which som men call *labores Herculis* '.

[3] J. Bruce from *Harl. MS.* 287, f. 1, in *Who was Will, my Lord of Leicester's jesting player ?* (*Sh. Soc. Papers*, i. 88).   Bruce thinks that ' Will ' might be Johnson, Kempe, or Sly, but not Shakespeare, whose ' earliest works bear upon them the stamp of a mind far too contemplative and refined ' for Sidney to call him ' knave ' and ' jesting player '.   I do not subscribe to the reasoning. W. J. Thoms, *Three Notelets on Shakespeare*, 120, upholds the Shakespeare theory, and attempts to support it by evidence of military knowledge in the plays.

[4] Wright, *Eliz.* ii. 268, from *Cott. MS. Galba* C. viii ; cf. *M. L. R.* iv. 88.

Kempe, went on to Dresden.   Some of them ultimately became Lord Strange's men.   But it seems to me very doubtful whether, as is usually suggested, they passed direct into his service from that of Leicester.[1] They did not leave Dresden until 17 July 1587.   But Leicester's were at Exeter on 23 March 1586.   They played at Court on 27 December 1586, and were in London about 25 January 1587.   They were at Abingdon, Bath, Lathom, Coventry, Leicester, Oxford, Stratford-on-Avon, Dover, Canterbury, Marlborough, Southampton, Exeter, Gloucester, and Norwich during 1586–7. Kempe may, of course, have been with them on these occasions; but if Stevens and the rest passed as Leicester's in the Low Countries, it is likely that they ceased to do so when they went to Denmark.

Finally, Leicester's men were at Coventry, Reading, Bath, Maidstone, Dover, Plymouth, Gloucester, York, Saffron Walden, and probably Exeter in 1587–8.[2] On 4 September they were at Norwich, and here William Stonage, a cobbler, was committed to prison at their suit, 'for lewd words uttered against the ragged staff '.[3]   As late as 14 September they did not yet know that the lord in whose name they wore this badge was dead, for on that day, unless the records are again in error, they were still playing at Ipswich.[4]

iii. LORD RICH'S MEN

Richard Rich ; *nat. c.* 1496 ; cr. 1st Baron Rich, 26 Feb. 1548 ; Lord Chancellor, 23 Oct. 1548—21 Dec. 1551 ; m. Elizabeth Jenks ; *ob.* 12 June 1567.

Robert, s. of 1st Baron ; *nat. c.* 1537 ; succ. as 2nd Baron, 1567 ; *ob.* 1581.

The company was at Ipswich on 3 May 1564, Saffron Walden in 1563–4, Maldon in 1564–5, York on 6 April 1565,

---

[1] Fleay, 82 ; but cf. Lee, 36, and pp. 124, 272.   The thing is complicated by the influence of Malone's suggestion (*Variorum*, ii. 166) that Shakespeare might have left Stratford with Leicester's men on a visit to the town. This assumes its most fantastic form in the suggestion of Lee¹, 33, that Shakespeare was already in London, but ' Shakespeare's friends may have called the attention of the strolling players to the homeless youth, rumours of whose search for employment about the London theatres had doubtless reached Stratford '.

[2] At Exeter they are called the Lord Steward's, certainly not the Marquis of Winchester's, as Murray, ii. 95, suggests, for he was never Steward of Elizabeth's household.

[3] *Norfolk Archaeology*, xiii. 11.

[4] J. M. Cowper, in *1 R. Hist. Soc. Trans.* i. 218, records a performance by ' my Lord of Leicester's men ' at Faversham in 1589–90 ; but I think this must be an error.

and Ipswich on 31 July 1567. Then it secured a footing in London, and appeared at Court during the Christmas of 1567-8, on 26 December 1568, and on 5 February 1570. On 2 February 1570 it played at the Lincoln's Inn Candlemas 'Post Revels'.[1] It was also at Canterbury in 1569, Saffron Walden in 1569-70, and Maldon in 1570. Presumably it was a later company to which Gabriel Harvey referred in 1579 (cf. p. 4), and the death of Lord Rich in 1581 might naturally have led to its disbandment or change of service.

iv. LORD ABERGAVENNY'S MEN

Henry Neville, s. of George, 3rd Lord Abergavenny ; succ. as 4th Lord, 1535 ; *ob.* 1586.

The only London record of this company is a civic licence for it of 29 January 1572 (App. D, No. xxi), but it is found in provincial records at Dover, Canterbury, Leicester, Bristol, and Faversham in 1571 and 1572, and at Ludlow in 1575-6.

v. THE EARL OF SUSSEX'S MEN

Thomas Radcliffe, s. of Henry, 2nd Earl ; *nat. c.* 1526 ; m. (1) Elizabeth, d. of Thomas Earl of Southampton, (2) Frances, d. of Sir William Sidney, 26 Apr. 1555 ; succ. as 3rd Earl, 17 Feb. 1557 ; Lord Chamberlain, 13 July 1572 ; *ob.* 9 June 1583.

Henry Radcliffe, s. of Henry, 2nd Earl ; *nat. c.* 1530 ; m. Honora, d. of Anthony Pound, before 24 Feb. 1561 ; succ. as 4th Earl, 1583 ; *ob.* 14 Dec. 1593.

Robert Radcliffe, s. of 4th Earl ; *nat. c.* 1569 ; m. (1) Bridget, d. of Sir Charles Morison, who *ob.* Dec. 1623, (2) Frances Shute ; succ. as 5th Earl, 1593 ; acting Earl Marshal, 1597, 1601 ; *ob.* 22 Sept. 1629.

The third Earl of Sussex had a company, which proved one of the most long-lived of the theatrical organizations of Elizabeth's time and held together, now in London and now in the provinces, under no less than three earls. It first makes its appearance at Nottingham on 16 March 1569, at Maldon in 1570, on 28 January 1571, and on 20 August 1572, at Ipswich in 1571-2, at Canterbury and Dover in 1569 and 1570, and in 1569-70 at Bristol, Gloucester, and Ludlow, where it was of six men. Sussex became Chamberlain in July 1572 and in the following winter his company came to the Court, whose Christmases it helped to enliven pretty regularly until the death of its first patron in 1583. As I have shown elsewhere (ch. vi), Sussex seems to have had occasional

---

[1] J. D. Walker, *The Black Books of Lincoln's Inn*, i. 374, gives the name as 'Lord Roche', but this is probably a mistake. Viscount Roche of Fermoy in Ireland is not likely to have had players in London.

deputies in Lord Howard of Effingham and Lord Hunsdon during his term of office, but it is probably justifiable to assume that, when the Chamberlain's men are referred to at any time during 1572–83, Sussex's men are meant, and in 1577 and 1581 there is clear evidence that the names are used synonymously. Oddly enough, Howard's men are also referred to in one record of 1577 (cf. p. 134) as the Chamberlain's, but that is probably a slip. The detailed history of the company during this period is as follows. In 1572–3 they were at Bath, in July 1573 at Leicester, on 14 September at Nottingham, in 1573–4 at Coventry, in 1574, on some date before 29 September, at Leicester again, on 13 July at Maldon, and in September at Wollaton (Francis Willoughby's). They rehearsed two Court plays for Christmas on 14 December, *Phedrastus* and *Phigon and Lucia*, but in the end did not give a performance. In 1574–5 they were at Gloucester, in 1575 at Maldon, and before 29 September at Leicester. They played at Court on 2 February 1576. Their payee was John Adams, the only actor whose name is recorded in connexion with the company. In 1575–6 they were at Ipswich, on 27 July 1576 at Cambridge, and between 29 July and 5 August at Bristol, where they played *The Red Knight*. On 2 February 1577 they played *The Cynocephali* at Court. In 1576–7 they were at Coventry and Bath, on 30 May 1577 at Ipswich, and on 31 August at Nottingham. On 2 February 1578 they played at Court. In 1577–8 they were at Bath, on 15 July 1578 at Maldon, in the same year at Bristol, and in 1578–9 at Bath. Thereafter their activities seem to have been mainly confined to London. They were named by the Privy Council to the Lord Mayor among the Court companies for the Christmas of 1578–9 (App. D, No. xl), and played *The Cruelty of a Stepmother* on 28 December 1578, *The Rape of the Second Helen* on 6 January, and *Murderous Michael* on 3 March 1579. In the following winter their pieces were *The Duke of Milan and the Marquess of Mantua* on 26 December, *Portio and Demorantes* on 2 February, and *Sarpedon* on 16 February 1580.[1] The names of their Court plays on 27 December 1580 and 2 February 1581 are unfortunately not recorded. On 14 September they recur in the provinces, at Nottingham.[2] They missed the next winter at Court, and made their last appearance there for a decade in *Ferrar* on 6 January 1583.

[1] J. de Perott (*Rev. Germ.* Feb. 1914) suggests that *Portio and Demorantes* may be the Lamorat and Porcia of the French version (1548) of *Amadis de Grecia* (1542), viii. 56.

[2] Murray, i. 307, and A. Clark (*10 N. Q.* xii. 41) add records for 1573–83.

Either the death of their patron in June 1583, or possibly the formation of the Queen's men in the previous March, eclipsed them, but in 1585 they reappear as a provincial company, visiting Dover on 15 May, Bath on 22 July and in May 1586, Coventry twice in 1585–6, Ipswich in 1586–7, York in 1587, Leicester before Michaelmas of the same year, and Coventry in September. Here they were playing under the name of the Countess of Sussex. In 1587–8 they were at Coventry and Bath, on 18 April 1588 at Ipswich, on 17 February 1589 at Leicester, on 1 March at Ipswich, on 19 November at Leicester again, in the course of 1589 at Faversham, and in 1588–9 at Aldeburgh. On 17 February 1590 they were at Ipswich. In the spring of 1591 they appear to have made a temporary amalgamation with a group of the Queen's men (q.v.) and appeared with them on 14 February at Southampton, on 24 March at Coventry, and during 1590–1 at Gloucester. This arrangement probably terminated in May, and on 11 August Sussex's were alone at Leicester.[1]

They enter the charmed London circle again with a Court performance on 2 January 1592.[2] It is possible that they had attracted the services of Marlowe, for Kyd in a letter, probably to be dated in 1593, speaks of himself as having been in the service of a lord for whose players Marlowe was writing, and there are some traces of connexion between Kyd and the house of Radcliffe. During the plague of 1593 the company were obliged to travel again, and on 29 April the Privy Council Register records the issue of

' an open warrant for the plaiers, servantes to the Erle of Sussex, authorysinge them to exercyse theire qualitie of playinge comedies and tragedies in any county, cittie, towne or corporacion not being within vij[en] miles of London, where the infection is not, and in places convenient and tymes fitt.' [3]

The company were at Ipswich, Newcastle, and York in 1592–3. They were at Winchester on 7 December 1593; then came to London under the patronage of the fifth Earl, and, although not at Court, had a season of about six weeks, beginning on 26 December and ending on 6 February, with Henslowe, probably at the Rose. The names and dates of their plays and sums received at each, probably by himself as owner of the theatre, are noted by Henslowe in his diary. The company performed on thirty nights, in twelve plays.

---

[1] Murray, i. 307, has additional provincial records for 1585–91.
[2] I do not agree with Fleay, *Sh.* 18, 184, that Sussex's were satirized in *A Midsummer-Night's Dream* ; cf. *infra*, s.v. Hertford's.
[3] Dasent, xxiv. 209.

Henslowe's receipts averaged £1 13s., amounting to £3 1s. on the first night and £3 10s. on each of the next two, and thereafter fluctuating greatly, from a minimum of 5s. to a maximum of £3 8s. This last was at the production of the one 'new' play of the season, *Titus Andronicus*, on 24 January. The enterprise was brought to an abrupt termination by a renewed alarm of plague, and a consequent inhibition of plays by the Privy Council on 3 February. *Titus Andronicus* was played for the third and last time on 6 February, and on the same day the book was entered for copyright purposes in the Stationers' Register. The edition published in the same year professes to give the play as it was played by 'the Earle of Darbie, Earle of Pembrooke, and Earle of Sussex their Servants'. I suppose it to have passed, probably in a pre-Shakespearian version, from Pembroke's to Sussex's, when the former were bankrupt in the summer of 1593 (cf. *infra*), and to have been revised for Sussex's by the hand of Shakespeare. If so, it is a plausible conjecture that certain other plays, which were once Pembroke's and ultimately came to the Chamberlain's men, also passed through the hands of Sussex's. Such were *The Taming of A Shrew*, *The Contention of York and Lancaster*, and perhaps the *Ur-Hamlet*, *1 Henry VI*, and *Richard III*. There is no basis for determining whether any of Shakespeare's work on the York tetralogy was done for Sussex's; but it is worth noting that one of their productions was *Buckingham*, a title which might fit either *Richard III* or that early version of *Henry VIII*, the existence of which, on internal grounds, I suspect. Of Sussex's other plays in this season, one, *George a Greene, the Pinner of Wakefield*, was published as theirs in 1599; another, Marlowe's *Jew of Malta*, probably belonged to Henslowe, as it was acted in turn by nearly every company which he financed; and of the rest, *God Speed the Plough*, *Huon of Bordeaux*, *Richard the Confessor*, *William the Conqueror*, *Friar Francis*, *Abraham and Lot*, *The Fair Maid of Italy*, and *King Lud*, nothing is known, except for the entry of *God Speed the Plough* in 1601 and an edifying tale related about 1608 by Thomas Heywood in connexion with an undated performance of *Friar Francis* by the company at King's Lynn.[1]

At Easter 1594 Henslowe records another very brief season of eight nights between 1 and 9 April, during which the Queen's and Sussex's men played 'together'. This suggests to Dr. Greg that the companies appeared on different nights, but to me rather that they combined their forces, as they seem to have already done at Coventry in 1591. Henslowe's

[1] Cf. App. C, No. lvii.

receipts averaged £1 17s. The repertory included, besides *The Fair Maid of Italy* and *The Jew of Malta, King Leare*, doubtless to be identified with *King Leire and his Three Daughters* (1605), *The Ranger's Comedy*, and *Friar Bacon and Friar Bungay*. The latter was published in 1594 as a Queen's play. Both it and *The Ranger's Comedy* were played at a later date by the Admiral's, and may have belonged to Henslowe. Strange's had played *Friar Bacon* in 1592–3.

Thereafter Sussex's men vanish from the annals; they may have been absorbed in the Queen's men for travelling purposes. Later players under the same name are recorded at Coventry in 1602–3, Dover in 1606–7, Canterbury in 1607–8, Bristol, Norwich, and Dunwich in 1608–9, Leicester on 31 August 1615, and Leominster in 1618, and it may be these to whom Heywood alludes as visiting King's Lynn. If so, their possession of *Friar Francis* suggests some affiliation to the earlier company.

vi. SIR ROBERT LANE'S MEN

Robert Lane, of Horton, Northants; *nat. c.* 1528; Kt. 2 Oct. 1553; m. (1) Catherine, d. of Sir Roger Copley, (2) Mary, d. of John Heneage.

I have not come across Sir Robert Lane's men except at Bristol in August 1570, and at Court during the Christmas of 1571–2. On 27 December 1571 they played *Lady Barbara* and on 17 February 1572 *Cloridon and Radiamanta*. The first performance was paid for by a warrant of 5 January to Laurence Dutton; the second by a warrant of 26 February, in which, according to the entry in the Privy Council Register, Dutton was again named.[1] But the Treasurer of the Chamber records the payment as made to John Greaves and Thomas Goughe. Probably this company is identical with that found next year in the service of the Earl of Lincoln.

vii. THE EARL OF LINCOLN'S (LORD CLINTON'S) MEN

Edward Fiennes de Clinton; s. of Thomas, 8th Lord Clinton and Saye, *nat.* 1512; m. (1) Elizabeth Lady Talboys, d. of Sir John Blount, 1534, (2) Ursula, d. of William Lord Stourton, *c.* 1540, (3) Elizabeth Lady Browne, 'the fair Geraldine,' d. of Gerald, 9th Earl of Kildare, *c.* 1552; succ. as 9th Baron, 1517; Lord High Admiral, 1550–3, and again 13 Feb. 1558; 1st Earl of Lincoln, 4 May 1572; ambassador to France, 1572; Lord Steward, 1581–5; *ob.* 16 Jan. 1585.

Henry Fiennes de Clinton, s. of Edward and Ursula; *nat. c.* 1541; m. (1) Catharine, d. of Francis, 2nd Earl of Huntingdon, Feb. 1557,

---

[1] Dasent, viii. 71, dating the warrant on 29 Feb.

(2) Elizabeth, d. of Sir Richard Morison and wid. of William Norreys, after 1579; Kt. 29 Sept. 1553; succ. as 2nd Earl, 16 Jan. 1585; *ob.* 29 Sept. 1616.

Players serving the Lord Admiral were at Winchester in 1566–7. A company under the name of the Earl of Lincoln and led by Laurence Dutton played at Court during the Christmas of 1572–3, and a company under that of Lord Clinton, and also led by Dutton, in *Herpetulus the Blue Knight and Perobia* on 3 January 1574, and on 27 December 1574 and 2 January 1575. For 1574–5 they rehearsed three plays, one of which was *Pretestus*. Probably these are the same company transferred by the Lord Admiral to his son. Dutton was with Sir Robert Lane's men in 1571–2 and with the Earl of Warwick's in 1575–6. The whole company may have taken service with Lincoln instead of Lane as a result of the statute of 1572 (App. D, No. xxiv), but it does not seem to have been altogether absorbed in Warwick's, as Lord Clinton's men are found at Southampton on 24 June 1577, when they were six in number, at Bristol in July, and at Coventry in 1576–7. A later company under the name of the Earl of Lincoln has a purely provincial record in 1599–1604. There is an isolated notice at Norwich in 1608–9.

viii. THE EARL OF WARWICK'S MEN

Ambrose Dudley, 3rd s. of John, 1st Duke of Northumberland; *nat. c.* 1528; m. (1) Anne Whorwood, (2) Elizabeth Talboys, *c.* 1553, (3) Anne, d. of Francis, Earl of Bedford, 11 Nov. 1565; Master of Ordnance, 12 Apr. 1560; Earl of Warwick, 26 Dec. 1561; Chief Butler of England, 4 May 1571; Privy Councillor, 5 Sept. 1573; *ob.* 20 Feb. 1590.

Dudley seems to have had players in London in January 1562, when they were rewarded by the Duchess of Suffolk.[1] They are also found in 1559–64 at Oxford, Gloucester, Bristol, Plymouth, Winchester, Dover, Canterbury, and Norwich. Their only Court performances upon record were two during the Christmas of 1564–5. In 1564–5 they were apparently at Canterbury.[2]

After an interval of ten years there are Warwick's men at Court on 14 February 1575 and also at Stratford in the course of 1574–5, at Lichfield between 27 July and 3 August during the progress,[3] and at Leicester before 29 September 1575. At the following Christmas they gave three plays at Court,

[1] *Ancaster MSS. (Hist. MSS.)* 466.
[2] *Hist. MSS.* ix. 1. 156. The payment is given as to the Earl of 'Waffyts' men. [3] Nichols, *Eliz.* i. 531.

on 26 December 1575 and 1 January and on 5 March 1576.
John and Laurence Dutton and Jerome Savage were their
payees.   Laurence Dutton and possibly others of the company
had been, a year before, in Lord Clinton's service.   During
the next four winters they appeared regularly at Court, and
are recorded at Leicester in 1576 and Nottingham on 1 September 1577.   On 26 December 1576 they played *The Painter's
Daughter*, and on 18 February 1577 *The Irish Knight*.   The
names of their plays on 28 December 1577 and 6 January
and 9 February 1578 are not preserved.   They were notified
by the Privy Council to the Lord Mayor as one of the Court
companies for the Christmas of 1578–9 (App. D, No. xl),
and played *The Three Sisters of Mantua* on 26 December and
The Knight in the Burning Rock on 1 March.   A play intended
for 2 February was not performed, but payment was made
to Jerome Savage.   Gabriel Harvey (cf. p. 4) mentions them
as a London company in the summer of 1579.   On 1 January
1580 they played *The Four Sons of Fabius*.   A Winchester
record of 'Lord Ambrose Dudley's' men in 1581–2 must be
an error.

   The Duttons were evidently a restless folk, and the disappearance of Warwick's men and the appearance of Oxford's
men in 1580 is to be explained by another transfer of their
services.   This is referred to in the following verses : [1]

The Duttons and theyr fellow-players forsakyng the Erle of Warwycke
theyr mayster, became followers of the Erle of Oxford, and wrot them-
selves his COMOEDIANS, *which certayne Gentlemen altered and made*
CAMOELIONS. *The Duttons, angry with that, compared themselves to*
any gentleman ; therefore these armes were devysed for them.

> The fyeld, a fart durty, a gybbet crosse-corded,
> A dauncing Dame Flurty of alle men abhorred ;
> A lyther lad scampant, a roge in his ragges,
> A whore that is rampant, astryde wyth her legges,
> A woodcocke displayed, a calfe and a sheepe,
> A bitch that is splayed, a dormouse asleepe ;
> A vyper in stynche, *la part de la drut,*
> Spell backwarde this Frenche and cracke me that nut.
>
> Parcy per pillery, perced with a rope,
> To slythe the more lytherly anoynted with sope ;
> A coxcombe crospate in token of witte,
> Two eares perforate, a nose wythe slytte.
> Three nettles resplendent, three owles, three swallowes,
> Three mynstrellmen pendent on three payre of gallowes,

----

[1] Wright and Halliwell, *Reliquiae Antiquae*, ii. 122, from *Harl. MS.*
7392, f. 97 ; cf. *M. L. R.* ii. 5.

Further sufficiently placed in them
A knaves head, for a difference from alle honest men.

The wreathe is a chayne of chaungeable red,
To shew they ar vayne and fickle of head ;
The creste is a lastrylle whose feathers ar blew,
In signe that these fydlers will never be trew ;
Whereon is placed the horne of a gote,
Because they ar chast, to this is theyr lotte,
For their bravery, indented and parted,
And for their knavery innebulated.

Mantled lowsy, wythe doubled drynke,
Their ancient house is called the Clynke ;
Thys Posy they beare over the whole earthe,
Wylt please you to have a fyt of our mirthe ?
But reason it is, and heraultes allowe welle,
That fidlers should beare their armes in a towelle.

In 1587–8 tumblers were at Bath under Warwick's name.
I do not understand the entry of his men in the Ipswich
accounts, as playing on 10 March 1592. Ambrose Dudley
died in 1590, and his doubtfully legitimate nephew, Sir Robert
Dudley, does not seem even to have claimed the title until
1597. The Ipswich records are unreliable, but possibly Lady
Warwick maintained a company for a while. The Corporation
of London were considering some ' cause ' of hers as to plays
in May 1594 (App. D, No. xcviii).

ix. THE EARL OF OXFORD'S MEN

John de Vere, s. of John, 15th Earl of Oxford ; *nat. c.* 1512 ; succ.
as 16th Earl and Lord Great Chamberlain, 21 Mar. 1540 ; m. Margaret
Golding, 1547 ; *ob.* 3 Aug. 1562.
  Edward de Vere, s. of John, 16th Earl of Oxford ; *nat.* 2 Apr. 1550 ;
succ. as 17th Earl and Lord Great Chamberlain, 3 Aug. 1562 ; m. (1)
Anne, d. of William Lord Burghley, Dec. 1571, (2) Elizabeth Trentham,
c. 1591 ; *ob.* 24 June 1604. Of his daughters by (1), Elizabeth m.
William Stanley, 6th Earl of Derby, 26 Jan. 1595 ; Bridget m. Francis,
Lord Norris ; Susan m. Sir Philip Herbert, afterwards Earl of Mont-
gomery, 27 Dec. 1604.

  The Earls of Oxford had their players as far back as 1492.[1]
A company belonging to the 16th Earl caused a scandal by
playing in Southwark at the moment when a dirge was
being sung for Henry VIII in St. Saviour's on 6 February
1547.[2] It is probably the same company which is traceable
in 1555–6 at Dover, in 1557–8 at Ipswich, in 1559–60 and

[1] *Mediaeval Stage*, ii. 222.   [2] Cf. ch. viii.

1560–1 at Maldon, and in 1561–2 at Barnstaple, Maldon, and Ipswich. Murray (ii. 63) adds a few notices. There is no sign of it at Court, and it is likely that the 17th Earl discontinued it soon after his succession. The last notices of it are at Leicester, Plymouth, and Ipswich in 1562–3.

At a later date, however, this Earl was clearly interested in things dramatic. He took part in a Shrovetide device at Court in 1579, and is recorded in Francis Meres's *Palladis Tamia* (1598) to have been himself a playwright and one of ' the best for comedy amongst us ' (App. C, No. lii). In 1580 the Duttons and the rest of the Earl of Warwick's men transferred themselves to his service, and thereby laid themselves open to satire upon their fickleness (cf. *supra*). I do not know whether it was their resentment at this that brought them into trouble, but on 12 April 1580 the Lord Mayor wrote to Sir Thomas Bromley, the Lord Chancellor, about a disorder at the Theatre two days before, which he understood to be already before the Privy Council; and on 13 April we find the Council committing Robert Leveson and Laurence Dutton, servants of the Earl of Oxford, to the Marshalsea for a fray with the Inns of Court. On 26 May the matter was referred to three judges for examination, and on 18 July Thomas Chesson, sometime servant to the Earl, was released on bail (App. D, Nos. xliii, xliv). These notices suggest that the company had arranged, possibly during the absence of Leicester's men from town, to occupy the Theatre. In view of their disgrace, it was no doubt better for them to travel, and on 21 June John Hatcher, Vice-Chancellor of Cambridge, wrote to Lord Oxford's father-in-law, Lord Burghley, to acknowledge recommendations received from him, as well as from the Lord Chancellor and Lord Chamberlain Sussex, that Oxford's men should be allowed to ' show their cunning in several plays already practised by them before the Queen's majesty ', and to explain that, in view of pestilence, the need for industry at commencement, a previous refusal to Leicester's men, and a Privy Council order of 1575 against assemblies in Cambridge, he had thought it better to give them 20s., and send them away unheard.[1] They are traceable provincially in 1580–3.[2] At Norwich (1580–1) the payment was made to ' the Earle of Oxenfordes lads ', and at Bristol (Sept. 1581) there were nine boys and a man. These were probably

---

[1] Ellis, i. 3, 32 ; Cooper, ii. 379 ; from *S. P. D. Eliz.* cxxxix. 26. The Privy Council letter of 30 Oct. 1575 (*M. S. C.* i. 195) forbids ' open shewes ' and ' assemblies in open places of multitudes of people ' within five miles of Cambridge.

[2] Murray, i. 348. I add Maldon (1581).

boys of the Earl's domestic chapel, travelling either with the Duttons or as a separate company.

The Duttons joined the Queen's company, John on its first establishment in 1583. It is in the following winter, however, that an Oxford's company first appears at Court. Here the Earl's 'servauntes' performed on 1 January and 3 March 1584. Their payee was John Lyly, who had probably been for some years in the Earl's service. Provincial performances continue during 1583–5, and in the records the company are always described as 'players' or 'men'.[1] On 27 December 1584 *Agamemnon and Ulysses* was played at Court by the Earl of Oxford's 'boyes'. For this the payee was Henry Evans, probably the same who in 1600 set up the Chapel plays. I do not feel much doubt that the companies under Lyly and Evans were the same, or that in 1583–4 they in fact consisted of a combination of Oxford's boys, Paul's and the Chapel, working under Lyly and Evans at the Blackfriars theatre.[2] This arrangement had, no doubt, to be modified when Sir William More recovered possession of the premises in the spring of 1584, and after the performance of December 1584 Oxford perhaps ceased to maintain boy players and contented himself with another company of his servants, who made an appearance at Court on 1 January 1585, under John Symons, in feats of activity and vaulting. These tumblers had apparently been Lord Strange's men in 1583, and by 1586 had returned into the service of the Stanley family.

An Oxford's company did not again perform at Court, but his 'plaiers' were at Norwich in 1585–6, and Ipswich in 1586–7,[3] and players under his name were notified to Walsingham amongst others setting up their bills in London on 25 January 1587 (App. D, No. lxxviii). They were at York in June 1587 and Maidstone in 1589–90. Finally, at the end of the reign, comes a letter from the Privy Council to the Lord Mayor on 31 March 1602, which informs him that at the Earl's suit the Queen has tolerated a new company formed by a combination of his servants and those of the Earl of Worcester, and that they are to play at the Boar's Head (App. D, No. cxxx). Oxford's men had probably then

---

[1] Murray, i. 348. I add Stratford (1583–4). Dr. Boas kindly informs me that the Oxford City Accounts for 1584–5 have a payment to Oxford's 'musytions'.

[2] Cf. ch. xii (Chapel).

[3] The payment was made to Richard Woderam, but he is more likely to have been an agent of the Corporation than a member of the company.

been established for some little time, as they are indicated as having played *The Weakest Goeth to the Wall* (1600, S. R. 23 October 1600) by the title-page, and *The History of George Scanderbarge* by the entry in the Stationers' Register (3 July 1601). Meres's reference to Oxford in 1598 suggests that they may have been in existence still earlier, as it is natural to suppose that he wrote comedies for his own men. Some of the writers, however, with whom Meres groups him belong to the early years of the reign, although others are contemporary. From 1602 the company was no doubt merged in Worcester's, which in its turn became Queen Anne's.

x. THE EARL OF ESSEX'S MEN

Walter Devereux, s. of Sir Richard Devereux and g.s. of Walter, Lord Bourchier and 1st Viscount Hereford ; *nat.* 1541 ; succ. as 2nd Viscount Hereford, 1558 ; m. Lettice, d. of Sir Francis Knollys, *c.* 1561 ; 1st Earl of Essex, 4 May 1572 ; *ob.* 22 Sept. 1576.

Lettice, Countess of Essex, b. *c.* 1541 ; m. (2) Robert, Earl of Leicester, 21 Sept. 1578, (3) Sir Christopher Blount, July 1589 ; *ob.* 25 Dec. 1634.

Robert Devereux, s. of 1st Earl of Essex ; b. 19 Nov. 1566 ; succ. as 2nd Earl, 1576 ; m. Frances, Lady Sidney, d. of Sir Francis Walsingham, 1590 ; Master of the Horse, 23 Dec. 1587 ; Earl Marshal, 28 Dec. 1597 ; Chancellor of Cambridge University, 10 Aug. 1598 ; rebelled, 8 Feb. 1601 ; executed, 25 Feb. 1601.

The Bourchiers, Earls of Essex, whom the Devereux succeeded through an heiress, had their players well back into the fifteenth century. In fact, the earliest household troop on record is that of Henry Bourchier, first earl of the senior creation, which is found at Maldon in 1468–9 and at Stoke-by-Nayland on 9 January 1482.[1]

Walter Devereux had a company, which visited Bath, Bristol, Gloucester, and Nottingham in 1572–3, Wollaton (Francis Willoughby's) in July 1574, Coventry on 29 August, and Leicester before 29 September 1574, Gloucester, Dover, and Coventry in 1574–5, Coventry and Leicester in 1575–6, Nottingham in September 1576, and Bristol in September 1577. On the Earl's death the Countess retained the company, and under her name it appeared at Coventry and Oxford in 1576–7. On 11 February 1578 it gave its only performance at Court, taking the place of Leicester's men, to whom that day had originally been assigned. It was included in the list of Court companies sent to the Lord Mayor in December

---

[1] *Mediaeval Stage*, ii. 186, 256. The 1469 entry has been since published by A. Clark in *10 N. Q.* vii. 181, ' Et solut. lusoribus domini comitis Essex ludentibus coram burgensibus infra burgum hoc anno, vs.'

1578 (App. D, No. xl), but gave no play that winter. The Privy Council described it as the Earl of Essex's men, and it played under that name at Coventry in 1577–8 and at Ipswich in 1579–80 ; but at Oxford, Coventry, and Stratford-on-Avon in 1578–9, and at Oxford in 1579–80, it is still called the Countess of Essex's. It could hardly have borne that name after August 1579, when the Countess's secret marriage with Leicester was revealed to Elizabeth, and doubtless her disgrace debarred it from any further Court favour.

Robert Earl of Essex had a provincial company from 1581 to 1596. In 1581–2 it was at Exeter, in July 1584 at Ludlow, in 1583–4 at Leicester, Stratford-on-Avon, and Ipswich, and in 1584–5 at Bath. On 26 June 1585 it played at Thorpe in Norwich, in spite of a prohibition by the Corporation, and was sentenced to be excluded from civic reward in future. In 1585–6 it was at Coventry and Ipswich, in 1586 before 29 September at Leicester, and possibly about May at Oxford, on 27 February 1587 at York, on 16 July at Leicester, and in the course of the year at Stratford-on-Avon. In 1587–8 it was at Coventry, Ipswich, Saffron Walden, and Leicester, in 1588–9 at Bath, Saffron Walden, and Reading, on 7 September 1589 at Knowsley, on 31 October at Ipswich, and in the same year at Faversham. It was also at Coventry and Faversham in 1589–90, at Maldon in 1590, and twice at Faversham in 1590–1, and is last recorded at Ludlow in April 1596. Murray adds some intermediate dates. A company of Essex's men which appeared at Coventry in 1600–1 is probably distinct. The execution of Essex on 25 February 1601 must have brought it to a premature end.

xi. LORD VAUX'S MEN

William Vaux, 3rd Lord Vaux ; *nat. c.* 1542 ; m. (1) Elizabeth Beaumont, (2) Mary Tresham ; *ob.* 20 Aug. 1595.
Edward Vaux, 4th Lord Vaux ; *nat.* 1588 ; *ob.* 1661.

These companies are extremely obscure. Gabriel Harvey mentions the first in 1579 (cf. p. 4) ; the second was at Leicester in October–December 1601, Coventry in 1603–4 and 1608, and Skipton in 1609.

xii. LORD BERKELEY'S MEN

Henry FitzHardinge Berkeley, Baron Berkeley ; succ. 1553 ; m. Catherine, d. of Henry Howard, Earl of Surrey ; *ob.* 1613 ; father of Thomas Berkeley, *nat.* 11 July 1575 ; m. Elizabeth, d. of Sir G. Carey, afterwards 2nd Baron Hunsdon, 19 Feb. 1596 ; *ob.* 22 Nov. 1611.

The only London record of this company is in July 1581, when some of them, including Arthur King and Thomas

Goodale, were committed to the Counter after a brawl with Inns of Court men. Lord Berkeley apologized to the Lord Mayor on their behalf, and said that they would go to the country (App. D, Nos. xlix, l). Their other appearances are all in the country, at Bristol between 6 and 12 July 1578, where they played *What Mischief Worketh in the Mind of Man*, at Bath on 11 July 1578 and on another day in 1578–9, at Abingdon in 1579–80, Stratford-on-Avon in 1580–1, Maldon in 1581, Stratford-on-Avon in 1582–3, Barnstaple in 1583–4, and Bath in 1586–7. Long after they, or a later company under the same name, reappear at Coventry in 1597–8, at Leicester in 1598 before Michaelmas, at Saffron Walden in 1598–9, and at Coventry and elsewhere in 1603–10. Lord Berkeley's name is sometimes misspelt in the account-books as ' Bartlett '.[1]

xiii. QUEEN ELIZABETH'S MEN

The origin of this company, the most famous of all the London companies during the decade of the 'eighties, can be dated with an extreme minuteness.[2]   The Revels Accounts for 1582–3 record an expenditure of 20s. in travelling charges by

' Edmond Tylney Esquire Master of the office being sente for to the Courte by Letter from Mr. Secretary dated the xth of Marche 1582. To choose out a companie of players for her maiestie.'[3]

The date then was 10 March 1583, and the business was in the hands of Sir Francis Walsingham. Lord Chamberlain Sussex, to whom it would naturally have fallen, was ill in the previous September[4] and died on the following 9 June. Walsingham's agency in the matter is confirmed in the account of the formation of the company inserted by Edmund Howes in the 1615 and 1631 editions of Stowe's *Annales* :

' Comedians and stage-players of former time were very poor and ignorant in respect of these of this time : but being now grown very skilful and exquisite actors for all matters, they were entertained into the service of divers great lords : out of which companies there were twelve of the best chosen, and, at the request of Sir Francis Walsingham, they were sworn the queens servants and were allowed wages and liveries as grooms of the chamber : and until this yeare 1583,

---

[1] *Variorum*, ii. 150.   The ' lord Cartleyes players ' recorded by B. S. Penley, *The Bath Stage*, 12, in 1580–1, 1582–3, and 1583–4 were perhaps Lord Berkeley's.   Murray, ii. 27, adds other provincial notices.

[2] This did not prevent Chalmers from giving the date 1581 and being set right by Malone (*Variorum*, iii. 442).   Collier, i. 247, gives 1583, but misdates Tilney's commission of 1581, and takes it for the instrument constituting the company.

[3] Feuillerat, *Eliz.* 359.   [4] Nicolas, *Hatton*, 271.

the queene had no players. Among these twelve players were two
rare men, viz. Thomas Wilson, for a quicke, delicate, refined, extemporall witt, and Richard Tarleton, for a wondrous plentifull pleasant
extemporall wit, he was the wonder of his time. He lieth buried in
Shoreditch church. [In a note] He was so beloved that men use his
picture for their signs.' [1]

Howes is not altogether accurate. ' Thomas ' is obviously
a mistake for ' Robert ' Wilson. Elizabeth had maintained
players before, the Interluders, although they had cut little
figure in the dramatic history of the reign, and the last of
them had died in 1580. Dr. Greg thinks that the players
were not appointed as grooms of the Chamber, on the ground
that their names do not appear in a list of these officers
appended to a warrant of 8 November 1586.[2] But Tarlton
is described as ' ordenary grome off her majestes chamber '
in the record of his graduation as a master of fence in 1587,
and both he and his ' fellow ', William Johnson, are described
as ' grooms of her majesties chamber ' in his will of 1588.
Their absence from Dr. Greg's list is probably due to their
treatment as a special class of grooms of the chamber in
ordinary without fee, who were not called upon to perform
the ordinary duties of the office, such as helping to watch
the palace.[3] That they had liveries, which were red coats,
is borne out by the particular mention of the fact that they
were not wearing them, in the depositions concerning a very
untoward event which took place in the first few months
of their service. On the afternoon of 15 June 1583 they were
playing at the Red Lion in Norwich. A dispute as to payment
arose between a servant of one Mr. Wynsdon and Singer,
who, in a black doublet and with a player's beard on, was
acting as gatekeeper. Tarlton and Bentley, who was playing
the duke, came off the stage, and Bentley broke the offender's
head with the hilt of his sword. The man fled, pursued by
Singer with an arming-sword which he took off the stage,
and by Henry Browne, a servant of Sir William Paston. Both
of them struck him, and one of the blows, but it was not
certain whose, proved mortal.[4]

Several other places, besides Norwich, received a visit
from the Queen's men during the first summer of their
existence. In April they were at Bristol, on 9 July at Cambridge, and between 24 July and 29 September at Leicester.

[1] Stowe, *Annales* (1615), 697, (1631), 698.
[2] Greg, *Henslowe*, ii. 79, citing *Addl. MS.* 5750, f. 113.
[3] Cf. ch. x.
[4] Halliwell, *Affray at Norwich in 1583 in which Queen Elizabeth's Players
were involved* (1864), and in *Illustrations of the Life of Shakespeare*, 118.

Their travels also extended to Gloucester, Aldeburgh, Nottingham, and Shrewsbury.[1]   In the winter they returned to London, and on 26 November the Privy Council wrote to the Lord Mayor to bespeak for them permission to play in the City and the liberties upon week-days until Shrovetide. The City accordingly licensed them to play at the Bull and the Bell, but with unwelcome limitations, for on 1 December it was necessary for Walsingham to write a personal letter, explaining that it was not the intention of the Council that the licence to play should be confined to holidays.   The City record gives the names of the twelve members of the company as Robert Wilson, John Dutton, Richard Tarlton, John Laneham, John Bentley, Thobye Mylles, John Towne, John Synger, Leonall Cooke, John Garland, John Adams, and William Johnson.   The company made its initial appearance at Court on 26 December, and played again on 29 December, and on 3 March 1584.   Their public performances probably continued through the spring, but in June there were disturbances in and around the Middlesex theatres, and the City obtained leave from the Council to suppress plays.   The Queen's submitted to an injunction from William Fleetwood, the Recorder; and their leader advised him to send for the owner of the Theatre, who was Lord Hunsdon's man, and bind him.   They travelled again, and are found in 1583-4 at Bath and Marlborough, and in October or November at Dover. When the winter came on, they once more approached the Council and requested a renewal of the previous year's privilege, submitting articles in which they pointed out that the time of their service was drawing near, and that the season of the year was past to play at any of the houses outside the City.   They also asked for favourable letters to the Middlesex justices.   The City opposed the concession, and begged that, if it were granted, the number and names of the Queen's men might be set out in the warrant, complaining that in the previous year, when toleration was granted to this company alone, all the playing-places were filled with men calling themselves the Queen's players.   The records do not show whether the Council assented.[2]   The company appeared four times at Court, giving *Phillyda and Corin* on 26 December, *Felix and Philiomena* on 3 January 1585, *Five Plays in One* on 6 January, and an antic play and a comedy on 23 February. They had prepared a fifth performance, of *Three Plays in One*, for 21 February, but it was not called for.   Mr. Fleay has conjectured that the *Five Plays in One* and the *Three*

[1] Murray, i. 20, and A. Clark in *10 N. Q.* xii. 41 (Saffron Walden) give other provincial records throughout.   An Ipswich one for 1581-2 must be misplaced.   [2] Cf. App. D, No. lxxv.

Plays in One may have been the two parts of Tarlton's *Seven Deadly Sins*.[1] The payment for this winter's plays was made to Robert Wilson.

There is no evidence that the company were travelling in 1585. They were at Court again on 26 December and on 1 January and 13 February 1586. During 1586 they were at Maidstone, in July at Bristol, on 22 August and later at Faversham, and before 29 September at Leicester. In 1585–6 they were also at Coventry. On 26 December 1586 and on 1 and 6 January and 28 February 1587 they were at Court, and in the same January a correspondent of Walsingham's names them amongst other companies then playing regularly in the City (App. D, No. lxxviii). During 1586–7 they were at Bath, Worcester, Canterbury, and Stratford-on-Avon, whence Malone thought that they might have enlisted Shakespeare.[2] They were at Bath again on 13 July 1587, and at Aldeburgh on 20 May and 19 July. Before 29 September they were at Leicester, on 9 September at York, where it is recorded that they ' cam in her Majesties lyvereys ', twice in September at Coventry, and at Aldeburgh on 16 December. They were at Court on 26 December 1587 and on 6 January and 18 February 1588.

A subsidy list of 30 June 1588 shows that Tarlton, Laneham, Johnson, Towne, Adams, Garland, John Dutton, Singer, and Cooke were then still household players.[3] It can, perhaps, hardly be assumed that the whole of the company is here represented. Mills, Wilson, and Bentley may have dropped out since 1583. But one would have expected to find the name of Laurence Dutton beside that of John, as he was certainly a Queen's man by 1589. Knell also acted with Tarlton in *The Famous Victories of Henry the Fifth*, and must have belonged to the company. He also may have been dead by 1588. And this must certainly be the case if he is the William Knell whose widow Rebecca John Heminges married on 10 March 1588. There is some reason to suppose that Heminges himself joined the Queen's men, perhaps in right of his wife. The composition of the list of 1583 generally bears out the statement of Howes, that the Queen's men were selected as the best out of the companies of divers great lords, for Wilson, Laneham, and Johnson belonged to Leicester's in 1572, Adams to Sussex's in 1576, and Dutton, after a chameleon past, to Oxford's in 1580. Mr. Fleay, who did not know either the list of 1583 or that of 1588, declares that the original members of the

---

[1] Fleay, 83.   [2] *Variorum*, ii. 166.
[3] *M. S. C.* i. 354, from *P. R. O. Lay Subsidies, Household*, 69/97.

company included James Burbadge and William Slaughter, and probably John Perkyn.[1] Of these William Slaughter is merely what the philologists would call a ' ghost '-name, for there is no evidence that any such actor ever existed.[2] Evidently James Burbadge did not join the Queen's men. Probably Mr. Fleay was biased by his knowledge that these men acted at the Theatre, which was Burbadge's property. But this could prove nothing, as the relations between particular companies and particular theatres were much less permanent than Mr. Fleay is apt to suppose. The Queen's seem to have been acting at the Theatre when Fleetwood suppressed them in June 1584, but the owner of the house, who can hardly be any other than James Burbadge, is specifically described as Lord Hunsdon's man, which of course does not necessarily signify that he was a player at all. Moreover, it is clear from the official correspondence of the following autumn, not only that, as we know from other sources, the companies regularly moved in from the suburban houses to the City inn-yards at the approach of winter, but also that the Queen's in particular had in the winter of 1583 dispersed themselves for their public performances over various play-places. The view that they did not exclusively

[1] Fleay, 34.
[2] The illustration of Mr. Fleay's methods of constructing stage history is delightful. In *The True Tragedie of Richard the Third*, a Queen's play, the murderers of the princes in the Tower are Will Slawter or Sluter, ' yet the most part calles him blacke Will ' (Hazlitt, *Sh. L.* v. 95), and Jack Denten or Douton. On this Mr. Fleay (ii. 316) comments, ' One of the actors in it, Sc. 11, is called Will Slaughter, " yet the most part calls him Black Will ", *i.e.* the Black Will of *Arden of Faversham*, q.v., which had no doubt been acted by the same man. Another actor is called Jack Donton (Dutton) or Denten, an accommodation of the Dighton of history to the actor's real name.' Obviously there is no need to suppose that the characters in *The True Tragedie* bore the names of their actors. John Dutton is not very likely to have taken a part of four speeches, and Will Slawter is evidently added to the John Dighton of Holinshed, to give Edward V the ' irony ' of a pun upon ' slaughter '. As for *Arden of Faversham*, it is not known to have been a Queen's play at all, and its ' Black Will ' is taken from Holinshed. Having gone so far, I do not know why Mr. Fleay stopped short of identifying Black Will's colleague ' Shakebag ' with the name of an actor. Of course, Mr. Fleay's blundering conjectures must be distinguished from the deliberate fabrications of Collier, who published in his *New Facts*, 11, from a forged document amongst the *Bridgewater MSS.*, a certificate to the Privy Council under the date ' Nov. 1589 ', from ' her Ma^{ts} poore playeres James Burbidge Richard Burbidge John Laneham Thomas Greene Robert Wilson John Taylor Anth. Wadeson Thomas Pope George Peele Augustine Phillippes Nicholas Towley William Shakespeare William Kempe William Johnson Baptiste Goodale and Robert Armyn being all of them sharers in the blacke Fryers playehouse '. On this cf. ch. xvii, and Ingleby, 249.

attach themselves to Burbadge's, or to any other one theatre, is further borne out by the indications in the *Jests* of Tarlton, which there is no reason to reject, however apocryphal they may be in detail, as evidence of the theatrical conditions under which the famous mime appeared. The *Jests* frequently speak of Tarlton as a Queen's man and never mention any other company in connexion with him.[1] And, as it happens, they record performances at the Curtain,[2] the Bell,[3] and the Bull,[4] but none at the Theatre. Nashe, however, tells us that Tarlton made jests of Richard Harvey and his *Astrological Discourse* of 1583 there ; [5] and an entry in the Stationers' Register makes it possible to add that shortly before his death he appeared at the Bel Savage.[6] The stage-keeper in *Bartholomew Fair* (1614), Ind. 37, gives us a reminiscence of a scene between Tarlton and John Adams, ' I am an Asse ! I ! and yet I kept the *Stage* in Master *Tarletons* time, I thanke my starres. Ho ! and that man had liu'd to haue play'd in *Bartholmew Fayre*, you should ha' seene him ha' come in, and ha' beene coozened i' the Cloath-quarter, so finely ! And *Adams*, the Rogue, ha' leap'd and caper'd vpon him, and ha' dealt his vermine about, as though they had cost him nothing. And then a substantiall watch to ha' stolne in vpon 'hem, and taken 'hem away, with mistaking words, as the fashion is, in the *Stage*-practice.'

Tarlton's own talent probably ran more to ' jigs ' and ' themes ' than to the legitimate drama. But the palmy days of the Queen's company were those that intervened between its foundation in 1583 and his death on 3 September 1588. To it belonged the men whom such an actor of the next generation as Thomas Heywood could remember as the

[1] Tarlton, 12, 13, 27, 29, 30, 31, 33, 37, ' while the queenes players lay in Worcester ', ' when the queenes players were restrained in summer, they travelled downe to S. James his fair at Bristow ', ' in the country where the queenes plaiers were accepted into a gentlemans house ', ' at Salisbury, Tarlton and his fellowes were to play before the maior and his brethren ', ' the queenes players travelling into the west country to play, and lodging in a little village some ten miles from Bristow '.

[2] Tarlton, 16, ' one in mockage threw him in this theame, he playing then at the Curtaine '.

[3] Tarlton, 24, ' Tarlton then, with his fellowes, playing at the Bel by . . . the Crosse-keyes in Gracious streete '.

[4] Tarlton, 13, ' at the Bull in Bishops-gate-street, where the queenes players oftentimes played '. It was here (Tarlton, 24) that Tarlton and Knell played *The Famous Victories of Henry the Fifth*.

[5] Nashe, *Pierce Penilesse* (*Works*, i. 197 ; cf. i. 308).

[6] Arber, ii. 526, ' A sorowfull newe sonnette intituled Tarltons Recantacon uppon this theame gyven him by a gentleman at the Bel savage without Ludgate (nowe or ells never) beinge the laste theame he songe '. The tract is not extant.

giants of the past,[1] and whose reputation Edward Alleyn's friends were ready to back him to excel.[2] From 1588 the future of the stage lay with Alleyn and the Admiral's men and Marlowe, and it may reasonably be supposed that the Queen's men were hard put to it to hold their own against their younger rivals. Adams probably survived Tarlton, and his name appears to be traceable as that of the clowns in *A Looking Glass for London and England* (*c.* 1590) and *James IV* (*c.* 1591). In 1587–8 the Queen's visited Coventry and Exeter, and in 1588 Dover, and on two occasions Faversham. On 19 July and 14 August they were at Bath. The Bath accounts for this year also show a payment ' to the quenes men that were tumblers '. Owing to Tarlton's death or to some other reason, the Queen's men prolonged their travels far into the winter. On 31 October they were at the Earl of Derby's house at New Park, Lancashire ; on 6 November ' certen of ' them were at Leicester; on 10 December they were at Norwich and on 17 December at Ipswich. But they reached the Court in time for the performance on 26 December, with which they seem to have had the prerogative of opening the Christmas season, and appeared again on 9 February. They must have had some share in the Martin Marprelate controversy, which raged during 1589. In the previous year, indeed, Martin was able to claim Tarlton as an ally who had ' taken ' Simony ' in Don John of London's cellar ', and was himself accused of borrowing his ' foolery ' from Laneham. But when the bishops determined to meet the Puritans with literary weapons like their own, they naturally turned to the Queen's men amongst others. About April 1589 *A Whip for an Ape* bids Martin's grave opponents to ' let old Lanam lash him with his rimes ', and although it cannot be assumed that, if the *May-game of Martinism* was in fact played at the Theatre, it was the Queen's men who played it, *Martin's Month's Minde* records in August the chafing of the Puritans at players ' whom, saving their liveries (for indeed they are hir Majesty's men . . .) they call rogues '. Influence was brought to bear to suppress the anti-Martinist plays. A pamphlet of October notes that *Vetus Comoedia* has been ' long in the country ' ; and this accords with the fact that the provincial performances of the Queen's men began at an unusually early date in 1589. They are found at Gloucester on 19 April, at Leicester on 20 May, at Ipswich on 27 May, at Aldeburgh on 30 May, and at Norwich on

---

[1] App. C, No. lvii. He names Knell, Bentley, Mills, Wilson, and Laneham.

[2] Cf. ch. xv, s.v. Alleyn, and ch. xviii.

3 June. On 5 July they were at the Earl of Derby's at Lathom, and on 6 and 7 September at another house of the Earl's at Knowsley. On 22 September Lord Scrope wrote from Carlisle to William Asheby, the English ambassador in Scotland, that they had been for ten days in that town. He had heard from Roger Asheton of the King's desire that they should visit Scotland, and had sought them out from ' the furthest parte of Langkeshire '.[1] One would be glad to know whether they did in fact visit Scotland. In any case they were back in England and at Bath by November. During 1588-9 they were also at Reading, at Nottingham, and twice at Coventry. Both the Nottingham records and those of Leicester furnish evidence that for travelling purposes they divided themselves into two companies. At Leicester the town account for 1588-9 shows ' certen of her Maiests playars ' as coming on 6 November, and ' others moe of her Mayestyes playars ' as coming on 20 May ; that of Nottingham for the same year has an entry of ' Symons and his companie, being the Quenes players ' and another of ' the Quenes players, the two Duttons and others '. The arrangement was of course natural enough, seeing that even in London the Queen's men were sufficiently numerous to occupy more than one inn-yard. Laurence Dutton was evidently by now a member of the company with his brother John. It is to be presumed that Symons is the John Symons who on not less than five occasions presented ' activities ' at Court, in 1582-3 with Strange's (q.v.), in 1585 with Oxford's, in 1586 with ' Mr. Standleyes boyes ', in 1587-8 with a company under his own name, and in 1588-9 either with the Admiral's or possibly with the Queen's itself.

Doubtless the incorporation of Symons into the Queen's service explains the appearance of the Queen's tumblers at Bath in 1589. Performances at Court, for which John Dutton and John Laneham received payment, took place on 26 December 1589 and 1 March 1590. During 1589-90 the company were at Coventry, Ludlow, Nottingham, Bridgnorth, and Faversham, on 22 April 1590 at Norwich, on 24 June under the leadership of ' Mr. Dutton ' at Knowsley, and on 30 October at Leicester. Acrobatic feats still formed a part of their repertory, and in these they had the assistance of a Turkish rope-dancer.[2] There were further Court performances on 26 December and on 1, 3, and 6 January, and 14 February 1591. It is to be noted that payment was made for the play of 1 January to ' John Laneham and his companye her maiesties players ' and for the rest by a separate warrant

---

[1] E. J. L. Scott in *Athenaeum* for 21 Jan. 1882.   [2] Cf. ch. xviii.

to ' Lawrence Dutton and John Dutton her maiesties players and there companye '; and that this distinction indicates some further development of the tendency to bifurcation already observed may be gathered from a study of the provincial records for 1590–1. On the very day of the performance of 14 February Queen's men were also at Southampton, and the form of the entry indicates that they were there playing in conjunction with the Earl of Sussex's men. This was the case also at Coventry on 24 March and at Gloucester during 1590–1.[1] At Ipswich during the same year there are two entries, of ' the Quenes players ' on 15 May 1591 and of ' another company of the Quenes players ' on 18 May. Obviously two groups were travelling this year and one had strengthened itself by a temporary amalgamation with Sussex's. Perhaps the normal combination was restored when the two groups found themselves on the same road at the end of May, for Queen's men are recorded alone at Faversham on 2 June 1591, at Wirkburn on 18 August, and at Coventry on 24 August and 20 October.

It was probably during this summer that Greene, having sold *Orlando Furioso* to the Queen's men for twenty nobles, resold it ' when they were in the country ' to the Admiral's for as much more. The winter of 1591–2 marks a clear falling-off in the position of the company at Court, since they were only called upon to give one performance, on 26 December, as against six assigned to Lord Strange's men, with whom at this date Alleyn and the Admiral's men appear to have been in combination. Yet it was still possible for the City, writing to Archbishop Whitgift on 25 February 1592, to suggest that Elizabeth's accustomed recreation might be sufficiently served, without the need for public plays, ' by the privat exercise of hir Ma^{ts} own players in convenient place '.[2] That they were again making use of the Theatre may perhaps be inferred from a passage in Nashe's *Summer's Last Will and Testament* of the following autumn, in which a Welshman is said to ' goe ae Theater, and heare a Queenes Fice, and he make hur laugh, and laugh hur belly-full '.[3] During 1591–2 they were at Nottingham, Coventry, Stratford-

---

[1] Murray, ii. 398 (Southampton), ' the Queenes maiesties & the Earle of Sussex players, xxx^s '; 240 (Coventry), ' the Quenes players & the Erle of Sussex players, xv^s '; 284 (Gloucester), ' the Queenes and the Earle of Sussex players, xxx^s '. At Faversham (Murray, ii. 274) separate payments of 1590–1 for the Queen's (20s.) and Essex's (10s.) are followed by ' to the Queen's Players and to the Earl of Essex's Players ' (20s.). It is conceivable that in this last entry ' Essex's ' may be a slip for ' Sussex's '.

[2] App. D, No. lxxxv.   [3] Nashe, *Works*, iii. 244.

on-Avon, twice at Aldeburgh, and twice at Bath. In 1592 they were at Rochester, on 27 May at Norwich, before 29 September at Leicester, and early in September at Chesterton close to Cambridge. Here they came into conflict with the authorities of Cambridge University, who were apprehensive of infection from the crowds assembled at Sturbridge fair, and forbade them to play. Encouraged by Lord North and by the constables of Chesterton, they disobeyed, set up their bills upon the college gates, and gave their performance. It is interesting to note that 'one Dutton' was 'a principale', and to remember that, twelve years before, the Duttons had gone to Cambridge as Lord Oxford's men and had been refused permission to play by the University authorities.[1] The outcome of the present encounter was a formal protest by the Vice-Chancellor and Heads of Houses to the Privy Council for which they requested Burghley's support as Chancellor of the University. After a further appeal about a year later, they succeeded in obtaining a confirmation of their privileges.[2] Another letter from the University to their Chancellor, written on 4 December 1592, is of a different character. Its object is to excuse themselves from accepting an invitation conveyed through the Vice-Chamberlain to present an English comedy before Elizabeth at Christmas. Sir Thomas Heneage appears to have given it as a reason for his request ' that her Maiesties owne servantes, in this time of infection, may not disport her Highnes wth theire wonted and ordinary pastimes '.[3]

On 11 October 1592 the Queen's men were at Aldeburgh, on the same day as, and conceivably in association with, Lord Morley's men, although the payments are distinct. They did not in fact appear at Court during the Christmas of 1592–3, although both Lord Pembroke's and Lord Strange's did. They were at Coventry and Stratford-on-Avon in the course of 1592–3, at Leicester in June 1593 and again after Michaelmas, at Bath on 22 August, and at York in September. On 6 January 1594 they returned to Court and gave what proved to be their last performance there. On 1 April they began to play at one of Henslowe's

---

[1] M. S. C. i. 190, from *Lansd. MSS.* 71, 75. The letters are both dated 18 Sept. 1592, and that to Burghley contained copies of the charters of Henry III and Elizabeth, of a Privy Council letter of 30 Oct. 1575 (cf. Dasent, ix. 39) forbidding shows within five miles of the University, and of the warrant of the Vice-Chancellor and other justices to the constables of Chesterton, dated 1 Sept. 1592.

[2] University Letter of 17 July 1593 in M. S. C. i. 200, from *Lansd. MS.* 75 ; Privy Council Act of 29 July 1593 in Dasent, xxiv. 427.

[3] M. S. C. i. 198, from *Lansd. MS.* 71.

theatres ' to geather '—that is to say, either alternately or in combination—with Sussex's men, who had already performed there for the six weeks between Christmas and Lent. Possibly this was a renewal of an earlier alliance of 1591. Only eight performances are recorded, and of the five plays given only *King Leire* can very reasonably be assigned to the repertory of the Queen's men. The others were *The Jew of Malta* and *The Fair Maid of Italy*, which Sussex's men had been playing in the winter, Greene's *Friar Bacon and Friar Bungay*, which was played for Henslowe by other companies both before and after, and was probably his property, and *The Ranger's Comedy*, the performances of which were being continued by the Admiral's men in the following autumn, but which it is possible that they or Henslowe may have acquired from the Queen's. For there can be no doubt that the Queen's men, whether because they had ceased to be modish, or because their finances had proved unable to stand the strain of the plague years, were now at the end of their London career. On 8 May 1594 the significant entry occurs in Henslowe's diary of a loan of £15 to his nephew Francis Henslowe ' to lay downe for his share to the Quenes players when they broke & went into the contrey to playe '.[1] This by itself would not perhaps be conclusive, as there are other years in which the company began its provincial wanderings as early as May. But from the present journey there is nothing to show that they ever returned, and it may fairly be reckoned as another sign of defeat that while *The Troublesome Reign of King John* (1591) was the only play certainly theirs which was printed before 1594, no less than nine found their way into the publishers' hands during that and the following year. These were, besides *Friar Bacon and Friar Bungay* (1594, S. R. 14 May 1594), with which they probably had only a recent connexion, *A Looking Glass for London and England* (1594, S. R. 5 March 1594), *King Leire* (1594, S. R. 14 May 1594), *James IV* and *The Famous Victories of Henry V* (1598, S. R. 14 May 1594), *The True Tragedy of Richard III* (1594, S. R. 19 June 1594), *Selimus* (1594), Peele's *Old Wive's Tale* (1595, S. R. 16 April 1595), and *Valentine and Orson* (S. R. 23 May 1595), of which no copy is known to be extant. Somewhat later came *Sir Clyomon and Clamydes* (1599).

The Queen's men were at Coventry on 4 July 1594, at

---

[1] Henslowe, i. 4. The date in the diary is ' 8 of Maye 1593 ', but I am prepared to accept Dr. Greg's view (ii. 80) that as Francis was pawn-broking for his uncle all through 1593, this must be an error of Henslowe's for ' 1594 '. He seems to have actually left London on 18 May 1594.

Bristol in August, and at Bath and Barnstaple, where they were unlucky enough to break down the ceiling in the Guild-hall, during 1593–4, and thereafter they are traceable right up to the end of the reign, at Coventry, Oxford, and Bath in 1594–5, at Leicester both before and after Michaelmas 1595, twice at Coventry and at Ludlow in 1595–6, at Stratford-on-Avon on 16 and 17 July 1596, at Bristol in August, at Leicester between October and December 1596, and at Faversham and Bridgnorth in the same year, at Coventry, at Dunwich, and twice at Bath in 1596–7, at Bristol again about Christmas 1597, at Nottingham on 8 July 1597, at Bristol about 25 July, at Bath in 1597–8, at Leicester on 9 January 1598, at Maldon in 1598, at Ipswich and Reading in 1598–9, at Maldon in 1599, at Dunwich in 1599–1600, at Ipswich on 2 June 1600, and at Leicester before 29 September in the same year, at Coventry and Bath in 1600–1, at York in July 1602, at Leicester on 30 September 1602, at Belvoir in August or September of the same year, and at Coventry in 1602–3. But little, naturally enough, is known of the *personnel* of the company during this period of its decay. On 1 June 1595 Francis Henslowe borrowed another £9 from his uncle ' to laye downe for his hallfe share wth the company wch he dothe playe wth all ',[1] and I see no particular reason to suppose that this was another company than the Queen's. The loan is witnessed by William Smyght, George Attewell, and Robert Nycowlles, each of whom is described as ' player '. It is likely enough that these were now fellows of Francis Henslowe. Attewell had been payee for Lord Strange's men in 1591. The earlier loan was witnessed by John Towne, Hugh Davis, and Richard Alleyn. Davis and Alleyn appear elsewhere in connexion with Henslowe, but Towne was certainly a Queen's man. He is in the 1588 list and is described as ' one of her Majesties plears ' when on 8 July 1597 he obtained a release of debts due to Roger Clarke of Nottingham.[2] The other men of 1588 had nearly all vanished. John Singer had joined the Admiral's by the autumn of 1594. I should not be surprised, however, to find that John Garland was still with the Queen's. He was an associate of Francis Henslowe in the Duke of Lennox's men in 1604, and was then ' owld ' Garland. Indeed, it seems probable that, when the Queen's men lost their last shred of claim to a livery on Elizabeth's death, they made an attempt still to hold together under the patronage of Lennox. John Shank was once a Queen's man.

---

[1] Henslowe, i. 6.   [2] W. H. Stevenson. *Nottingham Records*, iv. 244.

xiv. THE EARL OF ARUNDEL'S MEN

Henry Fitzalan, 12th Earl of Arundel ; *nat. c.* 1511 ; m. (1) Katherine, d. of Thomas Grey, Marquis of Dorset, before 1532, (2) Mary, Countess of Sussex, d. of Sir John Arundel, after 1542 ; succ. Jan. 1544 ; Lord Chamberlain, 1544 ; Lord Steward, 1553, and again 1558–64 ; *ob.* 24 Feb. 1580.

Philip Howard, 13th Earl of Arundel, s. of Thomas Howard, 4th Duke of Norfolk, attainted 1572, and Mary, d. and h. of 12th Earl ; *nat.* 28 June 1557 ; m. Anne, d. of Thomas, Lord Dacre, 1571 ; succ. Feb. 1580 ; sent to Tower, 25 Apr. 1585, and *ob.* there, 19 Oct. 1595.

The Earls of Arundel had players as far back as the fifteenth century.[1] The 12th Earl entertained Elizabeth with a mask at Nonsuch on 5 August 1559. He had players, who were rewarded by the Duchess of Suffolk, apparently during a London visit, in December 1561. The 13th Earl had a company in 1584. It was in London when plays were suppressed in June, and obediently submitted. It seems to have been located at the Curtain. It can be traced at Ipswich on 1 July, at Leicester before 29 September, at Aldeburgh in 1583–4, at Norwich in 1585–6, and thereafter no more.

xv. THE EARL OF HERTFORD'S MEN

Edward Seymour, s. of Edward, Protector and 1st and attainted Duke of Somerset ; *nat.* 25 May 1539 ; cr. Earl of Hertford, 13 Jan. 1559 ; m. (1) Lady Catherine Grey, d. of Henry, Duke of Suffolk, *c.* Nov. 1560, (2) Frances, d. of William, 1st Lord Howard of Effingham, before 1582, (3) Frances, d. of Thomas, Lord Howard of Bindon and widow of Henry Pranell, Dec. 1600 ; *ob.* 6 Apr. 1621.

These are among the most obscure of the companies. They appeared at Canterbury in 1582, Faversham in 1586, Newcastle in October 1590, Leicester on 22 November 1590, and Bath, Marlborough, and Southampton in 1591–2. During the progress of 1591 Elizabeth was entertained from 20 to 24 September by the Earl at Elvetham in Hampshire ' beeing none of the Earles chiefe mansion houses ' (cf. ch. xxiv). This was really a visit of reconciliation, for much of Hertford's life had been spent in disgrace, owing to his first marriage with the heiress, under Henry VIII's will, to Elizabeth's throne. The entertainment was very elaborate, and at its close Elizabeth protested to the Earl that it was so honourable ' as hereafter he should find the rewarde thereof in her especiall favour '. No doubt Hertford's players took a part, and shared the ' largesse ' which she

---

[1] *Mediaeval Stage*, ii. 186, 251.

bestowed upon the 'actors' of the pastimes before she departed. I think it must have also been their success on this occasion which earned them their only appearance at Court, on the following 6 January 1592. I have elsewhere tried to show that there is a special connexion between this Elvetham entertainment and *A Midsummer-Night's Dream*,[1] and if any special company is satirized in Bottom and his fellows, I feel sure that it must have been the Earl of Hertford's and not, as Mr. Fleay thinks, the Earl of Sussex's.[2]

Probably the company went under in the plague of 1592–4, and in 1595 Hertford was again in disgrace for presuming so far upon his favour as to claim a declaration of the validity of his first marriage. But there were players under his name at Coventry in 1596–7, at Ipswich in 1600–1, and on 8 May 1602, at Norwich in 1601, and at Bath in 1601–2, and this company appeared at Court on 6 January 1603. Their payee was Martin Slater, formerly of the Admiral's, and since then, possibly, an associate of Laurence Fletcher in his Scottish tours. In 1604–5 they were at Norwich. In 1606 they visited Leicester, on 9 July Oxford, and on 2 December the Earl of Derby wrote to the Mayor of Chester to bespeak for them the use of the town-hall. In 1606–7 they were at Coventry.

xvi. MR. EVELYN'S MEN (1588)

George Evelyn, of Wotton, Surrey ; *nat.* 1530 ; *ob.* 1603.

Collier gives no authority for the following rather puzzling statement :[3]

' In Feb. 1587, the Earl of Warwick obtained a warrant for the payment of the claim of George Evelyn of Wotton, for provisions supplied to the Tower, and for the reward of actors on Shrove Tuesday for a Play, the title of which is not given nor the name of the company by which it was performed : the whole sum amounted to only 12s.'

The date intended must be 1588, as in 1587 Shrovetide fell in March. But there is probably some misunderstanding, as no such payment occurs in the Treasurer of the Chamber's accounts, and the sum named is too small for a reward. Moreover, private gentlemen do not seem to have entertained Court companies at so late a date. The Revels Account for 1587–8 only records seven plays. Of these the Treasurer of the Chamber paid for six, and the seventh was presented by Gray's Inn.

---

[1] *Sh. Homage*, 154.   [2] Fleay, *Shakespeare*, 184.
[3] Collier, i. 259.

xvii. THE EARL OF DERBY'S (LORD STRANGE'S) MEN

Henry Stanley, s. of Edward, 3rd Earl of Derby ; *nat.* 1531 ; known as Lord Strange ; m. Margaret, d. of Henry, 2nd Earl of Cumberland, 7 Feb. 1555 ; succ. as 4th Earl, 24 Oct. 1572 ; Lord Steward, 1588 ; *ob.* 25 Sept. 1593.

Ferdinando Stanley, 2nd s. of Henry, 4th Earl of Derby ; *nat. c.* 1559 ; m. Alice, d. of Sir John Spencer of Althorp, 1579 ; summoned to Parliament as Lord Strange, 28 Jan. 1589 ; succ. as 5th Earl of Derby, 25 Sept. 1593 ; *ob.* 16 Apr. 1594.

William Stanley, s. of Henry, 4th Earl of Derby ; *nat.* 1561 ; succ. as 6th Earl of Derby, 16 Apr. 1594 ; m. Elizabeth, d. of Edward, 17th Earl of Oxford. 26 Jan. 1595 ; *ob.* 29 Sept. 1642.

The companies connected with the great northern house of Stanley present a history perhaps more complicated than that of any other group, partly because it seems to have been not unusual for the heir of the house to entertain players during his father's life-time. The 3rd Earl had a company in Henry the Eighth's reign. His successor had one as Lord Strange, which is only recorded in the provinces, in 1563–70.[1] Four years later he had again a company as Earl of Derby. The earliest mention of it is at Coventry in 1573–4. It was at Dover and Coventry in 1577–8, at Ipswich on 28 May 1578, at Nottingham on 31 August 1578, at Bristol in the same year, and at Bath in 1578–9. In the last three months of 1579 it was at Leicester ; and during the following Christmas it made its first appearance at Court with a performance of *The Soldan and the Duke of* —— on 14 February 1580. In 1579–80 it was at Stratford-on-Avon, Exeter, and Coventry, on 1 January 1581 at Court, in 1580–1 at Bath, Leicester, Nottingham, Exeter, and Winchester, in 1581–2 at Nottingham, Winchester, and Abingdon, in October to December 1582 at Leicester, and in 1582–3 at Bath, Norwich, and Southampton. Its last appearance at Court was in *Love and Fortune* on 30 December 1582.

I think that the Earl of Derby's players must be taken to be distinct from another company, which was performing during much the same period of years under the name of Lord Strange. These men are found in 1576–7 at Exeter, in 1578–9 at Bath, Ipswich, Rochester, Nottingham, Coventry, and Stratford-on-Avon. They also made their first appearance at Court in the winter of 1579–80. Their performance was on 15 January 1580, and they are spoken of, not as players, but as tumblers. On the other hand they appear as players

---

[1] Murray, i. 294. I add Maldon (1564–5). There is no proof that 'Beeston and his fellowes' at Barnstaple in 1560–1 were Strange's.

at Bath, side by side with Derby's men, in 1580–1 and 1582–3, and as players also at Bristol, Canterbury, and Gloucester in 1580–1, Plymouth in 1581–2, and Barnstaple in 1582–3 and 1583–4. With the tumbling at Court in 1580 begins a rather puzzling series of records. There are further Court entries of feats of activity by Lord Strange's men on 28 December 1581, and of feats of activity and tumbling on 1 January 1583. For this last occasion the payee of the company was John Symons. Two years later Symons and his 'fellows' were again at Court with feats of activity and vaulting, but they were then under the patronage, not of Lord Strange, but of the Earl of Oxford. There would be nothing extraordinary about such a transference of service, were it not that during the following Christmas, on 9 January 1586, tumbling and feats of activity are ascribed to John Symons and 'Mr. Standleyes boyes', and that by 'Mr. Standley' one can hardly help assuming either Ferdinando Stanley, Lord Strange, or some other member of his family to be intended. This inference is confirmed by a mention of Lord Strange's men at Faversham in 1585–6, and it becomes necessary to assume that, after attaching himself for a year to the Earl of Oxford, Symons thought better of it, and returned to his original master. Symons and his company again showed feats of activity on 28 December 1587. No patron is named on this occasion, but as Strange's men are traceable at Coventry during 1587–8, it is natural to assume that they were still holding together. Now a new complication comes in. There were activities again at Court in the winter of 1588–9, and Symons certainly took part in them.[1] But the only men companies to whom payments were made were the Queen's and the Admiral's, who now reappear at Court after absence during two winters, and it is only in the case of the Admiral's that the payment is specified to be for activities. If the restless Symons had joined the Admiral's men, it cannot have been for long, since in the course of 1588–9 he was leading one section of the Queen's men to Nottingham. Nor had Strange's yet entirely broken up, for on 5 November 1589, both they and the Admiral's, evidently playing as distinct companies, were suppressed by the Lord Mayor in the City.[2] Strange's, who were then at the Cross Keys, played contemptuously, and some of them were imprisoned.

[1] The Revels account for 1587–9 (Feuillerat, *Eliz.* 390) includes ' a paire of fflanell hose for Symmons the Tumbler ', which is not in the separate account for 1587–8 (Feuillerat, *Eliz.* 380).

[2] App. D, No. lxxxii. The forged list of Queen's men (q.v.) in 1589 is sometimes, by a further error, whose I do not know, assigned to Strange's.

A year later, the Admiral's were with Burbadge at the Theatre, and there I conceive that the residue of Strange's, deserted by Symons, had joined them. If they were too many for the house, we know that the Curtain was available as an 'easer'. After the quarrel with Burbadge in May 1591, the two companies probably went together to the Rose. The main evidence for such a theory is that, while the Privy Council record of play-warrants include two for the Admiral's men in respect of plays and feats of activity on 27 December 1590 and 16 February 1591, the corresponding Chamber payments are to George Ottewell on behalf of Strange's men.

This amalgamation of Strange's and the Admiral's, tentative perhaps in 1588–9, and conclusive, if not in 1589–90, at any rate in 1590–1, lasted until 1594. So far as Court records are concerned, the company seems to have been regarded as Strange's. But the leading actor, Edward Alleyn, kept his personal status as the Lord Admiral's servant, and it is to be observed that, for whatever reason, both the Admiral's and Strange's continue to appear, not only in combination, but also separately in provincial documents.[1] Of this various explanations are conceivable. One is that the municipal officials were not very precise in their methods, and when an amalgamated

---

[1] I had better give the complicated and in some cases uncertain notices in full; the unspecified references are to Murray: Cambridge (1591-2), 'my Lord Stranges plaiers' (Cooper, ii. 518), and so also (ii. 229, 284) Canterbury (13 July 1592) and Gloucester (1591-2) ; Bath (1591-10 June 1592), 'my Lord Admiralls players ' . . . ' my L. Stranges plaiers ' (ii. 202) ; Aldeburgh (1591-2), ' my Lord Admirals players ' (Stopes, *Hunnis*, 314) ; Shrewsbury (30 Sept. 1591-29 Sept. 1592), ' my L. Admeralls players ' . . . ' my l. Stranges and my l. Admyralls players ' (ii. 392, s. a. 1592-3, but the entries for the two years seem to be transposed ; *vide infra*) ; Coventry (10 Dec. 1591-29 Nov. 1592), ' the Lord Strange players ' (ii. 240) ; Leicester (19 Dec. 1592), ' the Lorde Admiralls Playars ' (ii. 305) ; Shrewsbury (30 Sept. 1592-29 Sept. 1593), ' The iii of Feb: 1592. Bestowed vppon the players of my Lorde Admyrall ' . . . ' my L. Darbyes men being players ' (ii. 392, s. a. 1591-2, but the detailed date and the name Derby make an error palpable) ; Bath (11 June 1592-10 Sept. 1593), ' my L. Stranges plaiers ' (ii. 203) ; Coventry (30 Nov. 1592-26 Nov. 1593), ' the Lo Admiralls players ' (ii. 240) ; York (April 1593), ' the Lord Admerall & Lord Mordens players ' (ii. 412) ; Newcastle (May 1593), ' my Lord Admiralls plaiers, and my Lord Morleis plaiers being all in one companye ' (G. B. Richardson, *Extracts from Municipal Accounts of N.*); Southampton (1592-3), ' my L. Morleys players and the Earle of Darbyes ' (ii. 398, ' *c.* 18 May ', but Strange became Derby on 25 Sept.) ; Leicester (Oct.-Dec. 1593), ' the Erle of Darbyes playors ' (ii. 306) ; Coventry (2 Dec. 1593), ' the Lo: of Darbyes players ' (ii. 240) ; Bath (11 Sept. 1593-1594), ' the L. Admiralls, the L. Norris players ' (ii. 203) ; Ipswich (7 March 1594), ' vnto therlle of Darbys players and to the Lorde Admirals players, the ij amongste ' (ii. 293, s. a. 1591-2, but on 7 March 1592 Strange was not yet Derby, and his men were playing for Henslowe).

company came before them, sometimes entered the name of one lord, sometimes of the other, sometimes of both. Another is that a few of the Admiral's men may have been left out of the amalgamation and have travelled separately under that name. We know, of course, that Richard Jones and others went abroad in 1592, but they may have spent some time in the provinces first. And thirdly, it is possible that, while the combined company performed as a whole in London, they found it more economical to take their authorities from both lords with them, when they went to the country in the summer, and to unite or divide their forces as convenience prompted. I am the more inclined to this third conjecture, in that the ' intollerable' charge of travelling with a great company and the danger of ' division and separacion' involved were explicitly put forward by Lord Strange's men in a petition to the Privy Council for leave to quit Newington Butts, where they had been commanded to play during a long vacation, and return to their normal quarters, doubtless at the Rose, on the Bankside. They particularly wanted to avoid going to the country, but Newington Butts did not pay, and they were backed by the Thames watermen, who lost custom when the Rose was not open. It is not clear whether this petition belongs to 1591 or 1592.[1] The provincial records show that the company probably travelled during 1592, but not 1591. If the petition belongs to 1592, it is obvious that the plague intervened, and I strongly suspect that the company's fears proved justified, and that the re-organization for provincial work did in fact lead to a ' division and separacion ', by the splitting off of some members of the combine as Pembroke's men (q.v.).

This, however, anticipates a little. To Alleyn's talent must be attributed the remarkable success of the company in the winter of 1591-2, during which they were called upon to give six performances at Court, on 27 and 28 December, 1 and 9 January, and 6 and 8 February, as against one each allotted to the Queen's, Sussex's, and Hertford's men. On 19 February 1592 the company began a season with Philip Henslowe, probably at the Rose, and played six days a week for a period of eighteen weeks, during which they only missed Good Friday and two other days. Henslowe records in his diary the name of the play staged at each of the hundred and five performances, together with a sum of money which probably represents his share of the takings.[2] If so, his

---

[1] App. D, No. xcii.
[2] Henslowe, i. 13. The account is headed, ' Jn the name of god Amen 1591 beginge the 19 of febreary my lord stranges mene a ffoloweth 1591 '.

average receipts were £1 14s. 0d.; but the daily amounts
fluctuated considerably, sometimes falling to a few shillings
and again rising to twice the average on the production of
a new or popular play or during the Easter or Whitsun
holiday. Twenty-three plays in all were given, for any
number of days from one to fifteen; the same play was
rarely repeated in any one week. Five of the plays are marked
in the diary with the letters *ne*, which are reasonably taken
to indicate the production of a new piece. These were
' Harey the vj ', probably Shakespeare's *1 Henry VI*, *Titus
and Vespasian*, probably the play on which was based
Shakespeare's *Titus Andronicus*, the *Second Part* of *Tamar
Cham*, *The Tanner of Denmark*, and *A Knack to Know a Knave*.
The eighteen old plays included Marlowe's *Jew of Malta*,
Greene's *Orlando Furioso* and *Friar Bacon and Friar Bungay*,
Greene and Lodge's *A Looking Glass for London* ; also *Muly
Mollocco* which might be Peele's *Battle of Alcazar*, *Four Plays
in One*, which is conjectured to be a part of Tarlton's *Seven
Deadly Sins*, and *Jeronimo*, which is almost certainly Kyd's
Spanish Tragedy. There was also a play, sometimes given
on the day before this last, under the varying titles of *Don
Horatio*, the *Comedy of Jeronimo*, or *The Spanish Comedy*,
which does not appear to have been preserved.[1] The same
fate has befallen the other ten plays, of which the names
were *Sir John Mandeville*, *Henry of Cornwall*, *Clorys and
Orgasto*, *Pope Joan*, *Machiavel*, *Bindo and Richardo*, *Zenobia*,
Constantine, *Jerusalem*, and *Brandimer*. From the financial
point of view, the greatest successes were *Titus and Vespasian*,
The Jew of Malta, *2 Tamar Cham*, *1 Henry VI*, and *The
Spanish Tragedy*. These averaged respectively for Henslowe
£2 8s. 6d. for seven days, £2 3s. 6d. for ten days, £2 1s. 6d.
for five days, £2 0s. 6d. for fifteen days, and £1 17s. 0d. for
thirteen days. The *Seven Deadly Sins* and perhaps also the
Looking Glass must have passed in some way into the hands
of Strange's or the Admiral's, or into Henslowe's, from the
Queen's.

The performances came to an end on 23 June, for on that
day the Privy Council inhibited all plays until Michaelmas.
Whether the Newington Butts episode and the watermen's
petition followed or not, at any rate plague intervened in
the course of the summer, and the company had to face the
disadvantages of travelling. They were afoot by 13 July
and still on 19 December. Ten days later, Henslowe resumed

---

[1] Cf. ch. xxiv, s.v. *1 Jeronimo*. Some marginal notes of sums of money
are not clearly intelligible, but may represent sums advanced by Henslowe
for the company.

his account, and the resemblance of the list of plays to that of the previous spring renders it reasonable to suppose that the actors were the same.[1] The season lasted to the end of January 1593, and a play was given on each of the twenty-six week-days of this period. *Muly Mollocco, The Spanish Tragedy, A Knack to Know a Knave, The Jew of Malta, Sir John Mandeville, Titus and Vespasian, Friar Bacon and Friar Bungay, 1 Henry VI,* and *2 Tamar Cham* all made their appearance again. In addition, there were a comedy called *Cosmo,* and two new plays, *The Jealous Comedy,* which may, I think, be *The Comedy of Errors,* and *The Tragedy of the Guise,* which is usually accepted as Marlowe's *Massacre of Paris.* The first representation of the former yielded Henslowe £2 4s. 0d., that of the latter £3 14s. 0d.; as in the spring, his daily takings averaged £1 14s. 0d. Besides their public performances, Strange's men were called upon for three plays at Court, on the evenings of 27 and 31 December 1592 and 1 January 1593.

The plague made a new inhibition of plays necessary on 28 January, but it does not seem to have been for some months that Strange's men made up their minds to travel. A special licence issued in their favour by the Privy Council on 6 May is registered in the following terms :

' Whereas it was thought meet that during the time of the infection and continewaunce of the sicknes in the citie of London there shold no plaies or enterludes be usd, for th' avoiding of th' assemblies and concourse of people in anie usual place apointed nere the said cittie, and though the bearers hereof, Edward Allen, servaunt to the right honorable the Lord Highe Admiral, William Kemp, Thomas Pope, John Heminges, Augustine Phillipes and Georg Brian, being al one companie, servauntes to our verie good the Lord the Lord Strainge, ar restrained their exercize of playing within the said citie and liberties thereof, yet it is not therby ment but that they shal and maie in regard of the service by them don and to be don at the Court exercize their quallitie of playing comodies, tragedies and such like in anie other cities, townes and corporacions where the infection is not, so it be not within seaven miles of London or of the Coort, that they maie be in the better readines hereafter for her Majesty's service whensoever they shalbe therunto called. Theis therfore shalbe to wil and require you that they maie without their lett or contradiccion use their said exercize at their most convenient times and places (the accustomed times of Devine praiers excepted).' [2]

The importance of this document is in the information which it gives as to the composition of the company. Presumably only the leaders are named, and of these Alleyn alone

[1] Henslowe, i. 15. [2] Dascnt, xxiv. 212.

is specially designated as an Admiral's man. Kempe, at any rate, and probably also Pope and Bryan, were in Leicester's service in the Low Countries during 1586, and all three were together during the same year in Denmark. Whether they had belonged, as has sometimes been supposed, to Leicester's long-enduring company of Court players is less certain. Pope and Bryan passed from Denmark to Germany, and may have joined the Admiral's or Strange's on their return. They also were acrobats as well as players.[1] Kempe, however, seems to have parted company from the others in Denmark, and may have joined Strange's independently, presumably before 10 June 1592, when *A Knack to Know a Knave*, in which he played ' merrimentes ', was produced. Heminges may possibly have been a Queen's man.

Some details of the 1593 tour and the names of two or three more members of the company are found in the familiar correspondence of Alleyn with his wife, whom he had married on 22 October 1592, and with Philip Henslowe, who was her step-father.[2] On 2 May he writes from Chelmsford, and on 1 August from Bristol. Here he had received a letter by Richard Cowley and he sends his reply by a kinsman of Thomas Pope. At the moment of writing he is ready to play *Harry of Cornwall.* He asks that further letters may be sent to him by the carriers to Shrewsbury, West Chester, or York, ' to be keptt till my Lord Stranges players com '. He does not expect to be home until All Saints' Day. A reply from Henslowe and Mrs. Alleyn on 14 August is in fact addressed to ' Mr. Edwarde Allen on of my lorde Stranges players '. This mentions an illness of Alleyn at Bath during which one of his fellows had had to play his part. With these letters is one written to Mrs. Allen on behalf of a ' servant ' of Alleyn's, whose name was Pige or Pyk, by the hand of Mr. Doutone, possibly Edward Dutton, but perhaps more probably Thomas Dowten or Downton, who was later a sharer among the Admiral's men. The provincial records, subject to the confusion of company nomenclature already noted, appear to confirm the visits to Bath, Shrewsbury, and York, to indicate others to Southampton, Leicester, Coventry, Ipswich, and Newcastle, and to show that some temporary alliance had been entered into with the purely provincial company of Lord Morley.[3] After 25 September 1593 Strange's men of course became Derby's men.

[1] Cf. W. W. Greg.in Henslowe, ii. 70.

[2] *Dulwich MSS.* i. 9–15 (*Henslowe Papers*, 34) ; cf. Henslowe, i. 3.

[3] Their patron was Edward Parker, Lord Morley (Murray, ii. 54). I suspect the Morden of the York entry and the Norris of the Bath entry

I now come to a difficult point. There exists amongst the Dulwich papers a 'plott' or prompter's abstract of a play called *The Second Part of the Seven Deadly Sins*, which an ingenious conjecture of Mr. Fleay has identified on internal evidence with the *Four Plays in One* included in the Strange's repertory of 1592.[1] In this leading parts were taken, not only by 'Mr. Pope', 'Mr. Phillipps', and 'Mr. Brian', but also by 'Richard Burbadge'; lesser ones by Richard Cowley, John Duke, Robert Pallant, John Sincler, Thomas Goodale, William Sly, J. Holland, and three others described only as Harry, Kitt, and Vincent; and female parts by Saunder, Nick, Robert, Ned, Will, and T. Belt, who may be presumed to have been boys.[2] Alleyn, Kempe, and Heminges are not named, but there are several parts to which no actors are assigned. What, however, is the date of the 'plott'? Not necessarily 1592, for the performance of *Four Plays in One* in that year was only a revival. The authorship of the *Seven Deadly Sins* is ascribed to Tarlton, and therefore the original owners were probably the Queen's men. They are not very likely to have parted with it before Tarlton's death in 1588 brought the first shock to their fortunes, but clearly it may have come into the possession of Strange's or the Admiral's or the combined company before ever they reached the Rose. And surely the appearance of Richard Burbadge suggests that the 'plott' was brought from the Theatre, and represents a performance there. He is very unlikely to have joined at the Rose the company which had just been driven there by a quarrel with his father. It is true that in the 'plott' of *Dead Man's Fortune*, which also probably dates from the sojourn of the Admiral's (q.v.) at the Theatre, he was apparently not playing leading parts but only a messenger. But the wording is obscure, and after all the absence of the prefix 'Mr.' from his name in the 'plott' of the *Sins* may indicate, in accordance with the ordinary usage of the Dulwich docu-

---

of being both transcriber's errors for Morley. No players of Lord Norris are on record, and those of Lord Mordaunt (Murray, ii. 90) only recur in 1585–6 and 1602.

[1] Text in *Henslowe Papers*, 130 ; on the nature of a 'plott', cf. App. N.

[2] The following rather hazardous identifications have been attempted by Greg (*loc. cit.*) and Fleay, 84 : 'Harry'=Henry Condell (Fleay, Greg) ; 'Kit'=Christopher Beeston (Fleay, Greg) ; 'Saunder'=Alexander Cooke (Fleay, Greg) ; 'Nick'=Nicholas Tooley (Fleay, Greg) ; 'Ro.' or 'R. Go.'=Robert Gough (Fleay, Greg) ; 'Ned'=Edward Alleyn or Edmund Shakespeare (Fleay) ; 'Will'=William Tawyer (Fleay), William Tawler (Greg). The object is, of course, to establish the connexion between Strange's and the Chamberlain's men. Both writers assign two of the unallocated parts to Heminges and Shakespeare.

ments, that he was not yet a sharer when it was drawn up. Apparently, then, at least four of Strange's men, as we find them in 1593, besides Alleyn, had been playing at the Theatre about 1590–1. These were Pope, Phillips, Bryan, and Cowley. Obviously we cannot say whether it was to the original Admiral's or the original Strange's that they belonged. One other point of *personnel* must not be overlooked. Shakespeare contributed to the repertory of Strange's in 1592 and perhaps also in 1593. Greene calls him a Shake-scene, but neither the 'plott' of 1590, nor the licence of 1593, nor the Alleyn correspondence of the same year, yields his name.[1]

Derby's men did not appear at Court during the winter of 1593–4. On 16 April 1594 Lord Derby died. On 16 May the company used the Countess's name at Winchester. It seems clear that during the summer there was some re-shuffling of the companies, that Alleyn took the leadership of a new body of Admiral's men, that several other members of the old combination, including Pope, Heminges, Kempe, and Phillips, joined with Burbadge, Shakespeare, and Sly, under the patronage of the Lord Chamberlain, Henry Lord Hunsdon, and that, after a short period of co-operation with each other and Henslowe, the two companies definitely parted. In the course of 1594 the name of Derby's men appeared upon the title-page of *Titus Andronicus*, probably because they had played it in its earlier form of *Titus and Vespasian* in 1592–3, before it passed to Pembroke's and from them to Sussex's. In the same year was published *A Knack to Know a Knave* (S. R. 7 January 1594) as played 'by Ed. Allen and his companie' and with 'merrimentes' by Kemp. This also belongs to the 1592–3 repertory, of the other plays in which *I Henry VI*, like *Titus Andronicus*, passed ultimately to the Chamberlain's men, and a considerable number, either as their own property or that of Henslowe, to the Admiral's. These included *Tamar Cham*, *The Battle of Alcazar*, *The Spanish Tragedy*, *The Jew of Malta*, *The Massacre of Paris*, *Friar Bacon and Friar Bungay*, and probably *Orlando Furioso*, of Orlando's part in which a transcript, with alterations in Alleyn's hand, is preserved at Dulwich.[2] The only play not named in Henslowe's diary which can be traced to the company is *Fair Em*, which bears the name of Lord Strange's men on its title-page, but of which the first edition is undated.

It is possible that those of the fifth Earl of Derby's men who did not take service with the Lord Chamberlain, passed into a provincial period of existence under his successor,

---

[1] For speculation as to Shakespeare's early career, cf. s.v. Pembroke's.
[2] Text in *Henslowe Papers*, 155.

the sixth Earl. A company bearing his name was at Norwich on 15 September 1594, at Dunwich in 1594-5 and 1595-6, at Coventry, Bath, and Stratford in 1595-6, at Leicester between October and December 1596, at Bath in 1596-7, at Maldon in 1597, at Coventry twice in 1597-8, at Leicester in 1597-8, and between October and December 1598, at Wollaton (Percival Willoughby's) on 7 October 1599, and at Leicester again on 16 October 1599. Letters of 30 June 1599 relate that the Earl of Derby was then ' busy penning comedies for the common players ', and it is perhaps natural to suppose that his own company were chosen as the exponents of his art.[1] This perhaps explains its appearance at Court during the winters of 1599-1600 and 1600-1. Four performances were given, on 3 and 5 February 1600 and 1 and 6 January 1601, and for these Robert Browne, who had been both with Worcester's men and the Admiral's, but much of whose dramatic career had been spent in Germany, was the payee. In an undated letter to Sir Robert Cecil, Lady Derby writes, ' Being importuned by my Lord to intreat your favor that his man Browne, with his companye, may not be bared from ther accoustomed plaing, in maintenance wherof they have con-sumde the better part of ther substance, if so vaine a matter shall not seame troublesum to you, I could desier that your furderance might be a meane to uphold them, for that my Lord taking delite in them, it will kepe him from moer prodigall courses '.[2] To this company are doubtless to be assigned *Edward IV*, perhaps by Heywood (1600, S. R. 28 August 1599), and the anonymous *Trial of Chivalry* (1605, S. R. 4 December 1604), both of which are credited to Derby's men on their title-pages. It again becomes provincial and is trace-able at Norwich on 27 February and 9 June 1602, at Ipswich on 4 June 1602, and thereafter up to 1618, chiefly at Coventry and at Gawthorpe Hall, the house of Derby's neighbours, the Shuttleworths.[3]

John Taylor, the water-poet, returned from his journey to Scotland in 1618 at the Maidenhead Inn, Islington, and here after supper on 14 October ' we had a play of the Life and Death of Guy of Warwick, played by the Right Honour-able the Earl of Derby his men '. Presumably this was Day and Dekker's play entered on the Stationers' Register in 1619, which Mr. Bullen declines to identify with the *Guy of Warwick* published as ' by B. J.' in 1661.[4]

[1] George Fanner to H. Galdelli and G. Tusinga in *S. P. Dom. Eliz.* cclxxi. 34, 35. I do not accept Mr. James Greenstreet's theory that W. Stanley was the real W. Shakespeare.   [2] *Hatfield MSS.* xiii. 609.

[3] Murray, i. 295.   [4] Taylor, *Penniless Pilgrimage* (ed. Hindley), 67.

xviii. THE EARL OF PEMBROKE'S MEN

Henry Herbert, s. of William, 1st Earl of Pembroke; *nat. c.* 1534; succ. as 2nd Earl, 17 Mar. 1570; m. (1) Catherine, d. of Henry Grey, Duke of Suffolk, 21 May 1553, (2) Catherine, d. of George Talbot, Earl of Shrewsbury, 17 Feb. 1563, (3) Mary, d. of Sir Henry Sidney, *c.* Apr. 1577; President of Wales, 1586; residences, Baynard's Castle, London, Wilton House, Wilts., Ludlow Castle, &c.; *ob.* 9 Jan. 1601.

[*Bibliographical Note.*—Halliwell-Phillipps collected provincial records and other notes on Pembroke's men in *A Budget of Notes and Memoranda* (1880). The Bill, Answer, and Replication in Shaw *et al.* v. Langley (1597–8, Court of Requests) are in C. W. Wallace, *The Swan Theatre and the Earl of Pembroke's Servants* (1911, *E. S.* xliii. 340).]

There is an isolated record of a Pembroke's company at Canterbury in 1575-6, hardly to be regarded as continuous with that which makes its appearance in the last decade of the century. Fleay, 87, puts the origin of the latter in 1589, and supposes it to be a continuation of Worcester's men after the death of their original patron in 1589, and to be the company ridiculed by Nashe (iii. 324) for playing *Delphrigus* and *The King of the Fairies*, in his preface to Greene's *Menaphon* (1589). But this Worcester's company is not in fact traceable during 1585-9, and Fleay's theory is only based on the allusion to *Hamlet* in the same preface (iii. 315), and the assumption that the *Ur-Hamlet*, like some other plays, passed to the Chamberlain's from Pembroke's, whereas it may just as well have passed to them from Strange's. As a matter of fact, there is no mention of Pembroke's before 1592 and no reason to suppose that it had an earlier existence. It will be well to detail the few facts of its history before attempting anything in the nature of conjecture. It was at Leicester in the last three months of 1592 and made its only appearances at Court on 26 December 1592 and 6 January 1593. In the following summer it travelled, and is found at York in June, at Rye in July, and in 1592-3 at Ludlow, Shrewsbury, Coventry, Bath, and Ipswich. But it had little success. Henslowe wrote to Alleyn on 28 September, 'As for my lorde a Penbrockes wch you desier to knowe wheare they be they ar all at home and hausse ben this v or sixe weackes for they cane not saue ther carges wth trauell as I heare & weare fayne to pane ther parell for ther carge'.[1] About the same time three of their plays came to the booksellers' hands. These were Marlowe's *Edward the Second* (1594, S. R. 6 July 1593), *The Taming of A Shrew*

---

[1] *Dulwich MS.* i. 14, in *Henslowe Papers*, 40.

(1594, S. R. 2 May 1594), and *The True Tragedy of Richard Duke of York* (1595). Probably the play to which this last is a sequel, *1 Contention of York and Lancaster* (1594, S. R. 12 March 1594) was also theirs, although the name of the company is not on the title-page. It is on the title-page of *Titus Andronicus* (1594), and its position suggests that the play passed to them from Strange's and from them before publication to Sussex's. All these plays, with the exception of *Edward II*, seem to have been worked upon by Shakespeare, and probably they ultimately became part of the stock of the Chamberlain's men. These men were playing *Titus Andronicus* and *The Taming of The Shrew* in June 1594, and that they also owned *The Contention* in its revised form of *2, 3 Henry VI* is suggested both by its inclusion in the First Folio and by the reference in the Epilogue to *Henry V* not only to the loss of France but also to the bleeding of England ' which oft our stage hath shown '.

I now enter a region of conjecture. It seems to me, on the whole, likely that the origin of Pembroke's men is to be explained by the special conditions of the plague-years 1592-3, and was due to a division for travelling purposes of the large London company formed by the amalgamation of Strange's and the Admiral's. Such a division had been fore-shadowed as likely to be necessary in the petition sent by Strange's men to the Privy Council during the summer of 1592 or earlier, and may actually have become necessary when, after all, the plague rendered travelling imperative. If this suggestion is well founded, it becomes not difficult to explain some of the transferences of acting rights in certain plays which seem to have taken place. Thus Strange's may have handed over *Titus Andronicus* in its earlier form of *Titus and Vespasian* to Pembroke's for the travels of 1593, and may also have handed over *The Contention of York and Lancaster*, if that was originally theirs, as is suggested by their production of *1 Henry VI*, which belongs to the same closely related series. This opens up a more important line of speculation. It is usual to assume that one of the members of Strange's from 1592 or earlier until its reconstitution as the Chamberlain's in 1594 was William Shakespeare, and there is no reason to doubt his authorship at any rate of the Talbot scenes, which we know from Nashe to have been staged as part of *1 Henry VI* in 1592. At the same time, the names of at least seventeen of Strange's and the Admiral's men in 1590-3 are otherwise known, and his is not one of them, and in particular his prominence amongst the Chamber-lain's men from the very beginning renders it extremely unlikely that, if he had been a member of the company in 1593, he would not have been mentioned in the Privy Council warrant of 6 May. Further, it seems to me impossible to resist the inference that the attribution to him of *Titus Andronicus* both by Francis Meres in 1598 and in the First Folio of 1623 can only be explained by his revision under that name of *Titus and Vespasian*, and that this was for the second production of the play as 'ne' for Henslowe by Sussex's men on 24 January 1594. There is, therefore, really some basis for the suggestion made long ago by Halliwell-Phillipps that he is to be looked for during these years in Pembroke's company until its collapse and then in Sussex's, and that it was from this rather than directly from Strange's that he went to the Chamberlain's.[1] On the other hand, it may be that for a time he was not attached as an actor to any company at all. It is possible that he took advantage of the plague-interval to travel in Italy and only resumed the regular exercise of his profession when the Chamberlain's company was formed. In any event, it must have been he who revised *The Contention* as *2, 3 Henry VI*, and the close stylistic relation of these plays to *1 Henry VI* makes it probable that the work on all three belongs to about the same date. The limitations of conjecture on so intricate a question are obvious, but I can conceive the order of events as being somewhat as follows. Shakespeare's first dramatic job, which earned him the ill will of Greene, was the writing or re-writing of *1 Henry VI* for Strange's, in the early spring of 1592. During the winter of 1592–3 he revised *The Contention* for Pembroke's and completed the series of his early histories with *Richard III*, and, as I am inclined to suspect, also an *Ur-Henry VIII*. He also wrote *The Jealous Comedy* or *Comedy of Errors* for Strange's. In the summer of 1593 Sussex's took over the plays of the bankrupt Pembroke's, including the Shakespearian histories *Titus and Vespasian* and *The Taming of A Shrew*. Some at least of these Pembroke's had themselves derived in 1592 or 1593 from Strange's. During the winter of 1593–4 Sussex's played either *Richard III* or *Henry VIII* as *Buckingham*, and also *Titus and Vespasian* revised for them by Shakespeare as *Titus Andronicus*. Alarmed at the further inhibition of plays in February, they allowed the revised *Titus* and unrevised texts of *The Taming of A Shrew* and *The Contention* to get into the hands of the booksellers. Whether Shakespeare had already revised *A Shrew* or did so later for the Chamberlain's (q.v.) I am

---

[1] *Outlines*, i. 122 ; ii. 329.

uncertain.   Finally, by the transfer of their plays to the
Chamberlain's men, who at once revived *A Shrew* and *Titus
Andronicus*, and by the incorporation of Strange's men in
the same company, the original stock of Strange's plays,
as distinct from the Admiral's, came together in the same
hands once more.   On the assumption that Shakespeare
never left Strange's, it is difficult to explain either the fortunes
of *Titus Andronicus*, or the absence from the lists of Strange's
plays in Henslowe's diary of *Richard III*, which must have
been written about 1592-4.   The silence as regards Strange's
both of the Court records and of Henslowe's diary during the
winter of 1593-4 makes it unlikely that they were in London,
and they would surely not produce a new play in the country.
    Nothing further is heard of a Pembroke's company for
three or four years.[1]   But in 1597 one appeared in London
about which we have rather full information, recently
increased by Mr. Wallace's discovery of a Court of Requests
suit in which they were concerned.   Towards the end of
February in that year Robert Shaw, Richard Jones, Gabriel
Spencer, William Bird *alias* Borne, and Thomas Downton,
who describe themselves in a suit of the following November
as Pembroke's servants, together with others their ' accom-
plices and associates ', entered into an agreement with Francis
Langley to play for twelve months ending on 20 February
1598 at the Swan.   Each man gave a bond of £100, which was
apparently to safeguard Langley against any failure by the
company as a whole or of Robert Shaw or a sufficient substi-
tute in particular to perform during this period, or against
any performance elsewhere, otherwise than ' in private
places ', within five miles of London.   Langley found £300
for apparel and, as he claimed, making ready of the play-
house, and was to receive a moiety of the takings of the
galleries and to be repaid for the apparel out of the other
moiety.   Of the men concerned, Jones and Downton had
been Admiral's men during 1594-7, and their transference
coincides with a three weeks' break in the performances of
the Admiral's at the Rose from 12 February onwards.
Mr. Wallace (*E. S.* xliii. 357) says that Shaw, Spencer, and
Bird were also of the Admiral's, but of this there is no evidence.
If Pembroke's had any continued life during 1594-7, they
may have shared it.   But this seems improbable, and on the
whole I am inclined to think that they came from the Chamberlain's (q.v.).   Plays were given at the Swan for some months,
and Langley took £100 from the galleries, and £100 more for

[1] Fleay, 136, ' Pembroke's men continued to act at the Curtain from
1589 to 1597 ' is guess-work.

apparel. Then came an inhibition of plays near London on 28 July 1597, caused by the production of *The Isle of Dogs*, as a result of which one of the authors, Nashe, fled, and the other, Jonson, together with Shaw and Spencer, was committed to the Marshalsea. The definite evidence that Shaw and Spencer were Pembroke's men at the Swan, now produced by Mr. Wallace, confirms my conjecture (*M. L. R.* iv. 411, 511) that *The Isle of Dogs* was an adventure of that house and not, as has sometimes been thought, of the Rose. Either in anticipation of a prolonged closing of the house or for some other reason, the company now desired to shake off their relations with Langley. Early in August Jones returned to Henslowe and made a new covenant with him. His example was followed by Shaw, Spencer, and Bird, and early in October by Downton. Their prescience was justified, for when in the course of October the chief offenders were released, and the inhibition, which was nominally terminable on 1 November, was in practice relaxed, it proved that, while Henslowe was able to get a new licence for the Rose, Langley could get none for the Swan. He urged them to try their fortunes without a licence, as others of their company were willing to do, but they not unnaturally refused, and Henslowe (i. 54) records, ' The xj of October begane my lord Admerals and my lord of Penbrockes men to playe at my howsse 1597'. He describes the company under the double name again on 21 and 23 October and 5 November, but on 1 December and thereafter as the Lord Admiral's (i. 68–70). A study of the Admiral's repertory for 1597–8 suggests that some or all of the plays *Black Joan, Hardicanute, Bourbon, Sturg-flattery, Branholt, Friar Spendleton, Alice Pierce*, and *Dido and Aeneas* may have been brought in by Pembroke's men.

The five seceders had not heard the last of Langley. He sued them at common law on the bonds given not to play in a rival house. They successfully applied to have the case transferred to the Court of Requests, and in the course of the pleadings maintained, firstly, that they were prevented from playing at the Swan by the restraint and Langley's failure to get a licence ; secondly, that Langley had orally assented to their transfer to Henslowe ; thirdly, that they could not appear at the Swan as a company, since Langley had ' procured from them ' two (or, as they afterwards said, three) of their associates, to whom he had returned their obligations ; and fourthly, that Langley had suffered no damage, since other men were occupying his house. They also complained that Langley had never handed over the apparel for which they had recouped him out of their gallery takings. The negotiations with Langley which they describe seem to have taken place during October. About the cove-nants entered into with Henslowe as far back as the beginning of August they said nothing, and whether either Langley or the court ever found out about these, and what the ultimate decision of the court on the main issue was, must remain uncertain. But certain loans entered in Henslowe's diary suggest that in March 1598 Langley was in a position to arrest Bird, and that in September of the same year some kind of agreement was arrived at, under which Langley received £35, as well as £19 or more for a rich cloak (i. 63, 72, 73, 95, 96). It is possible that a 'sewt agenste Thomas Poope' of the Chamberlain's, for which Henslowe (i. 72) made a personal advance of 10s. to William Bird on 30 August 1598, may also have been connected with the shiftings of companies in 1597.

The names of the two or three members of the company to whom Langley gave back their bonds are not stated in the pleadings. Perhaps one was Jonson, and the other two might conceivably have been Humphrey and Anthony Jeffes, since the name of 'Humfrey' stands with that of 'Gabriel' in stage-directions to *3 Henry VI*, and Henslowe's list of the reconstituted Admiral's company as it stood in October 1597–January 1598 contains 'the ij Geffes', who are not traceable in the 1594–7 company and may well have come in with the five Pembroke's men. Langley tells us that certain 'fellows' of his opponents had taken a more reasonable line than theirs and returned to the Swan. How long these men remained there we do not know, but probably they secured Pembroke's patronage after the five had been definitely merged in the Admiral's, for by the end of 1597 there was clearly a distinct Pembroke's company again. Provincial records yield the name, not only at Bath in 1596–7 and at Bristol in September 1597, which may point to a tour of the undivided Swan company during the period of restraint, but also at Bath in 1598–9, at Bristol in July 1598, at Leicester between October and December, at Dover on 7 October, at Coventry on 12 December, and at Bewdley on 22 December. They were at Norwich in April 1599, at Coventry on 4 July, and at Bristol in July. They were at York on 21 January 1600, Bristol in April, Marlborough in May, and Leicester before Michael-mas. In October they were in relationship with Henslowe, who notes 'my Lordes of Penbrockes men begane to playe at the Rosse', and records performances of *Like Unto Like* and *Roderick* on 28 and 29 October respectively.[1] The former

---

[1] Henslowe, i. 131 ; cf. ch. xxiii, s.v. Fulwell.

brought him 11s. 6d. and the latter 5s., and there apparently the experiment ended, and with it, so far as is known, the career of Pembroke's men. It is just possible that they were merged in Worcester's company, which arose shortly afterwards. Mr. Fleay expands this possibility into a definite theory that Kempe, Beeston, Duke, and Pallant left the Chamberlain's men for Pembroke's in 1599, and ultimately passed from these to Worcester's. This is improbable as regards Kempe, and unproved as regards the rest.[1]

xix. THE LORD ADMIRAL'S (LORD HOWARD'S, EARL OF NOTTINGHAM'S), PRINCE HENRY'S, AND ELECTOR PALATINE'S MEN

Charles Howard, s. of William, 1st Baron Howard of Effingham, g.s. of Thomas, 2nd Duke of Norfolk; *nat.* 1536; m. (1) Catherine Carey, d. of Henry Lord Hunsdon, Lady of the Privy Chamber, (2) Margaret Stuart, d. of James Earl of Murray, c. 1604; succ. as 2nd Baron, 29 Jan. 1573; Deputy Lord Chamberlain, 1574–5; Vice-Admiral, Feb. 1582; Lord Chamberlain, c. Dec. 1583; Lord High Admiral, 8 July 1585–1619; Earl of Nottingham, 22 Oct. 1596; Lord Steward, 1597; *ob.* 14 Dec. 1624.

Henry Frederick, s. of James VI of Scotland and I of England; *nat.* 19 Feb. 1594; cr. Duke of Rothesay, 30 Aug. 1594; succ. as Duke of Cornwall, 24 Mar. 1603; cr. Earl of Chester and Prince of Wales, 4 June 1610; *ob.* 6 Nov. 1612.

Frederick, s. of Frederick IV, Count Palatine of the Rhine; *nat.* 19 Aug. 1596; succ. as Frederick V, 1610; m. Princess Elizabeth of England, 14 Feb. 1613; elected King of Bohemia, 1619; *ob.* 1632.

[*Bibliographical Note.*—The material preserved amongst the papers of Philip Henslowe and Edward Alleyn at Dulwich has been fully collected and studied by W. W. Greg in *Henslowe's Diary* (1904–8) and *Henslowe Papers* (1907), which replace the earlier publications of Malone, Collier, and others from the same source. I have added a little from Professor Wallace's researches and elsewhere, and have attempted to give my own reading of the evidence, which differs in a few minor points from Dr. Greg's.]

It was perhaps his employment as deputy to the Earl of Sussex in the office of Lord Chamberlain which led Lord Howard to encourage players. A company, under the name of Lord Howard's men, appeared at Court for the first time at the Christmas of 1576–7. On 27 December they played *Tooley*, and on 17 February *The Solitary Knight.*[2] They came again for the last time in the following winter, and performed

---

[1] Cf. *infra* (Chamberlain's). Shank (cf. ch. xv) was once in Pembroke's.
[2] The Council Register assigns this performance to the Chamberlain's; cf. App. B.

on 5 January 1578. They were also at Kirtling on 3 December 1577, Saffron Walden in 1577–8, Ipswich on 24 October 1577, in 1578–9, and perhaps on 8 October 1581, Bristol, where they gave *The Queen of Ethiopia*, between 31 August and 6 September 1578, Nottingham on 19 December 1578, and Bath and Coventry in 1578–9.

Howard again had players at Court, after he became Admiral in 1585. The first record of them is at Dover in June 1585. Later in the year they were playing in conjunction with the Lord Chamberlain's (Lord Hunsdon's). ' The Lorde Chamberlens and the Lord Admirall's players ' were rewarded at Leicester in October–December 1585, and ' the servants of the lo: admirall and the lo: Chamberlaine ' for a play at Court on 6 January 1586.[1] During the same Christmas, however, the Admiral's played alone on 27 December 1585, and as Hunsdon's survived in the provinces, the two organizations may have been amalgamated for one performance only. The Admiral's were at Coventry, Faversham, Ipswich, and Leicester in 1585–6. They were reported to Walsingham amongst other London companies on 25 January 1587 (App. D, No. lxxviii), although they did not appear at Court during this winter. In 1586–7 they were at Cambridge, Coventry, Bath, York, Norwich, Ipswich, Exeter, Southampton, and Leicester. By November they were back in London, and on the 16th an accident at their theatre is thus related by Philip Gawdy to his father :[2]

' Yow shall vnderstande of some accydentall newes heare in this towne thoughe my self no wyttnesse thereof, yet I may be bold to veryfye it for an assured troth. My L. Admyrall his men and players having a devyse in ther playe to tye one of their fellowes to a poste and so to shoote him to deathe, having borrowed their callyvers one of the players handes swerved his peece being charged with bullett missed the fellowe he aymed at and killed a chyld, and a woman great with chyld forthwith, and hurt an other man in the head very soore. How they will answere it I do not study vnlesse their profession were better, but in chrystyanity I am very sorry for the chaunce but God his iudgementes ar not to be searched nor enquired of at mannes handes. And yet I fynde by this an old proverbe veryfyed ther never comes more hurte than commes of fooling.'

Possibly the company went into retirement as a result of this disaster ; at any rate nothing more is heard of them

---

[1] Fleay, *Sh.* 286, supposed Howard to be both Admiral and Chamberlain at this date, but this view was refuted by Halliwell-Phillipps in the *Athenaeum* for 24 April 1886, and resigned by Fleay, 31 ; cf. Greg, ii. 81.

[2] I. H. Jeayes, *Letters of Philip Gawdy* (Roxburghe Club), 23.

until the Christmas of 1588-9. They then came to Court, and were rewarded for two interludes and ' for showinge other feates of activitye and tumblinge ' on 29 December 1588 and 11 February 1589.[1] On 6 November 1589 they were playing in the City, and were suppressed by the Lord Mayor, because Tilney, the Master of the Revels, misliked their plays. Probably they had been concerning themselves with the Marprelate controversy. Strange's men, who were evidently performing as a separate company, shared their fate. It may have been this misadventure which led the Admiral's to seek house-room with James Burbadge at the Theatre (q.v.), where some evidence by John Alleyn, who, with James Tunstall, was of their number, locates them in November 1590 and May 1591. A relic of this period may be presumed to exist in the ' plot ' of *Dead Man's Fortune*, preserved with other plots belonging to the company at Dulwich, in which Burbadge, doubtless Richard Burbadge, then still a boy, appeared. Certainly there is nothing to connect Burbadge with the company at any other date. Other actors in the piece were one Darlowe, ' b[oy ?] Samme ', and Robert Lee, later of Anne's men. The Admiral's again showed ' feats of activitie ' at Court on 28 December 1589, and a play on 3 March 1590. In 1589-90 they were at Coventry, Ipswich, Maidstone, Marlborough, Winchester, and Gloucester, and in 1590-1 at Winchester and Gloucester. Marlowe's *Tamburlaine* was published in 1590 as ' shewed upon stages in the City of London ' by the Admiral's men. The Court records for the following winter present what looks at first sight like a curious discrepancy. The accounts of the Treasurer of the Chamber include payments for plays and activities on 27 December 1590 and 16 February 1591 to Lord Strange's men. The corresponding warrants, however, were made out, according to the Privy Council Register, for the Admiral's. Probably there is no error here, and the entries are evidence of an amalgamation between the two companies, which possibly dated from as far back as the winter of 1589, and which seems to have endured until the summer of 1594. Technically, it would seem that it was the Admiral's who were merged in Strange's men. It is the latter and not the former who generally appear in official documents during this period. I have therefore dealt with its details for both companies, with the question of the precise date of the amalgamation, and with the possibility that the plot of *The Seven Deadly Sins* and its list of actors also belong to a Theatre performance of about 1590, in my account of Strange's men,

---

[1] Stopes, *Hunnis*, 322, names payees in error.

and need only remark here that the name of the Admiral's does not altogether fall into disuse, especially in provincial records, and that the leading actor, Edward Alleyn, in particular, is shown by an official document to have retained his personal status as an Admiral's servant.

It is a question of some interest how early Alleyn's connexion with the Admiral's may be supposed to have begun. Was he, for example, the original Tamburlaine of 1587, and was it as an Admiral's man that Nashe referred to him, if it was he to whom Nashe referred, as the Roscius of the contemporary players in his *Menaphon* epistle of 1589? He is known to have been a member of Worcester's company in 1583. Dr. Greg is disposed to think that he remained with them until the death of the third Earl of Worcester on 22 February 1589, and then joined the Admiral's.[1] It is, however, to be observed that there is no trace of Worcester's men between 1584 and 1590, and that it is in 1585 that the Admiral's men begin to appear at Court. On the whole, it commends itself to me as the more probable conjecture that the first Earl of Worcester's company passed into Howard's service, when he became Admiral in 1585, and that the players of the fourth Earl of Worcester between 1590 and 1596 were distinct from those of his father. The issue concerns others besides Edward Alleyn himself. Amongst the members of Worcester's company in 1583 were Robert Browne, James Tunstall, and Richard Jones; and all three of these are found concerned with Alleyn in matters of theatrical business during 1589–91. The most important document is a deed of sale by 'Richarde Jones of London yoman' to 'Edwarde Allen of London gent' for £37 10s. of 'all and singuler suche share parte and porcion of playinge apparrelles, playe bookes, instrumentes, and other comodities whatsoeuer belonginge to the same, as I the said Richarde Jones nowe haue or of right ought to haue joyntlye with the same Edwarde Allen, John Allen citizen and inholder of London and Roberte Browne yoman'.[2] This is dated 3 January 1589. There are also three deeds of sale to Edward and John Alleyn of theatrical apparel between 1589 and 1591, and to two of these James Tunstall was a witness.[3] On Dr. Greg's theory as to the date at which Alleyn took service with the Lord Admiral, the organization in whose properties Richard Jones had an interest would naturally be Worcester's men; on mine it would be the Admiral's, and it would follow that Jones and Browne, as well as Alleyn, had joined that company.

[1] Henslowe, ii. 83.   [2] *Henslowe Papers*, 31.
[3] *Alleyn Papers*, 11, 12; cf. *Henslowe Papers*, 32.

We have seen that James Tunstall had done so by 1590–1. John Alleyn was an elder brother of Edward. There is nothing to connect him with Worcester's men. He was a servant of Lord Sheffield in November 1580 and of the Lord Admiral in 1589.[1] A letter of one Elizabeth Socklen to Edward Alleyn refers to a time 'when your brother, my lovinge cozen John Allen, dwelt with my very good lord, Charles Heawarde', and this rather suggests that his service was in some household capacity, and not merely as player.[2] If so, it may have been through him that Edward Alleyn and his fellows became Admiral's men. The first period of their activity seems to have lasted from 1585 to 1589, and it was no doubt Edward Alleyn's genius, and perhaps also his business capacity, which enabled them to offer a serious rivalry to the Queen's company. I suspect that in 1589 or 1590 they were practically dissolved, and this view is confirmed by the fact that their most important play was allowed to get to the hands of the printers. Alleyn, with the help of his brother, bought up the properties, and allied himself with Lord Strange's men, and so far as the Admiral's continued to exist at all for the next few years, it was almost entirely in and through him that it did so. After a financial quarrel with James Burbadge in May 1591, the combined companies moved to the Rose. There is nothing to show whether the Alleyns bought up Robert Browne's interest as well as that of Richard Jones. At any rate Browne began in 1590 that series of continental tours which occupied most of the rest of his career (cf. ch. xiv). Jones joined him in one of these adventures in 1592, and it is possible that John Bradstreet and Thomas Sackville, who went with them, were also old Admiral's men. But I do not think that it is accurate to regard this company, as Dr. Greg seems to be inclined to do, as being itself under the Admiral's patronage. It is true that they obtained a passport from him, but this was probably given rather in his capacity as warden of the seas than in that of their lord. His name is not mentioned in any of the foreign records of their pere-grinations. It is not possible to say which, other than Alleyn, of the members of the 1592–3 Strange's and Admiral's company, whose names have been preserved, came from each of the two contributing sources. They do not include either John Alleyn or James Tunstall, or Edward Browne, a Wor-cester's man of 1583, who reappears with Tunstall among the Admiral's after 1594. Nor is it possible to say how far the repertory of Strange's men, as disclosed by the

[1] *Alleyn Papers*, I, 5.   [2] Ibid. 54.

1592-3 entries in Henslowe's diary, included plays drawn from the Admiral's stock. This may have been the case with *The Battle of Alcazar*, which was printed as an Admiral's play in 1594, and with *Orlando Furioso*, which contemporary gossip represents Greene as selling first to the Queen's and then to the Admiral's. And it may have been the case with *1 Tamar Cham*, which passed to the later Admiral's. Neither *Tamburlaine* nor *The Wounds of Civil War*, printed like *The Battle of Alcazar* as an Admiral's play in 1594, is recorded to have been played by Strange's.

When the companies settled down again to a London life after the conclusion of the long plague in 1594, the Admiral's men reconstituted themselves as an independent company with Alleyn at its head, leaving the greater number of their recent comrades of the road to pass, as the Lord Chamberlain's men, under the patronage of Lord Hunsdon. The personal alliance between Alleyn and Henslowe, whose step-daughter, Joan Woodward, he had married on 22 October 1592, led to the institution of close business relations between the company and the pawnbroker, and the record of these in the famous diary enables us to follow with a singular minuteness the almost daily fortunes of the Admiral's men during the course of some nine or ten years, broken into two periods by a reconstruction of the company in 1597 and finally closing about the time of their conversion into Prince Henry's men in 1604. The precise nature of the position occupied by Henslowe has been carefully investigated by Dr. Greg,[1] and has already been briefly considered in these pages (ch. xi). He was not a member of the company, but its landlord, and, probably to an increasing extent, its financier. In the former capacity he received, after every day's performance, a fluctuating sum, which seems to have represented half the amount received for admission to the galleries of the house ; the other half, with the payments for entrance to the standing room in the yard, being divided amongst such of the players as had a share in the profits. Out of this, of course, they had to meet all expenditure other than by way of rent, such as the wages of hired men, payments for apparel and play-books, fees to the Master of the Revels for the licensing of plays, and the like. In practice it became convenient for Henslowe, who was a capitalist, while many of the players lived from hand to mouth, to advance sums to meet such expenditure as it fell due, and to recoup himself from time to time out of the company's profits. It seems likely that,

---

[1] Henslowe, ii. 127.

when the system was in full working, the moiety of the gallery money, which remained after the deduction of the rent, was assigned for the purpose of these repayments. During the period 1597–1604 Henslowe's entries in his diary are mainly in the nature of a running account of these advances and of the receipts set off against them; for 1594–7 similar entries occur irregularly, but the principal record is a daily list, such as Henslowe had already kept during his shorter associations with Strange's, the Queen's, and Sussex's companies in the course of 1592–4, of each performance given, with the name of the play and of the amount accruing to Henslowe himself in the form of rent. This list renders possible a very interesting analysis, both of the repertory of the company and of some at least of the financial conditions of their enterprise.

The entries start with the heading, 'In the name of God Amen begininge the 14 of Maye 1594 by my lord Admeralls men'. After three days, during which *The Jew of Malta*, *Cutlack*, and *The Ranger's Comedy*, all of which are found in the later repertory of the company, were given, they stop abruptly.[1] To about the same date may be assigned a fragmentary account, headed 'Layd owt for my Lorde Admeralle seruantes as ffoloweth 1594', and recording expenditure for coming and going to Court and to Somerset House, the residence of the Lord Chamberlain, 'for mackinge of our leater twise', and 'for drinckinge with the jentellmen', all evidently concerned with the initial business of forming and licensing the company.[2] On 5 June the account of performances is resumed with a fresh heading, 'In the name of God Amen begininge at Newington my Lord Admeralle men and my Lorde Chamberlen men as ffolowethe 1594'.[3] Henslowe's takings only averaged 9s. for the first ten days, probably on account of the distance of Newington Butts from London.[4] The takings for the three days in May averaged 41s., and it may perhaps be inferred that these May performances were at the Rose, and that some fear of renewed plague on the part of the authorities led to their being relegated to a safer quarter. The tentative character of these early performances is shown by the fact that the Admiral's were still sharing a theatre with the Chamberlain's. To the repertory of the latter it seems safe to assign three of the seven plays produced, *Titus Andronicus*, *Hamlet*, and *The Taming of A Shrew*, and probably also a fourth, *Hester and Ahasuerus*, as there is no later sign of this amongst the Admiral's plays. This leaves

[1] Henslowe, i. 17.   [2] Ibid. 198.   [3] Ibid. 17.
[4] Cf. the petitions assigned to 1592 (App. D, No. xcii).

three others to be regarded as the Admiral's contribution, *The Jew of Malta* and *Cutlack*, which they had played in May and were often to play again, and *Belin Dun*, to which are attached the letters ' ne ', Henslowe's normal indication of a new play.[1] There is nothing in the order in which the plays were taken to indicate an alternation of the two companies, and it is likely enough that neither was yet fully constituted, and that they actually joined forces in the same performances.

After the tenth play on 15 June, Henslowe drew a line across the page, and although the entries continue without any indication of a change in the conditions under which the performances were given, I can only concur in the conjecture of Mr. Fleay and Dr. Greg that at this point the Admiral's plays were transferred to the Rose, and the combination with the Chamberlain's ceased.[2] A sudden rise in the amount of Henslowe's takings, and the absence from the rest of the list of the four plays named above and of any other attributable to the Chamberlain's repertory, are alike strongly in favour of this view, which may be treated as a practical certainty. Henceforward the fortunes of the company seem to have followed a smooth course for the space of three years. Their proceedings may be briefly summed up as follows. They played for thirty-nine consecutive weeks from 15 June 1594 to 14 March 1595, appearing at Court during this season on 28 December, 1 January, and 6 January. After a break of thirty-seven days during Lent, opportunity of which was taken to repair the Rose, they played again for ten weeks from Easter Monday, 21 April, to 26 June 1595. Then came a vacation of fifty-nine days, with visits to Bath and Maidstone. They began again in London on 25 August 1595 and played for twenty-seven weeks to 28 February 1596, giving Court performances on 1 January, 4 January, and 22 and 24 February. This took them to the end of the first week in Lent. After forty-three days' interval, they played for fifteen weeks, from Easter Monday, 12 April, to 23 July 1596. Their summer vacation lasted for ninety-five days, and they are noted during 1595–6 at Coventry, Bath, Gloucester, and Dunwich. In the autumn they started playing on 27 October, but the receipts were low, and if the record is complete, they suspended performances between 15 and 25 November, and then went on to 12 February 1597, making up a season of about fourteen weeks in all. They do not seem to have played at Court at all this winter. This year they

---

[1] They may represent n[ew] e[nterlude], or merely ne[w].
[2] Fleay, 140 ; Henslowe, ii. 84.

rather disregarded Lent, stopping for eighteen days only, during a reconstruction of the company, and then playing three days a week until Easter, and then regularly until the end of July, in all twenty-one weeks. To certain irregularities at the close of this season it will be necessary to refer later. During the three years, then, there were three winter and three summer seasons of London playing, covering about a hundred and twenty-six weeks. Except in Lent or at the beginning or end of a season, or occasionally, probably for climatic reasons, at other times, especially in December, plays were given upon every week-day. It emerges from Dr. Greg's re-ordering of Henslowe's very inaccurate dates that there were no plays on Sundays.[1] On the other hand, a summons to play at Court in the evening did not necessarily entail a blank day in the afternoon. The total number of performances during the three years was seven hundred and twenty-eight. It is reasonable to assume that Henslowe's takings varied roughly with those of the company, although the reserve must be made that different plays might prove the most attractive to the galleries and to the yard respectively. The amounts entered range from a minimum of 3s. to a maximum of 73s. Dr. Greg calculates the average over ' certain typical periods of 1595 ' as 30s. ;[2] during the first half of 1597 it was 24s. The fluctuations are determined, partly by the popularity or novelty of the plays presented, partly by the season of the year, and doubtless the weather and the competition of other amusements. There were generally some high receipts during Christmas, Easter, and Whitsun weeks. Unfortunately there is no means of estimating the proportion which Henslowe's share bore to that which fell for division among the players. Some light is thrown upon the expenses by the subsidiary accounts of advances, which Henslowe began to keep from time to time in 1596. In May of that year he lent Alleyn ' for the company ' a total amount of £39 in several instalments, and recovered it by small sums of £1 to £3 at a time during the next three months.[3] A longer account extending from October 1596 to March 1597 reaches, with the aid of a miscalculation, a total of £52. Of this £22 was repaid during the same period, chiefly by deductions from the profits of first nights, and an acknowledgement given for the balance of £30.[4] The advances were made through various members of the company, and the purposes specified include apparel for three new plays, travelling expenses, and fees to playwrights. A third account, if I am

---

[1] Henslowe, ii. 324.
[3] Ibid. i. 126.
[2] Ibid. ii. 133.
[4] Ibid. i. 44.

right in the interpretation of some very disputable figures, shows an expenditure at the average rate of 31s. a day during the six months from 24 January to 28 July 1597, of which, however, nearly half was in fact incurred during the first twenty-four days of the period. In this case only the sums and not the purposes for which they were advanced are entered.[1]

During the three years the Admiral's men produced new plays to the total number of fifty-five, and at the average rate of one a fortnight. The productions were not at regular intervals, and often followed each other in successive weeks. There is, however, no example of two new productions in the same week.[2] These are the names and dates of the new plays:

Belin Dun (10 June 1594).
Galiaso (28 June 1594).
Philipo and Hippolito (9 July 1594).
2 Godfrey of Bulloigne (19 July 1594).
The Merchant of Emden (30 July 1594).
Tasso's Melancholy (13 Aug. 1594).
The Venetian Comedy (27 Aug. 1594).
Palamon and Arcite (18 Sept. 1594).
The Love of an English Lady (26 Sept. 1594).
A Knack to Know an Honest Man (23 Oct. 1594).
1 Caesar and Pompey (8 Nov. 1594).
Diocletian (16 Nov. 1594).
The Wise Man of West Chester (3 Dec. 1594).
The Set at Maw (15 Dec. 1594).
The French Comedy (11 Feb. 1595).
The Mack (21 Feb. 1595).
Olympo (5 Mar. 1595).[3]
1 Hercules (7 May 1595).

[1] Henslowe, i. 51 ; cf. Dr. Greg's explanation in ii. 129 and my criticism in *M. L. R.* iv. 409. Wallace (*E. S.* xliii. 361) has a third explanation, that the figures represent the sharers' takings. But (*a*) these would not all pass through Henslowe's hands, (*b*) the amounts are often less than half the galleries, and (*c*) the columns are blank for some days of playing.

[2] I include *Belin Dun*, produced just before the separation of the Admiral's and the Chamberlain's, in the fifty-five ; but I do not follow Dr. Greg in taking the sign ' j ', which Henslowe attaches to *Tamburlaine* (30 Aug. 1594) and *Long. Meg of Westminster* (14 Feb. 1595) as equivalent to ' ne '. Were it so, these would furnish two, and the only two, examples of a second new production in a single week. Probably ' j ' indicates in both instances the *First Part* of a two-part play. This view is confirmed by Henslowe's note on 10 March 1595, ' 17 p[laies] frome hence lycensed ' ; cf. my criticism in *M. L. R.* iv. 408.

[3] Variously entered as ' olimpo ', ' seleo & olempo ', ' olempeo & hengenyo ', &c. ; but apparently only one play is meant.

2 Hercules (23 May 1595).
1 The Seven Days of the Week (3 June 1595).
2 Caesar and Pompey (18 June 1595).
Longshanks (29 Aug. 1595).
Crack me this Nut (5 Sept. 1595).
The New World's Tragedy (17 Sept. 1595).
The Disguises (2 Oct. 1595).
The Wonder of a Woman (16 Oct. 1595).
Barnardo and Fiammetta (30 Oct. 1595).
A Toy to Please Chaste Ladies (14 Nov. 1595).
Henry V (28 Nov. 1595).
Chinon of England (3 Jan. 1596).
Pythagoras (16 Jan. 1596).
2 The Seven Days of the Week (23 Jan. 1596).
The Blind Beggar of Alexandria (12 Feb. 1596).
Julian the Apostate (29 Apr. 1596).
1 Tamar Cham (7 May 1596).
Phocas (20 May 1596).
2 Tamar Cham (11 June 1596).
Troy (25 June 1596).
The Paradox (1 July 1596).
The Tinker of Totnes (23 July 1596).
Vortigern, Valteger, or *Hengist* (4 Dec. 1596).
Stukeley (10 Dec. 1596).
Nebuchadnezzar (18 Dec. 1596).
That Will Be Shall Be (30 Dec. 1596).
Jeronimo (7 Jan. 1597).
Alexander and Lodowick (14 Jan. 1597).[1]
Woman Hard to Please (27 Jan. 1597).
Guido (21 Mar. 1597).
Five Plays in One (7 Apr. 1597).
A French Comedy (18 Apr. 1597).
Uther Pendragon (29 Apr. 1597).
The Comedy of Humours (11 May 1597).
The Life and Death of Henry I (26 May 1597).
Frederick and Basilea (3 June 1597).
The Life and Death of Martin Swart (30 June 1597).

Oblivion has overtaken the great majority of these plays. *Longshanks* is possibly Peele's *Edward I*, and *Jeronimo* certainly Kyd's *Spanish Tragedy*. The title of *The Wise Man of West Chester* agrees with the subject of Munday's *John a Kent* and *John a Cumber*, the manuscript of which is dated December 1595. One would be more willing to

---

[1] *Alexander and Lodowick* is actually entered for a second time as ' ne ' on 11 Feb. 1597, but I have assumed this to be a mistake.

identify *Henry V* with *The Famous Victories*, if the latter had not been printed in 1598 with the name of the Queen's men on its title-page. *A Knack to Know an Honest Man* was printed, as acted ' about the Citie of London ', but without any company name, in 1596 (S. R. 26 November 1595). *Stukeley* was also printed without a name, as *The Famous History of the Life and Death of Captain Thomas Stukeley*, in 1605 (S. R. 11 August 1600). *1 Tamar Cham* and *Frederick and Basilea* are extant in ' plots ' alone, and *Belin Dun*, or *Bellendon*, as Henslowe writes it, was entered in the Stationers' Register on 24 November 1595 as *The true tragicall historie of Kinge Rufus the first with the life and deathe of Belyn Dun the first thief that ever was hanged in England*, but is not known to be extant. The list also contains two of the early works of George Chapman, *The Blind Beggar of Alexandria* (1598, Admiral's, S. R. 15 August 1598), and *The Comedy of Humours*, which can be safely identified with *A Humorous Day's Mirth* (1599, Admiral's). Ingenious attempts have been made to trace in some of the remaining titles other plays by Chapman, or by Heywood, Dekker, and the like, or presumed early drafts of these, or the English originals of plays or titles preserved in German versions ; but in most cases the material available is so scanty as to render the game a hazardous one.[1] It appears, however, from Henslowe's notes of advances during 1596-7 that payment was made to Heywood for a book, from which it may be inferred that his activity as a dramatist for the company had already began. Payments to ' marcum ' and ' Mr. porter ' perhaps indicate the same of Gervase Markham and Henry Porter.[2]

It is evident that some of the plays marked ' ne ' by Henslowe cannot have been new in the fullest sense. This applies to *Jeronimo*, which had been played by Strange's

---

[1] It has been chiefly played by Fleay and Dr. Greg. The relations suggested are between *1 Caesar and Pompey* and Chapman's play of the same name, *Disguises* and Chapman's *May-day, Godfrey of Bulloigne* and Heywood's *Four Prentices of London, Olympo, 1, 2 Hercules*, and *Troy* and Heywood's *Golden, Silver, Brazen,* and *Iron Ages* respectively, *Five Plays in One* and some of Heywood's *Dialogues and Dramas, The Wonder of a Woman* and a supposed early version by Heywood of W. Rowley's *A New Wonder, or, A Woman Never Vexed, The Venetian Comedy* and both the German *Josephus Jude von Venedig* and Dekker's lost *Jew of Venice, Diocletian* and Dekker's *The Virgin Martyr, A Set at Maw* and Dekker's *Match Me in London, The Mack* and Dekker's *The Wonder of a Kingdom, Vortigern* and Middleton's *The Mayor of Quinborough, Uther Pendragon* and W. Rowley's *Birth of Merlin, Philipo and Hippolito* and both Massinger's lost *Philenzo and Hypollita* and the German *Julio und Hyppolita*. Full details will be found in Henslowe, ii. 165 sqq.

[2] Henslowe, i. 44, 128.

men as an old play during 1592–3, and to 2 *Tamar Cham,* which had been produced by the same company on 28 April 1592, and on that occasion also marked ' ne ' by Henslowe. It applies also to *Longshanks* and *Henry V,* if these are really the same as *Edward I* and *The Famous Victories.* And it may, of course, apply also in other cases, which cannot now be distinguished. Two explanations are possible. One is that plays were treated as new, for the purpose of Henslowe's entries, which were only new to the repertory of the particular company concerned, having been purchased by them or by Henslowe from the stock of some other company. There is, however, no indication that Henslowe received any special financial advantage from the production of a new play, such as would give point to such an arrangement. The other, and perhaps the most plausible, is that an old play was marked ' ne ' if it had undergone any substantial process of revision before revival. But it must be admitted that the problem set is one that we have hardly the means to solve.

In addition to their new and revised plays, the Admiral's had a considerable stock of old ones. Some of these they were playing, when they began their first season in June 1594. Several others were revived in the course of that season, and a few at later dates. The only new play of the repertory which reached the stage of revival during the three years was *Belin Dun,* which was originally produced on 10 June 1594, played to the end of the year, then dropped, and afterwards revived for a single performance on 11 July 1596, and for a series in the spring of 1597. But it is not likely that many new plays were written during the plague years, and probably most of the revived plays of 1594–5 were a good deal more than two or three years old. A list of the plays not marked ' ne ' by Henslowe, nineteen in number, follows. It is, however, possible that some of them are only plays in the list already given, masquerading under different names.

Cutlack.	*Dr. Faustus.*
The Ranger's Comedy.	*The Love of a Grecian Lady,*
The Guise, or, *The Massacre of*	or, *The Grecian Comedy.*[1]
Paris.	*The French Doctor.*
The Jew of Malta.	*Warlamchester.*
Mahomet.	*2 Tamburlaine.*
1 Tamburlaine.	*The Siege of London.*

[1] Possibly identical with *Mahomet,* if that was Peele's play. Dr. Greg's identification with *The Love of an English Lady* strikes me as rather arbitrary.

Antony and Valia.[1] *Osric.*
1 Long Meg of Westminster.[2] *Time's Triumph and Fortune's.*
The Welshman.[3] *The Witch of Islington.*
1 Fortunatus.

Five plays of Marlowe's are conspicuous in the list. *Mahomet* might be either Greene's *Alphonsus, King of Arragon* or Peele's lost *Turkish Mahomet and Hiren the Fair Greek*. *Fortunatus*, as revised by Dekker in 1599, is extant, but it is doubtful whether Dekker was writing early enough to have been the author of the original play. Conjectural identifications of some of the other titles have been attempted.[4] There is, perhaps, a natural inclination to eke out our meagre knowledge of the repertory of the earlier Admiral's men, as it was constituted before 1590, by the assumption that the old and the revised new plays of 1594–7 belong to that stock. But this can only be proved to be so in the case of *1 and 2 Tamburlaine*, where the title-page of the 1590 edition comes to our assistance. There is no trace between 1594 and 1597 of any of the other three plays, *The Battle of Alcazar*, *The Wounds of Civil War*, and *Orlando Furioso*, which there is independent evidence for connecting with the Admiral's. And it must be borne in mind that there were several other sources from which a supply of old plays might be drawn. Alleyn seems to have bought up the books and properties of the pre-1590 men, and we do not know how far he also retained rights in some or all of the plays produced during his alliance with Strange's. Moreover, there were plenty of opportunities for either Alleyn, Henslowe, or the Admiral's men as a whole, to acquire copies from one or more of the companies, Pembroke's, the Queen's, Sussex's, which went under in the plague years. *Henry V*, if identical with *The Famous Victories*, had certainly been a Queen's play; *The Ranger's Comedy* had been played for Henslowe by the Queen's and Sussex's in April 1594; *Jeronimo* and *The Guise* had been similarly played by Strange's in 1592–3; and the fact that Strange's, the Queen's, Sussex's, and the

---

[1] I assume that 'valy a for' entered on 4 Jan. 1595 is the same play. Conceivably it might be *Vallingford*, i. e. *Fair Em*, an old Strange's play.

[2] An allusion in Field's *Amends for Ladies*, ii. 1, shows that *Long Meg* still held the Fortune stage about 1611.

[3] Possibly identical with *Longshanks*.

[4] The relations suggested are between *The Love of a Grecian Lady* and the German *Tugend- und Liebesstreit*, *The French Doctor* and both Dekker's *Jew of Venice* and the German *Josephus Jude von Venedig*, *The Siege of London* and Heywood's *1 Edward IV*, *The Welshman* and R. A.'s *The Valiant Welshman*, *Time's Triumph and Fortune's* and Heywood's *Timon*. For details cf. Henslowe, ii. 165 *sqq*.

Admiral's, all in turn played *The Jew of Malta* leads to a strong
suspicion that it was Henslowe's property and placed by him
at the disposal of any company that might from time to time
be occupying his theatre.

The Rose was what is now known as a ' repertory ' house.
A very successful play might be repeated on the night after
its first production or revival, or in the course of the same week.
But as a rule one performance a week was the limit, and after
a play had been on the boards a few weeks, the intervals
between its appearances rapidly became greater. *The Wise
Man of West Chester*, which was presented thirty-two times
between December 1594 and July 1597, had a longer life
than any other new play during the three years. Next came
A Knack to Know an Honest Man, with twenty-one performances in two years, *1 Seven Days of the Week*, with twenty-one
performances in fifteen months, and *The Blind Beggar of
Alexandria*, with twenty-two performances in fourteen
months. *Belin Dun*, although not continuously upon the
stage for long together, achieved with the aid of its revival
a total of twenty-four performances. The only other new
plays, that outlived a year, were *2 Godfrey of Bulloigne* and
A Toy to Please Chaste Ladies. Even such highly successful
plays as *1 and 2 Hercules* ceased to be heard of after six
months. The usual run of a play was anything from six to
seventeen nights, but sixteen plays failed to obtain even
such a run, and several plays, which apparently did well
enough on the first night, were not repeated at all. As a rule
the first night of a play brought Henslowe the highest returns ;
but this was by no means invariably the case, and the success
of any play, which held the boards for as many as six nights,
can perhaps best be measured by its average returns. By
far the most fortunate was *The Comedy of Humours* which
averaged 53s. for the eleven nights available before the
summer season of 1597 closed. Next came *1 and 2 Hercules*
with 42s. and 43s. respectively, *1 Seven Days of the Week*
with 35s., and *The Wise Man of West Chester* with 34s. On
the other hand the average of *Henry I* was no more than
19s. and that of the second *French Comedy* no more than 16s.
The highest individual returns were those from the first
nights of *1 and 2 Hercules*, *2 Godfrey of Bulloigne*, and *1 Seven
Days of the Week*, which yielded 73s., 70s., 71s., and 70s.
respectively, and that from the sixth night of the *Comedy of
Humours*, which was also 70s. The booking for this play
shows a curious progress, being 43s., 55s., 58s., 64s., 66s.,
70s., for the first six nights. Similarly *The Wise Man of
West Chester*, which began with a bad first night of 33s.,

rose to a good average, while 2 *Godfrey of Bulloigne,* for all its start of 70s., ended with an average of only 28s. The worst first night taking was the 22s. of *Nebuchadnezzar,* and this affords another curious example of box-office fluctuations, for, though it achieved no higher average than 22s., it rose on its third night to 68s. The worst takings, on other than first nights, were 3s. for *Chinon of England,*[1] 4s. for *Vortigern,* and for *Olympo,* and 5s. twice over for *A Woman Hard to Please.* Probably these were due to weather or other accidents, as each play averaged enough to justify a reasonable run. The success of the old plays followed much the same lines as that of the new ones. They ran for anything from one night to twenty-four, this total being reached by *Dr. Faustus.* The best average returns were the 32s. and 38s. of *1 and 2 Tamburlaine,* the 30s. of *Mahomet,* the 29s. of *1 Long Meg of Westminster,* the 27s. of *The Guise,* and the 26s. of *The Jew of Malta* ; the best individual returns the 72s. and 71s. yielded by the respective first nights of *Dr. Faustus* and *1 Tamburlaine.* The persistent popularity of Marlowe's work comes out quite clearly from the statistics ; and the success of Chapman's first attempts is also not to be overlooked.

The *personnel* of the Admiral's men during 1594–7 can be determined with some approach to certainty. They were Edward Alleyn, John Singer, Richard Jones, Thomas Towne, Martin Slater, Edward Juby, Thomas Downton, and James Donstone. Their names are found in a list written in the diary, without any explanation of its object, amongst memoranda of 1594–6.[2] There can be little doubt that it represents the principal members of the company, and in most cases corroborative evidence is available. The books of the Treasurer of the Chamber indicate Alleyn, Jones, and Singer as payees for the Court money of 1594–5, and Alleyn and Slater for that of 1595–6. Alleyn, Slater, Donstone, and Juby are noted in Henslowe's subsidiary accounts for 1596 as responsible for advances made by him on behalf of the company.[3] Another advance was made to Stephen the tireman, and he is doubtless the Stephen Magett who also appears in personal financial relations with Henslowe during 1596.[4] Transactions by way of loan, sale, or pawn are also noted by Henslowe during 1594–7 with Slater, Jones, Donstone, Singer, and Towne, and also with Edward Dutton and

---

[1] This was on Whit-Tuesday 1596, and I rather suspect a mis-entry of *iij*s for *iij*ll, the exact amount taken for the plays of the Monday and Wednesday in the same week.

[2] Henslowe, i. 5.   [3] Ibid. 44.   [4] Ibid. 31, 45.

Richard Alleyn.[1] These latter were probably not sharers in
the company, but can be traced with others amongst its
subordinate members by means of the ' plot ' of *Frederick
and Basilea*, which it is reasonable to connect with the
performances of the play in June and July 1597, since it
was a new play on 3 June, and it is recorded in the diary that
Martin Slater, who figures in the ' plot ', left the company on
18 July. It is to be inferred from the plot that the principal
parts in *Frederick and Basilea* were taken by Mr. Alleyn,
Mr. Thomas Towne, Mr. Martin [Slater], Mr. Juby, Mr. Donstone, and R. Alleyn ; that minor male parts were taken by
Edward Dutton, Thomas Hunt, Robert Ledbetter, Black
Dick, Pigge, Sam, Charles, and the 'gatherers' or money-
takers and other ' attendants ' ; and that female parts were
taken by Edward Dutton's boy Dick and two other boys
known as Will and Griffen. Apparently the play, although
not employing all the principal actors, made considerable
demands on the minor staff. Dr. Greg may be right in
identifying Sam and Charles with the Samuel Rowley and
Charles Massey who became members of the company at a
later date.[2] It will be seen that the only name in Henslowe's undated list which cannot be verified as that of
a member of the company during 1594–7 is that of Thomas
Downton ; but it may safely be accepted. Downton had
accompanied Alleyn on the provincial tour with Strange's
men in 1593. So had Pigge or Pyk. Jones and Donstone,
who is the same as Tunstall, had belonged to Worcester's
men in 1583, and probably to the Admiral's men before 1590 ;
Jones had been abroad, as we have seen, during the plague
years. John Singer had been a member of the Queen's men
in 1588. The other names now come into the story for the
first time. Henslowe's advances for 1596 included sums ' to
feache Fletcher ' and ' to feache Browne '.[3] It can only be
matter of conjecture whether there is evidence here of
negotiations for the incorporation in the company of Robert
Browne and of Laurence Fletcher, at a later date a colleague
of Slater's, and if so, whether they led to any fruitful result.

The departure of Martin Slater on 18 July 1597 was only
one of several changes which profoundly modified the composition of the company in the course of that year.[4] In February

---

[1] Henslowe, i. 29, 31, 43, 44, 199–201.

[2] I see no reason to agree with Dr. Greg in identifying ' Black Dick '
with Jones, who would naturally have the ' Mr. ' ; and the suggestions
that ' Dick ' might be Dick Juby and that ' Will ' might be Will Barnes
or Will Parr are mere guesses based on the occurrence of these names
in other ' plots '. ' Will ' might just as well be Will Kendall.

[3] Henslowe, i. 45.

[4] Henslowe's entry is (i. 54), ' Martin Slather went for the company

Richard Jones and Thomas Downton went to the Swan as Pembroke's men, and the disturbance thereby caused probably accounts for the three weeks' cessation of playing during Lent. The Swan enterprise was brought to a disastrous conclusion after five months by the production of *The Isle of Dogs*, which not only brought personal trouble on the chief offenders, but also led to a restraint of plays at all the theatres. This event synchronizes with the first appearance in the diary of Nashe's collaborator in *The Isle of Dogs*, Ben Jonson. On 28 July Henslowe lent him no less a sum than £4, and took Alleyn and Singer as witnesses. On the same day he opened an account headed ' R of Bengemenes Johnsones share as ffoloweth ' with a first instalment of 3s. 9d.[1] On this very day of 28 July the Privy Council's inhibition fell, and Jonson went to prison and paid no more instalments. It is impossible to say whether his ' share ' was in the Admiral's company or in Pembroke's. In any event, although he continued to write for the Admiral's men after 1597, there is no further sign that he was either a ' sharer ', or indeed an actor in any capacity.

One result of the restraint was that Jones and Downton not merely returned to the Rose, but brought at least three other of Pembroke's men, Robert Shaw, Gabriel Spencer, and William Bird, known also by the *alias* of Borne, with them. Henslowe was thus enabled, almost immediately after playing stopped, to set about the reconstitution of his company, and the memoranda of agreement which he noted in his diary during the next fourteen months are so interesting for the light which they throw upon his relations with the actors, that I think it well, before discussing them, to transcribe them in full. There are in all eleven of them, as follows :[2]

i. (*Thomas Hearne*)

Memorandom that the 27 of Jeuley 1597 I heayred Thomas Hearne with ij pence for to searve me ij yeares in the qualetie of playenge for fyve shellynges a weacke for one yeare & vj⁸ viij⁴ for the other yeare which he hath covenanted hime seallfe to searue me & not to departe frome my companey tyll this ij yeares be eanded wittnes to this

John Synger.
Jeames Donston.
Thomas Towne.

of my lord admeralles men the 18 of July 1597 '. I think that ' for ' must be meant for ' from '. Elsewhere (i. 66) Henslowe writes ' for ' for ' from '.

[1] Henslowe, i. 47, 200.

[2] Ibid. 201–4 ; *Egerton MS.* 2623, f. 19 (a fragment from the Diary).

ii. (*John Helle*)

Lent John Helle the clowne the 3 of Aguste 1597 in redy money the some of x^s. At that tyme I bownd hime by ane a sumsett of ij^d to contenew with me at my howsse in playinge tylle Srafte tid next after the date a boue written yf not to forfytte vnto me fortipowndes wittneses to the same

E Alleyn John Synger Jeames Donstall.
Edward Jubey Samewell Rowley.

iii. (*Richard Jones*)

Memorandom that the 6 of Aguste 1597 I bownd Richard Jones by & a sumsett of ij^d to contenew & playe with the companye of my lord Admeralles players frome Mihelmase next after the daye a bowe written vntell the eand & tearme of iij yeares emediatly followinge & to play in my howsse only known by the name of the Rosse & in no other howse a bowt London publicke & yf restraynte be granted then to go for the tyme into the contrey & after to retorne agayne to London yf he breacke this a sumsett then to forfett vnto me for the same a hundreth markes of lafull money of Ingland wittnes to this E Alleyn & John Midelton.

iv. (*Robert Shaw*)

More over Richard Jones at that tyme [6 Aug. 1597] hath tacken one other ij^d of me vpon & asumset to forfet vnto me one hundrethe markes yf one Robart Shaee do not playe with my lordes Admeralles men as he hath covenanted be fore in euery thinge & time to the oter moste wittnes E Alleyn John Midellton.

v. (*William Borne*)

Memorandom that the 10 of Aguste 1597 William Borne came & ofered hime sealfe to come and playe with my lord Admeralles mean at my howsse called by the name of the Rosse setewate one the back after this order folowinge he hath receued of me iij^d vpon & a sumsette to forfette vnto me a hundrethe marckes of lafull money of Ingland yf he do not performe thes thinges folowinge that is presentley after libertie being granted for playinge to come & to playe with my lordes Admeralles men at my howsse aforsayd & not in any other howsse publicke a bowt London for the space of iij yeares beginynge imediatly after this restraynt is recaled by the lordes of the cownsell which restraynt is by the meanes of playinge the Jeylle of Dooges yf he do not then he forfettes this asumset afore or ells not wittnes to this E Alleyn & Robsone.

vi. (*Thomas Downton*)

Memorandom that the 6 of October 1597 Thomas Dowton came & bownd him seallfe vnto me in xxxx^{ll} in & a somesett by the receuing of iij^d of me before wittnes the covenant is this that he shold frome the daye a bove written vntell Sraftid next come ij yeares to playe in my howsse & in no other a bowte London publickely yf he do with owt my consent to forfet vnto me this some of money a bove written wittnes to this

E Alleyn   Robarte Shawe
Wm Borne   John Synger
Dicke Jonnes

vii. (*William Kendall*)

Memorandum that this 8th of December 1597 my father Philyp Hinshlow hierd as a covenauant servant Willyam Kendall for ij years after the statute of Winchester with ij single penc a to geue hym for his sayd servis everi week of his playng in London x^s & in the cuntrie v^s for the which he covenaunteth for the space of those ij years to be redye att all tymes to play in the howse of the sayd Philyp & in no other during the said terme.

Wittnes my self the writer of this   E Alleyn.

viii. (*James Bristow*)

Bought my boye Jeames Brystow of William Agusten player the 18 of Desember 1597 for viij^{li}.

ix. (*Richard Alleyn*)

Memorandom that this 25 of Marche 1598 Richard Alleyne came & bownde hime seallfe vnto me for ij yeares in & asumsette as a hiered servante with ij syngell pence & to contenew frome the daye aboue written vnto the eand & tearme of ij yeares yf he do not performe this covenant then he to forfette for the breache of yt fortye powndes & wittnes to this

Wm Borne.
Thomas Dowton.
Gabrell Spencer.
Robart Shawe.
Richard Jonnes.

x. (*Thomas Heywood*)

Memorandom that this 25 of Marche 1598 Thomas Hawoode came and hiered hime seallfe with me as a covenante searvante for ij yeares by the receuenge of ij syngell pence acordinge to the statute of Winshester & to begine at the daye a boue written & not to playe any wher publicke a bowt London not whille these ij yeares be expired but in my howsse yf he do then he doth forfett vnto me by the receuinge of these ij^d fortie powndes & wittnes to this

Antony Monday   Wm Borne
Gabrell Spencer   Thomas Dowton
Robart Shawe   Richard Jonnes.
Richard Alleyn.

xi. (*Charles Massey and Samuel Rowley*)

Memorandom that this 16 of November 1598 I hired as my covenant servantes Charles Massey & Samewell Rowley for a yeare & as mvche as to Sraftide begenynge at the daye a bove written after the statute of Winchester with ij syngell pence & for them they haue covenanted with me to playe in my howes & in no other howsse dewringe the thime publeck but in mine yf they dooe with owt my consent yf they dooe to forfett vnto me xxxx^{ll} a pece wittnes Thomas Dowton Robart Shawe Wm Borne Jubey Richard Jonnes.

Evidently the position of James Bristow is distinct from that of the other players. He was a 'boy' or apprentice, whose indentures had been transferred to Henslowe for a consideration by his former master. In the rest of the cases, the essence of the agreement appears to be the undertaking by the player under bond to play only with the Admiral's men at Henslowe's house. It is interesting to notice that in the agreement with Hearne Henslowe calls the company 'my company'; and the fact that its members were constituted Henslowe's covenant servants seems to argue a closer personal relation between the organization and its financier, than might on other grounds have been inferred. Dr. Greg, indeed, draws a distinction between the agreements with Jones, Shaw, Borne, and Downton, whom he regards as merely 'binding themselves to play at Henslowe's house like other sharers', and those with the rest, whom he regards as 'placing themselves in the position of covenant servants to him, which would seem to imply that they were merely hired men'.[1] But I do not think that there is any justification for this theory in the terms of the documents, and it immediately gets Dr. Greg into difficulties about Massey and Rowley, who, as we shall see, were in fact on the footing of full members of the company even before the date of their agreement. I do not mean that I deny the distinction between sharers and hired men, which is of course important, but that I do not think that it is relevant to the contractual relations set up by the agreements. I am not quite clear whether Henslowe's memoranda, which are written throughout, including the names of the witnesses, in his own hand or Alleyn's, constitute the formal instruments under which the agreements were effected, or are merely notes for his own information. But in either event their terminology is loose. They are not always expressed as being agreements of hiring, or for service, even in the cases of those men whom Dr. Greg does not suppose to have been sharers, and they are not careful to

[1] Henslowe, ii. 89, 101.

specify the considerations, other than the formal 2*d*. or 3*d*., which the actors were to receive. Wages are, in fact, provided for only in the agreements with Hearne and Kendall, and it is quite possible that, if we had the full terms before us, we should find that, while some of the others were also to receive wages, some were to find their recompense in a share of such profits as the company might make. It is probable that, even where Henslowe undertook to pay wages, the general agreement between him and the company provided for the shifting of that liability to them. They certainly had to pay him, at the rate of 3*s*. a week, for the services of his boy Bristow.[1] To a slightly later date belongs an agreement with an unnamed actor, in which the hirer is not Henslowe but Thomas Downton, and this I add in order to complete the series.[2]

xii.

Thomas Downton the 25 of Janewary 1599 ded hire as his couenante servante —— for ij yers to begyne at Shrofe Tewesday next & he to geue hime viij^s a wecke as longe as they playe & after they lye stylle one fortnyght then to geue hime hallfe wages   wittnes P H & Edward Browne & Charlles Masey.

The appearance of Jones as guarantee for Shaw is due to the fact that, as a result of *The Isle of Dogs*, the latter was languishing with Gabriel Spencer and Ben Jonson in the Marshalsea. Meanwhile some at least of the company travelled. Henslowe lent Alleyn 40*s*. for John Singer and Thomas Towne ' when they went into the contrey ' and noted that this was ' at ther last cominge '. There is another entry of a small loan to Singer on 9 August, so they cannot have started before that ; and they must have been back by 6 October, when Singer witnessed the agreement with Thomas Downton. Possibly Edward Dutton and Richard Alleyn, who also borrowed money from Henslowe, went with them.[3] The Privy Council warrants for the release of the prisoners in the Marshalsea were signed on 3 October,[4] and a few days later Henslowe, more successful than Langley of the Swan in getting the licence for his house renewed, even before the formal expiration of the restraint on 1 November, was in a position to resume his play list with the heading, ' The xj of Octobe begane my lord Admèrals & my lorde of Penbrockes men to play at my howsse 1597 '.[5] The entries of plays are few and irregular up to 5 November, and then stop.

---

[1] Henslowe, i. 105, 131, 134.
[2] Ibid. 40.
[3] Ibid. 199–201.
[4] App. D, No. cxii.
[5] Henslowe, i. 54 ; *E. S.* xliii. 351.

A note is appended that on 26 November the Master of the Revels was paid for four weeks. The performances included one new play, *Friar Spendleton*, and five old ones, *Jeronimo*, *The Comedy of Humours*, *Dr. Faustus*, *Hardicanute*, and *Bourbon*, of which the last two do not belong to the 1594–7 repertory, and may have been contributed by Pembroke's men. The diary also contains an account of weekly receipts running from 21 October 1597 to 4 March 1598, under the heading, ' A juste a cownte of all suche monye as I haue receyed of my lord Admeralles & my lord of Penbrocke men as foloweth be gynynge the 21 of October 1597 ', and some notes of individual advances and repayments, mainly through Robert Shaw and Thomas Downton, on behalf of the company, from 23 October to 12 December.[1] In the course of these the company is again described on 23 October and 5 November as ' the company of my lord Admeralles men & my lord Penbrockes ', but on 1 December as ' the companey of my lord Admeralles men ' ; and the substance of the whole of these advances is set out again, without any reference to Pembroke's men, at the beginning of a continuous account from 21 October onwards, which is headed, ' A juste a cownt of all suche money as I haue layd owt for my lord Admeralles players begynyng the xj of October whose names ar as foloweth Borne Gabrell Shaw Jonnes Dowten Jube Towne Synger & the ij Geffes '.[2] Nothing very certain is known of the previous career of Humphrey and Anthony Jeffes, but if the former is the ' Humfrey ' who appears with ' Gabriel ' [Spencer] in the stage-directions to *3 Henry VI* it is most likely that these men also came from Pembroke's.[3]

The responsible members of the Admiral's company at the beginning of the third period of their existence were, then, so far as their relations to Henslowe were concerned, Thomas Downton, Richard Jones, Edward Juby, Thomas Towne, John Singer, Robert Shaw, William Borne, who seems to have had the regular *alias* of William Bird, Gabriel Spencer, Humphrey Jeffes, and Anthony Jeffes. To these must probably be added a number of hired men, including Thomas Hearne, John Helle, William Kendall, Richard Alleyn, Thomas Heywood, and probably Charles Massey, Samuel Rowley, Thomas Hunt, and Stephen Maget the tireman, and of apprentices, including James Bristow and Pigge. Of the sharers Downton, Jones, Juby, Towne, and Singer had alone belonged to the earlier Admiral's men. Slater's departure involved the company in a law-suit, the nature of which is

---

[1] Henslowe, i. 68–70.   [2] Ibid. 82.   [3] Ibid. ii. 91 ; cf. p. 200.

not stated in the diary. Professor Wallace, however, has found an independent record of a Queen's Bench action by Thomas Downton to recover £13 6s. 8d., the value of a play-book which Downton had lost in the parish of St. Mary le Bow on 1 December 1597, and Slater had 'found', refused to surrender, and was alleged to have disposed of for his own profit. Damages of £10 10s. were awarded on 3 November 1598.[1] Donstone also seems to have dropped out or may have been dead; he witnessed Helle's agreement on 3 August 1597, and thereafter no more is heard of him. But incomparably the greatest loss was that of Edward Alleyn, who now retired from the stage and did not return to it for a period of three years.[2] From 29 December 1597 to 8 November 1598 Henslowe made notes of playing goods bought 'sence my sonne Edward Allen leafte [p]laynge', and it would appear that the company acknowledged a debt of £50 in respect of his interest on retirement.[3] In place of Alleyn, it would seem that the lead was taken by Robert Shaw and Thomas Downton, perhaps as representing the two elements of which the company was made up. These two were joint payees for the Court money of both 1597–8 and 1598–9. For 1599–1600 Shaw was sole payee. It was, moreover, most often, although by no means always, to one or other of these men that Henslowe's advances on behalf of the company were made. It must be added that some of the new-comers appear to have sought private assistance from Henslowe in order to enable them to take up their shares. On 14 January 1598, he opened an account of sums received 'of Humfreye Jeaffes hallfe share', entered seven instalments up to 4 March, amounting to a total of 60s. 6d., and then noted, 'This some was payd backe agayne vnto the companey of my lord Admeralles players the 8 of Marche 1598, & they shared yt amonste them'. There is a later account, running from 29 April to 21 July 1598, and amounting by small instalments to 35s., of 'all such money as I dooe receue for Umfrey Jeaffes and Antoney Jeaffes . . . of the companey'.[4] Possibly the brothers only held a single share between them. A similar transaction took place with Gabriel Spencer. On 20 April 1598 this actor gave an acknowledgement for £4 and between 6 April and 24 June Henslowe carried to an account headed 'R of Gabrell Spencer at severall tymes of his share in the gallereyes' a total of 25s. 6d., of which 5s. 6d. was paid over to Downton.[5] In addition, personal loans were negotiated

---

[1] Henslowe, i. 69, 73 ; Wallace in E. S. xliii. 382.
[2] Cf. p. 173.   [3] Henslowe, i. 81, 122.
[4] Ibid. 64, 67.   [5] Ibid. 63, 79.

from time to time by various members of the company, and
the reasons given for these indicate that in the course of 1598,
besides the dispute of the ex-Pembroke's men with Langley,
Bird and perhaps the company as a whole were engaged in
litigation with Thomas Pope, presumably the actor in the
Chamberlain's company.[1]

There does not seem to have been much further change
in the composition of the Admiral's men during 1597–1600.
An acknowledgement of the state of their account with
Henslowe between 8 and 13 March 1598 bears the signatures
of ' J. Singer, Thomas Downton, William Birde, Robt Shaa,
Richard Jones, Gabriell Spenser, Thomas Towne, Humfry
Jeffes, Charles Massye, and Samuell Rowlye '.[2] The last two
had evidently become sharers in the course of the year. Juby
and Anthony Jeffes do not sign, but this is probably due to
an accident, as they were certainly sharers both in 1597 and
in 1600.[3] Gabriel Spencer was killed by Ben Jonson (cf.
ch. xxiii) on 22 September 1598. On 26 September Henslowe
wrote to Alleyn at the Brill in Sussex, ' Now to leat you
vnderstand newes I will teall you some but yt is for me harde
& heavey. Sence you weare with me I haue loste one of my
company which hurteth me greatly ; that is Gabrell, for he
is slayen in Hogesden fylldes by the handes of Bengemen
Jonson bricklayer '.[4] No doubt Henslowe wrote from the
heart. Probably Spencer's share was not yet paid for, and
in addition small personal loans to the amount of 66s. stand
undischarged against him in the diary, of which the last was
on 19 May ' to bye a plume of feathers which his mane
Bradshawe feched of me '. Richard Bradshaw was an actor
and may have played as a hired man with the company.
A fragmentary ' plot ' of *Troilus and Cressida*, probably to
be dated in April 1599, yields the names of ' Mr. Jones ' and
his ' boy ', Thomas Hunt, Stephen, Proctor, and Pigge.
Mr. Jones's boy is shown by a note of 17 November 1599 in
the diary to have been called James.[5] Of Proctor no more is
known. Stephen is probably Stephen Magett, the tireman,
and Pigge was with Alleyn on the tour of Strange's men in

---

[1] Henslowe, i. 72, ' Lent Wm Borne to folowe the sewt agenste Thomas
Poope ' ; cf. i. 26, 38, 47–8, 56, 63–9, 71–8, 80, 201, 205 ; and s.v.
Pembroke's.   [2] Henslowe, i. 84.

[3] During 1599–1602 Henslowe sometimes enters advances as made to
the company through ' W^m ' Juby, and in two cases corrects the entry
by substituting ' Edward '. As there is no other evidence for a William
Juby as an actor, not to speak of a sharer, either Henslowe must have
persistently mistaken the name, or William must have been a relative
of Edward, acting as his agent (cf. Henslowe, ii. 290).

[4] *Henslowe Papers*, 48.   [5] Henslowe, i. 26.

1593. He is also mentioned, with Dobe, Whittcombe, and Anderson, who may have been actors, in some inventories of properties belonging to Alleyn or to the company in March 1598.[1] Thomas Downton also had in June 1600 a 'boye' who played in *Cupid and Psyche*.[2] Another acknowledgement of account, dated on 10 July 1600, only differs from the former one by the omission of Spencer's name and the inclusion of those of Juby and Anthony Jeffes.[3] The alleged manuscript notes to a copy of Dekker's *Shoemaker's Holiday* (q.v.), produced in January 1600, which are discredited by Dr. Greg, give the cast as composed of 'Jones, H. Jeffes, Rowley, Shawe, Massy, Dowton, Singer, Jewby, Towne, A. Jeffes, Birde, Wilson, Flower, Price, Day, Dowton's boy Ned and Alleine'; the last for a female part. Certainly nothing is known of Day or Wilson as actors for the Admiral's, or of Price at any such early date, or of Flower at all. But if the document is a forgery, it is a very pointless, and at the same time a very cautious one. And how did the forger, unless he were Collier or Cunningham, know that Day was an actor at all?

The records kept by Henslowe for the period 1597–1600 differ considerably in character from those for 1594–7. The diurnal list of plays performed and of rent-takings disappears altogether. On the other hand, the records of advances made, for the books and licensing of plays, for costumes and properties, and for certain miscellaneous items of expenditure, become full and systematic. A *per contra* account is also kept of weekly sums received by Henslowe in repayment of such advances, and from time to time a balance is struck, and the hands of the company taken to a settlement or acknowledgement of debt. Henslowe's book-keeping, however, if not exactly faulty, is not always sufficiently lucid to make the whole of the financial transactions perfectly clear. In the absence of the daily entries of performances, the weekly records of repayments make it possible to determine roughly the periods covered by the theatrical seasons.[4] The company played for twenty continuous weeks from 11 October 1597 to about 4 March 1598, apparently with some irregularity at the beginning and again about Christmas time. Their Court plays were on 27 December and 28 February. In Lent they had a three weeks' interval, during the course of which they met to read a book in New Fish Street, and 'played in Fleatstreet pryuat'.[5] Playing was resumed about 25 March and lasted for some fifteen weeks, until about 8 July, making

[1] *Henslowe Papers*, 113. [2] Henslowe, i. 122. [3] Ibid. 122.
[4] Ibid. 66, 68, 91, 108. [5] Ibid. 85.

thirty-five weeks in all for the year 1597–8.   The company
only took two weeks' vacation in the summer and are not
likely to have travelled, although on 27 September, after the
new season had begun, Borne is found riding to the Lord
Admiral at Croydon at the time of the Queen's visit there.[1]
They played for thirty-one weeks from about 22 July to
24 February 1599, with performances at Court on 27 December,
6 January and 18 February, and stopped for three weeks in
Lent.   The summer season lasted for eleven weeks from about
19 March to 3 June, making forty-four weeks playing for
1598–9.   On Easter Eve Towne and Richard Alleyn went
to Court for some unspecified purpose.   About the same time
Anthony Jeffes was making purchases against St. George's
Day.[2]   The interval of this summer was seventeen weeks, but
I have no evidence of any travelling.   The next season was
one of nineteen weeks from about 29 September 1599 to
10 February 1600, with Court performances on 27 December
and 1 January, and was followed by a Lenten interval of
about four weeks.   At the beginning of February they bought
a drum and trumpets ' when to go into the contry '.[3]   Whether
these were for use during the short break in Lent or not until
the following summer must remain uncertain; at any rate
the purchase confirms the view that there had been no provincial tour since 1596.[4]   Finally they played for nineteen
weeks from about 2 March to 13 July, thus completing
thirty-six weeks for 1599–1600.   Apparently the summer
season was diversified by a visit to Windsor for the Garter
installation of Henri IV of France on 27 April.[5]   In all they
seem to have played for about 115 weeks or something under
690 days in 1597–1600, as compared with 728 days in 1594–7.

The entries of sums paid for plays usually give the names of
the authors as well as those of the plays, and therefore furnish
a good deal of material for reconstituting the literary side of
the company's activity.   Henslowe's terminology is neither
precise nor uniform, but it is clear that, while the payments
were always entered as loans to the company, they were
often made direct by him to the playwrights, on the ' appointment ' of one or more of its members.   Sometimes they are

---

[1] Henslowe, i. 72.   [2] Ibid. 63, 104.   [3] Ibid. 118.
[4] I find ' Lorde Haywards ' men at Leicester during Oct.–Dec. 1599,
' Lord Howardes ' at Bristol in 1599–1600, ' Lord Heywardes ' at Bath
in the same year, ' Lord Howards ' at Coventry on 28 Dec. 1599, and
' Lord Haywards ' in 1602–3.   This must have been another company.
The Admiral's were playing in London at the time of the Leicester and
the earlier Coventry visits, and Lord Howard of Effingham became Earl
of Nottingham on 22 Oct. 1596.   They were at Canterbury in 1599–1600.
[5] Henslowe, i. 120.

expressed as being 'to bye a boocke of' a play; that is to say, for the purchase outright of an old or even a new manuscript. But a new play was generally commissioned, upon the strength of a sample or of an outline of the plot, and in such cases payment was made by instalments, of which the earlier ones were 'lent upon' or 'in earneste of' or 'in parte paymente of', and the last 'in full paymente of' the book. Portions of the manuscript were handed over as security for the earlier payments. Production was very rapid, and a play put together in two or three weeks often represented the collaboration of as many as four or even five or six authors. The procedure, which prevailed during the whole of the period covered by the diary, is illustrated by a small group of letters preserved amongst the miscellaneous papers found at Dulwich. Thus on 8 November 1599 Shaw writes with regard to *2 Henry Richmond*, 'Mr. Henshlowe, we haue heard their booke and lyke yt. Their pryce is eight poundes, which I pray pay now to Mr. Wilson, according to our promysse'; and accordingly Henslowe includes in his account, by an entry written and signed by Wilson, a sum of £8 'by a note vnder the hand of Mr. Rob: Shaw'.[1] On 14 June 1600 Shaw writes again, 'I pray you, Mr. Henshlowe, deliuer vnto the bringer hereof the some of fyue & fifty shillinges to make the 3ˡˡ fyue shillinges which they receaued before full six poundes in full payment of their booke called the fayre Constance of Roome, whereof I pray you reserue for me Mr. Willsons whole share which is xjˢ. which I to supply his neede deliuered him yesternight.' The diary duly records the payment to Drayton, Hathway, Munday, and Dekker 'at the a poynt-ment of Roberte Shawe' of 44*s*.[2] Similarly Samuel Rowley writes on 4 April 1601, 'Mr. Hinchloe, I haue harde fyue shetes of a playe of the Conqueste of the Indes & I dow not doute but it wyll be a verye good playe; therefore I praye ye delyuer them fortye shyllynges in earneste of it & take the papers into your one hands & on Easter eue thaye promyse to make an ende of all the reste'. The earnest and several supplementary earnests were paid to Day, Haughton, and Smith, but the completion of the play lagged until the following September.[3] An undated letter of Rowley's relates to the withdrawal of a play, 'Mr. Hynchlo, I praye ye let Mr. Hathwaye haue his papars agayne of the playe of John a Gante & for the repayement of the monye back agayne he is contente to gyue ye a byll of his hande to be payde at some

---

[1] *Henslowe Papers*, 49; Henslowe, i. 113.
[2] *Henslowe Papers*, 55; Henslowe, i. 122.
[3] *Henslowe Papers*, 56; Henslowe, i. 135, 147.

cartayne tyme as in your dyscressyon yow shall thinke good ; which done ye may crose it oute of your boouke & keepe the byll ; or else wele stande so much indetted to you & kepe the byll our selues '. Henslowe appears to have thought it safer to adopt the second alternative, as incomplete payments to the amount of £1 19s. 0d. for *The Conquest of Spain by John of Gaunt* still stand in his 'boouke '.[1] Other letters of the same kind concern *Six Yeomen of the West*, and *Too Good to be True*.[2] The normal price for a new play during 1597–1601 seems to have been £6, but sometimes it fell to £5 or possibly even £4, and sometimes the playwrights succeeded in squeezing out a few shillings more. One or two of them, notably Chapman, were able to secure a higher rate from the beginning ; and about 1599 a general tendency towards a higher scale of prices becomes discernible. The 'book' of an old play could generally be purchased for about £2.

In attempting to estimate the actual 'output' of the company, one is faced by the difficulty that some of the plays commissioned are not shown by the diary to have reached the stage of payment in full, and that it must, therefore, remain doubtful whether they were ever completed. It is possible that, as Dr. Greg thinks,[3] some of the payments were made direct by the company, instead of through Henslowe. But the correspondence just quoted rather suggests that any such arrangement would be exceptional ; and it would not be inconsistent with human nature, if the extremely out-at-elbows men of letters who hung about the Rose occasionally found it profitable to take their ' earnest ' for a play, and then to find plausible reasons for indefinitely delaying its completion. Probably in the long run they had to account for the advance, but the example of *The Conquest of Spain* shows that such a repayment would not necessarily find its way into Henslowe's account. This view is borne out by an examination of the affairs of one of the most impecunious of them all, Henry Chettle, during 1598–9. During the first six months of the year, he had a hand in half a dozen plays, all of which were completed and paid for in full. But on one of these, *I Black Bateman of the North*, Henslowe appears, perhaps by an oversight, to have paid him £1 too much. At the beginning of May £1 was lent to Chettle upon this play, and the loan does not appear to have been considered when, on 22 May, a further sum of £6 was laid out upon ' a boocke called Blacke Battmane of the North . . . which coste sixe powndes '. On 24 June Chettle borrowed 10s., not apparently on any

---

[1] *Henslowe Papers*, 56 ; Henslowe, i. 135.
[2] *Henslowe Papers*, 56–8.   [3] Henslowe, ii. 125.

particular play, and Henslowe seems then to have recalled
the overpayment, and noted against Chettle's name in the
diary, ' All his parte of boockes to this place are payde which
weare dew unto hime & he reastes be syddes in my deatte
the some of xxx⁸.' Chettle collaborated in several other
plays, which got completed during the year, but no deduction
seems to have been made from his share of the fees in respect
of this debt. In addition he had £5 upon *A Woman's Tragedy*,
upon condition ' eather to deliver the playe or els to paye
the mony with in one forthnyght '; he had 5s. in earnest
upon *Catiline's Conspiracy* ; and he had £1 14s. od. in earnest
upon *Brute*, probably a continuation of an older *1 Brute*
bought by the company. When the last payment on *Brute*
was made on 16 September Henslowe noted, ' Hary Cheattell
vntell this place owes vs viij¹¹ ix⁸ dew al his boockes &
recknynges payd '. This amount is precisely made up of
the 30s. due on 24 June and the sums paid on account of
these three plays. By ⸜22 October Chettle had completed
2 Brute and managed somehow to get £6 for it in full. On
the same day he gave Henslowe an acknowledgement of
a debt, not of £8 9s. od., but of £9 9s. od. In November he
got an earnest of £1 for *Tis no Deceit to Deceive the Deceiver*,
and £1 for ' mending' *Robin Hood*, and in January 1599 30s.
' to paye his charges in the Marshallsey '. Small loans of a
shilling or two are also noted in the margin of the book,
and appear to be quite distinct from the company's account
with him, and to indicate private generosities of Henslowe.
In February 1599 Chettle had finished *Polyphemus*, and it is
recorded that in full payment of £6 he got £2 10s. down,
' & strocken of his deatte which he owes vnto the companey
fyftye shelenges more '. A separate entry in the diary
indicates that he paid off yet another 10s. out of his fee for
The Spencers in March.[1] Material is not available for the
further tracing of this particular chain of transactions, but
the inference that credit obtained for an unfinished play had
sometimes to be redeemed out of the profits of a finished
one is irresistible. Chettle, at least, does not seem to have
been hardly treated, but obviously the unbusinesslike methods
of the playwrights kept down the price of plays, and a familiar
device of the modern Barabbas was anticipated when Henry
Porter was obliged, on the receipt of an earnest, to give
Henslowe ' his faythfulle promysse that I shold haue alle
the boockes which he writte ether him sellfe or with any other '.[2]
Whatever Henslowe's precise financial relations with the

---

[1] Henslowe, i. 84–107.   [2] Ibid. 103.

company may have been, by the way, he seems to h ve been in a position to pose as paymaster, so far as the poets were concerned.

On the whole, I think it must be concluded that, if the diary fails to record payments to the amount of at least £5 for a new play, there is *prima facie* evidence that that play never got itself finished. Occasionally, of course, apparently incomplete payments may be explained by the fact that the same play is entered under more than one name. Occasionally, also, a particular play may have been tacitly debited with payments not specifically expressed in the diary to have been made in respect of that play. Thus a sum of £2 paid on 4 February 1598 'to dise charge Mr. Dicker owt of the cownter in the Powltrey' was probably treated as an instalment of the price of *Phaethon* on which Dekker was then working, and for which otherwise only £4 is entered. Another sum of £3 10s. paid on 30 January 1599 'to descarge Thomas Dickers frome the a reaste of my lord Chamberlens men' seems similarly to have gone towards *The First Introduction of the Civil Wars of France*. And Haughton probably got 10s. less than he would otherwise have done for *Ferrex and Porrex*, because he had required a loan of that amount on 10 March 1600, 'to releace him owt of the Clyncke'.[1] The record, again, for a few plays is most likely rendered imperfect by the loss of a leaf or two from the manuscript, which once contained entries for the end of April and beginning of May 1599.[2] When these factors have been taken into consideration, the resultant total of possibly unfinished plays is not a very large one, amounting for 1597–1600 on my calculation to not more than twenty as against fifty-six new plays duly completed and paid for in full. Of these twenty it is very likely that some were in fact finished, either for other companies, or for the Admiral's men themselves, later than the period covered by the diary. It is, however, consonant with the literary temperament to suppose that some at least remained within the category of unrealized projects. The most puzzling problem is that of Haughton's *A Woman will have her Will*. For this it is impossible to trace payments beyond £2 10s., and these are not stated to be in full. Yet the play is not only now extant but was certainly extant in 1598. In this case I see no alternative to Dr. Greg's theory of direct payments by the company.

Henslowe's notes of advances to authors are not the sole material which is available for drawing up an account of

[1] Henslowe, i. 83, 101, 119.   [2] Ibid. ii. 124.

the repertory of the Admiral's men. There are also entries of the purchase of costumes and properties for certain plays, and of fees for the licensing of plays by the Master of the Revels. And there is a valuable series of inventories, formerly preserved at Dulwich, and dating from 1598, which record respectively the stock of apparel and properties in the hands of the Admiral's men during the second week of March, their play-books at the same date, and the additions made out of Henslowe's purchases up to about the following August.[1] The theory that some of the plays recorded in the diary were never finished receives confirmation from the absence of any corroborative proof of their existence in these subsidiary entries and documents, whereas such evidence exists in the case of a very large proportion of the plays for which the diary records payment in full. It must not, however, be assumed, either that every play completed necessarily got produced, although it is not likely that many were withheld, or that a play was necessarily not produced, because no special apparel or properties were bought for it, since it may have been quite possible to mount some plays out of the company's existing stock. The number of fees paid for licensing is so small in proportion to the number of plays certainly produced, that these fees cannot all be supposed to have passed through Henslowe's hands.

Subject to the difficulties discussed in the foregoing paragraphs, I think that the following is a fairly accurate account of the repertory of the company for the three years now in question.[2] During 1597–8 they purchased seventeen

---

[1] *Henslowe Papers*, 113, from Malone (1790), i. 2. 300 ; the manuscript is now lost. The various sections of the document are headed : (a) 'The booke of the Inventary of the goods of my lord Admeralles men, tacken the 10 of Marche in the yeare 1598 ' ; (b) ' The Enventary of the Clownes sewtes and Hermetes Swetes, with dievers others sewtes, as followeth, 1598, the 10 of March ' ; (c) ' The Enventary of all the aparell for my lord Admiralles men, tacken the 10 of Marche 1598—Leaft above in the tier-house in the cheast ' ; (d) ' The Enventary tacken of all the properties for my Lord Admeralles men, the 10 of Marche 1598 ' ; (e) ' The Enventorey of all the aparell of the Lord Admeralles men, taken the 13th of Marche 1598, as followeth' ; (f) ' A Note of all suche bookes as belong to the Stocke, and such as I have bought since the 3d of Marche 1598 ' ; (g) ' A Note of all suche goodes as I have bought for the Companey of my Lord Admirals men, sence the 3 of Aprell, 1598, as followeth '. A comparison of the book-list with the diary payments makes it clear that ' 1598 ' is 159⅞ and not 159⅜. The last book entered was bought in Aug. 1598. An undated inventory of Alleyn's private theatrical wardrobe is in *Henslowe Papers*, 52.

[2] It should be borne in mind that these lists are based in part upon a rather conjectural interpretation of evidence. Full details, for which I have not space, will be found in Henslowe, ii. 186 *sqq.* I have annotated a few points of interest.

new plays. These, with the names of their authors, were :

Mother Redcap (Drayton and Munday).
Phaethon (Dekker).
1 Robin Hood (Munday).
2 Robin Hood (Chettle and Munday).
The Triangle of Cuckolds (Dekker).[1]
The Welshman's Prize, or, The Famous Wars of Henry I and the Prince of Wales (Chettle, Dekker, and Drayton).[2]
1 Earl Godwin and his Three Sons (Chettle, Dekker, Drayton, and Wilson).
2 Earl Godwin and his Three Sons (Chettle, Dekker, Drayton, and Wilson).
King Arthur (Hathway).
Love Prevented (Porter).[3]
A Woman will have her Will (Haughton).
1 Black Bateman of the North (Chettle, Dekker, Drayton, and Wilson).
2 Black Bateman of the North (Chettle and Wilson).
The Madman's Morris (Dekker, Drayton, and Wilson).
The Funeral of Richard Cœur de Lion (Chettle, Drayton, Munday, and Wilson).
Hannibal and Hermes (Dekker, Drayton, and Wilson).[4]
Valentine and Orson (Hathway and Munday).

There is evidence of the actual performance of *Mother Redcap*, *Phaethon* (January), *1 and 2 Robin Hood* (March), *1 Earl Godwin* (April), *King Arthur* (May), *2 Earl Godwin* (June), *1 Black Bateman* (June). Properties were bought for *The Madman's Morris* in July, and the next season probably opened with it. To the new plays must be added *Friar Spendleton*, produced as ' ne ' on 31 October, and *Dido and Aeneas*. A loan of 30s. on 8 January ' when they fyrst played Dido at nyght ' suggests a supper, not a night performance. Either play may have been purchased at the end of 1596–7, or may have come from Pembroke's stock. The same applies to *Branholt* and *Alice Pierce*, which were probably new when properties were purchased for them in November and December. The company also bought on 12 December two jigs

---

[1] So called in the book-inventory ; in the diary it is *Triplicity of Cuckolds*.

[2] The first name appears in the inventory, the second in the diary.

[3] Only £4 was paid ' to by a boocke ', which is low for a new play and high for an old one. Possibly Porter was in debt to the company.

[4] Once described as ' other wisse called worsse feared then hurte ', whence Dr. Greg infers that the 1598–9 play of that name was a second part of it.

from two young men, for which they paid 6s. 8d. Hardly
any of the 1597–8 new plays are extant. The two parts of
Robin Hood are *The Downfall of Robert Earl of Huntingdon*,
and *The Death of Robert Earl of Huntingdon*, printed
without Munday's name as Admiral's plays in 1601. Haughton's *A Woman will have her Will* was entered on the
Stationers' Register on 3 August 1601, and printed with the
alternative title of *Englishmen for my Money* in 1616. *Phaethon*
probably underlies Dekker and Ford's *The Sun's Darling*,
and it is a plausible conjecture of Mr. Fleay's that *Love
Prevented* may be *1 The Two Angry Women of Abingdon*,
printed as an Admiral's play in 1599, and not to be traced
elsewhere in the diary. The payments for four plays during
the year, besides the puzzling *A Woman will have her Will*, were
incomplete. I take it that the £2 paid to Chettle, Dekker,
Drayton, and Wilson for *Pierce of Exton* was transferred to
the account for *2 Earl Godwin*, which otherwise lacks just
that amount of the full £6; that Chettle failed to deliver
A Woman's Tragedy; that Chapman's *Isle of a Woman* was
held over until 1598–9; and that a projected tragedy of
Ben Jonson's was similarly held over, and then indefinitely
postponed owing to the tragedy in real life of Spencer's
death. There are two entries with regard to this. On
3 December 1597, Henslowe lent Jonson 20s. ' vpon a boocke
which he showed the plotte vnto the company which he
promysed to deliver vnto the company at Cryssmas next '. On
23 October 1598, a month after the duel, not Jonson, but
Chapman, received £3 ' one his playe boocke & ij ectes of
a tragedie of Bengemenes plotte '. I think that Chapman's
own play was *The Four Kings* and that he finished it in 1599;
but I see no sign that he ever did anything with ' Bengemenes
plotte '.

Of older plays the Admiral's revived at the beginning of
the year Chapman's success of the previous spring, *The
Comedy of Humours*; also the perennial *Dr. Faustus*, and two
pieces which, as they formed no part of the 1594–7 repertory,
may have been brought in by Pembroke's men, *Hardicanute*
and *Bourbon*. They bought for £8 from Martin Slater
1 and 2 Hercules, *Phocas*, *Pythagoras*, and *Alexander and
Lodowick*, all of which had been produced between May 1595
and January 1597, and had evidently been retained by
Slater when he left the company. These books presumably
do not include that which became the subject of the law-suit
between Slater and the Admiral's men, and as they had
afterwards to buy back some of their old books in a precisely
similar way from Alleyn, it is probable that a retiring member

of the company had a right to claim a partition of the repertory. They also bought *The Cobler of Queenhithe*,[1] and from
Robert Lee, formerly of the Admiral's men and afterwards
of Queen Anne's, *The Miller*. But of these seven purchased
plays, the only one that they can be proved to have revived
is one of the *Hercules* plays, for which they bought properties
in July. The book-inventory shows that they had plays
called *Black Joan* and *Sturgflattery*,[2] also possibly from
Pembroke's stock ; and the property-inventories that they
had properties and clothes, if not in all cases books,[3] for *The
Battle of Alcazar* [4] and for a number of pieces staged during
1594–7, including *Mahomet*,[5] *Tamburlaine*,[6] *The Jew of Malta*,[7]
1 Fortunatus,[8] *The Siege of London*,[9] *Belin Dun*,[10] *Tasso's
Melancholy*,[11] *1 Caesar and Pompey*,[12] *The Wise Man of West
Chester*,[13] *The Set at Maw*,[14] *Olympo*,[15] *Henry V*,[16] *Longshanks*,[17]
Troy,[18] *Vortigern*,[19] *Guido*,[20] *Uther Pendragon*.[21] To these must
be added *Pontius Pilate*,[22] revived in 1601 and perhaps from
the Pembroke's stock, and others now unidentifiable.[23] As
the company revived *The Blind Beggar of Alexandria* in
1601 they probably had this also.[24]

[1] So in the book-inventory ; in the account it is only called *The Cobler*.
[2] Possibly *Strange Flattery*, but the manuscript is lost.
[3] They had to buy *Mahomet, The Wise Man of West Chester, Longshanks*, and *Vortigern* from Alleyn in 1601 and 1602.
[4] ' the Mores lymes ', ' iiij Turckes hedes ', ' j Mores cotte '.
[5] ' iiij genesareys gownes ', ' owld Mahemetes head '.
[6] ' Tamberlyne brydell ', ' Tamberlynes cotte, with coper lace ', ' Tamber-
lanes breches of crymson vellvet '.
[7] ' j cauderm for the Jewe '.   [8] ' j tree of gowlden apelles '.
[9] ' j whell and frame in the Sege of London '.
[10] ' Belendon stable '.   [11] ' Tasso picter ', ' Tasoes robe '.
[12] ' senetores gowne ' and ' capes '.   [13] ' Kents woden leage '.
[14] ' j mawe gowne of calleco for the quene '.
[15] ' j sewtte for Nepton ', ' Nepun forcke & garland '.
[16] ' Harey the fyftes dublet ' and ' vellet gowne ', ' j payer of hosse for
the Dowlfyn '.
[17] ' j longe-shanckes sewte '.   [18] ' j great horse with his leages '.
[19] ' Vartemar sewtte ', ' Valteger robe of rich tafitie ', ' j payer of hosse
& a gercken for Valteger ', ' ij Danes sewtes, and ij payer of Danes hosse '.
[20] ' j tome of Guido ', ' j cloth clocke of russete with coper lace, called
Guydoes clocke '.   [21] ' Merlen gowne, and cape '.
[22] ' my lord Caffes gercken & his hoose '.
[23] These include ' Argosse head ', ' Andersones sewte ', ' Will Sommers
sewtte ', ' ij Orlates sewtes ', ' Cathemer sewte ', ' j Whittcomes dublett
poke ', ' Nabesathe sewte ', ' j Hell mought ', ' the cloth of the Sone &
Mone ', ' Tantelouse tre ', ' Eves bodeyes '. Probably ' Perowes sewte
which Wm Sley were ' dated back to the days of Strange's men. After
3 April 1598 Henslowe bought, *inter alia*, ' a gown for Nembia ' and
' a robe for to goo invisibell '.
[24] It looks as if the book-inventory were not exhaustive ; perhaps it
only includes books more or less in current use.

The new plays purchased in 1598–9 were twenty-one in number:

Pierce of Winchester (Dekker, Drayton, and Wilson).
Hot Anger Soon Cold (Chettle, Jonson, and Porter).
Chance Medley (Chettle or Dekker, Drayton, Munday, and Wilson).[1]
Worse Afeared than Hurt (Dekker and Drayton).[2]
1 Civil Wars of France (Dekker and Drayton).
The Fount of New Fashions (Chapman).[3]
2 The Conquest of Brute, or, Brute Greenshield (Chettle).[4]
Connan, Prince of Cornwall (Dekker and Drayton).
2 Civil Wars of France (Dekker and Drayton).
3 Civil Wars of France (Dekker and Drayton).
The Four Kings (Chapman).[5]
War without Blows and Love without Suit (Heywood).[6]
First Introduction of the Civil Wars of France (Dekker).
2 Two Angry Women of Abingdon (Porter).
Joan as Good as my Lady (Heywood).
Friar Fox and Gillian of Brentford (Anon.).
The Spencers (Chettle and Porter).
Troy's Revenge and the Tragedy of Polyphemus (Chettle).
Troilus and Cressida (Chettle and Dekker).
Agamemnon, or, Orestes Furious (Chettle and Dekker).[7]
The World Runs on Wheels, or, All Fools but the Fool (Chapman).[8]

The property and licence entries only make it possible to trace the actual performance during the year of *Pierce of*

[1] There is a self-contradictory entry, ' to paye vnto Mr Willson Monday & Deckers . . . iiijli vs in this maner Willson xxxs Cheattell xxxs Mondy xxvs '.

[2] Regarded by Dr. Greg as *2 Hannibal and Hermes*.

[3] I agree with Dr. Greg that this, for which Chapman had £4 in 1598–9, is probably identical with *The Isle of a Woman*, for which he had had earnests of £4 or £4 10s. in 1597–8.

[4] I think the play licensed as *Brute Grenshallde* in March 1599 was a second part written by Chettle to an old *1 Brute* by Day, which would not need re-licensing.

[5] I do not see with what to identify the play licensed under this name in March 1599 except the unnamed ' playe boocke ' and ' tragedie ', for which Chapman had something under £9 in the previous Oct. and Jan.

[6] The title *War without Blows and Love without Strife* in one entry is probably an error.

[7] I agree with Dr. Greg that the entries point to two plays by Chettle and Dekker rather than one. They are probably incomplete owing to the hiatus in the manuscript.

[8] Dr. Greg makes two plays of this, but the entry ' his boocke called the world rones a whelles & now all foolles but the foolle ' seems unambiguous, and the total payments of £8 10s. are not too high for a play by Chapman.

Winchester (October), *1 and 2 Civil Wars of France* (October and November), *The Fount of New Fashions* (November), *2 Angry Women of Abingdon* (February), *2 Conquest of Brute* (March), *The Four Kings* (March), *The Spencers* (April), and *Agamemnon* (June). Probably, in view of the extant fragment of a ' plot ' *Troilus and Cressida* should be added. The production of *Troy's Revenge* was deferred until the following October. No one of this year's new plays is extant, unless, as is possible, *All Fools but the Fool* was an early form of Chapman's *All Fools*.[1] Earnests were paid in the course of 1598–9 for *Catiline's Conspiracy* (Chettle), *Tis no Deceit to Deceive the Deceiver* (Chettle), *William Longsword* [2] (Drayton), *Two Merry Women of Abingdon* (Porter), and an unnamed pastoral tragedy by Chapman, but there is no reason to suppose that any one of these was ever finished. On 9 August 1598 Munday had 10s. in earnest of an unnamed comedy ' for the corte ' and Drayton gave his word for the book to be done in a fortnight, but the project must have been dropped, as the entry was cancelled. Of old plays the company revived in August *Vayvode*, in November *The Massacre at Paris*, in which Bird played the Guise,[3] in December *1 The Conquest of Brute*, bought from John Day, and in March *Alexander and Lodowick*, bought from Martin Slater in the preceding year. As to *Vayvode*, the entries are rather puzzling. In August Chettle received £1 ' for his playe of Vayvode ', and the purchase of properties show that the production took place. But in the following January there was a payment of £2 to Alleyn ' for the playe of Vayvod for the company '. Possibly Alleyn had some rights in the manuscript, which were at first overlooked. On 25 November Chettle had 10s. ' for mendinge of Roben Hood for the corte '. Either *1* or *2 Robin Hood* was therefore probably the play given on 6 January 1599. At the beginning of the year the company bought *Mulmutius Dunwallow* from William Rankins and another old play called *Tristram of Lyons*, but it must be uncertain whether they played them. A reference in Guilpin's *Skialetheia* suggests that *The Spanish Tragedy* may have been on the boards of the Rose not long before September 1598.[4]

---

[1] No importance can be attached to Mr. Fleay's childish identifications of *War without Blows and Love without Suit, Joan as Good as my Lady,* and *The Four Kings* with *The Thracian Wonder,* Heywood's *A Maidenhead well Lost,* and *Sir Clyomon and Sir Clamydes* respectively.

[2] So called in Drayton's autograph receipt, but Henslowe calls it *William Longbeard.*

[3] Henslowe, i. 72, 78.　　　　[4] Cf. ch. xv, s.v. Alleyn.

The new plays completed during 1599–1600, twenty in all, were :

The Gentle Craft (Dekker).[1]
Bear a Brain (Dekker).[2]
Page of Plymouth (Dekker and Jonson).
Robert II, or, *The Scot's Tragedy* (Chettle, Dekker, Jonson, and Marston).[3]
The Stepmother's Tragedy (Chettle and Dekker).
1 Sir John Oldcastle (Drayton, Hathway, Munday, and Wilson).
Cox of Collumpton (Day and Haughton).
2 Henry Richmond (Wilson).
2 Sir John Oldcastle (Drayton, Hathway, Munday, and Wilson).
Patient Grissell (Chettle, Dekker, and Haughton).
The Whole History of Fortunatus (Dekker).
Thomas Merry, or, *Beech's Tragedy* (Day and Haughton).
Jugurtha (Boyle).[4]
The Seven Wise Masters (Chettle, Day, Dekker, and Haughton).
Ferrex and Porrex (Haughton).
Cupid and Psyche, or, *The Golden Ass* (Chettle, Day, and Dekker).
Damon and Pythias (Chettle).
Strange News out of Poland (Haughton and Pett).
1 Blind Beggar of Bethnal Green (Chettle and Day).
1 Fair Constance of Rome (Dekker, Drayton, Hathway, Munday, and Wilson).

[1] The only entry is of 15 July ' to bye a boocke ', but the hiatus in the manuscript probably conceals earlier payments.

[2] Here also the hiatus has only left an entry of £2 ' in full payment ' on 1 Aug. Dr. Greg, however, would identify *Bear a Brain* and *The Gentle Craft*.

[3] The entries are as follows : 2 Sept., ' Thomas Deckers Bengemen Johnson Hary Chettell & other Jentellman in earneste of a playe calle Robart the second kinge of Scottes tragedie ' ; 15 Sept., ' in earneste of a boocke called the Scottes tragedi vnto Thomas Dickers & Harey Chettell ' ; 16 Sept., ' Hary Chettell . . . in earneste of a boocke called the Scottes tragedie ' ; 27 Sept., ' Bengemen Johnsone in earneste of a boocke called the Scottes tragedie ' ; 28 Sept., ' vnto Mr Maxton the new poete in earneste of a boocke called [blank] '. Dr. Greg resists the fairly reasonable identification of ' Mr Maxton the new poete ' with the ' other Jentellman '. All the payments are called earnests, but the total is £6 10s. and therefore the play probably existed.

[4] ' Lent vnto me W Birde the 9 of Februarye to paye for a new booke to Will Boyle cald Jugurth xxxs which if you dislike Ile repaye it back.' The price is the lowest ever entered for a ' new ' book. Mr. Fleay's suggestion that Will Bird, who already had one alias in Will Borne, was also himself Will Boyle, is one of those irresponsible guesses by which he has done so much to make hay of theatrical history.

It is possible to verify the actual performance of *Page of Plymouth* (September), *1 Sir John Oldcastle* (November),[1] *Fortunatus* (December), *The Gentle Craft* (January), *Thomas Merry* (January), *Patient Grissell* (January), *2 Sir John Oldcastle* (March), *The Seven Wise Masters* (March), *Ferrex and Porrex* (May), *Damon and Pythias* (May), *Strange News out of Poland* (May), *Cupid and Psyche* (June). *Sir John Oldcastle* must of course be regarded as a counterblast to the *Henry IV* plays of the Chamberlain's men, in which the character of Falstaff originally bore the name of the Lollard hero. One infers that it had a considerable success, for the company gave 10s. for 'Mr. Mundaye and the reste of the poets at the playnge of Sr John Oldcastell the ferste tyme', and Henslowe notes in the margin that this was 'as a gefte'. It is with some hesitation that I have included *Fortunatus* in the list of new plays, because it is impossible to suppose that it was not based upon the earlier *Fortunatus*, already an old play in 1596, of the properties of which the Admiral's men certainly retained possession. But Dekker was paid on the scale of a new play, for he got a full £6 in the course of November for the book, together with an additional £1 'for the altrenge of the boocke' and £2 a fortnight later 'for the eande of Fortewnatus for the corte'. I take it that this was the Court play of 27 December. That of 1 January was another of Dekker's, *The Gentle Craft*, also called *The Shoemaker's Holiday*, which was published in the year '1600' as played before the Queen 'on New Year's Day at night last' by the Admiral's men. *Fortunatus*, *1 Sir John Oldcastle*,[1] *Patient Grissell*, and *1 Blind Beggar of Bethnal Green* have also been preserved, while the publication, also in the course of the twelve months ending on 24 March 1601, of *Look About You* as an Admiral's play must surely render plausible the hypothesis, rejected by Dr. Greg, of its identity with *Bear a Brain*. It would seem that *Thomas Merry* furnishes one of the two parallel plots of Robert Yarington's *Two Lamentable Tragedies*, and a notice by Simon Forman suggests that *Cox of Collumpton* was ultimately finished.[2] An outline of the opening scenes of *2 Henry Richmond* is among the Dulwich papers.[3] Publication was a form of popularity which the actors were apt to resent. The Admiral's men spent £2 on 18 March 1600 'to geue vnto the printer to staye the

---

[1] Both parts were entered on the Stationers' Register, but no copy of *2 Sir John Oldcastle* is known.

[2] *Bodl. Ashm. MS.* 236, f. 77ᵛ (c. 1600), has Forman's note of the 'plai of Cox of Cullinton and his 3 sons, Henry Peter and Jhon'.

[3] *Henslowe Papers*, 49.

printing of Patient Gresell '. This did not prevent the play
being entered on the Stationers' Register on 28 March, but
does perhaps explain why the earliest known edition is dated
1603. The unfinished plays of 1599–1600 were *The Poor
Man's Paradise* (Haughton), *The Orphans' Tragedy* (Chettle),[1]
an unnamed Italian tragedy by Day, *The Arcadian Virgin*
(Chettle and Haughton), *Owen Tudor* (Drayton, Hathway,
Munday, and Wilson), *Truth's Supplication to Candlelight*
(Dekker),[2] *The Spanish Moor's Tragedy* (Day, Dekker, and
Haughton),[3] *The English Fugitives* (Haughton), *The Devil
and his Dame* (Haughton),[4] *The Wooing of Death* (Chettle),
Judas (Haughton),[5] *2 Fair Constance of Rome* (Hathway),
and an unnamed play by Chettle and Day.[6] Except in so far
as *Fortunatus* was an old play, I find no trace of a revival
during 1599–1600, but it may be assumed that some of the
productions of the last two years still held the boards.

The year 1600 was another turning-point in the history of
the company. Probably at some date between 14 August,
when the first entry in a fresh account was made, and 28 October, when Pembroke's men were in occupation of the Rose,
they crossed the river, and took up their quarters at Alleyn's
recently built Fortune, on the north-west boundary of the
City. A more important event still was the return of Alleyn
himself to the stage, from which he had been absent for three
years. It is suggested in the Privy Council letter of 8 April
1600 to the Middlesex justices in favour of the Fortune
project, that this step was determined by the personal wish
of the Queen to see the great actor at Court with his fellows
again.[7] It is not quite clear on what terms he rejoined the

[1] This was taken up again in 1601, but still not finished. Dr. Greg,
however, thinks that it is identical with Day's Italian tragedy, and forms
half of *Two Lamentable Tragedies* (1601), and that Chettle's work in
1601 may have been the effecting of the combination with *Thomas Merry*.

[2] Dr. Greg, following Mr. Fleay, identifies this with Dekker's *Whore
of Babylon*, and as Time is a character in this play, cites the purchase of
' a Robe for tyme ' in April 1600 as a proof that it was then performed.
Time, however, might also have been a character in *The Seven Wise
Masters*.

[3] Possibly finished later and identical with the pseudo-Marlowesque
Lust's Dominion.

[4] The payment-entry is cancelled. The play may have been finished
for another company, and be identical with the extant *Grim, the Collier
of Croydon*, or, *The Devil and his Dame*.

[5] Possibly the basis of Bird and Rowley's *Judas* of 1601.

[6] It seems to me a little arbitrary of Dr. Greg to assume that the 10s.
entered as an earnest for this was really a bonus on *1 The Blind Beggar
of Bethnal Green*.

[7] *Henslowe Papers*, 51. I do not think that Dr. Greg recognizes the
full significance of this when he suggests (Henslowe, ii. 94) that Alleyn

company. There was a 'composicion' or agreement, in connexion with which a payment of £4 was made to him on 11 November. The next entry, which is undated, runs, 'P^d vnto my sonne Alleyn for the firste weckes playe the xj parte of xvij^{li} ix^s which came to therti & ij shellinges'. There are no further entries of the same kind until the date of a reckoning in February 1602, when Henslowe paid Alleyn 27s. 6d. 'dew to my sone out of the gallery money'. Probably this was a share of some small residue, the origin of which cannot now be traced. The earlier payment suggests that Alleyn received one full share of the actors' takings, for, if I am right in supposing that the brothers Jeffes only held half a share each, there would have been just ten sharers besides himself. Or possibly his share may have been limited to the actors' moiety of the gallery takings, and the outgoings may all have been charged to the receipts from the yard. Certainly Alleyn does not seem to have had any responsibility for these outgoings. His name is never put with those of other sharers to Henslowe's periodical reckonings, and if his play-books were used, they were bought from him. On the other hand, he sometimes, although not so often as some of his fellows, 'appointed' payments, and he received the Court money for the company, alike in 1601, 1602, and 1603. That his share did not pass through Henslowe's hands after the date of the first instalment is perhaps explained by the assumption that, as the owner and joint occupier with Henslowe of the Fortune, the appointment of a 'gatherer' for the gallery money may naturally have fallen to him.

Some such change in the financial arrangements may also account for the fact that, while Henslowe's record of advances continues on the same lines as that for 1597–1600, the notes of weekly repayments are now discontinued. As a result it is no longer possible to determine with any exactness the length of the theatrical seasons, since, naturally enough, the outgoings did not altogether stop while the house was closed. Their course, however, suggests intervals in February and March 1601, February to April 1602, August 1602 and January and February 1603. It is possible, although not very likely, that there was no cessation of playing during the summer of 1601. I find no evidence of further provincial travels before the end of the reign. These were, I think, years of prosperity. The players still required small personal

was back on the stage by 1598 ; cf. my criticism in *M. L. R.* iv. 410. Dr. Greg relies mainly on the appearance of his name in the plot of *The Battle of Alcazar*, which, he says, 'almost certainly belongs to 1598'. But I can find no reason why it should not belong to 1600–2 ; cf. p. 175.

advances from time to time, and Thomas Towne was reduced to pawning a pair of stockings on 13 March 1602.[1] But it is noticeable that about the previous June Henslowe opened an account under the heading, ' Begininge to receue of thes meane ther privet deates which they owe vnto me ', and was able to enter in it a series of repayments by Jones, Downton, Bird, and Shaw.[2] Bird, however, still owed £10 10s. on 12 March 1602, and Henslowe noted, ' He is cleere of all debtes & demaundes except theis debtes and such stocke & covenentes as I maie clayme & challendge of him by reason of his coniunction with the companie '.[3] Whether the playwrights reaped any benefit may be doubted. The tendency to a rise of prices which showed itself in 1599 was hardly maintained. Some of them were still impecunious enough. The company had, on more than one occasion to redeem a play which the unfortunate Chettle had pawned with one Bromfield, a mercer ; and in March 1602 he seems to have followed Porter's example and put his hand, for a consideration of £3, to an instrument binding him to write for them alone.[4] There were some legal troubles in the course of 1601. A sum of £21 10s. had to be paid on a bond to a Mr. Treheren during March, and in August there were fees to a jury and a clerk of assizes. The company had also to find 10s. in May ' to geatte the boye into the ospetalle which was hurt at the Fortewne '.[5] Information as to the composition of the company at some time between Alleyn's return and February 1602 is given by the ' plot ' of *The Battle of Alcazar*, although, as this is mutilated, it must not be treated as negative evidence, and in particular the names of W. Borne and John Singer are missing.[6] All the other sharers, however, are found in it—' Mr. Ed. Allen, Mr. Doughton, Mr. Juby, Mr. Shaa, Mr. Jones, Mr. Towne, Antony Jeffes, H. Jeffes, Mr. Charles [Massey], and Mr. Sam [Rowley] '. There are also Mr. Rich. Allen and Mr. Hunt, who were not sharers, but whose long service had apparently earned them the

---

[1] Henslowe, i. 56.   [2] Ibid. 162.   [3] Ibid. 141.
[4] Ibid. 144, 165, 174.   [5] Ibid. 134, 136, 140, 147.
[6] Dr. Greg puts it in 1598, on the assumption that Alleyn returned to the stage in that year. It might conceivably belong to 1597, between 18 Dec., when Bristow was bought, and 29 Dec., by which day Alleyn had left. It cannot be later than Feb. 1602, by which month Jones and Shaw had left. The prefix ' Mr ' allotted to Charles and Sam is in favour of a date after their agreements on 16 Nov. 1598. Dr. Greg's argument (*Henslowe Papers*, 138) that Kendall's agreement expired 7 Dec. 1599 is not convincing, as there was nothing in it to prevent him from staying on, and the satire of the play in Jonson's *Poetaster* of 1601, to which he refers, obviously tells in favour of a date nearer to 1601 than 1598.

dignity of the ' Mr.', W. Kendall, Jeames, who was possibly
Henslowe's apprentice James Bristow and possibly Jones's
boy of the same name, and Dob, who was probably the Dobe
of the 1598 inventory. The remaining names, all of which
are new, are those of W. Cartwright, who, however, had
witnessed a loan for Henslowe as far back as 21 April 1598,[1]
Dick Jubie, Ro. Tailor, George Somerset, Tho. Drum, [Thomas]
Parsons, Harry, and the ' boys ' of Mr. Allen and Mr. Towne.
The only important woman's part, that of Callipolis, is
assigned by the ' plot ' to Pisano, which does not look like
an actor's name and may be a mistake. The services of
Bristow were evidently leased out by Henslowe to the company or some one of its members, at a rate of 3s. a week.
Antony Jeffes paid two weeks' arrears ' for my boyes Jeames
wages' in August 1600, and Henslowe charged the company
£6 10s. on the same account in the following February.[2]
Another boy attached to the company about the same time
must have been ' Nick ', for whom hose ' to tumbell in be
fore the quen ' were bought on 25 December 1601. Hugh
Davis, for the mending of whose tawny coat ' which was
eatten with the rattes ' 6s. 7d. was paid in November 1601,
was perhaps a hired man. A list of the responsible members
of the company is attached by Henslowe to a reckoning
cast between 7 and 23 February 1602. They were then ' John
Singer, Thomas Downton, William Byrd, Edward Juby,
Thomas Towne, Humphrey Jeffs, Anthony Jeffs, Samuel
Rowley, and Charles Massy '.[3] A note is added that £50 had
been advanced ' to geve vnto Mr. Jonnes & Mr. Shaw at ther
goinge a waye '. This departure must have been quite
recent. Shaw had been agent for the company on the previous
21 January, and the list of continuing members is in fact in
his handwriting. The last instalment of Jones's private debt
had been paid off on 1 November. His three years' agreement
with Henslowe had expired at Michaelmas 1600. Richard
Alleyn must have died in November 1601, for on the 19th
of that month his widow borrowed £5 10s. to take her mantle
and sheet and face-cloth out of pawn.[4] Neither Shaw nor
Jones nor Richard Alleyn is in the plot of 1 Tamar Cham,
which may reasonably be assigned to a date in the vicinity
of the purchase of the book from Alleyn on 2 October 1602.
This is of interest, partly because it is complete, and partly
because there was a procession in the play, and the number
of supernumeraries required must have tried the resources

---

[1] Henslowe, i. 38.   [2] Ibid. 131, 134.
[3] Ibid. 164.   [4] Ibid. 205.

of the establishment to their utmost. All the principal members of the company appeared—'Mr. Allen, Mr. Denygten, Mr. Boorne, Mr. Towne, Mr. Singer, Mr. Jubie, H. Jeffs, A. Jeffs, Mr. Charles [Massey], and Mr. Sam [Rowley]'; and in addition Dick Jubie, W. Cart[wright], George [Somerset], Tho. Parsons, and Jeames [Bristow], who were in *The Battle of Alcazar*, and W. Parr, Tho. Marbeck, Jack Grigorie, Gedion, Gibbs, Tho. Rowley, Rester, 'old Browne', Ned Browne, 'the red fast fellow' and several boys, described, perhaps in some cases twice over, as Jack Jones, 'little Will', 'little Will Barne', who do not seem to be identical, 'Gils his boy', 'Mr. Denyghtens little boy', perhaps the same already recorded in 1600, and 'the other little boy'. 'Old Browne' can hardly be Robert Browne, who seems to have been in Germany; but Ned Browne may be the Edward Browne who, like Robert, was a member of Worcester's company in 1583. Little is added by the only other extant 'plot', the fragmentary one of *2 Fortune's Tennis*. This is difficult to date, but it must be later than Dekker's *1 Fortune's Tennis* of September 1600, and may not improbably be Munday's *Set at Tennis* of December 1602. The few names which it contains—Mr. Singer, Sam, Charles, Geo[rge Somerset], R. Tailor, W. Cartwright, Pavy—suggest proximity to *The Battle of Alcazar* and *1 Tamar Cham*. The only fresh one is that of Pavy, who may or may not be connected with the Salathiel Pavy of Ben Jonson's epitaph. Both *1 Tamar Cham* and *2 Fortune's Tennis* must be earlier than January 1603, a month which saw the retirement of the old Queen's man, John Singer. So at least may be inferred from the fact that he makes no further appearance in the diary after 13 January, when he received £5 'for his play called Syngers Vallentarey'. I take 'vallentarey' to mean 'valediction'. His name is absent from the next list of the company, which belongs to 1604. He probably left to become an ordinary Groom of the Chamber in the royal household, a post which he is found occupying at the time of Elizabeth's funeral.[1]

The succession of new plays was not quite so rapid during 1600–3 as in previous periods. I can only trace thirty-one in all, as against fifty-five in 1594–7 and sixty-two in 1599–1600. It may well have been the case that Alleyn, who had 'created' parts in the 'eighties and early 'nineties, had a tendency towards revivals. For 1600–1 the company bought only seven new books. These were:

1 Fortune's Tennis (Dekker).
Hannibal and Scipio (Hathway and Rankins).

[1] Cf. ch. x.

Scogan and Skelton (Hathway and Rankins).
All is not Gold that Glisters (Chettle).
2 Blind Beggar of Bethnal Green (Day and Haughton).
The Six Yeomen of the West (Day and Haughton).
King Sebastian of Portugal (Chettle and Dekker).

None of these plays is extant, but the purchase of properties testifies to the performance of *2 Blind Beggar of Bethnal Green* in April and *The Six Yeomen of the West* in July. Moreover, Day received a bonus of 10s. between 27 April and 2 May ' after the playinge of ' the former piece. Only £1 was paid for *1 Fortune's Tennis*, but the existence of a ' plot ' for *2 Fortune's Tennis* suggests that it must have been completed. Probably it was a short topical overture designed to celebrate the opening of the Fortune.[1] Unfinished plays were *Robin Hood's Pennyworths* (Haughton)[2] and *The Conquest of Spain by John of Gaunt* (Hathway and Rankins). The revivals included *Phaethon* (January), *The Blind Beggar of Alexandria* (May), and *The Jew of Malta* (May). Dekker had £2 for ' alterynge of ' *Phaethon* for the Court, and this was therefore the Admiral's play of 6 January 1601. They also appeared on 28 December and 2 February. *Dr. Faustus* was entered on 7 January; the earliest print (1604) bears their name. The new books of 1601–2 were fourteen in number, as follows :[3]

The Conquest of the West Indies (Day, Haughton, and Smith).
3 Blind Beggar of Bethnal Green (Day and Haughton).
The Life of Cardinal Wolsey (Chettle).[4]
1 The Six Clothiers (Hathway, Haughton, and Smith).
The Rising of Cardinal Wolsey (Chettle, Drayton, Munday, and Smith).
Friar Rush and the Proud Woman of Antwerp (Chettle, Day, and Haughton).
Judas (Bird and Rowley).[5]

[1] The entry is ' Thomas Deckers for his boocke called the fortewn tenes '. Collier read ' forteion tenes ' and interpreted *Fortunatus*. Mr. Fleay furnished the alternatives of *Fortune's Tennis* and *Hortenzo's Tennis*. I should add that Dr. Greg assigns the ' plot ' to this play.

[2] Dr. Greg thinks that this may be the same as Haughton's *The English Fugitives* of the previous April. If so, it was probably finished, as the payments amount to £6.

[3] As the account of advances is continuous, I have drawn the line between 1600–1 and 1601–2 at the beginning of Aug. 1601.

[4] *The Life* became *2 Cardinal Wolsey*, as *The Rising*, although written later, was historically *1 Cardinal Wolsey*. The entries are complicated. It is just possible that the playwrights were working on an old play, for the property-inventories of 1598 include an unexplained ' Will Sommers sewtte ' (cf. p. 168). A ' Wm Someres cotte ' was, however, bought for *The Rising* on 27 May 1602.

[5] Possibly based on Haughton's unfinished play of 1600.

Too Good to be True (Chettle, Hathway, and Smith).
Malcolm King of Scots (Massey).
Love Parts Friendship (Chettle and Smith).
Jephthah (Dekker and Munday).
Tobias (Chettle).
The Bristol Tragedy (Day).
Caesar's Fall, or, *The Two Shapes* (Dekker, Drayton, Middleton, Munday, and Webster).

At least ten of these appear to have been played: *2 Cardinal Wolsey* (August), *3 Blind Beggar of Bethnal Green* (September), *Judas* (January), *The Conquest of the West Indies* (January), *Malcolm King of Scots* (April), *Love Parts Friendship* (May), *1 Cardinal Wolsey* (June), *Jephthah* (July), and at uncertain dates, *Tobias* and probably *The Bristol Tragedy*.[1] None is now extant. The unfinished plays were *The Humorous Earl of Gloucester with his Conquest of Portugal* (Wadeson), *2 Tom Dough*[2] (Day and Haughton), *The Orphan's Tragedy* (Chettle),[3] *2 The Six Clothiers* (Hathway, Haughton, and Smith),[4] *The Spanish Fig* (Anon.),[5] *Richard Crookback* (Jonson),[6] *A Danish Tragedy* (Chettle),[7] and *A Medicine for a Curst Wife* (Dekker).[8] There was considerable activity of revival during the year. Six old plays belonging to the 1594–7 repertory, for some of which the company already held the properties,[9] were bought

---

[1] A note preserved at Dulwich (*Henslowe Papers*, 58) indicates that licensing fees were in arrear on 4 Aug. 1602 for ' baxsters tragedy, Tobias Comedy, Jepha Judg of Israel & the Cardinall, Loue parts frendshipp '. But of course Warner's identification of ' baxsters tragedy' with *The Bristol Tragedy* is conjectural.

[2] There is no *1 Tom Dough*, unless this was an intended sequel to *The Six Yeomen of the West*.

[3] Already begun by Chettle in 1599.

[4] This may be identical with *1 The Six Clothiers*, which is not called by Henslowe a ' first part ', if, as is possible, that was a sequel to *The Six Yeomen of the West*.

[5] Possibly finished later as Dekker and Rowley's *The Noble Spanish Soldier*. But it may have been an old play re-written, for C. R. Baskervill (*M. P.* xiv. 16) quotes from the preface to H. O.'s translation of Vasco Figueiro's *Spaniard's Monarchie* (1592), ' albeit it hath no title fetched from the Bull within Bishopsgate, as a figge for a Spaniard '.

[6] I suppose this was unfinished. The only entry is on 22 June 1602, ' vnto Bengemy Johnsone . . . in earneste of a boocke called Richard Crockbacke & for new adicyons for Jeronymo the some of x^{li} '. Jonson had already had £2 on 25 Sept. 1601 ' vpon his writtinge of his adicians in Geronymo '. Unless *Richard Crookback* was nearly complete, his prices must have risen a good deal.

[7] Possibly finished later as *Hoffman* (1631).

[8] The £4 paid was cancelled and then reinstated, but the book was evidently transferred to Worcester's men (cf. p. 227).

[9] Cf. p. 168.

from Alleyn at £2 each, *Mahomet* in August, *The Wise Man of West Chester* in September, *Vortigern* in November, and *The French Doctor*, *The Massacre at Paris*, and *Crack Me this Nut* in January. The first and the last three of these certainly were played, and the revival of *The Massacre at Paris* appears to have caused annoyance to Henri IV.[1] In addition, properties were bought for one of the *Hercules* plays in December, Dekker got 10s. for a prologue and epilogue to *Pontius Pilate*[2] in January, and Jonson wrote additions to *The Spanish Tragedy*, possibly those now extant, in September, although it may be doubted whether the further additions contemplated in the following June were ever made. There is nothing to show what was selected, other than Nick's tumbling, for the Admiral's only Court play of 1601–2, which took place on 27 December.

The season of 1602–3 was, of course, shortened by the death of Elizabeth and the outbreak of plague. The new plays numbered nine. They were:

Samson (Anon.).
Felmelanco (Chettle and Robinson).
Joshua (Rowley).
Randal Earl of Chester (Middleton).
Merry as May Be (Day, Hathway, and Smith).
The Set at Tennis (Munday).
1 The London Florentine (Chettle and Heywood).
Singer's Voluntary (Singer).
The Boss of Billingsgate (Day, Hathway, and another).[3]

It must be added that in September properties were bought for a ' new playe ' called *The Earl of Hertford*, which it seems impossible to identify with any of the pieces bought. This looks like one of the rare cases in which payment did not pass through Henslowe's hands. This and *Samson* are the only new plays of the year, the actual performance of which can be verified ; and none of these plays is extant.[4] I suspect, however, that Munday's *Set at Tennis* is the *2 Fortune's Tennis* of which a ' plot ' survives. The payment, of only £3, was ' in full ', and it may, like *1 Fortune's Tennis*, have been a short piece of some exceptional character, motived by the name of the theatre in which it was presented. Unfinished

---

[1] Cf. vol. i, p. 323. *The Massacre* was printed (N.D.) as an Admiral's play.

[2] The conjectural rendering of Henslowe's ' ponesciones pillet ' finds support from the presence of garments for ' Caffes ' or Caiaphas in the inventory of 1598 ; cf. p. 168.

[3] A payment to ' John Daye & his felowe poetes ' implies at least three collaborators.   [4] For *Samson* cf. p. 367.

plays at the end of the season were *The Widow's Charm* (Munday or Wadeson),[1] *William Cartwright* (Haughton), *Hoffman* (Chettle),[2] *2 London Florentine* (Chettle and Heywood), *The Siege of Dunkirk and Alleyn the Pirate* (Massey). The revival of old plays continued. Costumes for *Vortigern*, one of those bought from Alleyn in the previous year, were in preparation during September, and Alleyn's stock yielded three more, *Philip of Spain* and *Longshanks* in August and *Tamar Cham*, probably the second part, as the extant 'plot' testifies, in October. The last two of these belonged to the Admiral's repertory of 1594–7, but the origin of *Philip of Spain* is unknown. A book of *The Four Sons of Aymon*, for which £2 was paid to Robert Shaw, was probably also old, and was bought on condition that Shaw should repay the £2, unless the play was used by the Admiral's or some other company with his consent by Christmas 1604. Bird and Rowley had £4 in November for additions to *Dr. Faustus*. Dekker completed some alterations of *Tasso's Melancholy*, another 1594–7 play, in December, and in the same month Middleton wrote 'for the corte' a prologue and epilogue to Greene's *Friar Bacon and Friar Bungay*, which I should suppose to have been Henslowe's property, as it was played by Strange's men in 1592–3 and the Queen's and Sussex's in 1594. This probably served for the first of the three appearances made by the Admiral's at Court, on 27 December. The other two were on 6 March and on a date unspecified. For one of these occasions Chettle was writing a prologue and epilogue at the end of December, but the play is not named.[3] One of the new plays, *Merry as May Be*, was intended for Court, when the first payment on account of it was made on 9 November.

On 12 March 1603 Henslowe practically closes the detailed record which he had kept continuously in his diary since October 1597 of his financial transactions, otherwise than by way of rent, with the Admiral's men. A brief review of these is not without interest.[4] His advances from 21 October 1597 to 8 March 1598 amounted to £46 7s. 3d., and to this he took the signatures of the company, with the note, 'Thes men dothe aknowlege this deat to be dewe by them by seatynge

---

[1] All four entries merely show the payments as made to 'Antony the poyete'.

[2] Finished later and extant ; probably identical with the *Danish Tragedy* of 1601–2.

[3] I suppose that it was the play which Chettle 'layd vnto pane' to Mr. Bromfield, and which had to be redeemed for £1 (Henslowe, i. 174).

[4] The more so as I do not think that Dr. Greg's survey in Henslowe. ii. 135, is accurate.

of ther handes to yette '. By 28 July a further amount of
£120 15s. 4d. had been incurred, making a total of £166 17s. 7d.
for 1597–8.[1] During the same period he entered weekly
receipts from the company to a total of £125. These must have
gone to an old debt, for he did not balance them with the
payments for the year, but carried on the whole debit of
£166 17s. 7d. to 1598–9. Apparently, however, he was not
satisfied with the way in which expenditure was outstripping
income, for he headed a new receipts account, ' Here I begyne
to receue the wholle gallereys frome this daye beinge the
29 of July 1598 ', and the weekly entries become about double
what they were during 1597–8. On the other hand, there is
also a considerable increase in the rate of expenditure. It
is an ingenious and, I think, sound conjecture of Dr. Greg's,
that throughout 1594–1603 Henslowe was taking half the
gallery money for rent, and that, at different times, he also
took either the other half, or another quarter only, to recoup
himself for his advances.[2] The outgoings entered during
1598–9 reach £435 7s. 4d., but some items for March and
April 1599 are probably missing, owing to a mutilation of
the manuscript.[3] The receipts for the same period were
£358 3s. On 13 October 1599, about a fortnight after the
beginning of the 1599–1600 season, a balance was struck.
Henslowe credited the company with the £358 received from
the gallery money, and debited them with £632 advanced
by him. This includes £166 17s. 7d. for 1597–8, £435 7s. 4d.
for 1598–9, and £29 15s. 1d., which may reasonably be taken
as the sum of the missing entries for March and April 1599.
The balance of £274 remained as a debt from the company.
They did not, however, set their hands to a reckoning until
the end of the next year, on 10 July 1600. During 1599–1600
a fresh account had been running, on which Henslowe's
receipts were £202 10s. and his payments £222 5s. 6d.
At the reckoning the company's indebtedness is calculated
at £300, and is admitted by the formula, ' which some of
three hundred powndes we whose names are here vnder
written doe acknowledge our dewe debt & doe promyse
payment '. To this their signatures are appended. There
is, however, an unexplained discrepancy of £6 4s. 6d., as the

[1] Henslowe made the total £167 7s. 7d., but evidently the error was
detected, as only £166 17s. 7d. was carried forward.
[2] Henslowe, ii. 133. Apparently Henslowe reverted to the plan of
deducting three-quarters only, at the beginning of 1599–1600, but only
for a fortnight, as the receipts from 20 Oct. are headed, ' Heare I begane
to receue the gallereys agayne which they receued begynynge at Myhellmas
wecke being the 6 of October 1599 '.
[3] I have disregarded an error of 15s. made by Henslowe.

old debt of £274 and the 1599–1600 debit balance of £19 15s. 6d. only make up £293 15s. 6d.

From 1600 onwards there are no records of receipts. A continuous account of payments is kept up to 7 February 1602. The total amounts to £304 10s. 4d., but Henslowe sums it in error as £308 6s. 4d., and notes, ' Frome ther handes to this place is 308ll–06s–04d dewe vnto me & with the three hundred of owld is £608–06–04d '. He then adds the £50 paid to Jones and Shaw on retirement, ' which is not in this recknynge '. Above this summary comes a list of names, said by Dr. Greg to be in Shaw's hand, of those sharers who were continuing in the company, headed by the figures ' 211. 9. 0.' I think the interpretation is that £386 17s. 4d. of the £608 6s. 4d. was paid out of gallery money or other sources, leaving £211 9s., together with the £50 for Jones and Shaw, chargeable on the company. This is borne out by the remnant of the accounts, which is headed, ' Begininge with a new recknyng with my lord of Notingames men the 23 daye of Febreary 1601 as foloweth '. The expenditure on this new reckoning up to 12 March 1603 was, as calculated by Henslowe, £188 11s. 6d., and he adds to this total a sum of £211 9s. ' vpon band ', being evidently the residue of the debt as it stood at the close of the old reckoning, and makes a total of £400 0s. 6d. This, with the £50 for Jones and Shaw, was no doubt what the company owed when the detailed account in the diary closed. There was, however, an unstated amount of gallery receipts during 1602–3 to set against it ; and in fact a retrospect of the whole series of figures shows that there would have been a pretty fair equivalence of gallery money and advances throughout, but for the exceptionally heavy expenditure of 1598–9, £465 2s. 5d. in all, which left the company saddled with an obligation which they never quite overtook. This expenditure was more than half the total expenditure of £854 5s. 6d. for the triennium 1597–1600, and nearly as much as the whole expenditure of £493 1s. 10d. for the triennium 1600–3, during which it may be suspected that the business capacities of Alleyn brought about considerable economies.

The accounts may be looked at from another point of view. If the unanalysable sum of £29 15s. 1d. for the missing items of March and April 1599 be neglected, there was a total expenditure for the six years of £1,317 11s. 3d. Of this £652 13s. 8d., being about half, went in payments in respect of play-books ; £561 1s. 1d. for properties and apparel ; and £103 16s. 6d. in miscellaneous outgoings, such as licensing fees, legal charges, musical instruments, travelling expenses, merry-makings and the like. Thus, if the company supped together at Mr. Mason's of the Queen's Head, or met to read a 'book' at the Sun in New Fish Street, Henslowe would put his hand into his pocket to pay the score, and would not forget afterwards to debit the company with the amount in his diary.[1] It must, of course, be borne in mind that only part of this miscellaneous expenditure was incurred through Henslowe. He certainly did not, for example, pay all the fees for the licensing of new plays by the Master of the Revels. And of course there were many matters, in particular the wages of hired actors and servitors, for which the company had regularly to find funds in other ways. It is probable that only play-books, properties, and apparel were normally charged to his account, although the convenience of an occasional extension of his functions can readily be under-stood. Dr. Greg may be right in thinking that his position as agent for the company in its purchases was a natural development of his pawnbroking business.[2] But during the period under review he did not, as a rule, supply them with goods himself. A sale of 'A shorte velluett clocke wraght with bugell & a gearcken of velluet layd with brade coper sylver lace' for £4 on 28 November 1598 was exceptional. Usually the payments are to tradesmen, to the mercers Stone, Richard Heath, and Robert Bromfield, to ' him at the Eagell and Chylld' for armour, to Mrs. Gosson for head-tires, and for wigs to one Father Ogle, who is mentioned also in the Revels Accounts and in the play of *Sir Thomas More*. Sometimes ready-made garments, new or second-hand, were bought A doublet and hose of sea-water green satin cost £3 and a doublet and 'venesyons' of cloth of silver wrought with red silk £4 10s. But often stuffs were obtained in piece and made up by tailors, of whom the company employed two, Dover and Radford, the latter known, for the sake of distinction, as 'the little tailor'. These and William White, who made the crowns, probably worked at the theatre, in the tiring-house. The company gave 6s. a yard for russet broadcloth and the same for murrey satin, 12s. for other satins, 12s. 6d. for taffeties, and no less than £1 for 'ij pylle velluet of carnardyn'. Laces cost 1d. each; copper lace anything from 4s. a pound to 1s. 2d. an ounce. Of this they used quantities, and in the summer of 1601 they had run up a considerable 'old debt' to the copper lace-man, as well as another to Heath the mercer, which had to be paid off by degrees. The more expensive garments,

---

[1] Henslowe, i. 85, 145.　　　　　[2] Ibid. ii. 33.

such as a rich cloak bought of Langley for £19, were, of course, an investment on the part of the company, and were worn in their time by many sharers and hired men in different parts. But the principal actors had also, as Alleyn's inventory shows, their private wardrobes. Henslowe was prepared to furnish these on the instalment system. Thus Richard Jones bought in 1594 'a manes gowne of pechecoler in grayne' for £3 payable in weekly sums of 5s., and Thomas Towne in 1598 'a blacke clothe clocke layd with sylke lace' for 26s. 8d. at 1s. weekly. It was as hard to keep these glories as to procure them. On one occasion the company came to the rescue and lent Thomas Downton £12 10s., to fetch out of pawn two cloaks, 'which they exsepted into the stock'. The one was 'ashecolerd velluet embradered with gowld', the other 'a longe black velluet clocke layd with sylke lace'.[1]

The termination of the record of advances after 12 March 1603 indicates an interruption of performances, probably due to the increasing illness of Elizabeth, who died on the following 24 March. Thereafter there are only a few winding-up entries in the diary. The company must have immediately begun to travel under the leadership of Thomas Downton, who in the course of 1602–3 received a gift for them from the Corporation of Canterbury, 'because it was thought fitt they should not play at all, in regard that our late Queene was then very sicke or dead as they supposed'. London playing, if resumed at all, must have very soon been stopped again by the plague. There was some further small expenditure, of which the details are not given, before Henslowe noted that, in addition to the bond for £211 9s., 'Ther reasteth dew vnto me to this daye beinge the v daye of M ye 1603 when we leafte of playe now at the Kynges cominge all recknynges abated the some of a hundred fowerscore & sevntenepowndes & thirteneshellynges & fowerpence I saye dew—£197 13s. 4d. the fyftye powndes which Jonnes & Shawe had at ther goinge a way not reconed'. The company travelled again during the plague, being traceable as the Admiral's men in 1602–3 at Bath and York and on 18 August 1603 at Leicester, and as the Earl of Nottingham's in 1602–3 at Coventry. The tour was over by 21 October, on which date Joan Alleyn wrote to her husband at the house of Mr. Chaloner in Sussex, telling him amongst other things that 'all of your owne company ar well at theyr owne houses', that all the other companies had returned, that

---

[1] Henslowe, i. 29, 47, 81, 96, 97, 118, 124, 136, 138, 144, 146, 148, 152, 153, 166, 172, &c.

'Nicke and Jeames be well', and that 'Browne of the Boares head' had not gone into the country at all, and was now dead, '& dyed very pore'. This might be either Edward Browne, or the 'old Browne' who appeared with him in *I Tamar Cham* in the previous autumn. In any case, it is clear from the reference to him that he was not a regular member of Alleyn's company. 'Jeames' is no doubt James Bristow, who, as Henslowe's apprentice, would be likely to form part of his household; and 'Nicke', who seems to have been in the same position, may be supposed to be the Nick who tumbled before the Queen at Christmas 1601.

The Jacobean records of the company seem meagre in the absence of Henslowe's detailed register of proceedings. About Christmas 1603 they were taken into the service of Prince Henry, and are hereafter known as the Prince's players.[1] They are entered amongst other 'Officers to the Prince' as receiving four and a half yards of red cloth apiece as liveries for the coronation procession on 15 March 1604, and their names are given as 'Edward Allen, William Bird, Thomas Towne, Thomas Dowton, Samuell Rowley, Edward Jubie, Humfry Jeffes, Charles Massey, and Anthony Jeffes'.[2] Alleyn, even if not a 'sharer', was therefore a member of the company in its official capacity. He is also named as the Prince's servant, both in the printed account of the entertainment at which, dressed as a Genius, he delivered a speech, and in Stowe's description of a bear-baiting which formed part of the festivities.[3] It may, however, be inferred that he took an early opportunity of leaving a profession to which he had only been recalled by the personal whim of the late Queen.[4] He was joint payee with Juby in the warrant of 19 February, but Juby's name stands alone in another of 17 April and in those of all subsequent years up to 1615. And when the company received a formal licence by patent on 30 April 1606, Alleyn's name was omitted, and does not appear in any further list of its members. It is true that as late as 11 May 1611 he is still described in a formal document as the Prince's servant, but he may have held some other appointment, actual or honorific, in the household.[5] A note of his resources about 1605, however,

---

[1] The exact date is uncertain, as they do not appear to have had a patent until 1606; but it must lie between their visit to Leicester as the Admiral's on 18 Aug. 1603 and the making out of a warrant to them as the Prince's men on 19 Feb. 1604 for their Christmas plays.

[2] *N. Sh. Soc. Trans.* (1877–9), 17*, from *Lord Chamberlain's Books*, 58ᵃ.

[3] Cf. ch. xvi (Hope).

[4] On the legend that he had developed moral scruples about the stage, cf. s.v. Marlowe, *Dr. Faustus*.   [5] *Henslowe Papers*, 18.

includes 'my share of aparell, £100 '.[1] And he certainly remained interested in the company. They were his tenants at the Fortune, although an unexecuted draft of a lease to Thomas Downton dated in 1608 suggests that he may have taken steps to transfer the whole or a share of his direct interest to them. Under this lease Downton was to receive during thirteen years a thirty-second part of the daily profits accruing to Henslowe and Alleyn, and in return to pay £27 10s., a rent of 10s. annually and his proportionate share of repairs, and to bind himself to play in the house and not elsewhere without consent.[2] On 11 April 1612 Robert Browne is found writing to Alleyn on behalf of one Mr. Rose, lately 'entertayned amongst the princes men', to request his interest as one 'who he knowes can strike a greter stroke amongst them then this' to procure him a 'gathering place' for his wife.[3] Another letter from Bird to Alleyn, also about a gatherer, is amusing enough to quote in full. It is undated.

'Sir there is one Jhon Russell, that by yowr apoyntment was made a gatherer wth vs, but my fellowes finding often falce to vs, haue many tymes warnd him ffrom taking the box. And he as often, with moste damnable othes, hath vowde neuer to touch, yet not with standing his execrable othes, he hath taken the box, & many tymes moste vnconsionablye gathered, for which we haue resolued he shall neuer more come to the doore; yet for your sake, he shall haue his wages, to be a nessessary atendaunt on the stage, and if he will pleasure himself and vs, to mend our garmentes, when he hath leysure, weele pay him for that to. I pray send vs word if this motion will satisfie you ; for him his dishonestye is such we knowe it will not, Thus yealding our selues in that & a farr greater matter to be comaunded by you I committ you to god. Your loving ffrend to comaunde. W Birde.'[4]

With the exception of Alleyn, all the players of the 1604 list and no others appear in the patent of 1606, the text of which follows : [5]

De concessione licenciae pro Thoma Downton et aliis.

Iames by the grace of God &c. To all Iustices, Maiors, Sheriffes, bailiffes, Constables, headboroughes and other our officers and loving subiectes greeting. Knowe ye that wee of our especiall grace, certaine knowledge, and meere mocion haue licenced and auctorized, and by theis presentes doe licence and auctorize Thomas Downton, Thomas Towne, William Byrde, Edwarde Iuby, Samuell Rowle, Humfrey Ieffes, Charles Massey, and Anthonie Ieffes, Servauntes to our dearest sonne the Prince, and the rest of theire

---

[1] *Dulwich MS.* iii. 15.
[2] *Henslowe Papers*, 13 ; cf. ch. xvi, s.v. *Fortune*.
[3] *Henslowe Papers*, 63.   [4] *Ibid.* 85.
[5] *M. S. C.* i. 268, from *P. R. 4 Jac. I*, pt. 19 ; also printed by T. E. Tomlins, and dated in error 1607, in *Sh. Soc. Papers*, iv. 42.

Associates to vse and exercise the arte and facultie of playing Commedies, Tragedies, Histories, Enterludes, Moralls, Pastoralls, Stageplayes, and such other like as they haue alreadie studied or hereafter
shall vse or studie, aswell for the recreacion of our loving subiectes,
as for our solace and pleasure when wee shall thincke good to see them,
during our pleasure, And the said Commedies, Tragedies, histories,
Enterludes, Moralls, pastoralls, stageplaies, and suche like to shewe
and exercise publiquelie to their best Commoditie, aswell within theire
nowe vsuall house called the Fortune within our Countie of Middlesex,
as alsoe within anie Towne halls or Moutehalls or other convenient
places within the libertie and ffredome of anie other Cittie, vniversitie,
Towne, or Boroughe whatsoever, within our Realmes and Domynions,
willing and Commaunding you and everie of you, as you tender our
pleasure, not onelie to permitt and suffer them herein without anie
your lettes, hindraunces, or molestacions during our saide pleasure,
but alsoe to be aiding and assisting vnto them yf anie wrong be to
them offered, And to allowe them such former curtesies as hath been
given to men of theire place and quallitie, And alsoe what further
favour you shall shewe vnto them for our sake wee shall take kindelie
at your handes.   Prouided alwaies, and our will and pleasure ys, that
all auctoritie, power, priuiledges, and profittes whatsoever belonging
and properlie appertaining to the Maister of our Revells in respecte
of his office, and everie Clause, article, or graunte conteined within
the letteres patentes or Commission, which haue heretofore been
graunted or directed by the late Queene Elizabeth our deere Sister,
or by our selves, to our welbeloued servantes Edmonde Tilney, Maister
of the office of our said Revells, or to Sir George Bucke knighte, or to
either of them in possession or reversion, shall be remayne and abide
entire, and in full force estate and vertue, and in as ample sorte as yf
this our Commission had never been made.   In witnesse whereof etc.
Witnesse our selfe at Westminster the Thirtith daie of Aprill.   per
breve de priuato sigillo.

Between 1606 and 1610 it seems to have been thought
desirable to strengthen the composition of the company by
the introduction of new blood.   A list of ' Comedyanes and
Playores ', included in the establishment book drawn up
when Henry formed his own Household as Prince of Wales
in 1610, contains six names in addition to the eight of the
patent.[1]   They are ' Edward Colbrande, Wm. Parre, Rychard
Pryore, William Stratford, Frauncys Grace, and John Shanke '.
Of these William Parr, who is in the plot of 1 Tamar Cham in
1602, is alone traceable in the earlier records of the company.
Shank had been of Pembroke's and Queen Elizabeth's men.

Henslowe entered two more advances in his diary, one for
' facynge of a blacke grogren clocke with taffytye ', the other

¹ Birch, *Life of Henry*, 455 ;   Greg, *Gentleman's Magazine*, ccc. 67, from
Harl. MS. 252, f. 5, dated 1610.

to Dekker and Middleton in earnest of *The Patient Man and the Honest Whore*. This was entered in the Stationers' Register on 9 November 1604, and printed as *The Honest Whore* during the year. The name of Towne is in a stage-direction. On 14 March ' 1604 ', which may have been either 1604 or 1605, Henslowe had a final reckoning with the company and noted ' Caste vp all the acowntes frome the begininge of the world vntell this daye beinge the 14 daye of Marche 1604 by Thomas Dowghton & Edward Jube for the company of the prynces men & I Phillipe Henslow so ther reasteth dew vnto me P Henslow the some of xxiiij[ll] all reconynges consernynge the company in stocke generall descarged & my sealfe descarged to them of al deates '.[1] With this, so far as the extant book goes, the record of his transactions with the company practically ceases. The only exception is a note of receipts at the Fortune during the three days next after Christmas in 1608, which amounted to 25s., 45s., and 44s. 9d. respectively.[2] Something of the career of the Prince's men may be gleaned from other sources. They played at Court before James on 21 January and 20 February 1604, and before Henry on 4, 15, and 22 January ; and during the following Christmas before Anne on 23 November 1604 and before Henry on 24 November, 14 and 19 December, and on 15 and 22 January and 5 and 19 February 1605. On 8 February 1605 their play of *Richard Whittington*, of which nothing further is known, was entered on the Stationers' Register.[3] In the same year Samuel Rowley's *When You See Me, You Know Me*, was printed as played by them. During the Christmas of 1605–6 they gave three plays before James and three before Henry.[4] In 1604–5 they were at Maidstone and Winchester, in 1605–6 at Bath, on 17 July 1606 at Oxford, and on 17 October at Ipswich. During the Christmas of 1606–7 they gave six plays before James. Dekker's *Whore of Babylon* was entered on the Stationers' Register on 20 April 1607 and printed as theirs in the same year. In 1606–7 they were at Bath. During the Christmas of 1607–8 they gave four plays before James and Henry. In 1607–8 they were

---

[1] Henslowe, i. 175.   [2] Ibid. 214.

[3] There may be an allusion to this play in H. Parrot, *Laquei Ridiculosi, Springes for Woodcocks* (1613), ii. 162 :

> 'Tis said that *Whittington* was rais'd of nought,
> And by a cat hath divers wonders wrought :
> But *Fortune* (not his cat) makes it appear,
> He may dispend a thousand marks a year.

Dr. Greg (*Henslowe*, ii. 65) has dispersed Collier's myth of one Whittington ' perhaps a sleeping partner in the speculation of the Fortune '.

[4] Most of the play-dates of 1605–12 are in Apps. A and B.

at Maidstone and Saffron Walden, and on 1 October 1608 they were at Leicester; but a visit of the same year from 'the Princes players of the White Chapple, London' is rather to be assigned to the Duke of York's men (q.v.). They gave three plays before James and Henry during the Christmas of 1608–9, four before James during that of 1609–10, and four before James during that of 1610–11. Middleton and Dekker's *The Roaring Girl* was printed in 1611 as lately played by them at the Fortune, and Field's *Amends for Ladies* (*c.* 1610–11) names 'Long Meg and the Ship' as in their repertory. Presumably their *Long Meg of Westminster* of 1595 still held the boards.[1] In 1608–9 they were at Shrewsbury and Saffron Walden, in 1609–10 at Shrewsbury and Hereford, in 1610–11 at Shrewsbury and Winchester.

They played at Court before James on 28 and 29 December 1611, giving on the second night *The Almanac*, and before Henry in February and Elizabeth in April 1612. On 1 October 1612 the lewd jigs, songs, and dances at the Fortune are recited in an order of the Middlesex justices as tending to promote breaches of the peace. One of these may have been the occasion on which an obscure actor, Garlick by name, made himself offensive to the more refined part of his audience.[2] On the following 7 November Henry died and on 7 December his players figured in his funeral procession.[3]

They found a new patron in the Elector Palatine, then in England, and on entering his service got a new patent, which bears date 11 January 1613 and closely follows in its terms that of 1606.[4] The house specified for them was again the Fortune, which they had no doubt continuously occupied since its opening in 1600. The players named were 'Thomas Downton, William Bird, Edward Juby, Samuell Rowle, Charles Massey, Humfrey Jeffs, Frank Grace, William Cartwright, Edward Colbrand, William Parr, William Stratford, Richard Gunnell, John Shanck, and Richard Price'. Possibly Price may be the Pryor of the 1610 list. Cartwright and Gunnell are new since that list, but Cartwright had been in *The Battle of Alcazar* and *1 Tamar Cham* plots of 1601 and 1602. These two must be supposed to have taken the places of Thomas Towne and Antony Jeffes. Thomas Towne had enjoyed an annuity of £12 out of Alleyn's manor of Dulwich from

---

[1] *A. for L.* II. i. In III. iv a drawer says, 'all the gentlewomen [from Bess Turnup's] went to see a play at the Fortune, and are not come in yet, and she believes they sup with the players'.

[2] Cf. ch. xv, s.v. Garlick.   [3] Nichols, *James*, ii. 495.

[4] *M. S. C.* i. 275, from *P. R. 10 Jac. I*, pt. 25; also from signet bill in Collier, i. 366, and Hazlitt, *E. D. S.* 44. Greg (*Henslowe*, ii. 263) notes copies in *Addl. MS.* 24502, f. 60ᵛ, and *Lincoln's Inn MS.* clviii.

28 October 1608 to 15 January 1612, but on 5 November 1612
'widow Towne' is mentioned,[1] and further evidence of his
death is supplied by a letter from Charles Massey to Alleyn,
not dated, but from internal evidence written not very long
after the prince's death, to which reference is made. Massey
is in debt and wants £50. He offers two things as security.
One is 'that lyttell moete I have in the play hovsses';
from which it may be inferred that, like Downton, he had
obtained an interest in the Fortune, although what the
second house may have been can hardly be conjectured.
The other is his interest under 'the composisions betwene
ovre compenye that if any one give over with consent of
his fellowes, he is to receve three score and ten poundes
(Antony Jefes hath had so much) if any on dye his widow
or frendes whome he appoyntes it tow reseve fyfte poundes
(M^res Pavie and M^res Tovne hath had the lyke)'. In order
to be in a position to repay the loan at the end of the year
he undertakes to get Mr. Jube to reserve 'my gallery mony
and my quarter of the hovse mony' for the purpose, and
should it prove at the end of six months that this will be
insufficient, he will be prepared to surrender his whole share,
with the exception of 13s. 4d. a week for household expenses.[2]
From this letter it may also be gathered that Antony Jeffes
had retired, and apparently that Pavy, whose name is found
in the plot of 2 Fortune's Tennis, which I assign to 1602–3,
had at some time become a sharer in the company. One
other player, originally in 1597 a hired man, had evidently
reached some prominence between that date and 1614.
William Fennor, in the course of a rhyming controversy with
John Taylor, makes the following boast of his histrionic talent:

> And let me tell thee this to calme thy rage,
> I chaleng'd Kendall on the Fortune stage ;
> And he did promise 'fore an audience,
> For to oppose me. Note the accidence :
> I set up bills, the people throngd apace,
> With full intention to disgrace, or grace ;
> The house was full, the trumpets twice had sounded,
> And though he came not, I was not confounded,
> But stept upon the stage, and told them this,
> My aduerse would not come : not one did hisse,
> But flung me theames : I then *extempore*
> Did blot his name from out their memorie,
> And pleasd them all, in spight of one to braue me,
> Witnesse the ringing plaudits that they gaue me.[3]

[1] *Henslowe Papers*, 106.   [2] Ibid. 64.
[3] *Fennor's Defence, or I am Your First Man* (Taylor's *Works*, 1630,

As the Elector Palatine's men the company played at Court during the winter of 1613–14, twice before James and once before Charles. They were amongst the companies which performed irregularly in the Lent of 1615, and Humphrey Jeffes and Thomas Downton were summoned before the Privy Council to account for their misdoing. One of the irregular licences condemned by the Lord Chamberlain on 16 July 1616 was an exemplification of the patent of 1613, taken out by Charles Marshall, Humphrey Jeffes, and William Parr for provincial purposes.

xx. THE LORD CHAMBERLAIN'S (LORD HUNSDON'S) AND KING'S MEN

Henry Carey, s. of William Carey and Mary, sister of Anne Boleyn ; *nat. c.* 1524 ; cr. 1st Lord Hunsdon, 13 Jan. 1559 ; m. Anne, d. of Sir Thomas Morgan ; Warden of East Marches and Governor of Berwick, Aug. 1568 ; Lord Chamberlain, 4 July 1585 ; lived at Hunsdon House, Herts., and Somerset House, London ; *ob.* 22 July 1596.

George Carey, s. of Henry, 1st Lord Hunsdon ; *nat.* 1547 ; Kt. 18 May 1570 ; m. Elizabeth, d. of Sir John Spencer of Althorp ; Captain-General of Isle of Wight, 1582 ; succ. as 2nd Baron, 22 July 1596 ; Lord Chamberlain, 17 Mar. 1597 ; lived at Carisbrooke Castle, Hunsdon House, Drayton, and Blackfriars ; *ob.* 9 Sept. 1603.

A company of Lord Hunsdon's men was at Leicester in the last three months of 1564, at Norwich and Maldon in 1564–5, at Plymouth before Michaelmas in 1565, at Canterbury in the autumn of 1565, at Gloucester and Maldon in 1565–6, at Bristol in July 1566, and at Canterbury in the spring of 1567. Another makes its appearance at Ludlow on 13 July 1581, and at Doncaster in 1582. In the winter Lord Hunsdon was apparently deputy for the Earl of Sussex as Lord Chamberlain, and took occasion to bring his men to Court, where they acted *Beauty and Housewifery* on 27 December 1582. They did not again appear at Court, but when plays were temporarily suppressed on 14 June 1584 the owner of the Theatre, presumably James Burbadge, made a claim to be Lord Hunsdon's man. Meanwhile ' my L. Hunsdouns and my Lords Morleis players being bothe of one companye ' are recorded at Bristol in March 1583, and Lord

ed. *Spenser Soc.* 314). The 1659 print of the *Blind Beggar of Bethnal Green* has at l. 2177, ' Enter . . . Captain Westford, Sill Clark '. The title-page professes to give the play as acted by the Prince's men, but whether Clark was an actor of 1603–12 or not must remain doubtful.

Hunsdon's alone at Norwich in 1582–3, Bath in June 1583, and Exeter in July 1583. Hunsdon became Lord Chamberlain on 4 July 1585. Between October and December of that year, a visit was paid to Leicester by ' the Lord Chamberlens and the Lord Admiralls players ', and on 6 January 1586 ' the servants of the lo: Admirall and the lo: Chamberlaine ' gave a play at Court. These entries suggest an amalgamation of Hunsdon's men with those of Lord Admiral Howard, both of whom had perhaps been weakened by the formation of the Queen's men in 1583. But if so, it was only a partial or temporary one, for while the Admiral's men established themselves in London, the Chamberlain's are traceable in the provinces, at Coventry in 1585–6, at Saffron Walden in 1587–8, and at Maidstone in 1589–90.

An interval of four or five years renders improbable any continuity between this company and the famous Lord Chamberlain's company, which first emerged on the resorting of the plague-stricken mimes in 1594, passed under royal patronage in 1603, and prolonged an existence illumined by the genius of Shakespeare, Ben Jonson, Beaumont and Fletcher, Massinger and Shirley, until the closing of the theatres in 1642. The first notice of the new organization is in June 1594, when ' my Lord Admeralle men and my Lorde Chamberlen men ' played from the 3rd to the 13th of the month, either in combination or separately on allotted days, for Henslowe at Newington Butts.[1] Some of the plays given during this period can be traced to the subsequent repertory of the Admiral's men ; others, which cannot, may be assigned to the Chamberlain's. They are *Hester and Ahasuerus, Titus Andronicus, Hamlet*, and *Taming of A Shrew*, which, although so described, may of course have been really the *Taming of The Shrew*, Shakespeare's adaptation of the older play entered in the Stationers' Register on the previous 2 May. It is ingeniously, and I think rightly, inferred from a line drawn in Henslowe's account after 13 June, that from that date all the performances recorded are by the Admiral's men, probably at the Rose, and that his relations with the Chamberlain's men had ceased. The company is found at Marlborough about September, and on 8 October Lord Hunsdon wrote to the Lord Mayor, asking permission for ' my nowe companie ' to continue an occupation of the Cross Keys,[2] on which it seems to have already entered.

[1] Henslowe, i. 17 ; cf. p. 140.
[2] Cf. App. D, No. ci. It is not ' my newe companie ', as it is sometimes misprinted. But I do not think that either term can be interpreted as showing that the company had or had not a corporate existence before

Henceforward the company was regularly established in London, took the lead annually at Court, and except for brief periods of inhibition in 1596, 1597, and possibly 1601, does not appear to have travelled during the remainder of Elizabeth's reign. Whether Hunsdon's men got the Cross Keys for the winter or not, they probably had from the beginning the use of the Theatre for the summer seasons, for Richard Burbage, the son of the owner, was one of their leading members, and on 15 March 1595 appears as joint payee with William Kempe and William Shakespeare for two plays given at Court on 26 and 28 December 1594. These plays cannot be identified, but Shakespeare's *Love's Labour's Lost* and *Romeo and Juliet* may well have been produced this winter.[1] Most likely the date 28 December was entered in the payment warrant by mistake for 27 December, for the Admiral's men are also recorded as playing at Court on 28 December, and on the same night ' a company of base and common fellows ', with whom one is bound to identify the Chamberlain's men, played ' a Comedy of Errors ' as part of the Christmas revels of the Prince of Purpoole at Gray's Inn.[2] There seems to be some echo of *Romeo and Juliet* in the Pyramus and Thisbe interlude of *A Midsummer-Night's Dream*, which may very well have been given at Greenwich or Burghley House for the wedding of William Stanley, Earl of Derby, and Elizabeth Vere, daughter of the Earl of Oxford, on 26 January 1595. Another possible occasion for the production, however, is the wedding of Elizabeth, daughter of Sir George Carey and grand-daughter of Lord Hunsdon, to Thomas, son of Henry Lord Berkeley on 19 February 1596. This took place at Blackfriars, presumably in Sir George Carey's house there.[3]

To 1595 or thereabouts I also assign Shakespeare's *Two Gentlemen of Verona* and *King John* and *Richard II*.[4] The company played at Court on 26, 27, and 28 December 1595

it came under Hunsdon's patronage. The use which the company ' have byn accustomed ' to make of the inn is only related to ' this winter time '.

[1] The dates here assigned to Shakespeare's plays are mainly based on the conclusions of my article on Shakespeare in the *Encyclopaedia Britannica*.

[2] Cf. ch. xxiv, s.v. *Gesta Grayorum* and *M. L. R.* ii. 11.

[3] Cf. my paper on *The Occasion of A Midsummer-Night's Dream* in *Shakespeare Homage*, 154, and App. A.

[4] I have recently found confirmation of the date for *Rich. II* in a letter from Sir Edward Hoby inviting Sir R. Cecil to his house in Canon Row on 9 Dec. 1595, ' where, as late as shall please you, a gate for your supper shall be open, and K. Richard present himself to your view ' (*Hatfield MSS.* v. 487).

and 6 January and 22 February 1596. In the warrant for
their fees, dated on 21 December 1596, and made payable
to John Heminges and George Bryan, they are described as
'servauntes to the late Lord Chamberlayne and now servauntes to the Lorde Hunsdon'. It is clear that, when the
first Lord Hunsdon died on 22 July 1596, the players had
been retained by his son and heir, Sir George Carey. The
Lord Chamberlainship passed to Lord Cobham ; but he died
on 5 March 1597, and on 17 March the post was given to the
second Lord Hunsdon. The company, then, was properly
known as Lord Hunsdon's men from 22 July 1596 to 17 March
1597 ; before and after that period it was the Lord Chamberlain's men.

To 1596 I assign Shakespeare's *Merchant of Venice*. Evidence of the occupation of the Theatre about this time by
the company is to be found in Lodge's allusion to a revival
of *Hamlet* there, for this play is not likely to have been in
other hands.[1] It is not an unreasonable conjecture that
James Burbadge destined to their use the playhouse in the
Blackfriars, which he purchased in February, and had
converted for 'publique' use by November of this year.
If so, he and they were disappointed, for a petition of the
inhabitants, amongst the signatories to an alleged copy of
which Lord Hunsdon himself is somewhat oddly found, led
to an intervention of the Privy Council, who forbade plays
to be given within the liberty.[2] At this time also the Corporation seem to have succeeded in finally and permanently
expelling the players from the City inns which had long been
their head-quarters, and Nashe connects this persecution
with the loss of 'their old Lord', by whom he doubtless
means Henry Lord Hunsdon. It is possible that plays
were inhibited altogether during the summer of 1596, although
no formal order to that effect is preserved, for Hunsdon's went
to Faversham, and Nashe himself was disappointed of 'an after
harvest I expected by writing for the stage and for the presse'.[3]

In the following winter the company played at Court on

[1] T. Lodge, *Wits Miserie* (S. R. 5 May 1596), 56, ' the Visard of yᵉ
ghost which cried so miserably at yᵉ Theator, like an oister wife, Hamlet,
revenge '.

[2] Cf. ch. xvii (Blackfriars). There is a slight doubt as to the authenticity
of the text of the petition, which the inclusion of Lord Hunsdon's name
can only emphasize. But the fact of the petition and its result are vouched
for by a City document of later date. The counter-petition of the players
published by Collier, i. 288, in which they are misdescribed as the Lord
Chamberlain's men, is a forgery. The names given are those of Pope,
Burbadge, Heminges, Phillips, Shakespeare, Kempe, Sly, and Tooley.
There is nothing to connect Tooley with the company before 1605.

[3] Cf. App. D, No. cvi.

26 and 27 December 1596 and on 1 and 6 January and 6 and
8 February 1597. Their payees, for this and for the next two
years, were Thomas Pope and John Heminge. In 1597 began
the printing of plays written by Shakespeare for this company,
with a 'bad' quarto of *Romeo and Juliet*, bearing on its
title-page the name of Lord Hunsdon's men and 'good'
quartos of *Richard II* and *Richard III*, bearing that of the
Lord Chamberlain's.[1] From the text of *Richard II* was
omitted the deposition scene, which did not appear in print
until after the death of Elizabeth. The only Shakespearian
productions that can be plausibly ascribed to this year are
those of the two parts of *Henry IV*. The presentation of
Sir John Oldcastle in the original versions of these seems
to have led to a protest, and the character was renamed
Sir John Falstaff. It is not improbable that the offence taken
was by Lord Chamberlain Cobham, whose ancestress, Joan
Lady Cobham, Oldcastle had married.[2] It is impossible to
say whether either this scandal or any possible interpretation
of disloyalty put upon *Richard II* contributed to the inhibition
of plays on 28 July, of which the main exciting cause was
certainly the performance of *The Isle of Dogs* at the Swan
on the Bankside.[3] For the second time since their formation
in 1594, the company had to travel. They are traceable at Rye in August, at Dover between 3 and 20 September, at Marlborough, Faversham, and Bath during 1596–7,
and at Bristol about 29 September. This inhibition was
removed early in October. There is some reason to believe
that, when the Chamberlain's men resumed playing, it was
not at the Theatre, as to the renewal of the lease of which
the Burbadges were disputing with their ground landlord,
but at the Curtain. Marston, in one and the same passage
of his *Scourge of Villainy*, entered in the Stationers' Register
on 8 September 1598, alludes to the acting of *Romeo and
Juliet* and to 'Curtaine plaudeties', while almost simultaneously Edward Guilpin in his *Skialetheia*, entered on
15 September, speaks of 'the unfrequented Theater'. The
transfer may, however, not have taken place until 1598.[4]
    The company played at Court on 26 December 1597 and

---

[1] For the distinction between 'bad' and 'good' quartos, cf. ch. xxii.
[2] R. James (*c.* 1625), in the dedication to his manuscript *Legend of Sir
John Oldcastle* (quoted by Ingleby, *Shakespeare's Centurie of Praise*, 165),
says, 'offence beinge worthily taken by Personages descended from his
title'.
[3] Raleigh wrote to R. Cecil on 6 July 1597 that Essex was 'wonderful
merry at your conceit of Richard II' (Edwardes, ii. 169) ; for the later
history of the play, *vide infra*.
[4] Cf. ch. xvi (Curtain).

on 1 and 6 January and 26 February 1598.   It is conceivable
that one of these plays may have been a revised version of
Love's Labour's Lost, which was printed as ' newly corrected
and augmented ' and ' as it was presented before her Highnes
this last Christmas ' in 1598.   On the other hand, it is also
possible that this print may have been intended to replace
an earlier ' bad ' quarto, not now preserved, and if so, the
reference to the representation may have been carried on from
the earlier title-page.   In 1598 were also printed *1 Henry IV*,
and the anonymous *Mucedorus*, which may have already
belonged to the Chamberlain's repertory, as it was certainly
revised for them about 1610.   *The Merchant of Venice* was
entered in the Stationers' Register on 22 July, but with
a proviso that it must not be printed ' without lycence first
had from the Right honorable the lord chamberlen '.   On
7 September 1598 was entered in the Stationers' Register
the *Palladis Tamia* of Francis Meres, with its list of Shakespeare's plays up to date, including the mysterious *Love's
Labours Won*, which I incline to identify with the *Taming
of the Shrew*.[1]   The earliest play not mentioned by Meres is
probably *Much Ado about Nothing*, which may belong to
1598 itself.   Another production of this year was Jonson's
Every Man In his Humour, which was still a new play
about 20 September, when an Almain in the audience lost
300 crowns.   Possibly John Aubrey has this period in mind
when he says that Jonson ' acted and wrote, but both ill,
at the Green Curtaine, a kind of nursery or obscure play-
house, somewhere in the suburbes, I thinke towardes Shoreditch or Clarkenwell '.[2]   Jonson, however, was in prison
soon after the production of the play for the manslaughter
of Gabriel Spencer on 22 September in Hoxton Fields, and
there is no other evidence that he ever acted with the Chamberlain's men.   His own name is not in the list of the original
' principall Comoedians ' affixed to the text of *Every Man In
his Humour* in the folio of 1616.   This is of great value, as
being the earliest extant list of the company.   The ten names
given are :

Will. Shakespeare.	Ric. Burbage.
Aug. Philips.	Joh. Hemings.
Hen. Condel.	Tho. Pope.
Will. Slye.	Chr. Beeston.
Will. Kempe.	Joh. Duke.

[1] App. C, No. lii.
[2] Aubrey, ii. 12. The same writer is obviously confused when he says,
on the authority of Sir Edward Shirburn, that Jonson ' killed Mr Marlow
the poet, on Bunhill, comeing from the Green-Curtain play-house '.

It must not, of course, be assumed, either that the list is in itself quite complete, or that there had been no changes amongst the Chamberlain's men between 1594 and 1598; but as those named include five out of the six payees for that period, they may perhaps be taken, with the sixth payee, George Bryan, who does not re-appear after 1596, and was by 1603 an ordinary groom of the Chamber of the royal Household, as fairly representing the original constitution of the company.[1]   And an inference to its origin at once becomes possible, for of these eleven men five (Kempe, Pope, Heminges, Phillips, and Bryan) formed, with Edward Alleyn, the company of Lord Strange's men to whom Privy Council letters of assistance were granted in 1593, and at least six (Pope, Phillips, Bryan, Burbadge, Duke, and Sly) are to be found in the cast of 2 Seven Deadly Sins as performed by Strange's or the Admiral's or the two together about 1590–1. It will be remembered that the Strange's company of 1593, known as the Earl of Derby's after 25 September 1593, was apparently formed by a combination of the earlier Strange's and Admiral's men somewhere near the time of this performance, if not earlier, and that its composite character never wholly disappeared, Alleyn in particular, who was its leading member, retaining his personal status as an Admiral's man. It seems clear that in 1594 the combination broke up, that Alleyn became the nucleus of a new Admiral's company at the Rose, and that the group with whom he had been travelling took fresh service with the Lord Chamberlain. It is not, I think, quite accurate to treat this transaction as a mere continuance of Lord Derby's men under the style of Lord Chamberlain's, entailing no reconstruction other than a change of patron following upon Lord Derby's death on 16 April 1594. On the one hand a Derby's company continued in existence, and is traceable under the sixth earl from 1594 to 1617. On the other hand, while we do not know what business reconstruction there may have been, a very fundamental change is involved in the replacement of Alleyn as principal actor by Richard Burbadge, who is not at all likely to have played with Strange's men after the break between the Admiral's and his father at the Theatre in 1591. Except for Alleyn, all the more important members of the company, as it existed in 1593, seem to have been included

---

[1] Cf. ch. x. There is no reason to suppose that the Richard Hoope, Wm Blackwage, Rafe Raye, and Wm Ferney, to whom Henslowe lent money as ' my lord chamberlenes men ' in 1595 (Henslowe, i. 5, 6), were actors. In fact Raye was a ' man ' of Hunsdon's before the company was in existence at all (Henslowe, ii. 305).

in the transfer to Lord Hunsdon. It is, however, little more than conjecture that finds Henry Condell and Christopher Beeston in the ' Harry ' and ' Kitt ', or Alexander Cooke, Nicholas Tooley, and Robert Gough, who were numbered amongst the King's men at a later date, in the ' Saunder ', ' Nick ', and ' R. Go.' of the 2 *Seven Deadly Sins* plot. Alleyn's correspondence of 1593 adds Richard Cowley to the list of Lord Strange's men, and, as we shall find him acting as a payee for the Chamberlain's men in 1601, he may have been one of them from the beginning. In any case he had joined them by 1598, as the stage-directions of *Much Ado about Nothing* show that he played Verges to Kempe's Dogberry.[1]

There is, of course, one conspicuous Chamberlain's man who is not discoverable either in the Privy Council letter of 1593 or in the 2 *Seven Deadly Sins* of 1590–1. Even the audacity of Mr. Fleay has not attempted to identify the ' Will ' of the plot with Will Shakespeare. Some relations, if only as author, Shakespeare must have had with Lord Strange's men, when they produced *1 Henry VI* on 3 March 1592, and Greene's satire of him as a 'Shake-scene' in the same year must indicate that he was an actor as well as an author.[2] He may have stood aside altogether during the period of the provincial tours, and devoted himself to poetry, and perhaps, although this is very conjectural, to travel abroad. Or he may, as I have already suggested, have joined Lord Pembroke's men (q.v.), whom I suspect to have been an off-shoot for provincial purposes of the Strange's combination, and have passed from them to Lord Sussex's, ultimately rejoining his old fellows in 1594. The possibility of identifying certain minor members of the Chamberlain's company is also affected by this somewhat obscure problem of Pembroke's men. The most obvious of these is John Sincler or Sincklo, who was in the cast of 2 *Seven Deadly Sins* as played by the Admiral's or Strange's about 1590–1, and must have ultimately joined the Chamberlain's, as his name occurs in a stage-direction to Q_1 of 2 *Henry IV* (1600), and in the induction to *The Malcontent* (1604). It also occurs in stage-directions to *3 Henry VI* and the *Taming of The Shrew* in the Folio of 1623.[3] These both happen to be plays which passed through the hands of Pembroke's, and the inference may be that Sincler

---

[1] The order of the Shakespearian actors named in the 1623 Folio, and the omission of the names of Duke and Beeston, rather suggests that these two were hired men, and that there were ten original sharers, Shakespeare, Burbadge, Heminges, Phillips, Kempe, Pope, Bryan, Condell, Sly, and Cowley.

[2] App. C. No. xlviii.   [3] Cf. ch. xxii.

had also passed through this company. But this is far from
being conclusive.   It is the revised and not the unrevised
texts that yield the name, and although I think it likely,
on stylistic grounds, that the revision of *3 Henry VI* was
done for Pembroke's (q.v.), it is probable from the reference
in *Henry V*, epil. 12, to the loss of France and the civil wars,
'which oft our stage hath shown', that the play was revived
by the Chamberlain's, and it may have been in such a revival
that Sincler took part.   As to the *Shrew*, it is impossible
to say whether Shakespeare's work upon it was before or
after its transfer to the Chamberlain's.   In any case the
Chamberlain's were playing it in some form on 13 June 1594,
so that here again the appearance of Sincler's name cannot
ear-mark him as Pembroke's. We can now go a step farther.
The stage-directions to *3 Henry VI* contain not only Sincler's
name, but those of a certain 'Gabriel' and a certain 'Humfrey', not common Elizabethan names even separately, and
certainly suggesting, when found in combination, the Gabriel
Spencer and Humphrey Jeffes, who were fellows of the
Admiral's in 1597.   Now Spencer, and very likely also Jeffes,
had come from Pembroke's, the short-lived Pembroke's of
1597 at the Swan.   Had they been Pembroke's men ever
since 1593 ?   If so, it would be difficult to resist the conclusion
that the performance which brought their names into the
text of *3 Henry VI*, and with theirs John Sincler's, was one
by Pembroke's about that date.   The obstacle is that there
is no known evidence, in provincial records or elsewhere,
for any continuous existence of Pembroke's between 1593 and
1597.   Pending the discovery of any such evidence, it seems
better to assume that Sincler, Spencer, and Jeffes were all
Chamberlain's men before 1597, and that it was from a combination of discontented elements in that company and in the
Admiral's that the Pembroke's of the Swan arose.   If so,
the rest of the Pembroke's men not traceable as coming
from the Admiral's, namely Robert Shaw, William Bird *alias*
Borne, and probably Anthony Jeffes, may also have come
from the Chamberlain's ; and such an origin might explain
the suit with Thomas Pope in which Bird was entangled
in 1598.[1]   Two other minor actors in the company about
1597 were probably Harvey and Rossill, whose names appear
to have got into the text of *1 Henry IV* in place of those
of Bardolph and Peto, whom they represented.[2]   The list
of actors in Shakespeare's plays given by the editors of
the First Folio includes Samuel Crosse, of whom nothing

---

[1] Henslowe, i. 72.   [2] Cf. ch. xxii.

more is known except that he was of an early generation.
As the list in the Folio appears to be limited to Chamberlain's
and King's men, excluding for example Alleyn, who certainly
acted in Shakespearian plays, e.g. *1 Henry VI*, it may be
that Crosse was for a short time a member of the company
soon after 1594.

It is hardly possible to carry the analysis of origins any
further with profit, or to assume that the groups which
segregated themselves from the Strange-Admiral's combination in 1594 bore any close correspondence to the respective
contributions of Strange's and the Admiral's to that combination in 1589 or 1590. The only name that can be connected
with Strange's men before 1588 is John Symons and neither
he nor George Attewell, their payee in 1591, became a Chamberlain's man. Hypotheses have been framed, mainly in the hope
of affiliating Shakespeare to Lord Leicester's men, who are
supposed to have carried him away from Stratford-on-
Avon when they visited it in 1586-7, and ultimately to have
become Lord Strange's men.[1] So far as Shakespeare is concerned, the first record of him on the boards is in 1592, and the
interval since his hegira from Stratford may have been quite
otherwise spent. The proof of continuity between Leicester's
men and Strange's altogether fails, since the latter made their
appearance a decade before the former came to an end.
The only member of the Lord Chamberlain's company of
1594 who can be traced to Leicester's service was Kempe,
and he had left Leicester's men by the summer of 1586
and was in Denmark. With him were Bryan and Pope, who
afterwards spent a year in Germany, and may have joined
either Strange's or the Admiral's on their return. The only
other Chamberlain's man, who can be assigned to an earlier
company than Strange's, is Heminges, who was probably
at some time a Queen's man.

The Chamberlain's men evidently started business in 1594
with something of a repertory derived by inheritance or purchase from antecedent companies. Our knowledge of this is
mainly confined to plays with which Shakespeare was concerned as author or reviser. They certainly did not get all
the plays produced by Strange's men at the Rose during 1592
and 1593. Some of these were Henslowe's property; others
passed with Alleyn to the Admiral's men. But they got
The Jealous Comedy, if I am right in identifying this with
The Comedy of Errors. They probably got *1 Henry VI*, for
although the appearance of a Shakespearian play in the 1623

---

[1] Malone, *Variorum*, ii. 166 ; Fleay, *L. and W.* 8.

Folio is not perhaps, in view of the composition of the 1647
'Beaumont and Fletcher' Folio, absolute proof that the
King's men possessed the copy, their stage had often shown
both the loss of France and the bleeding of England before
Henry V was produced in 1599.[1] And they got *Titus and
Vespasian*, as revised, after passing through the hands of
Pembroke's men, for production by Sussex's under the title
of *Titus Andronicus*. Three other of Pembroke's men's plays
came to them, *The Taming of A Shrew* and *2 and 3 Henry VI*,
and probably *Hamlet* belongs to the same group. It is of
course only a guess of mine that these also went with Shakespeare to Sussex's men and came thence with him. *Titus
Andronicus* and *A Shrew*, indeed, became available in print
during 1594, but not *Hamlet*, and not *Henry VI*, except in
the obsolete version called *The Contention of York and Lancaster*. I think Shakespeare must also have brought
Richard III and possibly an early version of *Henry VIII*,
and that one or other of these had already been played by
Sussex's as *Buckingham*. Of the *provenance* of *Hester and
Ahasuerus* nothing can be said. It is not necessary to suppose
that the Chamberlain's acquired any plays from the stock
of the Queen's men. It is true that Shakespeare subsequently
made some use of *The Troublesome Reign of King John*,
The Famous Victories of Henry V, and *King Leire*, but these
were all in print before he needed them.[2] *Alphonsus, Emperor
of Germany*, published in 1654 as a play of the King's
men at the Blackfriars is believed by some to be an early
play, possibly by Peele, and if so, may belong to the repertory
of 1594.

I now return to the chronicle of the Chamberlain's men
from 1598 onwards. The restriction of the London companies
by the action of the Privy Council to two had left them in
direct rivalry with the Admiral's at the Rose. Disputes broke
out. Henslowe made a loan to William Bird of the Admiral's
on 30 August 1598 to follow a ' sewt agenste Thomas Poope ',
and another to Thomas Downton on 30 January 1599, ' to
descarge Thomas Dickers [Dekker] from the areaste of my
lord chamberlens men '.[3] The company played at Court on
26 December 1598 and 1 January and 20 February 1599.
During this winter they undertook the enterprise of finding
a new head-quarters on the Bankside. The disputes between

---

[1] *Hen. V*, epil. 12.
[2] That the *Famous Victories* was reprinted in 1617 as a King's men's
play proves nothing. It was to pass as *Henry V* ; obviously the King's
men never acted it, *Henry V* being in existence.
[3] Henslowe, i. 72, 101.

landlord and tenants as to the lease of the Theatre had reached
a crisis, and in December or January the Burbadges removed
the timber of the house across the Thames, to serve as material
for the construction of the Globe. The lease of the new site
was signed on 21 February 1599. Under it one moiety of the
interest was retained by Richard Burbadge and his brother
Cuthbert, who was not himself an actor; the other was
assigned to Shakespeare, Pope, Phillips, Heminges, and
Kempe.[1] Shortly afterwards Kempe made over his share to
the other four. Presumably he now quitted the company,
having first, as a stage-direction shows, played Peter in the
revised version of *Romeo and Juliet* printed in 1599. His
place was probably taken by Robert Armin, formerly of
Lord Chandos's men, who describes himself in two successive
issues of his *Fool upon Fool* (1600 and 1605), first as ' clonnico
del Curtanio', and then as 'clonnico del Mondo', and who had
therefore probably joined the Chamberlain's men before their
actual transfer to the Globe. As the Theatre had to be built,
this is not likely to have taken place until the autumn of
1599, and it must therefore remain doubtful which house was
the ' wooden O ' of *Henry V*, produced during the absence
of Essex in Ireland between 27 March and 28 September
1599. It was, however, certainly at the Globe that Thomas
Platter saw *Julius Caesar* on 21 September.[2] 'This fair-
filled Globe ', too, is named in the epilogue to Jonson's
Every Man Out of his Humour, which is ascribed in the Folio
of 1606 to 1599, although if this be correct, an apparent
allusion to Kempe's journey to Norwich in the spring of
1600 must, on the assumption that it is a real allusion, be an
interpolation. The ' principall Comoedians ' in this play were
Burbadge, Heminges, Phillips, Condell, Sly, and Pope.
Four of the 1598 names are missing. Shakespeare evidently
stood aside. Kempe had gone. Beeston and Duke may have
gone also, although it is only a conjecture of Mr. Fleay's
that they and Kempe now seceded to Pembroke's men at
the Rose, and they are not definitely heard of again until
they are found with Worcester's men in August 1602.[3]
Mr. Fleay thinks that another Worcester's man, Robert
Pallant, had accompanied them ; but, although Pallant was
with Strange's or the Admiral's about 1590, there is no

---

[1] For further details, cf. ch. xvi (Globe).
[2] Cf. ch. xvi, introd.
[3] Fleay, 138 ; cf. Murray, ii. 125 ; Greg, *Henslowe*, ii. 108. A loan of
21 Sept. 1600 by Henslowe (i. 132) to Duke is only slight evidence, and
the fact that Anne's men chose to revive the already printed *Edward II*,
once a Pembroke's play, even slighter.

evidence that he was ever a Chamberlain's man. Conceivably he may have joined the King's men about 1619, but that is another matter.[1] About November 1599 was published *A Warning for Fair Women*, which belonged to the company.

The Court plays called for from the Chamberlain's men during the following winter were on 26 December 1599 and on 6 January and 3 February 1600. Heminges was sole payee, and occupied the same position in every subsequent year, up to and beyond 1616, except in 1600–1, when Richard Cowley was associated with him, and for a special payment made to Burbadge in 1604. On 6 March 1600 the company had an opportunity of rendering direct service to their patron Lord Hunsdon, by playing *Henry IV*, still oddly called *Sir John Oldcastle*, after a dinner which he gave to the Flemish ambassador, Ludovic Verreyken, presumably at his house in the Blackfriars.[2] To 1600 I assign Shakespeare's *Merry Wives of Windsor*, not improbably prepared for performance, with the aid of the boys of Windsor Chapel, at the Garter Feast on 23 April, and also *As You Like It*. This was a year of some activity among the publishers and, as in 1598, the company had to take steps to protect their interests. In May John Roberts was prevented from printing their moral of *Cloth Breeches and Velvet Hose*, until he could bring proper authority, and in August a note was made in the Stationers' Register to stay the printing of *As You Like It*, *Henry V*, and *Much Ado about Nothing*.[3] The last two of these, but not the first, were in fact printed during the year, and so were *A Midsummer-Night's Dream*, *The Merchant of Venice*, *2 Henry IV*, *Every Man Out of his Humour*, and *An Alarum for London*, all plays belonging to the company.

The Chamberlain's men played at Court on 26 December 1600 and on 6 January and 24 February 1601. Shortly before this last performance, they had been involved in one of the tragedies of history. This was the abortive *coup d'état* of 8 February 1601 in which the Earl of Essex, smarting under the disgrace which his failure in Ireland had brought upon him, attempted to secure his position and get rid of Sir Walter Raleigh and other enemies by taking forcible possession of the person of Elizabeth and the palace of Whitehall. Some of his followers seem to have conceived the idea of predisposing the mind of the populace to their cause by a dramatic representation of the dangers of evil counsellors and the possible remedy of a deposition, as illustrated in the case of Elizabeth's predecessor Richard II, in whom for some

---

[1] Cf. ch. xv.   [2] Cf. ch. vii.   [3] Cf. ch. xxii.

obscure reason the political thought of the time was fond of finding an analogue to the Queen. Saturday, 7 February, the day before the outbreak, was chosen for the performance, and the players applied to were the Chamberlain's. A deposition by Augustine Phillips, taken before Chief Justice Popham and Justice Fenner during the subsequent inquiries, records the transaction.[1]

' The Examination of Augustine Phillips, servant unto the L. Chamberlain and one of his players, taken the xviij[th] of February, 1600, upon his oath.

' He saith that on Friday last was sennight or Thursday Sir Charles Percy Sir Josceline Percy and the Lord Mounteagle with some three more spoke to some of the players in the presence of this Examinate to have the play of the deposing and killing of King Richard the Second to be played the Saturday next, promising to get them xl*s.* more than their ordinary to play it. Where this Examinate and his fellows were determined to have played some other play, holding that play of King Richard to be so old and so long out of use that they should have small or no company at it. But at their request this Examinate and his fellows were content to play it the Saturday and had their xl*s* more than their ordinary for it, and so played it accordingly.'

The fact that Phillips speaks of the play as old and long out of use, which becomes in the narrative of Camden ' exoleta tragoedia ', hardly justifies the suggestion that it was something earlier than Shakespeare's *Richard II*. This, if produced in 1596, may well have been off the boards by 1601.

A good deal of misunderstanding has gathered round the connexion of the Chamberlain's men with this affair. Mr. Fleay is responsible for the theory that they fell into disgrace, had to travel, and were excluded from the Court festivities of the following Christmas.[2] As a matter of fact they played four times during that winter. This Mr. Fleay did not know, as he only had before him Cunningham's incomplete extracts from the accounts of the Treasurer of the Chamber. But he ought to have noticed that their last performance for 1600-1 was itself some days later than the examination of Augustine Phillips. Nor is any evidence that the company travelled in 1601 forthcoming from the provincial archives. Mr. Fleay's identification of them with Laurence Fletcher's

---

[1] *S. P. D. Eliz.* cclxxviii. 72, 78, 85. Accounts consistent with this are given in depositions of Sir W. Constable and Sir Gilly Meyrick (ibid.), Camden, *Annales*, 867, Cobbett, *State Trials*, i. 1445, and Bacon, *A Declaration of the Practices and Treasons attempted and committed by Robert late Earl of Essex and his Complices* (1601 ; *Works*, ix. 289).

[2] Fleay, 123, 136 ; cf. *M. L. R.* ii. 12.

Scottish company of that year merely rests upon the presence of Fletcher's name in the patent of 1603, and this will not bear the strain of the argument.[1] Thus remains, however, the possibly autobiographical passage in *Hamlet*, ii. 2. 346, which assigns an ' inhibition by the means of the late innovation ' as a cause of the travelling of players to Elsinore. The date of *Hamlet* may well be 1601, since the same passage refers to the theatrical competition set up by the establishment of boy companies at St. Paul's in 1599 and at the Chapel Royal in 1600. But it must be borne in mind that this competition is the only reason given for the travelling in the 1603 edition of the play. In the 1604 edition the only reason is the inhibition, while in the text of the 1623 Folio both reasons stand somewhat inconsistently side by side.[2] No doubt the text of 1603 is an imperfect piratical reprint. On the other hand that of 1604 almost certainly represents a revised version of the play, and the ' inhibition ' cited, if it had an historical existence at all, may be that of 1603, during which certainly the company travelled. I suppose that ' innovation ' might mean the accession of a new sovereign, although it does not seem a very obvious term. But then it does not seem a very obvious term for a seditious rising either.[3] On the whole, there is no reason to suppose that any serious blame was attached to the Chamberlain's men for lending themselves to Sir Gilly Meyrick's intrigue. It is certainly absurd to suggest, as has been suggested, that the ' adorned creature ', whose ingratitude instigated the comparison between Elizabeth and Richard, was not Essex but Shakespeare.[4] At the same time the company may, of course, have been told to leave London for a few weeks. At some time, as the 1603 title-page tells us, they took *Hamlet* both to Oxford and to Cambridge, and it is at least tempting to find a reminiscence of the Cambridge visit in the scene from *2 Return from Parnassus* cited below. It is possible that

[1] Cf. ch. xiv (Scotland).   [2] For the texts cf. ch. xi.
[3] W. H. Griffin in *Academy* for 25 April 1896, suggests that the ' innovation ' of 1604 was the same as the ' noveltie ' of 1603, i.e. the setting up of child actors. But I am afraid that this leaves ' inhibition ' without a meaning.
[4] Nichols, *Eliz*. iii. 552, prints, perhaps from a manuscript of Lord De La Warr's (*Hist. MSS*. iv. 300), a note by W Lambarde of a conversation with the Queen on 4 Aug. 1601, ' Her Majestie fell upon the reign of King Richard II, saying, I am Richard II, know ye not that ? *W. L.* Such a wicked imagination was determined and attempted by a most unkind Gent. the most adorned creature that ever your Majestie made. *Her Majestie.* He that will forget God, will also forget his benefactors ; this tragedy was played 40^{tie} times in open streets and houses '. The performances here referred to must have been in 1596–7, not 1601.

Phillips and his fellows, and even their relation to the Essex crisis itself, may be glanced at in the satirical picture of the Roman actors in Jonson's *Poetaster*, produced by the Chapel boys in the course of 1601.[1] Certainly the play betrays its author's knowledge of a counter-attack which the Chamberlain's men were already preparing for him in Dekker's *Satiromastix*. This play, in which Dekker may have had some help from Marston, was entered in the Stationers' Register on 11 November 1601, and had probably been on the stage not long before. It is noteworthy that it was produced by the Paul's boys, as well as by the Chamberlain's men. It was actually published in 1602. Another play which may reasonably be assigned to 1601 is *Twelfth Night*.

In the following winter the company played at Court on 26 and 27 December 1601 and on 1 January and 14 February 1602. They also gave *Twelfth Night* at the Middle Temple feast on 2 February;[2] and I have very little doubt that it was they who furnished the play at which Elizabeth and her maids of honour were present in the Blackfriars after dining with Lord Hunsdon on 31 December.[3] The alleged production of *Othello* before the Queen when Sir Thomas Egerton entertained her at Harefield from 31 July to 2 August 1602 rests on a forgery by Collier.[4] It is possible that, as Professor Wallace conjectures, the play was on the capture of Stuhl Weissenburg, seen by the Duke of Stettin on 13 September 1602, may have been a Globe production.[5] *Sir Thomas Cromwell*, a play of unknown authorship belonging to the company, was published in the course of 1602, with an ascription on the title-page to W. S., and to this year I assign Shakespeare's *All's Well that Ends Well* and *Troilus and Cressida*. If so, the portrait of Ajax in the latter play cannot very well have been the ' purge ' administered by Shakespeare to Jonson, to which reference is made in *2 Return from Parnassus*. This is a Cambridge Christmas piece, probably of 1601–2, and in it Burbadge and Kempe are introduced as in search of scholars to write for them. Perhaps the Cambridge author did not know that Kempe had ceased to be the ' fellow ' of Burbadge and Shakespeare in 1599, and was at the time playing with Worcester's men at the Rose. It is, however, just possible that after returning from his continental tour and before throwing in his lot with Worcester's, he may have rejoined the Chamberlain's for a while, and may

---

[1] Cf. ch. xi.   [2] J. Manningham, *Diary*, 18.   [3] Cf. App. A.
[4] Collier, *New Particulars*, 57, and *Egerton Papers*, 343, ' 6 August 1602 Rewardes . . . x^{li} to Burbidges players for Othello '; cf Ingleby, 262
[5] Wallace, ii. 108 ; cf. p. 367.

have accompanied them to Cambridge, if they did travel in 1601.[1]

The last performances of the company before Elizabeth took place on 26 December 1602 and 2 February 1603, and on the following 24 March the Queen died. Playing immediately ceased in London. Strictly speaking, the Chamberlain's men must have again become Lord Hunsdon's men for a month or so, for the Household appointments naturally lapsed with the death of the sovereign, and Hunsdon, being in failing health, was relieved of his duties on 6 April. On 9 September he died.[2] The company, however, had already passed under royal patronage.

A contemporary panegyrist records the graciousness of James in 'taking to him the late Lord Chamberlaines servants, now the Kings acters'.[3] The appointment was by letters patent dated 19 May 1603, of which the text follows.[4]

Commissio specialis pro Laurencio Fletcher & Willelmo Shackespeare et aliis

Iames by the grace of god &c. To all Iustices, Maiors, Sheriffes, Constables, hedborowes, and other our Officers and louinge Subiectes greetinge. Knowe yee that Wee of our speciall grace, certeine knowledge, & mere motion haue licenced and aucthorized and by theise presentes doe licence and aucthorize theise our Servauntes Lawrence Fletcher, William Shakespeare, Richard Burbage, Augustyne Phillippes, Iohn Heninges, Henrie Condell, William Sly, Robert Armyn, Richard Cowly, and the rest of theire Assosiates freely to vse and exercise the Arte and faculty of playinge Comedies, Tragedies, histories, Enterludes, moralls, pastoralls, Stageplaies, and Suche others like as theie haue alreadie studied or hereafter shall vse or studie, aswell for the recreation of our lovinge Subiectes, as for our Solace and pleasure when wee shall thincke good to see them, duringe our pleasure. And the said Commedies, tragedies, histories, Enterludes, Morralles, Pastoralls, Stageplayes, and suche like to shewe and exercise publiquely to theire best Commoditie, when the infection of the plague shall decrease, aswell within theire nowe vsual howse called the Globe within our County of Surrey, as alsoe within anie towne halls or Moute halls or other conveniente places within the liberties and freedome of anie other Cittie, vniversitie, towne, or Boroughe whatsoever within our said Realmes and domynions. Willinge and Commaundinge you and everie of you, as you tender our pleasure, not onelie to permitt and suffer them herein

---

[1] Cf. ch. xv (Kempe). [2] Cf. ch. ii.
[3] G. Dugdale, *Time Triumphant* (1604), sig. B.
[4] Printed in *M. S. C.* i. 264, from *P. R. 1 Jac. I, pars* 2, *membr.* 4 ; also in Rymer, xvi. 505, and Halliwell, *Illustr.* 83. Halliwell also prints the practically identical texts of the Privy Signet Bill, dated 17 May, and the Privy Seal, dated 18 May. The former is also in Collier, i. 334, Hazlitt, 38, and Halliwell-Phillipps ii. 82.

without anie your lettes hindrances or molestacions during our said
pleasure, but alsoe to be aidinge and assistinge to them, yf anie wronge
be to them offered, And to allowe them such former Curtesies as hath
bene given to men of theire place and quallitie, and alsoe what further
favour you shall shewe to theise our Servauntes for our sake wee shall
take kindlie at your handes. In wytnesse whereof &c. witnesse
our selfe at Westminster the nyntenth day of May
per breve de priuato sigillo &c.

Of the nine players named, eight are recognizable as the
principal members of the Lord Chamberlain's company
as it stood at the end of Elizabeth's reign. Only Thomas
Pope is not included. He was near his end. He made his
will on 22 July 1603, and it was proved on 13 February 1604.
In it he names none of his fellows, unless Robert Gough,
who has a legacy, was already of the company ; his interest
in the house of the Globe passed to legatees and was thus
alienated from the company. Laurence Fletcher, on the other
hand, whose name heads the list in the patent, is not discernible as a Chamberlain's man. His inclusion becomes readily
intelligible, when it is recalled that he had headed English
actors on tour in Scotland, and had already been marked
by the personal favour of James.[1] Whether he ever joined
the company in the full sense, that is to say, the association
of actors as distinct from the body of royal servants, seems to
me very doubtful. His name is not in the *Sejanus* list, or
in the Folio list of Shakespearian players, and that he was
described as a ' fellow ' by Phillips in 1605 hardly takes the
matter further. He may have held a relation to the King's
men analogous to that of Martin Slater to Queen Anne's
men. After 1605 nothing is heard of him.[2]

The terms of the patent imply that it was issued during
a suspension of playing through plague. Probably this had
followed hard upon the suspension at Elizabeth's death.
The company travelled, being found at Bath, Coventry, and
Shrewsbury in the course of 1602–3. A misplaced Ipswich
entry of 30 May 1602 may belong to 1603. The visits to
Oxford and Cambridge referred to on the title-page of the 1603
edition of *Hamlet* must also have taken place in this year, if
they did not take place in 1601. On 2 December 1603 the
company were summoned from Mortlake to perform before
the King at Lord Pembroke's house of Wilton.[3]

[1] Cf. ch. xiv (Scotland).
[2] Except in one of Collier's Blackfriars forgeries ; cf. ch. xvi.
[3] W. Cory (*Letters and Journals*, 168) was told on a visit to Wilton in
1865 that a letter existed there, naming Shakespeare as present and the
play as *As You Like It* ; but the letter cannot now be found.

During the winter of 1603–4 the company gave eight
more plays at Court, a larger number than Elizabeth had
ever called for. They took place on 26, 27, 28, and 30 December 1603 and on 1 January and 2 and 19 February 1604. On
New Year's Day there were two performances, one before
James, the other before Prince Henry. The plague had not
yet subsided by 8 February, and James gave his men £30
as a ' free gifte ' for their ' mayntenaunce and releife ' till
it should ' please God to settle the cittie in a more perfecte
health '. One of the plays of this winter was *The Fair Maid
of Bristow*. Another, produced before the end of 1603, was
probably Ben Jonson's *Sejanus*. For alleged popery and
treason in this play Jonson was haled before the Privy Council
by the Earl of Northampton, but there is nothing to show
that the players were implicated. The principal actors in
Sejanus were Burbadge, Shakespeare, Phillips, Heminges, Sly,
Condell, John Lowin, and Alexander Cooke. This is Shakespeare's last appearance in the cast of any play. He may
have ceased to act, while remaining a member of the company
and its poet. The names of Lowin and Cooke are new. Lowin
had been with Worcester's men in 1602–3. Cooke had
probably begun his connexion with the company as an
apprentice to Heminges. The identification of him with
the ' Sander ' of Strange's men in 1590 is more than hazardous.
The Induction to Marston's *Malcontent*, published in 1604,
records the names of Burbadge, who played Malevole, Condell,
Sly, Lowin, Sincler, and a Tireman. Sincler was probably
still only a hired man. Nothing further is heard of him.
This Induction seems to have been written by John Webster
to introduce the presentation by the King's men of *The
Malcontent*, which was really a Chapel play. The transaction
is thus explained : [1]

Sly. I wonder you would play it, another company having interest
in it ?

Condell. Why not Malevole in folio with us, as Jeronimo in decimo-
sexto with them ? They taught us a name for our play ; we call it
One for Another.

The play of *Jeronimo*, which the Chapel are here accused of
taking, cannot be *The Spanish Tragedy*, which was an Admiral's
play, and is not very likely to have been the ' comedy of
Jeronimo ' which Strange's men had in 1592, and which was
evidently related to *The Spanish Tragedy* and may be expected
to have remained with it. It might be the extant *First Part
of Jeronimo*, written perhaps for the Chamberlain's men

---

[1] Marston, *Malcontent*, Ind. 82.

about 1601–2, when Jonson was revising *The Spanish Tragedy* for the Admiral's. A reference in T. M.'s *Black Book* shows that *The Merry Devil of Edmonton*, which belonged to the company, was already on the stage by 1604.[1]

The coronation procession of James, deferred on account of the plague, went through London on 15 March 1604, and the Great Wardrobe furnished each of the King's players with four and a half yards of red cloth. The same nine men are specified in the warrant as in the patent of 1603, and their names stand next those of various officers of the Chamber. They did not, however, actually walk in the procession.[2] From 9 to 27 August 1604, they were called upon in their official capacity as Grooms of the Chamber to form part of the retinue assigned to attend at Somerset House upon Juan Fernandez de Velasco, Duke of Frias and Constable of Castile, who was in England as Ambassador Extraordinary for the negotiation of a peace with Spain. The descriptions of his visit, which have been preserved, do not show that any plays were given before him.[3]

The company were at Oxford between 7 May and 16 June 1604. About 18 December they had got into trouble through the production of a tragedy on *Gowry*, always a delicate subject with James.[4] But this did not interfere with a long series of no less than eleven performances which they gave at Court between 1 November 1604 and 12 February 1605, and of which the Revels Accounts fortunately preserve the names.[5] The series included one play, *The Spanish Maze*, of which nothing is known; two by Ben Jonson, *Every Man In his Humour* and *Every Man Out of his Humour*; and seven by Shakespeare, *Othello, The Merry Wives of Windsor, Measure for Measure, The Comedy of Errors, Henry V, Love's Labour's Lost*, and *The Merchant of Venice*, which was given twice. *Othello* and *Measure for Measure* had probably been produced for the first time during 1604, but

---

[1] Bullen, *Middleton*, viii. 36, ' Give him leaue to see the Merry Deuil of Edmonton or A Woman Killed with Kindness '.

[2] *N. S. S. Trans.* (1877–9), 15*, from *Lord Chamberlain's Records*, vol. 58ª, now ix. 4 (5) ; cf. Law (*ut infra*), 10. Collier, *Memoirs of Alleyn*, 68, printed a list headed ' Ks Company ' from the margin of the copy of the Privy Council order of 9 April 1604 at Dulwich. This is a forgery. To the nine genuine names Collier added those of Hostler and Day. The former joined the company some years later, the latter never ; cf. Ingleby, 269.

[3] App. B ; cf. E. Law, *Shakespeare as a Groom of the Chamber* (1910), and the Spanish narrative in *Colección de Documentos inéditos para la historia de España*, lxxi. 467.

[4] Cf. ch. x.

[5] For the exact dates and the difficult critical questions raised by the records, cf. App. B.

the rest of the list suggests that opportunity was being taken to revive a number of Elizabethan plays unknown to the new sovereigns. This is borne out by the terms of a letter from Sir Walter Cope to Lord Southampton with regard to the performance of *Love's Labour 's Lost*.[1]

Between 4 May 1605, when he made his will, and 13 May, when it was proved, died Augustine Phillips. Unlike Pope, he was full of kindly remembrances towards the King's men. He appointed Heminges, Burbadge, and Sly overseers of the will. He left legacies to his 'fellows' Shakespeare, Condell, Fletcher, Armin, Cowley, Cooke, and Nicholas Tooley; to the hired men of the company; to his 'servant' Christopher Beeston; to his apprentice James Sands, and to his late apprentice Samuel Gilburne. We have here practically a full list of the company. The name of Nicholas Tooley is new, unless indeed he was the 'Nick' of Strange's men in 1592. He speaks of Richard Burbadge in his will as his 'master' and may have been his apprentice. The use of the term 'fellow' suggests that Tooley and Cooke were now sharers in the company. On the other hand Lowin, who is not named among the 'fellows', may still have been only a hired man. Beeston's legacy is doubtless in memory of former service as hired man or apprentice; he was in 1605 and for long after with the Queen's men. Samuel Gilburne is recorded as a Shakespearian actor in the 1623 Folio, but practically nothing is known of him or of James Sands. The exact legal disposal of the interest held by Phillips in the Globe subsequently became matter of controversy, but in effect it remained from 1605 to 1613 with his widow and her second husband, and was thus alienated from the company.

On some date before Michaelmas in 1605 the King's men visited Barnstaple, and on 9 October they were at Oxford. This year saw the publication of *The Fair Maid of Bristow* and of *The London Prodigal*, which was assigned on its title-page to Shakespeare. To it I also assign Shakespeare's *Macbeth* and *King Lear*.

Ten Court plays were given in the winter of 1605–6, but the dates are not recorded. Three more were given in the summer of 1606 during the visit of the King of Denmark to James, which lasted from 7 July to 11 August, and then the company seem to have gone on tour. They were at Oxford between 28 and 31 July, at Leicester in August, at Dover between 6 and 24 September, at Saffron Walden and Maidstone during 1605–6, and at Marlborough in 1606. To

[1] Cf. App. B.

this year I assign Shakespeare's *Antony and Cleopatra* and *Coriolanus*, and to the earlier part of it Ben Jonson's *Volpone*, in which the principal actors were Burbadge, Condell, Sly, Heminges, Lowin, and Cooke.

Nine Court plays were given during the winter of 1606–7, on 26 and 29 December 1606, and on 4, 6, and 8 January and 2, 5, 15, and 27 February 1607. The entry in the Stationers' Register for *King Lear* and the title-page of Barnes' *The Devil's Charter*, both dated in 1607, show these to have been the plays selected for 26 December and 2 February respectively. In the same year were also published Tourneur's *The Revenger's Tragedy* and Wilkins' *The Miseries of Enforced Marriage*, and to it I assign the production of *Timon of Athens*. On 16 July 1607 Heminges lent his boy John Rice to appear as an angel of gladness with a taper of frankincense, and deliver an eighteen-verse speech by Ben Jonson as part of the entertainment of James by the Merchant Taylors at their hall.[1] During the summer the company travelled to Barnstaple, to Dunwich, to Oxford, where they were on 7 September, and possibly to Cambridge. *Volpone* had probably been given in both Universities before its publication about February 1607 or 1608.

During the winter of 1607–8 the company gave thirteen Court plays, on 26, 27, and 28 December 1606, and on 2, 6, 7, 9, 17, and 26 January, and 2 and 7 February 1607. On each of the nights of 6 and 17 January there were two plays. In 1608 was published *A Yorkshire Tragedy*, with Shakespeare's name on the title-page, and to it I assign the production of *Pericles*, in which Shakespeare probably had Wilkins for a collaborator. About May the company had to find their share of the heavy fine necessary to buy off the inhibition due to the performance of Chapman's *Duke of Byron* by the Queen's Revels.[2] The year was in many ways an eventful one for the King's men. They had, I suspect, to face a growing detachment of Shakespeare from London and the theatre; and the loss was perhaps partly supplied by the establishment of relations with Beaumont and Fletcher, whose earliest play for the company, *Philaster*, may be of any date from 1608 to 1610. About 16 August died William Sly, leaving his interest in the Globe to his son Robert and legacies to Cuthbert Burbadge and James Sands. Both he and Henry Condell had been admitted to an interest at some date subsequent to

[1] Clode, *Early Hist. of Merchant Taylors*, i. 290, 'To Mr Hemmyngs for his direccion of his boy that made the speech to his Maiestie 40ˢ, and 5ˢ given to John Rise the speaker'; cf. ch. iv.

[2] Cf. ch. x.

November 1606, the moiety of the lease not retained by the Burbadges having been redistributed into sixths to allow of this. The deserts of Pope, Phillips, and Sly are all commemorated in the *Apology* of Thomas Heywood, which, though not published until 1612, was probably written in 1608.[1] Sly's death complicated an important transaction in which the King's men were engaged. This was the acquisition of the Blackfriars, of which the freehold already belonged to the Burbadges, but which had been leased since 1600 to Henry Evans and occupied by the Children of the Revels. About July 1608 Evans was prepared to surrender his lease, and the Burbadges decided to take the opportunity of providing the King's men with a second house on the north side of the Thames, suitable for a winter head-quarters. As in the case of the Globe, they shared their interest as housekeepers with some of the leading members of the company. New leases were executed on 9 August 1608, by which the house was divided between a syndicate of seven, of whom five were Richard Burbadge, Shakespeare, Heminges, Condell, and Sly, while the other two, Cuthbert Burbadge and Thomas Evans, were not King's men. When Sly's death intervened, his executrix surrendered his interest and the number of the syndicate was reduced to six. Probably, however, the King's men did not enter upon the actual occupation of the Blackfriars until the autumn of the following year.[2] In fact the plague kept the London theatres closed from July 1608 to December 1609. The King's men were at Coventry on 29 October 1608 and at Marlborough in the course of 1607–8. The plague did not prevent them from appearing at Court during the winter of 1608–9, and they gave twelve plays on unspecified dates. But their difficulties are testified to by a special reward ' for their private practise in the time of infeccion ', which had rendered their Christmas service possible.

The plague led to an early provincial tour. The company were at Ipswich on 9 May, at Hythe on 16 May, and at New Romney on 17 May 1609. Their winter season was again interfered with, and a further grant was made in respect of six weeks of private practice. Amongst the plays so practised may, I think, have been *Cymbeline*. They gave thirteen plays at Court on unspecified dates during the holidays of 1609–10.[3] One of these may have been *Mucedorus*, the edition of which with the imprint

---

[1] App. C, No. lvii.   [2] Cf. ch. xii (Queen's Revels).

[3] Fleay, 173, and Murray, i. 152, are wrong in saying that there were no Court plays this year ; cf. *M. L. R.* iv. 154.

1610 represents a revised version performed at Court on the previous Shrove Sunday. This might be either 18 February 1610 or 3 February 1611. The epilogue contains an apology for some recent indiscretion of the company in a play of which no more is known, but which might conceivably be Daborne's *A Christian Turned Turk*, since this certainly brought its players into some disgrace. By April the company were at the Globe, playing *Macbeth* on 20 April, *Cymbeline* probably shortly before, and *Othello* on 30 April.[1] To this year I assign *The Winter's Tale* and Beaumont and Fletcher's *The Maid's Tragedy*. It also saw the production of Jonson's *Alchemist*, with a cast including Burbadge, Lowin, Condell, Cooke, Armin, Heminges, William Ostler, John Underwood, Tooley, and William Ecclestone. This is the last mention of Armin in connexion with the King's men, but it is sufficient to show that the production of his *Two Maids of Moreclack* by the King's Revels about 1608 did not involve any breach with his old company. Of Ecclestone's origin nothing is known.[2] Ostler and Underwood came from the Queen's Revels, probably when the Blackfriars was taken over in 1609. In fact an account of the transaction given by the Burbadges in 1635 suggests that the desire to acquire these boys was its fundamental motive. They say :

' In processe of time, the boyes growing up to bee men, which were Underwood, Field, Ostler, and were taken to strengthen the King's service ; and the more to strengthen the service, the boyes dayly wearing out, it was considered that house would bee as fitt for ourselves, and soe purchased the lease remaining from Evans with our money, and placed men players, which were Heminges, Condall, Shakspeare, &c.'

This narrative seems, however, to have antedated matters as regards Field. Or, if he did come to the King's men in 1609, he almost immediately returned to the Queen's Revels at Whitefriars, joining the King's again about 1616.[3] About 8 May 1610 some superfluous apparel of the company was sold by Heminges on their behalf to the Duke of York's

---

[1] Rye, 61, from narrative of tour of Lewis Frederick, Duke of Württemberg, ' Lundi, 30 [Apr.] S. E. alla au Globe, lieu ordinaire où l'on joue les Commedies, y fut representé l'histoire du More de Venise '. Forman's accounts of *Macbeth* from *Bodl. Ashm. MS.* 208, f. 207, and of *Cymbeline* from the preceding leaf, but undated, are printed in *N. S. S. Trans.* (1875–6), 417.

[2] Fleay, 190, says that Ecclestone came from the Queen's Revels. I think he must have confused him with Field.

[3] Perhaps his place between Ostler and Underwood in the actor-list of the 1623 Folio gives some confirmation to the statement of the Burbadges ; cf. p. 219.

men (q.v.). On 31 May Burbadge and Rice were employed by the City to make speeches on fish-back at the civic pageant of welcome to Prince Henry.[1] The autumn travelling took the company to Dover between 6 July and 4 August 1610, to Oxford in August, and to Shrewsbury and Stafford in 1609–10. During the following winter they gave fifteen Court plays on unspecified days. They were playing a piece on the story of Richard II, not now extant, at the Globe on 30 April 1611, and *A Winter's Tale* on 15 May.[2] During 1611 Jonson's *Catiline* was produced, with a cast similar to that of *The Alchemist*, except that Armin was replaced by Richard Robinson, whose earlier history is unknown. Robinson, playing a female part, and Robert Gough also appear in the stage directions of *The Second Maiden's Tragedy*, licensed for the stage by Sir George Buck on 31 October 1611. Gough was probably one of Strange's men in 1592. He appears in the wills of Pope in 1603 and of Phillips, who was his brother-in-law, in 1605, but with no indication that he belonged to the King's men. Beaumont and Fletcher's *A King and No King* was also licensed by Buck in 1611, and to this year I assign Shakespeare's *Tempest*. On 25 August 1611 the interest in the Blackfriars originally intended for Sly was assigned to Ostler. Ecclestone, on the other hand, later in the year than the production of *Catiline*, but before 29 August, left the company for the Lady Elizabeth's men.

The only provincial visit by the King's men recorded in 1610–11 was to Shrewsbury. They gave twenty-two plays at Court during a rather prolonged winter season extending from 31 October 1611 to 26 April 1612. Two of these, on 12 and 13 January, were joint performances with the Queen's men, and the plays used, Heywood's *Silver Age* and *Rape of Lucrece*, were from the repertory of the latter.[3] The King's men also gave *The Tempest* and *A Winter's Tale*, *A King and No King*, Tourneur's *The Nobleman*, and *The Twins' Tragedy*. On 20 February 1612 the actors' moiety of the Globe was again redistributed, into sevenths, so as to allow of the admission as a housekeeper of Ostler, who had married a daughter of Hemings. From the statement of the interests held by the parties to this transaction, it is to be inferred that Heminges and Condell had between them bought out since 1608 the representatives of Sly. On 21 April 1612 the company was at New Romney and at some date during 1611–12

---

[1] Cf. ch. iv.

[2] *N. S. S. Trans.* (1875–6), 415, from Simon Forman's notes in *Bodl. Ashm. MS.* 208, f. 200.

[3] For the precise dates and their difficulties, cf. App. B.

at Winchester. Heminges received a payment for services to the Lord Mayor's pageant of this year, which was Dekker's *Troja Nova Triumphans*.[1]

The actor-list attached to *The Captain* in the Beaumont and Fletcher Folio of 1679 probably belongs to the original production of the play between 1609 and 1612. It names Burbadge, Condell, Cooke, and Ostler. It was one of the plays selected for the Court season of 1612–13, during which, on 14 February, took place the wedding of the Elector Palatine Frederick and the Princess Elizabeth, and which was therefore singularly rich in plays, notwithstanding the interruption of the festivities due to the death of Prince Henry on 7 November 1612. Heminges lent a boy for Chapman's mask on 15 February. The twenty plays given this winter by the King's men, the exact dates of which are not upon record, were Shakespeare's *Much Ado about Nothing* (performed twice), *The Tempest*, *A Winter's Tale*, *Julius Caesar*, *Othello*, and *1 and 2 Henry IV*, Jonson's *Alchemist*, Beaumont and Fletcher's *Philaster* (also performed twice), *The Maid's Tragedy*, *A King and No King,* *The Captain* and the lost play of *Cardenio*, Tourneur's *The Nobleman*, and four plays of unknown authorship, *The Merry Devil of Edmonton*, *The Knot of Fools*, *The Twins' Tragedy*, and *A Bad Beginning Makes a Good Ending*. On 8 June there was a special perform-ance of *Cardenio* for the Savoyan ambassador. Some un-known cause seems to have brought Shakespeare back in 1613 to the assistance of his fellows, and he collaborated with Fletcher in *The Two Noble Kinsmen* and in *Henry VIII* or *All is True*, possibly a revision of the *Buckingham* which formed part of the repertory of Sussex's men in 1594. During a performance of *Henry VIII*, on 29 June 1613, the Globe was burnt to the ground. Some contemporary verses mention Burbadge, Heminges, and Condell as present on this occasion. A levy was called for from the housekeepers to meet the cost of rebuilding, and owing to the inability of the representatives of Augustine Phillips to meet the call upon them, Heminges was enabled to recover one of the alienated interests, which he divided with Condell.

The company was at Oxford before November in 1613, and also visited Shrewsbury, Stafford, and Folkestone during 1612–13. They played sixteen times at Court in the winter of 1613–14, on 1, 4, 5, 15, and 16 November and 27 December 1613, and on 1, 4, and 10 January, 2, 4, 8, 10, and 18 February and 6 and 8 March 1614. The rebuilding of the Globe was

---

[1] Clode, *Early Hist. of the Merchant Taylors*, i. 334.

complete by 30 June 1614, and in the course of 1613–14 the company visited Coventry. Cooke died in February 1614, being then a sharer. Ostler died on 16 December, and his interests in the Globe and Blackfriars became matter of dispute between his widow and her father, John Heminges. The ascertained dates of Ostler's career render it possible to assign to 1609–14, the period of his connexion with the King's men, three plays in which he took part. These are Webster's *Duchess of Malfi*, at the first production of which, if the actor-list of the 1623 edition is rightly interpreted, the parts of Ferdinand, the Cardinal, and Antonio were played respectively by Burbadge, Condell, and Ostler, Fletcher's *Valentinian*, played by Burbadge, Condell, Lowin, Ostler, and Underwood, and his *Bonduca*, played by Burbadge, Condell, Lowin, Ostler, Underwood, Tooley, Ecclestone, and Robinson. *Bonduca* must be either earlier than Ecclestone's departure for the Lady Elizabeth's men in 1611, or after he quitted that company and presumably rejoined the King's in 1613.

The King's men gave eight plays at Court on unspecified days during the winter of 1614–15. On 29 March 1615 they were in trouble with other companies for playing in Lent, and Heminges and Burbadge appeared on their behalf before the Privy Council. In April 1615 they were at Nottingham. They gave fourteen plays at Court between 1 November 1615 and 1 April 1616, and again the precise dates are not specified. They also appeared before Anne at Somerset House on 21 December 1615.

Shakespeare died on 23 April 1616, and with this event I must close my detailed chronicle of the fortunes of the company. A new patent was issued to them on 27 March 1619, probably to secure their right to perform in the Blackfriars, which was being challenged by the action of the City.[1] Since 1603 Shakespeare, Phillips, Sly, Cowley, Armin, and Fletcher have dropped out of the list, and are replaced by Lowin, Underwood, Tooley, Ecclestone, Gough, and Robinson, together with Nathan Field, Robert Benfield, and John Shank, who now appear for the first time as members of the company.[2] Benfield and Field are last traceable with the Lady Elizabeth's men in 1613 and 1615 respectively, Shank with the Palsgrave's men in 1613. The only names common to both patents are those of Burbadge, Heminges, and Condell.

---

[1] Text in *M. S. C.* i. 280, from Signet Bill in *Exchequer, Treasury of Receipt, Privy Seals*, 17 *Jac. I*, Bundle ix, No. 2 ; also in Collier, i. 400, and Hazlitt, *E. D. S.* 50.

[2] Tawyer, a ' man ' of Heminges's, played in some revival of *M. N. D.* before 1623, but not necessarily before 1619 (cf. ch. xv).

But in fact Burbadge died on 13 March 1619, while the patent
was going through its stages, and his place was almost immediately taken by Joseph Taylor, from Prince Charles's men.
About the same time Field left the company.[1] Heminges,
described as 'stuttering' in 1613, cannot be shown to have
acted since the *Catiline* of 1611. He had probably devoted
himself to the business management of the company, in which
he always appears prominent. Condell also seems to have
given up acting about 1619, and during the rest of the
history of the company up to its extinction in 1642, its
mainstays were Lowin and Taylor, who became depositaries
of the tradition of the great Shakespearian parts. John
Downes, who was prompter to the Duke of York's men after
the Restoration, relates how, when Betterton played Hamlet,
'Sir *William* [Davenant] (having seen *Mr. Taylor* of the
Black-Fryers Company Act it, who being instructed by the
Author *Mr. Shakespear*) taught *Mr. Betterton* in every
Particle of it'; and how Davenant was similarly able to act
as Betterton's tutor for Henry the Eighth, for he 'had it
from Old *Mr. Lowen*, that had his Instructions from *Mr. Shake-
spear* himself'.[2] When Heminges and Condell came to print
Shakespeare's plays in 1623, they prefixed 'the names of the
principall Actors in all these playes' as follows: 'William
Shakespeare, Richard Burbadge, John Hemmings, Augustine
Phillips, William Kempt, Thomas Poope, George Bryan,
Henry Condell, William Slye, Richard Cowly, John Lowine,
Samuell Crosse, Alexander Cooke, Samuel Gilburne, Robert
Armin, William Ostler, Nathan Field, John Underwood,
Nicholas Tooley, William Ecclestone, Joseph Taylor, Robert
Benfield, Robert Goughe, Richard Robinson, John Shancke,
John Rice.' The order is a little puzzling. The first ten
entries may be those of the original members of the Chamber-
lain's company in 1594; and if so, their order does not matter.
But it is difficult to believe that the other sixteen can represent either the order in which the men began to play for the
company, or the order in which they became sharers. Of
course, there may have been comings and goings known to
Heminges and Condell, but not now traceable. Thus Field
and even Taylor may have come for a short while and gone
again before 1611. But it seems impossible that Tooley,
who was 'fellow' to Phillips in 1605, could really have been
junior to the recruits from the Queen's Revels in 1609. On
the whole, one must suppose that, if Heminges and Condell

---

[1] *M. L. R.* iv. 395.
[2] Downes, 21, 24. Nevertheless, Taylor did not join the King's men
until three years after Shakespeare's death.

aimed at an exact chronology, their memory occasionally failed them. The omission from the Folio of Duke, Beeston, Sincler, and Sands may indicate that the list is confined to sharers. It is probable that Fletcher, who is also omitted, was not a sharer and did not act in any Shakespearian play.

xxi. THE EARL OF WORCESTER'S AND QUEEN ANNE'S MEN

William Somerset, *nat.* 1526 ; succ. as 3rd Earl of Worcester, 1548 ; m. Christian, d. of Edward, 1st Lord North ; *ob.* 22 Feb. 1589.

Edward Somerset, s. of William ; *nat.* 1553 ; Lord Herbert of Chepstow ; succ. as 4th Earl, 1589 ; m. Elizabeth, d. of Francis, 2nd Earl of Huntingdon ; Deputy Master of the Horse, Dec. 1597 ; Master of the Horse, 21 Apr. 1601 ; Earl Marshal, 1603 ; Lord Privy Seal, 2 Jan. 1616 ; *ob.* 3 Mar. 1628.

Henry Somerset, s. of Edward ; *nat.* 1577 ; Lord Herbert of Chepstow from 1589 ; m. 16 June 1600, Anne, d. of John, Lord Russell ; succ. as 5th Earl, 1628 ; cr. 1st Marquis of Worcester, 1642.

Anne, d. of Frederick II, King of Denmark and Norway; *nat.* 12 Dec. 1574 ; m. James VI, King of Scotland, 20 Aug. 1589 ; Queen Consort of England, 24 Mar. 1603 ; *ob.* 2 Mar. 1619.

[*Bibliographical Note.*—The records of Worcester's men in 1602–3 are printed and discussed by W. W. Greg in *Henslowe's Diary* (1904–8). The will of Thomas Greene (1612) was printed by J. Greenstreet in the *Athenaeum* (29 August 1895), and the Bill, Answer, and Orders in the Chancery suit of *Worth et al. v. Baskerville et al.* (1623–6) by the same in the *Athenaeum* (11 July and 29 August 1885) and *N. S. S. Trans.* (*1880–6*), 489. Both are reprinted in Fleay, 192, 271. The Court of Requests suit of *Smith v. Beeston et al.* (1619–20) is printed by C. W. Wallace in *Nebraska University Studies,* ix. 315.]

The first company under the patronage of this house had a long and wholly provincial career.[1] The earliest record of it is at Barnstaple in 1555. On 10 October 1563 it was at Leicester. On 13 and 14 January 1565 it was at Sir George Vernon's, Haddon Hall, Derbyshire, under the leadership of one Hamond.[2] It is further traceable in December 1565 at Newcastle, before Michaelmas 1566 at Leicester, in 1567–8 at Gloucester, in 1568–9 at Ipswich, Stratford-on-Avon, and Bath, on 11 August 1569 at Nottingham, in 1569–70 and 1570–1 at Gloucester and Barnstaple, in 1571 at Leicester and Beverley, on 9 January 1572 at Nottingham, before Michaelmas at Leicester, on 31 December 1572 at Wollaton, Notts. (Francis Willoughby's), on 6 January 1573 at Nottingham, in 1572–3 at Bath, in 1573–4 at Abingdon, and in January 1574 at Wollaton again. As the Earl of Worcester's

[1] Murray, i. 56, adds 1563–83 records. [2] G. Le B. Smith, *Haddon Hall*, 121.

eldest son bore the courtesy title of Lord Herbert, it is probably the same company which appeared at Leicester, after Michaelmas in 1574, as 'Lorde Harbards'. But it is named as Worcester's again in 1574-5 at Stratford-on-Avon, on 28 April 1575 at Nottingham, and after Michaelmas in the same year at Leicester, in 1575-6 at Coventry, in 1576-7 at Stratford-on-Avon and Bath, and on 14 June 1577 at Southampton, where it consisted of ten men. On 19 January 1578 it was at Nottingham, in 1577-8 at Coventry, in 1580-1 and 1581-2 at Stratford-on-Avon, in 1581-2 at Abingdon, on 15 June 1582 at Ipswich, in the same year at Doncaster.

Two incidents in successive years suggest that Worcester's men were not always quite so amenable, as vagrants should have been, to municipal discipline. The first was at Norwich on 7 June 1583. Here there was a fear of plague, and the company were given 26s. 8d., on a promise not to play. In spite of this they played in their host's house. The Corporation ordered 'that their lord shall be certified of their contempt', and that they should never again receive reward in Norwich, and should presently depart the town on pain of imprisonment. It was afterwards agreed, however, on submission and earnest entreaty, not to report the misdemeanour to the Earl of Worcester. The second occasion was in the following March in Leicester, and the entries in the Corporation archives are so interesting as to deserve reproduction in full.[1]

Mr Mayor
Mr J. Tatam
Mr Morton.

Tuesdaie the third daie of Marche, 1583, certen playors whoe said they were the seruants of the Quenes Maiesties Master of the Revells, who required lycence to play & for there aucthorytye showed forth an Indenture of Lycense from one Mr Edmonde Tylneye esquier Mr of her Maiesties Revells of the one parte, and George Haysell of Wisbiche in the Ile of Elye in the Countie of Cambridge, gentleman on the other parte.

The which indenture is dated the vjth daie of Februarye in the xxvth yere of her Maiesties raign &c.

In which Indenture there ys one article that all Justices, Maiores, Sherifs, Bayllyfs, Constables, and all other her officers, ministers & subiects whatsoeuer to be aydinge & assistinge vnto the said Edmund

---

[1] Kelly, 211, from *Leicester Hall Papers*, i, ff. 38, 42; *Hist. MSS.* viii. 1, 431. The latter part of the record, from the Earl's licence onwards, was given by Halliwell in *Sh. Soc. Papers*, iv. 145, but with the date 1586, due to a misprint of '28° Eliz.' for '25° Eliz.' in the licence. This has misled Fleay, 86, and other writers. Maas, 49, and M. Bateson, *Records of Leicester*, iii. 198, introduce fresh errors of their own.

Tilneye, his Deputies & Assignes, attendinge & havinge due regard
vnto suche parsons as shall disorderly intrude themselves into any
the doings and accions before mencioned, not beinge reformed, qualifyed
& bound to the orders prescribed by the said Edmund Tyllneye.
These shalbee therefore not only to signifye & geve notice vnto all
& euery her said Justices &c that none of there owne pretensed
aucthoritye intrude themselves & presume to showe forth any suche
playes, enterludes, tragedies, comodies, or shewes in any places
within this Realm, withoute the orderlye allowance thereof vnder the
hand of the sayd Edmund.

NOTA.   No play is to bee played, but suche as is allowed by the
sayd Edmund, & his hand at the latter end of the said booke they
doe play.

The forsed Haysell is nowe the chefe playor &c.

Fridaye the 6 of Marche.

Certen players came before Mr Mayor at the Hall there beinge present
Mr John Tatam, Mr George Tatam, Mr Morton & Mr Worship : who
sayed they were the Earle of Wosters men : who sayd the forsyd
playors were not lawfully aucthorysed, & that they had taken from
them there commyssion, but it is untrue, for they forgat there box
at the Inne in Leicester, & so these men gat yt & they sed the syd
Haysell was not here hymself and they sent the same to Grantom
to the syd Haysell who dwellith there.

William Earle of Worcester &c. hath by his wrytinge dated the
14 of Januarye Anno 25° Eliz. Reginae licensed his Seruants viz.
Robert Browne, James Tunstall, Edward Allen, William Harryson,
Thomas Cooke, Rychard Johnes, Edward Browne, Rychard Andrewes
to playe & goe abrode, vsinge themselves orderly &c. (in theise words
&c.)   These are therefore to require all suche her Highnes offycers
to whom these presents shall come, quietly & frendly within your
severall presincts & corporacions to permytt & suffer them to passe
with your furtherance vsinge & demeanynge themselves honestly &
to geve them (the rather for my sake) suche intertaynement as other
noble mens players haue   (In Wytnes &c.)

Mr Mayor	M^r Ja. Clarke	Mr Robt Heyrycke
M^r Jo. Heyrycke	Mr George Tatam	Mr Ellys
Mr Noryce	Mr Morton	Mr Newcome.

Memorandum that Mr Mayor did geve the aforesaid playors an
angell towards there dinner & wild them not to playe at this present :
being Fryday the vj^th of Marche, for that the tyme was not con-
veynyent.

The foresaid playors mett Mr Mayor in the strete nere Mr Newcomes
housse, after the angell was geven abowte a ij howers, who then
craived lycense ageyne to play at there inn, & he told them they shold
not, then they went away & seyd they wold play, whether he wold
or not, & in dispite of hym, with dyvers other evyll & contemptyous
words : Witness here of Mr Newcome, Mr Wycam, & William Dethicke.

More, these men, contrary to Mr Mayors comandment, went with their drum & trumppytts thorowe the Towne, in contempt of Mr Mayor, neyther wold come at his comandment, by his offycer, viz. Worship.

William Pateson my lord Harbards man ⎫ these ij
Thomas Powlton my lord of Worcesters man ⎭

were they which dyd so much abuse Mr Mayor in the aforesayd words.

NOTA. These sayd playors have submytted them selves, & are sorye for there words past, & craved pardon, desyeringe his worship not to write to there Master agayne them, & so vpon there submyssyn, they are lycensed to play this night at there inn, & also they have promysed that vppon the stage, in the begynyng of there play, to shoe vnto the hearers that they are licensed to playe by Mr Mayor & with his good will & that they are sory for the words past.

The latter part of this record is intelligible enough ; · evidently there was a repetition of the misrule at Norwich. But the earlier part, which refers to a different matter altogether, is distinctly puzzling. The ' theys ' in the first sentence of the Corporation minute of 6 March are complicated, and it has sometimes been supposed that there was really a company of Master of the Revels' men, and that it was Worcester's men who questioned the licence of these.[1] On the whole, I think that a different interpretation of the documents is the more natural one. No doubt Worcester's men had found it necessary, as a result of the powers granted to Tilney as Master of the Revels by the patent of 24 December 1581, to renew the authority under which they travelled. In addition to a fresh warrant from their lord licensing them to travel as his household servants, and dated 14 January 1583, they obtained on the following 6 February a further licence from Tilney, issued under the clause of his commission which appointed him to ' order and reforme, auctorise and put downe ' all players in any part of England, whether they were ' belonginge to any noble man ' or otherwise.[2] This licence, but not the other, they left at their inn in Leicester, while passing through on some previous occasion ; and here it was found by some unlicensed players, who appropriated it, and either throvgh misunderstanding or through fraud, imposed it upon the Corporation as an instrument constituting a Master of the Revels' company. There are two difficulties in this theory. One is that George Haysell, to whom Tilney's licence was issued, is not one of the actors named in the Earl of Worcester's warrant. But there are other cases in which the constitution of a company in the

¹ Gildersleeve, 53.   ² Cf. ch. ix and App. D, No. lvi.

eyes of its lord was not quite the same as its constitution from the point of view of business relations, and I should suppose that Haysell, who was evidently not himself acting at the time, was the financier of the enterprise, and gave the bonds which Tilney would probably require for the satisfaction of the covenants of his indenture of licence. The other difficulty is that Leicester is not the only place in which the presence of a Master of the Revels' company is recorded. Such a company was at Ludlow on 7 December 1583 and at Bath in 1583-4.[1] But, after all, this need mean no more than that the bogus company kept up their fraud for two or three months before they were exposed. If Tilney had really started a company of his own, it might have been expected to have a longer life. The establishment in 1583 of the Queen's men makes it the less probable that he did so.

The list of this provincial company, as it stood in January 1583, is interesting, because at least four of its members, Robert Browne, Richard Jones, James Tunstall, and above all Edward Alleyn, then only a lad of sixteen, were destined to take a considerable share in the stage history of the future. Edward Browne, too, was afterwards one of the Admiral's men. Of the rest, William Harrison, Thomas Cooke, Richard Andrewes, as well as of George Haysell (cf. ch. xv) and of the two players who were not named in the warrant, Thomas Powlton and William Pateson, Lord Herbert's man, nothing or practically nothing further is known.[2] It is possible that the escapades of the company at Norwich and Leicester came, after all, to Worcester's ears and aroused his displeasure. Visits are recorded to Coventry and Stratford in 1583-4, to Maidstone in 1584-5, to York in March 1585, and thereafter no more. It is also possible that the company passed from Worcester's service into that of Lord Howard, when the latter became Lord Admiral in 1585. If so, a conveyance by Richard Jones to Edward Alleyn on 3 January 1589 of his share in a stock of apparel, play-books, and so forth, held jointly with Edward and John Alleyn and Robert Browne, must relate, not to a break up of Worcester's men shortly before the death of the third earl, but to some internal change in the organization of the Admiral's men.[3] In any case Mr. Fleay's theory that Worcester's men, other than Alleyn, became Pembroke's in 1589 and only joined the

---

[1] Halliwell-Phillipps, *Notices of Players Acting at Ludlow* ; B. S. Penley, *The Bath Stage*, 12, from account for year ending 16 June 1584.

[2] Lord Herbert was, of course, Worcester's son ; not, as Dr. Greg (Henslowe, ii. 104) seems to think, one of the Pembroke family.

[3] *Henslowe Papers*, 31 ; cf. *supra* (Admiral's).

Admiral's in 1594 is quite gratuitous, as there is no evidence of the existence of Pembroke's men before 1592.[1] Whether there was a Worcester's company or not from 1585 to 1589, there was certainly one after the accession of the fourth earl. It is traceable at Coventry in 1589–90, at Newcastle in October 1590, at Leicester during the last three months of the same year, at Coventry and Faversham in 1590–1, at Leicester on 26 June 1591 and again in the last three months of the year, at Coventry and Shrewsbury in 1591–2, at Ipswich in 1592–3,· twice at Leicester in 1593, both before and after Michaelmas, twice at Bath in 1593–4, at Leicester before Michaelmas in 1595, at Ludlow on 3 December 1595, at Bath in 1595–6, at Leicester on 1 August 1596, at Bristol in August 1598, at York in April 1599, and at Coventry on 3 January 1600 and in 1600–1 and 1601–2.[2]

By the end of 1601 the Earl of Worcester was holding the Mastership of the Horse and other important offices at Court, and may have thought it consonant with his dignity to have London players under his patronage. On 3 January 1602 his company was at Court. On 31 March the Privy Council, after attempting for some years to limit the number of London companies to two, made an order that Oxford's and Worcester's men, ' beinge ioyned by agrement togeather in on companie ', should be allowed to play at the Boar's Head and nowhere else.[3] In the course of 1602 *How a Man may Choose a Good Wife from a Bad* was published as played by Worcester's men. By 17 August the company were in relations, under the style of ' my lorde of Worsters players ', with Henslowe, who opened an account of advances made for their play-books and apparel, on the same lines as that which he kept during 1597–1603 with the Admiral's men.[4] An early entry is of 9s. for a supper ' at the Mermayd when we weare at owre a grement '. The account was continued until the spring of 1603, when Henslowe's famous diary was disused. No theatre is named, but it is probable that, with or without leave from the Privy Council, the company moved to the Rose, which had been vacated by the Admiral's men on the opening of the Fortune

---

[1] Fleay, 87.   [2] Murray, i. 58, adds 1589–94 records.
[3] App. D, No. cxxx.
[4] Henslowe, i. 179. As Henslowe paid 7s. ' for my Loͬ Worsters mens warant for playinge at the cort vnto the clarke of the cown-selles for geatynge the cownselles handes to yt ' (*Henslowe Papers*, 108), and the only warrant to these men was dated 28 Feb. 1602, the connexion with Henslowe probably began while they were still at the Boar's Head.

in 1600. Certainly this was so by May 1603, when an acquittance for an advance entered in the account refers to a play to be written for 'the Earle of Worcesters players at the Rose '.[1] There is no complete list of the company in the diary. The names of those members incidentally mentioned, as authorizing payments or otherwise, are John Duke, Thomas Blackwood, William Kempe, John Thare, John Lowin, Thomas Heywood, Christopher Beeston, Robert Pallant, and a Cattanes whose first name is not preserved. The payees for the performance of 1601–2 were Kempe and Heywood. One Underell was in receipt of wages from the company, together with a tireman, who made purchases of stuffs for them. It is impossible to say which of these men had been with Worcester's and which with Oxford's before the amalgamation. Heywood, who was playwright as well as actor, had written for the Admiral's from 1596 to 1599, and had bound himself to play in Henslowe's house for two years from 25 March 1598. Pallant had been with Strange's or the Admiral's in 1590–1, and Duke, Kempe, and Beeston with the Chamberlain's in 1598. Since then Kempe had travelled abroad, returning in September 1601. It is little more than a guess that some of these men may have played with Henslowe as Pembroke's.[2] Several members of the company borrowed money from Henslowe, in some cases before their connexion with the Rose began. Duke had a loan as early as 21 September 1600, and Kempe on 10 March 1602.[3] Blackwood and Lowin borrowed on 12 March 1603 to go into the country with the company.[4] This was, no doubt, when playing in London was suspended owing to the illness of Elizabeth. A loan for a similar purpose was made on the same day to Richard Perkins, and suggests that he too was already one of Worcester's men. There is, indeed, an earlier note of 4 September 1602 connecting him with one Dick Syferweste, whose fellows were then in the country, while Worcester's were, of course, at the Rose. But this itself makes it clear that he was interested in a play of Heywood's, which can hardly be other than that then in preparation at the Rose, and perhaps Syferwest was an unfortunate comrade in Oxford's or Worcester's, who had been left out at the reconstruction.[5]

---

[1] Henslowe, i. 160, 190. [2] Cf. *supra* (Chamberlain's).
[3] Henslowe, i. 132, 163. [4] Ibid. 177.
[5] Ibid. 178, ' Lent vnto Richard Perckens the 4 of September 1602 to buy thinges for Thomas Hewode play & to lend vnto Dick Syferweste to ride downe to his felowes '. This is, of course, a private loan, and not in the company's account.

During the seven months of the account Worcester's men bought twelve new plays. These were :

A Medicine for a Curst Wife (Dekker).
Albere Galles (Heywood and Smith).
Marshal Osric (Heywood and Smith).
The Three Brothers (Smith).[1]
1 Lady Jane, or, *The Overthrow of Rebels*[2] (Chettle, Dekker, Heywood, Smith, and Webster).
Christmas Comes but Once a Year (Chettle, Dekker, Heywood, and Webster).
1 The Black Dog of Newgate (Day, Hathaway, Smith, and another).
The Blind Eats Many a Fly (Heywood).
The Unfortunate General (Day, Hathaway, and Smith).
2 The Black Dog of Newgate (Day, Hathaway, Smith, and another).
A Woman Killed with Kindness (Heywood).
The Italian Tragedy (Smith).

As a rule the price was £6 a play ; occasionally £1 or £2 more. Dekker had 10s. ' over & above his price of ' *A Medicine for a Curst Wife*. This had originally been begun for the Admiral's and was evidently transferred to Worcester's by arrangement. After buying *2 Black Dog of Newgate* for £7, the company apparently did not like it, and paid £2 more for ' adycyones '. It is possible to verify from the purchase of properties the performance of nine of the twelve plays. These are *Albere Galles* (September), *The Three Brothers* (October), *Marshal Osric* (November), *1 Lady Jane* (November), *Christmas Comes but Once a Year* (December), *1 Black Dog of Newgate* (January), *The Unfortunate General* (January), *2 Black Dog of Newgate* (February), and *A Woman Killed with Kindness* (March). The production of this last may, however, have been interfered with by Elizabeth's death. Two plays of the series are extant, *A Woman Killed with Kindness*, printed in 1607 and described in 1617 as a Queen's play, and *1 Lady Jane*, which may be reasonably identified with *Sir Thomas Wyatt*, also printed in 1607 as a Queen's play, and by Dekker and Webster. Dr. Greg regards Mr. Fleay's identification of *Albere Galles* with *Nobody and Somebody* as ' reasonable ' ; but it appears to rest on little, except the fact that the latter was also printed as a Queen's play (S. R. 12 March 1606) and the conjecture that the title of the former might

---

[1] Called in the earlier entries *The Two Brothers*.
[2] The two names do not occur together, but almost certainly indicate the same play.

be a corruption of *Archigallo*. Payments were made in respect
of a few contemplated plays, which apparently remained
incomplete at the end of the season. These were *2 Lady Jane*
(Dekker), an unnamed tragedy by Chettle, an unnamed play
by Middleton, and another unnamed play by Chettle and
Heywood. The company also produced some plays of earlier
date. *Sir John Oldcastle* was presumably transferred to them
from the Admiral's men, for Dekker had £2 10s. in respect of
new additions to it in August and September. Heywood
also had £1 in September for additions to a play called
Cutting Dick, as to the origin of which nothing is known;
and properties were bought in October for *Byron*[1] and for
Absalom. Possibly the latter is identical with *The Three
Brothers*. Worcester's men did not perform at Court in
1602–3, but they must have expected a summons, as on
1 January they bought head-tires of one Mrs. Calle ' for the
corte '. Amongst their tradesmen were also Goodman
Freshwater, who supplied ' a canvas sewt and skenes ',
apparently for a stage dog, and John Willett, mercer, on
whose arrest John Duke found himself in the Clink at the end
of the season. Their expenditure was at a fairly high rate,
amounting to a total of £234 11s. 6d. for the seven months.
Unlike the Admiral's men, they spent more on apparel and
properties than on play-books. Some of their purchases were
costly enough, ' a grogren clocke, ij veluet gerkens, ij dubletes
and ij hed tyres ' from Edward Alleyn for £20, ' a manes
gowne of branshed velluet & a dublett ' from Christopher
Beeston for £6, and ' iiij clothe clockes layd with coper lace '
from Robert Shaw, formerly of the Admiral's, for £16. On
this last transaction they had to allow Henslowe £1 as interest
on his money. A ' flage of sylke ', no doubt for the theatre
roof, cost them £1 6s. 8d.[2] In summing his account,
Henslowe made various errors, whereby he robbed himself
of £1 1s. 3d., and presented a claim to the company
for £140 1s. It may be inferred that they had already
repaid him £93 12s. 3d., but of this there is no record in the
diary. He prepared an acknowledgement to be signed by all
the members of the company, but the only signature actually
attached is Blackwode's.

On 9 May 1603 Henslowe notes ' Begininge to playe agayne
by the Kynges licence & layd out sense for my lord of
Worsters men as folowethe '; but the only entry is one of £2
paid in earnest to Chettle and Day for a play of *Shore's Wife*.

---

[1] Spelt ' Burone ' and ' Berowne ' in the entries.
[2] Henslowe, i. 180. 183, 185, 186, 187, 190.

If playing was actually resumed, it was not long before the plague drove the companies out of London again, and there is nothing more of Worcester's men in the diary. Two visits from them are recorded at Leicester in the course of 1603, and two at Coventry and one at Barnstaple, whence they departed without playing, during 1602–3. Early in the new reign the company was taken into the patronage of Queen Anne.[1] This change was probably effected by Christmas, and certainly by 19 February 1604, when John Duke obtained a warrant on account of plays performed before Prince Henry by ' the Queenes Majesties players ' on the previous 2 and 13 January. The Queen's men are named in the Privy Council letter permitting the resumption of playing on 9 April 1604, which indicates their house as the Curtain. A list of players is found amongst other ' officers to the Queene ' receiving four and a half yards of red cloth apiece for the coronation procession of 15 March 1604.[2] The names given are ' Christopher Beeston, Robert Lee, John Duke, Robert Palante, Richard Purkins, Thomas Haward, James Houlte, Thomas Swetherton, Thomas Grene, and Robert Beeston '. Evidently several leading members had left the company. Kempe was probably dead.[3] Thare and Black-wood were on tour in Germany; Lowin seems to have joined the King's men. Of Cattanes and Underell no more is known. The same ten names are found in a draft patent for a royal licence to the Queen's men, of which the text follows:[4]

Iames, by the grace of God kynge of England, Scotland, Fraunce and Irelande, defender of the faith &c: To all Iustices *of peace*, Maiors, Sherryfes, vicechancellours *of any our vniuersities*, *Bailiffes* [Constables], headboroughes, [and other our officers] *Constables, and to all other our Officers, mynisters* and lov[e]inge subiectes *to whome it may appertaine* Greeting. Knowe yee that wee of our speciall grace, certaine know-ledge, and mere motion haue lycensed and awthorised, and by these presentes doe lycence and awthorise Thomas Greene, Christopher

---

[1] Cf. p. 7. A further notice of the transfer is given by Thomas Hey-wood, Γυναικεῖον or *General History of Women* (1624), who says that he was one of Worcester's men, who at James's accession ' bestowed me upon the excellent princesse Queen Anne '.

[2] *N. S. S. Trans.* (1877–9), 16*, from *Lord Chamberlain's Books*, 58ᵃ. In August the company served as grooms of the chamber (App. B).

[3] In assigning Kempe to the Queen's Revels in 1605, Dr. Greg (Henslowe, ii. 108) has been tripped up by one of Collier's forgeries ; cf. my review in *M. L. R.* iv. 408.

[4] Printed in *M. S. C.* i. 265, from *S. P. D. Jac. I*, ii. 100 ; also by Collier, i. 336, and Halliwell-Phillipps, *Illustrations*, 106. It is a rough draft full of deletions, marked by square brackets, and of additions, printed in italics, in the text. The theory of Fleay, 191, that the document is a forgery is disposed of by Greg, *Henslowe's Diary*, ii. 107.

Beeston, Thomas Hawood, Richard Pyrkins, Robert Pallant, Iohn Duke, Thomas Swynerton, I[e]ames Ho[u]lt, Robert Beeston, & Robert Lee, servauntes vnto our deare*st* [and welbeloved] wyfe *the* Queene Anna, with the rest of there Associates, freely to vse and exercise the art and faculty of playinge Comedies, Tragedies, Histories, Enterludes, Morralls, Pastoralls, Stage plaies, and such other lyke as they haue already studied, or hereafter shall vse or stud[d]y, as well for the recreacion of our lovinge subiectes as for our solace and pleasure, when wee shall thinke good to see them, during our pleasure ; And the said Comedies, Tragedies, Histories, Enterludes, Morralls, Pastoralls, Stage plaies, and such like, to shew and exercise publikly, when the infeccion of the plague shall decrease to the number of thirty weekly within *our Citie of* London and the liberties *therof,* aswell within there now vsuall Howsen, called the Curtayne, and the Bores head, within our County of Middlesex, [or] *as in* any other play howse not vsed by others, by the said *Thomas* Greene elected, or by him hereafter to be builte, and also within any Towne Halls, or Mouthalls, or other convenyent places, within the liberties and freedomes of any Cittie, vniversitie, Towne, or Boroughe whatsoeuer, within our said Realmes and domynyons : Willing and Commaundinge yowe and euerie of yowe, as you tender our pleasure, not only to permytt and suffer them [herein] *to vse and exercise the said art of playinge* without any your Lettes hinderaunces or molestacions, duringe our said pleasure, but also to be aydinge and assistinge vnto them, yf any wronge be to them offered, and to allow them such [former] curtesies, as hath *heretofore* bene given vnto any men of theire qualitie : [And also what further favour, any of our subiectes shall shew to theise our deare and loveinge wyfes servauntes, for our sake, wee shall take kyndly at your handes. Yeouen at   the   daye of
In the   yere of our Raygne of England: &c:]

Gyuen &c.

[Endorsed] The Quenes Plaiers.

This draft is undated. But it was prepared during a plague, and located the Queen's men at the Boar's Head ; and as they may reasonably be supposed to have exchanged the Boar's Head for the Red Bull (q.v.) before the plague of 1606 began, it may be conjecturally assigned to that of 1603–4. Probably it never passed the Great Seal, for if it had there would have been no necessity, so far as one can judge, for a later patent of 15 April 1609, which is on the rolls, and which closely follows the earlier draft in its terms, except that it omits the reference to the plague, names the Red Bull instead of the Boar's Head as one of the company's regular houses, and adds a saving clause for the rights of the Master of the Revels. Here is the text :[1]

---

[1] Printed in *M. S. C.* i. 270, from *P. R. 7 Jac. I,* pt. 39 ; also from

Iames by the grace of God &c. To all Iustices,
Mayors, Sheriffes, Baylieffes, Constables, head-
borrowes and other our Officers and lovinge
Subiectes Greetinge. Knowe yee that wee of
our especiall grace certayne knowledge and meere mocion have lycenced
and aucthorised and by these presentes doe lycence and aucthorize
Thomas Greene, Christofer Beeston, Thomas Haywood, Richard
Pirkyns, Richard Pallant, Thomas Swinnerton, Iohn Duke, Robert
Lee, Iames Haulte, and Roberte Beeston, Servantes to our moste
deerely beloved wiefe Queene Anne, and the reste of theire Associates,
to vse and exercise the arte and faculty of playinge Comedies, Tragedies, historyes, Enterludes, Moralles, Pastoralles, Stageplayes and
suche other like, as they have already studied or heareafter shall vse
or studye, aswell for the recreacion of our loving Subiectes as for our
solace and pleasure when wee shall thinke good to see them, during our
pleasure. And the said Comedies, Tragedies, histories, Enterludes,
Moralles, Pastoralles, Stageplayes and suche like to shẹwe and exercise
publiquely and openly to theire beste commoditye, aswell within
theire nowe vsuall houses called the Redd Bull in Clarkenwell and the
Curtayne in Hallowell, as alsoe within anye Towne halles, Mouthalles
and other convenient places within the libertye and freedome of any
other Citty, vniuersitye, Towne or Boroughe whatsoever within our
Realmes and Domynions. Willing and Commaundinge you and every
of you, as you tender our pleasure, not only to permitt and suffer them
herein without any your lettes hinderances or molestacions during our
said pleasure, but alsoe to be aydinge [and] assistinge vnto them, yf
anye wronge be to them offered, and to allowe them suche former
curtesies as hath byn given to men of theire place and qualitye, and
alsoe what favoure you shall shewe to them for our sake wee shall
take kyndly at your handes. Prouided alwaies and our will and
pleasure is that all aucthoritye, power, priuiledges, and profyttes
whatsoeuer belonginge and properly appertayninge to Master of
Revelles in respecte of his Office and everye Cause, Article or graunte
contayned within the lettres Patentes or Commission, which have byn
heretofore graunted or directed by the late Queene Elizabeth our deere
Sister or by our selues to our welbeloued Servant Edmond Tylney
Master of the Office of our said Revelles or to Sir George Bucke knighte
or to eyther of them in possession or revercion, shalbe remayne and
abyde entyer and full in effecte, force, estate and vertue as ample sorte
as if this our Commission had never byn made. In witnes wherof &c.
Witnes our selfe at Westminster the fifteenth daye of Aprill.

*De concessione licen-
tie Thome Greene et
aliis.*

per breve de priuato sigillo &c.

It will be observed that the documents quoted disclose no
change in the composition of the Queen's official servants

P. R., but misdescribed as a Privy Seal, by T. E. Tomlins in *Sh. Soc.
Papers,* iv. 45. The Signet Bill is indexed under April 1609 in Phillimore,
104.

between 1604 and 1609. But the question of *personnel* is not really quite so simple as this, since the members of a company under a trade agreement were not always the same as those named in the authority under which it performed. Before discussing this complication, it will be simplest first to set out separately the notices of the Queen's men, which have been preserved in London and in provincial records respectively.

Queen's men played at Court on 30 December 1605, in Heywood's *How to Learn of a Woman to Woo*, which is not extant. They played also on 27 December 1606. For both years their payee was, as in 1604, John Duke. During 1607 Dekker and Webster's *Sir Thomas Wyatt* and Day, Wilkins, and Rowley's *Travels of Three English Brothers* were printed with their name on the title-pages. The latter play, according to the entry of 29 June 1607 in the Stationers' Register, was acted at the Curtain. But it is shown by a passage in *The Knight of the Burning Pestle* to have been also on the stage of the Red Bull. In this house Thomas Swinnerton, one of the men named in the patents, acquired an interest between 24 March 1605 and 23 March 1606, and all the evidence is in favour of a continuous sojourn of Queen's men there until 1617. The first quarto of Heywood's *A Woman Killed with Kindness*, also printed in 1607, does not bear their name, but it is on that of the 'third edition' of 1617. They are not named as playing at Court during the winter of 1607–8, but in the course of 1608 Heywood's *Rape of Lucrece* was printed, as played by them at the Red Bull. They gave five plays at Court in the winter of 1608–9, one on 27 December 1609, three on 10 and one on 27 December 1610. Heywood's *Golden Age* was printed, as played by them at the Red Bull, in 1611. The Court records of 1611–12 are a little confused.[1] But they appear to have played Cooke's *City Gallant* on 27 December, his *Tu Quoque*, which is in fact the same play, on 2 February, to have joined with the King's men in performances of Heywood's *Silver Age* and *Rape of Lucrece* on 12 and 13 January, and to have played unnamed pieces on 21 and 23 January. From 1609 to 1612 their payee was Thomas Greene. Webster's *White Devil* and Dekker's *If It be not Good, the Devil is in It*, were printed as theirs in 1612, the former with a laudation of the acting of 'my freind Maister Perkins', the latter as played at the Red Bull. They did not play at Court during the winter of 1612–13, but did on 24 December 1613 and 5 January 1614. *Tu Quoque* was printed as theirs in 1614. In the winter of 1614–15 they gave three plays at Court. Heywood's

[1] Cf. App. B.

Four Prentices of London was printed in 1615 as played by them at the Red Bull, and their name is also on *The Honest Lawyer*, registered on 14 August 1615 and printed in 1616. They gave four plays at Court during the winter of 1615–16. For all their Court plays from 1613–16 Robert Lee was payee, but Ellis Worth replaces him for a Somerset House performance before Queen Anne on 17 December 1615. When they were called with other companies before the Privy Council on 29 March 1615 to answer for playing in Lent, they were represented by Lee and Christopher Beeston. The records of the Middlesex justices contain a note of 4 October 1616 that Beeston and the rest of the players at the Red Bull were in arrears to the extent of £5 on an annual rate of £2 agreed to by them for the repair of the highways.

Provincial visits of Queen's men are recorded in November 1605 at Dover; in 1605 at Leicester; in 1605–6 at Bath, Coventry, Saffron Walden, and Weymouth; on 25 July 1606 at Ipswich; on 4 September 1606 at Ludlow; in 1606 at York; in 1606–7 at Bath (twice), Coventry, Exeter, and Ipswich; on 14 August 1607 at Oxford; on 12 September 1607 at Belvoir (Earl of Rutland's);[1] in 1607 at Barnstaple, Leicester, and Reading; in 1607–8 at Coventry, Oxford, Reading, and Shrewsbury; on 6 June and 26 September 1608 at Leicester;[2] in 1608–9 at Coventry,[3] Marlborough, and Shrewsbury; between 8 July and 9 August 1609 at Dover; on 15 October 1609 at Norwich; in 1609 at Canterbury; in 1609–10 at Shrewsbury and Stafford; about 23 March 1610 at Maidstone; on 2 November 1610 at Ipswich; on 31 December 1610 at Leicester; in 1610–11 at Shrewsbury and Southampton; on 27 February 1611 (for a week) at Norwich; between 11 April and 9 May and between 29 August and 29 September 1612 at Dover; on 14 June and 26 October 1612 at Leicester; in 1611–12 at Saffron Walden; in 1612–13 at Barnstaple, Coventry (perhaps twice), and Ipswich; on 18 February 1613 at Marlborough; on 16 March 1613 at Leicester; between 13 April and 15 May 1613 at Dover; on 2 November 1613 at Marlborough; on 22 December 1613 at Leicester; in 1613–14 at Saffron Walden, Marlborough, Oxford, and Shrewsbury; on 27 April 1614 (for three days) at

[1] *Rutland MSS.* iv. 461. They stayed two days, and gave four performances.

[2] Kelly, 248, 'Item the vj[th] of June given to the Queenes Players xl[s]. . . . Item the xxj[th] of Auguste given to the Children of the Revells xx[s]. Item the xxvj[th] of September given to one other Companye of the Queenes plaiors xx[s].'

[3] Murray, ii. 245, 'paid to the Queenes players to Thomas Swinerton xl[s]'.

Norwich; [1] between 3 and 29 September 1614 at Dover; in
1614–15 at Barnstaple and Doncaster (perhaps twice); on
15 April 1615 at Coventry; in April or May 1615 at Leicester;
on 6 May 1615 at Norwich; [2] on 16 October 1615 and again
later in 1615 and on 22 February 1616 at Leicester; [3] on
7 November 1615 at Marlborough; in 1615–16 at Barnstaple, Dunwich (thrice), Southampton, and Weymouth;
in January 1616 at Nottingham; between 20 January and
17 February 1616 and between 11 May and 8 June at Dover;
on 17 February 1616 at Coventry; on 22 February 1616 at
Leicester; between 1 and 6 April (four days) and on 29 May
1616 at Norwich; [4] on 26 October 1616 at Marlborough;
and on 6 February 1617 and again later in 1617 at Leicester. [5]

There were thus tours in each year, which sometimes
extended over periods during which the London theatres
must have been open. The Leicester notices of 1608, 1615,
and 1617 suggest that more than one company was at work,
and the explanation certainly is that some of the players
named in the patent, instead of joining the London organization, had recourse to making up companies of their own for
provincial purposes. Of this there is further evidence. The
Southampton archives contain a copy of the following
warrant from Queen Anne herself, dated on 7 March 1606: [6]

[1] Murray, ii. 340, from Mayor's Court Books (18 April 1614), ' Swynnerton one of the Quenes players in the name of himselfe & the rest of his
company desyred leaue to play in the cytty accordinge to his Maiesties
Lettres patents shewed forth, And Mr Maior & Court moved them to
play onely on Wednesday, Thursday & Fryday in Easter weke.'

[2] Murray, ibid. (6 May 1615), ' Thomas Swynnerton produced this day
Letters Patents dated the xth [? xv^th] of Aprill Anno Septimo Jacobi
whereby hee & others are authorised to play as the Quenes men, vidz.
Thomas Grene, Christofer Breston [? Beeston], Thomas Haywood, Richard
Pyrkyns, Robt. Pallant, Tho. Swynnerton, John Duke, Robt. Lee, James
Hoult, & Robt. Breston [? Beeston].'

[3] Kelly, 252, ' Item given to the Queenes Maiesties Highnes Playors
xl^s. . . . Item the xvj^th daye of October Given to the Queenes Playors xl^s.
Item given to one other Companye of the Queenes Playors xxx^s.'

[4] Murray, ii. 340 (30 March 1616), ' A Patent was this day brought
into the Court by Thomas Swynerton made to Thomas Grene . . . &
Robert Beeston Servants to Quene Anne & the rest of their associats
bearing Teste xv^o Aprilis Anno Septimo Jacobi. But the said Swynerton
confesseth that hee himselfe & Robert Lee only are here to play the rest
are absent . . .'; (29 May 1616), ' Thomas Swynerton came this day into
the Court & affirmed himselfe to be one of the players to the Quenes
Maiestie & bringinge with him no patent desyred to haue leaue to play
here . . . the same company had liberty to play here at Easter last. . . .'
Leave was refused on this occasion.

[5] Kelly, 253, ' Item the sixt of Februarye given to the Queenes Playors.
Item given to one other Companye of the Queenes Playors '.

[6] Hist. MSS. xi. 3. 26.

' Warrant from the Queenes Majestie of her Players. Anna Regina. Anne by the grace of God Queene of England, Scottland, Fraunce, and Ireland. To all Justices of the Peace, Maiors, Sheriffs, Bayliffes, and all other his Majestes Officers and loving subiectes to whom yt shall or may appertaine greetinge, Know yee that of our speciall grace and favour, Wee are well pleased to authorize under our hand and signett the bearers hereof our sworne servauntes Robert Lee, Martin Statier and Roger Barfield with theyr fellowes and associates being our Commedians vppon theyr humble Suite unto us for theyr better maintenaunce, Yf att annie time they should have occasion to travell into anie parte of his Majestes Dominions to playe Tragedyes, historyes, commedies and pastoralls as well in anie about the Cittye of London, and in all other cittyes vniversities and townes at all time anie times (the time of divine seruice onlye excepted) Theise are therefore to will and requier you vppon the sight hereofe quiettlye and favourably with your best favours, to permitt and suffer them, to use theyr sayd qualitye within your Jurisdiccions without anie of your molestacions or troubles, and also to affourd them your Townehalls and all other such places as att anie time have been used by men of theyr qualitye, That they maye be in the better readiness for our seruise when they shalbe thereunto commaunded, Nott doubtinge butt that our sayd servauntes shall find the more favour for our sake in your best assistaunce, Wherein you shall doe unto us acceptable pleasure. Given att the Court of Whitehall, the seaventh daye of Marche 1605.'

Of these three men, Lee, and Lee alone, appears in the London lists of 1603, 1604, and 1609. Of Barfield's career nothing more is known. Martin Slater, whose name can be divined under that of Statier, had left the Admiral's in 1597. He was probably in Scotland during 1599, and if so his patronage by Anne may be analogous to the patronage by James, which brought Laurence Fletcher's name into the King's men's patent. In 1603 he was payee for Hertford's men. Presumably the enterprise of 1606 did not last long, for in the spring of 1608 Slater became manager for the King's Revels. His place in the provinces may have been taken by Thomas Swinnerton, who was leading a company of Queen's men at Coventry in 1608–9, and whose departure from the London company is perhaps indicated by the fact that at about the same time he sold a share, which he had held in the house of the Red Bull. Swinnerton was travelling again in 1614–16 and using an exemplification of the patent of 1609. In 1616 he was accompanied by Robert Lee, who for two years before had been acting as payee for the London company. Lee came again with the exemplification to Norwich on 31 May 1617, and it was then noted to have been taken out on 7 January 1612. A few days later, on 4 June 1617, a copy was entered in the Norwich court-books of a warrant by the

Lord Chamberlain of 16 July 1616, condemning the use of such exemplifications, and specifying amongst others two taken out by Thomas Swinnerton and Martin Slater, ' beinge two of the Queens Maiesties company of Playors hauing separated themselves from their said Company '.[1] Slater had, therefore, returned to the provincial field, and there were now two travelling companies of Queen's men. I take it that in 1617 the Lord Chamberlain succeeded in suppressing them, and that the Queen's men who continued to appear in the provinces up to Anne's death on 2 March 1619 were the London company.[2] Lee joined the Queen's Revels as reorganized under a licence of 31 October 1617. Slater, about the same time, joined the Children of Bristol, for whom, with John Edmonds and Nathaniel Clay, he got letters of assistance in April 1618. In these all three are described as her Majesty's servants. Swinnerton apparently succeeded in keeping on foot a company of his own, which visited Leicester in 1619.[3] The Bristol company was in fact under Anne's patronage, but Lee and Swinnerton, no less than Slater and Edmonds, remained technically the Queen's servants, and are included with the London men in a list of the players who received mourning at her funeral on 13 May 1619.[4] These were Robert Lee, Richard Perkins, Christopher Beeston, Robert Pallant, Thomas Heywood, James Holt, Thomas Swinnerton, Martin Slater, Ellis Wroth, John Comber, Thomas Basse, John Blaney, William Robinson, John Edmonds, Thomas Drewe, Gregory Sanderson, and John Garret.

The list of seventeen names includes seven of the ten patentees of 1609. I do not know what had become of John Duke and Robert Beeston. Thomas Greene had died in August 1612, having made on 25 July a will, amongst the witnesses to which were Christopher Beeston, Heywood, and Perkins. The disposal of his property led many years after-wards to a lawsuit, which gives valuable information as to both the *personnel* and the organization of the London company. After providing for his family and making some small legacies, including one to John Cumber, and 40s. to ' my fellowes of the house of the Redd Bull, to buy gloves for them ', he left the residue to his widow and executrix, Susanna Greene, formerly wife of one Browne.[5] In June 1613 she took a third

[1] App. D, No. clviii ; cf. Murray, ii. 343.
[2] Murray, i. 204. [3] Kelly, 254.
[4] Collier, i. 397, from a manuscript at Bridgewater House.
[5] Fleay, 192, guesses that her first husband was Robert Browne of the 1583 Worcester's company. As Queen Anne's men played at the Boar's

husband, James Baskervile. The following is her account in 1623 of certain transactions with the company. Shortly before Greene's death had died George Pulham, a 'half sharer' in the company, which is described as being in 1612 'the companie of the actors or players of the late queenes majestie Queene Anne, then vsuallie frequentinge and playinge att the signe of the Redd Bull in St. Johns Street, in Clerkenwell parishe, in the county of Middlesex'. His representatives received £40 from the company in respect of his half-share. This was under an agreement formerly made amongst the company 'concerninge the part and share of euerie one of the sharers and half sharers of the said companie according to the rate and proporcion of their shares or half shares in that behalfe'. Under the same agreement Susanna Greene, whose husband was 'one of the principall and cheif persons of the said companie, and a full adventurer, storer and sharer of in and amongst them', claimed £80, together with £37 laid out by him before his death in 'diuers necessarie prouisions' for the company. In order to get satisfaction she had to appeal to Viscount Lisle, Chamberlain of the Queen's Household, 'who hadd a kind of gouernment and suruey ouer the said players'. It was arranged that Mrs. Greene should receive a half-share in the profits until the debt was paid. By the time, however, of her marriage with Baskervile, she had only received £6. In June 1615 negotiations took place between the Baskerviles and the company, who then included Worth, Perkins, and Christopher Hutchinson, *alias* Beeston, by which the Baskerviles agreed to invest £57 10s. in the enterprise and to accept in discharge of their claims a pension for their joint lives of 1s. 8d. a day 'for euerye of sixe daies in the weeke wherin they should play'. The company defaulted, and in June 1616 a second settlement was made, whereby the Baskerviles invested another £38, a further pension of 2s. a day was established, and the life of Susan's son, Francis Browne (or Baskervile), was substituted for her husband's. The players were Christopher Beeston, Thomas Heywood, Ellis Worth, John Cumber, John Blaney, Francis Walpole, Robert Reynolds, William Robins, Thomas Drewe, and Emanuel Read.[1] Again they defaulted, and moreover fell into arrear for the wages of

Head, he is very likely to have been the 'Browne of the Boares head' who 'dyed very pore' in the plague of 1603 (*Henslowe Papers*, 59).

[1] Murray, i. 193, appears to date this list *c.* 1612, and the allegation in the Bill (Fleay, 275) that the pensions were paid for five years supports this. But it cannot be earlier than 1613 as Read was still with the Lady Elizabeth's in that year. Nor does it include Lee, who was payee for the Queen's in 1614–16. It clearly belongs to the 1616 settlement.

another of Susan Baskervile's sons, William Browne, who played with them as a hired man. A third settlement, reassuring the pensions, and substituting William Browne for Francis, who was now dead, was made on 3 June 1617, when the company were ' now comme, or shortlie to comme from the said Playhowse called the Redd Bull to the Playhowse in Drurie Lane called the Cockpitt '; and to this the parties, so far as the company were concerned, were Beeston, Heywood, Worth, Cumber, Walpole, Blaney, Robins, and Drewe. Apparently Reynolds and Read, and also Perkins and Thomas Basse, although their names were recited in the deed, refused to seal. Some further light is thrown on this by allegations of Worth, Cumber, and Blaney, in opposition to those of Mrs. Baskervile in 1623. The company of 1617 contained some members ' new come into ' it, ' which were of other companyes at the tyme of graunting the first annuity '. The terms of the agreement were carefully looked into, and were found to bind the company to procure the subscription of any future new members to its terms. This was inconsistent with a proviso of 1616 that the pensions should only last so long as four of those then signing should play together ; and therefore, while some of the company signed and gave bonds by way of security on an oral promise by Mrs. Baskervile that this proviso should in fact hold good, others refused to do so. These were the wiser, for in 1623, when Worth, Cumber, and Blaney were the only three of the 1617 signatories who still held together, Mrs. Baskervile sued them on their bonds, and although they applied to Chancery for equitable enforcement of the alleged oral promise, Chancery held that the agreement, being made between players, was ' vnfitt to be releeued or countenaunced in a courte of equitie '. In some other respects the players' account of the transactions differs from Mrs. Baskervile's, and in particular they alleged that the Baskerviles had secured their interest by bribing Beeston, to whom ' your oratours and the rest of thier fellowes at that tyme and long before and since did put the managing of thier whole businesses and affaires belonging vnto them ioyntly as they were players in trust ', so that she knew well that whatever he promised the rest ' would allowe of the same '. This Mrs. Baskervile repudiates as regards the bribe, and does not wholly accept as regards Beeston's position in the company, although she admits that both before and after her husband's death they ' did putt much affiance in the said Huttchinson alias Beeston, concerninge the managing of their affaires '.

I am afraid that Beeston's character does not come

altogether unstained out of another suit brought by one John Smith in the Court of Requests during 1619 for a sum of £46 5s. 8d. in respect of ' tinsell stuffes and other stuffe ' delivered on Beeston's order to Worth, Perkins, Cumber, and others at the Red Bull between 27 June 1612 and 23 February 1617, since when they had ' fallen at variance and strife amongst themselves and separated and devided themselves into other companies '. He accuses these four men of conspiring to keep him out of payment. Worth, Perkins, and Cumber asserted that the liability was Beeston's. The company had ' required divers officers and that every of the said actors should take vpon them some place & charge '. Beeston was charged with the provision of furniture and apparel, which needed ' a thriueing man & one that was of abilitie & meanes '. He was to ' defaulke outt of the collec-cions and gatheringes which were made continually when-soeuer any playe was acted a certen some of money as a comon stock ', to pay for purchases out of this, and to account to the company for the balance. No one else was privy to his transactions. The arrangement lasted for seven or eight years, and they believe that he ' much enritched himself ', and rendered a false account for expenditure of £400. He is now conspiring with Smith and hoping for a chance to ' exclayme on ' them. If he incurred debt, he had certainly taken funds to meet it. From the beginning he had ' a greater care for his owne privatt gaine '. Now he has ' of late given over his coate & condicion & separated and devided himself ' from the company, carrying away all the furniture and apparel. Beeston says that he has long been ill. On Queen Anne's death he left the company and joined Prince Charles's men. The Queen's had ten sharers, and sometimes one, sometimes another, provided the clothes. He denies liability. Several witnesses, including William Freshwater, merchant tailor and ' a workman to the said company ', spoke to Beeston's liability.[1] One John King says that the company allowed Beeston ' one half of the profitt that came of the gallyryes ', and that they began to break up about three years ago. At a hearing on 16 June 1620 Beeston got the case deferred on the ground that Emanuel Read, a material witness, was in Ireland until Michaelmas. Elizabeth, the wife of Richard Perkins, said that Read had been there for two or three years, was over at Easter, and was not expected again. Smith got in a blow at Beeston's credit with an affidavit that he had said ' it was

---

[1] ' Goodman Freshwater ' was furnishing stuffs to Worcester's men in 1602–3 (Henslowe, i. 179, 187).

nothing for him to put in a false answere into the Court of Requestes, for that it was not punishable '. The result of the suit is unknown.

We may perhaps reach the following conclusions as to the composition of the London company after the deaths in 1612 of Pulham, presumably a recent comer since 1609, and Greene. Their nucleus consisted of two of the patented men, Christopher Beeston and Heywood, who probably remained with them throughout. Of the other patentees, Swinnerton kept to the provinces. Lee had rejoined them from the provinces by 1613 or 1614, and went back to the provinces about May 1616. Perkins was apparently not of their number in June 1616, but was in June 1617. Holt is not traceable; perhaps he also went to the provinces. Pallant joined the Lady Elizabeth's in 1614 and had passed to Prince Charles's by 1616. All these five men, however, appear with Beeston and Heywood as Anne's servants at her funeral. Here too are Slater and Edmonds, then of the Bristol, and apparently never of the London company; also Worth, Cumber, Blaney, Drewe, and Robinson, presumably identical with Robins, all of whom had joined the London company by June 1616, Basse, formerly of the Lady Elizabeth's, who joined it between June 1616 and June 1617, and Gregory Sanderson and John Garret, who, if they belonged to the London company at all, must have joined it after June 1617.[1] The list does not contain the names of two men who belonged to the company in 1616 and 1617. One was Emanuel Read, who joined it from the Lady Elizabeth's in 1613 or later; the other, Robert Reynolds, whose attachment to the company must have been rather loose, as he was travelling in Germany in July 1616 and again in 1618. Evidently, as the lawsuits suggest, the organization of the Queen's men during its later years was rather unstable. Into its attempts to hold together after Anne's death and the after-careers of its members, it is not necessary to go.

In June 1617 the Queen's were come, or shortly to come, from the Red Bull to the Cockpit. In fact they were at the Cockpit, then a new house, on 4 March 1617, when it was sacked by prentices in a Shrovetide riot.[2] But they may have returned to the Red Bull for a time, while the Cockpit was being repaired, as they did again after they lost it on the separation from Christopher Beeston, who seems to have been its owner, in 1619.

[1] Sanderson may be the ' Sands ' who played with ' Ellis ' [Worth] in Laborne's *Poor Man's Comfort* (q.v.), about 1617. Or James Sands, formerly a boy with the King's men, may have come to the Queen's.
[2] Adams, 351.

xxii. THE DUKE OF LENNOX'S MEN

Ludovic Stuart, s. of Esmé, 1st Duke of Lennox ; cousin and until 1594 heir presumptive of James ; *nat.* 29 Sept. 1574 ; succ. as 2nd Duke, 26 May 1583 ; Gentleman of Bedchamber, 1603 ; Earl of Richmond, 6 Oct. 1613 ; Lord Steward, Nov. 1615 ; Duke of Richmond, 17 Aug. 1623 ; o.s.p. 16 Feb. 1624.

The first notice of Lennox's men is on 13 October 1604, when he gave an open warrant of assistance in their behalf addressed to mayors, justices, and other local officers, some of whom had apparently refused the company permission to play (App. D, no. cxxxvii).   On 16 March 1605 Francis Henslowe gave his uncle Philip a bond of £60 to observe articles of an agreement he had entered into with John Garland and Abraham Savere ' his ffellowes, servantes to the most noble Prince the duke of Lennox ' ; and on 1 March 1605 Savere had given Francis Henslowe a power of attorney to recover £40 on a forfeited bond from John Garland of ' the ould forde ', securing delivery of a warrant made to Savere by Lennox (*Henslowe Papers*, 62).   Some   other traces point to a connexion between Savere and Francis Henslowe, which was ended by the latter's death in the middle of 1606 (Henslowe, ii. 277), and an undated loan of £7 by Philip Henslowe to his nephew ' to goyne with owld Garlland and Symcockes and Saverey when they played in the duckes nam at ther laste goinge owt ' (Henslowe, i. 160) makes it possible to add one more to the list of the company.   It does not seem to have played in London, but is traceable at Canterbury in 1603–4, Barnstaple, Coventry, and Norwich in 1604–5, and Coventry again in 1607–8.   Both Garland and Henslowe had been Queen Elizabeth's men, and it is possible that, when these men were left stranded by her death in 1603, they found a new patron in Lennox.   John Garland had joined the Duke of York's men by 1610, and it has been suggested that this company may have been a continuation of Lennox's.

xxiii. THE DUKE OF YORK'S (PRINCE CHARLES'S) MEN

The Duke of York's Men (1608–12) ; The Prince's Men (1612–16)

Charles, 2nd s. of James I ; *nat.* 19 Nov. 1600 ; Duke of Albany, 23 Dec. 1600 ; Duke of York, 16 Jan. 1605 ; Prince of Wales, 3 Nov. 1616 ; afterwards (27 Mar. 1625) Charles I.

[*Bibliographical Note.*—The documents bearing on the relations of the Duke of York's men with Alleyn are printed by W. W. Greg in *Henslowe*

Papers (1907); the Bill and Answers in the equity suit of *Taylor v. Hemynges* (1612) by C. W. Wallace in *Globe Theatre Apparel* (p.p., 1909).]

A company under the patronage of Prince Charles, then Duke of York, first makes its appearance during 1608. and in the provinces. A visit of 'the younger princes' men to Ipswich is recorded on 20 October. During 1608–9 the company was also at Bath, and it is at least possible that it was 'the Princes players of the White Chapple London' rewarded at Leicester in 1608. The Boar's Head (q.v.) may have been roughly spoken of as in Whitechapel, and although there is no proof that the Duke of York's men occupied it after the Queen's moved to the Red Bull, there is nothing to connect them during the earlier years of their career with any of the better-known London houses. On 30 March 1610 they received, like other London companies, a patent, of which the following are the terms:[1]

De licentia agendi Tragedias &c pro Johanne Garland & aliis.

Iames by the grace of God &c. To all Iustices, Mayors, Sheriffes, Baylies, Constables, hedboroughes and other our loveing subiectes and officers greetinge. Knowe ye that wee of our especyall grace, certen knowledge, and meere mocion haue lycensed and aucthorized, and by theis presentes doe lycence and authorise Iohn Garland, Willyam Rowley, Thomas Hobbes, Robert Dawes, Ioseph Taylor, Iohn Newton, and Gilbert Reason, alreadye sworne servauntes to our deere sonne the Duke of York and Rothesay, with the rest of their company, to vse and exercise the arte and quality of playing Comedyes, Tragedies, histories, Enterludes, Moralles, Pastoralles, Stagplayes, and such other like as they haue already studdied or hereafter shall studye or vse, aswell for the recreacion of our loveing subiectes, as for our solace and pleasure when wee shall thinke good to see them, and the said Enterludes or other to shewe and execise publiquely to their best aduantage and commoditie, aswell in and about our Cittye of London in such vsuall howses as themselues shall provide, as alsoe within anye Townehalles, Mootehalles, Guildhalles, Schoolehowses, or other convenient places within the lybertye and freedome of any other Cittye, vniversity, Towne, or Boroughe whatsoever within our Realmes and Domynions, willing and comaundinge you and everie of you, as you tender our pleasure, not onlye to permitt and suffer them herein without any your lettes, hindraunces, molestacions or disturbances during our said pleasure, but alsoe to be ayding and assisting vnto them, if any wronge be vnto them offered, and to allowe them such former curtesies as hath byne given to men of their place and quality, And alsoe what further favor you shall shewe them for our sake wee shall take yt kyndlye at your handes. Prouided alwaies and our will and pleasure is that all authority, power, privi-

---

[1] *M. S. C.* i. 272, from *P. R. 8 Jac. I*, p. 8; also printed by T. E. Tomlins in *Sh. Soc. Papers*, iv. 47.

ledg, and proffitt whatsoever belonging and properly apperteyninge
to the Master of our Revelles in respect of his Office and everie article
and graunt contayned within the lettres patentes or Commission,
which haue byne heretofore graunted or directed by the late Queene
Elizabeth our deere sister or by our selfe to our welbeloved servantes
Edmond Tillney Master of the said Office of the said Revelles, or to
Sir George Bucke knight, or to eyther of them, in possession or Revercion, shall remayne and abyde entire and in full force, estate and
vertue and in as ample sort as if this our commission had never bene
made. Witnes our selfe att Westminster the thirtith daye March.

per breve de priuato sigillo &c.

The only member of the Duke of York's men, of whose previous
history anything is known, is John Garland. He was of
the Duke of Lennox's men in 1605. Perhaps the whole
company was taken over from the Duke of Lennox. Mr. Fleay
says that the Duke of York's men arose ' immediately after
the disappearance of the King's Revels Children ',[1] and appears
to suggest a continuity between the two companies ; but he
must have overlooked the fact that the Duke of York's were
already performing in the provinces, while the King's Revels
were in all probability still at Whitefriars.[2]

Some reconstruction doubtless took place about the date
of the issue of the patent, for the pleadings in the equity
suit of *Taylor v. Hemynges* in 1612 recites an agreement of
15 March 1610, which provided for the continuance of
fellowship during three years and the forfeiture of the interest
in a common stock of 'apparrell goodes money and other
thinges ' of any member, who left without the consent of the
rest. It was made between Garland on the one side and
Taylor, Rowley, Dawes, and Hobbes on the other, and these
four gave Garland a bond of £200 as security. On 8 May the
five bought some ' olde clothes or apparrell which formerly
weare players clothes or apparrell ' from John Heminges of
the King's men for £11, and gave a bond of £20 for payment.
Apparently payment had not been made by Easter 1611,
when Taylor ' by the licence and leave of his said Master the
Duke vpon some speciall reason . . . did give over and leave
to play in the company '. Under the agreement the apparel
passed to his fellows, and according to Taylor they paid
Heminges the £11 or otherwise satisfied him, and then
' havinge conceaued some vndeserued displeasure ' against
Taylor for leaving them, conspired with Heminges to defraud
him of £20 on the bond. According to Heminges no payment

---

[1] Fleay, 188.
[2] Murray, i. 239, confuses the Duke's with Lord Aubigny's men.

was made, and he sued Taylor as ' the best able to paye and discharge the same '. Taylor was arrested and in February 1612 brought his suit in equity to stay the common law proceedings. The result is unknown.

The company frequently played at Court, but, as it would seem, only before the younger members of the royal family. Their first appearance was before Charles and Elizabeth on 9 February 1610. In 1610–11 they were at Saffron Walden. They came before Charles and Elizabeth on 12 and 20 December 1610 and 15 January 1611, and before Henry, Charles, and Elizabeth on 12 and 28 January and 13 and 24 February 1612. On this last occasion they played William Rowley's *Hymen's Holiday, or Cupid's Vagaries*. After Henry's death, on 7 November 1612, they became entitled to the designation of the Prince's players. In 1612–13 they were at Barnstaple and Ipswich. On 2 and 10 March 1613 they gave the two parts of *The Knaves*, perhaps by Rowley, before Charles, Elizabeth, and the Palsgrave. In 1613–14 they were at Barnstaple, Dover, Saffron Walden, and Coventry. They were not at Court for the winter of 1613–14. In November 1614 they were at Oxford, Leicester, and Nottingham. At the Christmas of 1614–15 they gave six plays before Charles, and on 11 February they were at Youghal in Ireland. Ten days later R. A.'s *The Valiant Welshman* was entered and in the course of the year published as theirs. Their leader seems to have been Rowley. He both wrote plays for them and acted as payee for all their court rewards from 1610 to 1614. In 1611 they lost Taylor and in 1614 Dawes to the Lady Elizabeth's men ; and these transferences seem to have led to a temporary amalgamation of the two companies, which Mr. Fleay and Dr. Greg place in 1614, but for which their distinct appearances at Court in the following winter suggest 1615 as the more likely date.[1] On 29 March 1615 William Rowley and John Newton were called with representatives of other companies before the Privy Council to answer for playing in Lent. No separate representation of the Lady Elizabeth's is indicated by the list. In 1614–15 the Prince's were at Norwich, Coventry, Winchester, and Barnstaple. In the winter of 1615–16 they gave four plays before Prince Charles, and the payee was not Rowley, but Alexander Foster, formerly

[1] A letter, probably originally from Dulwich, but now *Egerton MS.* 2623, f. 25 (printed in *Sh. Soc. Papers*, i. 18, and *Henslowe Papers*, 126), is signed by William Rowley, as well as by Taylor and Pallant, and must therefore be later than this amalgamation, and not, as Dr. Greg suggests, from the Lady Elizabeth's c. 1613. It confirms a purchase of clothes from Henslowe for £55.

of the Lady Elizabeth's. Rosseter's patent of 3 June 1615 for a second Blackfriars theatre contemplates its use by the Prince's men and the Lady Elizabeth's, as well as by the Queen's Revels, and Field's *Amends for Ladies* was actually played in the Blackfriars, probably in this house before it was suppressed, by the two first-named companies. After Henslowe's death on 6 January 1616, the combination, whatever its nature, was probably broken up, and separate companies of Prince's men and Lady Elizabeth's men were again formed. But both of the original companies continued to be represented in one which remained at the Hope. This is shown by an agreement entered into with Alleyn and Meade on 20 March 1616, and signed in the presence of Robert Daborne and others by William Rowley, Robert Pallant, Joseph Taylor, Robert Hamlen, John Newton, William Barksted, Thomas Hobbes, Antony Smith, William Penn, and Hugh Attwell.[1] This recites that the signatories and others had given bonds to Henslowe and Meade for the repayment of sums lent them by Henslowe, for a stock of apparel worth £400, and for the fulfilment of certain Articles of Agreement ; and that at their entreaty Alleyn had agreed to accept £200 in discharge of their full liabilities. They covenant to pay the £200 by making over to Alleyn one-fourth of the daily takings of the whole galleries at the Hope or any house in which they may play, and to carry out the Articles with Alleyn and Meade by so playing. Alleyn and Meade agree to cancel the bonds when the £200 is paid, except any which may relate to private debts of any of the men to Henslowe, and also to make over to them any apparel which they had received from Henslowe, Alleyn, or Meade. The rights of Alleyn and Meade against any bondsmen not taking part in the new agreement are to remain unaffected. That the signatories to this document used the name of Prince Charles's men seems pretty clear from the reappearance of several of their names in two later lists of the Prince's men, one in Rowley and Middleton's *Mask of Heroes* (1619), the other in the records of King James's funeral on 20 May 1625.[2] This last contains also the name of Gilbert Reason, who is not one of the signatories of 1616, but was in that year travelling the provinces with an irregularly obtained exemplification of

---

[1] Text in Collier, *Memoirs of Alleyn*, 127 ; abstract in *Henslowe Papers*, 90.

[2] *N. S. S. Trans. 1877–9*, 19* ; cf. Fleay, 265. Collier, i. 406, has an elegy by William Rowley on Hugh Attwell, servant to Prince Charles, who died 25 Sept. 1621.

the 1610 patent.[1] An undated letter from Pallant, Rowley,
Taylor, Newton, Hamlen, Attwell, and Smith to Alleyn,
which may belong to some time in 1616 or 1617, shows that,
in spite of the easy terms which the company seem to have
received by the agreement, the subsequent relations were not
altogether smooth. They write to excuse their removal from
the Bankside, where they had stood the intemperate weather,
until 'more intemperate Mr. Meade thrust vs over, taking
the day from vs wch by course was ours'. They ask Alleyn
to find them a house and in the meantime to lend them £40,
on the security that 'we haue to receiue from the court
(wch after Shrouetide wee meane to pursue wth best speede)
a great summe of monie', amounting to more than twice the
loan desired.[2] It is to be presumed that the 'course' to
which they refer was some distribution of days between
playing and bear-baiting. In 1619 the company was joined
by Christopher Beeston, formerly of the Queen's, and his
house of the Cockpit became available for their use.

xxiv. THE LADY ELIZABETH'S MEN

Elizabeth, e. d. of James I ; *nat. c.* 19 Aug. 1596 ; m. Frederick V,
Elector Palatine (Palsgrave), 14 Feb. 1613 ; Queen of Bohemia,
7 Nov. 1619 ; known as Queen of Hearts ; *ob.* 13 Feb. 1662.

[*Bibliographical Note.*—Nearly all the material is to be found among
the extracts from the Dulwich MSS. printed by W. W. Greg in *Henslowe
Papers* (1907) and summarized in Henslowe, ii. 137.]

This company seems to have come into existence in 1611
under the following patent of 27 March :[3]

De licencia speciali
pro Iohanne Townsend
& Iosepho Moore & aliis.

Iames by the grace of god &c. To all Iustices,
Maiors, Sheriffes, Bailiffes, Constables, hed-
borroughes, and other our louving Subiectes
and officers greetinge. Knowe ye that wee
of our especiall grace, certaine knowledge, and meere mocon have
licenced and authorised, and by these presente do licence and authorize Iohn Townsend and Joseph Moore, sworne servantes to our deere
daughter the ladie Elizabeth, with the rest of theire Companie, to vse
and exercise the Arte and qualitie of playinge Comedies, histories,
Enterludes, Morralls, pastoralls, stage playes, and such other like as
they haue alreadie studied or hereafter shall studie or vse, aswell for
the recreacion of our loving Subiectes, as for our solace and pleasure
when wee shall thinke good to see them, And the said enterludes or
other to shewe and exercise publiquelie to their best commoditie in
and about our Cittie of London in such vsuall howses as themselues

---

[1] App. D, No. clviii.   [2] *Henslowe Papers*, 93.
[3] *M. S. C.* i. 274, from *P. R. 9 Jac. I*, p. 20.

shall prouide, And alsoe within anie Towne halles, mootehalles, Guyld-
halles, Schoolehowses or other convenient places within the libertye
and freedome of anie other Cittie, vniuersitie, Towne or Burroughe
whatsoeuer within our Realmes and Domynions, willinge and comaundinge you and everie of you, as you tender our pleasure, not onelie to
permitt and suffer them herein without any your lettes, hinderances,
molestacions or disturbances during our said pleasure, but alsoe to be
ayding and assistinge vnto them, if anie wronge be vnto them offred,
And to allowe them such former curtesies as hath byne given to men
of their place and qualitie, And alsoe what further fauour you shall
shewe them for our sake wee shall take yt kindelie at your handes.
Prouided alwayes and our will and pleasure is that all authoritie,
power, priveledge, and profitt whatsoever belonginge or properlie
apperteyning to the maister of the Revelles in respecte of his office
and euerie Article and graunte conteyned within the letters Pattentes
or Comission, which haue byne heretofore graunted or directed by
the late queene Elizabeth our deere sister or by our selfe to our welbeloued Servantes Edwarde Tylney Maister of the saide Revells, or
to Sir George Bucke knighte, or to eyther oi them, in possession or
reuercon, shall remayne and abide entire and in full force, effecte and
vertue, and in as ample sorte as if this our Comission had neuer byne
made   In witnesse wherof &c.   Witnesse our selfe at Westminster
the seaven and Twentith daye of Aprill.

per breve de priuato sigillo &c.

The company is first traceable in the country, at Bath during
1610–11 and at Ipswich on 28 May 1611. The names of
Moore and Townsend render possible its identification with
an unnamed company, which on 29 August 1611 gave
duplicate bonds of £500 to Henslowe for the observance of
certain articles of agreement of the same date. Unfortunately the articles themselves are not preserved, but it is
likely that they contained an arrangement for the housing
and financing of the company by Henslowe.[1] The signatories
to both bonds include John Townsend, Joseph Taylor,
William Ecclestone, Thomas Hunt, John Rice, Robert Hamlen,
Joseph Moore, William Carpenter, Thomas Basse, and
Alexander Foster. To these one adds Giles Gary and William
Barksted and the other Francis Waymus. The names recited
in the bodies of the documents agree with the signatures,
except that Gary appears in both. Several of these men
now come into London theatrical history for the first time,
but Gary is probably the Giles Cary who with Barksted played
in *Epicoene* for the Queen's Revels in 1609, Taylor came from
the Duke of York's, and Rice from the King's. One Hunt,
whose Christian name is unknown, was with the Admiral's

---

[1] *Henslowe Papers*, 18, 111.

in 1601. Alexander Foster received payment on behalf of the Lady Elizabeth's men for three plays given at Court during the Christmas of 1611–12. The first was on 19 January 1612 before Elizabeth and Henry; the second was *The Proud Maid's Tragedy*, on 25 February before James; and the third was on 11 March, again before Elizabeth and Henry. In 1611–12 the company were at Dover and Coventry, and on 30 July 1612 at Leicester. On 20 October they played before Elizabeth and the Palsgrave, shortly after the latter's arrival in England, in the Cockpit. This was perhaps the play paid for out of the private funds of Elizabeth, as the result of a wager with Mr. Edward Sackville.[1] During Christmas they played twice before Charles, Elizabeth, and the Palsgrave, showing Marston's *The Dutch Courtesan* on 25 February and *Raymond Duke of Lyons* on 1 March. For 1612–13 Joseph Taylor was payee.

The names of Taylor and Ecclestone are found in another document in the Dulwich collection, which pretty clearly belongs to the Lady Elizabeth's men, and which shows that about the spring of 1613 their business relations with Henslowe entered upon a somewhat troubled phase. This is shown by internal evidence to have been written in the course of 1615. It is here reproduced:[2]

Articles of [   ]uaunce against
M[   ] Hinchlowe

Imprimis in March 1612 vppon M^r. Hynchlowes Joyninge Companes with M^r. Rosseter the Companie borrowed 80^{ll} of one M^r. Griffin and the same was put into M^r. Hinchlowes debt which made itt sixteene score poundes; whoe [a]fter the receipt of the same or most parte thereof in March 1613 hee broke the saide Comp[any a]gaine and Ceazed all the stocke, vnder Culler to satisfie what remayned due to [him]; yet perswaded M^r. Griffyne afterwardes to arest the Companie for his 80^{ll}, whoe are still in daunger for the same; Soe nowe there was in equitie due to the Companie . . . . 80^{ll}:

Item M^r. Hinchlowe having lent one Taylor 30^{ll} and 20^{ll} to one Baxter fellowes of the Companie Cunninglie put theire said privat debts into the generall accompt by which meanes hee is in Conscience to allowe them . . . . 50^{ll}:

Item havinge the stock of Apparell in his handes to secure his debt he sould tenn poundes worth of ould apparrell out of the same without accomptinge or abatinge for the same; heare growes due to the Companie . . . . 10^{ll}:

[1] Cf. App. B.
[2] *Henslowe Papers*, 86, from *Dulwich MS.* i. 106; also printed in *Variorum*, xxi. 416, and Collier, *Alleyn Papers*, 78.

Also vppon the departure of one Eglestone a ffellowe of the Companie
hee recovered of him 14[11] towardes his debt which is in Conscience
likewise to bee allowed to the Companie   .   .   .   . 14[11] :

In March 1613 hee makes vpp a Companie and buies apparrell of one
Rosseter to the value of 63[11], and valued the ould stocke that remayned
in his handes at 63[11], likewise they vppon his word acceptinge the same
at that rate, which being prized by M[r]. Daborne iustlie, betweene his
partner Meade and him, Came but to 40[11] : soe heare growes due to
the Companie .   .   .   . 23[11] :

Item hee agrees with the said Companie that they should enter bond
to plaie with him for three yeares att such house and houses as hee
shall appointe and to allowe him halfe galleries for the said house
and houses, and the other halfe galleries towardes his debt of 126[11],
and other such moneys as he should laie out for playe apparrell
duringe the space of the said 3 yeares, agreeinge with them in Consideracion theareof to seale each of them a bond of 200[11] to find them
a Convenient house and houses, and to laie out such moneies as fower
of the sharers should think fitt for theire vse in apparrell, which att
the 3 yeares, being paid for, to be deliuered to the sharers ; whoe
accordinglie entered the said bondes ; but M[r]. Henchlowe and M[r].
Mead deferred the same, an[d] in Conclusion vtterly denied to seale
att all.

Item M[r]. Hinchlowe havinge promised in Consideracion of the Companies lying still one daie in forteene for his baytinge to give them 50[s],
hee havinge denied to bee bound as aforesaid gave them onlie 40[s], and
for that M[r]. Feild would not Consent therevnto hee gave him soe
much as his share out of 50[11] would have Come vnto ; by which meanes
hee is dulie indebted to the Companie   .   .   .   .   . x[11] :

In June followinge the said agreement, hee brought in M[r]. Pallant and
short[l]ie after M[r]. Dawes into the said Companie, promisinge one 12[s]
a weeke out of his part of the galleries, and the other 6[s] a weeke out
of his parte of the galleries ; and because M[r]. Feild was thought not
to bee drawne therevnto, hee promissed him six shillinges weekelie
alsoe ; which in one moneth after vnwilling to beare soe great a
Charge, he Called the Companie together, and told them that this
24[s] was to bee Charged vppon them, threatninge those which would
not Consent therevnto to breake the Companie and make vpp a newe
without the[m]. Whearevppon knowinge hee was not bound, the three-
quarters sharers advauncinge them selves to whole shares Consented
therevnto, by which meanes they are out of purse 30[11], and his parte
of the galleries bettred twise as much   .   .   .   .   . 30[11] :

Item havinge 9 gatherers more then his due itt Comes to this yeare
from the Companie .   .   .   . 10[11] :

Item the Companie paid for [Arra]s and other properties 40[11], which
M[r]. Henchlow deteyneth .   .   .   . 40[11] :

In Februarie last 1614 perceav[ing]e the Companie drewe out of his
debt and Called vppon him for his accompts hee brooke the Companie

againe, by withdrawinge the hired men from them, and selles theire stocke (in his hands) for 400^{ll}, givinge vnder his owne hand that hee had receaved towardes his debt . . . . . . 300^{ll} :

Which with the iuste and Conscionable allowances before named made to the Companie, which Comes to .   267^{ll}, makes . . 567^{ll} :

Articles of oppression against
M^r. Hinchlowe.

Hee Chargeth the stocke with . . . 600^{ll} : and odd, towardes which hee hath receaved as aforesaid . . . 567^{ll} of vs ; yet selles the stocke to strangers for fower hundred poundes, and makes vs no satisfacion.

Hee hath taken all boundes of our hired men in his owne name, whose wages though wee have truly paid yet att his pleasure hee hath taken them a waye, and turned them over to others to the breaking of our Companie.

For lendinge of vj^{ll} to p[ay] them theire wages, hee made vs enter bond to give him the profitt of a warraunt of tenn poundes due to vs att Court.

Alsoe hee hath taken right gould and silver lace of divers garmentes to his owne vse without accompt to vs or abatement.

Vppon everie breach of the Companie hee takes newe bondes for his stocke and our securitie for playinge with him ; Soe that hee hath in his handes bondes of ours to the value of 5000^{ll} and his stocke to ; which hee denies to deliuer and threatens to oppresse us with.

Alsoe havinge apointed a man to the seeinge of his accomptes in byinge of Clothes (hee beinge to have vj^s a weeke) hee takes the meanes away and turnes the man out.

The reason of his often breakinge with vs hee gave in these wordes ' Should these fellowes Come out of my debt, I should have noe rule with them '.

Alsoe wee have paid him for plaie bookes 200^{ll} or thereaboutes and yet hee denies to give vs the Coppies of any one of them.

Also within 3 yeares hee hath broken and dissmembred five Companies.

It is not quite possible to trace all the five breakings of companies referred to in the closing sentence ; but the statement is sufficient to give a fairly clear outline of the history of the Lady Elizabeth's men during the years which it covers, and, as it happens, there is a good deal of other evidence from which to supplement it. It appears that in March 1613 Henslowe joined companies with Rosseter ; that is to say, that an amalgamation took place between the Lady Elizabeth's men and the Children of the Queen's Revels, who had been acting at the Whitefriars under the patent to Rosseter

and others of 4 January 1610. One of these children was
Robert Baxter, if he is the Baxter named in the Articles
of Grievance as a fellow of the company with Taylor between
March 1613 and March 1614.[1] During the same period it
appears that William Ecclestone left the company. He
afterwards joined the King's men. But, before he went, he
took a part in *The Honest Man's Fortune*, which is stated in
the *Dyce MS.* to have been played in 1613, while its ' principal
actors ' are named in the 1679 folio of Beaumont and Fletcher
as ' Nathan Field, Robert Benfield, Emanuel Read, Joseph
Taylor, Will. Eglestone and Thomas Basse '. This particular
combination seems to point clearly to the Lady Elizabeth's
men as the original producers of the play. A very similar
cast is assigned in the same folio to *The Coxcomb*, namely,
' Nathan Field, Joseph Taylor, Giles Gary, Emanuel Read,
Richard Allen, Hugh Atawell, Robert Benfeild, and William
Barcksted '; and I think that this also must belong to a per-
formance by the Lady Elizabeth's men about 1613. *The
Coxcomb* had certainly been played at Court by the Queen's
Revels in 1612, but it seems impossible that Taylor can then
have been a member of that company.[2] The new blood
brought in from Rosseter's company will, then, have included
Field, Attwell, Richard Allen, Benfield, Reade, and perhaps
Robert Baxter, of whom the first three had played in Jonson's
Epicoene for the Revels in 1609. When it is remembered that
Cary and Barksted had been in the same cast, it will be
realized that the Lady Elizabeth's men, as constituted in
1613, were very much the Queen's Revels over again.

I think there can be no doubt that the Lady Elizabeth's
men was the company principally referred to in the long
series of letters from Robert Daborne to Henslowe, which
runs from 17 April 1613 to 31 July 1614.[3] Daborne had been

---

[1] Greg, *Henslowe Papers*, 58, 87, thinks that the ' Baxter ' of the
Grievances was William Barksted or Backstede. It may be so.

[2] Thorndike, 66, thinks that the list belongs to an earlier production
by the Queen's Revels before 30 March 1610, when Taylor joined the
Duke of York's. But there is no evidence that he was ever in the Queen's
Revels.

[3] *Henslowe Papers*, 65, 125 ; A. E. H. Swaen, *Robert Daborne's Plays*
(*Anglia*, xx. 153). The account in Fleay, i. 75, is full of inaccuracies.
The documents now form separate articles of *Dulwich MS.* 1. All, unless
otherwise specified below, are letters or undertakings from Daborne to
Henslowe. Most of them are dated, and I think that the following ordering,
due to Dr. Greg, is reasonable : (i) Art. 70, 17 Apr. 1613 ; (ii) Art. 71,
17 Apr. 1613 ; (iii) Art. 72, 25 Apr. 1613 ; (iv) Art. 73, 3 May 1613 ;
(v) Art. 74, 8 May 1613 ; (vi) Art. 75, 16 May 1613 ; (vii) Art. 77,
19 May 1613 ; (viii) Art. 78, 5 June 1613 ; (ix) Art. 79, 10 June 1613 ;
(xi) Art. 80, 18 June 1613 ; (xii) Art. 81, 25 June 1613 ; (xiii) ? Art. 100,

one of the patentees for the Queen's Revels in 1609, and some
letters apparently belonging to the same series show Field
as interested, either as writer or actor, in some of the plays
which Henslowe was purchasing from Daborne, with a view
to reselling them to this company. Further confirmation is
to be obtained for this view from the signature of Hugh
Attwell as witness to one of Henslowe's advances to Daborne,[1]
and from the mention of Benfield,[2] of Pallant who, as will be
seen, joined the company in 1614,[3] and of *Eastward Ho!*
which their repertory had inherited from that of the Queen's
Revels.[4] That ' Mr. Allin ' was hearing Daborne's plays with
Henslowe in May 1613 need cause no difficulty.[5] It is true
that Edward Alleyn is not known to have had any relations
with the Lady Elizabeth's men, but John Alleyn, a nephew
of Edward, is amongst Henslowe's witnesses about this time,[6]
and Richard Allen, who may not have belonged to the same
family, was himself one of the Lady Elizabeth's men, and
perhaps served as their literary adviser. The correspondence
makes it possible to recover the names of a series of plays on
which Daborne was engaged, either alone or in collaboration
with others, during the period over which it extends, and all
of which seem to have been primarily meant for the Lady
Elizabeth's men, although he occasionally professes, as an aid
to his chaffering, to have an alternative market with the King's
men.[7] From April to June 1613 he was writing a tragedy of
Machiavel and the Devil, and this is probably the ' new play ',
of which he suggests the performance on Wednesday in
August, to follow one of *Eastward Ho!* on the Monday.[8]

Field to Henslowe, N.D.; (xiv) ? Art. 69, Field to Henslowe, N.D.;
(xv) ? Art. 68, Field, Daborne, and Massinger to Henslowe, N.D.; (xvi)
Art. 82, 16 July 1613; (xvii) Art. 83, 30 July 1613; (xviii) ? Art. 76,
N.D.; (xix) ? Art. 99, Daborne to Edward Griffin (Henslowe's scrivener),
N.D.; (xx), Art. 84, 23 Aug. 1613; (xxi) Art. 85, 14 Oct. 1613; (xxii) Art. 86,
29 Oct. 1613; (xxiii) Art. 87, 5 Nov. 1613; (xxiv) Art. 88, 13 Nov. 1613;
(xxv) Art. 89, 13 Nov. 1613; (xxvi), Art. 90, 27 Nov. 1613; (xxvii) Art. 91,
9 Dec. 1613; (xxviii) Art. 92, 10 Dec. 1613; (xxix) Art. 93, 24 Dec. 1613;
(xxx) ? Art. 95, N.D.; (xxxi) Art. 94, 31 Dec. 1613; (xxxii) Art. 96, 11 Mar.
1614; (xxxiii) Art. 97, 28 Mar. 1614; (xxxiv), Art. 98, 31 July 1614.
    [1] *Henslowe Papers*, 68.
    [2] *Sh. Soc. Papers*, i. 16; *Henslowe Papers*, 125, from *Egerton MS.* 2623,
f. 24. This document cannot be dated, but it has probably been detached
from the Dulwich series.
    [3] *Henslowe Papers*, 82.
    [4] Ibid. 71. I should suppose this, rather than, with Dr. Greg, *Bartholomew
Fair*, to be the ' Johnsons play ' contemplated on 13 Nov. (*Henslowe
Papers*, 78), but others of Jonson's plays may also have been revived.
    [5] Ibid. 69, 70.   [6] Ibid. 71, 103, 111.
    [7] Ibid. 76, 77, 78.   [8] Ibid. 71.

For this Henslowe covenanted to pay him £20. In June he was also completing *The Arraignment of London*, of which he had given an act to Cyril Tourneur to write; and to this *The Bellman of London*, for which he and a colleague, perhaps again Tourneur, asked no more than £12 and ' the overplus of the second day ' in August, was probably a sequel.[1] This may be the play which he had delivered to Henslowe about the beginning of December. About July he seems also to have been occupied upon a play in collaboration with Field, Fletcher, and Massinger. This is not named, and Mr. Fleay's identification of it with *The Honest Man's Fortune* is rather hazardous.[2] In December he began *The Owl*, for which his price fell to £10; and on 11 March 1614 he had finished this, and was beginning *The She Saint* and asking ' but 12¹ a play till they be playd '. The correspondence has a gap between the middle of August and the middle of October 1613. Probably the company were on tour; they are found at Coventry, Shrewsbury, and Marlborough in 1612–13, Canterbury on 4 July 1613, Dover between 12 July and 7 August, and Leicester on 13 October. In the spring they had been at Bristol and Norwich. On 12 December they repeated one of their plays of the preceding winter, Marston's *The Dutch Courtesan*, before Charles, and on 25 January 1614 gave *Eastward Ho!* which they had been playing in public during the summer, before James. Taylor was again their payee for this Christmas.

The statement of grievances indicates another reconstruction of the company in March 1614. In this transaction, which apparently involved the buying out of Rosseter's interest, Meade was in partnership with Henslowe, and Field was presumably in some position of authority on behalf of the players, as it is alleged that Henslowe bribed him, in order to obtain his assent to the modification of a covenant under which he was to make an allowance for a withdrawal of the theatre once a fortnight for baiting. The terms recited agree with those of an undated and mutilated agreement between Henslowe and Jacob Meade on one side and Field on behalf of an unnamed company of players on the other. The text of this follows:[3]

---

[1] Dr. Greg (*Henslowe Papers*, 75) makes them the same play, founded on Dekker's tracts, *The Bellman of London* (1608) and *Lanthorn and Candlelight, or the Bellman's Second Night-walk* (1609), but *The Arraignment* seems to have been too nearly finished on 5 June for this identification (*Henslowe Papers*, 72).

[2] Still more so the ascription (Fleay, i. 81) of *The Faithful Friends* to Daborne and the Lady Elizabeth's men.

[3] *Henslowe Papers*, 23; also in Collier, *Memoirs of Alleyn*, 118. A few

Articles of agreement made, concluded, and agreed vppon, and which are on the parte and behalfe of Phillipp Henslowe Esquier and Jacob Meade Waterman to be perfourmed, touchinge & concerninge the Company of players which they haue lately raised, vizt

Imprimis the saide Phillipp Henslowe and Jacob Meade doe for them, their executours and administratours, Covenante, promise, and graunt by theis presentes to and with Nathan Feilde gent., That they the saide Phillipp Henslowe and Jacob Meade or one of them shall and will duringe the space of Three yeares at all tymes (when noe restraynte of playinge shalbe) at their or some of their owne proper costes and charges fynde and provide a sufficient howse or howses for the saide Company to play in, And also shall and will at all tymes duringe the saide tearme disburse and lay out all suche somme & somes of monny, as ffower or ffive Shareres of the saide Company chosen by the saide Phillipp and Jacob shall thinck fittinge, for the furnishinge of the said Company with playinge apparrell towardes the settinge out of their newe playes, And further that the saide Phillipp Henslowe and Jacob Meade shall and will at all tymes duringe the saide tearme, when the saide Company shall play in or neare the Cittie of London, furnish the saide Company of players, aswell with suche stock of apparrell & other properties as the said Phillipp Henslowe hath already bought, As also with suche other stock of apparrell as the saide Phillipp Henslowe and Jacob Meade shall hereafter provide and buy for the said Company duringe the saide tearme, And further shall and will at suche tyme and tymes duringe the saide tearme, as the saide Company of Players shall by meanes of any restraynte or sicknes goe into the Contrey, deliuer and furnish the saide Company with fitting apparrell out of both the saide stockes of apparrell. And further the saide Phillipp Henslowe and Jacob Meade doe for them, their executours and administratours, convenante and graunt to and with the saide Nathan Feilde by theis presentes in manner and fourme followinge, that is to say, That they the saide Phillipp Henslowe and Jacob Meade or one of them shall and will from tyme to tyme duringe the saide tearme disburse and lay out suche somme or sommes of monny as shalbe thought fittinge by ffower or ffive of the Shareres of the saide Company, to be chosen by the saide Phillipp & Jacob or one of them, to be paide for any play which they shall buy or condicion or agree for ; Soe alwaies as the saide Company doe and shall truly repaye vnto the saide Phillipp and Jacob, their executores or assignes, all suche somme & sommes of monny, as they shall disburse for any play, vppon the second or third daie wheron the same play shalbe plaide by the saide Company, without fraude or longer delay ; And further that the saide Phillipp Henslowe and Jacob Meade shall and will at all tymes, vppon request made by the Maior parte of the Sharers of the saide Company v[nder

additional lines, much mutilated, appear to have provided for the allocation of half the daily takings of the galleries to the discharge of a debt of £124 due to Henslowe and Meade and of any further disbursements by them. This agrees with the Dawes articles *infra*, but the Articles of Grievance refer to a debt of £126.

their] handes, remove and putt out of the saide Company any of the saide Company of playeres, if the saide Phillipp Henslowe and Jacob Meade shall fynde [the s]aide request to be iust and that ther be noe hope of conformety in the partie complayned of ; And further that they the saide Phillipp Henslowe and Jacob Mea[de shall] and [will] at all tymes, vppon request made by the saide Company or the maior parte therof, pay vnto them all suche somes of monny as shall comme vnto their handes v[ppon   of] any forfectures for rehearsalles or suche like paymentes ; And also shall and will, vppon the request of the said Company or the maior parte of the[m], sue [ ] ar[   ] persons by whom any forfecture shalbe made as aforesaid, and after or vppon the recovery and receipte th[ero]f (their charges disbursed about the recovery [b]einge first deducted and allowed) shall and will make satisfaccion of the remaynder therof vnto the said Company without fraude or guile.

Mr. Fleay and Dr. Greg think that at the time of this recon-struction the company was further strengthened by the incorporation of the Duke of York's, now the Prince's, men.[1] This I doubt, as the Prince's men continued to play at Court, as a company quite distinct from the Lady Elizabeth's, during the winter of 1614–15. It is true that Robert Dawes, who had been one of the Duke of York's in 1610, joined the Lady Elizabeth's, but it was precisely one of the grievances that this man and Robert Pallant were introduced by Henslowe, by means of a financial adjustment unfavourable to the sharers, in June 1614. Pallant had passed through several companies, and is traceable with Queen Anne's men in 1609. He was still technically a servant of the Queen at her death in 1619.[2] A letter from Daborne on 28 March 1614 shows that he was then expecting an answer to some proposal made to Henslowe, which the latter had neglected.[3] Articles between Robert Dawes and Henslowe and Meade are on record, and bear the date 7 April 1614.[4] The following is the text :

Articles of Agreement,] made, concluded, and agreed uppon, and which are to be kept & performed by Robert Dawes of London, Gent. unto and with Phillipp Henslowe Esqre and Jacob [Meade Waterman] in manner and forme followinge, that is to say

Imprimis. The said Robert Dawes for him, his executors, and administrators doth covenante, promise, and graunt to and with the said Phillipp Henslowe and Jacob Meade, their executors, admini-strators, and assynes, in manner and formme followinge, that is to

---

[1] Fleay, 187 ; Greg, *Henslowe Papers*, 87, *Henslowe's Diary*, ii. 138.
[2] Cf. p. 240.   [3] *Henslowe Papers*, 82.
[4] Ibid. 123, from *Variorum*, xxi. 413 ; also in Collier, *Alleyn Papers*, 75. The original, formerly at Dulwich, is now missing.

saie, that he the said Robert Dawes shall and will plaie with such company, as the said Phillipp Henslowe and Jacob Meade shall appoynte, for and during the tyme and space of three yeares from the date hereof for and at the rate of one whole share, accordinge to the custome of players ; and that he the said Robert Dawes shall and will at all tymes during the said terme duly attend all suche rehearsall, which shall the night before the rehearsall be given publickly out ; and if that he the saide Robert Dawes shall at any tyme faile to come at the hower appoynted, then he shall and will pay to the said Phillipp Henslowe and Jacob Meade, their executors or assignes, Twelve pence ; and if he come not before the saide rehearsall is ended, then the said Robert Dawes is contented to pay Twoe shillings ; and further that if the said Robert Dawes shall not every daie, whereon any play is or ought to be played, be ready apparrelled and——to begyn the play at the hower of three of the clock in the afternoone, unles by sixe of the same company he shall be lycenced to the contrary, that then he, the saide Robert Dawes, shall and will pay unto the said Phillipp and Jacob or their assignes Three [shillings] ; and if that he, the saide Robert Dawes, happen to be overcome with drinck at the tyme when he [ought to] play, by the judgment of ffower of the said company, he shall and will pay Tenne shillings ; and if he, [the said Robert Dawes], shall [faile to come] during any plaie, having noe lycence or just excuse of sicknes, he is contented to pay Twenty shillings ; and further the said Robert Dawes, for him, his executors, and administrators, doth covenant and graunt to and with the said Phillipp Henslowe and Jacob Meade, their executors, administrators, and asignes, by these presents, that it shall and may be lawfull unto and for the said Phillipp Henslowe and Jacob Meade, their executors or assignes, during the terme aforesaid, to receave and take back to their own proper use the part of him, the said Robert Dawes, of and in one moyetie or halfe part of all suche moneyes, as shal be receaved at the Galleries & tyring howse of such house or howses wherein he the saide Robert Dawes shall play, for and in consideration of the use of the same howse and howses ; and likewis shall and may take and receave his other moyetie .   .   .   .   . the moneys receaved at the galleries and tiring howse dues, towards the pa[ying] to them, the saide Phillip Henslowe and Jacob Meade, of the some of one hundred twenty and fower pounds, being the value of the stock of apparell furnished by the saide company by the saide Phillip Henslowe and Jacob Meade .   .   . the one part of him the saide Robert Dawes or any other somes .   .   . . to them for any apparell hereafter newly to be bought by the [said Phillip Henslowe and Jacob Meade, until the saide Phillip Henslowe and Jacob Meade] shall therby be fully satisfied, contented, and paid. And further the said Robert Dawes doth covenant, [promise, and graunt to and with the said Phillip Henslowe and Jacob Meade, that if he, the said Robert Dawes], shall at any time after the play is ended depart or goe out of the [howse] with any [of their] apparell on his body, or if the said Robert Dawes [shall carry away any propertie] belonging to the said company, or

shal be consentinge [or privy to any other of the said company going
out of the howse with any of their apparell on his or their bodies, he,
the said] Robert Dawes, shall and will forfeit and pay unto the said
Phillip and Jacob, or their administrators or assignes, the some of
ffortie pounds of lawfull [money of England] . . . . .
and the said Robert Dawes, for him, his executors, and administrators
doth [covenant promise and graunt to with the said] Phillip Henslowe
and Jacob Meade, their executors, and administrators [and assigns]
that it shall and may be
lawfull to and for the said Phillip Henslowe and Jacob Meade, their
executors, and assignes, to have and use the playhows so appoynted
[for the said company   one day of] every fower daies, the said
daie to be chosen by the said Phillip and [Jacob]
Monday in any week, on which day it shalbe lawful
for the said Phillip [and Jacob, their administrators], and assignes, to
bait their bears and bulls ther, and to use their accustomed sport and
[games]   and take
to their owne use all suche somes of money, as thereby shall arise and
be received
    And the saide Robert Dawes, his executors, administrators, and
assignes, [do hereby covenant, promise, and graunt to and with the
saide Phillip and Jacob,] allowing to the saide company daye the
some of ffortie shillings money of England . . . [In testimony] for every
such whereof, I the saide Robert Dawes haue hereunto sett my hand
and seal this [sev]enth daie of April 1614 in the twelfth yeare [of the
reign of our sovereign lord &c.]

Robert Dawes.

It must be mainly matter of conjecture at what theatres
the Lady Elizabeth's had played from 1611 to 1614. Possibly
they may have begun at the Swan. Middleton's *A Chaste
Maid in Cheapside* was published as ' often acted at the
Swan on the Banke-side by the Lady Elizabeth her Seruants ', and although this publication was not until 1630,
it is rather tempting to identify the play with *The Proud Maid*
of 1611–12. Probably the association of the company with
Henslowe led to a transfer to the Rose ; and after the joining
of forces with Rosseter in March 1613, the Whitefriars must
have been available for the combination. That there were
alternatives open in 1613 is shown by two passages in
Daborne's letters.[1] On 5 June he says that the company were
expecting Henslowe to conclude ' about thear comming over
or goinge to Oxford ', and by ' comming over ' may most
naturally be understood crossing the Thames. On 9 December
he claims that a book he is upon will ' make as good a play
for your publique howse as ever was playd ', and the inference

<hr>

[1] *Henslowe Papers*, 72, 79.

is that at the time Henslowe was interested in a ' private '
as well as in a ' public ' house. Certainly the Watermen's
complaint in the spring of 1614 indicates that there were then
no plays on Bankside, and both the Swan and the Rose
must therefore have been deserted. But by the autumn
the Lady Elizabeth's men were in the Clink, occupying
the newly built Hope on the site of the old Bear-garden;
and that the use of this theatre was contemplated in the
agreements of the previous spring is shown both by the
presence of Meade, who is not known to have been interested
in any other house, as a party, and by the reservation of one
day in fourteen for the purpose of baiting.[1] It was at the
Hope that William Fennor failed to appear to try his challenge
with John Taylor on 7 October, and the Lady Elizabeth's
men were presumably the players—

> And such a company (I'll boldly say)
> That better (nor the like) ne'er played a play—

who came to the rescue and saved the occasion from fiasco.
And it was at the Hope and by the Lady Elizabeth's men,
as the Induction and the title-page show, that Jonson's
Bartholomew Fair was produced on 31 October. There is
a reference in the text of the play to Taylor's adventure,[2]
and a compliment to Field, which puts him on a level with
Burbadge of the King's men.[3] *Bartholomew Fair* was presented on the very next day before James at Court. This
performance, for which Field was payee on 11 June, was
the only one by the company during the winter festivities of
1614–15. In February 1615 there was a breach between
Henslowe and the company, as a result of which the Articles
of Grievance were drawn up. According to the Articles
Henslowe ' brooke the companie '; but it is not quite clear
what exactly took place. In some form the Lady Elizabeth's
men certainly continued to exist. They visited Nottingham
in March 1615, and a letter from Lord Coke to the Mayor
of Coventry shows that they also contemplated a visit to
that town in the same month.[4] My impression is that they
subsequently patched up another reconstruction with Henslowe, and that on this occasion the process did entail some

---

[1] I agree with Dr. Greg that the ' fower ' in Dawes's articles is probably
a mistake for ' fourteen '.

[2] *Bartholomew Fair*, v. 3, ' I thinke, one Taylor, would goe neere to
beat all this company, with a hand bound behinde him '.

[3] Ibid. *Cokes.* Which is your Burbage now?
Lanterne. What meane you by that, Sir?
Cokes. Your best Actor. Your Field?

[4] Murray, ii. 254. This, however, was probably Long's company; v. *infra*.

kind of amalgamation with Prince Charles's men. Field, however, probably now joined the King's men. The Lady Elizabeth's do not appear to have been separately represented when the Privy Council called the London companies before them for a breach of Lent on 29 March 1615. It is true that they may have been alone in not offending, but it is more probable that William Rowley and John Newton, who were summoned, answered for the amalgamation. The Prince's men are recorded as playing at Court during the Christmas of 1615–16 and the Lady Elizabeth's men are not. Yet the payee for their four plays, of which the dates are not specified, was Alexander Foster, who had been a Lady Elizabeth's man and not a Prince's man. But it is probable that both this amalgamation and the earlier one between the Lady Elizabeth's and the Queen's Revels, although effective as a business operation from Henslowe's point of view, did not amount to a complete merging of identities, such as would entail a surrender of one or other of the official patents. Certainly the Lady Elizabeth's, the Prince's and the Revels were in some sense distinct, and yet in the closest relationship in 1615. So much is clear from Rosseter's patent of 3 June to build in the Blackfriars, which contemplated that all three companies would share in the use of the new house. That the joint user extended also to plays is suggested by the title-page of Field's *Amends for Ladies* (1618) which declares it to have been 'acted at the Blacke-Fryers, both by the Princes Seruants and the Lady Elizabeths'. Perhaps this indicates alternative rather than combined playing. Whatever the arrangement, it was probably altered again on or before Henslowe's death on 6 January 1616.[1] A company containing many of the former Lady Elizabeth's men remained at the Hope. But they went under Prince Charles's patronage, and it is not until 1622, when we find them at Christopher Beeston's house of the Cockpit or Phoenix, that we can be sure of the presence of Lady Elizabeth's men in London once more.[2] But they had held together in the provinces. Possibly the nucleus of the provincial company had been formed of men left out by the Henslowe-Rosseter negotiations of 1613–14. They first appear at Norwich on 2 March 1614 under Nicholas Long, who in 1612 had been travelling with Queen's Revels boys. They came again on 27 May 1615 with an exemplification of the 1611 patent dated 31 May 1613, and again on 5 June 1616 under John Townsend, and again

[1] Robert Pallant, one of the company, is noted (Henslowe, ii. 20) as visiting Henslowe on his death-bed.

[2] *Variorum*, iii. 59.

on 7 June 1617 under Henry Sebeck.   In the same year
Joseph Moore was acting as an agent of the Lord Chamberlain
and Master of the Revels in clearing the provinces of irregularly
licensed players, not improbably in the interests of the
Lady Elizabeth's themselves, whose original patent was now
set free, through changes in London, for provincial use in
place of a mere exemplification.[1]   The company is also
traceable at Leicester, Coventry, Nottingham, Marlborough,
and elsewhere from 1614,[2] and on 11 July 1617 Townsend
and Moore received a warrant for £30 in respect of three
plays given before James during his journey to Scotland.[3]
On 20 March 1618 Townsend and Moore, with Alexander
Foster and Francis Waymus, obtained a new licence under the
royal signet.[4]   This authorized them to play in London, and
their actual return there may have been earlier than 1622.

[1] App. D, No. clviii.
[2] Murray, i. 263 ; ii. 4.   I add Belvoir on 1 March 1614.
[3] Cunningham, xliv.   [4] Murray, ii. 344.

XIV

INTERNATIONAL COMPANIES

i. ITALIAN PLAYERS IN ENGLAND

[*Bibliographical Note.*—The wanderings of the Italian companies in Italy tself and in France are recounted in A. D'Ancona, *Origini del Teatro Italiano* (ed. 2, 1891), and A. Baschet, *Les Comédiens italiens à la Cour de France* (1882), but without much knowledge of the few English records. W. Smith, *Italian and Elizabethan Comedy* (*M. P.* v. 555) and *The Commedia dell' Arte* (1912), deals more fully with these. The literary influence of Italian comedy is discussed by L. L. Schücking, *Die stofflichen Beziehungen der englischen Komödie zur italienischen bis Lilly* (1901), and R. W. Bond, *Early Plays from the Italian* (1911).]

THE England of Elizabeth and James was a lender rather than a borrower of players. No records have been disinterred of French actors in this country between 1495 and 1629;[1] and although there are a few of Italian actors, their visits seem to have been confined to a single brief period.[2] The head-quarters of Italian comedy during the middle of the sixteenth century was at the Court of Mantua, and when Lord Buckhurst went as ambassador to congratulate Charles IX of France on his wedding, it was by Louis Gonzaga, Duke of Nevers and brother of the Duke of Mantua, that he was entertained on 4 March 1571 'with a comedie of Italians that for the good mirth and handling thereof deserved singular comendacion'.[3] In the following year the Earl of Lincoln was at Paris from 8 to 22 June in order to conclude a treaty, and letters relate how he saw at the Louvre 'an Italian playe, and dyvers vauters and leapers of dyvers sortes verie excellent', and how later, when he visited the King at the Chateau de Madrid, 'he had some pastyme showed him by Italian players, which I was at with hym'.[4] It may perhaps have been encouragement from one or both of these nobles, which led an Italian company not long afterwards to make its way across the Channel. The first notice of it is at Nottingham

---

[1] Lawrence, i. 128 (*Early French Players in England*). One can hardly, I suppose, assume that the Turkish acrobat of 1589–90 (cf. ch. xviii) was a real Turk.

[2] J. A. Lester, *Italian Players in Scotland* (*M. L. N.* xxiii. 240), traces *histriones*, whom he unjustifiably assumes to be actors, and *tubicines* in 1514–61.

[3] *S. P. F.* (1569–71), 413.

[4] Nichols, *Eliz.* i. 302.

in September 1573, when a reward was 'gevin to the Italyans for serteyne pastymes that they shewed before Maister Meare and his brethren '.[1] In 1574 the Revels Accounts include expenditure 'for the Italyan players that ffollowed the progresse and made pastyme fyrst at Wynsor and after-wardes at Reading '. Elizabeth was at Windsor on 11 and 12 July ; on 15 July she removed to Reading and remained there to 22 July. At Windsor the Italians used 'iij devells cotes and heades & one olde mannes fries cote ' ; at Reading, where they performed on 15 July, the provisions included staves, hooks, and lambskins for shepherds, arrows for nymphs, a scythe for Saturn, and 'horstayles for the wylde mannes garment '. Professor Feuillerat appears to suggest that they may have been playing Tasso's *Aminta*, produced at Ferrara on 31 July 1573. But there were other pastorals.[2] The Italians are probably the comedians commended to the Lord Mayor on 22 July, and in November Thomas Norton calls special attention to 'the unchaste, shamelesse and unnaturall tomblinge of the Italian weomen '. How long this company remained in England is unknown. There was an Italian acrobat at the Kenilworth festivities on 14 July 1575, but the description suggests that he was a solitary per-former.[3] The Treasurer of the Chamber paid 'Alfruso Ferrabolle and the rest of the Italian players ' for a play at Court on 27 February 1576, to the consideration of which I shall return. In April 1577 there was an Italian play before the Council at Durham Place.[4] Finally, on 13 January 1578, the Privy Council addressed a letter to the Lord Mayor, requiring him to permit 'one Drousiano, an Italian, a commediante and his companye ', to play until the first week of the coming Lent. I take it that the company was also at Court, since the Chamber Accounts for 1577–8 include an item 'for a mattres hoopes and boardes with tressells for the Italian Tumblers '. The company to which the visit of 1573–4 was due cannot be identified with any certainty. Presumably it came through France, and ought to have left signs there. There seem to have been three Italian companies in France during 1571. The first, in February, was that of Giovanni Tabarin. The second, that seen by Lord Buckhurst in Paris, was the famous Compagnia de' Gelosi, of which one Signora Vittoria, of Ferrara, known on the stage as Fioretta, was the prima donna. This, however, had returned to Milan by the spring of 1572 and its subsequent movements hardly render a visit to England in 1573 plausible. A third

---

[1] Murray, ii. 374. [2] Feuillerat, *Eliz.* 225, 227, 458.
[3] Furnivall, *Robert Laneham's Letter*, 18. [4] Cf. App. B.

company, that of Alberto Ganassa, a Zanni or clown from Bergamo, reached Paris in the autumn of 1571.[1] It was sent away by the Parlement on account of its high charges for admission, but returned in 1572 and played at the wedding of Henri of Navarre and Marguerite of Valois on 18 August. Nothing is heard of Ganassa in France after October 1572, but during the summer of 1574 he seems to have been in Madrid; so he also is not available for the English visit. It may very likely have been his company which the Earl of Lincoln saw. But it may also have been that led by Soldino of Florence and Anton Maria of Venice, which was performing ' commedies et saults ' before Charles IX at Blois on 25 March 1572, and subsequently made its way to Paris. My authorities say nothing further about Soldino and Anton Maria, so we are at liberty to believe that Lincoln invited them to try their fortune across the sea.[2]

The ' Drousiano ' of 1578 offers less difficulty. He must have been Drusiano, son of Francisco Martinelli, of Mantua, who in after years won a considerable reputation, although less than that of his brother Tristano Martinelli, as Arlecchino in the *commedia dell' arte*.[3] There is no other notice of him before 1580, when he subscribes himself as ' marito di Mª Angelica ', who appears to have been one Angelica Alber-ghini, and the company with which he was associated in 1578 is not known.[4] But it may very well have been the Gelosi. This company paid in 1577 their second visit to France, upon the invitation of Henri III, and remained there at least until July. They seem to have been in Florence fairly early in 1578, but some or all of them may have found time for an English trip in the interval. Direct proof that Drusiano Martinelli ever belonged to the Gelosi is lacking. But they are the only Italian company known to have been in France in the summer of 1577, and players are not likely to have passed from Italy to England without leaving some traces of their presence in France.[5]

[1] Smith, 148, makes him then head of the Gelosi, but the authorities she cites do not bear her out.

[2] Baschet, 18, 25, 34, 43 ; D'Ancona, ii. 455, 457, 459 ; Rennert, 28, 479.

[3] R. B. McKerrow (*Nashe*, iv. 462) suggests that Tristano may have been ' that famous Francatrıp Harlicken ' represented in the dedication of *An Almond for a Parrat* (1590) as asking questions at Venice about Kempe. But Francatrippa seems to have been the stage name of Gabriello Panzanini da Bologna of the Gelosi (D'Ancona, ii. 469, 511).

[4] Is this ' the nimble, tumbling Angelica ' of Marston's *Scourge of Villainy* (1598), xi. 101 ? If so, a later visit may be suspected. Drusiano Martinelli was comedian to the Duke of Mantua, to whose son Angelica had been mistress, in 1595 (D'Ancona, ii. 518).

[5] Baschet, 72, 82, 90, 194, 199 ; D'Ancona, ii. 464, 479, 504, 518, 523,

The professional Italian actors of the second half of the sixteenth century played both the popular *commedia dell' arte* and the literary *commedia erudita*, or *commedia sostenuta*. The former, with its more or less improvised dialogue upon *scenarii*, which revolved around the amorous and ridiculous adventures of the *zanni*, the *arlecchino*, the *dottore*, and other standing types, was probably best adapted to the methods of wandering mimes in an alien land.[1] The latter was common to professionals and amateurs. And I suspect that the Court play of 27 February 1576, although it earned its reward from the Treasurer of the Chamber, was an amateur performance. The ' Alfruso Ferrabolle ' of the account-book can hardly be other than a clerical perversion of the name of Alfonso Ferrabosco, the first of three generations of that name, father, son, and grandson, who contributed in turn to the gaiety of the English Court. The eldest Ferrabosco was certainly in this country by 1562 when he was granted an annuity of 100 marks. His service terminated after various interruptions in 1578.[2] He is doubtless the ' Mr. Alphonse ' who took part in the preparation of a mask in June 1572.[3] In connexion with the same mask, a reward was paid to one ' Petrucio ', while for a later mask of 11 January 1579 ' Patruchius Ubaldinas ' was employed to translate speeches into Italian and write them out fair in tables.[4] This was Petruccio Ubaldini, another of Elizabeth's Italian pensioners, who was both a literary man and an illuminator, and made his residence in England from 1562 to 1586.[5] It is quite possible that the performance of 1576 may be referred to in the following undated letter from Ubaldini to the Queen, in which he makes mention of Ferrabosco.[6] If so, it came off after all.

526 ; Smith, 147. The main body of the Gelosi passed about this time under the leadership of Flaminio Scala, fifty of whose *scenarii* are printed in *Il Teatro delle Fauole rappresentatiue* (1611).

[1] Cf. ch. xviii as to traces of improvised comedy in England.

[2] G. E. P. Arkwright, *Notes on the Ferrabosco Family* (*Musical Antiquary*, iii. 221 ; iv. 42) ; G. Livi, *The Ferrabosco Family* (ibid. iv. 121). I may add that he was evidently the Bolognese groom of the chamber, favoured by the Queen as a musician, who dropped a hint for a Venetian embassy in 1575 (*V. P.* vii. 524). He left an illegitimate son, Alfonso, in England, who also was a Court musician by 1603, and was succeeded in turn by sons, Alfonso and Henry, in 1627 (Lafontaine, 45, 63).

[3] Feuillerat, *Eliz.* 159, 160.

[4] Ibid. 160, 301.

[5] Cunningham, 221 ; cf. *D. N. B.* ; *M. L. N.* xxii. 2, 129, 201.

[6] *Magdalene College, Cambridge, Pepys MS.* ii. 663 (cf. *Hist. MSS. Comm. Report*, 190). The letter is endorsed, ' To Q. Elizabeth : Ubaldino an Italian Musitian I suppose '.

Sacra Serenissima Maiesta,

Perché à i giorni passati io haveva promesso à M. Claudio Cavallerizzo,
et a M. Alfonso Ferrabosco, d'esser contento di recitare ad una piacevol
Comedia Italiana ; per compiacere alla Maiesta Vostra ; et non si
trovando di poi altri, che tre ò quattro, che fusser contenti d' accettar
tal carico ; ho voluto che l' Altezza Vostra conosca da me stesso il
pronto animo, ch' io ho per la mia parté di servirla, et di compiacerla
in ogni attioné, che me sia comandata ò da lei, ò in suo nomé, non
solamente comé servitore giurato, ch' io gli sono ; ma comé desidero-
sissimo di far conoscere, che la divotioné, ch'io porto allé sue Reali
qualità, supera ogn' altro rispetto ; desiderandogli io contentezza, et
felicità non meno, che qualunqué altro suo servitore gli desideri : la
cui bontà Dio ci prosperi.

Di Vostra Sacra Serenissima Maiesta.

Of Claudio Cavallerizzo I regret to say that I know nothing.
A statement that Venetian actors were in England in 1608
rests upon a misreading of a record.[1]

ii. ENGLISH PLAYERS IN SCOTLAND

The interlude players of Henry VII, under John English,
accompanied the Princess Margaret to Scotland for her
wedding with James IV in 1503, and ' did their devoir '
before the Court at Edinburgh.[2] It is the best part of a century
before any similar adventure is recorded. In the interval
came the Scottish reformation, which was no friend to
courtly pageantry. Yet in Scotland, as elsewhere, Kirk
discipline had to make some compromise with the drama.
In 1574 the General Assembly, while utterly forbidding, not
for the first time, ' clerk playes, comedies or tragedies maid
of ye cannonicall Scriptures ', went on to ordain ' an article
to be given in to sick as sitts upon ye policie yat for uther
playes comedies tragedies and utheris profaine playes, as are
not maid upon authentick pairtes of ye Scriptures, may
be considerit before they be exponit publictlie and yat they
be not played uppon ye Sabboth dayes '.[3] It was once more
a royal wedding that led to a histrionic courtesy between
England and Scotland. In the autumn of 1589 James VI
was expecting the arrival of his bride Anne of Denmark,
a sensuous and spectacle-loving lady, who had already had
experience of English actors at her father's Court in 1586.[4]
And being then, two years after his mother's execution, actively engaged in promoting friendly relations with

---

[1] Cf. my letter in *T.L.S.* for 12 May 1921.
[2] Cf. ch. xiii (Interluders) ; *Mediaeval Stage*, ii. 187.
[3] *Variorum*, iii. 461 ; cf. *Mediaeval Stage*, ii. 202.   [4] Cf. p. 272.

Elizabeth, he sent a request through one Roger Ashton to Lord Scrope, the Warden of the English West Marches, ' for to have her Majesties players for to repayer into Scotland to his grace '. In reply Scrope wrote from Carlisle on 20 September to William Ashby, the English ambassador at Edinburgh, begging him to notify the King, that he had sent a servant to them, ' wheir they were in the furthest parte of Langkeshire, whervpon they made their returne heather to Carliell, wher they are, and have stayed for the space of ten dayes '.[1] After all, the Lapland witches and their winds delayed Anne's crossing for some months, and James had himself to join her in Denmark. It is, I think, only a conjecture that the players whose ' book ' was submitted on 3 June 1589 for the licence of the Kirk Session at Perth, in accordance with the order of 1574, were Englishmen.[2] But certainly ' Inglis comedianis ' were in Scotland in 1594, probably for the baptism of Henry Frederick on 30 August, and received from James the generous gift of £333 6s. 8d. out of ' the composicioun of the escheit of ye laird of Kilcrewch and his complices '.[3] Probably Laurence Fletcher was at the head of this expedition, for on 22 March 1595 George Nicolson, the English agent at Edinburgh, wrote to Robert Bowes, treasurer of Berwick, that, ' The King heard that Fletcher, the player, was hanged, and told him and Roger Aston so, in merry words, not believing it, saying very pleasantly that if it were true he would hang them also '.[4] In any case, Fletcher appears to have been the leader of a company whose peregrinations in Scotland a few years later, much favoured by James, were also much embarrassed by the critical relations which then existed between the Sovereign and the Kirk. It 's only a conjecture that this was the company which was refused leave to play at St. Andrews on 1 October 1598.[5] But of greater troubles, which took place

---

[1] E. J. L. Scott in *Athenaeum* for 21 Jan. 1882. I am sorry to say that Mr. Scott suggests that Shakespeare was of the company.

[2] J. Scott, *An Account of Perth*, in Sir J. Sinclair, *Statistical Account of Scotland*, xviii (1796), 522.

[3] J. C. Dibdin, *Annals of the Edinburgh Stage* (1888), 20, from *Accounts* of the Lord High Treasurer of Scotland. *A True Accompt of the Baptism of Prince Henry Frederick*, printed in 1594 (*Somers Tracts*, ii. 171), records plays amongst other festivities, but does not say that English actors took part.

[4] *Scottish Papers*, ii. 676. I suppose that this document is the authority on which P. F. Tytler, *Hist. of Scotland*, ix. 302, describing the events of 1599, says of Fletcher, ' He had been there before, in 1594; and on his return to England, had suffered some persecution from his popularity with James '.

[5] D. H. Fleming, *St. Andrews Kirk Session Register*, ii. 870, ' Ane

at Edinburgh a year later, we are very well informed. They are detailed from the Kirk point of view in the more or less contemporary chronicle of David Calderwood.[1]

The King Chargeth the Kirk of Edinburgh to Rescind an Act.

Some English comedians came to this countrie in the moneth of October. After they had acted sindrie comedeis in presence of the King, they purchassed at last a warrant or precept to the bailliffes of Edinburgh, to gett them an hous within the toun. Upon Moonday, the 12th of November, they gave warning by trumpets and drummes through the streets of Edinburgh, to all that pleased, to come to the Blacke Friers' Wynd to see the acting of their comedeis. The ministers of Edinburgh, fearing the profanitie that was to ensue, speciallie the profanatioun of the Sabbath day, convocated the foure sessiouns of the Kirk. An act was made by commoun consent, that none resort to these profane comedeis, for eshewing offence of God, and of evill exemple to others ; and an ordinance was made, that everie minister sould intimat this act in their owne severall pulpits. They had indeed committed manie abusses, speciallie upon the Sabboth, at night before. The King taketh the act in evill part, as made purposelie to crosse his warrant, and caused summoun the ministers and foure sessiouns, *super inquirendis*, before the Secreit Counsell, They sent doun some in commissioun to the King, and desired the mater might be tryed privatlie, and offered, if they had offended, to repair the offence at his owne sight ; and alledged they had the warrant of the synod presentlie sitting in the toun. The King would have the mater to come in publict. When they went doun, none was called upon but Mr. Peter Hewat and Henrie Nisbit. After that they were heard, the sentence was givin out against all the rest unheard, and charge givin to the ministers and foure sessiouns to conveene, within three houres after, to rescind their former ordinance, and to the ministers, to intimat the contrarie of that which they intimated before. They craved to be heard. Loath was the King, yitt the counsell moved him to heare them. Mr. Johne Hall was appointed to be their mouth. ' We are summouned, Sir,' said Mr. Johne, ' and crave to understand to what end.' ' It is true', said the King, ' yee are summouned, and I have decerned alreadie.' Mr. Johne made no reply. Mr. Robert Bruce said, ' If it might stand with your good pleasure, we would know wherefore this hard sentence is past against us.' ' For contraveening of my warrant,' said the King. ' We have fulfilled your warrant,' said Mr. Robert, ' for your warrant craved no more but an hous to them, which they have gottin.' ' To what end, I pray you, sought I an hous,' said the King, ' but onlie that the people might resort to their comedeis ? ' ' Your warrant beareth not that end,' said Mr. Robert, ' and we have good

Jnglishman haveing desyrit libertie of the session to mak ane publik play in this citie, it was voted and concludit that he suld nocht be permitted to do the samin '.

[1] Calderwood, *Historie of the Kirk of Scotland* (Wodrow Soc.), v. 765.

reasoun to stay them from their playes, even by your owne acts of parliament.' The King answered, ' Yee are not the interpreters of my lawes.' ' And farther, the warrant was intimated but to one or two,' said M^r. Robert, and, therefore, desired the King to retreate the sentence. The King would alter nothing. ' At the least, then,' said M^r. Robert, ' lett the paine strike upon us, and exeeme our people.' The King bade him make away. So, in departing, M^r. Robert turned, and said, ' Sir, please you, nixt the regard we ow to God, we had a reverent respect to your Maiestie's royall person, and person of your queene ; for we heard that the comedians, in their playes, checked your royall person with secreit and indirect taunts and checkes ; and there is not a man of honour in England would give such fellowes so much as their countenance '. So they departed.

They were charged, at two houres, by sound of trumpet, the day following, at the publict Croce, about ten houres, to conveene themselves, and rescind the acts, or ellis to passe to the horne immediatly after. The foure sessiouns conveene in the East Kirk. They asked the ministers' advice. The ministers willed them to advise with some advocats, seing the mater tuiched their estate so neere. M^r. William Oliphant and M^r. Johne Schairp, advocats, came to the foure sessiouns. The charge was read. The advocats gave their counsell to rescind the act, by reasoun the King's charge did not allow slanderous and undecent comedeis ; and farther, shewed unto them, that the sessiouns could doe nothing without their ministers, seing they were charged as weill as the sessiouns, and the mater could not passe in voting, but the moderator and they being present. They were called in, and after reasouning they came to voting. M^r. Robert Bruce being first asked, answered ' His Majestie is not minded to allow anie slanderous or offensive comedeis ; but so it is that their comedeis are slanderous and offensive ; therefore, the king, in effect, ratifieth our act. The rest of the ministers voted after the same maner. The elders, partlie for feare of their estats, partlie upon informatioun of the advocats, voted to the rescinding of the act. It was voted nixt, whether the ministers sould intimat the rescinding of the act ? The most part voted they sould. The ministers assured them they would not. Henrie Nisbit, Archibald Johnstoun, Alexander Lindsey, and some others, tooke upon them to purchasse an exemptioun to the ministers. They returned with this answere, that his Majestie was content the mater sould be passed over lightlie, but he would have some mentioun made of the annulling of the act. They refuse. Their commissioners went the second tyme to the king, and returned with this answere, ' Lett them nather speeke good nor evill in that mater, but leave it as dead.' The ministers conveened apart to consult. M^r. Robert Bruce said it behoved them ather to justifie the thing they had done, or ellis they could not goe to a pulpit. Some others said the like. Others said, Leave it to God, to doe as God would direct their hearts. So they dissolved. M^r. Robert, and others that were of his minde, justified it the day following, in some small measure, and yitt were not querrelled.

Several other documents confirm this narrative. The Privy Council register contains an order of 8 November for an officer at arms to call upon the sessions by proclamation to rescind their resolution and a further proclamation of 10 November reciting the submission made by the sessions.[1] The Lord High Treasurer's accounts contain payments to Walter Forsyth, the officer employed, as well as gifts to ' ye Inglis comedianis ' of £43 6s. 8d. in October, of £40 in November ' to by tymber for ye preparatioun of ane house to thair pastyme ', and of a further £333 6s. 8d. in December.[2] It is George Nicolson, in a letter of 12 November forwarding the proclamation of 8 November to Sir Robert Cecil, who identifies the players for us as ' Fletcher and Mertyn with their company '.[3] The bounty of James, although it must be borne in mind that the sums were reckoned in pounds Scots, probably left them disinclined to quit Edinburgh in a hurry. Another gift of £400 reached them through Roger Ashton in 1601 ; [4] and on 9 October in the same year they visited Aberdeen with a letter of recommendation from the King, and with the style of his majesty's servants, and the town council gave them £22 and spent £3 on their supper ' that nicht thaye plaid to the towne '. Nay, more, another entry in the burgh register tells us that the players came in the train of ' Sir Francis Hospital of Haulszie, Knycht, Frenschman ', and one of those ' admittit burgesses ' with the foreign visitor was ' Laurence Fletcher, comediane to his Majesty '.[5]

Laurence Fletcher's name stands first in the English patent of 1603 to the King's men, and the inferences have been drawn that the company at Aberdeen was the Chamberlain's men, that their visit was due to a proscription from London on account of their participation in the Essex ' innovation ', that Shakespeare was with them, and that he picked up local colour, to the extent of ' a blasted heath ' for Macbeth.[6] To this it may be briefly replied that, as the

[1] Acts of the Privy Council of Scotland, vi. 39, 41. Calderwood seems to have put the whole business a week too late.   [2] Dibdin, 22.

[3] Lee, 83, from S. P. D. Scotland (R. O.), lxv. 64 ; cf. summary in Scottish Papers, ii. 777, ' Performances of English players, Fletcher, Martin, and their company, by the King's permission ; enactment of the [Fower] Sessions, and preaching of the ministers against them. The bellows blowers say that they are sent by England to sow dissension between the King and the Kirk '.   [4] Dibdin, 24.

[5] J. Stuart, Extracts from the Council Register of the Burgh of Aberdeen (Spalding Club), ii. xxi, xxii, 222.

[6] Fleay, 136 ; cf. Furness, Macbeth, 407. Fleay goes so far as to ' hazard the guess ' that the ' speciall letter ' of recommendation from James produced at Aberdeen was ' the identical letter that James wrote to Shakespeare with his own hand ', as recorded by Oldys.

Chamberlain's men were at Court as usual in the winter of 1602, any absence from London, which their unlucky performance of *Richard II* may have rendered discreet, can only have been of short duration ; that the most plausible reading of the Scottish evidence is that Fletcher's company were in the service of James as Court comedians from 1599 to 1601 ; and that there is nothing whatever to indicate that Fletcher ever belonged to the Chamberlain's company at all. In fact, very little is known of him outside Scotland, although it is just possible that he may have been the object of two advances made by Henslowe to the Admiral's men about October 1596, and described respectively as ' lent vnto Martyne to feache Fleacher ' and ' lent the company to geue Fleatcher '.[1] If Fletcher was the King's man in Scotland, it was not unnatural that he should retain that status when James came to England ; and it is very doubtful whether the insertion of his name in the patent in any way entailed his being taken into business relations with his ' fellows '. I strongly suspect that his companion at Edinburgh, Martin, was put into a precisely similar position amongst Queen Anne's men, for who can Martin be but Martin Slater, who is often, as in the passage quoted above, called Martin *tout court* in Henslowe's *Diary*, and who certainly left the Admiral's men in 1597 ?

iii. ENGLISH PLAYERS ON THE CONTINENT

[*Bibliographical Note.*—The earliest comprehensive study of the foreign travels of English actors is that of A. Cohn, *Shakespeare in Germany in the Sixteenth and Seventeenth Centuries* (1865). Much material has been collected, mostly since Cohn wrote, in a number of local histories and special studies, of which the most important are : C. M. Plümicke, *Entwurf einer Theatergeschichte von Berlin* (1781) ; D. C. von Rommel, *Geschichte von Hessen* (1820–38) ; J. E. Schlager, *Über das alte Wiener Hoftheater* in *Sitzungsberichte der phil.-hist. Classe der Kaiserlichen Akad. der Wissenschaften*, vi (1851), 147 ; M. Fürstenau, *Zur Geschichte der Musik und des Theaters am Hofe der Kurfürsten von Sachsen* (1861) ; E. Mentzel, *Geschichte der Schauspielkunst in Frankfurt am Main* (1882) ; O. Teuber, *Geschichte des Prager Theaters* (1883) ; J. Meissner, in *Shakespeare-Jahrbuch*, xix. 113 (Austria), and *Die englischen Comoedianten zur Zeit Shakespeares in Oesterreich* (1884) ; K. Trautmann in *Archiv für Litteraturgeschichte*, xii. 319 (Munich, Augsburg) ; xiii. 34 (Suabia), 315 (Ulm) ; xiv. 113 (Nuremberg), 225 (Suabia) ; xv. 209 (Ulm, Stuttgart, Tübingen) ; in *Zeitschrift für Vergleichende Litteraturgeschichte*, vii (Rothenburg) ; and in *Jahrbuch für Münchener Geschichte*, iii. 259 ; J. Crüger in *Archiv für Litteraturgeschichte*, xv. 113 (Strassburg) ; Duncker, *Landgraf Moritz von Hessen und die englischen Komödianten* in *Deutsche Rundschau*, xlviii (1886), 260 ; A. Cohn in *Shakespeare-Jahrbuch*, xxi. 245 (Cologne) ; J. Bolte in *Shakespeare-Jahrbuch*, xxiii. 99 (Denmark and Sweden), and *Das Danziger Theater im*

---

[1] Henslowe, i. 45

16. und 17. Jahrhundert (1893) ; J. Wolter in *Zeitschrift des Bergischen Geschichtsvereins*, xxxii. 90 (Cologne) ; A. Wormstall in *Zeitschrift für vaterländische Geschichte und Altertumskunde Westfalens*, lvi (1898), 75 (Münster) ; G. Witkowski in *Euphorion*, xv. 441 (Leipzig). A collection of records from the earlier of these and from more scattered sources is in K. Goedeke, *Grundriss der deutschen Dichtung aus den Quellen*[2] (1886), ii. 524, and valuable summaries are given in W. Creizenach, *Schauspiele der englischen Komödianten* (1889), and E. Herz, *Englische Schauspieler und englisches Schauspiel zur Zeit Shakespeares in Deutschland* (1903). The excursus of F. G. Fleay in *Life and Work of Shakespeare* (1886), 307, is misleading. Additional material, which has become available since Herz wrote, is recorded by C. F. Meyer in *Shakespeare-Jahrbuch*, xxxviii. 196 (Wolgast), and C. Grabau in *Shakespeare-Jahrbuch*, xlv. 311 (Leipzig). Useful special studies are by C. Harris, *The English Comedians in Germany before the Thirty Years' War : the Financial Side* (*Publ. of Modern Language Association*, xxii. 446), A. Dessoff, *Über englische, italienische und spanische Dramen in den Spielverzeichnissen deutscher Wandertruppen* (1901, *Studien für vergleichende Litteraturgeschichte*, i), and on the problem of staging (cf. ch. xx) C. H. Kaulfuss-Diesch, *Die Inszenierung des deutschen Dramas an der Wende des sechzehnten und siebzehnten Jahrhunderts* (1905). A collection of plays and jigs, in German, but belonging to the repertory of an English company, appeared as *Engelische Comedien und Tragedien* (1620) ; some of the plays have been edited by J. Tittmann, *Die Schauspiele der englischen Komödianten in Deutschland* (1880), and the jigs by J. Bolte, *Die Singspiele der englischen Komödianten und ihrer Nachfolger in Deutschland, Holland und Scandinavien* (1893). German plays written under English influences are to be found in J. Tittmann, *Die Schauspiele des Herzogs Heinrich Julius von Braunschweig* (1880), and A. von Keller, *Jacob Ayrers Dramen* (1865). Cohn prints, with translations, Ayrer's *Sidea* and *Phaenicia, Julio and Hyppolita* and *Titus Andronicus* from the 1620 volume, and early German versions of *Hamlet* (*Der bestrafte Brudermord*) and *Romeo and Juliet* from manuscripts. The literary records and remains of the English players are fully discussed by Creizenach and Herz, and their relation to Ayrer by W. Wodick, *J. Ayrers Dramen in ihrem Verhältniss zur einheimischen Literatur und zum Schauspiel der englischen Komödianten* (1912).

The material for the Netherlands, some of which was gathered by Cohn, may be studied in J. A. Worp, *Geschiedenis van het Drama en van het Tooneel in Nederland* (1904–8), who also deals with the Dutch versions of English dramas. The contemporary stage conditions in France are best treated by E. Rigal, *Le Théâtre français avant la période classique* (1901), and those in Spain by H. A. Rennert, *The Spanish Stage in the Time of Lope de Vega* (1909), who uses the results of recent researches by C. Pérez Pastor, which have added much to the information furnished by C. Pellicer, *Tratado histórico sobre el origen y progresos de la Comedia y del Histrionismo en España* (1804).]

Thomas Heywood records, about 1608, that ' the King of Denmarke, father to him that now reigneth, entertained into his service a company of English comedians, commended unto him by the honourable the Earl of Leicester '.[1] This King of Denmark was Frederick II (1559–88), father of Christian IV (1588–1648), and of Queen Anne of England. English

---

[1] App. C, No. lvii.

'instrumentister', Johann Krafftt, Johann Personn, Johann Kirck or Kirckmann, and Thomas Bull, were at the Danish Court as early as 1579–80, and in 1585 certain unnamed English played (*lechte*) in the courtyard of the town-hall at Elsinore, when the press of folk was such that the wall broke down. These may be the same men who played and vaulted at Leipzig on 19 July 1585, and are the earliest English players yet traced in Germany.[1] But the particular comedians referred to by Heywood were probably another company who had accompanied Leicester to Holland, when he took the command of the English forces in 1585, and had given a show, half dramatic, half acrobatic, of *The Forces of Hercules* at Utrecht on 23 April 1586. Certainly Leicester had in his train one Will, a 'jesting plaier', who is now usually identified with William Kempe, and in August and September 1586 the Household Accounts of the Danish Court record the presence of 'Wilhelm Kempe instrumentist', and of his boy Daniell Jonns. It is not clear what were the precise relations between Kempe and five other 'instrumentister och springere', Thomas Stiwens, Jurgenn Brienn, Thomas Koning, Thomas Pape, and Robert Persj, who were at Court from 17 June to 18 September 1586, and for whom the same accounts record a payment to Thomas Stiuens of six thalers a month apiece, at the end of that period. If he had, as is probable, been their fellow up to that point, he did not accompany them in their further peregrinations.[2] These took them to the Court of Frederick's nephew, Christian I, Elector of Saxony (1586–91), as a result of correspondence, still extant, between the sovereigns, in which the offer of salaries at the annual rate of 100 thalers overcame the reluctance of the Englishmen to face the perils of an unknown tongue. They started with an interpreter on 25 September, and shortly after their arrival at Waidenhain on 16 October received instructions from Christian to follow him with mourning clothes to Berlin, where he was then sojourning. Christian's own capital was Dresden, and here they held a formal appointment in his service, under which they were bound to follow him in his travels, and to entertain him with performances after his banquets, and with music and 'Springkunst', and were entitled, beyond their pay, to

---

[1] *Sh.-Jahrbuch*, xlv. 311, ' 5 Thaler den englischen Spielleuten, so ufm Rathaus ihr Spiel mit Springen und allerlei Kurzweil getrieben '.

[2] The inevitable attempt to show that Shakespeare ' must ' have been of the party was made by J. Stefansson, *Shakespeare at Elsinore*, in *Contemporary Review*, lxix. 20, and disposed of by H. Logeman, *Shakespeare te Helsingör* in *Mélanges Paul Fredericq* (1904) ; cf. *Sh.-Jahrbuch*, xli. 241.

board, livery, and travelling expenses, and a lodging allowance of forty thalers each. The Dresden archives give their names as Tomas Konigk, Tomas Stephan or Stephans, George Beyzandt, Tomas Papst, and Rupert Persten. Their departure from Court is recorded on 17 July 1587.[1] In all these notices music and acrobatic feats are to the fore, but that the men were actors there can be no doubt, for two of them, Thomas Pope and George Bryan, reappear amongst Strange's men, and thereafter as fellows of Shakespeare in the Chamberlain's company. Of Stevens, King, and Percy no more is known. Kempe was abroad again, in Italy and Germany, during 1601, and returned to England on 2 September. It is not certain whether he took a company with him, or went as a solitary morris dancer. But it is noteworthy that on the following 26 November an English company, under one Johann Kemp, reached Münster, after a tour which had taken them to Amsterdam, Cologne, Redberg, and Steinfurt. They played in English, and had a clown who pattered in German between the acts.[2]

The man, however, who did most to acclimatize the English actors in Germany was Robert Browne, who paid several visits to the country, and spent considerable periods there between 1590 and 1620. With him he took relays of actors, some of whom split off into independent associations, and account for most, although not all, of the groups of ' Engländer ' who became familiar figures at the Frankfort spring and autumn fairs and even in out-of-the-way corners of northern Europe. Of some of these groups the wanderings can be traced in outline, although the frequent failure of the archives to record individual names is responsible for many *lacunae*, which the conjectural ingenuity of literary historians has done its best to fill. Many of these anonymous performances I must pass over in silence.

Robert Browne first appears as one of Worcester's men, with Edward Alleyn, in 1583, and in 1589 these two, probably as Admiral's men, still held a common stock of apparel with John Alleyn and Richard Jones.[3] His career abroad begins with a visit to Leyden in October 1590.[4] This was

---

[1] Fürstenau, 69 ; Cohn, xxiii ; Bolte, *Sh.-Jahrbuch*, xxiii. 99. Herz, 5, endeavours to show traces of a visit to Danzig by this company.

[2] M. Röchell, *Chronik*, in J. Janssen, *Gesch. des Bisthums Münster* (1852), iii. 174 ; Cohn, cxxxiv (misdated 1599) ; *Sh.-Jahrbuch*, xxxvi. 274.

[3] *Henslowe Papers*, 31. Greg, *Henslowe*, ii. 8, disposes of the confusion between Robert Browne and Alleyn's step-father, John Browne.

[4] Cohn, xxxi. There seems nothing to connect the Andreas Röthsch who appeared at Leipzig in July 1591 with Browne, or even to justify the conjecture (*Sh.-Jahrbuch*, xlv. 311) that he was English.

perhaps only tentative, for in February 1592 he was preparing
to cross the seas again, and to this end obtained for himself,
John Bradstreet, Thomas Sackville, and Richard Jones, the
following passport to the States-General of the Netherlands
from the Lord Admiral:

Messieurs, comme les présents porteurs, Robert Browne, Jehan
Bradstriet, Thomas Saxfield, Richard Jones, ont deliberé de faire
ung voyage en Allemagne, avec intention de passer par le païs de
Zelande, Hollande et Frise, et allantz en leur dict voyage d'exercer
leurs qualitez en faict de musique, agilitez et joeux de commedies,
tragedies et histoires, pour s'entretenir et fournir à leurs despenses
en leur dict voyage. Cestes sont partant vous requerir monstrer et
prester toute faveur en voz païs et jurisdictions, et leur octroyer en
ma faveur vostre ample passeport soubz le seel des Estatz, afin que
les Bourgmestres des villes estantz soubs voz jurisdictions ne les
empeschent en passant d'exercer leurs dictes qualitez par tout.
Enquoy faisant, je vous demeureray à tous obligé, et me treuverez
très appareillé à me revencher de vostre courtoisie en plus grand cas.
De ma chambre à la court d'Angleterre ce xme jour de Febvrier 1591.

Vostre tres affecsionné à vous fayre plaisir et sarvis,
C. Howard.[1]

Presumably the Lord Admiral gave this passport in his
official capacity, as responsible for the high seas, and it is
not necessary to infer that the travellers were in 1592 his
servants.[2]

There are not many clear notices of Browne and his company during this tour. They were at Arnhem, with a licence
from Prince Maurice of Orange-Nassau, in 1592.[3] Thereafter
they may have gone into residence at some Court, Wolfenbüttel or another. They can hardly have been the English
'comoedianten und springer' who came to Nyköping in
Sweden for the wedding of Duke Karl of Sweden and Princess
Christina of Holstein on 28 August 1592[4]; for it was only
two days later that Browne approached the Frankfort
magistrates for leave to play at the autumn fair, where
they gave *Gammer Gurton's Needle* and some of Marlowe's
plays.[5] It was on this occasion that Fynes Moryson, the
traveller, visited the fair and noted the great vogue of the

---

[1] L. Ph C. van den Bergh, *'s Gravenhaagsche Bijzonderheden* (1857), 51
from Hague Archives; Cohn, xxviii. A letter from R. Jones to Alleyn
(*Henslowe Papers*, 33), often assigned to this date, seems to me probably
to belong to 1615: cf. p. 287.

[2] Another Admiral's passport is printed in Rye, 47.

[3] G. van Hasselt, *Arnhemsche Oudheden*, i (1803), 244, naming Robert
Bruyn, Johan Bradsdret, Thomas Saxwiell, Richardus Jonas, and Everhart Sauss.

[4] Bolte in *Sh.-Jahrbuch*, xxxiii. 104.   [5] Mentzel, 23.

English actors amongst the merchants.[1] Englishmen played at Cologne in October and November 1592,[2] and at Nuremberg in August 1593;[3] but in view of the Nyköping company it can hardly be assumed that these were Browne and his fellows, and indeed the leader at Nuremberg is called 'Ruberto Gruen', which may, but on the other hand may not, be a blunder for Browne's name. The Cologne players are anonymous. At any rate 'Robert Braun, Thomas Sachsweil, Johan Bradenstreit und consorten' were all at Frankfort in August 1593,[4] where they played scriptural dramas, including *Abraham and Lot* and *The Destruction of Sodom and Gomorrha*. Thereafter the company seems to have broken up. Richard Jones certainly went home before 2 September 1594, when he bought a gown ' of pechecoler in grayne' from Henslowe.[5] He had doubtless already joined the Admiral's men.

Thomas Sackville and John Bradstreet probably went to Wolfenbüttel. This was the capital of Henry Julius, Duke of Brunswick-Wolfenbüttel (1589–1613), himself the author of plays, mostly printed during 1593 and 1594, in which an English influence is perceptible. The Duke married Elisabeth, daughter of Frederick II of Denmark, and his wedding at Copenhagen in February 1590 was attended by his brother-in-law, afterwards James I of England. It is possible that his earliest play, *Susanna*, was written either for this occasion or for the repetition of his wedding ceremony at Wolfenbüttel. In this piece the jester, a conventional personage, bears the name ' Johan Clant', in the later plays ' Johan Bouset'; and in the *Ehebrecherin* (1594) Bouset says, quite irrelevantly to his dramatic character, ' Ich bin ein Englisch Mann'. Both names are in fact of English origin, from the words ' clown' and ' posset' respectively. Evidently the Duke must in some way have been in touch with the English stage at a date even earlier than Browne's second German visit in 1592. It is not, therefore, necessary to conjecture, as has been conjectured, that Wolfenbüttel was the first objective of this visit.[6] Unfortunately the Brunswick household accounts for 1590–1601 are missing, and with them all direct evidence of the first formation of his English company by the Duke has probably gone. The company existed by 1596, when

---

[1] Cf. vol. i, p. 343.   [2] *Sh.-Jahrbuch*, xxi. 247.
[3] *Archiv*, xiv. 116.   [4] Mentzel, 25.   [5] Henslowe, i. 29.
[6] Cohn, xxxiii, xxxviii; Goedeke, ii. 519; Herz, 8. A conventional clown, variously called ' Jahn Clam', ' Jahn Posset', ' Jahn der Engel-ländische Narr', &c., also appears in plays, from 1596 onwards, by Jacob Ayrer of Nuremberg, who has other debts, including the ' jig', to the English players (Cohn, lxi; Goedeke, ii. 545).

the 'furstelige comoedianten och springers' of the Duke
paid a month's visit to Copenhagen for the coronation of
his brother-in-law, Christian IV of Denmark, on 29 August.[1]
In the following year we find ' Jan Bosett und seine Gesellen '
at Nuremberg, ' Thomas Sackfeil und Consorten ' at Augsburg
in June, ' Johann Busset' and Jakob Behel at Strassburg
in July and August, and ' Thomas Sackville, John Bouset
genannt ', Johann Breitenstrasse and Jacob Biel at the
Frankfort autumn fair.[2] The identity of this company with
the Wolfenbüttel court comedians may perhaps be inferred
from Sackville's use of John Bouset as a stage name, and from
a reference, in this same year 1597, to ' Thomas Sackefiel,
princely servant at Wolfenbüttel '.   Another member of
the company may have been Edward Wakefiel, with whom
Sackville, also in 1597, had a brawl in a Brunswick tavern.[3]
No more is heard of them until 1601, when John Bouset
was expected to join his old friend Robert Browne for the
Frankfort Easter fair.[4] The Brunswick household accounts
are extant for 1602 and 1608, and from 1614 onwards.
Thomas Sackville appears frequently. On 30 August 1602 he
took a payment for the English comedians. Later references
to him from 1 October 1602 to 1617 are mainly in connexion
with purchases for the ducal wardrobe. It seems clear that,
while remaining a ducal servant, and possibly even an
actor, he went into business and prospered therein.[5] He
is said to have been selling silk at Frankfort in 1604, and
in 1608 Thomas Coryat, the Odcombian traveller and oddity,
records :

' The wealth that I sawe here was incredible. The goodliest shew
of ware that I sawe in all Franckford, saving that of the Goldsmithes,
was made by an Englishman one Thomas Sackfield a Dorsetshire man,
once a servant of my father, who went out of England but in a meane
estate, but after he had spent a few yeares at the Duke of Bruns-
wicks Court, hee so inriched himselfe of late that his glittering shewe

---

[1] Sh. Jahrbuch, xxiii. 103.
[2] Archiv, xii. 320 ; xiii. 316 ; xiv. 118 ; xv. 115 ; Mentzel, 26, 37.
Herz, 34, points out that about this date the Duke of Brunswick's Ehe-
brecherin and Vincentius Ladislaus were played in Frankfort, probably by
these men. They are referred to at length by Marx Mangoldt, Markschiffs-
Nachen (1597), in a passage beginning :
                Da war nun weiter mein Intent,
                Zu sehen das Englische Spiel,
                Dauon ich hab gehört so viel.
                Wie der Narr drinnen, Jan genennt,
                Mit Bossen wer so excellent.
Herz, 34, also assigns to the company anonymous appearances at Ulm,
Munich, and Tübingen in 1597 (Archiv, xii. 319 ; xiii. 316 ; xv. 212).
[3] Cohn, xxxiv.   [4] Cf. p. 279   [5] Cohn, xxxiv.

of ware in Franckford dit farre excell all the Dutchmen, French, Italians, or whomsoever else.'[1]

John Bradstreet's name appears in 1604 with that of Sackville in the album of Johannes Cellarius of Nuremberg. He died in 1618 and Sackville in 1628, leaving a library of theology and English literature. Edward Wakefield reappears in the Brunswick accounts for 1602, not specifically as a player. But certainly the playing company continued to exist. The accounts mention it in 1608, and Thomas Heywood notes its existence about the same date. There were English players at Wolfenbüttel in May 1615 and at Brunswick in 1611 and 1617, but no names are recorded, and it can hardly be assumed that these were the original ducal company. Henry Julius himself died in 1613.[2]

Robert Browne's own movements are uncertain after the break-up of his company in 1593. He is not traceable for a year or so either in Germany or in England, where his wife and all her children and household died of plague in Shore-ditch about August 1593.[3] But sooner or later he found his way to Cassel. This was another of the literary courts of Germany, the capital of Maurice the Learned, Landgrave of Hesse-Cassel (1592–1627). Maurice himself wrote an 'Anglia Comoedia' and other plays in Terentian Latin, which were performed by the pupils of the Collegium Mauritianum, but are unfortunately not preserved. He also composed music and, like the Duke of Brunswick, gave a welcome to John Dowland on one of his several foreign tours.[4] Possibly Dowland was one of the two lutenists who are recorded to have spent fifteen weeks at Cassel in 1594.[5] In the following year there were performances by players and acrobats at Maurice's castle of Wilhelmsburg at Schmalkalden, and in the same year Maurice wrote to his agent at Prague to give assistance to his comedians in the event of their visiting that city.[6] To 1594 or 1595 may, therefore, be plausibly ascribed undated warrants by which Robert Browne and Philip Kiningsmann receive appointments from the Landgrave, undertaking to do him service with their company in vocal

---

[1] Herz, 37 ; T. Coryat, Crudities, ii. 291. Cf. also Ein Discurss von der Frankfurter Messe (1615) :

Der Narr macht lachen, doch ich weht,
—Da ist keiner so gut wie Jahn begeht—
Vor dieser Zeitt wol hat gethan,
Jetzt ist er ein reicher Handelsmann.

[2] Cohn, xxxiv ; Sh.-Jahrbuch, xl. 342.   [3] Henslowe Papers, 37.
[4] Cohn, xviii, lvii ; Goedeke, ii. 522 ; Duncker, Landgrave Moritz von Hessen und die Englischen Komödianten in Deutsche Rundschau, xlviii. 260.
[5] Sh.-Jahrbuch, xiv. 361.   [6] Cohn, lviii ; Herz, 13.

and instrumental music and in plays to be supplied either by
Maurice or by themselves, and not to leave Cassel without
his permission.[1]   Certainly Browne was the Landgrave's
man by 16 April 1595, when a warrant was issued allowing
the export of a consignment of bows and arrows which
he had been sent over to bring from England to Cassel.[2]
The 'fürstlich hessische Diener und Comoetianten' were
at Nuremberg on 5 July 1596, and a company under
Philip Konigsman were at Strassburg in the following
August.[3]   Festivities were now in preparation at Cassel for
the christening of Maurice's daughter, one of whose god-
mothers was Queen Elizabeth, on 24 August 1596.   Brown
and one John Webster were on duty at Cassel during the
visit of the Earl of Lincoln, who came from England to stand
proxy for Elizabeth.[4]   Payments to the English comedians
and performances by them at Melsungen, Weissenstein, and
Rothenburg, in the Landgrave's territory, are recorded in
the Cassel archives during 1597 and 1598.   A proposed loan
of them in 1597 to Landgrave Louis of Marburg seems to
have fallen through, but in 1598 they left Cassel for the Court
of the Palsgrave Frederic IV at Heidelberg, with a liberal
Abfertigung or vail of 300 thalers and a travelling allowance of
20 thalers, which was entrusted to George Webster.[5]   From
Heidelberg they went to Frankfort towards the end of 1599,
but were refused leave to play, owing to the prevalence of
plague.[6]   Robert Browne, Robert Kingman, and Robert
Ledbetter were then of the company.   Ledbetter must have
recently joined them, as he is in the cast of *Frederick and
Basilea* as played by the Admiral's men in 1597.   Frankfort
having failed them, they fell back upon Strassburg, and here
they seem to have remained until the spring of 1601.[7]   Browne
was their leader at their arrival, but he then seems to have
left them and returned to England, where he came to Court
as manager of the Earl of Derby's men during the winters of

[1] Könnecke in *Z. f. vergleichende Litteraturgeschichte*, N. F. i. 85.

[2] *Hatfield MSS.* v. 174.   Browne was also the agent for a similar transaction licensed on 11 July 1597 (*S. P. D. Eliz.* cclxiv).

[3] *Archiv*, xiv. 117 ; xv. 114.

[4] Rommel, vi. 390, from Cassel archives, 'Robert Brown und John
Wobster begleiteten ihn'.   The payment therefore on behalf of the
Admiral's men about Oct. 1596 'to feache Browne' (Henslowe, i. 45) is
not very likely to refer to Robert.

[5] Cohn, lviii ; Duncker, 265.

[6] Mentzel, 41.

[7] *Archiv*, xv. 115.   Herz, 17, assigns to them, conjecturally, performances
by 'Englishmen' at Memmingen, Cologne, Munich, Ulm, and Stuttgart
during 1600.   But the wording of the Strassburg documents suggests
a continuous stay.

1599–1600 and 1600–1.[1] By Easter 1601, however, he had started on his fourth tour, and appeared once more at Frankfort, possibly in Kyd's *Spanish Tragedy*. With him were Robert Kingmann and Robert Ledbetter, and they were expecting to be joined by ' Johannen Buscheten und noch andere in unsere Companie gehörige Comödianten '. The old association of 1592 between Robert Browne and Thomas Sackville was, therefore, still in some sense alive.[2]

Meanwhile, Maurice of Hesse had not been wholly without English actors, since Browne and his fellows left Cassel in 1598. It would seem that George Webster returned from Heidelberg, or perhaps from Strassburg, to his service. The ' fürstlich-hessischen Komödianten · und Musikanten ' were at Frankfort in March, at Nuremberg in April 1600, and at Frankfort again at Easter 1601. The names recorded are those of George Webster, John Hill or Hüll, Richard Machin, and at Nuremberg Bernhardt Sandt.[3] Upon his second visit to Frankfort Webster would have met his old leader, now become his rival, Robert Browne. The Hessian company were for a third time at Frankfort in the autumn of 1601.[4] In the following year they left the Landgrave's service, not altogether to the regret of some of his subjects, who resented a patronage of foreign arts at the cost of their pockets.[5] Webster and Machin, with whom was then one Ralph Reeve, were still using their former master's name when they visited Frankfort at Easter 1603.[6] Thereafter they dropped it. Of Webster no more is heard. Machin is conjectured to have joined for a short time an English company in the service of Margrave Christian William, a younger son of the Elector Joachim Frederick of Brandenburg, which came to Frankfort for the Easter and autumn fairs of 1604.[7] The Margrave was administrator of the diocese of Magdeburg, and kept his

---

[1] On 21 Oct. 1603 Joan Alleyn wrote to Edward Alleyn (*Henslowe Papers*, 59), ' All the companyes be come hoame & well for ought we knowe, but that Browne of the Boares head is dead & dyed very pore, he went not into the countrye at all '. Obviously this is not Robert Browne, who lived many years longer. But it may have been a relative, as Lord Derby's men are very likely to have preceded Worcester's at the Boar's Head. There was at least one other actor of the name, Edward Browne, and possibly more (cf. ch. xv).

[2] Mentzel, 46.

[3] Mentzel, 45, 48 ; *Archiv*, xiv. 119. A performance at Dresden in Oct. 1600, assigned to them by Herz, 38, is anonymous.

[4] Mentzel, 48.

[5] Duncker, 267, from chronicle of Wilhelm Buch, ' Anno 1602 hat er die Engländer alle mit einander von sich gejagt und des springens und tanzens müde geworden '.

[6] Mentzel, 50.   [7] Mentzel, 51 ; Bolte, *Das Danziger Theater*, 34.

Court at Halle. His company is traceable from 1604 to 1605, but I do not find any evidence of Machin's connexion with it. In May 1605 he appeared at Strassburg, and there claimed as his credentials only his four years' service with Maurice of Hesse.[1] Shortly before, he had been at the Frankfort Easter fair with Reeve, and the two returned to Frankfort in the autumn, and again at Easter 1606.[2]

Robert Browne, for some years after the opening of his fourth tour at Frankfort in the spring of 1601, does not appear to have attached himself to any particular Court. He is found at Frankfort, with Robert Jones, in September 1602, at Augsburg in the following November and December, at Nuremberg in February 1603, and at Frankfort for the Easter fair of the same year.[3] With him were then, but it would seem only temporarily, Thomas Blackwood and John Thare, late of Worcester's men, who had doubtless just come out from England, when Elizabeth's illness and death closed the London theatres.[4] He is probably the 'alte Komödiant', whose identity seems to have been thought sufficiently described by that term at Frankfort in the autumn of 1604.[5] He returned to Frankfort on 26 May 1606, and was at Strassburg in the following June and July.[6] Here he was accompanied by John Green. On this or some other visit to Strassburg, the company probably lost Robert Kingman, who, like Thomas Sackville, found business more profitable than strolling. He became a freeman of Strassburg in 1618, and in that year was able to befriend his old 'fellow' Browne, and in 1626 other actors on their visits to the city.[7] In the course of 1606 Browne seems to have entered the service of Maurice of Hesse, who in the previous year had built a permanent theatre, the *Ottonium*, at Cassel, and had now again an English company for the first time since 1602. This is to be inferred from an application for leave to play submitted to the Frankfort town council on 26 August 1606, and signed by 'Robert Braun', 'Johann Grün', and 'Robert Ledbetter' as 'Fürstlich Hessische Comödianten'. Earlier

---

[1] *Archiv*, xv. 117.   [2] Mentzel, 52.

[3] Mentzel, 50 ; *Archiv*, xiv. 122.

[4] The Frankfort archives call them ' Thomas Blackreude ' and ' Johannes Fheer ', which has prevented their identity with Worcester's men from being noticed.   [5] Mentzel, 51.

[6] Mentzel, 53 ; *Archiv*, xv. 117. Herz, 18, assigns to Browne anonymous appearances by Englishmen at Strassburg in June 1601, Ulm in Nov. 1602, Nördlingen in May 1605, and Ulm in May and June 1605. At Nördlingen a play from the prophet Jonah, possibly Greene and Lodge's *Looking Glass for London and England*, was given.

[7] *Archiv*, xv. 120. Coryat, ii. 183, saw him at Strassburg in 1608.

in August the same men had been at Ulm.[1] They visited
Nuremberg with a letter of recommendation from their
lord in November, and then settled down at Cassel for the
winter.[2] But their service did not last long. On 1 March
1607 a household officer wrote to the Landgrave that the
English found their salaries inadequate, and after performing
the comedy of *The King of England and Scotland* had declared,
either in jest or earnest, that it was their last play in Cassel.[3]
Probably they were in earnest. Browne and Green went to
Frankfort, for the last time as the Hessian comedians, on
17 March.[4] Browne's name now disappears from German
records for a decade. In 1610 he was a member of the
Queen's Revels syndicate in London, and on 11 April 1612
he wrote a letter to Edward Alleyn from Clerkenwell.[5] But
whether Browne left them or not, the company held together
for a while longer. Green was at Danzig and Elbing in the
course of 1607.[6] Thereafter it seems probable that he tried
a bold flight, and penetrated to the heart of Catholic Germany
in Austria. In November 1607 an English company was with
the archducal court of Ferdinand and Maria Anna at Gräz
in Styria. A performance by them of *The King of England
and the Goldsmith's Wife* is recorded.[7] They followed Ferdinand
to Passau, where they gave *The Prodigal Son* and *The Jew*,
and possibly also to the Reichstag held in January 1608 at
Regensburg. By 6 February they were back at Gräz, and
a letter from Ferdinand's sister, the Archduchess Maria
Magdalena, then just betrothed to the Grand Duke Cosimo II
of Florence, gives a lively account of their performances and
of the assistance which they rendered in the revels danced
at Court.[8] Their repertory included *The Prodigal Son,
A Proud Woman of Antwerp, Dr. Faustus, A Duke of Florence
and a Nobleman's Daughter, Nobody and Somebody, Fortunatus,
The Jew, King Louis and King Frederick of Hungary, A King
of Cyprus and a Duke of Venice, Dives and Lazarus.*[9] It is
not absolutely certain that the company referred to in these
notices was Green's. No name is in fact mentioned. But
the probability suggested by the resemblance of the above

---

[1] Mentzel, 53 ; Meissner in *Sh.-Jahrbuch*, xix. 125 ; *Archiv*, xiii. 320 ;
Duncker, 268. The *Ottonium* was named after Maurice's son Otto, the
friend of Prince Henry Frederick, who paid a visit to England in 1611
(Rye, 141).   [2] *Archiv*, xiv. 124.
[3] Cohn, lviii ; R. P. Wülcker in *Sh.-Jahrbuch*, xiv. 360.
[4] Mentzel, 53.   [5] *Henslowe Papers*, 63.
[6] Bolte, 35.   [7] This might be Heywood's *King Edward IV.*
[8] F. von Hurter, *Gesch. Kaiser Ferdinands II*, v. 395.
[9] *The Proud Woman of Antwerp* might be the lost piece by Day and
Haughton.

play-list to those of 1620 and 1626, with which Green was
certainly connected, is confirmed by the existence of a German
manuscript of *Nobody and Somebody* with a dedication by
Green to Ferdinand's brother the Archduke Maximilian, who
was certainly present at the Gräz performances, and by
a letter which tells us that a company visiting Austria in
1617 was the same as that which had played at Gräz in the
lifetime of the Archduchess Maria, who died in 1608. Unfortunately the identification of this company of 1617 with
Green's is itself a matter of high probability, rather than of
absolute certainty.[1] The end of the visit to Gräz was marked
by a duel in which one of the English actors, ' the man with
long red hair, who always played a little fiddle ', killed
a Frenchman.[2] Green now, like Browne, drops for some
years out of the German records.

The Court functions at Cassel surrendered by Browne in
1607 were resumed by his predecessors, in whose leadership
Reeve had now succeeded Machin; and the appearance of
the Hessian company is recorded at Frankfort during both
the fairs of 1608 and 1609, the Easter fair of 1610, the autumn
fair of 1612, and the Easter fair of 1613. A proposed appearance for the coronation of the Emperor Mathias in June 1612
was prohibited, because the mourning for his predecessor
Rudolph II was not yet over.[3] It is perhaps something of
an assumption that the company was the same one throughout
all these years. Reeve was in charge up to the autumn of
1609; after that no individual name is mentioned. The
intervals between the fairs were presumably spent in the
main at Cassel. In the summer of 1609 the company visited
Stuttgart and Nuremberg and possibly other places, with
a letter of recommendation from their lord.[4] In the autumn

---

[1] Meissner, 74, and in *Sh.-Jahrbuch*, xix. 128 ; cf. pp. 284–6. The
text of *Nobody and Somebody* is printed from a manuscript at Rein by
F. Bischoff in *Mittheilungen des hist. Vereins für Steiermark*, xlvii. 127.
I think it is just possible that the companies of 1608 and 1617 may have
been Spencer's. There seem to have been *Saxoni*, as well as *Angli*, playing.
These do not seem to have constituted a distinct company, and are perhaps
more likely to have been with Spencer than with Green. Spencer, as well
as Green, was in relations with the imperial court in 1617 ; cf. p. 290.
But I think that the evidence of the Rein manuscript is fairly decisive
in favour of Green.

[2] This may have been Green himself. A drawing of a red-haired actor,
in the traditional get-up of Nobody, is on the Rein manuscript.

[3] Mentzel, 54, 55, 56, 58.

[4] *Archiv*, xiv. 125 ; xv. 215. Herz, 41, ascribes to them anonymous
appearances at Ulm, Nördlingen, and Augsburg. John Price, afterwards
well known as a musician at Dresden and Stuttgart, is said to be recorded
at Stuttgart in 1609 (Cohn, cxxxviii), and may have been with the Hessian
company.

of the same year John Sigismund, Elector of Brandenburg
(1608–19), who often entertained a company of his own,
but appears to have been temporarily without one, wrote
to Maurice to borrow them for the wedding of his brother
at Berlin.[1] In April 1610 they may not improbably, though
there is no evidence of the fact, have followed Maurice to
the Diet at Prague.[2] In 1611 they are said to have been at
Darmstadt.[3] They certainly played at the wedding of the
Margrave Joachim Ernest, uncle of the Elector of Brandenburg, at Anspach in October 1612, and later in the same
month paid a visit to Nuremberg.[4] No more is heard of them,
or of any other English actors in the service of Maurice of
Hesse-Cassel, after 1613.[5] Reeve was a member of Rosseter's
syndicate for the building of the Porter's Hall theatre at
Blackfriars in 1615, and with him were associated Philip
Kingman and Robert Jones, the last notices of whom in
Germany are as 'fellows' of Robert Browne in 1596 and
1602 respectively.

The appearance of Blackwood and Thare, late of Worcester's
men, in company with Browne at the Frankfort Easter fair
of 1603, has already been noted. The only further record
of either of them is of Thare at Ulm and Augsburg in the
following December.[6] But by a series of conjectures, to which
I hesitate to subscribe, they have been identified with a
company which came to Stuttgart in September 1603 in the
train of Lord Spencer and Sir William Dethick, ambassadors
from England carrying the insignia of the Garter to Frederick
Duke of Württemberg, and there gave a play of *Susanna*[7];
with a company which visited Nördlingen and other places
in January 1604 under the leadership of one Eichelin, apparently a German, but with a repertory which included a *Romeo
and Juliet* and a *Pyramus and Thisbe*[8]; with a company

---

[1] Cohn, lix ; Duncker, 272.

[2] Meissner, 46 ; Duncker, 272. Herz, 41, ascribes to them anonymous
appearances at the wedding of the Margrave John George, brother of the
Elector of Brandenburg, and the Princess Christina of Saxony at Jägern-
dorf in July, and at Nuremberg and Ulm in November.

[3] Cohn, lix, without reference. Herz, 41, adds an anonymous performance of *The Merchant of Venice* at the Court of Margrave Christian of
Brandenburg at Halle.

[4] *Archiv*, xiv. 126.   [5] Duncker, 273.

[6] *Archiv*, xiii. 319. If this is the company which, according to Alvens-
leben, *Allgemeine Theaterchronik* (1832), No. 158, played *Daniel, The Chaste
Susanna*, and *The Two Judges in Israel* at Ulm in 1602, the identification
with the company found at Nördlingen and Rothenburg is assisted.

[7] Cohn, lxxvii, from Erhard Cellius, *Eques Auratus Anglo-Wirtembergicus*
(1605) ; cf. Rye, cvii.

[8] *Archiv*, xi. 625 ; xiii. 70. They also played *Daniel in the Lions' Den,*

which held letters of recommendation from the Duke of Würtemberg at Nuremberg in February 1604;[1] and with a company which took a repertory closely resembling the Nördlingen one to Rothenburg is 1604 and 1606.[2] This is all very ingenious guesswork.[3]

All trace of John Green is lost for several years after 1608. An isolated notice at Utrecht in November 1613 suggests that he may have spent part of this interval in the Netherlands.[4] A year or two later he returned to Germany. He was at Danzig in July 1615 and again, with Robert Reinolds, late of Queen Anne's men, in July 1616, having paid an intermediate visit to Copenhagen.[5] In 1617 he was at Prague for the coronation of the Archduke Ferdinand as King of Bohemia, and in July of the same year at Vienna.[6] The comparative infrequency with which English actors visited Austrian territory perhaps justifies the assumption that his is the company mentioned in a letter of recommendation sent by Ferdinand's brother, the Archduke Charles, at Neiss to the Bishop of Olmütz on 18 March 1617, as having played at Gräz before his mother the Archduchess Maria, who died in 1608, and having recently spent some months at the Court of Poland in Warsaw.[7] In 1618 Green's old leader, the indefatigable veteran Robert Browne, came out with a new company on his fifth and last visit to the Continent. He is first noted at Nuremberg on 28 May.[8] My impression is that the two men joined forces. Green's name does not appear in the records for a couple of years. But Reinolds, who had been with him at Danzig in 1616, was with Browne at Strassburg

Susanna (? by Henry Julius of Brunswick or another version), *The Prodigal Son, A Disobedient Merchant's Son* (? *The London Prodigal*), *Charles Duke of Burgundy, Annabella a Duke's Daughter of Ferrara* (? Marston's *Parasitaster*), *Botzarius an Ancient Roman,* and *Vincentius Ladislaus* (? by Henry Julius of Brunswick). Three of these plays (*Romeo and Juliet, The Prodigal Son,* and *Annabella*) are in the repertories of John Green ; cf. p. 285.

[1] *Archiv,* xiv. 122.

[2] *Zeitschrift für vergleichende Litteraturgeschichte,* N. F. vii. 61. They played in 1604 *Daniel in the Lions' Den, Melone of Dalmatia, Lewis King of Spain, Celinde and Sedea, Pyramus and Thisbe, Annabella a Duke's Daughter of Montferrat* ; and in 1606 *Charles Duke of Burgundy, Susanna, The Prodigal Son, A Disobedient Merchant's Son, An Ancient Roman, Vincentius Ladislaus.* The Nördlingen and Rothenburg companies must be the same. *Celinde and Sedea,* however, is found in a repertory, not of Green, but of Spencer ; cf. p. 289.

[3] Herz, 42, 65.   [4] A. van Sorgen, *De Tooneelspeelkunst in Utrecht.*

[5] Bolte, 41, 47. Herz, 27, conjectures that these may have been the English players at Wolfenbüttel in May 1615 ; cf. p. 277.

[6] Schlager, 168 ; Meissner in *Sh.-Jahrbuch,* xix. 139.

[7] Cohn, xciii ; cf. p. 282 as to the inference that Green was at Gräz in 1607–8.   [8] *Archiv,* xiv. 129.

in June and July 1618.[1] Later in the year Browne was at the autumn fair at Frankfort.[2] There is no definite mention of him during the next twelve months, but it is not improbable that the combined company was that which visited Rostock in May and Danzig in July 1619.[3] At any rate Browne appeared at Cologne in October;[4] and then went for the winter to Prague, where the Elector Palatine and the Lady Elizabeth of England, now King and Queen of Bohemia, had set up their Court.[5] They were but a winter King and Queen. In 1620 the Thirty Years' War broke out, and Germany had other things to think of than English mumming. Browne was at Nuremberg in February and at Frankfort for the Easter fair.[6] That is the last we hear of him. But Green reached Cologne and Utrecht later in April, and was probably discreetly taking the company home.[7] In 1626 he came out again with Robert Reinolds, who made a reputation as a clown under the name of Pickleherring.[8] The details of this later tour lie beyond the scope of the present inquiry. Pickleherring is the clown-name also in a volume of *Engelische Comedien und Tragedien*, printed in 1620, which probably represents an attempt of Browne and Green to turn to profit with the printers their repertory of 1618–20, now rendered useless by their return to England.[9] The plays contained in this volume, in addition to two farces and five jigs, in most of which Pickleherring appears, are *Esther and Haman, The Prodigal Son, Fortunatus, A King's Son of England and a King's Daughter of Scotland, Nobody and Somebody, Sidonia and Theagenes, Julio and Hyppolita*, and *Titus Andronicus*.[10] The first five of these reappear in a list of plays forming the repertory of Green at Dresden during the visit of 1626 referred to above. If the titles can be trusted, two of the plays in this list had already been played by Browne at Frankfort and Cassel in 1601 and 1607, three by an unknown company, possibly that of Blackwood and Thare, at Nördlingen and

---

[1] *Archiv*, xv. 120.   [2] Mentzel, 60.   [3] Bolte, 51.
[4] Herz, 22, from Wolter, 97.   [5] Mentzel, 61 ; Meissner, 65.
[6] *Archiv*, xiv. 130 ; Mentzel, 61.
[7] Herz, 30, from Wolter, 97 ; A. van Sorgen, *De Tooneelspeelkunst in Utrecht*.   [8] Herz, 30.
[9] Goedeke, ii. 543, could find no copy of *Musarum Aoniarum tertia Erato* (Hamburg, 1611), the title-page of which claims ' etlichen Englischen Comedien ' as a source.
[10] The last two plays have some kind of relation to Shakespeare's *Two Gentlemen of Verona* and *Titus Andronicus*. *Sidonia and Theagenes* is a prose version of Gabriel Rollenhagen's *Amantes Amentes* (1609). A supplement to the 1620 collection, with six other plays and two jigs, appeared as *Liebeskampff oder Ander Theil der Englischen Comödien und Tragödien* (1630), but none of these are traceable before the Thirty Years' War.

Rothenburg in 1604 and 1606, and eight by Green himself at Passau and Gräz in the winter of 1607–8.[1] They number thirty in all, as follows: *Christabella, Romeo and Juliet,*[2] *Amphitryo,*[3] *The Duke of Florence,*[4] *The King of Spain and the Portuguese Viceroy,*[5] *Julius Caesar, Crysella,*[6] *The Duke of Ferrara,*[7] *Nobody and Somebody,*[8] *The Kings of Denmark and Sweden,*[9] *Hamlet,*[10] *Orlando Furioso,*[11] *The Kings of England and Scotland,*[12] *Hieronymo the Spanish Marshal,*[13] *Haman and Esther,*[14] *The Martyr Dorothea,*[15] *Doctor Faustus,*[16] *The King of Arragon,*[17] *Fortunatus,*[18] *Joseph the Jew of Venice,*[19] *The Clever Thief,*[20] *The Duke of Venice,*[21] *Barabbas Jew of Malta, The Dukes of Mantua and Verona, Old Proculus, Lear King of England, The Godfather, The Prodigal Son,*[22] *The Count of Angiers, The Rich Man.*[23]

The lists of 1620 and 1626 do not bear out Fleay's assumption that the repertories they represent were wholly made up of plays taken out by Browne in 1592.[24]

[1] Cf. pp. 279, 281, 283.   The Dresden list is in Cohn, cxv.

[2] Played at Nördlingen in 1604.   Cohn, 309, prints a German version from a Vienna manuscript.

[3] Possibly Heywood's *The Silver Age.*

[4] Green played at Gräz in 1608 ' Von ein Herzog von Florenz der sich in eines Edelmann's Tochter verliebt hat '.   This seems too early for Massinger's *Great Duke of Florence,* but suggests the same story.

[5] Possibly *1 Jeronimo.*   [6] Possibly Dekker's *Patient Grissel.*

[7] Played at Nördlingen and Rothenburg in 1604.   Bolte, 177, prints from a Danzig manuscript a later German version based on Marston's *Parasitaster.*

[8] Played by Green at Gräz in 1608, in a version extant in a Rein manuscript ; a later one is in the 1620 collection.   Cf. p. 282.

[9] Possibly *Clyomon and Clamydes.*

[10] Cohn, 236, prints a German version from a late copy.

[11] Possibly Robert Greene's play.

[12] Played by Browne at Cassel in 1607 ; a text is in the 1620 collection.

[13] Probably Kyd's *Spanish Tragedy,* played by Browne at Frankfort in 1601.   [14] Printed in the 1620 collection.

[15] Probably Dekker's *Virgin Martyr.*

[16] Played by Green at Gräz in 1608.

[17] Possibly Robert Greene's *Alphonsus, King of Arragon* or *Mucedorus.*

[18] Played by Green at Gräz in 1608.   A version, related to Dekker's *Old Fortunatus,* is in the 1620 collection.

[19] Played by an anonymous company at Halle in 1611 ; cf. p. 283. *The Jew,* played by Green at Passau and Gräz in 1607–8, might be either this play or *The Jew of Malta.*   Dekker wrote a *Jew of Venice,* now lost ; but a German version, printed by Meissner, 131, from a Vienna manuscript, is in part based on *The Merchant of Venice.*

[20] Could this be *The Winter's Tale* ?

[21] Green played *The King of Cyprus and Duke of Venice* at Gräz in 1608.

[22] Played at Nördlingen in 1604 and Rothenburg in 1606 and by Green at Passau and Gräz in 1607–8.   A version is in the 1620 collection.

[23] Green played *Dives and Lazarus* at Gräz in 1608.

[24] Fleay, *Sh.* 307.

Another member of Browne's last expedition can perhaps
be identified. With him in 1592 had been Richard Jones,
who afterwards became one of the Admiral's men in 1594
and left that company in 1602. He was again associated
with Browne in Rosseter's Queen's Revels syndicate of 1610.
The following undated letter to Edward Alleyn is preserved
at Dulwich:[1]

Mr Allen, I commend my love and humble duty to you, geving you
thankes for your great bounty bestoed vpon me in my sicknes, when
I was in great want, God blese you for it, Sir, this it is, I am to go over
beyond the seas with Mr Browne and the company, but not by his
meanes, for he is put to half a shaer, and to stay hear, for they ar all
against his goinge. Now good Sir, as you have ever byne my worthie
frend, so healp me nowe. I have a sut of clothes and a cloke at pane
for three pound, and if it shall pleas you to lend me so much to release
them I shalbe bound to pray for you so longe as I leve, for if I go over
and have no clothes, I shall not be esteemed of, and by godes help the
first mony that I gett I will send it over vnto you, for hear I get
nothinge, some tymes I have a shillinge a day, and some tymes nothinge,
so that I leve in great poverty hear, and so I humbly take my leave,
prainge to god I and my wiffe for your health and mistris Allenes,
which god continew,

Your poor frend to command
Richard Jones.

[*Endorsed*] Receved of master Allen the   of February the somme
of   [*and by Alleyn*] Mr Jones his letter wher on I lent hym 3^l.

This has generally been dated 1592. But Alleyn's first
recorded marriage was in October of that year, and the
reference to Browne as not going with the company has
always been a puzzle. I suspect that it was written in or
near 1615, and that Jones was one of the actors who started
in advance of Browne under John Green. That he did travel
about this time is shown by two other letters to Alleyn about
a lease of the Leopard's Head in Shoreditch held by his
wife.[2] The first, from Jones himself, is not dated, but a
mention of Henslowe shows that it was written before the
latter's death on 6 January 1616, or at least before Jones had
heard of that event. The writer and his wife were then out
of England. The second, from Harris Jones, was written
from Danzig on 1 April 1620. Mrs. Jones was then expecting
to join her husband, who was with ' the prince ', whoever
this may have been. If Jones had travelled with Browne's
men, he cut himself adrift from them on their return, for in
1622 he entered as a musician the service of Philip Julius,

[1] *Henslowe Papers,* 33.   [2] Ibid. 94.

Duke of Wolgast in Pomerania (1592–1625), who had twice visited England, and whose presence at more than one London theatre is recorded in 1602.[1] Two petitions from Jones are in the Stettin archives.[2] On 30 August 1623 he asked permission, with his fellows Johan Kostrassen and Robert Dulandt (Dowland?), to return from Wolgast to England. Behind them they appear to have left Richard Farnaby, son of the better-known composer Giles Farnaby.[3] On 10 July 1624 Jones wrote to the Duke that his hopes of profitable employment under the Prince in England had been disappointed, and asked to be taken back into his service.

All the groups of actors hitherto dealt with seem to have had their origin, more or less directly, in the untiring initiative of Robert Browne. There is, however, another tradition, almost as closely associated with the houses of Brandenburg and Saxony, as the former with those of Hesse-Cassel and Brunswick. Some give and take between Cassel and the Courts of some of the Brandenburg princes has from time to time been noted.[4] But Berlin, where the successive Electors of Brandenburg, Joachim Frederick (1598–1608) and John Sigismund (1608–9), had their capital, was during a long period of years the head-quarters from which an Englishman, John Spencer, undertook extensive travels, both in Protestant and in Catholic Germany. Of Spencer's stage-career in London, if he ever had one, nothing is known. Possibly he betook himself to the Brandenburg Court during the English plague-year of 1603. At any rate, comedians holding a recommendation given by the Elector on 10 August 1604 and confirmed by the Stadtholder of the Netherlands, Maurice Prince of Orange Nassau, in the following December, were at Leyden in January and The Hague in May 1605.[5] It is reasonable to identify them with the company under John Spencer, who received a recommendation from the Electress Eleonora of Brandenburg to the Elector Christian II of Saxony (1591–1611) in the same year.[6] At Dresden they possibly remained for some time, for although there are several anonymous appearances, including the famous ones at Gräz in the winter of 1607–8, which can be conjecturally assigned to them,[7] they do not clearly emerge until April 1608, when a visit of the Electoral players of Saxony is recorded at

[1] Cf. ch. xvi, introd. [2] C. F. Meyer in *Sh.-Jahrbuch*, xxxviii. 208.
[3] *D. N. B.* s.v. Giles Farnaby. [4] Cf. pp. 279, 283.
[5] Cohn, lxxviii. [6] Fürstenau, i. 76.
[7] Cf. p. 282. Herz, 44, identifies them with ' English ' at The Hague (June 1606), Cologne (Feb. 1607), The Hague (April), Ulm (May), Nördlingen (June), and Munich (July).

Cologne.[1] Subsequently they waited upon Francis, Duke of Stettin and by him were recommended to the new Elector of Brandenburg, John Sigismund, who passed them on once more to the Elector of Saxony on 14 July 1609.[2] Being in need of comedians for his brother's wedding in the same year, he applied, as has been noted, for a loan of those of Maurice of Hesse.[3] Dresden remained the head-quarters of Spencer's men again during the next two years, but in 1611 they were back in John Sigismund's service. Christian II of Saxony died in this year. In July and August they visited Danzig and Königsberg, and in October and November they attended the Elector to Ortelsburg and Königsberg for the ceremonies in connexion with the acknowledgement of him as heir to his father-in-law, Duke Albert Frederick of Prussia. On this occasion Spencer was at the head of not less than nineteen actors and sixteen musicians, and produced an elaborate Turkish ' Triumph-comedy '.[4] In April 1613 Spencer left Berlin on a tour which was to take him to Dresden once more.[5] The company were at Nuremberg in June, still using the name of the Elector of Brandenburg and playing *Philole and Mariana, Celinde and Sedea, The Fall of Troy, The Fall of Constantinople*, and *The Turk*.[6] In July and August they were at Augsburg, and in September they returned to Nuremberg, now describing themselves as the Elector of Saxony's company.[7] This Elector was John George I (1611–56), the third of his house to entertain an English company. In October they played *The Fall of Constantinople* at the Reichstag held by the Emperor Mathias at Regensburg. Spencer was their leader, but they no longer claimed any courtly status.[8] After an unsuccessful attempt to pay a third visit for the year to Nuremberg, they went to Rothenburg, and so to Heidelberg, whither the Elector Palatine Frederick V had just brought his English bride. Here they spent the winter, and left to attend the Frankfort fair of Easter 1614.[9] In May their service with the Elector of Brandenburg, although

---

[1] Wolter, 93.

[2] L. Schneider, *Geschichte der Oper in Berlin*, Beilage, lxx. 25 ; Fürstenau, i. 77.

[3] Cf. p. 283.   [4] Cohn, lxxxiv.   [5] Ibid. lxxxvii.

[6] *Archiv*, xiv. 128. *Philole and Mariana* may be Lewis Machin's *The Dumb Knight*, and *The Turk* Mason's play of that name. *Celinde and Sedea* had formed part of a repertory at Rothenburg in 1604 apparently related to those of Green ; cf. p. 284. Spencer is not recorded to have played any other piece found in Green's repertories.

[7] *Archiv*, xii. 320 ; xiv. 128.

[8] Schlager, 168 ; Elze in *Sh.-Jahrbuch*, xiv. 362 ; Meissner, 53, and in *Sh.-Jahrbuch*, xix. 120.

[9] *Archiv*, xiv. 129 ; *Zeitschrift für vergl. Litt.* vii. 64 ; Mentzel, 58.

now none of the most recent, helped them to get a footing in Strassburg, where they stayed until July and again played *The Fall of Constantinople*, as well as a play of *Government*.[1] In August they were at Augsburg and possibly Ulm.[2] In October they projected a return visit to Strassburg, but were rejected, ' so dies Jar hie lang genug super multorum opinionem gewessen '.[3] Possibly they fell back upon Stuttgart.[4] In February 1615 they were in Cologne, and here a queer thing happened. The whole company, with Spencer's wife and children, was converted to Catholicism by the eloquence of a Franciscan friar. The event is recorded in the town archives and also in a manuscript Franciscan chronicle preserved in the British Museum:[5]

' Twentie fowre stage players arrive out of Ingland at Collen : all Inglish except one Germanian and one Dutchman. All Protestants. Betwixt those and father Francis Nugent disputation was begunne and protracted for the space of 7 or eight dayes consecutively ; all of them meeting at one place together. The chiefe among them was one N. Spencer, a proper sufficient man. In fine, all and each of them beeing clearlie convinced, they yielded to the truth ; but felt themselves so drie and roughharted that they knew not how to pass from the bewitching Babylonian harlot to their true mother the Catholic church, that always pure and virginal spouse of the lamb.'

It need hardly be said that in so Catholic a city as Cologne this singular act of grace gave the performances of the English comedians an extraordinary vogue. In June and July 1615 Spencer was at Strassburg, in company with one Christopher Apileutter, who may have been the Germanian or the Dutchman of the Cologne notice.[6] He attended the autumn fair at Frankfort, using an imperial patent, perhaps given him at Regensburg in 1613.[7] During the winter of 1615–16 he was again in Cologne, still profiting by his conversion.[8] This, however, had not made of him such a bigot, as to be unable to render acceptable duty in the Protestant courts where his earliest successes had been won. For a year his movements became obscure. But in August 1617 he was playing before the Elector of Saxony and the Emperor Matthias at Dresden.[9] And in the following year he once more entered the Brandenburg service. During the interval which had elapsed since

---

[1] *Archiv*, xv. 118. [2] Ibid. xii. 320 ; xiii. 322.
[3] Ibid. xv. 119. Ibid. xv. 215 ; cf. Herz, 48.
[5] Wolter, 96 ; Cohn in *Sh.-Jahrbuch*, xxi. 260 ; Cohn, xci, from *Harl.*
MS. 3888, *The Evangelic Fruict of the Seraphicall Franciscan Order*.
[6] *Archiv*, xv. 119. [7] Mentzel, 59.
[8] Cohn in *Sh.-Jahrbuch*, xxi. 261 ; Wolter, 96.
[9] Meissner, 59, and in *Sh.-Jahrbuch*, xix. 122.

1613, John Sigismund had entertained another company. Early in 1614 he engaged William, Abraham, and Jacob Pedel, Robert Arzschar, Behrendt Holzhew, and August Pflugbeil.[1] The names hardly sound English ; but Jacob Pedel is probably the Jacob Behel or Biel who was travelling with Sackville in 1597, William Pedel appeared as an English pantomimist at Leyden in November 1608, and Arzschar, whose correct name was doubtless Archer, is also described as an Englishman at Frankfort in the autumn of 1608.[2] He was then in company with Heinrich Greum and Rudolph Beart. A Burchart Bierdt appeared as ' Englischer Musicant ' at Cologne in December 1612.[3] Archer perhaps came from Nuremberg. He was at Frankfort again in the autumn of 1610, and at the Reichstag held by the Emperor Matthias at Regensburg in September 1613.[4] It must have been this new company under Archer which visited Wolfenbüttel in September 1614 and Danzig in 1615, styling themselves the Brandenburg comedians.[5] The only names given at Danzig are Johann Friedrich Virnius and Bartholomeus Freyerbott, and in fact the Pedels, Holzhew, and Pflugbeil left Berlin at Easter 1615. Archer himself remained with the Elector until May 1616. The field,. then, was clear at Berlin for the enterprise of Spencer. On 17 March 1618 John Sigismund made a payment ' to one Stockfisch ' for bringing the English comedians from Elbing. Further payments to the English are recorded in the following November, and in June 1619 for plays at Königsberg and Balge in Prussia, of which the Elector had become Duke on the death of his father-in-law Albert Frederick in the preceding August.[6] In July 1619 the Elector of Brandenburg's comedians are heard of at Danzig.[7] On 23 December 1619 John Sigismund himself died, and in 1620 Hans Stockfisch addressed an appeal for certain arrears of salary to Count Adam von Schwartzenberg, an officer at the court of the new Elector George William (1619–40), in which he claimed to have enjoyed the Count's protection for more than fifteen years. In reply George William describes the petitioner as ' den Englischen Junkher Hans Stockfisch, wie er sich nennet '.[8] There can be little doubt that Hans Stockfisch was none other than John Spencer, for the period of fifteen years precisely takes us back to his first appearance as a Brandenburg comedian in 1605. His fish name corre-

[1] Cohn, lxxxviii.   [2] Ibid. lxxxiii ; Mentzel, 54.
[3] Cohn in Sh.-Jahrbuch, xxi. 257 ; Wolter, 95.
[4] Archiv, xiv. 124 ; Mentzel, 54 ; Schlager, 168 ; Herz, 53.
[5] Cohn, xxxv ; Bolte, 41.   [6] Cohn, xcii.   [7] Bolte, 51.
[8] Cohn, xcii ; Meissner, 38, and in Sh.-Jahrbuch, xix. 122.

sponds to, and was perhaps motived by, that of Pickleherring adopted by Robert Reinolds of the chief rival English company about the same date. Both had their prototype in Sackville's John Bouset.[1] The Elector George William was no friend to actors, and to Spencer, as to others, the Thirty Years' War closed many doors. In February 1623 he came to Nuremberg with Sebastian Schadleutner, but was not allowed to play.[2] And that is the last that is heard of him.

A few isolated records indicate the presence from time to time in northern Europe of players not yet mentioned, and not obviously connected either with the Browne or with the Spencer tradition. An English company under Peter de Prun of Brussels visited Nuremberg in April 1594. The name of the leader does not sound very English, and a company, not improbably the same, is described as ' niederländische ' at Ulm in the following August. Heywood, however, speaks of an English company as in the pay of the Cardinal and Archduke Albert, Governor of the Spanish Netherlands, about 1608.[3] Maurice of Orange-Nassau, Stadtholder of the Dutch Netherlands (1584–1625), who gave a recommendation to Spencer in .1605, had also an English company of his own, which visited Frankfort at Easter 1611, and then claimed to be strange in Germany.[4] To Augsburg in June 1602 came Fabian Penton and his company;[5] to Leyden in September 1604 John Woods and his company,[6] and to Leipzig in April 1613 Hans Leberwurst with his boys.[7] Of none of these is anything further known, nor of William Alexander Blank, a Scottish dancer, who performed at Cologne in April 1605.[8]

Traces of English players in southern Europe are few and far between. That Kempe's travels of 1601 took him to Italy has already been noted.[9] There were some English acrobats at Madrid in January 1583.[10] On 25 May 1598 the Confrères de la Passion leased their theatre in Paris,

[1] Cf. pp. 275, 285.　　　　　　　　　　　[2] Archiv, xiv. 131.
[3] Ibid., xiii. 316; xiv. 116; Heywood, 60.
[4] Mentzel, 55. H. Chardon, La Troupe du Roman comique, 32, notices Maurice of Nassau's company at Nantes in 1618 and Paris in 1625, but does not say that they were English.
[5] Archiv, xiii. 317; xiv. 121.　　　　　　[6] Cohn, lxxvii.
[7] Sh.-Jahrbuch, xlv. 311.　　　　　　　　[8] Cohn in Sh.-Jahrbuch, xxi. 253.
[9] Cf. p. 273.
[10] Pellicer, i. 80, citing the records of the Madrid hospital, ' en 11 de Enero de 1583 voltearon unos ingleses en el Corral de la Pacheca '. The original record is probably lost, as it is not with those of 1579–82, 1590, and 1601–2 published from the Archivo de la Diputacion provincial de Madrid by C. Pérez Pastor in the Bulletin Hispanique (1906) and reprinted by Rennert, 345.

the Hôtel de Bourgogne, to ' Jehan Sehais comédien Anglois ', and on 4 June obtained judgement in the court of the Châtelet, ' tant pour raison du susdit bail que pour le droit d'un écu par jour, jouant lesdits Anglais ailleurs qu'audit Hôtel '.[1] I do not know whether I am justified in finding under the French disguise of ' Jehan Sehais ' the name of one John Shaa or Shaw, conceivably related to Robert Shaw of the Admiral's men, who witnessed an advance by Henslowe to Dekker on 24 November 1599.[2] In 1604 another English company was in France, and gave a performance on 18 September in the great hall at Fontainebleau, the effect of which upon the imagination of the future Louis XIV, then a child of four, is minutely described in the singular diary of his tutor and physician, Jean Héroard.[3]

' Mené en la grande salle neuve ouïr une tragédie représentée par des Anglois ; il les écoute avec froideur, gravité et patience jusques à ce qu'il fallut couper la tête à un des personnages.'

On 28 September, Louis was playing at being an actor, and on 29 September, says Héroard :

' Il dit qu'il veut jouer la comédie ; " Monsieur," dis-je, " comment direz-vous ? " Il repond, " Tiph, toph," en grossissant sa voix. À six heures et demie, soupé ; il va en sa chambre, se fait habiller pour masquer, et dit : " Allons voir maman, nous sommes des comédiens." '

Finally, on 3 October :

' Il dit, " Habillons-nous en comédiens," on lui met son tablier coiffé sur la tête ; il se prend à parler, disant : " Tiph, toph, milord " et marchant à grands pas.'

It has been suggested on rather inadequate grounds that the play seen by Louis may have been 2 *Henry IV*. Possibly the princely imagination had merely been smitten by some comic rough and tumble.[4] But it is also conceivable that the theme may have been the execution of John Tiptoft, Earl of Worcester, at the restoration of Henry VI in 1470.[5]

[1] E. Soulié, *Recherches sur Molière*, 153 ; cf. Rigal, 46 ; Jusserand, *Shakespeare in France*, 51.   [2] Henslowe, i. 114.
[3] Soulié et de Barthélemy, *Journal de Jean Héroard*, i. 88, 91, 92.
[4] H. C. Coote in *Intermédiaire des Chercheurs et Curieux*, ii. 105 ; cf. 5 *N. Q.* ix. 42. The idea was that ' Tiph, toph ' represented a reminiscence of 2 *Henry IV*, II. i. 205, ' This is the right fencing grace, my lord ; tap for tap, and so part fair '. The phrase ' tiff toff ' occurs in brackets in a speech of Crapula while he beats Mendacio in *Lingua* (Dodsley,[4] ix. 434). Collier explains it as hiccups ; Fleay, ii. 261, on the authority of P. A. Daniel, as an Italian term for the thwack of stage blows.
[5] E. Fournier, *Chansons de Gaultier Garguille*, lix, and *L'Espagne et ses Comédiens en France au xviiᵉ Siècle* (*Revue des Provinces*, iv. 496), cites

It would be rash to assume that these records of 1598 and 1604 represent all the visits of English actors to France during the Elizabethan period; and it is not improbable that a search in the municipal archives of Picardy and Normandy, as thorough as that which has been carried out for Germany, might yield notable results. Some general evidence that tours in France did take place can be cited. John Green, dedicating his version of *Nobody and Somebody* to the Archduke Maximilian about 1608, says that he had been in that country.[1] His, indeed, so far as dates go, might have been the company of 1604. And France, no less than Germany, is referred to as scoured by the English comedians about 1613.[2]

H. Ternaux in *Revue Françoise et Étrangère*, i. 78, for statements that the head of the English at Fontainebleau was Ganassa, who in Spain had had a mixed company of English, Italians, and Spanish, and on 11 Jan. 1583 had a share in the receipts of a troupe of English *volteadores*. I have not been able to see the work of M. Ternaux, who does not inspire confidence by calling Ganassa Juan instead of Alberto. There seems to be nothing to connect Ganassa with the *volteadores* of 1583, except the fact that the Corral de la Pacheca where they played was leased to him for nine or ten years in 1574 (Rennert, 29), and they may therefore have paid him rent. His troupe in 1581–2, as given by Rennert, 479, consisted entirely of Italians, with two Spanish musicians. He is said to have been in Spain in 1603 (Pellicer, i. 57, 72 ; Rennert, 30), but there is nothing to show that, if so, he went on to France. But Héroard tells us that there was a Spanish rope-dancer at Fontainebleau in 1604, and a very obscure passage in his diary suggests that this Spaniard was really an Irishman. Irish marauders (*voleurs*) were then giving trouble in Paris, which led Louis to say ' Ce voleur qui voloit sur la corde étoit Irlandois ? ' and Héroard comments, ' Il étoit vrai ; il accommoda le mot de voleur à l'autre signification, il l'avoit vu voler à Fontainebleau ' (*Journal*, i. 90, 126).

[1] F. Bischoff in *Mittheilungen des hist. Vereins für Steiermark*, xlvii. 127 ; cf. p. 282.

[2] De Bry, *India Orientalis* (1613), xii. 137, ' Angli ludiones per Germaniam et Galliam vagantur '.

XV

ACTORS

[*Bibliographical Note.*—I include a few managers who were not necessarily themselves actors. The earlier studies of stage biography were mainly concerned with the Chamberlain's and King's men in the list of ' The Names of the Principall Actors in all these Playes ', prefixed to the Shakespearian F₁ of 1623. The statements about them in [J. Roberts] *Answer to Mr. Pope's Preface to Shakespeare* (1729) are conjectural and not, as sometimes supposed, traditional. A good deal was collected from wills and registers by E. Malone (*Variorum*, iii. 182), G. Chalmers (ibid. iii. 464), and J. P. Collier, *Memoirs of the Principal Actors in the Plays of Shakespeare* (1846, *Sh. Soc.* revised edition in *H. E. D. P.* iii. 255), and is summarized by K. Elze, *William Shakespeare* (tr. 1888), 246. New ground was broken by F. G. Fleay, *On the Actor Lists, 1578–1642* (*R. Hist. Soc. Trans.* ix. 44), and in the list in *Chronicle History of the London Stage* (1890), 370. Here he criticizes Collier's claim to have a list of 500 actors, as he cannot find ' that any list at all was found among his papers , and suggests that a forgery was planned. I am glad to have an opportunity for once of defending Collier, even if it is only against Fleay. The fifth report (1846) of the *Sh. Soc.* shows that ' a volume of the original actors in plays by writers other than Shakespeare was in preparation, and *Bodl. MS.* 29445 contains a number of rough extracts made by Collier and P. Cunningham from London parochial registers, with a digest of these and other material, entitled ' Old Actors. Collections for the Biography of, derived from Old Books & MSS. Alphabetically arranged '. I have used this manuscript and cite it as ' Bodl.' or ' B.'. The information is mainly from the registers of St. Saviour's, Southwark, St. Andrew's Wardrobe, St. Anne's, Blackfriars, St. Leonard's, Shoreditch, St. Giles', Cripplegate, and other churches. It appears to be reliable, except perhaps in one or two points. One would, of course, prefer to have the registers themselves in print, but with the exception of those of St. James's, Clerkenwell (*Harl. Soc.*), and A. W. C. Hallen's *Registers of St. Botolph's, Bishopsgate*, the published London Registers, as shown by A. M. Burke, *Key to the Ancient Parish Registers of England and Wales* (1908), are precisely those of least theatrical interest. The Southwark registers in particular, and the other records of that parish, including the ' token-books ' or annual lists, street by street, of communicants, ought to be made available. Some notes from them are in W. Rendle, *Bankside* (1877, Harrison, Part ii). Southwark marriages (1605–25) are in *Genealogist* (n. s. vi–ix). In these records ' man ' clearly means ' player'. Extracts from other registers may be found in parochial histories and elsewhere. Some from St. Giles's, Cripplegate, are in J. P. Malcolm, *Londinium Redivivum* (1802–7), iii. 303, J. J. Baddeley, *St. Giles, Cripplegate* (1888), and W. Hunter's *Addl. MS.* 24589. C. C. Stopes, *Burbage*, 139, gives a full collection from St. Leonard's, Shoreditch. An interesting list of actors and their addresses *c.* 1623 is in C. W. Wallace, *Gervase Markham, Dramatis!* (1910, *Sh.-Jahrbuch*, xlvi. 345), cited as ' J '· The citations ' H ' and ' H. P ' are from Greg's editions of Henslowe's *Diary* and *Henslowe Papers*.]

ABYNGDON, HENRY. Master of Chapel, 1455–78.

ADAMS, JOHN. Sussex's, 1576; Queen's, 1583, 1588. He possibly played the clown Adam in *A Looking Glass* and Oberon in *James IV*. It would hardly be justifiable to conjecture that he lived to join Hunsdon's and play Adam in *A. Y. L.*

ALDERSON, WILLIAM. Chapel, 1509–13.

ALLEYN, EDWARD, was born on 1 September 1566 in the parish of St. Botolph, Bishopsgate.[1] His father was Edward Alleyn of Willen, Bucks, Innholder and porter to the Queen, who died in 1570 ; his mother, Margaret Townley, for whom he claimed a descent from the Townleys of Lancashire which modern genealogists hesitate to credit, re-married with one John Browne, a haberdasher, between whom and other Brownes who appear in theatrical annals no connexion can be proved. Edward Alleyn is said by Fuller in his *Worthies* to have been ' bred a stage player '. In formal deeds he is generally described as ' yeoman ' or ' gentleman ', and once, in 1595, as ' musician '.[2] In January 1583 he was one of Worcester's players ; at some later date he joined the Admiral's men, and had as ' fellow ' his brother John, with whom during 1589–91 he was associated in purchases of apparel. On 22 October 1592 he married Joan Woodward, step-daughter of Philip Henslowe, with whom he appears ever after in the closest business relations. A Dulwich tradition that he was already a widower probably rests on a mention of ' Mistris Allene ' in an un-dated letter about a German tour by Richard Jones, which is com-monly assigned to February 1592, but is more probably of later date.[3] Alleyn is specifically described as the Admiral's servant in the Privy Council letter of assistance to Strange's men (q.v.), with whom he travelled during the plague of 1593. Some of the letters passing between him and his wife and father-in-law during this tour are preserved at Dulwich, and are full of interesting domestic details about his white waistcoat and his orange tawny woollen stockings, the pasturing of his horse, his spinach bed, and the furnishing of his house.[4] His ' tenants ' are mentioned and his ' sister Phillipes & her husband '. He had by this time a high reputation as an actor, as

[1] Alleyn's life is more fully dealt with than is here possible in G. F. Warner and F. Bickley, *Catalogue of Dulwich MSS.* (1881, 1903) ; G. F. Warner in *D. N. B.* (1885) ; W. Young, *History of Dulwich College* (1889) ; W. W. Greg, *Henslowe Papers* (1907), *Henslowe's Diary*, vol. ii (1908). An earlier treatment of the material is that by J. P. Collier, *Memoirs of Edward Alleyn* (1841), *Alleyn Papers* (1843). On an account by G. Steevens in *Theatrical Review* (1763) with a forged letter from Peele to Marlowe, cf. Lee, 646.

[2] *Dulwich Muniments*, 106.   [3] Cf. ch. xiv.

[4] *Henslowe Papers*, 34, from *Dulwich MSS.*, i. 9–15 ; Edward to Joan Alleyn, 2 May 1593 ; Henslowe to Edward Alleyn, 5 July 1593 ; Edward to Joan Alleyn, 1 August 1593 ; Henslowe to Edward Alleyn, c. August 1593 ; Henslowe to Edward Alleyn, 14 August 1593 ; Henslowe to Edward Alleyn, 28 September 1593 ; John Pyk (Alleyn's ' boy ') to Joan Alleyn, c. 1593. Later letters of 4 June and 26 September 1598 from Henslowe to Edward Alleyn and of 21 October 1603 from Joan to Edward Alleyn are in *Henslowe Papers*, 47, 59, 97.

witnessed by Nashe in his *Pierce Penilesse* of 1592, where he classes
him with Tarlton, Knell, and Bentley, and says, ' Not Roscius nor
Aesope, those admyred tragedians that haue liued euer since before
Christ was borne, could euer performe more in action than famous
Ned Allen '; and in his *Strange Newes* of the same year, where he says
of Edmund Spenser that ' his very name (as that of Ned Allen on the
common stage) was able to make an ill matter good '.[1] An undated
letter at Dulwich, written to him by an admirer who signs himself W. P.,
offers a wager in which ' Peele's credit ' was also in some way concerned,
and in which Alleyn was to have the choice of any one of Bentley's
or Knell's plays, and promises that, even if he loses, ' we must and will
saie Ned Allen still '.[2] In 1594 *The Knack to know a Knave* is ascribed,
quite exceptionally, on its title-page, not to the servants of a particular
lord, but to ' Ed. Allen and his Companie '. From 1594 to 1597 Alleyn
was one of the Admiral's men (q.v.) at the Rose. He then ' leafte
playnge', but resumed at the request of the Queen, although apparently
without becoming a full sharer of the company, when the Fortune (q.v.),
which he had built for them, was opened in the autumn of 1600. He
became a servant of Prince Henry with the rest of his fellows in 1604,
and at the coronation procession on 15 March appeared as the Genius
of the City and delivered a ' gratulatory speech ' to James ' with
excellent action and a well-tun'de, audible voyce '.[3] Further testi-
monies to his talent are rendered by John Weever;[4] by Ben Jonson,
Epigram lxxxix (1616), who equals him to Aesop and Roscius, and
himself to Cicero, who praised them; by Heywood, who says, ' Among
so many dead let me not forget one yet alive, in his time the most
worthy, famous Maister Edward Allen';[5] and by Fuller, who says, ' He
was the Roscius of our age, so acting to the life that he made any part
(especially a majestic one) to become him.'[6] Of his parts are recorded
Faustus,[7] Tamburlaine, Barabas in *The Jew of Malta*,[8] and Cutlack in a

[1] *Works*, i. 215, 296.
[2] *Henslowe Papers*, 32.   The verses on the same theme in Collier,
Memoirs, 13, are forged.   [3] Dekker, *Plays*, i. 280.
[4] *Epigrammes* (1599), iv. 23 :

In Ed: Allen.

Rome had her *Roscius* and her Theater,
Her *Terence, Plautus, Ennius* and *Me*[*n*]*ander*,
The first to *Allen, Phoebus* did transfer
The next, *Thames* Swans receiu'd fore he coulde land her,
Of both more worthy of we by *Phoebus* doome,
Then t' *Allen Roscius* yeeld, to *London Rome*.

[5] Heywood, *Apology*, 43.
[6] Fuller, *Worthies* (ed. 1840), ii. 385.
[7] S. Rowland, *Knave of Clubs* (1609), 29 :

The gull gets on a surplis
With a crosse upon his breast,
Like Allen playing Faustus,
In that manner he was drest.

[8] Heywood, *Epistle* to *The Jew of Malta* (1633), ' the part of the Jew
presented by so vnimitable an Actor as M[r] Allin '; and *Prologue*,
     And He, then by the best of Actors [*in margin* ' Allin '] play'd :
.   .   .   .   in Tamberlaine,

play of that name revived by the Admiral's men in 1594 and now lost,[1] while that of Orlando in Greene's *Orlando Furioso* is amongst the papers at Dulwich.[2] Heywood, writing about 1608, speaks of Alleyn's playing in the past. He probably retired finally soon after the beginning of the new reign. In 1605 he valued his ' share of aparell ' at £100 ; but his name is not in the patent to the Prince's men of 30 April 1606, although as late as 1611 he still retained his personal rank as servant to the prince. It is difficult to give much credit to the legend that his withdrawal was due to remorse, or, as one version has it, to an apparition of the devil when he was playing Faustus.[3] Certainly he continued to hold an interest in the Fortune, and conceivably in the Red Bull (q.v.) also. And certainly remorse did not prevent him from continuing to exercise the functions of Master of the Game of Paris Garden, a post which he acquired jointly with Henslowe in 1604, having already been interested in the Beargarden itself since 1594. At this after it became the Hope (q.v.) he was still about 1617 entertaining players. But the time of his retirement synchronizes with the first beginnings of his foundation of a school and hospital by the name of the College of God's Gift at Dulwich. By 1605 he was a wealthy man, with income from substantial investments in leasehold property as well as the profits from his enterprises, and on 25 October he took the first step in the purchase of the manor of Dulwich, which was completed by 1614 at a total cost of nearly £10,000. Here about 1613 he made his residence, moving from Southwark, where he had been churchwarden of St. Saviour's in 1610. In 1613 also he began the building of the college, which was opened in 1617. Alleyn himself acted as manager and was in a position to spend upon the college and his own household some £1,700 a year. The endowment of the college included, besides house property in London, the freehold of the Fortune. Henslowe had died in January 1616 and his widow in the following year, and his papers passed to Alleyn and remain at Dulwich. Here, too, is Alleyn's own diary for 1617–22, and this and his correspondence show him as a friend of persons of honour, and the patron of writers and the members of his own former profession. Alleyn's wife Joan died on 28 June 1623 and on the following 3 December he married Constance, daughter of John Donne, dean of St. Paul's, settling on her £1,500. A letter of 23 July 1624 indicates that he was then desirous of obtaining ' sum further dignetie '. He died on 25 November 1626.

ALLEYN, JOHN. Admiral's, 1589–91. Edward Alleyn had an elder brother John, who was born in 1556–7, and is described as servant to Lord Sheffield and an Innholder in 1580, and as servant to the Lord

> This Jew, with others many, th' other wan
> The Attribute of peerelesse, being a man
> Whom we may ranke with (doing no one wrong)
> Proteus for shapes, and Roscius for a tongue,
> So could he speake, so vary.

[1] E. Guilpin, *Skialetheia* (1598), *Epig.* xliii,
> *Clodius* me thinks lookes passing big of late,
> With *Dunston's* browes, and *Allens Cutlacks* gate.

[2] *Henslowe Papers*, 155.   [3] For this myth, cf. ch. xxiii, s.v. Marlowe.

Admiral in 1589. He died about May 1596, being then of St. Andrew's, Holborn, and left a widow Margaret and son John. Presumably he was the Admiral's player. But there was also an Allen family of St. Botolph's, Bishopsgate, one of whom, John, was a player. Here a John was baptized on 17 October 1570, a Lowin, son of John, baptized on 15 December 1588, a Joan buried on 13 May 1593, and a John on 18 May 1593. On 26 July 1596 is this curious baptismal entry: 'Bennett, reputed daughter of J^no Allen, which J^no went with S^r Fr. Drake to the Indians in which time the child was got by a stage-player.' Finally, on 18 October 1597, 'Jone uxor Joh^is Allen player was buried with a still born child' (H. ii. 239 ; Bodl.)

ALLEYN, RICHARD. Queen's, (?) 1594 ; Admiral's, 1597–1600. His daughters Anna and Elizabeth were baptized at St. Saviour's, Southwark, on 13 May 1599 and 17 May 1601 respectively. Here he is traceable in the token-books during 1583–1601, and was buried on 18 November 1601, leaving a widow (Rendle, *Bankside*, xxvi ; H. ii. 239 ; Bodl.).

ALLEYN (ALLEN), RICHARD. Revels, 1609 ; Lady Elizabeth's, 1613.

ANDREWE, HENRY. Chapel, 1509.

ANDREWES, RICHARD. Worcester's, 1583.

ANDROWES, GEORGE. Whitefriars lessee, 1608.

APILEUTTER, CHRISTOPHER. Germany, 1615.

ARCHER, RICHARD. *Vide* ARKINSTALL.

ARCHER ? (ARZSCHAR, ERTZER), ROBERT. Germany, 1608–16.

ARKINSTALL, JOHN. A common player of interludes under licence, with Richard Archer, Barker, and Anthony Ward as his fellows. He was at Hastings on 25 March 1603, and on 30 March laid an information of the proclamation of Lord Beauchamp as king by Lord Southampton (*Hist. MSS.* xii. 4. 126).

ARMIN, ROBERT, is said to have been apprentice to a goldsmith in Lombard Street, and to have been encouraged as a 'wag' by Tarlton (*ob.* 1588), who prophesied that he should 'enjoy my clownes sute after me'. He 'used to' Tarlton's plays, and in time became himself a player 'and at this houre performes the same, where, at the Globe on the Banks side men may see him'.[1] But his earliest reputation was as a writer. He wrote a preface to *A Brief Resolution of the Right Religion* (1590) and probably other things now unknown, for he is referred to as a son of Elderton in Nashe's *Foure Letters Confuted* of 1592 (*Works*, i. 280). R. A. wrote verses to Robert Tofte's *Alba* (1598), and R. A. compiled *England's Parnassus* (1600) ; the latter is generally taken to be Robert Allot. The first dramatic company in which Armin can be traced is Lord Chandos's men. In an epistle to Mary, widow of William Lord Chandos (1594–1602) prefixed to his kinsman Gilbert Dugdale's *True Discourse of the Practises of Elizabeth Caldwell*, &c. (1604), he says, 'Your good honor knowes Pinck's poor heart, who

[1] Tarlton, 22, 'How Tarlton made Armin his adopted sonne, to succeed him'. The earliest extant edition of *Tarlton's Jests* is that of 1611, but the Second Part, here quoted, was entered in S. R. on 4 Aug. 1600.

in all my services to your late deceased kind lord, never savoured of flatterie or fixion.' In his *Foole upon Foole, or Six Sortes of Sottes* (1600) he tells an incident which took place at Pershore in Worcestershire, during a tour of ' the Lord Shandoyes players ', at which he was himself present, not improbably playing the clown ' Grumball '.[1] By 1599, however, he had probably joined the Chamberlain's men, for in the first edition of *Foole upon Foole* he describes himself as ' Clonnico de Curtanio Snuffe '. In a later edition of 1605 this becomes ' Clonnico del Mondo Snuffe '. Both issues are anonymous, but Armin put his name to an enlargement entitled *A Nest of Ninnies* (1608).[2] ' Clunnyco de Curtanio Snuffe ' is also on the title-page of *Quips upon Questions* (1600), which must therefore be by Armin and not by J. Singer, whose autograph Collier (*Bibl. Cat.* ii. 203) said that he found on a copy. This is a book of quatrains on stage ' themes ' (cf. ch. xviii). It was written, as a reference to 28 December as on a Friday shows, in 1599. The author serves a master at Hackney (A ij). Later editions of 1601 and 1602 are said to have been in the Harley collection, and there is a reprint by F. Ouvry (1875). His name is in the 1603 licence for the King's men and in the Coronation list of 1604. In 1605 Augustine Phillips left him 20s. as his ' fellow '. Collier's statement that in the same year he and Kempe (q.v.) were in trouble for libelling aldermen cannot be verified. He is a King's man on the title-page of his *Two Maids of Moreclacke* (1609), produced by the King's Revels, and on the title-page and in the S. R. entry on 6 February 1609 of his *Phantasma, the Italian Tailor and his Boy*. This is a translation from Straparola and is dedicated to Lord and Lady Haddington. In it he claims to have been ' writ down an ass in his time ' and refers to ' his constableship ', from which it is inferred that he played Dogberry in *Much Ado about Nothing*. Fleay, *L. of S.* 300, finds a pun on ' armine ' (= wretch) in *London Prodigal* (*c.* 1603), v. i. 179, and suggests that Armin played Matthew Flowerdale. There is a clown Robin in *Miseries of Enforced Marriage* (1607), and a clown Grumball in *If it be not Good* (1610–12), but this was a play of Anne's men. He is in the actor-list of Jonson's *Alchemist* (1610). An epigram on ' honest gamesome Robert Armin ' is in John Davies of Hereford's *Scourge of Folly* (S.R. 8 October 1610). He is not in the actor-list of Jonson's *Catiline* (1611), nor has any later notice of him been found. That Armin is the R. A. whose play *The Valiant Welshman* was published in 1615 is only a conjecture. He is in the Folio list of actors in Shakespeare's plays. It is possible that a woodcut on the title-page of the *Two Maids* (q.v.) gives his portrait.

ARTHUR, THOMAS. Interluders, 1528.

ATTEWELL (OTTEWELL, OTWELL), GEORGE. Strange's, 1591 ; Queen's, (?) 1595. 'Mr Otwell ' lived in St. Saviour's Close in 1599. He is perhaps more likely than the following to be the author or singer

---

[1] Extract in Halliwell-Phillipps, i. 321 ; the unique copy of this edition is described in his *Calendar of Shakespeare Rarities* (1887), 145.
[2] Reprinted in the Shakespeare Society's *Fools and Jesters* (1842).

of 'Mʳ Attowel's Jigge : betweene Francis, a Gentleman ; Richard, a farmer; and their wives', printed in A. Clark, *Shirburn Ballads*, lxi (H. ii. 240 ; B. 147).

ATTWELL (OTTEWELL), HUGH. Revels, 1609 ; Lady Elizabeth's, 1613 ; Charles's, 1616–21 ; *ob.* 25 September 1621.

AUGUSTEN (AGUSTEN), WILLIAM. A 'player', from whom Henslowe bought his 'boy' Bristow in 1597 (H. ii. 240).

AYNSWORTH, JOHN. A 'player' buried at St. Leonard's 28 September 1581 (B. 153).

BAKER, HARRY. Performer of Vertumnus in *Summer's Last Will and Testament*, 1567.

BANASTER, GILBERT. Master of Chapel, 1478–83 (?).

BARFIELD, ROGER. Anne's, 1606. His d. Isabell was baptized at St. Giles's on 2 January 1611, and his d. Susan buried there on 3 July 1614 (B. 157).

BARKER. *Vide* ARKINSTALL.

BARKSTED (BACKSTEAD), WILLIAM. King's Revels (?), 1607 ; Revels, 1609; Lady Elizabeth's, 1611, 1613; Charles's, 1616; also a dramatist (cf. ch. xxiii) and a poet. His *Poems*, edited by A. B. Grosart as Part II of *Choice Rarities of Ancient English Poetry* (1876), were *Myrrha* (1607), which has commendatory verses by his kinsman Robert Glover and I. W., Lewes Machin, and William Bagnall, and *Hiren* (1611), which has sonnets to Henry Earl of Oxford, and Elizabeth Countess of Derby. On the title-page he describes himself as 'one of the servants of his Maiesties Revels'. The surmise of Fleay, i. 29, that this was repeated from an earlier edition of *c.* 1607 now lost may receive some confirmation from the connexion of Machin with the King's Revels ; but it must also be remembered that the Whitefriars Revels' company appears to be occasionally described as the King's Revels in provincial records of *c.* 1611. A trivial anecdote of him is in J. Taylor, *Wit and Mirth* (1629).

BARNE, WILLIAM. Admiral's, 1602.

BARRY, DAVID (LORD). Whitefriars lessee, 1608, and dramatist.

BARTLE (?). Alexander Bartle, son of '—— a player', was baptized at St. Saviour's on 27 February 1603 (B. 165).

BARTON, ONESIPHORUS. A 'player', buried at St. Giles's on 9 March 1608 (B. 167).

BASSE, THOMAS. Lady Elizabeth's, 1611, 1613 ; Anne's, 1617–19.

BAXTER, ROBERT. Chapel, 1601 ; Lady Elizabeth's (?), 1613. Greg, *H. P.* 58, 87, however, thinks that the 'Baxter' of 1613, whose Christian name is not given, may be Barksted. Neither man is likely to have written the 'Baxsters tragedy' of 1602 (*H. P.* 58).

BAYLYE, THOMAS. Shrewsbury's (provincial), 1581. J. Hunter, *Hallamshire* 80, and Murray, ii. 388, print from *College of Arms, Talbot MS.* G. f. 74, a Latin letter written by him to Thomas Bawdewin from Sheffield on 25 April 1581, in which he mentions a brother William, thanks him for a tragedy played by the company on St. George's day, and begs him to procure 'librum aliquem brevem, novum, iucundum, venustum, lepidum, hilarem, scurrosum, nebulosum,

rabulosum, et omnimodis carnificiis, latrociniis et lenociniis refertum
... qua in re dicunt quod Wilsonus quidam Leycestrii comitis servus
(fidibus pollens) multum vult et potest facere '.

BAYLYE. Paul's chorister, >1582.

BEART, RUDOLF. Germany, 1608.

BEESTON, CHRISTOPHER, has been conjectured to be the ' Kit '
who played a Lord and a Captain in 2 Seven Deadly Sins for Strange's
or the Admiral's about 1590–1. The actor-list of Every Man in his
Humour shows that he belonged to the Chamberlain's men in 1598.
He is not, however, named as a performer of Shakespeare's plays in
the Folio of 1623. Probably he was at one time the hired man of
Augustine Phillips who left him 30s. as his ' servant ' in 1605. By
1602 he had passed to Worcester's men, and with this company, afterwards Queen Anne's, he remained until it was reconstituted on the
Queen's death in 1619, taking a prominent part in the management of
the company, after the death of Thomas Greene in 1612. He seems
to have built or acquired the Cockpit theatre, and to have successively
housed there Queen Anne's men (1617–19), Prince Charles's men
(1619–22), Lady Elizabeth's men (1622–5), Queen Henrietta's men
(1625–37), and ' the King's and Queen's young company ', also known
as ' Beeston's boys ' (1637). By 1639 he had been succeeded as
' Governor ' of this company by his son William Beeston, and was
doubtless dead. The Cockpit had passed by June 1639 to ' Mrs. Elizabeth Beeston, alias Hutcheson '.[1] It appears from the lawsuit of 1623,
in which Queen Anne's men were concerned, that Christopher Beeston
also bore the alias of Hutcheson or Hutchinson. But if Elizabeth was
his widow, she must have been a second wife, for the records of the
Middlesex justices for 1615–17 record several true bills for recusancy
as brought against a wife Jane. In these records Beeston, whose alias
is also given, is described as a gentleman or yeoman, and as ' late of
St. James-at-Clerkenwell ', or in one case ' of Turmil streete '. In
1617 his house was burgled by Henry Baldwin and others.[2] The registers
of St. James's, Clerkenwell, record the baptism of a daughter Anne on
15 September 1611, and the burial of a servant on 1 July 1615.[3] But
at an earlier date Beeston lived in St. Leonard's, Shoreditch, where his
sons Augustine, Christopher, and Robert were baptized, and the first
two buried between 16 November 1604 and 15 July 1610. Robert also
was buried there on 26 December 1615, but Christopher was then
described in the register as of Clerkenwell. Possibly he afterwards
returned to Shoreditch, as Collier states that his name is traceable in
the register up to 1637.[4] His son William, also a suspected recusant,
was living in Bishopsgate Without just before his death in 1682.[5] An
earlier William Beeston, with whom Christopher may have had some
connexion, is the ' Maister Apis Lapis ' and ' Gentle M. William ', to
whom Nashe addressed his Strange Newes (1592).[6]

[1] Variorum, iii. 159, 241, 242; M.S.C. i. 345.
[2] Jeaffreson, ii. 107, 110, 114, 120, 128, 220.
[3] Harleian Soc. Registers, ix. 62 ; xvii. 131.
[4] Collier, Actors, xxxi.   [5] M.S.C. i. 344.   [6] McKerrow, Nashe, i. 255.

BEESTON, ROBERT. Anne's, 1604, 1609.

BEESTON. A player at Barnstaple in 1560–1 (Murray, ii. 198).

BELT, T. Strange's (?), 1590–1.

BENFIELD, ROBERT, is first named in the actor-lists of Beaumont and Fletcher's *The Coxcomb* and *The Honest Man's Fortune*, both of which probably represent performances by the Lady Elizabeth's men in 1613. Subsequently he joined the King's men, but at what date is uncertain. It may have been upon the death on 16 December 1614 of William Ostler, whom he succeeded in the part of Antonio in Webster's *Duchess of Malfi*. He is in the actor-list of *The Knight of Malta* (1616–19) and in the patent of 1619. He seems to have been a member of the company to the end, as he signed the dedication of the Beaumont and Fletcher Folio in 1647. He is in the Folio list of actors in Shakespeare's plays. Collier found some late records of his family (B. 181).

BENTLEY, JOHN. Queen's, 1583. He is named by Heywood as before his time, lauded by Nashe, *Pierce Penilesse* (1592) (*Works*, i. 215) with Tarlton, Alleyn, and Knell, coupled with Knell in the undated challenge to Alleyn (q.v.) to play one of their parts, and placed by Dekker in *A Knight's Conjuring* (1607) in the company of the poets, Watson, Kyd, and Achelow, ' tho he had ben a player molded out of their pennes, yet because he had been their louer and register to the muse, inimitable Bentley'. He may be the John Bentley whose poems are mentioned by Ritson, *Bibliographia Poetica* (1802), 129.

BIERDT, BURCHARD. Germany, 1612.

BILLINGESLY, JOHN. Payee for Westminster boys, 1572.

BIRCH, GEORGE. Interluders, 1538–59.

BIRCH, JOHN. Interluders, 1547–56.

BIRD, *alias* BORNE, WILLIAM. Chamberlain's (?), 1597 ; Pembroke's, 1597 ; Admiral's–Henry's–Palsgrave's, 1597–1622. Many personalia of his family and debts are recorded in Dulwich manuscripts and church registers (H. ii. 241 ; B. 204).

' BLACK DICK.' Admiral's, 1597.

BLACKWOOD, THOMAS. Worcester's, 1602–3 ; Germany, 1603–6 (?). The conjecture of Fleay, i. 290, that an earlier German tour is referred to in *How to Choose a Good Wife from a Bad* (1602) is baseless (H. ii. 244).

BLANEY, JOHN. Revels, 1609 ; Anne's, 1616–19. He lived near the Red Bull in St. John's Street in 1623 (J. 347).

BLANK, WILLIAM ALEXANDER. A Scottish dancer in Germany, 1605.

BOONE, WILLIAM. A ' player ' mentioned in books of St. Saviour's, *c*. 1600 (Rendle, *Bankside*, xxvi). Possibly an error for Borne.

BORNE, WILLIAM. *Vide* Birde.

BOWER, RICHARD. Master of Chapel, 1545–61, and possibly author of *Apius and Virginia* (1575) ; cf. ch. xxiv.

BOWRINGE, GREGORY. Paul's chorister, >1582.

BRADSHAW, RICHARD. Edward, Lord Dudley's (provincial),

1595. He was Gabriel Spencer's 'man' in 1598, and concerned in financial transactions with Henslowe during 1598–1601. He may be the same Richard Bradshaw who had a provincial company, with a licence to which his title was dubious, in 1630–33 (H. ii. 245 ; Murray, ii. 42, 106, 163).

BRADSTREET, JOHN. Germany, 1592–7, 1604. He *ob.* in 1618.

BRETTEN, WILLIAM. Chapel, >1546.

BRISTOW, JAMES. Augusten's boy, 1597 ; Admiral's, 1597–1602 (H. ii. 245).

BROMEHAM. Paul's, >1582.

BROWNE, EDWARD. Worcester's, 1583 ; Admiral's, 1602. He was a witness for Henslowe in 1599 (H. ii. 246).

BROWNE, JOHN. Interluders, 1551–63.

BROWNE, JOHN. Revels (?), 1608.

BROWNE, ROBERT. Worcester's, 1583 ; Holland, 1590 ; Germany, 1592–3, 1594 (?)–9 ; Derby's, 1599–1601 ; Germany, 1601–7 ; Revels patentee, 1610 ; Germany, 1618–20. His wife and family died at Shoreditch in the plague of 1593, but a son Robert and daughter Elizabeth were baptized at St. Saviour's on 19 October 1595 and 2 December 1599. On 11 April 1612 he wrote to Alleyn from Clerkenwell (*H. P.*, 37, 63 ; B. 229 ; Rendle, *Bankside*, xxvi).

BROWNE, WILLIAM. Anne's, *c.* 1616.

BROWNE. It is not safe to identify the Browne whom Henslowe paid to 'feach' for the Admiral's in 1596 (H. i. 45), or the 'old Browne' who, as well as Edward, played in *1 Tamar Cham* for the Admiral's in 1602 (*H. P.* 148), or 'Browne of the Boares head' who, according to Alleyn's wife on 21 Oct. 1603, 'is dead & dyed very pore, he went not into the countrye at all' (*H. P.* 59). The last may be the man whose widow married Thomas Greene (q.v.).

BRYAN, GEORGE, was one of the English company which visited Helsingör in Denmark and Dresden in Germany during 1586–7. He is one of the three actors distinguished as 'Mr.' in the plot of Tarlton's *The Seven Deadly Sins* as played by Strange's or the Admiral's about 1590–1, and is named in the Privy Council warrant for the travelling of Strange's in 1593. He was payee for the Chamberlain's men on 21 December 1596, but is not in the *Every Man in his Humour* actor-list of 1598 or traceable at any later date amongst the Chamberlain's or King's men. Probably he left to take up duty as an ordinary Groom of the Chamber, as he is found holding this post at Elizabeth's funeral in 1603 and still held it (*Chamber Accounts*) in 1611–13. His son George was baptized at St. Andrew's Wardrobe on 17 February 1600.[1] He is in the Folio list of actors in Shakespeare's plays.

BUCKE, PAUL. A 'player' whose d. Sara was buried on 23 July 1580 and his bastard son Paul buried on 23 July 1599 at St. Anne's (B. 237). It is apparently his name which, for whatever reason, appears at the end of Wilson's *Three Ladies of London* (1584). 'Paule Bucke's praier for Sir Humfrey Gilberte' was entered in S. R. on 17 July 1578.

---

[1] Collier, iii. 364.

BUGBY, JOHN. Grammar Master of Chapel, 1401.
BULL, JOHN. Chapel, 1572 (?)->1586.
BULL, THOMAS. Denmark, 1579–80.
BURBADGE, JAMES. The Shakespearo-centric tendencies of
literary historians have led them to suggest a regional connexion
between the dramatist and the family of his most famous interpreter.[1]
There was a Warwickshire family of Burbadge, of whom John was
bailiff of Stratford-on-Avon in 1555, and Malone was thus led
(*Var.* iii. 187) to ' suspect ' that James Burbadge was Shakespeare's
countryman. Collier (iii. 258) having learnt that the arms claimed by
Cuthbert Burbadge at the London visitation of 1634, ' crest, a boar's
head ; and three boars' heads on a shield ' (*Harleian Soc.* xv), were those
of a Hertfordshire family, attempted the explanation that the two
families ' were in some way related '. He committed himself deeply
by publishing in 1835 (*New Facts*, 32 ; cf. Ingleby, 256) a forged letter
from H. S. to Sir Thomas Egerton, containing the statement that
Shakespeare and Richard Burbadge are ' both of one countie, and
indeede almost of one towne '. Burbadges are traceable in various
parts of England, including Somerset, Oxfordshire, and Durham
(Halliwell-Phillipps, ii. 344 ; Stopes, 134, 243), and the conjecture has
about as much value as Malone's derivation of the name (*Var.* iii. 182)
from ' Borough-bridge ', or Chalmers's from ' Boar's badge '. Nor is any
connexion known between James Burbadge and various other Burbadges—Robert, John, and Edward—who appear in contemporary
documents (Collier, iii. 282 ; Stopes, 152), although A. Wood (*Fasti
Oxon.* i. 303) makes himself responsible for the statement that one
John Burbadge, of Lincoln College, was nearly related to the actor.
The name is indifferently spelt Burbadge, Burbage, or Burbege by
contemporaries, but usually Burbadge in family signatures (Wallace,
61, 63 ' James Burbage ', 252 ; Collier, iii. 294 ; *Malone Soc. Coll.*
ii. 69, 76). James sealed the Blackfriars indentures of 1596 with a
griffin.
   James was about sixty on 16 February 1591 (Wallace, 61) and was
therefore born in 1530–1. He was ' by occupacion a joyner and
reaping but a small lyving by the same, gave it over and became a
commen player in playes ' (Wallace, 141). He was one of Leicester's
men in 1572, 1574, and 1576, and apparently continued a ' fellow ' of
this or some other company for a year or two after he established the
Theatre in 1576 (Wallace, 142). In this year he was a poor man, and
of small credit, not worth above 100 marks (Wallace, 134, 141, 153),
but he had enlisted the capital of John Brayne, whose sister Ellen he
had married (Wallace, 40, 139). His business history thereafter is
bound up with that of the Theatre (q.v.) and of the Blackfriars, which
he planned, but probably never used, during the last years of his life.
Cuthbert Burbadge says of him (*Blackfriars Sharers Papers*, 1635)

---

[1] The biographical material collected by C. C. Stopes, *Burbage and
Shakespeare's Stage* (1913), is supplemented by the lawsuit records in
C. W. Wallace, *The First London Theatre, Materials for a History* (1913,
Nebraska University Studies, xiii. 1).

that he ' was the first builder of playhowses, and was himselfe in his younger yeeres a player '. He was described as ' joyner ' in the lease of the Theatre site in 1576, but in later years usually as ' yeoman ' or ' gentleman '. Presumably he went to live in Shoreditch in 1576, as entries for his family then begin in the registers of St. Leonard's (Stopes, 139). They testify to the baptism (17 March 1576) of a daughter Alice, mentioned as Alice Walker in the will of Nicholas Tooley (q.v.) in 1623, and the burial (18 August 1582) of a daughter Joan. Another daughter, Helen, was buried at St. Anne's, Blackfriars, on 15 December 1595 (*Bodl.*). Besides Alice and Helen he had in 1588 (Wallace, 39) two sons, Cuthbert and Richard, who would both have been born before 1576. James himself was buried at Shoreditch on 2 February 1597 and his widow on 8 May 1613. The registers generally give the family residence as ' Halliwell Street ', and the ' Halliwell ' which appears in 1597 and 1601 is perhaps an accidental variant. But the lawsuits suggest that James had built himself a house in the old inner cloister yard of the priory, which lay a little north of Halliwell Street, if that is the same as Holywell Lane (Wallace, 232, 236). They also represent him as a man of violent temper and not over-honest, while an independent record (App. D, No. lxxiv) refers to him as ' a stubburne fellow '. Before his death he seems to have made over his interest in the Blackfriars to his son Richard, while that in the Theatre had passed by redemption of a mortgage to Cuthbert (Wallace, 55, 73, 108, 145, 278).

Cuthbert Burbadge, the elder son of James, was not an actor, although as holder of the leases of the Theatre and afterwards of the Globe (q.v.) he was concerned during the greater part of his life with theatrical management. On 16 February 1591 he was servant to Walter Cope, gentleman usher to Lord Burghley. He was then twenty-four, and must have been born in 1566–7. He was then probably living in the Strand (Stopes, 152), but the subsidy rolls for 1597 (Stopes, 195) show him as assessed at 10s. 8d. in Holywell Street, and the registers of St. Leonard's have the records of his children, Walter (bapt. 22 June 1595), James (bur. 15 July 1597), and Elizabeth (bapt. 30 December 1601). Of these only Elizabeth, the wife first of Amias Maxey and secondly of George Bingley, was alive in 1634 and her son Amias had been adopted by his grandfather. Cuthbert himself was buried at Shoreditch on 17 September 1636, and his widow Elizabeth, daughter of John Cox, on 1 October 1636 (Stopes, 134, 140). His friendship with members of the King's company is commemorated by notices in the wills of William Sly (1608), Richard Cowley (1618), and Nicholas Tooley, who died in his house in 1623. Collier (iii. 285) identified him with Cuthbert Burby the stationer, but Burby was in fact the son of Edmund Burby of Beds., husbandman (Arber, ii. 127). Possibly, however, the families were related, since Burby's name is given at least once in the Stationers' Register (Arber, ii. 612) as ' Burbidge '.

BURBADGE, RICHARD, makes his first appearance, picturesquely enough, in the brawl at the Theatre which followed upon the Chancery

Order of 13 November 1590, restoring a moiety of the profits of the
house to the widow Brayne (cf. p. 392). John Alleyn deposed (Wallace,
101) that he ' found the foresaid Ry. Burbage the yongest sone of the
said James Burbage there, w^t a broome staff in his hand, of whom when
this deponente asked what sturre was there, he answered in laughing
phrase hew they come for a moytie. But quod he (holding vppe the
said broomes staff) I haue, I think, deliuered him a moytie with this
& sent them packing.' Nicholas Bishop (Wallace, 98, 115), one of
Mrs. Brayne's agents, adds the confirmatory detail that ' the said
Ry. Burbage scornfully & disdainfullye playing with this deponentes
nose, sayd, that yf he delt in the matter, he wold beate him also, and
did chalendge the field of him at that tyme '. Very possibly Richard
was then playing with the Admiral's men at the Theatre. His exact
age is unknown, but he was younger than Cuthbert, born in 1566-7,
and as Cuthbert, long after, spoke of the ' 35 yeeres paines, cost, and
labour ' out of which his brother ' made meanes to leave his wife and
children some estate ' in 1619 (*Sharers Papers*), it may perhaps be
inferred that his histrionic career began as early as 1584. The ' plot '
of *The Dead Man's Fortune*, wherein the doubtful direction (cf. p. 125)
' Burbage a messenger ' suggests that he played a minor part, may belong
to a performance by the Admiral's *c.* 1590. It is a little more difficult
to suppose that at a date when the Queen's men were still active the
Admiral's or Strange's had already acquired Tarlton's *Seven Deadly
Sins*, in the ' plot ' of which ' R. Burbadg ' is cast for the important
characters of Gorboduc and Terens. But perhaps it is even less
probable that, after the breach of the Admiral's with his father in
1591, he took part in the performances of the same play by the amalgamated Admiral's and Strange's men at the Rose in 1592. His name
does not appear amongst those of the Strange's men who were travelling
in 1593. But when the amalgamation broke up, and the Chamberlain's
company was formed, with some of its elements as a nucleus, in 1594,
he joined that company, and became a prominent member, often
acting as its representative or payee, both before and after its metamorphosis into the King's men, and to the end of his own life. His
name is constant in its lists (cf. ch. xiii), and his personal relations
with his fellows are reflected in the wills of Augustine Phillips in 1605,
Shakespeare in 1616, and Nicholas Tooley, whose ' master ' he had
been, in 1623. It would appear that in the somewhat irregular disposition of James Burbadge's theatrical interests the Blackfriars
freehold fell primarily to Richard. The leases of 1608 were made by
him as lessor to his brother and other members of the King's men's
syndicate as lessees. This, however, was doubtless a mere family
arrangement, for Cuthbert spoke of the Blackfriars in 1635 as ' our
inheritance ', and the two brothers shared in the supplementary
transactions which rounded off the original purchase (cf. ch. xvii).
At the Globe, on the other hand, Cuthbert and Richard held in common
a moiety of the housekeepers' interest under the lease from Nicholas
Brend (cf. ch. xvi). They continued to live as close neighbours in
Halliwell Street, Shoreditch, where they shared the misfortune of

having their houses burgled in 1615 (Jeaffreson, ii. 108) and where
the registers of St. Leonard's (Stopes, 139) record Richard's children :
Richard (bur. 16 August 1607), Julia or Juliet (bapt. 2 January 1603,
bur. 12 September 1608), Frances (bapt. 16 September and bur.
19 September 1604), Anne (bapt. 8 August 1607), Winifred (bapt.
10 October 1613, bur. 14 October 1616), a second Julia (bapt. 26 December 1614, bur. 15 August 1615), William (bapt. 6 November 1616), and
a posthumous Sara (bapt. 5 August 1619, bur. 29 April 1625). 'Richard
Burbadge, player' was himself buried on 16 March 1619. He had died,
not as Camden records in his *Annals* on 9 March, but on 13 March,
after making the day before a nuncupative will (Collier, iii. 293),
witnessed by his brother and by Nicholas Tooley and Richard Robinson
of the King's men, in which he left his wife Winifred sole executrix.
She subsequently married Richard Robinson, and was still alive, as
was Burbadge's son William, in 1635 (*Sharers Papers*). According to
the gossip of the day he left 'better than £300 land to his heirs' (Collier,
iii. 297).

Burbadge had a high reputation as a player, both in life and after
death. A note of 13 March 1602 by John Manningham (*Diary*, 39)
records how his impersonation of Richard III touched the heart of a
citizen's wife, and how Shakespeare prevented him at a resultant
assignation. John Davies of Hereford coupled him with Shakespeare
in 1603 (*Microcosmos*) among players whom he loved 'for painting,
poesie', and in 1609 (*Civile Warres of Death and Fortune*) amongst
those whom Fortune 'guerdond not, to their desarts'. He is introduced *in propria persona* into 2 *Return from Parnassus* (1602) and into
Marston's induction to *The Malcontent* (1604). Probably he is the
'one man' of the London stage with whom the player in *Ratseis Ghost*
(1605 ; cf. ch. xviii) is advised 'to play Hamlet for a wager'. Jonson,
in *Bartholomew Fair* (1614), v. iii, makes Cokes ask the master of the
puppets, 'which is your *Burbage* now ? . . . your best *Actor*. Your
Field ?' He was apparently the model for the *Character of an Actor*
in the *Characters* of 1615 (App. C, No. lxi). And other evidences of
his fame can be traced down to Restoration days in Richard Corbet's
Iter Boreale, in Sir Richard Baker's *Chronicle* and *Theatrum Redivivum*,
and in Richard Flecknoe's *Short Discourse of the English Stage* and his
Euterpe Restored (cf. Collier, iii. 279 ; Stopes, 121 ; *Shakespeare's
Centurie of Prayse*, N.S.S., 128, 250).

Shortly after Burbadge's death, on 20 May 1619, the Earl of Pembroke wrote to Lord Doncaster in Germany of a great supper given
the same night by the Duke of Lennox to the French ambassador, and
adds that the company were now at the play, 'which I being tenderharted could not endure to see so soone after the loss of my old acquaintance Burbadg' (E. J. L. Scott in *Athenaeum* (1882), i. 103). Several
epitaphs and elegies upon Burbadge are preserved. The shortest—
'Exit Burbadge'—was printed in Camden's *Remaines* (1674), 541.
Another is by Middleton (Collier, iii. 280, 296). A third, which begins

Some skillfull limner helpe mee, yf not soe,
Some sad tragedian, to expresse my woe,

has been the subject of much controversy (cf. Halliwell-Phillipps, ii. 88 ; C. M. Ingleby, *The Elegy on Burbadge*, in *Shakespeare, the Man and the Book*, ii. 169). It exists in two versions, one of 86 lines, the other of 124 lines. Of the shorter version several undoubtedly genuine manuscripts are known, and it is probably only by accident that one of these omits ll. 2–5 of the following passage, which is given completely by all the rest :

> Hee 's gone & with him what a world are dead,
> Which he reuiud, to be reuiued soe.
> No more young Hamlett, ould Heironymoe.
> Kind Leer, the greued Moore, and more beside,
> That liued in him, haue now for ever dy'de.
> Oft haue I seene him leap into the graue,
> Suiting the person which he seem'd to haue
> Of a sadd louer with soe true an eye,
> That theer I would haue sworne, he meant to dye.
> Oft haue I seene him play this part in ieast,
> Soe liuely, that spectators, and the rest
> Of his sad crew, whilst he but seem'd to bleed,
> Amazed, thought euen then hee dyed in deed.

In the longer version ll. 2–5 are not only omitted, but are replaced by an interpolation of many lines, detailing a number of parts, some of which belonged to other companies than the King's, and are not likely to have been played by Burbadge. No manuscript of this version is forthcoming, and there can be little doubt that the interpolation is due to Collier, who referred to the version in his *New Particulars* (1836), 27, and published it in his *Memoirs of the Actors* (1846), 52, professedly from a manuscript in the possession of Richard Heber. Of the shorter version I can add to what has been recorded by others that in *Stowe MS.* 962, f. 62ᵛ, I have found a copy of it, with the title ' An Elegie on the death of the famous actor Rich: Burbage, who died 13 Martij Aᵒ. 1618 ', and an ascription to ' Jo ffletcher '. Other copies also give the date of Burbadge's death, or refer, as do the opening lines themselves, to the fact that he was skilled not only as an actor but as a limner. John Davies testifies to this in the verses of 1603 already cited. The accounts of the Earl of Rutland for the birthday tilt of 1613 contain the entry, ' 31 Martij, To Mʳ. Shakspeare in gold, about my Lordes impreso, 44ˢ. To Richard Burbage for paynting and makyng yt, in gold, 44ˢ ' ; and those for the tilt of 1616, ' 25 Martij, 1616, paid given Richard Burbidg for my Lordes shelde and for the embleance, 4ˡⁱ 18ˢ ' (*H. M. C. Rutland MSS.* iv. 494, 508). The gallery at Dulwich contains a picture presented by William Cartwright, which is described in his catalogue as ' a womans head on a boord done by Mʳ. Burbige yᵉ actor '. The inveterate tendency of mankind to guess has led to suggestions that he may have painted the portrait of himself in the same gallery, the Chandos portrait of Shakespeare, or the original of the Droeshout print.

One other record of Burbadge, apart from his company, may be noted. On 31 May 1610 he was employed by the City, with his fellow James Rice, to deliver a speech to Prince Henry at a water-pageant on the Thames (cf. ch. iv). Presumably he represented Amphion, ' a grave and judicious Prophet-like personage ', and Rice Corinea.

BURGES, ROBERT. A ' player ' buried at St. Bennet's, Grace-church, 14 April 1559 (B. 251).

CANDLER, JAMES. Leader of a company at Ipswich, 1569–70 (*Hist. MSS*. ix. 1. 248).

CARIE (GARY), GILES. Revels, 1609 ; Lady Elizabeth's, 1611, 1613.

CARLETON, NICHOLAS. Paul's, >1582.

CARPENTER, WILLIAM. Lady Elizabeth's, 1611 ; Charles's, 1619, 1625. He was apparently porter at the Marshalsea in 1623 (J. 347).

CARTWRIGHT, WILLIAM. Admiral's–Henry's, 1598–1622 (H. ii. 247). He lived at the upper end of White Cross Street in 1623 (J. 347).

CASTLE, THOMAS. A ' player ', whose son Nicholas and daughter Hester were baptized at St. Giles's on 9 October 1608 and 15 April 1610 (B. 262).

CATTANES. Worcester's, 1602 (H. ii. 248).

CAVALLERIZZO, CLAUDIO. Italians, 1576 (?).

CHAPPELL, JOHN. Chapel, 1600–1.

CHESSON, THOMAS. Oxford's (?), 1580.

CLARK, SILL. Prince's, 1603< >1641.

CLARKE, ROBERT. A ' player ' whose son Ezekiel was buried at St. Giles's, 7 November 1617 (B. 268).

CLARKE, THOMAS. Leicester's, 1572.

CLAY, NATHANIEL. Anne's, 1618 ; Chamber of Bristol, 1618.

CLEMENT, WILLIAM. London player, 1550 (App. D, No. v).

CLIFTON, THOMAS. Kidnapped for Chapel, 1600.

COBORNE, EDWARD. A ' player ' whose son John was baptized at St. Giles's on 23 Nov. 1616. Of other family entries, 1613–25, some are for Edward Coborne ' gentleman ' (*Bodl*.). He may be identical with COLBRAND.

COKE, RICHARD. Interluders, 1547–56.

COLBRAND, EDWARD. Palsgrave's, 1610–13.

COLE. Paul's, 1599.

COLMAN, WILLIAM. Chapel, 1509.

CONDELL, HENRY, has been conjectured to be the ' Harry ' cast for Ferrex and a Lord in the ' plot ' of *The Seven Deadly Sins*, as played by Strange's or the Admiral's about 1590–1. The first definite notice of him is in the cast of Jonson's *Every Man in his Humour*, as played by the Chamberlain's men in 1598. Thereafter he appears in all formal lists of the Chamberlain's and King's men, up to the Caroline patent of 1625, including the list in the First Folio of 1623, of which, with Heminges, he acted as editor. He is also in all the casts up to *The Humourous Lieutenant* (c. 1619). About this date he presumably ceased to play ; his part of the Cardinal in *The Duchess of Malfi* had passed to Richard Robinson by 1623. The fact that he took this part somewhat discredits the conjecture of John Roberts (*Answer to Pope*, 1729) that he was a comedian ; nor can the statement of the same writer that he was a printer be verified. He is staged with other members of the company in Marston's *Malcontent* (1604), and appears

as ' Henry Condye ' in the verses on the burning of the Globe in 1613.
He is assigned 26s. 8d. to buy a ring as Shakespeare's ' fellowe ' in his
will of 1616, and appears also as a legatee in the will of Augustine
Phillips in 1605, as trustee in that of Alexander Cooke in 1614, as
executor and joint residuary legatee in that of Nicholas Tooley in 1623,
under which also his wife and his daughter Elizabeth receive legacies,
and as executor in that of John Underwood in 1625. By 1599 he was
married and apparently settled in St. Mary Aldermanbury, where he
held various parochial offices during 1606–21, and the register records
his children : Elizabeth (bapt. 27 February 1599, bur. 11 April 1599),
Anne (bapt. 4 April 1601, bur. 16 July 1610), Richard (bapt. 18 April
1602), Elizabeth (bapt. 14 April 1603, bur. 22 April 1603), Elizabeth
(bapt. 26 October 1606), Mary (bapt. 30 January 1608, bur. from
Hoxton at St. Leonard's, Shoreditch, 24 March 1608), Henry (bapt.
6 May 1610, bur. 4 March 1630), William (bapt. 26 May 1611), Edward
(bapt. 22 August 1614, bur. 23 August 1614).[1] Subsequently he had
a ' country house ' at Fulham, at which on 10 September 1625 a
pamphlet written by certain players on their travels during the plague,
as a reply to Dekker's *A Rod for Run-awayes*, under the title of *The
Run-awayes Answer*, was addressed to him, with an expression of
gratitude for a ' free and noble farewell' which he had given the
writers. At Fulham, too, on 13 December 1627, he made his will,
leaving to his widow Elizabeth, his sons Henry and William, and his
daughter Elizabeth, wife of Herbert Finch, much household property
at Aldermanbury and elsewhere in London, including ' rents and
profits' by ' leases and terms of years' of ' messuages houses and places '
in Blackfriars and on the Bankside, which were to pass for a time to
William and ultimately to the widow.[2] Condell had not been an
original sharer in the house of the Globe, but by 1612 had acquired
an interest jointly with Heminges ; of the Blackfriars house he was
an original sharer in 1608. The *Sharers Papers* of 1635 indicate that
Mrs. Condell had held four-sixteenths of the Globe and one-eighth
of the Blackfriars, but had transferred two-sixteenths of the Globe
when Taylor and Lowin were admitted as sharers. A minor legacy
in Condell's will is to his old servant, Elizabeth Wheaton, of her
' place or priviledge' in the Globe and Blackfriars. Heminges and
Cuthbert Burbadge are named as overseers. Condell was buried on
29 December 1627, and his widow on 3 October 1635, both at St. Mary
Aldermanbury.[3]

COOKE, ALEXANDER, has been conjectured to be the ' Sander ' who
is cast in the ' plot ' of *The Seven Deadly Sins* as played by Strange's
or the Admiral's about 1590–1, for the parts of Videna in *Envy* and
Progne in *Lechery*. But, as far as this goes, he might just as well be
the ' San.' who took the part of a player in *Taming of a Shrew* (1594),
ind. 1, which was a Pembroke's play. Malone ' presumes ', with some

---

[1] *Variorum*, iii. 199, 476 ; Collier, iii. 367 ; P. C. Carter, *Hist. of
St. Mary Aldermanbury*, 9, 11, 21, 58, 86, 87.
[2] *Variorum*, iii. 200, from P. C. C. ; Collier, iii. 376.
[3] Collier, iii. 376, 380.

rashness, that he performed 'all the principal female characters' in Shakespeare's plays.[1] It must be doubtful whether he was on the stage as early as 1592. He is traceable as a member of the King's men in the casts of *Sejanus* (1603), *Volpone* (1605), *Alchemist* (1610), *Catiline* (1611), and *The Captain* (1612–13). The fact that in the first two of these his name occurs at the end of the lists has been somewhat hazardously accepted as an indication that he played women's parts. He is also in the First Folio list of performers in Shakespeare's plays. Augustine Phillips left him a legacy as his 'fellow' in 1605.

'Mr. Cooke and his wife' commend themselves to Alleyn in his wife's letter of 21 October 1603.[2] The token-books of St. Saviour's, Southwark, show an Alexander Cooke in Hill's Rents during 1604, 1607, 1609, and 1610 ; and the parish register, recording the baptism of Francis Cooke, son of Alexander, 'a player', on 27 October 1605, makes an identification possible. There were three more children, Rebecca (bapt. 11 October 1607), Alice (bapt. 3 November 1611), Alexander (bapt. 20 March 1614). This last was posthumous ; the register records Alexander Cooke's burial on 25 February 1614.[3] His will, dated 3 January 1614, leaves £50 each to Francis, Rebecca, and the unborn child, and the residue to his wife.[4] He owned £50 'which is in the hand of my fellowes, as my share of the stock'. He appoints 'my master Hemings', to whom he had presumably been apprenticed, and Condell trustees for his children, and mentions brothers Ellis and John, of whom the latter is conjectured by Collier to be the author of *Greene's Tu Quoque*.

COOKE, EDWARD. Chapel, 1509.

COOKE, LIONEL. Queen's, 1583, 1588.

COOKE, THOMAS. Worcester's, 1583.

COOKE, WILLIAM. Whitefriars lessee, 1608.

CORNISH, JOHN. Gentleman of Chapel, and pageant-master at wedding of Arthur in 1501.

CORNISH, KIT. A 'ghost-name' in Chapel records.

CORNISH, WILLIAM. Master of Song School, Westminster, 1479–80.

CORNISH, WILLIAM. Master of Chapel, 1509–23. Conceivably identical with the last, and in any case probably of the same family.

COWLEY, RICHARD, was of Strange's men in 1593. He had played minor parts with that company or the Admiral's in *The Seven Deadly Sins* of 1590–1, and is mentioned in Alleyn's correspondence as travelling with the company. He joined the Chamberlain's men, probably on their formation in 1594, and was payee for the company in 1601. The stage-directions to the Quarto (1600) and Folio texts of *Much Ado about Nothing*, IV. ii, show that he played Verges. He is in the 1603 and 1604 lists of the King's men, and received a legacy from Augustine Phillips as his 'fellow' in 1605, but does not appear to have been a sharer in the houses of the Globe or Blackfriars. He is in the Folio list of performers in Shakespeare's plays. He dwelt in

[1] *Variorum*, iii. 211.   [2] *Henslowe Papers*, 61.

[3] Collier, iii. 406 ; Rendle, *Bankside*, xxvi.

[4] *Variorum*, iii. 482, from P. C. C. ; Collier, iii. 409.

Holywell, or for a short period in Alleyn's Rents, both in the parish of St. Leonard's, Shoreditch, whose register records his children, Robert (bapt. 8 March 1596, bur. (?) 20 March 1597), Cuthbert (bapt. 8 May 1597), Richard (bapt. 29 April 1598, bur. 26 February 1603), Elizabeth (bapt. 2 February 1602), as well as the funeral of his wife Elizabeth on 28 September 1616, and his own on 12 March 1619.[1] His will, dated on 13 January 1618, appoints his daughter Elizabeth Birch executrix and is witnessed by Heminges, Cuthbert Burbadge, Shank, and Thomas Ravenscroft, perhaps the madrigalist.[2]

CRANE, JOHN. A London player in 1550 (App. D, No. v).

CRANE, WILLIAM. Master of Chapel, 1523–45.

CROSSE, SAMUEL, is named amongst the performers of Shakespeare's plays in the First Folio, but in no list of the Chamberlain's or King's men. Probably, therefore, he belongs to the very beginning of Shakespeare's career, and is to be identified with the Crosse named by Heywood amongst famous actors of a generation before his time.[3]

CUMBER, JOHN. Anne's, 1616–19. He lived in Aldermanbury in 1623, and died in that year (J. 347 ; Fleay, 279).

CURTEYS, JAMES. Chapel, 1509.

CUTLER, JAMES. Chapel, > 1605.

DABORNE, ROBERT. Revels patentee, 1610, and dramatist.

DANIEL, JOHN. Chamber of Bristol patentee, 1615–17.

DANIEL, SAMUEL. Allower of Revels' plays, 1604, and dramatist.

DARLOWE. Admiral's, >1590.

DAVIES, HUGH. Admiral's (?), 1601 (H. ii. 255).

DAWES, ROBERT. Duke of York's, 1610 ; Lady Elizabeth's, 1614.

DAY, JOHN. Admiral's (?), c. 1600. John, son of John Day, 'player', was baptized at St. Saviour's, 3 June 1604 (B. 308 ; cf. ch. xxiii).

DAY, THOMAS. Chapel, 1601, 1602.

DOB. Admiral's, 1598–1601.

DOWNTON (DOWTON, DOUTON (?), DOWTEN, DOWGHTON, DENYGTEN, DOUBTON), THOMAS. Strange's, 1593 ; Admiral's–Henry's–Palsgrave's, 1594–c. 1618. The St. Saviour's registers record various family events, including the baptism of Christopher, son of Thomas Dowton 'musycyon' on 27 December 1592 and that of Thomas Dowton 'baseborne, the supposed son of Thomas Dowton, a player', 25 May 1600. He apparently married a vintner's widow on 15 February 1618, became a vintner, and was still alive on 18 August 1622 (B. 316 ; H. ii. 262, 265). Dr. Greg regards him as one of the Dutton family.

DRAKE, ROBERT. A London player in 1550 (cf. App. D, No. v).

DRAYTON, MICHAEL. Whitefriars lessee, 1608, and dramatist.

DREWE, BARTHOLOMEW. A 'player', whose son George was baptized at St. Saviour's on 12 November 1614 (B. 314).

DREWE, THOMAS. Anne's, 1616–19.

DROM, THOMAS. Admiral's, 1601.

---

[1] Collier, iii. 389.
[2] H. R. Plomer in 10 N. Q. vi. 368, from *London Archdeaconry Wills*, vi, f. 22.
[3] Heywood, *Apology*, 43.

DRUSIANO. *Vide* MARTINELLI.

DUKE, JOHN. Strange's (?), 1590–1 ; Chamberlain's, 1598 ; Worcester's–Anne's, 1602–9. Four children were baptized at St. Leonard's, where he lived in Holywell Street, from July 1604 to January 1609 (H. ii. 265 ; Collier, *Actors*, xxxi).

DULANDT (DOWLAND ?), ROBERT. Musician in Germany, 1623.

DUTTON, EDWARD. Admiral's, 1597, with a boy ' Dick '. Children of his were baptized at St. Saviour's during 1600–2 (B. 326).

DUTTON, JOHN. Warwick's, 1575–6 ; Oxford's, 1580 ; Queen's, 1583, ·1588–91. Lincoln's Inn paid him for musicians in 1567–8 (Walker, i. 362). There are family records of a John Dutton at St. Botolph's, who is called ' player ' in the entry of a daughter Elizabeth's baptism of 3 July 1586 (B. 328).

DUTTON, LAURENCE. Lane's, 1571–2 ; Clinton's, 1572–5 ; Warwick's, 1575–6 ; Oxford's, 1580 ; Queen's, 1589–91. It is curious that a John and a Laurence Dutton also appear as Court Messengers. I find a payment on 23 May 1578 to John for carrying letters to Antwerp (*Pipe Office, Chamber Declared Account* 541, m. 211ᵛ), and Laurence was paid for ' sondry jorneys ' in 1561–2 (ibid. m. 39) and was during 1576–82 one of the regular Messengers of the Chamber in attendance on the Privy Council (Dasent, ix. 223, x. 223, 228, xi. 437, xii. 23, xiii. 135, 392, etc.). The ' Edward ' Dutton of the last entry may be an error. In 1592 the Council (xxii. 493) recommended John the son of Laurence who had ' of long tyme served her Majestie ' as Messenger, for admission as a Queen's Scholar at Westminster. But this Laurence can hardly have been the actor, for he was acting as Messenger on 20 May 1580, while the affray for which Laurence the actor had been committed to the Marshalsea on 13 April was still uninquired into. Somewhat earlier a Thomas Dutton was employed as a post between Edward VI's Council and Thomas Gresham in Antwerp, and was Gresham's agent in Hamburg, *c.* 1571 (Burgon, *Gresham*, i. 109 ; ii. 421). It is easier again to conjecture than to prove a connexion between the actors and the house of Dutton of Dutton, which had a hereditary jurisdiction over minstrelsy in Cheshire (cf. ch. ix), although in this the names John and Laurence both appear. It is perhaps an accident that two of the recorded visits of the Queen's men to Lord Derby's northern seats in 1588–90 synchronize with visits by a Mr. Dutton (Murray, ii. 296).

ECCLESTONE, WILLIAM, appears as a King's man in the casts of *The Alchemist* (1610) and *Catiline* (1611). Mr. Fleay's statement that he joined the company from the Queen's Revels in 1609 rests upon a confusion with Field.[1] In 1611 he became a member of the Lady Elizabeth's men, but left them in 1613 after playing in *The Honest Man's Fortune* during that year. He returned to the King's, and his name is found in the official lists of the company for 1619 and 1621 and in most of the casts of their plays, from *Bonduca* in 1613–14 to *The Spanish Curate* in 1622, as well as in the First Folio list of performers in Shakespeare's plays. Nicholas Tooley forgave him a debt

[1] Fleay, 190 ; cf. *The Sharers Papers*.

in his will of 3 June 1623. As he is not in the Caroline patent of 1625, he had probably died or retired by that date. He may be the W. E. who writes commendatory verses to *The Wild-goose Chase* in 1652. If he is also the 'William Eglestone' whose marriage to Anne Jacob is recorded in the register of St. Saviour's, Southwark, on 20 February 1603, he lived to be an old man.[1]

EDMONDS, JOHN. Globe lessee, 1612 ; Chamber of Bristol, 1618–19. The St. Saviour's registers record the marriage of a John Edmonds to Margaret Goodyere on 22 February 1600 and the baptism of children of John Edmonds, 'player', from 6 January 1605 to 17 July 1615 (B. 334). Probably the two are not identical and the player is the John Edmans who seems to have married his fellow-legatee, Mary Clarke, of the will of Thomas Pope (q.v.) in 1604.

EDWARDES, RICHARD. Master of Chapel, 1561–6, and dramatist.

EICHELIN. Germany, 1604.

ELDERTON, WILLIAM. One Elderton, dressed as a fool, played the part of one of the Lord of Misrule's sons in George Ferrers's Christmas revel of 1552–3 (Feuillerat, *Edw. and Mary*, 120 ; cf. *Mediaeval Stage*, i. 407). Conjecture may identify him with the Elderton who brought the Eton boys to Court on 6 January 1573 and the William Elderton who brought the Westminster boys on 1 January 1574, and with the rhyming William Elderton, some of whose ballads are preserved and reprinted in Collier, *Old Ballads from Early Printed Copies* (1842, *Percy Soc.*), 25, 45 ; H. Huth, *Ancient Ballads and Broadsides* (1867, *Philobiblon Soc.*) ; and H. L. Collman, *Ballads and Broadsides* (1912, *Roxburghe Club*) ; or recorded, with ballads against him, in the Stationers' Register (Arber, i. 179, 180, 181, 199, 384, 403, 439 ; ii. 338, 363, 369, 388, 396, 399 ; cf. v. lxxvi), while his 'ale-crammed nose' and 'rymes lying a steepe in ale' are subject for much humour among the pamphleteers (Lyly, iii. 398 ; Nashe, i. 197, 256, 280 ; iii. 123, 133, 177, 354). Stowe (*Survey*, i. 272) makes him an attorney in the sheriff's courts at the Guildhall about 1568, but he can hardly be the 'master Elderton' who sat as a justice at the Guildhall in a coining case of 1562 (Machyn, 290). He appears to have been dead by 1592 (Harvey, i. 163 ; Nashe, i. 280). A recent paper on Elderton by H. E. Rollins is in *S. P.* xvii (1920), 199.

ENGLISH, JOHN. Interluders, 1494–1531.

EVANS, HENRY. Blackfriars lessee, 1583, 1600–8 ; payee for Oxford's, 1584 ; manager of Chapel, 1600–3. He was a scrivener, and overseer to the will of Sebastian Westcott, Master of Paul's, in 1582.

EVANS, THOMAS. Blackfriars lessee, 1608.

EVESEED, HENRY. Chapel, >1585.

FARNABY, RICHARD. Musician in Germany, 1623.

FARRANT, RICHARD. Master of Children of Windsor, 1564–80 ; Acting Master of Chapel and Blackfriars lessee, 1576–80.

FERRABOSCO, ALFONSO. Italians, 1576, and Court musician (cf. ch. ii).

---

[1] Collier, iii. 457 ; Rendle, *Bankside*, xxvi.

FETHERSTON, WILLIAM. Of Danby, Yorks., unlicensed player, 1612 (cf. ch. ix, p. 305).

FIDGE, WILLIAM. H. R. Plomer (3 *Library*, ix. 252) cites from a Canterbury record of 1571, ' William Fidge and Whetstone owe the said [Robert] Bettes [a painter] for their portions in buying of certen playebookes 35*s*. 4*d*.'

FIELD, NATHAN, was the son of John Field, preacher and castigator of the stage (cf. App. C, No. xxxi), and was baptized at St. Giles's, Cripplegate, on 17 October 1587 (Collier, iii. 425). His name is always spelt Nathan in formal contemporary documents, although he was familiarly known as Nat or Nid. But he appears in many reputable modern works of learning as Nathaniel. This error perhaps originated with the compilers of the 1679 Folio of Beaumont and Fletcher, who in four out of the six actor-lists in which his name is found used the form Nathan and in two (*Loyal Subject* and *Mad Lover*) Nathanael. It was certainly encouraged by a muddle of Collier, who finding in the Cripplegate registers that another son of John Field had been baptized Nathaniel on 13 June 1581, and not realizing that a cranky theological father might quite well use the names as distinct, thought it necessary to assume that this Nathaniel had died before 1587. As a matter of fact, he survived, was apprenticed to a stationer at Michaelmas 1596, took up his freedom on 3 June 1611, and between 1624 and 1627 published some books, including two sermons by a third brother, Theophilus Field, Bishop of Llandaff (McKerrow, *Dict.* 101). I need hardly linger over the suggestion that Nathan Field lived a double life as actor and bookseller. At this time of the apprenticeship he was not yet nine years old, and he was still a scholar of St. Paul's Grammar School when, not earlier than 1600, he was impressed by Nathaniel Giles and his deputies to serve as one of the Children of the Chapel (*Clifton v. Robinson* in Fleay, 128). His education was not entirely interrupted, for he fell into the hands of Ben Jonson, who told Drummond in 1619 that ' Nid Field was his schollar, and he had read to him the Satyres of Horace, and some Epigrames of Martiall ' (Laing, 11). Field remained a member of the Chapel and the Queen's Revels throughout the vicissitudes of the company from 1600 to 1613. He is in the actor-lists of *Cynthia's Revels* (1600), *The Poetaster* (1601), and *Epicoene* (1609), and presumably played Humfrey in *K. B. P.* (1607).[1] With his fellows he became absorbed into the Lady Elizabeth's in March 1613, contracted with Henslowe and Meade on behalf of this company (*Henslowe Papers*, 23), acted as their payee in 1615, and appears in the actor-lists of *The Coxcomb*, *The Honest Man's Fortune*, and *Bartholomew Fair* (1614), in the text of which Jonson compliments him (v. 3) as follows :

> *Cokes.* Which is your *Burbage* now ?
> *Lanterne.* What meane you by that, Sir ?
> *Cokes.* Your best Actor. Your *Field* ?

He seems to have been suspected by the company of taking bribes from Henslowe to connive at transactions contrary to their interest

[1] *K. B. P.* i. 104, ' Were you neuer none of Mr. Monkesters schollars ? '

(*Henslowe Papers*, 88). Certainly he was in financial straits and on more than one occasion appealed to Henslowe to secure his release from an arrest (*Henslowe Papers*, 66, 67). Perhaps it was as a result of this friction with his fellows that he abandoned their amalgamation with Prince Charles's men in 1615. Instead he joined, at or about this date, the King's men, and appears as one in the actor-lists of *The Loyal Subject*, *The Knight of Malta*, *The Queen of Corinth*, and *The Mad Lover*. It must, I think, have been by a slip that Cuthbert Burbadge, in the *Sharers Papers* of 1635, spoke of him as joining the King's with Ostler and Underwood in 1608 or 1609. It seems probable that Field brought with him to the King's a share of the plays which had formed the repertory of the joint Lady Elizabeth's and Queen's Revels, including Chapman's *Bussy D'Ambois*, in which a King's prologue vaunts his success as Bussy. He did not stay with the company very long, for though he is in the patent of 27 March and the livery list of 19 May 1619, he is replaced by John Rice in the livery list of 7 April 1621. And as he does not appear and Rice does appear amongst the actors named in the stage-directions to *Sir John von Olden Barnevelt* in August 1619, it is probable that he had left in the course of the summer (*M. L. R.* iv. 395). If so, his departure synchronizes with a scandal which attached itself to his name. His moral character was hardly becoming to the son of a preacher. More than one manuscript commonplace book (e. g. *Ashm. MS.* 47, f. 49, which appears from the spelling of the name to be a late copy) contains an epigram with some such heading as *On Nathaniell Feild suspected for too much familiarity with his M^{ris} Lady May*. And on 5 June 1619 Sir William Trumbull wrote from Brussels to Lord Hay (E. J. L. Scott in *Athenaeum* (1882), i. 103) that he was told that the Earl of Argyll had paid for the nursing of a child, ' which the world sayes is daughter to my lady and N. Feild the Player '. Lady Argyll was Anne, daughter of Sir William Cornwallis of Brome. Field's later life is obscure. There is an unimportant jest about him in John Taylor's *Wit and Mirth* (1629). He was married to a wife Anne, and had children baptized and buried at St. Anne's, Blackfriars, during 1619–25. If another epigram, printed by Collier, iii. 437, can be trusted, he very properly suffered from jealousy. In relevant register entries the name is given as Nathan. The Black-friars registers give children both of Nathan and of Nathaniel Field, and on 20 February 1633 occurs the burial of Nathaniel Field, whom, if the entry does not indicate that the confusion of persons had already begun, we are bound to take to be the bookseller. There is no reason why both brothers should not have resided in Blackfriars.

Field was dramatist, as well as actor. In addition to the two plays published under his single name, he collaborated with Massinger in *The Fatal Dowry*, which was a King's play and not likely, therefore, to fall outside the dates 1616–19. And as the Henslowe correspondence (*Henslowe Papers*, 65, 84) show him as collaborating also with Fletcher, Massinger, and Daborne for the Lady Elizabeth's, he has been con-jectured as a possible sharer in the authorship of several of the plays of the Beaumont and Fletcher series. He also, about the time of his joining the King's, wrote a defence of the stage, in the form of a remonstrance to Mr. Sutton, a preacher of St. Mary Overies (App. C, No. lxiii). A portrait of Field is at Dulwich.

FLETCHER, LAWRENCE. Scotland, 1595, 1599, 1601; Admiral's (?), 1596; King's, 1603. Although included as a King's man in the royal patent, there is no reason to suppose that Fletcher ever joined the company acting at the Globe; the absence of his name from the actor-list in the Shakespeare F_1 of 1623 is strong evidence that he did not. He lived in St. Saviour's, where he had a homonym, a victualler, who survived him. One of the two is shown by the token-books as housed in Hunt's Rents, Maid Lane, during 1605–7; probably this was the actor, who was buried on 12 September 1608. The description 'Lawrence Fletcher, a man : in the church' of the register is amplified in a fee-book to 'Lawrence Fletcher, a player, the King's servant, buried in the church, with an afternoon's knell of the great bell, 20s.' (Collier, *Memoirs of the Actors*[1], x; Rendle, *Bankside*, xxvii).

FLOWER. Admiral's (?), c. 1600.

FOSTER, ALEXANDER. Lady Elizabeth's, 1611, 1618; Charles's, 1616.

FREYERBOTT, BARTHOLOMEUS. Germany, 1615.

FRITH, MOLL. It appears to be suggested in the Epilogue to *The Roaring Girl* (cf. ch. xxiii, s.v. Dekker) that this lady was to appear in person on the Fortune stage, c. 1610.

FROST, JOHN. Chapel, 1601.

GARLAND, JOHN. Queen's, 1583, 1588; Lennox's, 1605; Duke of York's, 1610. He appears to have dwelt in 1605 at 'the ould forde' (H. ii. 267).

GARLICK. In I. H., *This World's Folly* (1615), an actor of this name is apparently said to have personated himself on the Fortune stage, 'behung with chaynes of Garlicke' (App. C, No. lix); cf. Dekker, *If This be not a Good Play* (1610–12), sc. x (ed. Pearson, iii. 325), 'Fortune fauours no body but Garlicke, nor Garlike neither now, yet she has strong reason to loue it; for tho Garlicke made her smell abhominably in the nostrills of the gallants, yet she had smelt and stuncke worse but for garlike'; H. Parrot, *Laquei Ridiculosi* (1613), Epig. 131, '*Greene's Tu Quoque* and those Garlicke Jigs'; in Tailor, *Hog Hath Lost his Pearl* (1614, ed. Dodsley[4], p. 434), a jig will draw more whores 'than e'er Garlic had'.

GARRET, JOHN. Anne's, 1619.

GEDION. Admiral's, 1602.

'GERRY.' King's Revels, 1607.

GEW. A blind player, referred to in *1 Ant. Mellida* (1599), ind. 142, ''t had been a right part for Proteus or Gew. Ho! blind Gew would ha' done 't rarely, rarely'; E. Guilpin, *Skialetheia* (1598), *Sat.* v, 'One that for ape tricks can put Gue to schoole', and *Epig.* xi, 'Gue, hang thy selfe for woe, since gentlemen Are now grown cunning in thy apishness'; Jonson, *Epig.* cxxix, 'Thou dost out-zany Cokely, Pod; nay, Gue.' Pod was a puppet-showman.

GIBBS. Admiral's, 1602.

GIBSON, RICHARD. Interluders, 1494–1508; afterwards Yeoman of the Revels.

GILBURNE, SAMUEL, is recorded in the First Folio list of performers in Shakespeare's plays. All that is known of him beyond this is that Augustine Phillips left him as his 'late apprentice' in his will of 1605 the sum of 40s., various garments, and a bass viol. Collier's inference that he could play on the viol is a fairly harmless example of biographical conjecture.[1] The identification of him with the ' b[oy ?] Sam ' of the ' plot ' of *The Dead Man's Fortune,* a play probably belonging to the Admiral's, and of a date not later than 1591, is more dangerous.[2]

GILES, NATHANIEL. Master of Windsor Choir, 1595–1634 ; Master of Chapel, 1597–1634.

GILES, THOMAS. Master of Paul's, 1585–1590 < ; Instructor in Music to Henry, 1606, and Charles, 1613.

GOODALE, BAPTISTE. ' Ghost-name ' (?) in Queen's list (1589) forged by Collier, *New Facts,* ii.

GOODALE, THOMAS. Berkeley's, 1581 ; Strange's (?), 1590–1 ; Chamberlain's (?) at date of *Sir Thomas More* (cf. ch. xxiv). If he is the Thomas Goodale, mercer, who entered with John Alleyn and Robert Lee into a bond to Edward Alleyn on 18 May 1593 (H. ii. 295, from *Dulwich MS.* iv. 29), he was not improbably connected with the Admiral's >1590.

GOUGHE or GOFFE, ROBERT, was probably the ' R. Go.' entered in the ' plot ' of *The Seven Deadly Sins,* as playing Aspasia in *Sloth* for the Admiral's or Strange's men about 1590–1. Probably he belonged at an early date to the King's men. He is a legatee in Thomas Pope's will of 22 July 1603, and witnessed that of Augustine Phillips on 4 May 1605, in which Phillips names a sister Elizabeth Goughe, doubtless the Elizabeth —— recorded in the register of St. Saviour's, Southwark, as marrying Robert Gough on 13 February 1603. The token-books of St. Saviour's indicate Gough's residence in Hill's Rents during 1604, Samson's Rents during 1605 and 1606, and Austin's Rents in 1612–22 ; and the registers, which generally call him a ' player ', record his children Elizabeth (bapt. 30 May 1605), Nicholas (bapt. 24 November 1608), Dorothy (bapt. 10 February 1611, bur. 12 January 1613), Alexander (bapt. 7 August 1614), and his own burial on 19 February 1624.[3] His son Alexander became in his turn a player. A stage-direction to l. 1723 of *The Second Maiden's Tragedy* (1611) shows that he played Memphonius. He also played Leidenberch in *Sir John von Olden Barnevelt* in 1619, and appears in the official lists of the King's men for 1619 and 1621 and in the First Folio list of performers in Shakespeare's plays.

GOUGHE, THOMAS. Lane's, 1572.

GRACE, FRANCIS. Henry's–Palsgrave's, 1610–22. He lived at George Alley, Golden Lane, in 1623 (J. 347).

GRAUNGER, JOHN. Chapel, 1509.

---

[1] Collier, iii. 411.   [2] Fleay, 85 ; Greg, *Henslowe Papers,* 133.
[3] Collier, iii. 473 ; Rendle, *Bankside,* xxvii.

GREAVES, JOHN. Lane's, 1572.

GREEN, JOHN. Germany, 1608; France, >1608; Holland, 1613; Germany, 1615–20, 1626. On his verses and portrait, 1608, cf. ch. xxiv, s.v. *Nobody and Somebody*. He may have been brother of the following.

GREENE, THOMAS. Anne's, 1604–12. In R. Braithwaite, *Remains after Death* (1618) are four epigrams on him, one of which says that he 'new come from sea, made but one face and dide'. A couplet on his death, signed W. R., is in Cooke's *Greene's Tu Quoque*. I. H., *World's Folly* (1615), mentions his performance of a baboon (cf. App. C, No. lix). He was of St. James's, Clerkenwell, in 1612, when he made his will (Fleay, 192), naming his wife Susan, daughter Honor, sons-in-law (i. e. stepsons) Robert and William Browne, daughters-in-law Susanna, Elizabeth, and Anne Browne, brothers John and Jeffery Greene, and sister Elizabeth Barrett. A conjecture that he was of Stratford origin has no foundation (Lee, 54).

GREUM, HENRY. Germany, 1608.

GRIFFEN. Admiral's, 1597.

GRIGORIE, JACK. Admiral's, 1602.

GRYMES, THOMAS. Chapel, 1600–1.

GUNNELL, RICHARD. Palsgrave's, 1613–22. Family notes appear in the registers of St. Giles's, 1614–30 (B. 409).

GYLLOME, FOKE. Player (?) to Alexander Houghton, 1581 (cf. ch. ix, p. 280).

GYRKE, RICHARD. A London player in 1550 (App. D, No. v).

HALLAWAIE, 'the younger'. Paul's, 1580.

HAMLEN (HAMLETT), ROBERT. Lady Elizabeth's, 1611–13; Charles's, 1616, 1625.

HAMMOND, JOHN. Interluders, 1494.

HAMOND. Worcester's, 1565.

HARRISON, JOHN. A 'player' whose daughter Suzanna by wife Anne was baptized at St. Helen's on 10 January 1602.

HARRISON, WILLIAM. Worcester's, 1583.

HARVEY. Chamberlain's, 1597.

HAWKINS, ALEXANDER. Blackfriars lessee, 1601; Revels patentee, 1604.

HAYNE, WILLIAM. Head Master of Merchant Taylors', 1599–1625.

HAYSELL, GEORGE. Worcester's, 1583. For a possible notice of the same man, cf. ch. xxiv, s.v. *Misogonus*.

HEARNE, THOMAS. Admiral's, 1597.

HELLE, JOHN. Admiral's, 1597.

HEMINGES, JOHN, whose name is variously spelt, appearing, for example, as 'Heminge' in his signature to the dedication of the First Folio of Shakespeare's plays, and as 'Hemmings' in the actor-list in the same volume, is known to have had a wife Rebecca, and may fairly be identified with the 'John Hemminge, gent.' of St. Mary Cornhill, who was married on 10 March 1588 to Rebecca Knell, widow, relict of William Knell, gent., late of St. Mary Aldermanbury. In the same parish William Knell had married Rebecca Edwards on

30 January 1586, and an older William Knell had been buried on 24 September 1578.[1] One of these was not improbably the early actor celebrated by Heywood. Malone found a family of Heming at Shottery, and conjectured that of this family John was born at some date earlier than the opening of the Stratford-on-Avon register in 1558.[2] But this is rendered improbable by a confirmation of arms in 1629 to ' John Hemings of London Gent. of long tyme Servant to Queen Elizabeth of happie Memory, also to King James hir Royal Successor and to King Charles his Sonne ', in which he is described as ' Sonne and Heire of George Hemings of Draytwiche in the Countye of Worcester Gent.'[3] There seems little reason to doubt that this John Hemings is the player. He very probably began his theatrical career with the Queen's company, to which also Knell had belonged. By May 1593, however, he had joined Strange's men, from whom he passed to the Chamberlain's men, probably on the original formation in 1594. Of this company, afterwards the King's men, he remained a member to the end of his career. He appears in all the official lists of the company up to 1629, and regularly acted as their payee for Court performances, generally with a colleague from 1596 to 1601, and thereafter alone. This and his prominence in the negotiations of the company and the law-suits arising out of them, suggest that he acted as their business manager. As an actor he appears in all the casts up to Catiline in 1611, but not thereafter ; possibly he may have resigned acting, and devoted himself to business. The unreliable John Roberts, Answer to Pope (1729), conjectures that he was a ' tragedian '. Malone had seen a statement in some tract of which he had forgotten the title, that he was the original performer of Falstaff.[4] The lines on the burning of the Globe in 1613 thus describe him :

> Then with swolne eyes, like druncken Flemminges,
> Distressed stood old stuttering Heminges.

He is ' old Master Hemings ' in Jonson's Masque of Christmas (1616). He lent his ' boy ' John Rice (q.v.) to the Merchant Taylors for their entertainment of James on 16 July 1607, and another ' boy ' for Chapman's mask of 1613. He is named as a legatee and overseer in the will of Augustine Phillips in 1605, and as executor in the event of the widow's re-marriage ; also as a trustee in the will of Alexander Cooke, who calls him his ' master ', in 1614 ; as a witness in that of Richard Cowley in 1618 ; as a legatee in that of Shakespeare in 1616 ; and as a legatee and overseer in those of Underwood in 1624 and of Condell in 1627. He was appointed a trustee for Shakespeare's Blackfriars property in 1613,[5] and acted with Condell as editor of the First Folio of the plays in 1623. This fact is probably the origin of the statement of Roberts that he was engaged with Condell in business as a printer. He filled various parochial posts from 1608 to 1619 in St. Mary's, Aldermanbury, and the registers contain records of the

---

[1] Variorum, iii. 472 ; Chester, London Marriage Licenses.
[2] Variorum, iii. 187.   [3] Ibid. 188.
[4] Ibid. 187.   [5] Halliwell-Phillipps, i. 31.

following children : Alice (bapt. 10 November 1590, married John Atkins 11 February 1612), Mary (bapt. 26 May 1592, bur. 9 August 1592), Judith (bapt. 29 August 1593), Thomasine (bapt. 15 January 1595), Joan (bapt. 2 May 1596), John (bapt. 12 August 1599), Beavis (bapt. 24 May 1601), William (bapt. 3 October 1602), George (bapt. 12 Feb. 1604), Rebecca (bapt. 4 February 1605), Elizabeth (bapt. 6 March 1608), Mary (bapt. 21 June 1611, bur. 23 July 1611).[1] In the same parish ' John Heminge, player ' was himself buried on 12 October 1630, beside his wife Rebecca, who preceded him on 2 September 1619. He is registered as a ' stranger ', and was therefore probably residing elsewhere. In his will, made on 9 October, he describes himself as ' citizen and grocer of London ', appoints his son William executor and trustee for his unmarried and unadvanced children, and Cuthbert Burbadge and ' Mr. Rice ', possibly the actor, overseers, and leaves legacies to his daughters Rebecca, wife of Captain William Smith, Margaret, wife of Mr. Thomas Sheppard, who is not mentioned in the register, Elizabeth, and Mrs. Merefield, and to his son-in-law Atkins ' and his now wife ', and his grandchild Richard Atkins. He also leaves 10s. for a ring ' unto every of my fellows and sharers, his majesties servants.[2] William Heminges went to Westminster and Christ Church, and became a playwright.[3] Unnamed in the will is Thomasine, who. may have been dead, but certainly had quarrelled seriously with her father. She had married William Ostler of the King's men in 1611 and her son Beaumont was baptized at St. Mary's, Aldermanbury, on 18 May 1612. Ostler died intestate on 16 December 1614 in possession of shares in the leases both of the Globe and the Blackfriars. These passed of right to Thomasine as his administratrix, and formed all the provision left for her maintenance and her husband's debts. The leases, however, passed into the hands of Heminges, who retained them and asserted that Ostler had created a trust, of which Thomasine declared that she knew nothing. On 20 September 1615 she entered a bill in Chancery against her father, and subpœnaed him to appear during the coming Michaelmas term. On 26 September Heminges promised that if she would withdraw her suit, and would also ' doe her dutie ' to him and to her mother Rebecca, he would satisfy her to the value of the shares. Thomasine states that on the same day kneeling and in tears she made her submission at her father's house in Aldermanbury. She also stayed her suit, but Heminges, although called upon to fulfil his promise on 5 October, failed to do so, and on 9 October Thomasine brought a common law action against him for damages to the amount of £600, which she estimated to be the value of the shares.[4] The issue of the case is unknown, but it would seem probable from the *Sharers Papers* of 1635 that Heminges succeeded in retaining the shares, and that at his death they passed

---

[1] *Variorum*, iii. 198, 475 ; Collier, iii. 308; P. C. Carter, *St. Mary, Aldermanbury*, 11, 58, 86, 87. Malone misread Beavis as Beatrice. An earlier John (1598) and a Swynnerton (1613) died as infants.

[2] *Variorum*, iii. 191. [3] *D. N. B.* s.v. ; Wood, *Athenae*, iii. 277.

[4] *O. v. H.* 16 ; cf. C. W. Wallace, in *The Times* for 2 and 4 Oct. 1909.

to his son William.   Professor Wallace states that in 1616 Thomasine
Ostler was involved in another law-suit with Walter Raleigh, son of
Sir Walter, and obtained a verdict of £250 against him for insult and
slander.   One way and another, Heminges seems to have acquired a
considerable financial interest in the Globe and Blackfriars.   He had
an original seventh of a moiety of the Globe lease in 1599, and an
original seventh of the Blackfriars lease in 1608.   But as executor to
Phillips (q.v.) and otherwise he had opportunities of adding to these
holdings.   The *Sharers Papers* show that at his death he had four
sixteenths of the Globe and probably two eighths of the Blackfriars ;
and these, or some of them, he had enjoyed ' thirty yeeres without
any molestacion, beeing the most of the sayd yeeres both player and
houskeeper, and after hee gave over playing diverse yeeres '.   In
Witter v. Heminges and Condell he is described as being in 1619 of
' greate lyveinge wealth and power '.[1]   The playhouse shares seem to
have been the chief part of the property left by his will.   They passed
to William Heminges as his executor.   He seems to have gradually
disposed of them, first selling one share in the Globe by arrangement
with the company to Taylor and Lowin, and later, by transactions
which some of his fellows resented, one share in each house to John
Shank during 1633 for £156, and the remaining shares also to John
Shank during 1634, for £350.   He was then in difficulties, and Shank
disbursed additional small sums to him in prison.   It was these sales
to Shank which brought about the petition to the Lord Chamberlain
recorded in the *Sharers Papers*.

HENSLOWE, FRANCIS.   Queen's, 1594 ; Lennox's, 1605.   He was
son of Richard and nephew of Philip Henslowe, and various entries in
the diary and other Dulwich MSS. record his imprisonments, more
than once on criminal charges, his employment during 1593-4 in his
uncle's pawnbroking, and his loans, one of which on 1 June 1595 was
of £9 ' to laye downe for his hallfe share with the company which he
dothe playe with all ' (H. i. 6), conceivably, as Dr. Greg suggests, some
company other than the Queen's, in which he had already acquired a
half share in 1594.   He dwelt in the Clink in 1594, took a house called
the Upper Ground on Bankside in 1597, and was of St. George's,
Southwark, in 1606, in which year, between 30 March and 6 October,
both he and his wife died (H. ii. 277).

HENSLOWE, PHILIP.   Owner of Rose, Fortune, Hope, and perhaps
lessee of Whitefriars ; cf. ch. xi.

HERIOT, HENRY.   Interluders, 1547-52.

HEYWOOD, JOHN.   For his possible connexion with Paul's, cf.
ch. xii, s.v. Chapel.

HEYWOOD, THOMAS.   Admiral's, 1598 ;   Worcester's Anne's,
1602-19, and dramatist.

HINSTOCK, ROBERT.   Interluders, 1538-51.

HOBBES, THOMAS.   Charles's, 1610, 1616-25.   He lived at the upper
end of Shoreditch in 1623 (J. 348).

[1] *N. U. S.* x. 311.

HOLE, RICHARD. Interluders, 1526–30.

HOLLAND, J. Strange's (?), 1590–1.

HOLT, JAMES. Anne's, 1604–19.

HOLT, JOHN. A 'momer', who helped the Westminster boys in 1561, probably identical with the Yeoman of the Revels of that name (cf. ch. iii), who helped them in 1564–5.

HOLZHEW, BEHRENDT. Germany, 1614–15.

HOVELL, WILLIAM. Licensee for 2 King's Revels, 1615.

HOWARD, THOMAS. A 'player' named in St. Saviour's records *c.* 1600 (Rendle, *Bankside*, xxvi).

HUDSON, RICHARD. Weaver of Hutton Bushell, Yorks, unlicensed player, 1612 (cf. ch. ix, p. 305).

HÜLL, JOHN. Germany, 1600–1.

HUNNIS, JOHN. A 'ghost-name' by an error for the following.

HUNNIS, WILLIAM. Master of Chapel, 1566–97, and dramatist.

HUNT (HONTE), THOMAS. Admiral's, 1599, 1602; Lady Elizabeth's, 1611 (H. ii. 285).

HUNTLEY, DICK. Actor in *Summer's Last Will and Testament* (*vide* l. 14).

HUSE, RICHARD. Paul's chorister, >1582.

IVY, NICHOLAS. Chapel, 1509.

JEFFES, ANTHONY. Chamberlain's (?), 1597; Pembroke's, 1597; Admiral's–Henry's, 1597->1613. Anthony, son of Richard Jeffes, baptized at St. Saviour's, Southwark, on 14 December 1578, may be the same who married Faith Jones there on 19 February 1601. Children of Anthony Jeffes 'player' are recorded in the registers of St. Giles's, Cripplegate, from 11 June 1602 to 1 May 1609; in later entries from 30 May 1610 to 30 October 1616, Anthony is called 'brewer' (H. ii. 286; *Bodl.*).

JEFFES, HUMPHREY. Chamberlain's (?), 1597; Pembroke's, 1597; Admiral's–Henry's–Palsgrave's, 1597–1616<. He was buried at St. Giles's, 21 August 1618. A daughter Mary was baptized at St. Saviour's, 25 January 1601 (H. ii. 287; Collier, *Actors*, xxx).

JOHNSON, WILLIAM. Leicester's, 1572–4; Queen's, 1583, 1587–8. The baptismal entries at St. Giles's include on 10 February 1587 'Comedia, base-borne daughter of Alice Bowker, and, as she saithe, the father's name is William Johnson, one of the Queen's plaiers', and the burials on 3 March 1593 'Comedia, daughter of William Johnson, player'. Is he the William Johnson, vintner, who was trustee of Shakespeare's Blackfriars property 1613–18 (Lee, 459, 493)?

JONES, RICHARD. Worcester's, 1583; Admiral's (?), >1589; Germany, 1592–3; Admiral's, 1594–6; Pembroke's, 1597; Admiral's, 1597–1602; Revels patentee, 1610; Germany (?), 1615; Germany, 1620, 1622–4. His wife Harris inherited a lease of the Leopard's Head in Shoreditch from her father in 1620. A Richard Jones is traceable in the Southwark token-books from 1588 to 1607 and may or may not be the same who married Anne Jube there on 14 February 1602 (H. ii. 288; *H. P.* 94; *Bodl.*).

JONES, ROBERT. Germany, 1602; Porter's Hall patentee, 1615.

JONNS, DANIEL. Denmark, 1586.

JONSON, BENJAMIN. Pembroke's (?), 1597 ; Chamberlain's (?), *c.* 1598 ; and dramatist.

JUBY, EDWARD. Admiral's–Henry's–Palsgrave's, 1594–1618, Fortune lessee, 1618. An Edward Juby is traceable during 1598 to 1619 in the token-books of St. Saviour's, Southwark. In the last year he is marked ' dead ', and his burial was registered on 20 November 1618. In 1610 and 1614 he filled parish offices. He may fairly be identified with the ' player ' whose children occur in the registers from 3 June 1599 to 15 September 1614. His widow Francis held his share of the Fortune lease in 1622 (H. ii. 290 ; Rendle, *Bankside*, xxvi ; *Bodl.*).

JUBY, RICHARD. Admiral's, 1602. His son Richard was baptized at St. Saviour's, Southwark, on 1 May 1602 (*Bodl.*).

JUBY, WILLIAM (?). Admiral's, 1599–1602 (H. ii. 290).

JUGLER, RICHARD. A London player in 1550 (cf. App. D, No. v).

KEMP, JOHN. Germany, 1601.

KEMPE, WILLIAM, cannot be securely identified or connected with any one of various homonyms who have been traced in *D. N. B.* and elsewhere.[1] He probably emerges as one of Leicester's men in the Low Countries during 1585–6 and thence made his way to Denmark. He was in London and had already won a comic reputation by 1590 when the dedication of *An Almond for a Parrat* (Nashe, iii. 341), ' To that most Comicall and conceited Caualeire Monsieur du Kempe, Jest-monger and Vice-gerent generall to the Ghost of Dicke Tarlton,' tells how the anonymous author, possibly Nashe, had been asked by ' that famous Francatrip' Harlicken ' at Bergamo in the previous summer, whether he knew ' any such Parabolano here in London as Signior Chiarlatano Kempino ' of whose ' pleasance ' Harlicken had heard ' report '. In *Four Letters Confuted* (1592) Nashe says of an action of Harvey's, ' Will Kempe, I mistrust it will fall to thy lot for a merriment, one of these dayes ' (i. 287). An example of Kempe's merriments is to be found in sc. xii of *A Knack to Know a Knave* (1594) played by Strange's men, to whom Kempe belonged by 1593. He was also famous for his jigs. Four of these are entered in the Stationers' Register during 1591–5 (cf. ch. xviii) but are not preserved, and ' Kemps jiggs ' is the heading to some music collected by John Dowland and preserved in *Camb. Univ. Libr. MS.* Dd. ii. 11 (cf. Halliwell, *MS. Rarities*, 8). Marston (iii. 372), *Scourge of Villainy* (1598), sat. xi. 30, ' the orbs celestial Will dance Kempe's jig,' and E. Guilpin, *Skialetheia* (1598), sat. v, ' Whores, bedles, bawdes, and sergeants filthily Chaunt Kemps Jigge, or the Burgonians tragedy,' show his vogue.

---

[1] *Kemps Nine Daies Wonder. Performed in a Daunce from London to Norwich* (1600) is reprinted with a biography by A. Dyce (1840, *Camden Soc.*) and in Arber, *English Garner*[2], ii (*Social England*), 139, and E. Goldsmid, *Collectanea Adamantea*, ii (1884). Dissertations are J. Bruce, *Who was ' Will, my Lord of Leycester's Jesting Player ' ?* (1844, *Sh. Soc. Papers*, i. 88) ; B. Nicholson, *Kemp and the Play of Hamlet* (*N. S. S. Trans. 1880–6*, 57) ; *Will Kemp* (1887, *Sh.-Jahrbuch*, xxii. 255).

In 1594–5 he was one of the recently constituted Chamberlain's men and the intrusion of his name into stage-directions to *R. J.* iv. 5. 102 (Q₂) and *M. Ado*, iv. 2, shows that he played Peter in the one play and Dogberry in the other. Oddly enough, one of his speeches (iv. 2. 4) in *M. Ado* is assigned to 'Andrew', possibly a generic name for a clown or 'merry-Andrew'. He is in the actor-list of *Every Man in his Humour* (1598) but not in that of *Every Man out of his Humour* (1599), and this fact, together with his sale of his share in the Globe soon after the lease of 21 February 1599 was signed, points to his leaving the company. 'Would I had one of Kemps shooes to throw after you,' says a speaker in *E. M. O.* iv. v (q.v.). This may be an allusion to some clownery by Kempe, perhaps in a performance with some other company at the Curtain in the autumn of 1599 after the Chamberlain's left that house; or, less probably, to Kempe's famous morris-dance for a wager from London to Norwich, at the end of which he hung his buskins in the Guildhall, for this began on 11 February 1600 and ended on 11 March, the year being fixed by the mayoralty (1599–1600) of Roger Weld at Norwich. Another allusion to 'Kemps morice' is in *Jack Drum's Entertainment* (1600), i. 45. Dudley Carleton wrote to John Chamberlain on 13 October 1600 (*S. P. D. Eliz.* cclxxv. 93) that on his way from Witham to Englefield 'we met a company of mad wenches, whereof Mrs. Mary Wroughton and young Stafford were ringleaders, who travelled from house to house, and to some places where they were little known, attended with a concert of musicians, as if they had undertaken the like adventure as Kemp did from London to Norwich'. Kempe's own account of his adventure was entered in the Stationers' Register as 'Kemps morris to Norwiche' on 22 April 1600 (Arber, iii. 160). In the Epistle to Anne Fitton, whom, possibly by confusion with her sister Mary, he describes as maid of honour to Elizabeth, he refers to unentered ballads on the subject, and when he says that 'I haue daunst my selfe out of the world' is not improbably jesting on his departure from the Globe. At the end he foreshadows crossing to Calais, which he no doubt did. A John Kemp, who was in charge of a touring company, which had been in Holland and reached Münster by November 1601, may have been a relative. But William Kempe had returned to England, after visiting Italy as well as Germany, on 2 September 1601, as is shown by the following interpolation in a diary of one William Smith of Abingdon, in *Sloane MS.* 414, f. 56 (wrongly cited by Halliwell, *Ludus Coventriae* 410, as *Sloane MS.* 392, f. 401; cf. F. J. Furnivall in *N. S. S. Trans.* 1880–6, 65):

'Sep. 2. Kemp, mimus quidam, qui peregrinationem quandam in Germaniam et Italiam instituerat, post multos errores, et infortunia sua, reversus: multa refert de Anthonio Sherley, equite aurato, quem Romae (legatum Persicum agentem) convenerat.'

Possibly Kempe rejoined the Chamberlain's for a while. In *3 Parnassus* (? January 1602), iv. 3, he is introduced as a fellow of Burbadge and Shakespeare, and greeted with allusions to his 'dancing the morrice ouer the Alpes' and 'the Emperour of Germany'. But on 10 March

1602 he had a loan from Henslowe, and during the winter of 1602–3 he was certainly one of Worcester's men. The dates do not lend support to the suggestion of Fleay, ii. 20, that he had already in 1599–1600 been at the Rose with Pembroke's men. After the end of Elizabeth's reign he is not traceable, and he is mentioned as dead in Heywood, *Apology* (*c.* 1608), and dead or retired in Dekker, *Gull's Hornbook* (1609), 11, ' Tarlton, Kemp, nor Singer, nor all the litter of fools that now come drawling behind them, never played the clown more naturally.' A William Kempe is recorded in token-books of St. Saviour's, Southwark, as living in Samson's Rents in 1595, 1596, 1598, and 1599, in Langley's New Rents in 1602, and later near the old play-house (Collier, iii. 351, and *Bodl.* ; Rendle, *Bankside*, xxvi). Collier, but not Rendle, gives the date ' 1605 ' for the last entry, probably with a view to supporting his notice of Kempe, as playing with Armin at the Blackfriars (q.v.) in 1605, which is doubtless a fabrication. On the other hand, though the date is plausible, the notice of ' Kempe a man ' as buried at St. Saviour's on 2 November 1603 (Rendle, xxvii) is not so worded as to be absolutely conclusive. The name was a common one, and Collier, *Actors*, xxxvi, gives notices of it from other parishes. In T. Weelkes, *Ayres on Phantasticke Sprites* (1608), it is said of Kempe that ' into France He took pains to skip it '. His visit to Venice and meeting with Sherley are dramatized in *Travels of Three English Brothers* (1607) and apparently misdated after the *Englands Joy* of November 1602. Finally, an epitaph upon him is in R. Braithwaite, *Remains after Death* (1618), sig. F 8ᵛ, which suggests that he died not long after his morris.

KENDALL, THOMAS. Blackfriars manager, 1602 ; Revels patentee, 1604. He died in 1608.

KENDALL, WILLIAM. Admiral's, 1597–8 ; Henry's–Palsgrave's, >1614. His son John was baptized at St. Saviour's, Southwark, on 5 January 1615 (*Bodl.*).

KEYSAR, ROBERT. Revels manager, 1606–10 (?) ; Blackfriars lessee, 1606–8. To him was written the epistle to *K. B. P.*

KING, ARTHUR. Berkeley's, 1581.

KING, THOMAS. Denmark–Germany, 1586–7.

KINGMAN (KINGSMAN), PHILIP. Germany, 1596 ; Porter's Hall patentee, 1615. ' Mʳ Kyngman the elder ' was a witness for Henslowe on 16 April 1599 (H. i. 205).

KINGSMAN, ROBERT. Germany, 1599, 1601 ; afterwards a tradesman in Strassburg, 1606 (?), 1618, 1626.

KIRCK (KIRCKMANN), JOHN. Denmark, 1579–80.

KIRKHAM, EDWARD. Chapel manager, 1602 ; Revels patentee, 1604–6. He is probably the Yeoman of the Revels (cf. ch. iii).

KITE, JOHN. Gentleman of Chapel, 1508 ; afterwards Abp. of Armagh.

KNAGGES, RICHARD. Of Moorsham, Yorks, unlicensed player, 1612 (cf. ch. ix, p. 305).

KNELL, WILLIAM (?). Queen's, >1588. A Rebecca, widow of William Knell, married John Heminges (q.v.), 10 March 1588.

Heywood notes Knell as before his time. Nashe, *Pierce Penilesse* (1592, *Works*, i. 215), names him with Tarlton, Alleyn, and Bentley, and he is coupled with Bentley in the undated challenge to Alleyn (q.v.) to play one of their parts.

KNIGHT, ROBERT. Paul's chorister, >1582.

KOSTRESSEN, JOHAN, musician. Germany, 1623.

KRAFFT, JOHN. Denmark, 1579–80.

LANEHAM, JOHN. Leicester's, 1572–4 ; Queen's, 1583, 1588–91. Heywood notes him as before his time. Was he related to Robert Laneham, Keeper of the Council Chamber door, who described the Kenilworth entertainment (cf. ch. xxiv) in 1575 ?

LANMAN, HENRY. Owner of Curtain, 1581–92. Adams, 80, suggests, apparently from the similarity of the names, that he was a brother of John Laneham.

LEBERWURST, HANS. Germany, 1613.

LEDBETTER, ROBERT. Admiral's, 1597 ; Germany, 1599, 1601, 1606.

LEE, ROBERT. Admiral's (?), >1591 ; Anne's, 1604–19 ; Revels Company, 1622. He had a business transaction with Edward and John Alleyn and Thomas Goodale (q.v.) in 1593. He lived in Clerkenwell Close in 1623 (H. ii. 294 ; J. 347 ; Murray, i. 198).

LEEKE, DAVID. Possibly an actor at Canterbury, *c.* 1571 (*3 Library*, ix. 253).

LEVESON, ROBERT. Oxford's, 1580.

LISTER, EDWARD. Weaver of Allerston, Yorks, unlicensed player, 1612 (cf. ch. ix, p. 305).

LONG, NICHOLAS. Revels (provincial) manager, 1612, 1617 ; Lady Elizabeth's, 1614–15. For his later career, cf. Murray, i. 192, 361 ; ii. 101. He was buried at St. Giles's, Cripplegate, on 21 January 1622 (*Bodl.*).

LOVEKYN, ARTHUR. Chapel, 1509–13.

LOWIN, JOHN, was a member of Worcester's company during their season of 1602–3 with Henslowe at the Rose. On 12 March 1603 Henslowe lent him money to go into the country with the company, but during the course of the year he must have transferred his services to the King's men, presumably as a hireling, since, although in the cast of *Sejanus* (1603) and the Induction to *Malcontent* (1604) he is not in the official lists of 1603 and 1604. A portrait of him in the Ashmolean Museum at Oxford, has the inscription ' 1640, Aetat. 64 ', and he may therefore be identified with the John, son of Richard Lowen, baptized at St. Giles's, Cripplegate, on 9 December 1576. If so, his father seems to have been a carpenter, and he had a sister Susan and a brother William.[1] He remained through a long life with the King's men, appearing in most of the casts, in the actor-list of the First Folio, and in the official lists from 1619 onwards. He played Bosola in *The Duchess of Malfi*. A pamphlet entitled *Conclusions upon Dances* (1607) has a dedication to Lord Denny, dated 23 November 1606, and signed

---

[1] Collier, iii. 391.

ACTORS

'I. L. *Roscio*'. Collier claims to have found in a copy of this the note 'By Jhon Lowin. Witnesseth Tho. D. 1610 '.[1] A John Lowen married Joan Hall, widow, by licence, in St. Botolph's, Bishopsgate, on 29 October 1607.[2] Shortly afterwards a John Lowin was paying a poor-rate of 2*d.* weekly in the liberty of the Clink. The Southwark token-books attest his residence 'near the playhouse' and in other parts of the parish at various dates from 1601 to 1642.[3] He was overseer of Paris Garden in 1617–18.[4] But in 1623 he lived in Lambeth (J. 348). He is named as a legatee and overseer in the will of his 'fellow' John Underwood in 1624. It appears from the *Sharers Papers* that he had no interest in the play-houses until after the death of Heminges in 1630, when he was admitted to purchase two sixteenths of the Globe and one eighth of the Blackfriars. From this time onwards he seems to have shared the business responsibilities of the company with Joseph Taylor. He was also prominent as an actor.[5] Wright enumerates amongst his parts Shakespeare's Falstaff; but when Roberts adds Hamlet and Henry VIII, he is presumably guessing that Lowin was 'fat and scant of breath'. He may have been the original Henry VIII, for Downes reports that Betterton was instructed in the part by Sir William Davenant, 'who had it from old Mr. Lowen, that had his instructions from Mr. Shakespeare himself'.[6] Wright tells us that at the outbreak of civil war he was 'superannuated', and 'in his latter days kept an inn (the Three Pigeons) at Brentford, where he dyed very old (for he was an actor of eminent note in the reign of King James the First), and his poverty was as great as his age '.[7] He signed with Taylor the dedication to Fletcher's *The Wild-goose Chase* in 1652, the publication of which was an attempt to relieve their necessities. A 'John Lewin' who left a widow Martha, was buried at St. Martin's-in-the-Fields on 18 March 1659, and a 'John Lowen' at St. Paul's, Covent Garden, on 16 March 1669.[8] Probably a G. Lowin who played Barnaveldt's daughter to Lowin's Barnaveldt in 1619 was his son.

LYLY, JOHN. Blackfriars lessee, 1583; Oxford's payee, 1584; and dramatist.

MACHIN, RICHARD. Germany, 1600–3, 1605–6.

MAGETT, STEPHEN. Admiral's tireman, 1596, 1599 (?) (H. ii. 295).

MARBECK, THOMAS. Admiral's, 1602.

MARSHALL, CHARLES. Palsgrave's (provincial), 1616.

MARSTON, JOHN. Blackfriars lessee, 1603–8, and dramatist.

MARTINELLI (?), ANGELICA. Italians, >1598.

MARTINELLI, DRUSIANO. Italians, 1578.

MARTON, THOMAS. Chapel, 1602.

MARTYN, WILLIAM. Payee for a company at Ipswich, 20 February 1572 (Murray, ii. 290).

[1] Ibid. 395.　　　　　　　　　　[2] Ibid. 396.
[3] Ibid. 397; *Bodl.*; Rendle, *Bankside*, xxvi.
[4] Norman, 91.
[5] For further details of his later career, cf. Collier and *D. N. B.*
[6] Downes, 24.　　　　　　　　　[7] Wright, 10.
[8] *Variorum*, iii. 211; Collier, iii 403.

MASON, JOHN. Whitefriars lessee, 1608, and dramatist.

MASSEY (MASSYE), CHARLES. Admiral's–Henry's–Palsgrave's, 1597->1635 (?); Fortune lessee, 1618->1635; and dramatist (cf. ch. xxiii). He is probably the Charles Marcy or Mercy, variously described as 'player', 'gentleman', and 'yeoman' in the registers of St. Giles's, Cripplegate, from 30 December 1610 to 20 July 1625. He died before 6 December 1635, leaving a widow Elianor, and had a cousin Ned Collins (H. ii. 296; *Bodl.*).

MAXE, ROBERT. Chapel, 1509->1513.

MAY, EDWARD. Interluders, 1494–1503.

MAY, NATHAN. Licensee for 2 King's Revels, 1615. Possibly the name, as given in Murray, ii. 340, may be a mistake for Clay (q.v.).

MAYLER, GEORGE. Interluders, 1525–40.

MEADE, JACOB. Keeper of the Bears, by 1599, and partner with Henslowe in the Bear Garden and Hope. He was buried at St. Saviour's on 9 July 1624 (*Bodl.*).

MELYONEK, JOHN. Master of Chapel (?), 1483–5.

MERYELL, HENRY. Chapel, 1509.

MILS (MYLLES), TOBIAS. Queen's, 1583. Heywood notes him as before his time. He was buried as 'one of the Queenes Maiesties players' at St. Olave's, Southwark, on 11 July 1585, and his sons William and Toby were baptized on 3 January 1584 and 5 September 1585 (*Bodl.*). Probably, therefore, 'one Myles, one of my lord of Summersettes players', whose testimony to the value of Bath waters for the gout is cited in a hydropathic treatise of 1557 (Collier, i. 139), was of an older generation. Somerset was beheaded on 22 January 1552. Robert Cecil had a Secretary Milles, whose son Tobias was buried at Chelsea on 9 April 1599 (R. Davies, *Chelsea Old Church*, 296).

MOON, PETER. Payee for a company of players at Ipswich, 1562 (Murray, ii. 287).

MOORE, JOSEPH. Lady Elizabeth's, 1611; 1616–29. He livéd at the Harrow in Barbican in 1623 (Murray, i. 252; J. 347).

MOTTERAM, JOHN. Chapel, 1600–1.

MUFFORD, JOHN. Beauchamp's, 10 June 1590 (Murray, ii. 337).

MULCASTER (MONCASTER), RICHARD. Head Master of Merchant Taylors, 1561–86; of St. Paul's Grammar School, 1596–1608.

MUNDAY, ANTONY. A player before 1582, according to a contemporary pamphlet, possibly with Oxford's, whose 'servant' he was in 1580, and dramatist (cf. ch. xxiii).

NASION. Paul's chorister, >1582.

'NED.' Musician (?) in *Summer's Last Will and Testament, prol.* 7.

'NED.' Strange's (?), 1590–1.

NETHE, JOHN. A London player in 1550 (cf. App. D, No. v).

NETHERSALL, JOHN. A London player in 1550 (cf. App. D, No. v).

NEWARK, WILLIAM. Master of Chapel, 1493–1509.

NEWMAN, JOHN. Blackfriars lessee, 1581–3.

NEWTON, JOHN. Charles's, 1610, 1616, 1619, 1625.

'NICK.' Admiral's, 1601–3. See also TOOLEY.

NILL, JOHN. A 'player' whose daughter Alice was baptized at St. Saviour's on 13 August 1601 (*Bodl.*).

NORWOOD. Paul's, 1599.

NYCOWLLES, ROBERT. A 'player' who witnessed a loan to Francis Henslowe on 1 June 1595 (H. i. 6).

OFFLEY, THOMAS. Paul's, *c.* 1522.

OSTLER, WILLIAM, began his career as a boy actor in the Chapel company. He took a part in Jonson's *Poetaster* in 1601. From the *Sharers Papers* we learn that on growing up he was, like Field and Underwood, 'taken to strengthen the King's service'.[1] He first appears amongst the King's men in the cast of Jonson's *The Alchemist* in 1610, and played also in *Catiline, The Captain, The Duchess of Malfi,* in which he took the part of Antonio, *Valentinian,* and *Bonduca.* The following epigram in John Davies, *Scourge of Folly* (*c.* 1611), attests his fame and his participation in some forgotten brawl:

> *To the Roscius of these Times, Mr. W. Ostler.*
>
> Ostler, thou took'st a knock thou would'st have giv'n,
> Neere sent thee to thy latest home : but O !
> Where was thine action, when thy crown was riv'n,
> Sole King of Actors ! then wast idle ? No :
> Thou hadst it, for thou would'st bee doing ? Thus
> Good actors deeds are oft most dangerous ;
> But if thou plaist thy dying part as well
> As thy stage parts, thou hast no part in hell.

Ostler married Thomasine, daughter of John Heminges, in 1611. His son Beaumont was baptized at St. Mary's, Aldermanbury, on 18 May 1612.[2] He acquired shares in the Blackfriars on 20 May 1611, and the Globe on 20 February 1612, and died on 16 December 1614, leaving his shares a subject for litigation between his widow and Heminges (q.v.).

PAGE, OLIVER. A London player in 1550 (App. D, No. v).

PALLANT, ROBERT. Strange's (?), 1590–1 ; Worcester's–Anne's, 1602–19 ; Lady Elizabeth's, 1614 ; Charles's, 1616 ; King's, 1619, unless, indeed, the R. Pallant who played the female part of Cariola in *Duchess of Malfi* was of a younger generation. This is not unlikely, for while the St. Saviour's registers record the burial of Robert Pallant, 'a man,' on 4 September 1619, the token-books give the name in 1621 as well as in 1612 and 1616. Ephraim and Hanburye, sons of Robert Pallant 'player', were baptized there on 1 January 1611 and 3 July 1614 respectively. There were others earlier. Pallant wrote commendatory verses for Heywood's *Apology* (1612), and is noted as visiting Henslowe on his death-bed on 6 January 1616 (H. ii. 20, 300 ; *Bodl.*).

PANT, THOMAS. Unlicensed player, 1607–10 (cf. ch. ix, p. 304).

PARR, WILLIAM. Admiral's–Henry's–Palsgrave's, 1602–20.

PARROWE (PARLOWE), RICHARD. Interluders, 1538–45.

PARSELEY, RICHARD. A London player in 1550 (cf. App. D, No. v).

---

[1] Halliwell-Phillipps, i. 317.   [2] Collier, iii. 423.

PARSONS, THOMAS. Admiral's, 1597, 1602 (H. ii. 301).

PATESON, WILLIAM. Worcester's, 1584.

PAVY. Admiral's, 1602.

PAVY, SALATHIEL (SALMON). Chapel, 1600–3. An epitaph on him is in Jonson's *Epigrams* (1616), cxx, which gives his age at death, after three years of playing, as 13. He was ' apprentice to one Peerce ', when he was pressed for the Chapel. This is not likely to have been the Master of Paul's, from whom it would have been rash to take a boy.

PAYNE, ROBERT. Revels patentee, 1604.

PEACOCKE, ROBERT. A London player in 1550 (cf. App. D, No. v).

PEARCE (PIERS), EDWARD. Gentleman of Chapel, 1589 ; Master of Paul's, 1600.

PEDEL, ABRAHAM. Germany, 1614–15 ; Palsgrave's, 1623. He lived at George Alley in Golden Lane in 1623 (J. 348, 350).

PEDEL (BEHEL, BIEL), JACOB. Germany, 1597, 1614–15.

PEDEL, WILLIAM. Holland, 1608 ; Germany, 1614–15. Children of a William Peadle, variously described as ' tumbler ' and ' gentleman ', were baptized at St. Saviour's, Southwark, in 1610, 1617, and 1629 (*Bodl.*).

PENN, WILLIAM. Revels, 1609 ; Charles's, 1616, 1625. He lived at George Alley, Golden Lane, in 1623 and had children baptized and buried at St. Giles's, Cripplegate, in 1636 (J. 347 ; *Bodl.*).

PENTON, FABIAN. Germany, 1602.

PEPEREL, GILES. Possibly an actor in the *Bugbears* of John Jeffere (cf. ch. xxiii).

PERKIN, JOHN. Leicester's, 1572–4. Is he the Parkins who assisted George Ferrers as Lord of Misrule in 1552–3 (Feuillerat, *Edw. and Mary*, 120) ?

PERKINS, RICHARD. Worcester's–Anne's, 1602–19 ; for his later history, cf. Murray, i. 198, 200, 266. He wrote commendatory verses for Heywood's *Apology* (1612), and Webster praises his acting in *The White Devil* (1612) in a note at the end of the print. His portrait is at Dulwich. He lived at the upper end of St. John's Street in 1623 (H. ii. 301 ; J. 347).

PERRY, WILLIAM. Licensee for 2 King's Revels, 1615 ; Queen's Revels manager, 1617.

PERSJ (PERSTEN), ROBERT (RUPERT). Denmark–Germany, 1586–7.

PERSONN, JOHANN. Denmark, 1579–80.

PERY, ROBERT. Chapel, 1529–31.

PERY, WILLIAM. Chapel, 1530.

' PETER ' (?). King's. At *Taming of the Shrew*, iv. 4. 68, F₁ has the s.d. ' Enter Peter ', apparently a servant of Tranio, who does not speak.

PFLUGBEIL, AUGUST. Germany, 1614–15.

PHILIP, ROBERT. Chapel, 1514.

PHILLIPPE, ROBERT. A ' momer ', buried at St. Leonard's, on 9 April 1559 (Collier, *Actors*, 79). He might be identical with the foregoing.

PHILLIPS, AUGUSTINE, is included in the 1593 list of Strange's men, and played for them or the Admiral's in 2 *Seven Deadly Sins* about 1590–1 as 'Mr. Phillipps'. Probably he joined the Chamberlain's men on their formation in 1594. He appears in the actor-lists of 1598 and 1599, was one of the original Globe shareholders of 1599, and on 18 February 1601 gave evidence as to the performance of *Richard II* by the company before the Essex rising. He is also in the official lists of the King's men in 1603 and 1604, in the actor-list of *Sejanus* in 1603, and in that of the First Folio of Shakespeare's plays. 'Phillips his gygg of the slyppers' was entered in the Stationers' Register on 26 May 1595 (cf. p. 552). It has been conjectured that Phillips was a brother-in-law of Alleyn, to whom Henslowe wrote on 28 September 1593, ' Your sister Phillipes & her husband hath leced two or thre owt of ther howsse, yt they in good health & doth hartily comend them unto you.' If so, his wife was probably Elizabeth Woodward. But it is also possible that the family in question was that of one Edward Phillipes, who was also in relations with Henslowe and Alleyn.[1] An Augustine Phillipps buried at St. Saviour's, Southwark, in 1592, was probably a relative of the actor, whose children the register of the same parish records as Magdalen (bapt. 29 September 1594), Rebecca (bapt. 11 July 1596), and Austen or Augustine (bapt. 29 November 1601, bur. 1 July 1604). The father is designated *histrio*, ' player,' or ' player of interludes '. The parish token-books show that he dwelt in Horse-shoe Court during 1593 and 1595, thereafter near the Swan in Paris Garden, in Montagu Close during 1601, in ' Bradshaw's Rents ' during 1602, and in Horse-shoe Court again during 1604.[2] But by 4 May 1605, when he made his will, he was of Mortlake, Surrey, where he had a house and land of which he had lately purchased the lease.[3] Doubtless he had prospered. A note of heraldic irregularities delivered by William Smith, Rouge dragon, to the Earl of Northampton as commissioner for the Earl Marshal states that ' Phillipps the player had graven in a gold ring the armes of Sr Wm Phillipp, Lord Bardolph, with the said L. Bardolph's cote quartred, which I shewed to M^r. York at a small gravers shopp in Foster Lane '.[4] The will mentions Phillips's wife, whose name was not Elizabeth but Anne, his daughters Magdalen, Rebecca, Anne, and Elizabeth, his mother Agnes Bennett, his brothers William and James Webb, his sister Margery Borne, and her sons Miles and Philipps, and his sister Elizabeth Gough. Elizabeth had been married at St. Saviour's in 1603, to Robert Gough (q.v.) of the King's men, who witnesses the will.[5] Margery Borne may have been the wife of William Borne *alias*

[1] Henslowe, ii. 302 ; *Henslowe Papers*, 36, 41.
[2] Collier, iii. 322, 325 ; Rendle, *Bankside*, xxv.
[3] *Variorum*, iii. 470.
[4] S. Lee in *Nineteenth Century* for May 1906, quoting a manuscript by Smith in private hands, with the title *A Brief Discourse of ye causes of Discord amongst ye Officers of arms and of the great abuses and absurdities comitted by painters to the great prejudice and hindrance of the same office.* Northampton did not get his title until 1604.   [5] Collier, iii. 323.

Bird (q.v.) of the Prince's men. Presumably the Webbs were his brothers-in-law, in which case his wife was obviously not a Woodward. There are legacies of £5 to ' the hyred men of the company which I am of ', of 30s. pieces to his ' fellows ' William Shakespeare and Henry Condell, and his ' servant ' Christopher Beeston, of 20s. pieces to his ' fellows ' Laurence Fletcher, Robert Armin, Richard Cowley, Alexander Cook and Nicholas Tooley, of silver bowls to John Hemings, Richard Burbadge, and William Sly, and of £20 to Timothy Whithorne. Samuel Gilburne, ' my late apprentice ' is to have 40s. and ' my mouse colloured velvit hose and a white taffety dublet, a blacke taffety sute, my purple cloke, sword, and dagger, and my base viall '.   James Sands ' my apprentice ' is to have 40s. and ' a citterne, a bandore and a lute '.   The widow is appointed executrix, but if she re-marries she is to have ' no parte or porcion of my goods or chattells ', and is to be replaced by the overseers of the will, Hemings, Richard Burbadge, Sly, and Whithorne.   After proving the will on 13 May 1605, the widow did in fact re-marry, with John Witter, and it was proved again by John Hemings on 16 May 1607.   His share in the Globe was subsequently the subject of litigation.[1]   Heywood (c. 1608) praises his deserts with those of other dead actors.

PICKERING, JAMES. Mason of Bowlby, Yorks, unlicensed player, 1612 (cf. ch. ix, p. 305).

PLUMMER, JOHN. Master of Chapel, 1444–55.

POKELEY, RICHARD. A London player in 1550 (cf. App. D, No. v).

POLE. Gate-keeper at Paul's, 1582.

POPE, THOMAS, was one of the English players, who visited Denmark and Germany in 1586 and 1587. He is in the 1593 list of Strange's men and played as ' Mr. Pope ' for them or the Admiral's in 2 Deadly Sins about 1590–1. He joined the Chamberlain's men, probably on their foundation in 1594, was joint payee for them with Heminge from 1597–9, and appears in the actor-lists of 1598 and 1599. On 30 August 1598, William Bird borrowed 10s. of Henslowe, ' to folowe the sewt agenst Thomas Poope '.[2] In 1600 he is mentioned, with Singer of the Admiral's, by Samuel Rowlands in The Letting of Humour's Blood in the Head-Vein, sat. iv :

> What meanes Singer then,
> And Pope, the clowne, to speak so boorish, when
> They counterfaite the clownes upon the Stage ?

He had an original fifth share of a moiety of the Globe, increased to a fourth on the retirement of Kempe. But he does not appear in the lists of the King's men, and had therefore probably retired by 1603. On 22 July of that year he made his will, which was proved on 13 February 1604.[3] He leaves his interests in the Globe and Curtain to Mary Clark, alias Wood, and Thomas Bromley, and legacies to Robert Gough and John Edmans. He mentions the house in South-

---

[1] N. U. S. x. 308, 312 ; cf. ch. xvi (Globe).
[2] Henslowe, i. 72.   [3] Variorum, iii. 506 ; Collier, iii. 363.

wark, in which he dwelt, held with other tenements of the late Francis Langley; also his brothers John and William Pope, and his mother Agnes Webbe. This hardly justifies Collier in connecting him with the Webbes of Snitterfield, Shakespeare's kin. Bazell Nicholl, scrivener, and John Wrench, are left executors. As in 1612 a sixth of the Globe was in the hands of Basil Nicoll and John and Mary Edmonds, it is probable that John Edmonds married Mary Clark. It appears from the Southwark token-books that one Pope lived in Blamer's Rents during 1593, in Wrench's Rents during 1595, and in Mr. Langley's New Rents during 1596, 1598, 1600, and 1602.[1] Dr. Greg thinks that Thomas Pope, rather than a Morgan Pope who also had interests in Southwark, was the 'Mr. Pope' with whom Henslowe had an interview on 25 June 1603, 'at the scryveners shope wher he lisse', concerning the renewal of the lease of the Rose.[2] But Thomas Pope clearly lived in his own house. Collier (*Actors*, xxxvi) gives a marriage of a Thomas Pope and Elizabeth Baly at St. Botolph's on 20 December 1584, but the indications of the will do not suggest a married man. William Smith complains that 'Pope the player would have no other armes but the armes of Sir Thomas Pope, Chancelor of ye Augmentations'.[3] Heywood mentions the 'deserts' of Pope in his *Apology*. He is included in the actor-list of the First Folio Shakespeare.

POWLTON, THOMAS. Worcester's, 1584.

PRICE, JOHN. Musician in Germany, 1609.

PRICE (PRYOR?), RICHARD. Admiral's–Henry's–Palsgrave's, 1600 (?), 1610, 1613, 1622. He lived in White Cross Street in 1623, and records of his children are in the registers of St. Giles, Cripplegate, from 1620 to 1627, where he is variously entered as 'gentleman', 'yeoman', and 'player' (J. 348; Bodl.).

PROCTOR. Admiral's, 1599.

PRUN, PETER DE. Germany, 1594. He was of Brussels.

PUDSEY, EDWARD. Germany, 1626. He was presumably the owner of the manuscript note-book from which extracts are given in R. Savage, *Stratford upon Avon Notebooks* (1888), i; cf. ch. xxiii, s.v. Chapman, *Blind Beggar of Alexandria*.

PULHAM, GEORGE. Anne's, 1612.

PYE, JOHN. A 'momer', whose son Samuel was baptized at St. Leonard's, Shoreditch, on 28 May 1559 (*Bodl.*).

PYK (PIK, PYGE, PIGGE), JOHN. Strange's, 1593; Admiral's, 1597–9 (H. ii. 303).

PYKMAN, PHILIP. Chapel, 1600–1.

RADSTONE, JOHN. A London player in 1550 (cf. App. D, No. v).

RASTALL, WILLIAM. Chapel manager, 1602. He died in 1608.

RAWLYNS, JOHN. A London player in 1550 (cf. App. D, No. v).

READE, EMANUEL. Lady Elizabeth's, 1613; Anne's, 1613 (?)–17.

READING, WILLIAM. Interluders, 1559–63 (cf. App. D, No. v).

REASON, GILBERT. Charles's, 1610, 1616, 1625.

[1] Collier, iii. 358; Rendle, *Bankside*, xxvi.
[2] Henslowe, i. 178; ii. 303.   [3] Cf. s.v. Phillips.

REDFORD, JOHN. Master of Paul's, *c.* 1540, and dramatist (cf. *Mediaeval Stage*, ii. 454).

REEVE, RALPH. Germany, 1603–9; Revels manager (provincial), 1611; Porter's Hall patentee, 1615.

REYNOLDS, ROBERT. Anne's, 1616–17; Germany, 1616, 1618–20, 1626. He was known in Germany by the clown-name Pickleherring. He and his wife Jane were indicted for non-attendance at church in 1616 and 1617 (Jeaffreson, ii. 120, 127).

RICE, JOHN, was 'boy' to Heminges when he delivered a speech in Merchant Taylors' hall on 16 July 1607, and must have been still with the King's men when he took part as Corinea with Burbadge in the water-pageant of 31 May 1610. He became one of the original Lady Elizabeth's men in 1611, and seems to have joined the King's men again in 1619. The Southwark token-books indicate a John Rice as a resident in 1615, 1619, 1621, and 1623, with an 'uxor' in 1621, and another record names John Rice 'of the Bankside' amongst players in 1623.[1] He is not in the official list of May of that year, but played in *Sir John van Olden Barnavelt* about August, and is in the official list of 1621. He is traceable up to the list of 1625, but is not in that of 1629. It is not improbable that he retired, and went into Orders, for Heminges, in his will of 1630, leaves 20s. to 'John Rice, clerk, of St. Saviour's in Southwark', and also names 'Mr. Rice' as overseer. Rice is in the actor-list of the First Folio Shakespeare.

'ROBIN.' Chapel, 1518.

ROBINS (ROBINSON), WILLIAM. Anne's, 1616–19. He lived on Clerkenwell Hill in 1623 (J. 348).

ROBINSON, JAMES. Chapel manager, 1600.

ROBINSON, RICHARD, first appears in the *Catiline* actor-list of the King's men in 1611, and as playing the Lady in a stage direction (l. 1929) to *The Second Maiden's Tragedy* of the same year. In *The Devil is an Ass* (1616), ii. 8. 64, Merecroft describes 'Dicke Robinson' as a lad, and as masquerading 'drest like a lawyer's wife'. I think it not impossible that he was a son of James Robinson, who was a member of the Children of the Chapel syndicate in 1600. If so, he may have been a Blackfriars boy. He played in *Bonduca* (*c.* 1613), is in the 1619 patent to the King's men, and in the actor-list of the First Folio Shakespeare, and is traceable as a King's man up to the Beaumont and Fletcher Folio of 1647. He may have married Richard Burbadge's widow, who held shares in the Globe and Blackfriars as Mrs. Robinson in 1635. He owed Tooley £29 13s. when the latter made his will in 1623. According to Wright he was a comedian. The same author states that he took up arms for the King, and was killed by Major Harrison at the taking of Basing House, on 14 October 1645. A contemporary report of this event by Hugh Peters confirms the death of 'Robinson, the player, who, a little before the storm, was known to be mocking and scorning the Parliament'. There were, however, other actors named Robinson, and probably this was one of them. If

[1] Collier, iii. 488; J. 348; *Bodl.*

Richard had been killed in 1645, he could not have signed the dedication of the Beaumont and Fletcher plays in 1647. Moreover, the
register of St. Anne's, Blackfriars, records the burial of ' Richard
Robinson, a player ' on 23 March 1648.[1] He seems to have lived at
the upper end of Shoreditch in 1623 (J. 347).

ROBINSON, THOMAS. Germany, 1626.

ROLL (ROE), JOHN. Interluders, 1530. He died in 1539.

RONNER, JOHN. A London player in 1550 (cf. App. D, No. v).

ROSE. Henry's, 1612, where his wife became (?) a gatherer (H. P. 63).

ROSSETER, PHILIP. Whitefriars lessee, 1609–15 ; Revels patentee,
1610 ; Porter's Hall patentee, 1615 ; Revels manager, 1617. He was
one of the royal lutenists from Midsummer 1604 to Easter 1623, and
published A Booke of Ayres (1601) with Campion, who left him his property in 1620. He died on 5 May 1623 (D. N. B. ; Chamber Accounts).

ROSSILL. Chamberlain's, 1597.

ROWLEY, SAMUEL. Admiral's–Henry's–Palsgrave's, 1597–1624 (?),
and dramatist (cf. ch. xxiii ; H. ii. 307).

ROWLEY, THOMAS. Admiral's, 1602.

ROWLEY, WILLIAM. Charles's, 1610–19 ; King's, 1623–5. But
he remained technically a Prince's man until the death of James in
1625 (Murray, i. 162, 172, table).

RUSSELL, JOHN. Gatherer for Palsgrave's, c. 1617 (H. P. 28, 29, 85).

RUTTER, WILLIAM. Interluders, 1503.

SACKVILLE, THOMAS. Germany, 1592–3, 1597–1602. He used
the clown-name Johannes Bouset, was a merchant in Frankfort,
1604–17, and died in 1628.

' SAM.' Admiral's, >1591.

SANDERSON, GREGORY. Anne's, 1617–19.

SANDS, JAMES. King's, 1605 ; Anne's, c. 1617 ? He received
legacies from Augustine Phillips (q. v.), to whom he was apprentice, in
1605 and from William Sly (q. v.) in 1608. A James Sands appears in
the Southwark token-books in 1596, 1598, and 1612 (Bodl.).

SANDT, BERNHARDT. Germany, 1600–1.

SAUNDERS, WILLIAM. Chapel, >1517.

SAUSS, EVERHART. Netherlands, 1592.

SAVAGE, JEROME. Warwick's, 1575–9.

SAVEREY, ABRAHAM. Lennox's, 1605.

SCHADLEUTNER, SEBASTIAN. Germany, 1623.

SCARLETT, JOHN. A ' player ' whose son Richard was baptized at
St. Giles's on 1 September, and buried on 19 September 1605 (Bodl.).

SCARLETT, RICHARD. A ' player ', buried on 23 April 1609 at
St. Giles's, where his daughter Susan had been baptized on 11 Febru-
ary 1607 and his wife Marie buried on 12 February 1607. Several
Scarletts were royal trumpeters—Edward, William, and William the
younger in 1483, John in 1509, Arthur in 1559–1603, John in 1677–9
(Bodl. ; Chamber Accounts ; Lafontaine, i, 3, 325, 341).

---

[1] Variorum, iii. 514 ; P. Cunningham in Sh. Soc. Papers, ii. 11 ; Collier,
iii. 478.

SCOTT, JOHN. Interluders, 1503-28.

SEBECK, HENRY. Lady Elizabeth's, 1617.

SEHAIS, JEHAN. France, 1598. Possibly the John Shaa, who witnessed an Admiral's payment to Dekker, 24 November 1599 (H. i. 114). ' John' appears for ' Robert ' Shaw, probably by an error, in a play warrant of 1600 as given in the P. C. Acts (cf. App. B).

SHAKESPEARE, EDMOND. The burials at St. Saviour's include, on 31 December 1607, ' Edmond Shakespeare, a player : in the church,' which is expanded in a fee-book as ' Edmund Shakespeare, a player, buried in the church, with a forenoone knell of the great bell, 20s. (Collier, *Actors*, xiv). Presumably this is the brother of William.

SHAKESPEARE, EDWARD. The baptisms at St. Giles's include, on 12 August 1607, ' Edward, sonne of Edward Schackspeere, Player : base borne ' (Collier, *Actors*, xv ; J. Hunter in *Addl. MS.* 24589, f. 24).

SHAKESPEARE, WILLIAM. Strange's, 1592 ; Pembroke's (?), 1593 ; Sussex's (?), 1594 ; Chamberlain's–King's, 1594-1616 ; and dramatist.

SHAKSHAFTE, WILLIAM. Player (?) to Alexander Houghton, 1581 (cf. ch. ix, p. 280).

SHANBROOKE, JOHN. A ' player ' buried on 17 Sept. 1618 at St. Giles's, where his children appear in the registers from 10 June 1610 to 4 June 1618 (*Bodl.*).

SHANK, JOHN, or SHANKS, for the name is variously spelt, describes himself to Lord Chamberlain Pembroke in the *Sharers Papers* of 1635 as ' beeing an old man in this quality, who in his youth first served your noble father, and after that the late Queene Elizabeth, then King James, and now his royall Majestye '.[1] Presumably the Pembroke's company in question was that of 1597-1600, and the Queen Elizabeth's men the travelling company of the latter years of the reign. Shank's account of his own career may be amplified from the records of his name in the 1610 list of Prince Henry's men and in the patent issued to the same company when they became the Elector Palatine's men in 1613. He lived in Rochester Yard, Southwark, in 1605, but the register of St. Giles's, Cripplegate, shows him later in Golden Lane, and records several baptisms and burials of his children between 1610 and 1629.[2] He had joined the King's men between 1613 and 1619, as his name is in the patent of the latter year. It recurs in the official lists of the company up to 1629, but occasionally only in actor-lists up to 1631, including that of the First Folio Shakespeare. Amongst his ' boyes ' or apprentices were Thomas Pollard, John Thompson, John Honiman, and Thomas Holcome. Thompson cost him £40 ; for other boys he had spent by 1635 as much as £200. After the death of John Heminges, Shank bought from his son William, surreptitiously, as his fellows averred, two shares in the Blackfriars and three in the Globe, for a total sum of £506. It was these transactions, which took place between 1633 and 1635, that led to the petition of Benfield, Swanston, and Pollard to the Lord Chamberlain recorded in the *Sharers Papers*.

---

[1] Halliwell-Phillipps, i. 314.
[2] Collier, iii. 482 ; Rendle, *Bankside*, xxvi.

As a result Shank was directed to transfer one share in each house to the petitioners. He, however, complained that he could not get satisfactory terms from them, and that they restrained him from the stage. The Cripplegate register records Shank's burial on 27 January 1636.[1] James Wright calls him a ' comedian ',[2] and the following verses, signed W. Turner, and quoted by Collier from Turner's *Dish of Stuff, or a Gallimaufry*, may perhaps be taken as confirming this [3] :

> That 's the fat fool of the Curtain,
>   And the lean fool of the Bull :
> Since Shancke did leave to sing his rhimes,
>   He is counted but a gull :
> The players on the Bankside,
>   The round Globe and the Swan,
> Will teach you idle tricks of love,
>   But the Bull will play the man.

The verses are dated 1662, but the theatres named indicate a much earlier date.

SHAW (SHAA, autograph), ROBERT.   Chamberlain's (?), 1597 ; Pembroke's, 1597 ; Admiral's, 1597–1602. John, son of Robert Shaw, ' player ', was baptized on 10 April 1603, at St. Saviour's, and Robert Shaw, ' a man ', buried on 12 September 1603 (H. ii. 309 ; *Bodl.*).

SHEALDEN.   A ' player ', who witnessed a loan for Henslowe on 24 August 1594 (H. i. 76).

SHEPARD.   Paul's door-keeper, 1582.

SHEPPARD, WILLIAM.   A ' player ', whose son Robert by his wife Johane was baptized at St. Helen's, 26 November 1602.

SIBTHORPE, EDWARD.   Whitefriars lessee, 1608.

SIMPSON, CHRISTOPHER.   Shoemaker of Egton, Yorks, recusant and unlicensed player in 1610–12 (cf. ch. ix, p. 305).

SIMPSON, CUTHBERT.   Of Egton, recusant and unlicensed player, 1616 (*ibid.*).

SIMPSON, JOHN.   Of Egton, recusant and unlicensed player, 1616 (*ibid.*).

SIMPSON, RICHARD.   Of Egton, recusant and unlicensed player, 1616 (*ibid.*).

SIMPSON, ROBERT.   Shoemaker of Staythes, Yorks, recusant and unlicensed player, 1612, 1616 (*ibid.*).

SINCLER (SINKLO, SINCKLO), JOHN.   Strange's (?), 1590–1 ; Pembroke's (?), 1592–3 ; Chamberlain's, 1594 (?)–1604.

SINGER, JOHN.   Queen's, 1583, 1588 ; Admiral's, 1594–1603. He became an ordinary Groom of the Chamber in 1603. A John Singer in 1571 owed money to a Canterbury citizen, who had also debts from players (H. R. Plomer in *3 Library*, ix. 253). Children of John Singer, ' player ', appear in the St. Saviour's register from 1 August 1597 to 5 October 1609, and his name is in the token-books from 1596 to 1602 (*Bodl.*). The *Quips upon Questions* (1600) of Armin (q.v.) has been ascribed to Singer in error. Rowlands couples him as a clown with Pope (q.v.) in 1600, and Dekker, *Gull's Horn Book*

---

[1] Collier, iii. 483.   [2] App. I (ii).   [3] Collier, iii. 481.

(1609), says, ' Tarlton, Kemp, nor Singer, nor all the litter of fooles that now come drawling behind them, never played the clowns more naturally than the arrantest sot of you all shall '. Heywood praised him as dead in the same year (H. ii. 310).

SKINNER, RICHARD. Interluders, 1547–58.

SLATER (SLAUGHTER), MARTIN. Admiral's, 1594–7 ; Scotland, 1599 ; Hertford's, 1603 ; Anne's, 1606 ; King's Revels manager, 1608 ; Chamber of Bristol, 1618–19. He is sometimes recorded by his Christian name only. He had a wife on 22 July 1604, and is described as a citizen and ironmonger in 1608. His name is in the Southwark token-books from 1595 to 1602, and Martin Slawter, ' a servant ', was buried there on 4 August 1625 (H. ii. 310 ; Bodl.).

SLAUGHTER, WILLIAM. ' Ghost-name ' evolved by Mr. Fleay for a supposed Queen's man.

SLEE (SLYE), JOHN. Queen Jane's, >1537 ; Interluders, 1539–40.

SLY, WILLIAM, was doubtless of Strange's men or the Admiral's about 1590–1, when he played in 2 Seven Deadly Sins. On 11 October 1594 Henslowe sold him ' a jewell of gowld seat with a whitte safer ' for 8s. to be paid for at the rate of 1s. weekly.[1] But apparently he never paid more than 6s. 6d. An inventory of garments belonging to the Admiral's men on 13 March 1598 includes ' Perowes sewt, which Wm Sley were '.[2] Presumably this had come from Strange's men, as Sly is never traceable as a member of the Admiral's company. Probably he joined the Chamberlain's men on their formation in 1594. He is in all the lists of this company from 1598 to 1605, and in the Induction to The Malcontent (1604). He is also in the actor-list of the First Folio Shakespeare. The fact that ' Christopher Sly, old Sly's son of Burton Heath ' is the name given to the beggar in The Taming of the Shrew (c. 1594), led Collier to suggest that he migrated from Warwickshire about the same time as Shakespeare. But the beggar in A Shrew is already Sly, and the name occurs in various parts of London. The Southwark token-books show a William Sly in Norman's Rents during 1588, in Horseshoe Court during 1593, and in Rose Alley during 1595 and 1596.[3] In 1605 he was named as one of the overseers and residuary executors, with a legacy, in the will of Augustine Phillips. The register of St. Giles's, Cripplegate, records the baptism on 24 September and the burial on 4 October 1606 of John, base-born son of William Sly, player, by Margaret Chambers ; and the register of St. Leonard's, Shoreditch, records his own burial on 16 August 1608, from Halliwell Street. His nuncupative will was made on 4 August 1608. He left legacies to Cuthbert Burbadge, and James Sandes, and the rest of his property to Robert and Cecily Browne and their daughter Jane. Robert is to have his part of the Globe, and Cecily is appointed executrix. The will was witnessed by several illiterate women, and disputed by a relative named William Sly, but proved on 24 August.[4] He was not one of the original shareholders in the Globe, but was admitted to a share in 1605 or later. On 9 August 1608, between the date of his will and that of his death, he was granted a lease of a seventh share in the Blackfriars, and this his executrix afterwards surrendered to Richard Burbadge.[1] Heywood names Sly (*c.* 1608) amongst other dead players, whose ' deserts ' he commemorates.

SMITH, ANTONY. Charles's, 1616, 1625.

SMITH, JOHN. Interluders, *c.* 1547–80. Is he the John Smith who assisted George Ferrers as Lord of Misrule in 1552–3 (Feuillerat, *Edw. and Mary*, 120) ?

SMITH, JOHN. Revels, 1609.

SMYGHT, WILLIAM. A ' player ' who witnessed a loan from Philip to Francis Henslowe on 1 June 1595 (H. i. 6 ; ii. 312).

SOMERSET, GEORGE. Admiral's, 1601–2. See also JOHN WILSON.

SOUTHEY, THOMAS. Interluders, 1547–56.

SOUTHYN, ROBERT. A London player in 1550 (cf. App. D, No. v).

SPENCER, GABRIEL. Chamberlain's (?), 1597 ; Pembroke's, 1597 ; Admiral's, 1598. He was slain by Ben Jonson (cf. ch. xxiii) on 22 September 1598, and was buried on the next day but one at St. Leonard's, where the register records him as from Hogge Lane (Collier, *Actors*, xxii). On 3 December 1596 a coroner's inquest found that he had himself slain James Feake with a rapier in the house of Richard East, barber, in St. Leonard's (Jeaffreson, i. xlv, 234). Henslowe sometimes describes him merely as ' Gabriel ', and under this name Heywood praises him (H. ii. 312).

SPENCER, JOHN. Germany, 1605–23. He was known by the clown-name of Hans Stockfisch.

SQUIRE, LAWRENCE. Master of Chapel, 1486–93.

STEVENS, THOMAS. Denmark–Germany, 1586–7.

STOKEDALE, EDMUND. A London player in 1550 (cf. App. D, No. v).

STRATFORD, WILLIAM. Henry's–Palsgrave's, 1610–23. He lived at the upper end of White Cross Street in 1623. His children appear in the St. Giles's register in that year, and he was buried as a ' player ' there on 27 August 1625 (J. 348, 350 ; *Bodl.*).

STROWDEWIKE, EDMUND. Interluders, 1559–68.

SUDBURY, THOMAS. Interluders, 1530.

SUTTON, ROBERT. A London player in 1550 (cf. App. D, No. v).

SWANSTON, ELIARD. Lady Elizabeth's, 1622; King's, 1624–42 (Murray, i. 172, 255).

SWINNERTON (SWETHERTON), THOMAS. Anne's, 1604–19 ; for his later career cf. Murray, ii. 101, 105.

SYFERWESTE, RICHARD. Worcester's (?), 1602 (H. ii. 314).

SYMCOCKES. Lennox's, 1605.

SYMONS, JOHN. A tumbler. Strange's, 1583 ; Oxford's, 1585 ; Strange's, 1586–8 (?) ; Queen's, 1588 (?)–9.

TAILOR, ROBERT. Admiral's, 1601–2.

---

[1] *N. U. S.* x. 317 ; *O. v. H.* 32.

TARBUCK, JOHN. Revels patentee, 1610.

TARLTON, RICHARD, first appears in the ' Q^d Richard Tarlton ' at the end of a ballad called *A very lamentable and wofull discours of the fierce fluds . . . the 5. of October, 1570* (Arber, i. 440).[1] This is preserved (Halliwell, 126 ; Collier, *Old Ballads,* 78 ; H. L. Collman, *Ballads and Broadsides,* 265). The Stationers' Registers also record in 1576 ' a newe booke in Englishe verse intituled Tarltons Toyes ' (Arber, ii. 306), in 1578 ' Tarltons Tragical Treatises conteyninge sundrie discources and pretie conceiptes bothe in prose and verse ' (Arber, ii. 323), and in 1579 ' Tarltons devise upon this unlooked for great snowe ' (Arber, ii. 346) ; but these are all lost. *Tarltons Jigge of a horse loade of Fooles* (Halliwell, xx) should, if it is genuine, date from about 1579, as the jest at the Puritan fool ' Goose son ' is obviously aimed at Stephen Gosson ; but it reads to me like a fake, and Halliwell took it from a manuscript belonging to Collier, who had already quoted it in his tainted *New Facts,* 18. It is improbable that Richard is the ' one Tarlton ' whose house in Paris Garden is included in a list of suspected papist resorts sent by Richard Frith to Alderman Martin at some date not earlier than 1585 (Wright, *Eliz.* ii. 250). The first mention of him is by Gabriel Harvey (cf. p. 4) in 1579, when he had already acquired some reputation. He became an original member of the Queen's men (q. v.) in 1583, and remained their principal comedian until his death in 1588. For this company he wrote *The Seven Deadly Sins* (q. v.) in 1585. Music for some of his jigs is in existence (Halliwell, *Cambridge Manuscript Rarities,* 8) and his facility as a jester made him, until he pushed it too far, a *persona grata* in Elizabeth's presence. Bohun, 352, says that the Queen admitted ' Tarleton, a famous comedian, and a pleasant talker, and other such like men, to divert her with stories of the town and the common jests or accidents, but so that they kept within the bounds of modesty and chastity '. He adds, ' Tarleton, who was then the best comedian in England, had made a pleasant play, and when it was acting before the Queen, he pointed at Sir Walter Raleigh and said " See, the Knave commands the Queen ", for which he was corrected by a frown from the Queen ; yet he had the confidence to add that he was of too much and too intolerable a power ; and going on with the same liberty, he reflected on the overgreat power and riches of the Earl of Leicester, which was so universally applauded by all that were present, that she thought best to bear these reflections with a seeming unconcernedness. But yet she was so offended, that she forbad Tarleton and all her jesters from coming near her table, being inwardly displeased with this impudent and unseasonable liberty.' An anecdote of Tarlton ' playing the God Luz with a flitch of bacon at his back ', fighting the Queen's little dog Perrico de Faldes with sword and long staff, and exchanging chaff with the Earl of Sussex (Halliwell, *Death-bed,* 30, from *S. P. Dom. Eliz.* ccxv, 89) might have some point

---

[1] J. O. Halliwell, *Tarlton's Jests . . . With . . . some Account of the Life of Tarlton* (1844, *Sh. Soc.* ; the Jests are reprinted with a few additions in Hazlitt, *Jest-Books,* ii. 189) and *Papers respecting Disputes which arose from Incidents at the Death-bed of Richard Tarlton, the Actor* (1866).

if Luz was a take-off of Leicester. On 27 October 1587 Tarlton was
allowed as a Master of Fence, and is described as an ' ordenary grome
off her majestes chamber ' (*Sloane MS.* 2530, f. 6). The same description recurs in his will, which was signed on 3 September 1588, the
actual day of his burial at St. Leonard's, Shoreditch, from Halliwell
Street. He left his property to his son Philip, as whose guardians he
appointed his mother Katharine, then a widow, his friend Robert
Adams, and his fellow of the Queen's men, William Johnson. One of
the witnesses, Charles Barnard, was his sister's husband. This will
was disputed by Katharine Tarlton, who brought a bill in Chancery,
alleging that after signing it and making over property worth £700 to
Adams, Tarlton repented, tried in vain to recall the will, and made
another. A rejoinder by Adams accuses Katharine of acting under
the influence of another son-in-law, Thomas Lee, a butcher, and
describes how Adams was called to Tarlton's death-bed in the house
of one Emma Ball in Shoreditch, ' of a very bad reputacion '. Some
colour is given to his mother's complaint by a death-bed petition from
Tarlton to Walsingham, begging his protection for Philip, who was
Sidney's godson, against 'a sly fellow, on Addames' (*S. P. Dom. Eliz.*
ccxv. 90). There is no mention of Tarlton's wife; the boy was six years
old. Robert Adams was apparently a lawyer, and to be distinguished
from John Adams of the Queen's men, who is referred to as a fellow
of Tarlton's by the stage keeper in *Bartholomew Fair* (Induction 38),
' I kept the Stage in Master *Tarletons* time, I thanke my starres. Ho !
and that man had liu'd to haue play'd in *Bartholmew Fayre,* you should
ha' seene him ha' come in, and ha' beene coozened i' the Cloath-
quarter, so finely. And *Adams,* the Rogue, ha' leap'd and caper'd
vpon him, and ha' dealt his vermine about, as though they had cost
him nothing.' After Tarlton's death, several pamphlets, ascribed
to him or otherwise exploiting his popularity, came to the press ; in
1588 ' a ballad intituled Tarltons Farewell ' (Arber, ii. 500) ; in 1589
' a sorowfull newe sonnette, intituled Tarltons Recantacon uppon this
theame gyven him by a gentleman at the Bel savage without Ludgate
(nowe or ells never) beinge the laste theame he songe ' (Arber, ii. 526) ;
in 1589 ' Tarltons repentance of his farewell to his frendes in his
sicknes a little before his deathe ' (Arber, ii. 531) ; in 1590 ' a pleasant
dyttye dialogue wise betwene Tarltons ghost and Robyn Good Fellowe '
(Arber, ii. 559). These are lost, unless, indeed, *Tarltons Farewell* is
identical with ' A pretie new ballad, entituled Willie and Peggie, to
the tune of Tarlton's Carroll ', printed in *Archiv.* cxiv. 341, and
A. Clark, *Shirburn Ballads,* 351, from *Rawl. Poet. MS.* 185, f. 10. This
ends ' qd. Richard Tarlton ', but it is in fact a lament over the death
of Tarlton under the name of Willie, as is clearly shown by lines 23
' None would be wery to see him one stage ', 41 ' A groome of her
chamber my Willie was made ', 55 ' To singe them their themes he
never denied '. These verses support the theory, based upon a contemporary note in a copy of Spenser (cf. *6 N. Q.* xi. 417 ; Halliwell-
Phillipps, ii. 394), that Tarlton is the ' pleasant Willy ' mourned as
dead in the *Tears of the Muses* (1591), 208, and if he is also the Yorick

of *Hamlet*, v. 1. 201, he was sufficiently honoured. Another ballad in the same manuscript on the Armada (*Archiv.* cxiv. 344 ; *Ballads from MS.* ii. 92) also claims to be to the tune of Tarlton's ' carroll ' ; the ' Carroll ' itself is unknown. *Tarltons Newes out of Purgatorie. Onelye such a jest as his Jigge, fit for Gentlemen to laugh at an houre, &c. Published by an old companion of his, Robin Goodfellow* ' (n.d., but entered in S.R. 26 June 1590 ; Arber, ii. 553) is a volume of *novelle*, put into the mouth of Tarlton's ghost. The writer describes him as only superficially seene in learning, having no more but a bare insight into the Latin tung ', and physically as ' one attired in russet, with a buttond cap on his head, a great bag by his side, and a strong bat in his hand '. Similarly, Henry Chettle, who put into his mouth a defence of plays forming a section of *Kind-hartes Dreame* (1592 ; cf. App. C, No. xlix), knew him in a dream ' by his sute of russet, his buttond cap, his taber, his standing on the toe, and other tricks '. *The Cobler of Caunterburie or an Invective against Tarltons Newes out of Purgatorie* (1590) is also a volume of *novelle*, and has practically nothing about Tarlton. On the other hand, *Tarltons Jests* at least claims to be biographical, although its material, like that of Peele's *Jests*, largely consists of the flotsam and jetsam of all the jest-books. The earliest extant edition is of 1611. But it was transferred from one publisher to another in 1609 (Arber, iii. 402), the second of its three parts, which mentions the Globe (Halliwell, 23), was entered in S. R. on 4 August 1600 (Arber, iii. 168), and probably therefore the first part was already in print in the sixteenth century. It speaks of Tarlton as a Queen's man (Halliwell, 13, 27, 29, 30, 33), as playing at the Bull in Bishopsgate (13, 24), where he did both the clown and the judge in ' Henry the Fifth ' (*The Famous Victories*) to Knell's Harry, the Curtain (16), and the Bell in Gracechurch Street (24), as singing themes (16, 27, 28, 40), and as jesting in clown's apparel in the royal presence or in the Great Chamber at Court (7, 8). It also tells us, for what the statements are worth, that his father lived at Ilford (40), that he had a wife Kate of light character (17, 19), that he kept the Saba tavern in Gracechurch Street, where he was scavenger of the ward (15, 21, 22), and an ordinary in Paternoster Row (21, 26), and that he had a squint (12) and a flat nose (28). A woodcut on the title-page confirms these peculiarities of feature, and represents a short, broad-faced, cunning-looking man, with curly hair, an elaborate moustache and a starved beard, wearing a cap, and a bag or money-box slung at his side, and playing on a tabor and a pipe. This appears to be taken from a drawing by John Scottowe in an initial letter to some verses on Tarlton's death in *Harl. MS.* 3885, f. 19. Nashe, *Pierce Penilesse* (1592, *Works*, i. 188), gives us a hint of his stage methods in describing how at a provincial performance, as the Queen's men ' were now entring into their first merriment (as they call it) the people began exceedingly to laugh, when *Tarlton* first peeped out his head ', and how a ' cholericke wise Iustice ' laid his staff about their pates, ' in that they, being but Farmers & poore countrey Hyndes, would presume to laugh at the Queenes men, and make no more account of her cloath in his presence '. According to Fuller (*Worthies*, iii. 139) Tarlton was born at Condover in Shropshire, and kept his father's swine there, until a servant of the Earl of Leicester, struck with his witty replies, brought him to Court. On the other hand, in the *Three Lords and Three Ladies of London* (1590), by his fellow Robert Wilson, Simplicity produces his picture, and says he was ' a prentice in his youth of this honorable city : . . . when he was yoong he was leaning to the trade . . . waterbearing : I wis he hath tossed a tankard in Cornehil er now ' (sign. c^v). Halliwell (xxx) has collected a large number of allusions to Tarleton and his humours, lasting well into the middle of the seventeenth century. Taverns were named after him, and one is said to have still stood in Southwark in 1798. Much of the action of W. Percy's *Cuck-Queanes and Cuckolds Errants* (q. v.) takes place at the Tarlton Inn, Colchester, of which he is said to have been the ' quondam controller and induperator '. Tarlton himself speaks the prologue to the play. George Wilson, *The Commendation of Cockes and Cock-fighting* (1607), records that on 4 May 1602 there fought at Norwich ' a cocke called Tarleton, who was so intituled, because he alwayes came to the fight like a drummer, making a thundering noyse with his winges, which cocke fought many batels with mighty and fierce adversaries '.

TAWYER, WILLIAM. At *M. N. D.* v. 1. 128, F_1 has the s. d. ' Tawyer with a Trumpet before them '. The St. Saviour's burials give in June 1625, ' William Tawier, Mr Heminges man '.

TAYLOR, JOHN. Choir Master at St. Mary's, Woolnoth, 1557; at Westminster, 1561–7.

TAYLOR, JOSEPH, is conjectured by Collier to be the Joseph Taylor who was baptized at St. Andrew's by the Wardrobe in Blackfriars on 6 February 1586, the Joseph Taylor who married Elizabeth Ingle, widow, at St. Saviour's, Southwark, on 2 May 1610, and the Joseph Taylor who is shown by the Southwark token-books as dwelling in ' Mr Langley's new rents, near the playhouse ' during 1607, in Austen's Rents during 1612 and 1615, as ' gone ' in 1617, and as dwelling ' near the playhouse ' in 1623 and 1629, ' on the Bankside' in 1631, and in Gravel Lane during 1633. ' Joseph Taylor, player,' is entered in the St. Saviour's registers as the father of Elsabeth (bapt. 12 July 1612), Dixsye and Joseph (bapt. 21 July 1614), Jone (bapt. 11 January 1616), Robert (bapt. 1 June 1617), and Anne (bapt. 24 August 1623).[1] On the other hand, a Joseph Taylor, not improbably a player, was living in Bishopsgate near the Spittle in 1623 (J. 347). He was a member of the Duke of York's company in 1610, but left them without the consent of his fellows for the Lady Elizabeth's in 1611, and thereby involved himself during the same year in a lawsuit with John Heminges.[2] He is in the actor-lists of *The Honest Man's Fortune* (1613) and of *The Coxcomb*, as played by the Lady Elizabeth's men about the same date, and is also named in the text of their *Bartholomew Fair* (1614). There seems to have been some sort of amalgamation between the

---

[1] Collier, iii. 460 ; Rendle, *Bankside*, xxvi.
[2] C. W. Wallace, *Globe Theatre Apparel* (1909).

Duke of York's, now Prince Charles's, and the Lady Elizabeth's in 1615, and when this terminated in the following year, Taylor became again a member of the Prince's company. He was still with them between 6 January and 2 February 1619, when he appeared as Dr. Almanac in Middleton and Rowley's *Mask of Heroes*, but on 19 May 1619 he appears in a livery warrant issued for the King's men. As he is not in their patent of the previous 27 March, it is to be supposed that he joined them to replace Burbadge, who had died on 13 March.[1] The rest of his stage career was spent with the King's men. He succeeded Burbadge in several of his characters, including Ferdinand in the *Duchess of Malfi* and Hamlet, although the incidence of dates must cast some doubt upon the statement of Downes that he was instructed in the part 'by the Author Mr Shakespear'.[2] Wright says that he played it 'incomparably well', and praises him also as Iago in *Othello*, Truewit in *Epicoene*, and Face in *The Alchemist*.[3] He is included in the First Folio list of performers in Shakespeare's plays. In 1623 Nicholas Tooley left him £10 to pay a debt for which Tooley had become his surety. With Lowin he seems to have assumed the leadership of the company in succession to Heminges and Condell, and after Heminges's death in 1630 he was admitted to two shares in the ' house ' of the Globe and one in that of the Blackfriars, which he still held in 1635. About 1637 he petitioned for a waiter's place in the Custom House of London,[4] and on 11 November 1639 he obtained the post of Yeoman of the Revels, probably through the influence of Sir Henry Herbert, with whom he had been in frequent contact as representative of his company.[5] After the closing of the theatres he joined his fellows of the King's men in publishing the First Folio of Beaumont and Fletcher's plays in 1647, and for his benefit and Lowin's *The Wild-goose Chase* was added in 1652. He died at Richmond and was there buried on 4 November 1652.[6] The ascription to his brush of the ' Chandos ' portrait of Shakespeare is now discredited.

THARE (THAYER), JOHN. Worcester's, 1602–3; Germany, 1603–6 (?).

TILBERY, JOHN. Chapel, 1405.

TOMSONE, JOHN. A ' player ' who borrowed 5s. from Henslowe on 22 December 1598 (H. i. 40).

TOOLEY, NICHOLAS, appears in the 1619 patent to the King's men, but not in that of 1603. He probably joined the company about 1605, as he received a legacy under the will of Phillips on 4 May as his ' fellow '. He is not in the actor-list of *Volpone* in that year, but is in most of the later actor-lists from *The Alchemist* (1610) to *The Spanish Curate* (1622), and in that of the First Folio Shakespeare. In 1619 he witnessed Richard Burbadge's will. He made his own will as Nicholas Tooley, Gentleman, on 3 June 1623. After legacies to charity, to the families of ' my good friend Mr. Cuthbert Burbadge (in whose house

[1] *M. L. Review*, iv. 395, from *Hist. MSS.* iv. 299.   [2] Downes, 21.
[3] Wright, *Hist. Hist.* 405.   [4] *S. P. D.* 1637–8, p. 99.
[5] Cunningham, l.; *Variorum*, iii. 238.
[6] Cunningham, l.; Wright, *Hist. Hist.* 411.

I do now lodge) ', of ' my late Mr. Richard Burbadge deceased ', and of ' my good friend Mr. Henry Condell ', and to Joseph Taylor, and remissions of debt to John Underwood and William Ecclestone, but not to Richard Robinson, he ends by making Burbadge and Condell his executors and residuary legatees. By a codicil of the same date, signed as Nicholas Wilkinson *alias* Tooley, he guards against any danger of invalidity due to his failure to use the name of Wilkinson.[1] Presumably, therefore, Wilkinson, and not Tooley, was his original name. The name of Tooley was fairly common in London, and more than one Nicholas Wilkinson has been traced. He may have been the Nicholas, son of Charles Wilkinson, baptized at St. Anne's, Black-friars, on 3 February 1575.[2] There seems no reason to connect him with a Nicholas Tooley found on the Warwickshire muster-book in 1569.[2] His reference to Richard Burbadge as his ' master ' suggests that he was his apprentice. It is tempting, but arbitrary, to identify him with the ' Nick ' who played with Strange's men in *2 Seven Deadly Sins* about 1592, or the ' Nycke ' who tumbled before Elizabeth for the Admiral's in 1601 and is commended by Joan to Edward Alleyn on 21 October 1603.[3] The register of St. Giles's, Cripplegate, records the burial of ' Nicholas Tooley, gentleman, from the house of Cuthbert Burbidge, gentleman ', on 5 June 1623.[4]

TOTTNELL, HARRY. A ' player ' whose daughter Joan was baptized at St. Saviour's on 20 March 1591 (*Bodl.*).

TOWNE, JOHN. Queen's, 1583, 1588, 1594-7. Greg (H. ii. 315) rather arbitrarily suggests that Henslowe's note of him as a witness to a loan to Francis Henslowe of the Queen's on 8 May 1593 (H. i. 4) is by an error for Thomas (q. v.).

TOWNE, THOMAS. Admiral's–Henry's, 1594-1610. His name is in a s. d. to *1 Honest Whore* (1604). Alleyn's papers record a widow Agnes. Towne's name is in the Southwark token-books during 1600-7, and Thomas Towne ' a man ' was buried on 9 August 1612. Towne's will of 4 July 1612 names his wife, whom he calls Ann, and his brother John, of Dunwich in Suffolk (' if he be still living ') and leaves £3 to his fellows Borne, Downton, Juby, Rowley, Massey, and Humphrey Jeffes, ' to make them a supper when it shall please them to call for it ' (H. ii. 316 ; *Bodl.*, citing will in P. C. C.).

TOWNSEND, JOHN. Lady Elizabeth's, 1611, 1616-32 (?) ; for his later career, cf. Murray, i. 252-60 ; ii. 8.

TOY. The performer of Will Summer in *Summer's Last Will and Testament*.

TREVELL, WILLIAM. Whitefriars lessee, 1608, 1621.

TRUSSELL, ALVERY. Chapel, 1600-1.

TUNSTALL (DONSTALL, DONSTONE), JAMES. Worcester's, 1583 ; Admiral's, 1590-1, 1594-7. Guilpin, *Skialetheia* (1598), refers to him in conjunction with Alleyn (q. v.). The variation in his name is made more, rather than less, puzzling by the baptism at St. Botolph's of Dunstone Tunstall on 20 August 1572 (H. ii. 261).

---

[1] *Variorum*, iii. 484, from *P. C. C.*   [2] Collier, iii. 447.
[3] Henslowe, i. 152 ; *Henslowe Papers*, 61.   [4] Collier, iii. 451.

UBALDINI, PETRUCCIO. Italians, 1576 (?).

UNDERELL. Worcester's, 1602. A Thomas Underell was a royal trumpeter in 1609–24 (*Chamber Accounts*).

UNDERWOOD, JOHN, was a Chapel boy in the year 1601, and continued at Blackfriars until, as the *Sharers Papers* state, on growing up to be a man, he was taken to strengthen the King's service. This was in 1608 or a little later. He is not in the Queen's Revels actor-list of *Epicoene* (1609), and is in the King's men's actor-list of *The Alchemist* (1610), and thereafter in the official lists and most of the actor-lists of the company, including that of the First Folio Shakespeare, up to 1624. Tooley in his will of 1623 forgave him a debt. His own will was made on 4 October 1624 and has a codicil appended on 10 October, doubtless from his oral directions, but after his death. He describes himself as ' of the parish of Saint Bartholomew the Less, in London, gent.', and leaves his shares in the Blackfriars, Globe, and Curtain to his executors, of whom Henry Condell is one, in trust for his five children, all under twenty-one—John, Elizabeth, Burbage, Thomas, and Isabel. The executors and his ' fellowes ', Mr. John Heminges and John Lowin, who are appointed overseers, have 11s. each for rings.[1] The baptism of his son John on 27 December 1610 is in the register of Saint Bartholomew the Less, West Smithfield.[2] The trust was still unexpired at Condell's death in 1627, and was handed on by him to his wife. The *Sharers Papers* of 1635 show one share in the Blackfriars still in the hands of an Underwood ; but apparently a third of it had been parted with about 1632 to Eliart Swanston.[3]

VINCENT. Strange's (?), 1590–1.

VIRNIUS, JOHANN FRIEDRICH. Germany, 1615.

WAKEFIELD, EDWARD. Germany, 1597, 1602.

WALPOLE, FRANCIS. Anne's, 1616–17.

WARD, ANTHONY. Vide ARKINSTALL.

WAYMUS (WAMBUS), FRANCIS. Lady Elizabeth's, 1611, 1617–24.

WEBSTER, GEORGE. Germany, 1598, 1600–3.

WEBSTER, JOHN. Germany, 1596. Is he identical with the dramatist ?

WESTCOTT, SEBASTIAN. Master of Paul's, 1557–82. He is sometimes described by his Christian name alone.

WHETSTONE, *c*. 1571. Cf. s.v. FIDGE. Plomer suggests that he might be George Whetstone (cf. ch. xxiii).

WHITELOCKE, JAMES, afterwards Sir James. Merchant Taylors, 1575–86.

WILDER, PHILIP VAN. Gentleman of the Privy Chamber and lutenist, commissioned to raise a royal company of young minstrels in 1550 ; cf. ch. xii, s.v. Chapel.

' WILL.' Strange's, 1590–1.

' WILL.' Admiral's, 1597.

WILLIAMS, JOHN. Chapel, 1509.

---

[1] *Variorum*, iii. 214. [2] Collier, iii. 443.
[3] Halliwell-Phillipps, i. 313.

WILSON, JOHN. In *Much Ado*, ii. 3. 38, for the 'Enter Balthaser
with musicke' of Q_1, F_1 has 'Enter . . . Iacke Wilson', who therefore, at
some date before 1623, sang 'Sigh no more, ladies !' He is probably
the son of Nicholas Wilson, 'minstrel', baptized at St. Bartholomew's
the Less on 24 April 1585. He had an elder brother Adam, and buried
a wife Joan on 17 July 1624, and an unnamed son on 3 September 1624
at St. Giles's from the house of George Sommerset, musician (Collier,
Actors, xviii). He seems to have become a city 'wait' about 1622 and
to have still held his post in 1641, and has been confused (Collier in
Sh. Soc. Papers, ii. 33 ; E. F. Rimbault, *Who was Jacke Wilson ?*, 1846)
with another John Wilson, born in 1595, a royal lutenist and musician
of distinction (cf. *D. N. B.*). One or other of them was concerned with
a performance of *M. N. D.* in the house of John Williams, Bishop of
Lincoln, on 27 September 1631, which gave offence to the Puritans
(Murray, ii. 148).

WILSON, ROBERT, was one of Leicester's men in 1572, 1574, and
1581. A reference in Gabriel Harvey's correspondence of 1579 suggests
that he was conspicuous amongst the actors of the day, and Lodge's
praise about the same date in the *Defence of Plays* of his *Shorte and
Sweete*, 'the practice of a good scholler,' shows that he was also a playwright. This piece Lodge compares with Gosson's *Catiline's Conspiracies*, and it may have been on the same theme. Further evidence of
his reputation is in the letter of 1581 from T. Baylye (q. v.). In 1583
he joined the Queen's men, and is described by Howes in his account
of the formation of that company as a 'rare' man 'for a quicke,
delicate, refined, extemporall witt'. He is not in the Queen's list of
1588. This may not be quite complete ; on the other hand he may
by then have left the company. I see no solid foundation for the conjectures of Fleay, ii. 279, that he was the player of *Greenes Groatsworth
of Wit* (cf. App. C, No. xlviii) who penned the *Moral of Man's Wit* and
the *Dialogue of Dives*, that he wrote *Fair Em*, that he left the Queen's
for Strange's in 1590 and thereby incurred Greene's hostility, that he
is the Roscius of Nashe's *Menaphon* epistle, that he died of the plague
in 1593. It is extremely unlikely that he died in 1593, for in his
Palladis Tamia of 1598, after lauding Tarlton as famous for 'extemporall verse', Meres continues, 'And so is now our wittie Wilson, who
for learning and extemporall witte in this facultie is without compare
or compeere, as to his great and eternall commendations he manifested
in his chalenge at the Swanne on the Banke side.' The common use
by Meres and Howes of the phrase 'extemporall witte' renders it
almost impossible to suppose that they are not speaking of the same
man. It is true that, in the *Apology for Actors*, Heywood, whose
knowledge of the stage must have gone back at least to 1594, classes
Wilson with the older generation of actors, whom he never saw, as
being before his time, and I take it the explanation is that, at or before
the virtual break-up of the Queen's men in the plague of 1592-3,
Wilson gave up acting, and devoted himself to writing, and occasional
extemporizing on themes. He is generally supposed to be the R. W.
of *The Three Ladies of London* (1584) and *The Three Lords of London*

(1590), and the ' Robert Wilson, Gent.' of *The Cobbler's Prophecy* (1594). The ' Gent.' is hardly an insuperable obstacle to identifying him with the ' Robert Wilson, yoman (a player)', who was buried at St. Giles's, Cripplegate, on 20 November 1600 (Collier, *Actors*, xviii). A Wilson is in the suspected Admiral's cast of *c*. January 1600. But now comes the real difficulty. Meres, also in the *Palladis Tamia* and without any indication that he has another man in mind, includes ' Wilson ' in a group of ' the best for comedy amongst vs ', which is composed of the principal writers for the Admiral's in 1598, and amongst these writers, as shown by Henslowe's papers, was a Robert Wilson, who collaborated in eleven plays during 1598, and in three more during 1599 and 1600. He is last mentioned in a letter of 14 June 1600. This is generally taken to be a younger man than the Queen's player, possibly a Robert Wilson who was baptized at St. Botolph's, Bishopsgate, on 22 September 1579, and married Mary Eaton there on 24 June 1606, possibly the Robert Wilson (not described as ' a player and the younger ' as Collier suggests in *Bodl.*) whose son Robert was baptized at St. Leonard's on 15 January 1601 (Stopes, *Burbage*, 141), possibly the Robert Wilson whose burial is recorded at St. Bartholomew's the Less on 21 October 1610. On the whole, I am inclined to think that, in view of the character of Meres' references, of the use of Catiline as a play-theme both about 1580 and in 1598 (cf. ch. xxiii), and of the sudden disappearance of Wilson from Henslowe's diary in the year of the ' player's ' death, the balance of evidence is in favour of one playwright rather than two. The undefined share of the Admiral's man in the extant *1 Sir John Oldcastle* does not really afford a basis for stylistic comparison with the more old-fashioned manners of the 1584–94 plays. There is nothing to show that the Bishopsgate man had any connexion with the stage, still less that he was a son of the Queen's player, as has been suggested.

WINTER, RICHARD. Possibly an actor at Canterbury, *c.* 1571 (*3 Library*, ix. 253).

WODERAM, RICHARD. Oxford's, 1586–7 (?).

WOODFORD, THOMAS. Whitefriars lessee, 1608, 1621.

WOODS, JOHN. Holland, 1604.

WORTH, ELLIS. Anne's, 1615–19 ; for his later career, cf. Murray, i. 198, 218. He is described as ' gentleman' in the register of St. Giles's at the baptism of his daughter Jane on 19 July 1613, and as ' player ' at that of his son Elizeus on 12 March 1629 (*Bodl.*).

WYLKYNSON, JOHN. A London ' coriour ', who maintained players in his house in 1549 (cf. App. D, No. ii).

YOUNG, JOHN. Queen Jane's, >1537 ; Interluders, 1539–53 (?). He seems to have been still alive in 1569–70.

BOOK IV

THE PLAY-HOUSES

The world the stage, the prologue tears,
The acts vain hope and varied fears :
The scene shuts up with loss of breath,
And leaves no epilogue but death.
HENRY KING.

XVI

INTRODUCTION: THE PUBLIC
THEATRES

[*Bibliographical Note.*—Some notes in the *Gentleman's Magazine* for 1813–16 by Eu. Hood [Joseph Haslewood] are reprinted in *The Gentleman's Magazine Library*, xv (1904), 86, and in *Roxburghe Revels* (ed. J. Maidment, 1837). J. P. Collier, *History of English Dramatic Poetry*, iii. 79, has *An Account of the Old Theatres of London*, and chronological sections on the subject are in F. G. Fleay, *A Chronicle History of the London Stage* (1890). T. F. Ordish, *Early London Theatres* (1894), covers the Shoreditch and Bankside theatres ' in the Fields ' other than the Globe ; a companion volume on the urban houses has never appeared. The Bankside houses are also dealt with by W. Rendle, *The Bankside, Southwark, and the Globe* (1877), being Appendix I to F. J. Furnivall, *Harrison's Description of England*, Part II (*N. Sh. Soc.*), and in *Old Southwark and its People* (1878) and *The Playhouses at Bankside in the Time of Shakespeare* (*Walford's Antiquarian*, 1885, vii. 207, 274 ; viii. 55). J. Q. Adams, *Shakespearean Playhouses* (1917), is a comprehensive and valuable work, which reached me when this chapter was practically complete. I am glad to find that our results so generally agree. The chief London maps have been reproduced by the *London Topographical Society* and on a smaller scale by G. E. Mitton, *Maps of Old London* (1908). Some are also given as illustrations in G. P. Baker, *The Development of Shakespeare as a Dramatist* (1907). They are classified by W. Martin, *A Study of Early Map-Views of London* in *The Antiquary*, xlv (1909), 337, 406, and their evidence for the Bankside analysed by the same writer, with partial reproductions, in *The Site of the Globe Playhouse of Shakespeare* (1910, *Surrey Archaeological Collections*, xxiii. 149).

The evidence of the maps as to the position of the theatres is obscured, partly by uncertainties as to the dates and authorships both of the engravings and of the surveys on which they were based, and partly by the pictorial character of the topography. They are not strict plans in two dimensions, such as modern cartographers produce, but either drawings in full perspective, or bird's-eye views in diminished perspective. The imaginary standpoint is always on the south, and the pictorial aspect is emphasized in the foreground, with the result that, while the Bankside theatres, but not those north of the river, are generally indicated, this is rarely with a precision which renders it possible to locate them in relation to the thoroughfares amongst which they stand. This is more particularly the case since, while the general grouping of buildings, gardens, and trees appears, from a comparison of one view with another, to be faithfully given, it is probable that the details are often both conventionally represented and out of scale. The following classification is mainly borrowed from Dr. Martin : (*a*) Pre-Reformation representations of London throwing no light on the theatres ; (*b*) *Wyngaerde*, a pictorial drawing (*c.* 1543–50) by A. Van der Wyngaerde (*L. T. Soc.* i ; Mitton, i) ; (*c*) *Höfnagel*, a plan with little perspective by G. Höfnagel, from a survey of *c.* 1554–7 (cf. A. Marks in *Athenaeum* for 31 March 1906), published

(1572) with the title *Londinum Feracissimi Angliae Regni Metropolis* in
G. Braun and F. Hohenburg, *Civitates Orbis Terrarum* (L. T. Soc. ii ;
Mitton, iv) ; (*d*) *Agas*, an engraving with more perspective, but generally
similar to that of Höfnagel and possibly from the same survey, but drawn
after 1561, and assigned by G. Vertue, who reproduced it (1737), to Ralph
Agas (L. T. Soc. xvii ; Mitton, ii) ; (*e*) *Smith*, a coloured drawing by
William Smith, possibly based on Höfnagel or Agas, in *B. M. Sloane MS.*
2596, reproduced in H. B. Wheatley and E. W. Ashbee, *W. Smith, The
Particular Description of England, 1588* (1879), and in G. P. Baker, *The
Development of Shakespeare as a Dramatist* (1907), 18 ; (*f*) *Bankside Views*,
small representations of the same general character as (*c*), (*d*), and (*e*),
used as backgrounds to pictures and described by W. Martin in *Antiquary*,
xlv. 408 ; (*g*) *Norden*, engravings in slight perspective of ' London ' and
' Westminster ' by P. Van den Keere in J. Norden, *Speculum Britanniae*
(1593), from survey of about the same date (L. T. Soc. vii ; Mitton, v, vi ;
Furnivall, *Harrison's Description of England*, Part I, with notes on p. lxxxix
by H. B. Wheatley, reprinted by L. T. Soc. in *Record*, ii) ; (*h*) *Delaram
Group*, perspective views as backgrounds to portrait (*c.* 1616) of James I
by F. Delaram (1620), reproduced by W. Martin in *Surrey A. Colls.*
xxiii. 186, and other portraits probably based on some original of *c.* 1603 ;
(*i*) *Hondius Group*, (i) drawing by P. D. Hondius (1610) in J. Speed,
Theatre of the Empire of Great Britain (1611), as inset to map of Britain
(*L. T. Record*, ii, with notes by T. F. Ordish ; Baker, *f. p.*), (ii) engraving
on title-page of R. Baker, *Chronicle* (1643), reproduced by Martin in
Surrey A. Colls. xxiii. 187, (iii) engraving on title-page of H. Holland,
Herωologia Anglica (1620), (iv) engraving of triumphal arch at coronation
entry of James I by W. Kip in S. Harrison (cf. ch. xxiv), *The Arches of
Triumph* (1604), all perhaps based on the same original or survey ;
(*k*) *Visscher*, engraving in perspective by Nikolaus Janssen Visscher (1616),
' Amstelodami, ex officina Judoci Hondii ', with mutilated text from
Camden's *Britannia*, reproduced from unique copy in Brit. Mus. (L. T.
Soc. iv, with notes by T. F. Ordish in *L. T. Record*, vi ; also W. Martin
in *Surrey A. Colls.* xxiii. 188, and in Ordish, *Shakespeare's London, f. p.*
and elsewhere) ; (*l*) *Merian Group*, (i) engraving in perspective by M. Merian
in J. L. Gottfried, *Neuwe Archontologia Cosmica* (1638), 290, reproduced
by Martin, 191, and Adams, 256, and copied in (ii) *f. p.* to James Howell,
Londinopolis (1657), reproduced by Baker, 154, and (iii) R. Wilkinson,
Londina Illustrata (1819) ; (*m*) ' *Ryther* ' *Group*, (i) engraving in very
slight perspective from drawing unfinished as regards the Bankside in
Crace Collection, No. 32, without date, imprint, or indication of authorship, reproduced by W. J. Loftie, *History of London*, ii. 282,
C. L. Kingsford, *Chronicles of London*, (1905) *f. p.*, and Baker,
36, 125, 135, and ascribed to Augustine Ryther in 1604, but prob-
ably of about 1636–45 (cf. *4 N. Q.* ix. 95 ; *6 N. Q.* xii. 361, 393 ;
7 N. Q. iii. 110 ; vi. 297 ; vii. 498) in view of (ii) another version in Crace
Coll., No. 31, with the Bankside complete, bearing the imprint of ' Cornelis
Danckerts grauer of maps ' in Amsterdam (*c.* 1631–56), and possibly by
Hollar, who worked for Danckerts, and was in England 1636–45, (iii) map
by T. Porter (*c.* 1666), based on (i) with later additions (reproduced
L. T. Soc. v) ; (*n*) *Hollar*, engraving in perspective by W. Hollar (in
London 1635–43), published by Cornelius Danckerts in 1647 (L. T. Soc.
xix ; section by Martin in *Surrey A. Colls.* xxiii. 194) ; (*o*) *Faithorne and
Newcourt*, engraving in conventional perspective by William Faithorne
from drawing by Richard Newcourt, published in 1658 (L. T. Soc. xviii ;
Mitton, vii). Of the various maps of post-conflagration London the most
useful are that of Leeke and Hollar (*c.* 1666), of which a section is repro-

duced by Martin in *Survey A. Colls*. xxiii. 191, and those of John Ogilby and W. Morgan (1677, Mitton, viii), John Ogilby and W. Morgan (1682, L. T. Soc. xv), and John Rocque (1746, L. T. Soc. xxxiv, xxxv, xxxvii ; Mitton, ix ; section in Martin, *ut supra*, 197). Rendle, *Bankside*, has attempted to indicate the sites of the Bankside theatres upon a reconstructed map based on Rocque, and Martin in *Survey A. Colls*. xxiii. 155, 202, gives parts of the Bankside area as it now stands from the Ordnance Survey map (1896) and a plan of the Anchor Brewery (1909).]

A. INTRODUCTION

The detailed notices, which will form the greater part of this chapter, may with advantage be prefaced with some general observations upon the historical sequence of the theatres and their distribution at different periods over the London area. The earlier Tudor London knew no theatre, in the sense of a building specially planned and maintained for public dramatic performances, although Yarmouth had its ' game-house ' by 1538, and a *theatrum* at Exeter was the scene of satirical farces far back in the fourteenth century. The miracle plays, not in London processional, were given in the open air, and probably on temporary scaffolds. Similar stages may sometimes have been used for the interludes, but these were ordinarily represented in the winter-time, and sought the kindly shelter of a hall.[1] In the provision of specialized buildings, the drama appears to have been anticipated by the ruder sport of baiting. Höfnagel's pre-Elizabethan map already shows on the Southwark side of the river the two rings, with open centres and roofed seats for spectators, which are repeated later on by Agas and by Smith. They stand in yards or gardens lined with dog-kennels. One is lettered ' The Bowll bayting ', the other ' The beare bayting '. When the first Elizabethan theatres were built in 1576, it was the hall on the one hand, and the ring on the other, which determined the general structure of the two types of auditorium that came simultaneously into being.[2] The ' private ' house, roofed and lit, and with its seats arranged in tiers along three sides of a long room, and the ' public ' house, generally circular, with covered stage and galleries, and a central yard or ' pit ' open to the day, co-existed for more than half a century, and finally merged in the post-Restoration type

---

[1] *Mediaeval Stage*, i. 383 ; ii. 184, 190, 380. It is, of course, doubtful whether the ' theatrum nostrae civitatis ' at Exeter was permanent.

[2] Ordish, 12, attempts to affiliate the ring type of baiting-place and theatre to Roman amphitheatres, Cornish ' rounds ', and other circular places used for mediaeval entertainments. But a ring is so obviously the form in which the maximum number of spectators can see an object of interest, that too much stress must not be laid upon it as an evidence of folk ' tradition '.

of theatre which has come down to our own day. The distinction between ' private ' and ' public ' is an unessential one, depending probably upon some difference in the methods of paying for admission necessitated by the regulations of the City or the Privy Council.[1] The performances in all the houses were public in the ordinary sense. There was, however, another important factor, besides the baiting ring, which greatly affected the structure of the open-air theatre. This was the inn-yard. Long before 1576, interludes had been given in public, as well as in the private halls of the great, and even the need for some kind of permanent, or quasi-permanent, installation had been felt. No doubt there were halls in London which could be hired. The keeper of the Carpenters' Hall in Shoreditch was prosecuted towards the end of Henry VIII's reign for procuring a Protestant interlude ' to be openly played '.[2] Fees for the letting of Trinity Hall for plays occur among the ' casuall recepts ' of the churchwardens of St. Botolph without Aldersgate in 1566-7.[3] A jest-book of 1567 records a play at Northumberland Place.[4] But an even more convenient hospitality was afforded by the great court-yards of the City inns, where there was sack and bottle-ale to hand, and, as the Puritans averred, chambers ready for deeds of darkness to be done, when the play was over.[5] In these yárds, approached by archways under the inn buildings from one or more streets, and surrounded by galleries with external staircases giving access to the upper floors, an audience could quickly gather, behold at their ease, and escape payment with difficulty. The actors could be accommodated with a tiring-room on the ground floor, and perform as on a natural stage between the pillars supporting the galleries. An upper gallery could be used to vary the scene. The first performances in London inns upon record were at the Saracen's Head, Islington, and the Boar's Head, Aldgate, both in 1557.[6] By the beginning of Elizabeth's reign the use of them was normal. Plays ' in hostels and taverns ' were

---

[1] Cf. ch. xviii. [2] *Mediaeval Stage*, ii. 221.

[3] G. Fothergill in *10 N. Q.* vi. 287, from *Guildhall MS.* 1454, roll 70, ' And wyth 22ˢ 2ᵈ for money by them receyved for the hyer of Tryntie Halle for playes, the warmanthe [ward-moot] inquest and other assemblyes within the time of this accompt '.

[4] Cf. ch. xxiii, s.v. Vennar.

[5] Several galleried inns are illustrated in W. Rendle and P. Norman, *The Inns of Old Southwark* (1888), and by Ordish, 119 (Tabard), Baker, 200 (Four Swans), Adams, 4 (White Hart). Probably, however, none of these are pre-Restoration. The only ones still extant are the George in Southwark and a much later one in Theobalds Road (*V. H. Surrey*, iv. 128).

[6] *Mediaeval Stage*, ii. 190, 223.

specified for prohibition by the proclamation of April 1559, and the City regulations of 1574 are clearly aimed at the control of the ' greate innes, havinge chambers and secrete places adjoyninge to their open stagies and gallyries ', and impose obligations for the sake of good order upon inn-keepers and tavern-keepers in the fore-front of those regarded as likely to harbour plays.[1] It is not reading too much between the lines to suggest that the owners of particular houses specially laid themselves out to secure the attraction of public entertainments, entered into regular contracts with players, and probably even undertook structural alterations which in fact converted their yards into little less than permanent theatres.[2] We have, indeed, the record of a trade dispute about the workmanship of play-scaffolds at the Red Lion in Stepney as far back as 1567. The Red Lion stood outside the jurisdiction of the City. Within it, and so far as we can judge, much more important in the history of the stage were the Bell and the Cross Keys, both in Gracechurch Street, the Bull in Bishopsgate Street, and the Bel Savage on Ludgate Hill. No one of these four is in fact mentioned by name as a play-house earlier than 1575, and although they must have been hard hit by the regulations of 1574, it is clear that they did not go altogether out of use, especially during the winter, when climatic conditions rendered the suburbs unattractive, for another twenty years. Stockwood, in 1578, speaks of six or eight ' ordinarie places ' where plays were then performed.[3] Nevertheless the action of the City, and the enterprise of James Burbadge, whose descendants claimed for him the honour of being ' the first builder of playhowses ', led to a shifting of the dramatic focus. The Theatre and the Curtain, both built in or about 1576, stood in ' the fields ' to the north of London proper, and were perhaps soon followed by Newington Butts on the south side of the river, beyond St. George's Fields ; while the Blackfriars, adapted in the same year (1576) by Richard Farrant to house the perform-ances of children, occupied an old monastic building in the precinct of a ' liberty ' which, although within the walls, was largely exempt from the jurisdiction of the Corporation. This became the home of the Children of the Chapel, while the Paul's boys played in their own ' song-school ', either

---

[1] Cf. ch. ix.

[2] Flecknoe tells us c. 1664 (App. I) that the actors, ' about the beginning of Queen Elizabeth's reign . . . set up Theaters, first in the City (as in the Inn-yards of the Cross-Keyes, and Bull in Grace and Bishops-Gate Street at this day is to be seen) '.

[3] Cf. App. C, No. xvii.

the church of St. Gregory or some other building in the neighbourhood of St. Paul's. How long this arrangement had existed, or whether any company of children had played in public at all before the date of Farrant's experiment, we do not know. From 1576 onwards, it is the Theatre and the Curtain which have to bear the brunt of the Puritan attack, and the luxury of these, as compared with the primitive accommodation of the inn-yards, arouses a special indignation. ' The sumptuous Theatre houses, a continual monument of Londons prodigalitie and folly ', wails Thomas White in 1577. Stockwood in 1578 discommends ' the gorgeous playing place erected in the fieldes ' ; and William Harrison, perhaps about the same time, finds it ' an evident token of a wicked time when plaiers wexe so riche that they can build such houses '.[1] Presently the theatres became notable amongst the sights which foreign travellers must see in London. Lupold von Wedel in 1584 says nothing of them, although he records the baiting and its rings.[2] But they are noticed in the following year by Samuel Kiechel, a merchant of Ulm, who writes : [3]

' Comedies are given daily. It is particularly mirthful to behold, when the Queen's comedians act, but annoying to a foreigner who does not know the language, that he understands nothing. There are some peculiar houses, which are so made as to have about three galleries over one another, inasmuch as a great number of people always enters to see such an entertainment. It may well be that they take as much as from 50 to 60 dollars [£10 to £12] at once, especially when they act anything new, which has not been given before, and double prices are charged. This goes on nearly every day in the week ; even though performances are forbidden on Friday and Saturday, it is not observed.'

The Theatre and the London inns were still the chief playing-places, when at some date between 1576 and 1596 William Lambarde illustrated his account of the pilgrimages

---

[1] App. C, Nos. xv, xvii ; App. D, No. xxii.   [2] Cf. s.v. Hope.
[3] K. D. Hassler, *Die Reisen des Samuel Kiechel* (1866) 29, ' Werden auch täglichen commedien gehalten, sonderlichen ist lustig zu zusehen, wann der Königen comedianten agiren, aber einem frembden, der düe sprach nicht kan, verdrüslich, das ers nicht verstöth ; es hat öttliche sonderbare heüser, wölche dozu gemacht sein, das ettwann drey genng ob ein ander sein, derowegen stöts ein grosse menge volckhs dohin kompt, solcher kurzweil zuzusehen. Es begibt sich wol, das süe uf einmal 50 in 60 dalr ufhöben ; sonderlichen wann süe was neyes agiren, so zuvor nicht gehalten worden, mues mann doppelt gelt gebenn, und wehrt solchs vast alle tag durch düe wochen, onangesehen es freytag wüe auch samstags zu halten verbotten, würt es doch nicht gehalten.' Cf. Rye, 87. Kiechel appears to have been in London from 12 Sept. to about 29 Oct. and from 14 to 17 Nov. 1585.

to Boxley, by explaining that those who visited the shrine
did not get off scot-free—

'no more than such as goe to Parisgardein, the Bell Sauage, or Theatre,
to beholde Beare baiting, Enterludes, or Fence play, can account of
any pleasant spectacle, unlesse they first pay one pennie at the gate,
another at the entrie of the Scaffolde, and the thirde for a quiet
standing.' [1]

Paris Garden was the generic name given to the successive
places for bear-baiting which lay on the Surrey side of the
river, not in Southwark proper, which was in the jurisdiction
of the City, but in the Liberty of the Clink, which stretched
in a westerly direction along the Bankside, or still farther
to the west, in the Manor of Paris Garden itself. In Surrey,
no less than in London, plays had established themselves at
an early date. A performance was going on in Southwark,
while the priests of St. Saviour's sang *Dirige* for Henry VIII's
soul in 1547.[2] The Privy Council ordered the Surrey justices
to suppress plays in the Borough and the adjoining places
during 1578; and it seems probable that a regular play-
house had been built south of the river at a date not much
later than that of the Theatre itself. It stood far back
behind Southwark, in the village of Newington, divided from
the river by St. George's Fields. The distance and the
bad roads were against it; and it was not until the Rose
was built in the Clink about 1587, that the Bankside became
a serious rival to the 'fields' in the north as the home of
theatres. The Swan, in Paris Garden, was built in 1595.
Newington is too far to the south to appear in the maps, but
Norden's map of 1593 shows two round buildings, standing
between Bankside and an unnamed road, which may safely
be identified with that called Maiden Lane. One is lettered
'The Beare howse', the other, more to the east and the south,
'The play howse'; and this must clearly be the Rose.

In 1596 the City appear to have at last obtained the
assent of the Privy Council to the complete exclusion of plays
from the area of their jurisdiction. This is probably the
proceeding described, with no precise indication of date, in
the following passage from Richard Rawlidge's *A Monster
Lately Found out and Discovered, or the Scourging of Tipplers*
(1628): [3]

'*London* hath within the memory of man lost much of hir pristine

---

[1] Lambarde, *Perambulation of Kent* (1596), 233. The passage is not in
the first edition of 1576.

[2] *Mediaeval Stage*, ii. 222; cf. ch. xiii (Oxford's).

[3] P. 2. Malone, in *Variorum*, iii. 46, refers the event to a date soon
after 1580; but there is no justification for this in the text.

lustre, . . . by being . . . filled with . . . sinnes, which . . . are . . . maintained, in Play-houses, Ale-houses, Bawdy-houses, Dising-houses, . . . All which houses, and traps for Gentlemen, and others, of such Receipt, were formerly taken notice of by many Citizens, and well disposed graue Gentlemen . . . wherevpon some of the pious magistrates made humble suit to the late Queene Elizabeth of ever-liuing memorie, and her priuy Counsaile, and obteined leaue from her Majesty to thrust those Players out of the Citty and to pull downe the Dicing houses : which accordingly was affected, and the Play-houses in *Gracious street*, *Bishops-gate-street*, nigh *Paules*, that on *Ludgate* hill, the *White-Friars* were put down, and other lewd houses quite supprest within the Liberties, by the care of those religious senators, . . . and surely had all their successors followed their worthy stepps, sinne would not at this day haue beene so powerfull, and raigning as it is.'

The play-houses in Gracious or Gracechurch Street, Bishops-gate Street, and Ludgate Hill were presumably the Bell and the Cross Keys, the Bull, and the Bel Savage. By the house 'nigh Paul's' Rawlidge possibly meant the choir song-school ; but in fact there had been no plays by the Paul's boys since 1590. If there was really a Whitefriars house at so early a date, this is the only notice preserved of it. It may be suspected that Rawlidge confused it with the Blackfriars, which James Burbadge was apparently prevented, upon representations by the City, from reopening in 1596. The claim of the City to exercise any control over the old religious precincts of the Blackfriars and the Whitefriars was a doubtful one ; and although they ultimately secured jurisdiction, they were not able to prevent the so-called 'private' theatres from establishing themselves in these 'liberties'.[1] With these exceptions, however, and possibly that of the Boar's Head, which seems to have been used for a few years after 1602, but was more likely just outside the bars, 1596 probably saw the last of playing within the actual gates of the City.

Londoners had now to look wholly to the suburbs for their dramatic entertainment. Prince Lewis of Anhalt-Cöthen found four theatres in 1596.[2] These were doubtless the Theatre and the Curtain on the north and the Rose and the Swan on the south of the river. The Newington house was still used in 1594, but even before that had long been out of fashion. It was probably also about 1596 that John

---

[1] Cf. p. 477.
[2] Rye, 216, from *Itinerarium* in Beckmann, *Accessiones Historiae Anhaltinae* (1716), 165 :

'Hier besieht man vier spielhäuser,
Darinnen man fürstelt die Fürsten, Könge, Keyser,
In rechter lebens gröss', in schöner kleider pracht,
Es wird der thaten auch, wie sie geschehn, gedacht.'

de Wit twrote his *Observationes Londinenses*. He too mentioned the four theatres, together with the baiting house, and was particularly struck by the newest, and as he avers, the largest and fairest of them, the Swan, of the interior of which he attached a rough sketch to his manuscript. This manuscript is lost, but fortunately an extract survives, copied into a commonplace book by Arend van Buchell of Utrecht. The following is the complete text:[1]

EX OBSERVATIONIBUS LONDINENSIBUS JOHANNIS DE WITT.

De phano D. Pauli. Huic Paulino phano adheret locus ab asservandis sacratioribus vestimentis Sacristi dictus, omnino observatione dignus,

[1] Text by H. B. Wheatley, *On a Contemporary Drawing of the Interior of the Swan Theatre, 1596 (N. S. S. Trans. 1887–92, 215)*, from *Utrecht Univ. Library MS. Var.* 355, ff. 131ᵛ, 132, with facsimile reproduction of drawing. The passage was first made known by K. T. Gaedertz, *Zur Kenntniss der altenglischen Bühne* (1888). The reproduction of the drawing published by Gaedertz and further reproduced from him in many modern books is not an exact facsimile; the only material difference is that the engraver has made the figure at the door of the loft rather more obviously a man than it is in the original. Letters of the early part of the seventeenth century from de Witt to Buchell, who was his fellow-student at Leyden in 1583, are also in the Utrecht Library (Gaedertz, 57). The last sentence of the passage appears from ' narrabat ' to be a report by Buchell either of something not directly copied by him or of de Witt's conversation; but the rest is pretty clearly from ' ea quae alio loco a me notata sunt ' a verbatim extract from a manuscript of de Witt's own. If so, ' adpinxi ' further shows that the eye-witness of de Witt and not the imagination of Buchell is the source of the drawing. Gaedertz, 63, indeed suggests that the drawing is an original given by de Witt to Buchell, but as Wheatley, 219, points out, this is impossible, as the paper is the same as that used in the rest of the volume. There remains the question of date. De Witt is traceable at Amsterdam in Nov. 1594, at Utrecht in the winters of 1595 and 1596, and in 1599, and at Amsterdam again in March 1604 (Gaedertz, 58). His visit to London obviously falls between Nov. 1594, when the Swan was still only an intention, and Dec. 1598, when the Theatre was pulled down. Gaedertz, 55, puts it in the summer of 1596, largely because Shakespeare, whom he thinks de Witt would certainly have mentioned if he had met him, may have been in Stratford about that time. This is hopeless. Nor does the further suggestion of Gaedertz that a lameness from which de Witt was suffering in Dec. 1596 was due to his travels carry much conviction. But he is not likely, before that year, to have appended the words ' Aᵒ. 1596 ' to his notice of Sir John Burgh's tomb. If this is intended to be the date, not of his visit, but of the tomb, it is an error. Camden, *Reges . . . in Ecclesia . . . Westmonasterii sepulti* (1600), gives the final words of the inscription as ' G. B. A. M. P. anno Dom. 1595 ', and although the tomb itself has disappeared since 1868 and some modern guides date it 1594 or 1598, Camden is confirmed by J. C[rull], *Antiquities of Westminster* (1711), 198. Burgh's death, also given on the monument, was 7 March ' 1594 '. On the whole 1596 is the most probable date for de Witt's visit. Arend van Buchell was himself a traveller, and his *Diarium* has been edited (1907) by G. Brom and L. A. van Langeraad. But he did not visit England.

quippe quo DIANAE delubrum fuisse ferunt. Sacellum est rotundum, hemyphericum, concameratum, cuius structura Romanam antiquitatem referre videtur. Aiunt cum fundamenta templi iacerentur effossam ante huius aediculae fores innumeram cervinorum capitum copiam ; inde colligi Dianae sacrificia (cui cervis litabatur) ibi olim peracta esse eique hanc aedem sacratam fuisse ; in eodem phano sunt epitaphia et sepulcra varia praeter ea quae alio loco a me notata sunt, Guilelmi Herberti Penbrochiae comitis Walliae praesidis qui obijt A° aetat. lxiii Christi vero 1569.

Ibidem in aede Westmonasteriensi sunt monumenta cum suis elogiis : Guill. Thynne armigeri ex antiqua Bottevillorum familia, Joannis Thynne fratris qui obijt 14 Martii 1584, item Joannis Bourgh Duisburgi gubernatoris A° 1596.

Amphiteatra Londinij sunt iv visendae pulcritudinis quae a diversis intersigniis diuersa nomina sortiuntur : in iis varia quotidie scaena populo exhibetur. Horum duo excellentiora vltra Tamisim ad meridiam sita sunt, a suspensis signis ROSA et Cygnus nominata : Alia duo extra vrbem ad septentrionem sunt, viâ quâ itur per Episcopalem portam vulgariter Biscopgat nuncupatam. Est etiam quintum, sed dispari [vsu ?] et structura, bestiarum concertationi destinatum, in quo multi vrsi, tauri, et stupendae magnitudinis canes, discretis caueis & septis aluntur, qui [drawing occupies rest of page] ad pugnam adseruantur, iocundissimum hominibus spectaculum praebentes. Theatrorum autem omnium prestantissimum est et amplissimum id cuius intersignium est cygnus (vulgo te theatre off te cijn [off te swan]),[1] quippe quod tres mille homines in sedilibus admittat, constructum ex coaceruato lapide pyrritide (quorum ingens in Britannia copia est) ligneis suffultum columnis quae ob illitum marmoreum colorem, nasutissimos quoque fallere possent. Cuius quidem formam quod Romani operis vmbram videatur exprimere supra adpinxi.

Narrabat idem se vidisse in Brittannia apud Abrahamum de lyndeley [?] mercatorem Alberti Dureri omnia opera cartacea elegantissima et absolutissima.

The account of Paul Hentzner, who was in London from 31 August to 8 September 1598, lays less stress upon the theatres than upon the baiting, and is not altogether consistent with that of de Witt as to the structure of the Swan, which was the nearest house to the moorings of the royal barge at the west end of Paris Garden.[2] Hentzner writes :

'Sunt porro Londini extra Urbem Theatra aliquot, in quibus Histriones Angli Comoedias & Tragoedias singulis fere diebus, in magna hominum frequentia agunt, quas variis etiam saltationibus, suavissima adhibita musica, magno cum populi applausu finire solent.

---

[1] The emendation is due to Wallace (E. S. xliii. 356). Adams, 168, suggests that ' cijn ' is Flemish for ' swan ', but the dictionary gives ' zwaen ', which is perhaps what de Witt wrote.

[2] Cf. plan of the manor in Rendle, Bankside, i.

INTRODUCTION

Non longe ab uno horum theatrorum, quae omnia lignea sunt, ad Thamesim navis est regia, quae duo egregia habet conclavia, fenestris perlucidis, picturis & sculpturis eleganter exornata, in sicco & quidem sub tecto collocata, propterea, ut a pluviis & coeli injuria immunis sit.'

Hentzner then describes the baiting.[1] He concludes:

' Utuntur in hisce spectaculis sicut & alibi, ubicunque locorum sint Angli, herba Nicotiana, quam Americano idiomate Tabacam nuncupant (Paetum alii dicunt) hoc modo frequentissime ; Fistulae in hunc finem ex argilla factae, orificio posteriori, dictam herbam probe exiccatam, ita ut in pulverem facile redigi possit, immittunt, & igne admoto accendunt, unde fumus ab anteriori parte ore attrahitur, qui per nares rursum, tanquam per infurnibulum exit, & phlegma ac capitis defluxiones magna copia secum educit. Circumferuntur insuper in hisce theatris varii fructus venales, ut poma, pyra, nuces & pro ratione temporis, etiam vinum & cerevisia.'[2]

It is perhaps natural that foreign visitors should be more struck by the English theatres at a time when the English stage was serving as a model to northern Europe, than was the case with a native chronicler of grave and slightly Puritanic tendencies. John Stowe, when he published his *Survey of London* in 1598, had nothing to say of the Bankside houses, and but little of those in Middlesex. After writing of the miracle plays, he says:

' Of late time in place of those Stage playes, hath beene vsed Comedies, Tragedies, Enterludes, and Histories, both true and fayned : For the acting whereof certaine publike places as the Theater, the Curtine, &c., haue been erected' [*in margin*, 'Theater and Curten for Comedies & other shewes '].[3]

In another place, at the end of a description of Holywell, he adds:

' And neare therevnto are builded two publique houses for the acting and shewe of Comedies, Tragedies, and Histories, for recreation. Whereof the one is called the Courtein, the other the Theatre : both standing on the Southwest side towards the field.'[4]

Even these scanty references were pruned in the second edition of 1603, after the Theatre had disappeared at the end of 1598 and the Chamberlain's men had left the Curtain.

[1] Cf. p. 456.   [2] Hentzner, 196.
[3] *Survey* (ed. Kingsford), i. 93. In 1603 the words ' as the Theater, the Curtine, &c.' are omitted from the body of the passage.
[4] *Survey*, ii. 73. This passage was omitted altogether in 1603. The early draft in *Harl. MS.* 538 (Kingsford, ii. 369) runs, ' Neare adjoyning are builded two houses for the shewe of Activities, Comedies, tragedies and histories, for recreation. The one of them is named the Curtayn in Holy Well, the other the Theatre.'

And of the Globe, built during the earlier half of 1599, to which they migrated, Stowe takes no notice. The Globe, however, appears, although unnamed, together with two other theatres, of which one must be the Curtain, in the next foreign account, a very full one by Thomas Platter of Basle, who was in England from 18 September to 20 October 1599.[1] I translate the passage, of which sufficient use has not been made by historians of the stage:

[1] G. Binz in *Anglia*, xxii. 456 (from Platter's narrative written in 1604–5 of his travels in 1595–1600, now in the Basle University Library):
' Den 21 Septembris nach dem Imbissessen, etwan umb zwey vhren, bin ich mitt meiner geselschaft v̇ber dz wasser gefahren, haben in dem streü-winen Dachhaus die Tragedy vom ersten Keyser Julio Caesare mitt ohngefahr 15 personen sehen gar artlich agieren ; zu endt der Comedien dantzeten sie ihrem gebrauch nach gar v̇berausz zierlich, ye zwen in mannes vndt 2 in weiber kleideren angethan, wunderbahrlich mitt ein-anderen.
Auf ein andere Zeit hab ich nicht weit von unserem wirdtshaus in der Vorstadt, meines behaltens an der Bischofsgeet, auch nach essens ein Comoedien gesehen, da presentierten sie allerhandt nationen, mit welchen yeder zeit ein Engellender vmb ein tochter kempfete, vndt vber-wandt er sie alle, aussgenommen den teütschen, der gewan die tochter mitt kempfen, satzet sich neben sie, trank ihme deszwegen mit seinem diener ein starken rausch, also dasz sie beyde beweinet wurden, vndt warfe der diener seinem Herren den schu an kopf, vnndt entschliefen beyde. Hiezwischen stige der engellender in die Zelten, vnndt entfuhret dem teütschen sein gewin, also v̇berlistet er den teütschen auch. Zu endt dantzeten sie auch auf Englisch vnndt Irlendisch gar zierlich vnndt werden also ale tag vmb 2 vhren nach mittag in der stadt London zwo biszweilen auch drey Comedien an vnderscheidenen örteren gehalten, damitt einer den anderen lustig mache, dann welche sich am besten verhalten, die haben auch zum meisten Zuhörer. Die örter sindt dergestalt erbauwen, dasz sie auf einer erhöchten brüge spilen, vnndt yederman alles woll sehen kan. Yedoch sindt vnderscheidene gäng vnndt ständt da man lustiger vnndt basz sitzet, bezahlet auch deszwegen mehr. Dann welcher vnden gleich stehn beleibt, bezahlt nur 1 Englischen pfenning, so er aber sitzen will, lasset man ihn noch zu einer thür hinein, da gibt er noch 1^d, begeret er aber am lustigesten ort auf kissen ze sitzen, da er nicht allein alles woll sihet, sondern auch gesehen kan werden, so gibt er bey einer anderen thüren noch 1 Englischen pfenning. Vnndt tragt man in wehrender Comedy zu essen vndt zu trinken vnder den Leüten herumb, mag einer vmb sein gelt sich also auch erlaben.
Die Comedienspiler sindt beim allerkostlichsten vnndt zierlichsten be-kleidet, dann der brauch in Engellandt, dasz wann fürnemme herren oder Ritter absterben, sie ihren dieneren vast die schönesten kleider verehren vndt vergaben, welche, weil es ihnen nicht gezimpt, solche kleider nicht tragen, sondern nachmahlen, den Comoedienspileren vmb ein ringen pfenning ze kaufen geben.
Was für zeit sie also in dem Comoedien lustig alle tag können zubringen, weisset yeglicher woll, der sie etwan hatt sehen agieren oder spilen. . . .
. . . Midt solchen vndt viel anderen kurtzweilen mehr vertreiben die Engellender ihr zeit, erfahren in den Comedien, wasz sich in anderen Landen zutraget, vndt gehendt ohne scheüchen, mann vndt weibs per-

' After dinner on the 21st of September, at about two o'clock, I went with my companions over the water, and in the strewn roof-house saw the tragedy of the first Emperor Julius with at least fifteen characters very well acted. At the end of the comedy they danced according to their custom with extreme elegance. Two in men's clothes and two in women's gave this performance, in wonderful combination with each other. On another occasion, I also saw after dinner a comedy, not far from our inn, in the suburb ; if I remember right, in Bishopsgate. Here they represented various nations, with whom on each occasion an Englishman fought for his daughter, and overcame them all except the German, who won the daughter in fight. He then sat down with him, and gave him and his servant strong drink, so that they both got drunk, and the servant threw his shoe at his master's head and they both fell asleep. Meanwhile the Englishman went into the tent, robbed the German of his gains, and thus he outwitted the German also. At the end they danced very elegantly both in English and in Irish fashion. And thus every day at two o'clock in the afternoon in the city of London two and sometimes three comedies are performed, at separate places, wherewith folk make merry together, and whichever does best gets the greatest audience. The places are so built, that they play on a raised platform, and every one can well see it all. There are, however, separate galleries and there one stands more comfortably and moreover can sit, but one pays more for it. Thus anyone who remains on the level standing pays only one English penny : but if he wants to sit, he is let in at a further door, and there he gives another penny. If he desires to sit on a cushion in the most comfortable place of all, where he not only sees everything well, but can also be seen, then he gives yet another English penny at another door. And in the pauses of the comedy food and drink are carried round amongst the people, and one can thus refresh himself at his own cost.

' The comedians are most expensively and elegantly apparelled, since it is customary in England, when distinguished gentlemen or knights die, for nearly the finest of their clothes to be made over and given to their servants, and as it is not proper for them to wear such clothes but only to imitate them, they give them to the comedians to purchase for a small sum.

' What they can thus produce daily by way of mirth in the comedies, every one knows well, who has happened to see them acting or playing.'

Platter then describes the Cock-pit and the baiting. He concludes :

' With such and many other pastimes besides the English spend their time ; in the comedies they learn what is going on in other lands, and this happens without alarm, husband and wife together in

sonen an gemelte ort, weil mehrtheils Engellender nicht pflegen viel ze reysen, sondern sich vergnügen zehausz frembde sachen ze erfahren vnndt ihre kurtzweil ze nemmen.'

a familiar place, since for the most part the English do not much use to travel, but are content ever to learn of foreign matters at home, and ever to take their pastime.'

A year later than Platter, another traveller thus describes a visit to the Bankside: [1]

' 1600 die Lunae 3 Julii. Audivimus comoediam Anglicam ; theatrum ad morem antiquorum Romanorum constructum ex lignis, ita formatum ut omnibus ex partibus spectatores commodatissime singula videre possint. In reditu transivimus pontem magnificis aedificiis ornatum e quibus uni adhuc affixa cernuntur capita quorundam comitum et nobilium, qui laesae Majestatis rei supplicio affecti sunt.'

When Lewis of Anhalt and de Witt wrote, there were four theatres, exclusive of the City inn-yards, which were probably already closed. Platter found two, and sometimes three, performances being given daily. This agrees with the evidence available from other sources. After the scandal of *The Isle of Dogs* in 1597, the Privy Council decreed a limitation of the London companies to two, the Chamberlain's men and the Admiral's. The former played at the Curtain until 1599, when they destroyed the Theatre and built the Globe. The latter played at the Rose until 1600, when they migrated to the newly built Fortune. But it is clear that the ordinance of the Privy Council was not strictly observed. An intruding company was playing in February 1598, either at the Theatre or the Swan. Platter's three houses in 1599 included the Curtain, together presumably with the Globe and the Rose. When the Council sanctioned the opening of the Fortune in 1600, they understood that the Curtain was to be ' either ruinated or applied to some other good use ', but it was still the scene of plays in 1601. Finally, in the spring of 1602 Elizabeth ordered the Council to tolerate a third company, that of the Earl of Worcester, Master of the Horse. This was then playing at the Boar's Head, a short-lived house of which practically nothing is known ; in the autumn it moved to the Rose. The Swan possibly went out of use, except for the occasional performances of acrobats and fencers, or of amateurs. On the other hand, Lord Hertford's men were in London during the winter of 1602–3, in addition to the three privileged companies, and they must have practised somewhere.

To the above must be added, for the closing years of Eliza-

[1] C. A. Mills in *The Times* (11 April 1914) from the travels of ' a foreign nobleman, to be published by J. A. F. Orbaan from a *Vatican MS.*'. Mills says that the visit was to the Globe, but the passage quoted does not exclude the Rose or Swan.

beth's reign, the 'private' houses; Paul's reopened in the winter of 1599, the Blackfriars in that of 1600. Of these Platter knows nothing, but Duke Philip Julius of Stettin-Pomerania, in the autumn of 1602, in addition to performances at the Fortune and another theatre, saw also, doubtless at the Blackfriars, the *Kinder-comoedia*. The following is an extract from the diary of the visit kept by the duke's secretary, Frederic Gerschow:[1]

'13 [September] On the thirteenth a comedy was played, of the taking of Stuhl-Weissenberg, firstly by the Turks, and thereafter back again by the Christians.

14. In the afternoon was played a tragicomedy of Samson and the half tribe of Benjamin.'[2]

On 16 September the duke and his retinue saw the baiting. On 18 September they visited the Blackfriars, and Gerschow wrote an account of the organization of the Children of the Chapel and of the nature of their performances.[3]

The Globe and the Fortune continued in regular use, as the houses of the King's men, and the Prince's men respectively, during the new reign, and endured to the closing of the theatres in 1642. Each was destroyed by fire and rebuilt; the former in 1613, the latter in 1621. Queen Anne's men at first used the Boar's Head and the Curtain, but migrated from the Boar's Head to the Red Bull, which had been built by 1606. This became their principal house, and they cannot be shown to have used the Curtain after 1609. These were the only companies of men players in London during 1603-8, and the Globe, the Fortune, and the Red Bull are obviously the 'three houses' whose rivalry is referred to by Dekker in the following passage from his *Raven's Almanack* of 1608:[4]

'Another ciuill warre doe I finde wil fal betweene players, who albeit at the beginning of this fatall yeare, they salute one another like sworne brothers, yet before the middle of it, shall they wish one anothers throate cut for two pence. The contention of the two houses, (the

---

[1] G. von Bülow in *2 R. Hist. Soc. Trans.* (1892), vi. 6, 10, from MS. *penes* Count von der Osten of Plathe, Pomerania; cf. Wallace, *Blackfriars*, 105, who identifies the *Samson* play, rightly, with that of the Admiral's men at the Fortune (cf. p. 180), and that at the Blackfriars, wrongly I think, with Chapman's *The Widow's Tears*. He assumes that the theatre visited on 13 Sept. was the Globe, but it might have been the Rose.

[2] '13. Den 13 ward eine comedia agirt, wie Stuhl-Weissenburg erstlich von den Türken, hernacher von den Christen wiederum erobert . . .

14. Auf den Nachmittag ward eine tragica comoedia von Samsone und dem halben Stamm Benjamin agirt. Als wir zu dem Theatro gingen . . .'.

[3] Cf. ch. xii (Chapel).

[4] Grosart, *Dekker*, iv. 210 (S. R. July 1608, printed 1609). The 'two houses' are, of course, those of York and Lancaster. Note the final puns.

gods bee thanked) was appeased long agoe, but a deadly warre betweene the three houses will I feare burst out like thunder and lightning. For it is thought that Flag will be aduanced (as it were in mortall defiance against Flag), numbers of people will also bee mustred and fall to one side or other, the drums and trumpets must be sounded, partes will then (euen by the chiefest players) bee taken : words will passe to and fro : speeches cannot so bee put vp, handes will walke, an alarum be giuen, fortune must fauour some, or els they are neuer able to stand : the whole world must sticke to others, or else al the water in the theames wil not serue to carrie those away that will bee put to flight, and a third faction must fight like wilde Buls against Lyons, or else it will be in vaine to march vp into the field.'

There were, however, more than three London companies about 1608. M. de la Boderie tells us how one fell into disgrace during that year, and how four others subscribed to buy off the consequent inhibition of plays.[1] The reconciliation is simple. Dekker has in mind only the ' public ' and not the 'private' houses. Of these Paul's was closed in 1606; it was made worth its Master's while not to reopen it. The Blackfriars was used by the successive boy companies, known generically as the Queen's Revels, until 1608 or 1609, when it passed to the King's men, who thereafter maintained it as a winter house, to supplement the Globe. The Queen's Revels then moved to the Whitefriars, a private house built at some time before 1608, and occupied in that year by the ephemeral company of the King's Revels.

An increase in the number of adult companies now made fresh demands upon theatrical house-room. It is presumably the Duke of York's men who were described at Leicester in 1608 as ' the Princes players of the White Chapple, London '. The description suggests that they used the Boar's Head, but if so, nothing more is heard of it, and it is conceivable that they soon succeeded to the Curtain. The Lady Elizabeth's, who came into existence in 1611, are traceable at the Swan, which Henslowe may have taken over to succeed the Rose, disused, if not pulled down, by 1606. The following lines are in John Heath's *Two Centuries of Epigrammes* (1610), but may of course, especially as the Red Bull is not named,

---

[1] Cf. ch. x. Fynes Moryson says in his *Itinerary*, iii. 2. 2 (*c.* 1605–17). ' The Theaters at London in England for Stage-plaies are more remarkeable for the number, and for the capacity, than for the building,' and in the continuation (*c.* 1609–26, C. Hughes, *Shakespeare's Europe*, 476), ' The Citty of London alone hath foure or fiue Companyes of players with their peculiar Theaters capable of many thousands, wherein they all play euery day in the weeke but Sunday. . . . As there be, in my opinion, more Playes in London than in all the partes of the worlde I haue seene, so doe these players or Comedians excell all other in the worlde.'

date back to the period when the Curtain was still in the hands
of the Queen's men:

> Momus would act the fooles part in a play,
> And cause he would be exquisite that way,
> Hies me to London, where no day can passe
> But that some playhouse still his presence has;
> Now at the Globe with a judicious eye
> Into the Vice's action doth he prie.
> Next to the Fortune, where it is a chaunce
> But he marks something worth his cognisance.
> Then to the Curtaine, where, as at the rest,
> He notes that action downe that likes him best.[1]

A foreign traveller again gives us help. The relation of the
visit of Prince Lewis Frederick of Württemberg in 1610 merely
records that he went to the Globe, and Justus Zingerling,
who was in London at about the same date, has the briefest
note of the existence of 'theatra comoedorum et in quibus
ursi et tauri cum canibus committuntur'.[2] But the itinerary
of Prince Otto of Hesse-Cassel in the following year is more
expansive. The compiler writes:

'In London there are seven theatres, where daily, except on Sundays,
comedies are performed, whereof the most important is the Globe,
which lies over the water. The theatre, where the children play, is on
the hither side of the water; they play at three o'clock, but only from
Michaelmas to Easter. Here it only costs half a shilling to enter, but
for the other places at least half a crown. These play only with lights,
and are the best company in London.'[3]

---

[1] *Epigram* 39. Both Curtain and Swan are named by W. Turner in
Turners Dish of Stuffe, or a Gallimaufry (1662), but this cannot be dated;
cf. ch. xv (Shank):

> That's the fat fool of the Curtain,
> And the lean fool of the Bull:
> Since Shancke did leave to sing his rhimes,
> He is counted but a gull:
> The players on the Bankside,
> The round Globe and the Swan,
> Will teach you idle tricks of love,
> But the Bull will play the man.

[2] Jodocus Sincerus, *Itineris Anglici brevissima delineatio* in *Itinerarium
Galliae* (1617), 370; cf. Rye, 131, who gives the first edition as 1616.

[3] K. Feyerabend in *E. S.* xiv. 440, from manuscript in Cassel Library
(cf. Rye, 143), 'Zu Londen sind 7 theatra, da tägliche, die sonntäge
ausgenommen, comoedien gehalten werden, unter welchen die vornehmste
der glbs [*sic*, for *globus*], so über dem wasser liegt. Das theatrum, da die
kinder spielen, ist auf diesseit des wassers, spielen um 3 uhr, aber nur
von michaelis bis auf ostern; hier kostet der eingang einen halben schilling
nur, da an andern orten wohl eine halbe kron. Diese [nämlich der Globus,
Ed., but surely in error] spielen nur bei lichtern und is die beste Cumpani
in London.' The baiting is also mentioned; cf. p. 457.

In addition to the Globe and the Whitefriars, the tale of seven
theatres is probably made up by the Blackfriars, the Fortune,
the Red Bull, the Curtain, and the Swan.

Henslowe's correspondence with Daborne shows that he
still had a ' publique howse ', probably the Swan, in December
1613, and also that in June of that year his company was only
just thinking of ' comming over ' for a summer season, presumably from the Whitefriars, as he had recently carried out
an amalgamation between the Lady Elizabeth's men and
the Queen's Revels.[1] In the following year occurred an
episode which curiously emphasizes the constant shifting of
the focus of theatrical interest during the whole of the period
with which we are concerned. Originally stageland was in
the heart of the City itself. With the building of the first
theatres, it was transferred to the Fields of the northern
suburbs. During the last decade of the sixteenth century
the Fields in their turn gave way to the Bankside. The
Rose, the Swan, and the Globe successively made their
appearance, and the vestry of Southwark began to echo the
earlier outcry of the City against the iniquities of players,
until their mouths were stopped with tithes. But the transpontine period proved a brief one. Hardly was the Globe
up, before Alleyn's choice of a site for the Fortune set the
fashion veering again, and opened up a new theatrical region
in the western suburbs. This was convenient for the Court
and the great houses along the Strand and for the lawyers in
the Temple and at Westminster, as well as for the City proper,
and its tradition has endured until quite recent years. The
Red Bull and the Whitefriars followed in the same area.
On the other hand, the Rose had vanished, and the King's
men, although they did not desert the Globe, acknowledged
the change of venue by taking up their winter quarters in
the Blackfriars hard by. One result was that men who had
ridden to the Fields and been ferried to the Bankside, now
walked or drove in their coaches to the theatre door. During
the spring of 1614 things were probably at their worst. Both
the Globe, after its fire, and the Hope were still in the builder's
hands, and if the Lady Elizabeth's lingered again at the
Whitefriars, there can have been no plays across the water
at all. The watermen, who twenty years before had exercised
the influence of their patron, the Lord Admiral, to induce the
Privy Council to revoke an inhibition on the Bankside houses,
sent up a bitter cry of protest. John Taylor, the ' water-
poet ', whom they chose as their spokesman, tells the story.[2]

---

[1] *Henslowe Papers*, 72, 79.
[2] Taylor, *The True Cause of the Watermen's Suit concerning Players,*

A petition to the King was prepared, to the effect that no
play-house might be permitted ' in London or in Middlesex,
within four miles of the City on that side of the Thames ',
and with this Taylor pursued James to Theobalds, New-
market, and Royston.   It recited the service done by watermen in the navy during the Armada invasion of 1588 and in
such expeditions as those of Essex in 1596 and 1597.   And
it proceeded :

' Afterwards the players began to play on the Bankside and to leave
playing in London and Middlesex (for the most part), then there went
such great concourse of people by water that the small number of
watermen remaining at home were not able to carry them, by reason
of the court, the terms, the players, and other employments, so that
we were enforced and encouraged (hoping that this golden stirring
would have lasted ever) to take and entertain men and boys.'

It was calculated that the number of watermen and their
dependants between Windsor and Gravesend had now by
1614 reached 40,000 :

' The cause of the greater half of which multitude hath been the
players playing on the Bankside, for I have known three companies
besides the bear-baiting, at once there ; to wit, the Globe, the Rose,
and the Swan. And it is an infallible truth that, had they never played
there, it had been better for watermen by the one half of their living,
for the company is increased more than half by their means of playing
there in former times.'

Foreign employment had now come to an end :

' And the players have all (except the King's men) left their usuall
residency on the Bankside, and do play in Middlesex far remote from
the Thames, so that every day in the week they do draw unto them
three or four thousand people, that were used to spend their monies
by water.'

Such, Taylor assures us, was the effect of the petition.   It was
referred by James to ' his commissioners for suits ', that is
to say, the Court of Requests, composed of Sir Julius Caesar,
Sir Thomas Parry, Sir Francis Bacon, Sir Henry Montagu,
Sir Walter Cope, George Calvert, and Baron Sotherton.   The
King's men exhibited a counter-petition, and the case came
on for hearing. .

' Sir Francis Bacon very worthily said that so far as the public weal
was to be regarded before pastimes, or a serviceable decaying multitude

and the reasons that their Playing on London side is their extreame hindrances.
With a Relation how farre that suit was proceeded in, and the occasions that
it was not effected, reprinted by Hindley, ii, No. 15, from Taylor's Works
(1630), probably originally printed in 1614.

before a handful of particular men, or profit before pleasure, so far was
our-suit to be preferred before theirs.'

The players appealed to the Earl of Somerset, who became
Lord Chamberlain and in that capacity their official protector
on 10 July 1614, but he proved well affected towards the
watermen.   The hearing was adjourned and never resumed,
owing to the death of Cope on 31 July, the promotion of
Caesar to the Mastership of the Rolls on 1 October, and the
consequent dissolution of the commission.   Ill feeling broke
out between Taylor and his fellows the watermen, who
declared that he met the players at supper at the Cardinal's
Hat on Bankside, and took bribes of them to let the suit
fall.   Taylor, therefore, wrote his pamphlet to vindicate his
position.[1]   The completion of the new Globe and the Hope
during the progress of the dispute had probably eased matters
temporarily for the watermen, but the growing tendency of
things theatrical towards Middlesex was not permanently
checked.   Some of the minor companies used the Hope until
1617, and then left it to the bears again.   The Globe survived,
but will be found to have occupied during the Caroline period
a distinctly secondary position to the Blackfriars in the
economy of the King's men.   For this there was another
reason besides the geographical superiority of Middlesex over
Surrey.   The acquisition of the Blackfriars, even though only
for winter purposes, in 1608 was an acknowledgement of the
advantages for adult companies of the ' private ' or roofed
type of theatre, hitherto used only by boys.   Once these
advantages were realized, the doom of the old ' ring ' type,
with its central opening, was written.   Probably the Hope
was the only new house constructed on these lines after 1608,
and obviously the Hope required free ventilation to get rid
of the stink of bears and dogs.   In 1615 Philip Rosseter and
others obtained sanction for the conversion of Porter's Hall
in the Blackfriars into a theatre.   This was to be used by
children as well as adults, and was probably roofed.   It was
pulled down again by what seems a somewhat arbitrary
decision in 1617.   About the same time, the roofed Cockpit
in Drury Lane was converted into a theatre, under the name
of the Phoenix, for the occupation of the Queen's men, who
migrated to it from the Red Bull.   Whether or not the

---

[1] It cites Caesar's promotion and describes the agitation by the watermen as taking place in ' January last, 1613 ', i.e. 1613¾.   Probably it was
written in the winter of 1614, and touched up before 1630, since it refers
to Bacon and Somerset as ' then ' Attorney-General and Lord Chamberlain
respectively.   Bacon's term of office was from 27 Oct. 1613 to 7 March
1617, Somerset's from 10 July 1614 to 2 Nov. 1615.

Fortune was given a roof at the rebuilding of 1623, or the Red Bull at somewhat the same time, is uncertain; but at any rate the Salisbury Court theatre, built near the Whitefriars in 1629, perhaps to replace the old Whitefriars theatre, was a roofed house.[1] This was the last new theatre built before the civil wars. The Blackfriars, the Cockpit, and Salisbury Court were the most important of the Caroline stages, and in the post-Restoration houses, although these were on a larger scale than the ' private ' houses of the past, the roofed model was invariably adopted.

Soon after the completion of Salisbury Court, Edmund Howes, who had already edited the fourth edition of John Stowe's *Annales* in 1615, was again revising the text for the fifth edition of 1631, and took occasion to append to his account of the burnings of the Globe and the Fortune the following summary of theatrical enterprise since 1569: [2]

' In the yeere one thousand six hundred twenty nine, there was builded a new faire Play-house, neere the white Fryers. And this is the seauenteenth Stage, or common Play-house, which hath beene new made within the space of threescore yeeres within London and the Suburbs, viz.

' Fiue Innes, or common Osteryes turned to Play-houses, one *Cockpit*, S. *Paules* singing Schoole, one in the *Black-fryers*, and one in the *White-fryers*, which was built last of all, in the yeare one thousand six hundred twenty nine, all the rest not not named, were erected only for common Play-houses, besides the new built Beare garden, which was built as well for playes, and Fencers prizes, as Bull bayting ; besides, one in former time at *Newington* Buts ; Before the space of threescore yeares aboue-sayd,.I neither knew, heard, nor read, of any such Theaters, set Stages, or Play-houses, as haue beene purposely built within mans memory.'

This passage serves as a fair summary of the detailed investigations set out in this chapter. Howes only allows one house to the Blackfriars and one to the Whitefriars, and must therefore be leaving out of account the abortive Porter's Hall house,

[1] There is, I suppose, no reason why Randolph's *Muses Looking Glass*, I. i. 55, should not have been written before Salisbury Court was built. Herein a ' brother ' is said to pray—

> That the Globe,
> Wherein (quoth he) reigns a whole world of vice,
> Had been consum'd : the Phoenix burnt to ashes :
> The Fortune whipp'd for a blind whore : Blackfriars,
> He wonders how it 'scaped demolishing
> I' th' time of reformation : lastly, he wish'd
> The Bull might cross the Thames to the Bear Garden,
> And there be soundly baited.

[2] Stowe, *Annales* (1631), 1004. In the extract in Harrison, ii. 49*, the period covered is given in error as 1553-1613.

and treating Salisbury Court as a continuation of the earlier Whitefriars. The Hope and Newington Butts are after-thoughts, and make his seventeen into nineteen. We can identify his five inns as the Bull, the Bell, the Cross Keys, the Bel Savage, and probably the Red Lion, although this just antedates his period of sixty years; while his balance of eight unnamed common play-houses must be the Theatre, the Curtain, the Rose, the Swan, the Globe, the Fortune, the Boar's Head, and the Red Bull.

Prynne, in his *Histriomastix* (1633), records six ' divels chappels ' as then in use, and these are doubtless the six houses, the Blackfriars, Globe, Cockpit, Salisbury Court, Fortune, and Red Bull, which are also noted by the Restoration writers on the stage, John Downes and James Wright, as surviving up to the cataclysm of the civil wars.[1]

Somewhat more confused and vague in their datings are the reminiscences about 1660 of the Marquis of Newcastle in his letter of advice to Prince Charles, under the head of ' Devertismentes for your Matie People ' :[2]

' Firste for London Paris Garden will holde good for the meaner People.

' Then for severall Playe Houses as ther weare five att leaste In my Time,—

' Black-Friers, the Cock-Pitt, Salsburye Courte, the Fortune, & the Redd Bull,—Ther weare the Boyes thatt played at Black-Friers, & Paules, & then the Kinges Players played att the Globe—which is nowe calde the Phenixe [!]—Some Played, att the Bores heade, & att the Curtin In the feildes & some att the Hope whiche Is the Beare Garden, and some at White Friers,—Butt five or Sixe Playe Houses Is enough for all sortes off Peoples divertion & pleasure In thatt kinde.'

The marquis is the only one of the chroniclers who definitely records the Boar's Head.

A manuscript continuation of Stowe's *Annales*, found in a copy of the 1631 edition, narrates the havoc wrought by Puritans and ground-landlords :[3]

' Play Houses. The Globe play house on the Banks side in South-warke, was burnt downe to the ground, in the yeare 1612. And now built vp againe in the yeare 1613, at the great charge of King Iames, and many Noble men and others. And now pulled downe to the ground, by Sir Matthew Brand, On Munday the 15 of April 1644, to make tenements in the room of it.

' The Blacke Friers players play house in Blacke Friers, London, which

---

[1] Cf. App. I.   [2] S. A. Strong, *Catalogue of Letters at Welbeck*, 226.
[3] Harrison, iv. 212, from *Phillipps MS.* 11613, f. 16, *penes* J. F. P. Fenwick, of Thirlestane House, Cheltenham, written about 1656–8. The writer is not quite accurate in some of his earlier dates.

had stood many yeares, was pulled downe to the ground on Munday the 6 day of August 1655, and tennements built in the rome.

'The play house in Salsbury Court, in Fleetstreete, was pulled downe by a company of souldiers, set on by the sectuaries of these sad times, on Saturday the 24 day of March 1649.

'The Phenix in Druery Lane, was pulled downe also this day, being Saterday the 24 day of March 1649, by the same souldiers.

'The Fortune Playhouse betweene White Crosse streete and Golding Lane was burnd downe to the ground in the yeare 1618. And built againe with brick worke on the outside in the yeare 1622. And now pulled downe on the inside by the souldiers this 1649.

'The Hope, on the Banks side in Southwarke, commonly called the Beare Garden, a Play House for Stage Playes on Mundayes, Wedens-dayes, Fridayes, and Saterdayes, and for the baiting of the Beares on Tuesdayes and Thursdayes, the stage being made to take vp and downe when they please. It was built in the year 1610, and now pulled downe to make tennementes, by Thomas Walker, a peticoate maker in Cannon Streete, on Tuesday the 25 day of March 1656. Seuen of M^r. Godfries beares, by the command of Thomas Pride, then hie Sheriefe of Surry, were then shot to death, on Saterday the 9 day of February 1655, by a company of souldiers.'

Downes and Wright do not mention the Hope, as they were not discussing baiting. On the other hand, the annalist says nothing of the fate of the Red Bull, which in fact appears to have escaped destruction, to have been occasionally used for 'drolls' during the Commonwealth, and to have served once more, with the Cockpit and Salisbury Court, the demoli-tion of which was probably limited to the interior fittings, for the first entertainments of the Restoration. The building of Vere Street in 1660, Lincoln's Inn Fields in 1661, and Drury Lane in 1663 made them obsolete.[1]

These records leave ambiguous the fate of the Curtain and the Swan. The Curtain is traceable in occasional use up to about 1627, and is figured as a roundish building in the 'Ryther' maps, which are probably of a decade later.[2] It cannot, therefore, have vanished long before the civil wars, and was the most long-lived of all the theatres. It may, of course, have been rebuilt, later than its original foundation in 1576, but as to this there is no evidence. The 'Ryther' maps also show the Fortune. No other maps give any of the theatres on the north of the river. Of the Bankside houses, the Swan is shown by a decagonal ground-plan, with the inscrip-tion 'Old Play house', in the Paris Garden Manor survey of 1627.[3] And it is described as still existing side by side with

[1] Ward, iii. 280 ; Lawrence, ii. 138.
[2] Baker, 135, gives an enlarged reproduction under the name of the Theatre ; but that is an obvious mistake.   [3] Rendle, *Bankside*, 1.

the Globe and the Hope, but clearly also as derelict, in the following passage from *Holland's Leaguer* (1632) :

'Especially, and aboue all the rest, she was most taken with the report of three famous *Amphytheators*, which stood so neere scituated, that her eye might take view of them from the lowest *Turret*, one was the *Continent of the World*, because halfe the yeere a World of *Beauties*, and braue *Spirits* resorted vnto it ; the other was a building of excellent *Hope*, and though *wild beasts* and *Gladiators* did most possesse it, yet the Gallants that came to behold those combats, though they were of a mixt Society, yet were many Noble worthies amongst them ; the last which stood, and as it were shak'd handes with this Fortresse, beeing in times past as famous as any of the other, was now fallen to decay, and like a dying *Swanne*, hanging downe her head, seemed to sing her owne dierge.'[1]

I turn now to the maps of the Bankside, which, had they been datable, and drawn with cartographical precision, ought not only to have furnished valuable evidence as to the duration of the theatres, but also to have indicated accurately the position of each amongst the streets and lanes of the district. Neither condition is, however, fulfilled.   Even where the date of an engraving is known, the date of the survey on which it was based can, as a rule, be only approximately determined.   And the constant intrusion of pictorial elements, which gives the maps the character of perspective views rather than of plans, is naturally emphasized on the Bankside, which has to serve as a foreground to the design.   The main topographical features which have to be borne in mind are simple, and can easily be related to those in John Rocque's map of 1746, as interpreted by Strype's *Survey* of 1720, or in a modern Ordnance map.   The whole region concerned lies roughly between the southern approaches to London and Blackfriars Bridges.   It underwent a good deal of development during one period, especially in the area of the Clink, a liberty lying between Southwark on the east and another liberty of Paris Garden on the west, and affording a convenient suburban resort outside the jurisdiction of the City.   Stowe's account of the neighbourhood in 1598 is perhaps a little misleading.   He describes no more than the Bankside proper, ' a continuall building of tenements ' on the riverside, extending about half a mile west of London Bridge.   Here he places, from west to east, the bear gardens, the former stews, the prison of the Clink, Winchester House, and the church of St. Mary Overie in Southwark.[2]   This agrees pretty well with

---

[1] [Nicholas Goodman ?] *Hollands Leaguer or an historical Discourse of the Life and Actions of Dona Britanica Hollandia the Arch-Mistris of the wicked women of Evtopia* (1632), sig. F 2 ; cf. C. W. Wallace in *Engl. Stud.* xliii. 392.   [2] Stowe, *Survey*, ii. 52.

the maps of Agas (*c.* 1561) and Norden (1593), except that
there was already a group of houses falling outside Stowe's
purview, which stood on the river near Paris Garden Stairs and
practically continued the Bankside westwards. But there
was also, which Stowe does not mention, a marshy *hinterland*
to the Bankside, of ponds and gardens, among which Agas,
and still more Norden, show a good many scattered houses.
By the end of the century there was a fairly definite north to
south street known as Deadman's Place, which debouched
from the east end of the Bankside, and from which in its turn
struck out one called Maid or Maiden Lane, which went in an
irregular line westwards over the marshes, and was finally
joined by two divergent ways, Love Lane and Gravel (afterwards Holland) Lane, to the Paris Garden group of houses.
Thus was formed a rough parallelogram, half a mile long, and
from 200 to 350 feet deep, within or near which all the theatrical
sites are placed by the maps. In Norden's map of 1593, both
the Bear House and the Play House, which must be the Rose,
stand considerably to the west of Deadman's Place. The Bear
House is the most westerly of the two, and is about half-
way between the Bankside houses on the north and Maid
Lane on the south. The Rose is a good deal nearer Maid Lane.
In the Delaram views (1603–20) there are three flagged, but
unnamed, structures. One which stands well back from the
river and, after allowing for the view-point, appears slightly
the most easterly of the three, is cylindrical; the upper half
is alone windowed, and has a smaller diameter than the
lower half. It is placed amongst trees and meadows. There
is nothing which obviously indicates Maid Lane.[1] The two
other buildings stand much nearer the river's edge, amongst
houses; they are angled, probably octagonal, and not
cylindrical. The ' Hondius ' views repeat the cylindrical
building and the most westerly of the two angled buildings
much in the same relative position; the intermediate one
has disappeared. It seems obvious that the cylindrical
building must be the Globe, and the other two the Bear
Garden, afterwards the Hope, to the west, and the Rose,
left out of the ' Hondius ' group, because it disappeared in
1605, in the centre. The Delaram and ' Hondius ' views do
not extend far enough west to include the Swan. It is shown
by Visscher in 1616, and named. So are the Bear Garden and
the Globe, both of which appear as angled buildings, octagonal

---

[1] I cannot agree with Dr. Martin (*Surrey Arch. Colls.* xxiii. 186), who
sees, both in the Delaram and the ' Hondius ' engravings, an east to west
highway running north of the cylindrical building, which he takes for
Maid Lane.

or hexagonal, about equidistant from the Bankside houses, and north of Maid Lane, the angle of which next Deadman's Place is shown.[1]   As the change from a cylindrical to an angled representation of the Globe coincides with the rebuilding of the house in 1614, we may perhaps infer that the structural form is not a mere cartographic convention.[2]   It is rather singular that in the Merian maps (circa 1638) there are four houses again, including the Swan, well to the west. This, with two of the three houses in the eastern group, is named by the engraver.   A third unnamed house stands between the Globe on the east and the Bear Garden on the west, which is approximately where the Rose used to stand. It is distinctly nearer the river than the other two, but all three are north of Maid Lane, from which the Bear Garden is slightly more remote than the Globe.[3] If the Rose had actually a second term of existence, it was probably only a brief one.[4]   The fullest of the Ryther maps (c. 1636–45) has two angled build-ings, one to the west, rather nearer to Bankside than to Maid Lane; the other to the east, and south of Maid Lane, standing in an angle between that and a track running from north-west to south-east. There are no names, but obviously the eastern house is the Globe, and the western the Hope, and indeed the dogs can be made out. The track joining Maid Lane may be Globe Alley. The Hollar view of 1647 shows two cylindrical, not angled, buildings. One lettered 'The Globe' is on the extreme brink of the river; the other, to the east and south of it, is lettered 'Beere bayting'. Faithorne and Newcourt, in 1658, give no theatres proper, but only a ring marked 'Beare garden'. Finally, Leeke and Hollar about 1666 give a single unnamed roundish theatre, south of Maid Lane. Presumably it is the Globe, but copied from a survey of earlier date, as the Globe had been pulled down for tenements in 1644.

On the whole, the maps are disappointing guides. It seems

[1] The somewhat wanton suggestion of Dr. Martin (loc. cit. 188) that the engraver mistook the Rose for the Globe is sufficiently refuted by the fact that the Rose was extinct or at least long disused.

[2] I do not know on what ground Adams, 458, says that Visscher's view was drawn several years before it was printed, ' and represents the city as it was in or before 1613 '.

[3] Martin, loc. cit. 192, again suggests that the houses are misnamed. He thinks that the Rose has been called the Globe in error and the Globe the Bear Garden, and that the unnamed house is the Globe. I cannot follow him in thinking that Merian represents the western house of the group as south of Maid Lane ; all three are clearly to the north.

[4] Adams, 458, thinks that Merian worked upon Visscher, ' with addi-tions from some other earlier view not yet identified '. If so, this might perhaps go back to 1605.

more probable than has quite been recognized, that the singular two-storied structure shown by Hondius and Delaram really represents the earlier, the Shakespearian, Globe. And the representation of a fourth house by Merian, even if he did not know its name, gives support to the view that the Rose may have had some kind of existence at a later date than the Sewers records indicate. But as regards the alinement, the distance from the river, and the relation to Maid Lane, of the three houses in the Clink, it is clear that no consistent story is told. The general impression one gets is that the Hope stood farthest to the west, then the Rose, and then the Globe; and that the Rose stood nearest to the river, then the Hope, and then the Globe. Nor is this inconsistent with documentary evidence, which in particular indicates that the parcel of land, on which the latest of the Bear Gardens was built, was contiguous on the west to that known as ' the little Rose '.[1] Bear Garden and Rose Alley, running side by side from the Bankside into Maid Lane or Park Street, are traceable in eighteenth-century maps and in the modern Ordnance map.[2] Did one judge by the maps alone, one would probably, in spite of the dissenting testimony of ' Ryther ' and of Leeke and Hollar, come to the conclusion that the Globe stood to the north of Maid Lane. The balance of other evidence points unmistakably in the other direction.[3]

B. THE PUBLIC THEATRES

i. The Red Lion Inn.
ii. The Bull Inn.
iii. The Bell Inn.
iv. The Bel Savage Inn.
v. The Cross Keys Inn.
vi. The Theatre.
vii. The Curtain.
viii. Newington Butts.

ix. The Rose.
x. The Swan.
xi. The Globe.
xii. The Fortune.
xiii. The Boar's Head.
xiv. The Red Bull.
xv. The Hope.
xvi. Porter's Hall.

i. THE RED LION INN

The following record appears in the court books of the Carpenters' Company:[4]

Courte holden the xv[th] daie of Julie 1567, Annoque Regni Reginae Eliz. nono by M[r] William Ruddoke, M[r] Richard More, Henrye Whreste & Richard Smarte wardeins, & M[r] Bradshawe.

Memorandum that at courte holden the daie & yeare abovesayd that, whear certaine varyaunce, discord & debate was betwene Wyllyam

---

[1] Cf. p. 463.   [2] Rendle, *Bankside*, xxx.   [3] Cf. p. 433.
[4] B. Marsh, *Records of the Worshipful Company of Carpenters*, iii. 95 I have to thank Mr. Marsh for this reference.

Sylvester carpenter on thone partie & John Brayne grocer on thother partie, yt is agreed, concluded & fullie determyned by the saide parties, by the assent & consent of them bothe, with the advise of the M^r & wardeins abovesayd that Willyam Buttermore, John Lyffe, Willyam Snellinge & Richard Kyrbye, Carpenters, shall with expedicon goe & peruse suche defaultes as are & by them shalbe found of in & aboute suche skaffoldes, as he the said Willyam hathe mad at the house called the Red Lyon in the parishe of Stebinyhuthe, & the said Willyam Sillvester shall repaire & amend the same with their advize substan-cyallie, as they shall thinke good. And that the said John Brayne, on Satterdaie next ensuenge the date above written, shall paye to the sayd Willyam Sylvester the some of eight poundes, tenne shillinges, lawfull money of England, & that after the playe, which is called the storye of Sampson, be once plaied at the place aforesaid the said John shall deliver to the said Willyam such bondes as are now in his custodie for the performaunce of the bargaine. In witnesse whereof both parties hereunto hathe sett their handes.

by me John Brayne grocer.
[Sylvester's mark.]

This is the only notice of the Red Lion playing-inn which has been preserved, but John Brayne, grocer, is doubtless the same who financed his brother-in-law, James Burbadge, in the far more important enterprise of the Theatre in 1576. Stebunheth or Stepney was a parish in Middlesex, lying to the east of the City, beyond Whitechapel, and, although near enough to be in a sense a suburb, was outside the civic jurisdiction.

ii. THE BULL INN

The first notice of the Bull is on 7 June 1575 when the playing of a 'prize' there is recorded in the register of the School of Defence. It appears to have been the most popular of all localities for this purpose and there are fourteen similar notices of its use in the register, ending with one on 3 July 1590.[1] Florio refers to it as a place for plays in 1578.[2] Stephen Gosson in his *Schoole of Abuse* (1579) exempts from his ordinary condemnation of plays *The Jew* and *Ptolemy* ' shown at the Bull '.[3] On 1 July 1582 the Earl of Warwick asked permission from the Lord Mayor for his servant John David to play his provost prizes at ' the Bull in Bishopsgatestrete or some other conuenient place to be assigned within the liberties of

London '. This was refused, much to Warwick's annoyance, on the ground that an inn was a place ' somewhat to close for infection ', and David appointed to play ' in an open place of the Leaden hall '.[1] The Bull, with the Bell, was assigned by a civic order of 28 November 1583 to the Queen's men for their first winter season. Tarlton and the Queen's men are said in the *Jests* to have played ' oftentimes ' at ' the Bull in Bishops-gate-street ', and here their play of *The Famous Victories of Henry the Fifth*, with Tarlton in the parts of the judge and the clown and Knell in that of Henry, was given.[2] This must, of course, have been between 1583 and Tarlton's death in 1588. In 1592 the translator of *The Spaniard's Monarchie* disclaims any ' title fetched from the Bull within Bishopsgate, as a figge for a Spaniard '. I do not know whether any old play underlying the Admiral's (q.v.) *Spanish Fig* of 1601–2 can be referred to. The house was still in use during 1594, for in April or May of that year Anthony Bacon settled in Bishopsgate, to the vexation of his mother, ' on account of its neighbourhood to the Bull-inn, where plays and interludes were continually acted, and would, she imagined, corrupt his servants '.[3] Richard Flecknoe mentions the Bull in Bishopsgate Street, with the Cross-Keys, as one of the inns turned into theatres at the beginning of Queen Eliza- beth's reign, as was ' at this day to be seen ' in 1664.[4] The site was at No. 91 on the west of Bishopsgate Street, and is shown in Hatton's map of 1708, and the Ordnance Survey maps of 1848–51 and 1875.

iii. THE BELL INN

This inn existed in 1560, for on 12 June of that year ' the wyff of the Bell in Gracyous-strett ' was carted as a bawd and whore.[5] Plays must have been used there in 1576–7, in the Revels Account for which year an item of 10*d*. is included ' ffor the cariadge of the partes of ye well counterfeit from the Bell in Gracious strete to St. Iohns to be performed for the play of Cutwell '.[6] With the Bull, it was assigned to the

---

[1] App. D, Nos. lx–lxii.   [2] Tarlton, 13, 24.
[3] Birch, *Elizabeth*, i. 173, from *Lambeth MS.* ; Spedding, viii. 314.
[4] Cf. App. I.   [5] Machyn, 238.
[6] Feuillerat, *Eliz.* 277. The play may have only been rehearsed, so that the identification of it by Fleay, 36, with *The Irish Knight* shown at Court by Warwick's men on 18 Feb. 1577 is untenable, and with it vanishes all ground for the assignment of the inn by Fleay, 40, to Rich's men in 1568–70, Lane's in 1571–3, Warwick's in 1575–80, and Hunsdon's in 1582–3.

Queen's men by a civic order of 28 November 1583 for their first winter season. *Tarlton's Jests* also mention Tarlton and ' his fellowes ', probably the Queen's men, as performing at the Bell ' by ' the Cross Keys which was also in Gracious Street, and this must have been before Tarlton's death in 1588.[1] Both houses may be included in Rawlidge's reference to play-houses in Gracious street and elsewhere ' put down ' by the City in Elizabeth's time. I suppose that the site is that of Bell Yard at No. 12 on the west of Gracechurch Street.[2]

iv. THE BEL SAVAGE INN

The Bel Savage is named as an early London play-house in the 1596 edition of Lambarde's *Perambulation of Kent*. This inn, of which the name is still preserved on Ludgate Hill, where it stood until 1873 (Harben, 63), must be distinguished from another in Gracechurch Street once kept by Tarlton, which in his time was known as the Saba.[3] The origin of the name is obscure ; a deed of 1452 refers to an ' inn . . . called Savages Inn, otherwise called the Bell on the Hoop, in the parishe of St. Bride in Fleet Street ' (*L. T. R.* ii. 71). Probably therefore the notion of the Belle Sauvage is a later perversion. Gascoigne, in the prologue to his *Glass of Government* (1575), repudiates the 'worthie jests' and ' vain delights ' of ' Bellsavage fair '.[4] Gosson, in 1579, excepts from his general condemnation of plays ' the two prose books, played at the Belsavage, where you shall find never a word without wit, never a line without pith, never a letter placed in vain '.[5] A play-house ' on Ludgate Hill ' is included by Rawlidge in his list of those ' put down ' in Elizabeth's time. Probably the Queen's men were acting at the Bel Savage in 1588, for after the death of Tarlton in that year was published ' a sorowfull newe sonnette, intituled Tarltons Recantacion uppon this theame gyven him by a gentleman at the Bel-savage without Ludgate (nowe or els never) beinge the laste theame he songe '.[6] Prynne's reference to *Dr. Faustus* (q.v.) at the Bel Savage suggests that at some time the Admiral's also played there. It was also occasionally used for the playing of ' prizes ' ; the earliest recorded date in

---

[1] Tarlton, 24.   [2] Harben, 65.
[3] Tarlton, 21. Apparently the Queen of Sheba, and not Pocahontas, was the original *Belle Sauvage*.
[4] App. C, No. xiv.
[5] App. C, No. xxii. The description reads like a compliment to Lyly, but does not justify the inference of Fleay, 39, that the Chapel boys played at the Bel Savage from 1559 to 1582.
[6] Arber, ii. 526.

the Register of the School of Defence being in 1575–7 and the latest on 31 January 1589.[1]

v. THE CROSS KEYS INN

This inn may have been the play-house, or one of the play-houses, ' in Gracious Street ' said by Rawlidge to have been ' put down ' under Elizabeth. The first notice of it dates from 23 June 1579, on which day James Burbadge was arrested at the suit of John Hynde for £5 1s. 1d., ' as he came down Gracious Street towards the Cross Keys there to a play '. The house is described as the dwelling-house of Richard Ibotson, citizen and brewer of London.[2] It was in use as a place of popular amusement during the life of Tarlton, who died in 1588, for one of the Jests relates how he came from the Bell, where he was playing to ' the Crosse-Keyes in Gracious streete ' to see Banks's performing horse there.[3] A company can first be definitely located at it in 1589, on 5 November of which year Lord Strange's men, as reported by Lord Mayor Hart to Burghley, disobeyed an admonition to forbear playing, and ' went to the Crosse Keys and played that afternoon '. In 1594 Strange's men were absorbed in Lord Hunsdon's, and on 8 October 1594 Hunsdon wrote to the Lord Mayor to obtain toleration for ' my nowe companie of players ' who had been accustomed ' to plaie this winter time within the citye at the Crosse Kayes in Gracious street '.[4] How long Shakespeare's fellows continued to use the Cross Keys as a winter house is unknown ; presumably it ceased to be available in 1596. The adaptation of the inn as a theatre was still visible at the Restoration, and is assigned by Richard Flecknoe to ' about the beginning of Queen Elizabeth's reign '. The site is shown in Ogilby and Morgan's map of 1677 and the Ordnance Survey map of 1848–51 : it is on the west of Gracechurch Street.

vi. THE THEATRE

[*Bibliographical Note.*—Material is available in the records of four litigations : (a) *Peckham v. Allen* (Wards and Liveries, 1589) as to the title to the site ; (b) *Burbadge v. Ames et al.* (Coram Rege, 1596–9) and *Earl of Rutland v. Allen and Burbadge* (Exchequer, 1599–1602) as to the title to a neighbouring plot ; (c) *Burbadge v. Brayne* (Chancery, 1588–95),

---

[1] *Sloane MS.* 2530, ff. 7, 10, 11, 14 ; cf. the quotation from G. Silver, *Paradoxe of Defence* (1599), in Adams, 13.

[2] Wallace, *N. U. S.* xiii. 82, 89.   [3] Tarlton, 23.

[4] App. D, No. ci. Fleay, 89, has no other material than these notices and an unjustifiable assumption of identity between the two companies for assigning the house to Leicester's (1586–8) and Strange's (1589–91).

Brayne (afterwards *Miles*) *v. Burbadge* (Chancery, 1590–5), and *Miles
v. Burbadge* (Requests, 1597), as to the profits of the house; (d) *Allen
v. Street* (Coram Rege, 1600), *Burbadge v. Allen* (Requests, 1600), *Allen v.
Burbadge* (Queen's Bench, 1601–2), and *Allen v. Burbadge et al.* (Star Chamber,
1601–2), as to the removal of the fabric. A few documents from these,
some of which he supposed to relate to the Blackfriars, were printed by
Collier in *Memoirs of the Actors* (1846 and *H. E. D. P.* iii. 257) and in
Original History of the Theatre in Shoreditch (1849, *Sh. Soc. Papers*, iv. 63).
A large number were used by Halliwell-Phillipps for his excursus on *The
Theatre and Curtain* (*Outlines*, i. 345), and in C. C. Stopes, *Burbage and
Shakespeare's Stage* (1913), where abstracts of (a) and (b) may be con-
sulted. The full texts of (c) and (d) are printed in C. W. Wallace, *The
First London Theatre, Materials for a History* (1913, *Nebraska University
Studies*, xiii. 1). The exact locality of the site has been carefully investi-
gated by W. W. Braines in *Holywell Priory and the Site of the Theatre,
Shoreditch* (1915, *Indication of Houses of Historical Interest in London*,
xliii), and again in *The Site of the Theatre, Shoreditch* (1917, *L. T. R.* xi. 1).]

The following statement as to the beginnings of theatrical
enterprise in London is made by Cuthbert Burbadge and his
family in the so-called *Sharers Papers* of 1635 : [1]

'The father of us, Cutbert and Richard Burbage, was the first
builder of playehowses, and was himselfe in his younger yeeres a
player. The Theater hee built with many hundred poundes taken up
at interest. The players that lived in those first times had onely the
profitts arising from the dores, but now the players receave all the
commings in at the dores to themselves and halfe the galleries from
the houskepers. Hee built this house upon leased ground, by which
meanes the landlord and hee had a great suite in law, and, by his death,
the like troubles fell on us, his sonnes ; wee then bethought us of
altering from thence, and at like expence built the Globe.'

The accuracy of this is fully borne out by the records of the
various legal proceedings in connexion with the Theatre,
which a painful investigation has exhumed, and the topographical indications furnished by the evidence in some of
these have made it possible to locate with some precision the
site of London's first regular play-house.

The Theatre stood in the Liberty of Halliwell or Holywell,
part of the Middlesex parish of St. Leonard's, Shoreditch,
immediately outside the Bishopsgate entrance to the City.[2]

---

[1] Halliwell-Phillipps, i. 317 ; cf. p. 425.

[2] Stowe, *Survey* (ed. Kingsford, ii. 262, 369), ends his account of Holywell
in the 1598 edition, ' And neare therevnto are builded two publique houses
for the acting and shewe of Comedies, Tragedies, and Histories, for recreation. Whereof the one is called the Courtein, the other the Theatre : both
standing on the Southwest side towards the field '. This is omitted from
the 1603 edition, probably not so much, as has been suggested, because
Stowe shared the Puritan dislike of the stage, as because in 1603 the
Theatre was gone and the Curtain little used. Stowe's draft (*c.* 1598) in

The name of the Liberty was derived from an ancient holy well, which has now disappeared, and its status from the fact that it had been the property of a priory of Benedictine nuns. The buildings of the priory lay between Shoreditch High Street, leading north from Bishopsgate, on the east and the open Finsbury fields on the west. Its southern gate was in a lane leading from the High Street to the Fields, then and still known as Holywell Lane or Street, on the south of which lay the Prioress's pasture called the Curtain. Part of this south end of the liberty, lying on both sides of Holywell Lane, had been leased in 1537 and 1538 to the Earls of Rutland, who continued to hold it from the Crown after the dissolution in 1539, and obtained a renewed lease in 1584.[1] The rest of the property, including the main conventual buildings, was sold in 1544 to one Henry Webb, whose daughter Susan and her husband Sir George Peckham sold it in 1555 to Christopher Bumsted, and he in the same year to Christopher Allen and his son Giles. The alienation of 1555 was challenged as illegal by Susan Peckham's heirs in 1582, and ultimately, but not until about thirty years later, they appear to have made good their claim.[2] In the meantime Giles Allen had leased a part of the property, which became the site of the Theatre, to James Burbadge on 13 April 1576.[3] This was bounded to the north by the wall of Allen's own garden, probably corresponding to the main cloister of the convent, on the east or south-east by the Earl of Rutland's holding, and on the west by a ditch dividing it from the open Finsbury fields. Within the ditch and divided from it by a strip of void ground, was the old brick wall of the precinct. On the extreme south was a bit of void ground lying between an Oat Barn occupied by Rutland and another Great Barn included in the lease. The Oat Barn and the void ground were in fact debatable property claimed both by Allen and Rutland. North of the Great Barn, and immediately to the

---

Harl. MS. 538 runs, ' Neare adjoyning are builded two houses for the shewe of Activities, Comedies, tragedies and histories, for recreation. The one of them is named the Curtayn in Holy Well, the other the Theatre.' No contemporary map shows the Theatre, although that of Agas (*c.* 1561) gives a good idea of the Halliwell district before it was built. The representation from the seventeenth-century ' Ryther ' map, given as the Theatre by Baker, 135, is presumably the Curtain.

[1] Braines (1915), 4 ; Stopes, 185.

[2] Halliwell-Phillipps, i. 345 ; Braines (1915), 5, 21.

[3] Latin translations of parts of the lease are recited in pleadings of 1600 and 1602 (Wallace, 166, 268), and the description of parcels agrees with that in the draft lease of 1585, similarly recited in 1600 (Wallace, 169) ; cf. Braines (1915), 8.

east of the precinct wall was more void and garden ground ; farther to the east the ' inner court yarde ' of the convent. This held tenements backing upon Allen's garden to the north, and others, including a mill-house, backing on the garden ground to the west. In this yard was a well, probably the eponymous ' Holywell ', which fed a horsepond by Rutland's stable on the south-east, and then drained away through the debatable ground to the Finsbury ditch.[1] Since Burbadge's barn is known to have been shored up to the Theatre, it is evident that this must have been constructed in the void and garden ground between the tenements and the precinct wall, and as there was no right of way through Rutland's holding from Holywell Lane, an entrance was made through the wall direct from Finsbury fields. The Theatre itself, indeed, was sometimes loosely spoken of as ' in the fields '.[2] Working from later title-deeds of the locality, Mr. Braines has successfully located the precise site of the building in the angle now formed by Curtain Road, which occupies the strip of void ground between the precinct wall and Finsbury ditch, and New Inn Yard, which occupies a strip of the ' debateable ground ' and a strip also of the site of the Great Barn. The site is now part of the premises of the Curtain Road Elementary School.[3]

[1] The position of the well in Chassereau's *Survey of Shoreditch* (1745) seems to me to bear out this identification, although, as Braines (1915), 4, points out, we do not know Chassereau's authority. Under Burbadge's lease all Giles Allen's tenants in Holywell were to have access to the well. Stowe, *Survey*, i. 15, describes the holy well as ' much decayed and marred with filthinesse purposely laide there, for the heightening of the ground for garden plots '. It is clearly distinct from Dame Agnes a Cleere's well, which was outside Holywell, towards the north (Stowe, *Survey*, i. 16 ; ii. 273 ; Stopes, 192).

[2] *Tarlton's News out of Purgatory* (S. R. 26 June 1590), in *Tarlton*, 54, 105, ' I would needs to the Theatre to a play, where when I came, I founde such concourse of unrulye people, that I thought it better solitary to walk in the fields, then to intermeddle myselfe amongst such a great presse. Feeding mine humour with this fancie, I stept by dame Anne of Cleeres well, and went by the backside of Hogsdon, where, finding the sun to be hotte, and seeing a faire tree that had a coole shade, I sat me downe to take the aire, where after I had rested me a while, I fell asleepe. . . . And with that I waked, and saw such concourse of people through the fields that I knew the play was doon.'

[3] Braines (1915), 27. Halliwell-Phillipps, i. 351, put the site on the present Deane's Mews, but this is too far south, and does not allow for the interposition of Rutland's holding between Holywell Lane and Allen's. The shoring up of the barn to the Theatre is testified to in Wallace, 227, 231, 243. The exact site therefore cannot have been far east of the Curtain Road, which apparently occupies the strip of void land held by Burbadge between the old priory wall and the ditch bordering Finsbury fields.

Burbadge's lease was for a term of twenty-one years from Lady Day 1576. He was to pay a fine of £20 and an annual rent of £14. He covenanted to spend £200 within the first ten years in improving the existing buildings, and in return Allen covenanted to make a new lease for twenty-one years at any time within the first ten years, and also to allow the tenant at any time within the term of either lease ' to take down such building as should within the sayd tenne yeeres be erected on the sayd voyde growndes for a theater or playinge place '. It was also agreed that Allen and his wife and family ' vpon lawfull request therfore made ' should be entitled ' to enter or come into the premisses and their in some one of the vpper romes to have such convenient place to sett or stande to se such playes as shalbe ther played freely without any thinge therefore payeinge soe that the sayd Gyles hys wyfe and familie doe com and take ther places before they shalbe taken vpp by any others '. Burbadge, a joiner as well as a player, had probably the technical qualifications for his enterprise. But he was a man of small means, not worth above 100 marks, and had no credit.[1] He found a partner in his brother-in-law, John Brayne, a well-to-do grocer of Bucklersbury, who had already been connected with a play-house speculation at the Red Lion inn. The association proved a calamitous one, and its history can only be traced through the dubious *ex parte* statements of later litigation. Burbadge, in ar, unfortunately mutilated document, appears to have alleged that Brayne acquired an interest by means of a promise, which he afterwards evaded, to leave it to his sister's children.[2] Robert Miles, of the George Inn, Whitechapel, a friend of Brayne, who supported and ultimately inherited the case of his widow, told a different story.[3] He had heard Burbadge ' earnestlie insynuate ' Brayne to join in the transaction, as one which ' wold grow to ther contynual great profitt and commodytie '. Brayne was ' verye loth to deale in the matter ', and complained later to Miles that it was ' his vtter vndoing ', and that he would never have touched it, but for the ' swete and contynuall ' persuasions of Burbadge. His brother-in-law had assured him that the cost of erecting the play-house would not exceed £200, and after it had already cost £500, urged that ' it was no matter ', and that the profits ' wold shortlie quyte the cost vnto them bothe '. Obviously Brayne was out for profits, and had to take his risks. But if the account of Miles is to be trusted, he had also definite grievances against his partner. Burbadge's small contribution to the outlay was partly made

Wallace, 134, 141, 153.   [2] Ibid. 39.   [3] Ibid. 139.

in material, for which he overcharged at the rate of sixpence for a groat's worth. When funds ran short, Brayne and his wife worked as labourers on the structure, while Burbadge, if he set his hand to a job, took the regular rate of wages for it. And there is some corroboration of a more serious charge of ' indyrect dealing ', after the house was opened, about the ' collecting of the money for the gallories '.[1] Miles alleged that during a space of two years Burbadge used a secret key made by one Braye, a smith in Shoreditch, to filch from ' the commen box where the money gathered at the said playes was putt in ', thus cheating ' his fellowes the players ' as well as Brayne. He would also ' thrust some of the money devident betwene him and his said ffellowes in his bosome or other where about his bodye '. The Theatre was in use by 1 August 1577, as it is mentioned by name in the Privy Council inhibition of that date.[2] But it was opened before the work was completed, and the last stages were paid for out of the profits.[3] Moreover, in addition to what Brayne and Burbadge could find, money had to be raised on mortgage, with the result that Brayne never got full security for his interest in the undertaking. He was not a party to the original lease, thinking that if a joint lease were entered into, the survivor would take all.[4] When a draft assurance of a moiety of the profits to him was prepared on 9 August 1577, it could not be executed because the lease was at pawn, and ultimately, on 22 May 1578, Burbadge gave him a bond of £400 to assure in due course.[5] An assurance was, however, never made. The friction between the partners led to violent disputes. On one occasion, after high words in a scrivener's shop, ' Burbage did there strike him with his fist and so they went together by the eares in somuch that this deponent could herdly part them '.[6] On 12 July 1578 they submitted their differences to arbitrators, who decided that, with the exception of 10s. weekly for Brayne's housekeeping and 8s. for Burbadge's out of the profits of ' such playes as should be playd there vpon Sundaies ', the first charge upon the rents and profits of the property should be the repayment of debts due upon the theatre. Thereafter Brayne should take them ' till he shuld be answered suche somes of money which he had lade out for and vpon the same Theatre more then the said Burbage had done '. And when this claim too was discharged, the rents and profits should ' go in devydent equallye betwene them '. Should it be necessary to raise

[1] Wallace, 142 (Miles), 152 (Nicoll).   [2] App. D, No. xxxiv.
[3] Wallace, 135.   [4] Ibid. 140.
[5] Ibid. 151 (Nicoll).   [6] Ibid. 152 (Nicoll).

money on mortgage, it should be a joint mortgage, and its redemption would then come in as the first claim on the rents and profits. Burbadge gave Brayne a further bond of £200 for the keeping of this award.[1] On 26 September 1579 a mortgage was in fact entered into for a loan of £125 from John Hyde, grocer, to be repaid in a year. The amount, however, was not forthcoming, and although Hyde made an arrangement to take £5 a week out of the profits, he only got it for four or five weeks. In June 1582 he arrested Burbadge and got £20 out of him. Shortly afterwards he claimed forfeiture of the lease, and as Burbadge warned him that Brayne ' wold catch what he cold ', appointed one of his own servants with Burbadge ' to gather vp v^li wekely during the tyme of playes '. In this way he got back another £20 or £30. There was, however, still at least £30 outstanding when Brayne died in August 1586.[2] His widow Margaret claimed a moiety of the interest under the lease as his heir. At first, we hear, Burbadge allowed her ' half of the profittes of the gallaries ', but only so long as she could lay out money ' to the necessary vse of the said playe howsse ', and when she had so spent £30, he said that he must take all the profits until the debts were paid, made her gather as a servant, and finally thrust her out altogether.[3] Meanwhile Hyde was getting impatient for his money. He had promised Mrs. Brayne that, if he were satisfied, he would reassure the lease to her and Burbadge jointly, but not to either party separately. But now he said that he must convey it to whichever would pay him first, and being approached through Walter Cope, the master of Burbadge's son Cuthbert, he did in fact, on some promise that Mrs. Brayne should not be wronged, take his £30 and make over the lease to Cuthbert Burbadge on 7 June 1589.[4] Henceforward Cuthbert, and not his father, was the ostensible tenant of the property. This transaction stimulated Mrs. Brayne to assert her claims. About a year before the Burbadges had brought an action against her in Chancery, apparently in the hope of enforcing the alleged promise of Brayne to leave his interest to his sister's children ; and she now retorted with a counter-action against James and Cuthbert, in which she claimed to have an assignment of a moiety of the lease.[5] Her chief

[1] Wallace, 73 (Bett), 102, 119 (Ralph Miles), 137 (Collins), 143 (Robert Miles), 152 (Nicoll), 157.

[2] Ibid. 53, 107, 111 (Hyde), 73 (Bett), 143 (Robert Miles), 103, 120 (Ralph Miles). Brayne's will was proved 10 Aug. 1586 (Wallace, 14).

[3] Ibid. 104 (Ralph Miles), 146 (Robert Miles).

[4] Ibid. 16, 55, 108 (Hyde), 73 (Bett), 145 (Miles).

[5] Ibid. 46.

witness was the Robert Miles on whose statements this
narrative has already drawn. He was not of unimpeachable
reputation. His long association with Brayne had ended
in a quarrel. Brayne had ' charged Miles with his deathe,
by certaine stripes geven him by Miles '. The widow had
accused him before the coroner and procured his indictment
as ' a comon barreter '. Afterwards they had become friends,
and he was now maintaining Mrs. Brayne in her suit.[1] Much
of his evidence, however, received corroboration from his
son Ralph, from William Nicoll, a notary who had prepared
the deeds connected with the partnership, and from Edward
Collins, who had acquired Brayne's grocery business in
Bucklersbury. Burbadge, on the other hand, relied largely
on one Henry Bett, who had had an opportunity of perusing
Mrs. Brayne's papers, and had then transferred his services
to the other side. We cannot perhaps assume that all the
evidence in the cross-suits is preserved. So far as what we
have goes, there seems to have been no attempt on Burbadge's
part to defend himself against the charge of indirect dealing
during the early years of partnership. Nor were the main
facts as to the history of the lease much in dispute. The
chief issue was as to Mrs. Brayne's equitable claim to an
interest in it, and this of course turned largely on the state
of the account between Brayne and Burbadge at the death
of the former. Miles asserted that the expenditure on the
building of the Theatre in cash and credit had been practically all Brayne's, that he had started as a rich man, but had
had to sell his lease and stock in Bucklersbury and pawn his
own wardrobe and his wife's to get the work finished, that he
was ruined, and that Mrs. Brayne was now ' vtterlye vndone '
by the suit, and owed 500 marks to her friends.[2] On the other
side it was claimed that Brayne's wealth, variously reputed
at from £500 to £1,000, had been exaggerated, that he was
already involved when he took the Theatre in hand, and
that his downfall was largely due to unfortunate investments
outside the partnership, especially in a soap-making business
carried on with Miles at the George, where in fact Burbadge
had incurred losses in helping him.[3] Bett, moreover, said that,
while Brayne ' would never plainlie declare ' what his profits
on the Theatre had been, ' yt seemed by his taulke, that he
had gayned and receyved a grete deale of monye, more than
he had disbursed '.[4] The actual figures produced in the course

[1] Wallace, 86 (Bett), 115 (Bishop), 122 (Ralph Miles).
[2] Ibid. 109 (Hyde), 134 (Griggs), 137 (Collins), 106 (Ralph Miles), 139,
148 (Robert Miles).
[3] Ibid. 83 (Bett), 88 (Gascoigne), 90 (James).
[4] Ibid. 87 (Bett).

of the case, which are sufficient to enable us to arrive at a fair estimate of the main position, do not quite bear out this suggestion. Towards the original outlay Burbadge seems to have found about £50; Brayne as much and £239 more, which he claimed as due to him from the partnership. In addition there were outside debts outstanding at the time of his death to the amount of at least £220. Something, moreover, had already been spent out of takings before 1586 in payments on Hyde's mortgage. So that we may perhaps reasonably accept the total cost of the building as being some-where about the 1,000 marks (£666) at which common repute estimated it.[1] A certain amount of building material worth perhaps 100 marks, was still in hand. All that Brayne could be shown to have received as against his considerable outlay was a sum of £135 1s., for which his receipt was produced. What Burbadge had received it is difficult to say. A comparison of various estimates suggests that after Brayne's death it may have been between £100 and £200 a year.[2] On the other hand, he had paid off the debt of £220 which Brayne had left outstanding. And throughout he had been responsible, without aid from Brayne, for certain outgoings independent of the structure of the Theatre, for which he was entitled to claim credit. He had paid £230 in rent and laid out at least £220 in putting the tenements in order, as well as at least £30 early in 1592 on the repair of the Theatre itself.[3]

The fortunes of the case in Chancery were various. In 1590 the Court seemed inclined to grant a sequestration of half the profits; but instead made an order that the arbitrament of 1578 should be observed.[4] On the strength of this Mrs. Brayne and Miles came to the Theatre on more than one occasion, and claimed to appoint collectors, including one

[1] Griggs (Wallace, 134) puts Brayne's expenditure at 1,000 marks and Burbadge's at under £100; Collins (Wallace, 137) agrees as to Brayne's and puts Burbadge's at about £50; Miles (ibid. 141) says Brayne spent £600 or £700 in cash or credit and Burbadge about £50 in cash and material; Lanman (ibid. 148) had heard that the building cost 1,000 marks; Giles Allen (ibid. 164) valued it at £700 in 1599.

[2] Robert Miles put Burbadge's total profits from tenements and play-house in eight or nine years before 1592 at 2,000 marks, but in 1600 he only put the aggregate profits of James and Cuthbert from the playhouse by itself at 1,000 marks (Wallace, 147, 263). Giles Allen (ibid. 198) put them at £2,000. Ralph Miles in 1592 had heard that Burbadge had received £700 or £800 in rents and profits since Brayne's death in 1586 (ibid. 106). John Alleyn, a more disinterested witness, confirms this estimate, putting the figure at £100 or 200 marks a year for the five years before 1592 (ibid. 102).

[3] Wallace, 76 (Ellam), 77 (Hudson). [4] Ibid. 47.

Nicholas Bishop, who was asked to stand ' at the door that goeth vppe to the gallaries of the said Theater to take and receyve for the vse of the said Margarett half the money that shuld be gyven to come vppe into the said gallaries at that door '. They were, however, refused access, and on 16 November 1590 there was a row royal, of which independent witness was borne by John Alleyn, of the Admiral's men, who were then playing at the Theatre. James Burbadge, ' looking out at a wyndoe vpon them ', joined his wife in reviling them as a murdering knave and whore, and expressed his contempt for the order of Chancery ; Cuthbert, who came home in the middle of the fray, backed him up ; while Richard Burbadge, the youngest son, snatched up a broom-staff, and as he afterwards boasted, paid Robert Miles his moiety with a beating. He also threatened Nicholas Bishop, ' scornfully and disdainfullye playing with this deponentes nose '. James said that at their next coming his sons should provide pistols charged with powder and hempseed to shoot them in the legs.[1] Both Cuthbert and James were summoned on 28 November for contempt before the court, which instead of dealing with this charge proceeded to take the whole case into further consideration.[2] This was something of a triumph for Burbadge, who continued to resist the order, and repeated with oaths that twenty contempts and as many injunctions would not force him to give up his property. This was heard by John Alleyn in the Theatre yard about May 1591, and about eight days later ' in the Attyring housse or place where the players make them ready ', on the occasion of a dispute with the Admiral's men about some of ' the dyvydent money between him and them ' which he had detained, Burbadge was equally irreverent before Alleyn and James Tunstall about the Lord Admiral himself, saying ' by a great othe, that he cared not for iij of the best lordes of them all '.[3] Margaret Brayne died in 1593, leaving her estate to Miles, who thus became a principal in the suit.[4] And on 28 May 1595 the court

---

[1] Wallace, 59 (C. Burbadge), 62 (J. Burbadge), 97, 114 (Bishop), 100, 126 (Alleyn), 105, 121 (Ralph Miles).

[2] Ibid. 49, 66.

[3] Ibid. 101, 127 (Alleyn). The two depositions are not quite consistent as to dates. From that of 6 Feb. 1592, one would infer that the dispute between Burbadge and the Admiral's was at the time of the contempt of 16 Nov. 1590. The second, of 6 May 1592, apparently corrects the first, by giving the date of the insult to the Lord Admiral as ' about a yere past '. The point is of importance, as bearing upon the length of the stay of the Admiral's and Strange's (cf. ch. xiii) at the Theatre. No doubt Mrs. Brayne, who came ' dyvers tymes ' to the Theatre, continued her applications after laying her affidavit of contempt.

[4] Wallace, 153.

came to the decision that it could not entertain the case, until Miles had endeavoured to obtain relief at common law, by suing on the two bonds which Burbadge had given to Brayne in 1578.[1] He does not seem to have thought it worth while to do this, probably because he saw very little chance of recovering money from James Burbadge, while Cuthbert, who now held the lease, was not a party to the bonds.[2]

It is the personality of Burbadge rather than the conduct of the Theatre that these details illumine. But we may gather that the building was constructed mainly of timber with some ironwork, that it had a tiring-house and galleries, one at least of which was divided into upper rooms, where spectators could sit as well as stand, and that money was taken by appointed gatherers, placed in locked boxes, and subsequently shared out amongst those entitled to it.[3] From other sources it appears that 1d. was charged for admission to the building and 1d. or 2d. more for a place in the galleries.[4] Apparently the players took the entrance fee and the owners of the house the whole or an agreed proportion of the gallery money. In the winter of 1585 an interesting arrangement was entered into between Burbadge and Brayne on the one hand and Henry Lanman, owner of the neighbouring Curtain, on the other, by which during a period of seven years the Curtain was taken ' as an Esore ' to the Theatre, and the profits of both houses pooled and equally divided between the two parties. This arrangement was still operative in 1592.[5] Kiechel tells us that the number of galleries was three, and De Witt that the shape was that of an ' amphitheatrum '.[6] It is impossible to trace with any certainty the successive occupation of the Theatre by various companies of players or to reconstruct the list of plays produced upon the boards. Its occupants were Burbadge's ' fellows ' at the time of his frauds of 1576–8, and may reasonably be identified with Leicester's, of whom he was certainly one in 1574.[7] Stephen Gosson tells us in 1579 that amongst plays then ' vsually

[1] Wallace, 156.
[2] Ibid. 161, 263. Miles still held Burbadge's bonds in 1600.
[3] Ibid. 137, ' iron worke which the said Braynes bestowed vppon the same Theater '.   [4] Cf. ch. xviii.
[5] Wallace, 62 (Burbadge), 88 (Bett), 125 (Alleyn), 149 (Lanman).
[6] Cf. pp. 358, 362. This evidence outweighs the rather slight grounds on which T. S. Graves, The Shape of the First London Theatre (South Atlantic Quarterly, xiii. 280), conjectures that it may have been rectangular.
[7] G. Harvey, Letter Book, 67, suggests in 1579 that he may be asked by Leicester's, Warwick's, Vaux's or Rich's men, or ' sum other freshe startenup comedanties ' for ' sum malt conceivid comedye fitt for the Theater, or sum other paintid stage ' (cf. p. 4). It is a pity he was not more precise.

brought in to the Theater ', were *The Blacksmith's Daughter*
and his own *Catiline's Conspiracies*, and in 1582 assigns to
the same house Lodge's, if it was Lodge's, *Play of Plays and
Pastimes* given on the last 23 February, the play of *The Fabii*
and possibly the history of *Caesar and Pompey*.[1] Presumably
The Fabii is *The Four Sons of Fabius*, presented by Warwick's
men at Court on 1 January 1580. Warwick's men had therefore probably replaced Leicester's at the Theatre, and it was
the same men, then in the service of the Earl of Oxford, who
were concerned in a riot at the Theatre on 10 April 1580.[2]
In 1582 came the controversy between Edmund Peckham
and Giles Allen about the freehold of the Theatre site, as
a result of which Burbadge was ' disturbed and trobled in his
possession ', and ' the players for sooke the said Theater
to his great losse '.[3] So there was probably another change
at this time. And in 1583 there was a complete reshuffling
of all the London companies on the formation of the Queen's
men. Professor Wallace, who is primarily considering that
part of the evidence which he has himself discovered, says
that the Queen's did not act at the Theatre.[4] But most
certainly they did. It is true that, when an inhibition against
the Theatre and Curtain was obtained on 14 June 1584, the
owner of the Theatre, ' a stubburne fellow ', described himself as Lord Hunsdon's man. Nevertheless the only companies
named as concerned are the Queen's and Arundel's, and
Burbadge may not himself have been then acting.[5] And as
to the presence of the Queen's in the Theatre at some date
there is no doubt. Tarlton is not traceable in any other
company than the Queen's, and it was at the Theatre that
Tarlton made jests of Richard Harvey's *Astrological Discourse
upon the Conjunction of Saturn and Jupiter*, published in
1583.[6] The Queen's certainly did not confine themselves to

---

[1] Cf. App. C, Nos. xxii, xxx. Fleay, 40, 88, 145, identifies *The Play
of Plays* in which Delight was a character with the *Delight* shown at Court
by Leicester's on 26 Dec. 1580, and *Caesar and Pompey*, which Gosson
does not quite clearly assign to the Theatre at all, with the *Pompey* shown
by Paul's on 6 Jan. 1581 ; and conjectures successive occupations by
Leicester's (1576–83), Paul's (1582), Queen's and Hunsdon's (1584), Queen's
and Oxford's (1585), Queen's (1586–93), Chamberlain's (1594–7). He was
unlucky in omitting the Admiral's from his guesses.

[2] Cf. App. D, Nos. xliii, xliv.

[3] Wallace, 201 (Cuthbert Burbadge), 239 (Smith), 240 (May), 242 (Tilt).

[4] Ibid. 11.   [5] Cf. App. D, No. lxxiv.

[6] Nashe, *Pierce Penilesse* (*Works*, i. 197). Harington, *Metamorphosis
of Ajax* (1596), speaks of a vulgar word ' admitted into the Theater with
great applause by the mouth of Mayster Tarlton, the excellent comedian '.
It was near the Theatre that the writer of *Tarltons Newes of Purgatorie*
(Tarlton, 54) had his dream of the dead actor.

the Theatre; but that they were there again in 1589 may be inferred from a mock testament of Martin Marprelate in *Martins Month's Mind*, in which he is made to admit that he learned his twittle tattles ... at the Theater of Lanam and his fellows '. A marginal note in the same pamphlet indicates that it was at the Theatre that the 'Maygame' representing the 'launcing and worming' of Martin was staged, and there is other evidence that Laneham, then one of the Queen's men, was one of the players who took a part in the ribald controversy.[1] Gabriel Harvey's scoff at Lyly as 'the Foolemaster of the Theatre' may perhaps indicate his authorship of plays for the house. In 1590–1 it is clear that the Admiral's men, probably already associated with Strange's, were at the Theatre, and their quarrel with Burbadge doubtless led them to cross the river and join Henslowe at the Rose. After the reconstitution of the companies in 1594, James Burbadge's son Richard became a leading member of the Chamberlain's men, and it is probable that, when this company left the Rose about the middle of June, it was to the Theatre that they went. Here *Hamlet*, which certainly belonged to them, was being acted in 1596.[2] It must be added that the Theatre was not strictly reserved for the purposes of the legitimate drama. It was built for 'activities', amongst other things, according to Stowe, and prizes of the School of Defence were played at it between 1578 and 1585.[3] On 22 February 1582, there took place at the Theatre 'a scurvie play set oot al by one virgin, which there proved a fyemarten without voice, so that we stayed not the matter'.[4]

It was a natural consequence of the success of Burbadge's new departure that the Theatre and its immediate successor, the Curtain, had to bear the brunt of the Puritan denunciations of the stage. These incidentally bore witness to the costly elaborateness of the new accommodation provided for the players.[5] Apart from the moral corruption

[1] Cf. App. C, No. xl.

[2] Lodge, *Wits Miserie* (1596), ' pale as the visard of the ghost which cried so miserably at the Theator, like an oister wife, Hamlet, revenge '. In T. M., *Black Book* (1604), is a mention of ' one of my divells in Dr Faustus, when the olde Theatre crackt and frighted the audience '. This was presumably before 1592, as *Dr. Faustus* seems to have been continuously in Henslowe's hands from the beginning of that year. Halliwell-Phillipps, i. 363, quotes an allusion of Barnaby Rich in 1606 (*Faultes Faults, and Nothing Else but Faultes*, 7) to ' Gravets part at the Theatre ', but this must not be pressed as a reference to the long-destroyed house.

[3] *Sloane MS.* 2530, ff. 6, 11, 12, 46 ; cf. App. D, Nos. lxii, lxviii.

[4] Cf. ch. xi, p. 371.

[5] T. W., *Sermon at Paul's Cross* (3 Nov. 1577), ' Beholde the sumptuous

upon which the Puritans laid most stress, there is some evidence that the position of the Theatre, with a great space of open ground before it, made it a natural focus for the disorderly elements of society. As early as 5 October 1577, just after the resumption of plays for the autumn, the Mayor and Recorder Fleetwood were listening to ' a brabell betwene John Wotton and the Leuetenuntes sonne of the one parte, and certain ffreholders of Shordyche, for a matter at the Theater '. There was serious trouble in the course of 1584. Fleetwood wrote to Burghley how on 8 June, ' very nere the Theatre or Curten, at the tyme of the playes, there laye a prentice sleping upon the grasse and one Challes *alias* Grostock dyd turne upon the too upon the belly of the same prentice ; whereupon the apprentice start up, and after wordes they fell to playne bloues '; and how on 10 June, ' one Browne, a serving man in a blow coat, a shifting fellowe, having a perrelous witt of his owne, entending a spoile if he cold have browght it to passe, did at Theatre doore querell with certen poore boyes, handicraft prentises, and strooke some of theym; and lastlie he with his sword wondend and maymed one of the boyes upon the left hand ; whereupon there assembled nere a ml. people'.[1] Unscrupulous characters might find congenial companions in the throng. Somewhere in 1594 a diamond, which had gone astray from the loot of a Spanish vessel, was shown in Finsbury Fields by a mariner

Theatre houses ' ; Northbrooke (S. R. 2 Dec. 1577), 85, ' places . . . builded for such Playes and Enterludes, as the Theatre and Curtaine is ' ; Stockwood, *Sermon at Paul's Cross* (24 Aug. 1578), ' the Theatre, the Curtayne, and other places of Playes in the Citie . . . the gorgeous Playing place erected in the fieldes . . . as they please to have it called, a Theatre ' ; *News from the North* (1579), ' the Theaters, Curtines . . . and such places where the time is so shamefully mispent ' ; T. Twyne, *Physic for Fortune* (1579), i. xxx, 42, ' the Curteine or Theater ; which two places are well knowen to be enimies to good manners : for looke who goeth thyther evyl, returneth worse ' ; Stubbes (S. R. 1 March 1583), i. 144, ' flockyng and runnyng to Theaters and Curtens . . . Venus pallaces ' ; Field (1583), ' the distruction bothe of bodye and soule that many are brought unto by frequenting the Theater, the Curtin and such like ' ; Rankins (1587), f. 4, ' the Theater and Curtine may aptlie be termed for their abhomination, the chappell *adulterinum* ' ; Harrison, *Chronologie* (1588), i. liv, ' It is an evident token of a wicked time when plaiers wexe so riche that they can build suche houses '.

[1] App. D, Nos. xxxv, lxxiv. It appears to have been thought a good example to frequenters of the Theatre that the locality should occasionally be used for a public execution. Stowe, *Annales* (1615), 749, 750, records the hanging of W. Gunter, a priest from beyond the seas, ' at the Theater ' on 28 Aug. 1588, and of W. Hartley, another priest, ' nigh the Theator, on 1 Oct. 1588 ; cf. Halliwell-Phillipps, i. 351, from *True Report of the Inditement of Weldon, Hartley, and Sutton, who Suffred for High Treason* (1588).

to certain goldsmiths, who said that they had met him by chance at a play in the Theatre at Shoreditch.[1] But James Burbadge had obtained for himself a tactical advantage by building outside the jurisdiction of the City and within that, less organized or more easy-going, of the Middlesex magistrates. The Corporation were powerless, except in so far as, directly by persuasion, or indirectly by invoking the Privy Council, they could stir the county bench to action. They lost no opportunity, which brawls or plague afforded, of attempting this.[2] An exceptionally troublous year was 1580. It began with an indictment of John Brayne and James Burbadge 'yeomen' of Shoreditch, at the Middlesex sessions, for bringing unlawful assemblies together on 21 February and other days ' *ad audienda et spectanda quaedam colloquia sive interluda vocata* playes or interludes' by them and others ' *exercitata et practicata* ' at the Theatre in Holywell, with the result of affrays and tumults leading to a breach of the peace.[3] On 6 April was the great earthquake, which threw down chimneys in Shoreditch, and according to one account 'shaked not only the scenical Theatre, but the great stage and theatre of the whole land '.[4] Four days later was the riot between Lord Oxford's men and the Inns of Court, and the two events gave the Lord Mayor an excellent opportunity of pointing out to the Council that the players of plays which were used at the Theatre were ' a very superfluous sort of men ' and of securing a suspension of performances until after Michaelmas. The riot of 8 June 1584 similarly led to the inhibition by the Council and Fleetwood already noticed, although it is clear that this was not so permanent as the City probably hoped, when the authority for ' the suppressing and pulling downe of the Theatre and Curten ' reached them. Matters came to a crisis again in 1597 with the production of *The Isle of Dogs* on the Bankside, and an appeal of the City on 28 July was answered on the same day by mandates of the Council, of which one was addressed to the Middlesex justices, and

---

[1] Sir A. Ashley to Sir R. Cecil (*Hatfield MSS.* vii. 504).

[2] Cf. ch. ix. In addition to the occasions described above, the Theatre and Curtain are particularly referred to in the City's complaint to Walsingham on 3 May 1583, and in the Council's inhibitions of 29 Oct. 1587, where the ' Liberty ' of Holywell is clearly pointed at in the allusion to ' places priviledged ', and 23 June 1592 (App. D, Nos. lxix, lxxx, xc).

[3] App. D, No. xlii. The County records also contain entries of a recognisance by ' James Burbage of Shorditch gent.', Henry Bett, and [Cuthbert] Burbage in the Strond, yeoman ', on 6 April 1592, for the former's appearance at the next Middlesex sessions, and a similar recognisance of ' James Burbage of Hallywell, yeoman ', on 11 Sept. 1593 (Jeaffreson, i. 205, 217) ; but there is nothing to show the nature of the proceedings.

[4] Cf. App. C, No. xxv.

directed them to send for the owners of the Theatre and Curtain, and enjoin them to ' plucke downe quite the stages, gallories and roomes that are made for people to stand in, and so to deface the same as they maie not be ymploied agayne to suche use '.[1]

It is unlikely that the Theatre was ever opened again. It is certain that the Chamberlain's men had moved to the Curtain before the end of 1597, and the abandonment of the old house is referred to unmistakably enough in a satire published in 1598.[2] The explanation is to be found in the relations of the Burbadges to their ground landlord, Giles Allen. The following account is taken in the main from Cuthbert Burbadge's allegations in litigation of 1600. On 1 November 1585, shortly before the termination of the first ten years of the lease, James Burbadge, as he was entitled to do, presented Allen with a draft of a new twenty-one years' lease. This Allen evaded signing, apparently alleging that it was not in verbatim agreement with the old lease, and probably also that some of Burbadge's covenants under the old lease had remained unfulfilled.[3] By way of precaution, Burbadge thought it desirable to put on record in his account-book some evidence that he had spent the £200 in improving the tenements, upon which his right to remove the structure of the Theatre depended. He called in expert craftsmen, and took two ' views ', one on 20 November 1585, another, after some further work had been done, on 18 July 1586. The first estimate was £220, the second £240. This last was later confirmed by a third view taken in connexion with the Brayne litigation in July 1591.[4] The money had been spent, partly on ordinary repairs, partly on converting the old barn into tenements, partly on putting up two new houses, one of which was for Burbadge's own occupation.[5] The matter of the new lease now slumbered until the expiration of the old one on 13 April 1597 drew near. In 1596 negotiations took place between landlord and tenant, and a compromise was mooted, by which the new lease was to be granted, but for an increased rent of £24 instead of £14. Allen afterwards asserted and Cuthbert Burbadge denied that there was a proviso that after five years the building should be converted to some other use

---

[1] App. D, No. cx.
[2] E. Guilpin, *Skialetheia*, sat. v :

        ' but see yonder,
    One, like the unfrequented Theater,
    Walkes in darke silence and vast solitude '.

[3] Wallace, 169, 183, 191, 214, 218.
[4] Ibid. 72, 76, 226.   [5] Ibid. 232, 235.

than that of a play-house.[1] Cuthbert continued the negotiations after James Burbadge's death in February 1597, but
they finally broke down, and for a year or so the tenancy
was only on sufferance.[2] Finally, in the autumn of 1598,
when Cuthbert had agreed to demands which he thought
extortionate, Allen refused to accept his brother Richard as
security, and all hope of a settlement disappeared.[3] Cuthbert
now resolved to avail himself of the covenant of the expired
lease, under which the tenant was entitled to pull down and
remove the Theatre. This he began to do, in spite of a protest
from Allen's representative, on 28 December 1598, with the
concurrence of his mother and brother, and the financial
aid of one William Smith of Waltham Cross.[4] The work was
still in progress on 20 January 1599, when Burbadge's agent,
Peter Street, carpenter, entered the close with ten or twelve
men, and carried the timber to the other side of the river
for use in the erection of the Globe. For this act Allen brought
an action of trespass against Street in the Queen's Bench,
alleging that he had trampled down grass in the close to the
value of 40s., and claiming damages for £800 in all, of which
£700 represented his estimate of the value of the Theatre.[5]
Burbadge applied to the Court of Requests to stop the common
law suit, alleging in effect that he was equitably entitled to
act upon the covenant, even though the lease had expired,
on account of the unreasonable refusal of Allen to grant the
new lease when applied for, under the terms of the old one,
in 1585.[6] The issue really turned upon whether this refusal
was reasonable. Allen said that James Burbadge had been
a troublesome tenant, that he had converted the barn into
eleven tenements, whose inhabitants became a nuisance
to the parish by begging for their 20s. rents, that he had
not repaired the building but only shored it up, that he had
not spent the stipulated £200, and that £30 rent was in

---

[1] Wallace, 195, 203, 212, 216, 220, 238. Robert Miles took occasion of
the negotiations to renew his old claim by petitioning in the Court of
Requests for an interest in the new lease. The proceedings, so far as
preserved, are inconclusive (ibid. 158). Meanwhile Cuthbert Burbadge
was co-operating with Giles Allen in defending a claim made by the Earl
of Rutland to the ' debateable ' ground, and remained a party to the
consequent litigation in 1602, long after the Theatre had disappeared
(Stopes, 184). [2] Wallace, 184, 196, 204. [3] Ibid. 221.
[4] Ibid. 164, 179, 197, 217, 222, 238, 278. The dates are not quite
certain ; possibly the 20 Jan. of *Allen v. Street* was an error. Allen's
Answer in the Court of Requests places the whole transaction ' aboute
the feast of the Natiuitie ', and this in his Star Chamber suit becomes
' aboute the eight and twentyth day of December ', without any suggestion
that more than one day was occupied.
[5] Ibid. 163. [6] Ibid. 181.

arrear at the time of the application of 1585 and was still unpaid.[1] Probably these last two were the only allegations to which the court attached importance. Allen claimed that he had no remedy against James Burbadge's estate, for he had made deeds of gift to his sons of his property, and his widow and administratrix was without funds. Burbadge, however, produced evidence of the estimates of 1585 and 1586, and suggested that his father had a counter-claim against the rent in the expense to which he had been put in maintaining his possession at the time of Peckham's claim to the freehold. On 18 October 1600 the Court decided in his favour.[2] Allen brought a Queen's Bench action against him in 1601 for breach of agreement, and in 1601 complained to the Star Chamber of perjury on the part of the expert witnesses and other wrongs done him in the course of the earlier proceedings; but, although the conclusions of these suits are not on record, it is not likely that he succeeded in obtaining a favourable decision.[3]

vii. THE CURTAIN

[*Bibliographical Note.*—Some rather scanty material is brought together by T. E. Tomlins, *Origin of the Curtain Theatre and Mistakes regarding it* in *Sh. Soc. Papers*, i. 29, and Halliwell-Phillipps, *The Theatre and Curtain* (*Outlines*, i. 345).]

The Curtain is included with the Theatre in Stowe's general description of Holywell as 'standing on the South-west side towards the field'. That it was somewhat south of the Theatre is indicated by a reference to it in 1601 as in Moorfields, a name given to the open fields lying south of and adjacent to Finsbury Fields. But, although it stood in the parish of Shoreditch and the liberty of Holywell, it was not, like the Theatre, actually within the precinct of the dissolved priory. *Curtina* is glossed by Ducange as ' *minor curtis, seu rustica area, quae muris cingitur* ', and the description is sufficiently met by the piece of land lying outside the southern gate of the priory, and on the other side of Holywell Lane into which that gate opened.[4] A priory lease to the Earl

---

[1] Wallace, 186, 215, 220.   [2] Ibid. 285.   [3] Ibid. 267, 275.

[4] Aubrey, ii. 12, on the authority of J. Greenhill, says that Ben Jonson ' acted and wrote, but both ill, at the Green Curtaine, a kind of nursery or obscure playhouse, somewhere in the suburbes (I thinke towards Shoreditch or Clarkenwell) ', and on that of Sir Edward Shirburn that Jonson killed Marlowe, ' on Bunhill, comeing from the Green-Curtain play-house '. Hoxton, where Jonson killed Gabriel Spencer, is of course not far from Bunhill, and both are in the Holywell neighbourhood. Probably Aubrey, in giving a name to the theatre, is babbling of green frieze, rather than green fields. Steevens and Malone (*Variorum*, iii. 54) committed themselves to the view that ' the original sign hung out at this playhouse was the painting of a curtain striped '.

of Rutland of his town house in 1538 described it as ' *infra muros et portas eiusdem monasterii* ', and part of the holding consisted of stables and a hay-loft ' *scituata et existentia extra portas eiusdem monasterii prope pasturam dictae Priorissae vocatam* the Curtene '. Post-dissolution conveyances refer to a ' house, tenement or lodge' called the Curtain, and to a parcel of ground, enclosed with a wall on the west and north, called the Curtain close, which lay south of the Earl of Rutland's house, and on which by 1581 stood various tenements, which were described as ' sett, lyeng and being in Halliwell Lane '. The property in question formed part of the possessions of Sir Thomas Leigh of Hoxton at his death in 1543 and had formerly been conveyed to him by Lord Wriothesley. Through Leigh's daughter Katharine it passed to her husband Lord Mountjoy. On 20 February 1567 it was sold for £40 to Maurice Long and his son William, being then in the occupation of one Wilkingeson and Robert Manne. On 23 August 1571 Maurice Long conveyed it for £200 to Sir William Allen, then Lord Mayor, possibly by way of mort-gage in connexion with building speculations, since on 18 March 1581 it was in the hands of William Long, who then sold it to Thomas Herbert. There had evidently been an increase in the number of tenements on the site, and Thomas Wilkinson, Thomas Wilkins, Robert Medley, Richard Hicks, Henry Lanman, and Robert Manne are named as tenants.[1] As Henry Lanman or Laneman had the profits of the theatre in 1585, there can be little doubt that it stood on part of the land dealt with in the conveyances. Halliwell-Phillipps thinks that it must have been situated ' in or near the place which is marked as Curtain Court in Chassereau's plan of Shoreditch, 1745 ',[2] and is now known as Gloucester Street. If so, it was very near the boundary between Holywell and Moorfields, much along the line of which now runs Curtain Road. But it must be remembered that Curtain Court may also have taken its name from the ' house, tenement or lodge ' which already existed in 1567 and is mentioned as the Curtain House in the Shoreditch registers as late as 1639 ; and certainly in Ryther's map (*c.* 1636–45) the theatre, though still bordering on Moorfields, is shown a good deal farther,

---

[1] Thomas Wilkins was perhaps related to George Wilkins the dramatist, who was buried at Shoreditch 9 Aug. 1613. Sir William Allen is not known to have had anything to do either with Edward Alleyn or with Giles Allen, the ground-landlord of the Theatre. Lanman was 54 on 30 July 1592. We cannot assume that the name is merely an orthographic variant of that of Laneham.

[2] Reproduced in Ordish, 40.

both to the east and the south, than the point indicated by Halliwell-Phillipps.[1]

The Burbadges claimed that James was the first builder of play-houses, but the Curtain must have followed very soon after the Theatre. It is not mentioned by name with its predecessor in the Privy Council order of 1 August 1577, but is in Northbrooke's treatise of the following December. Up to 1597 its history is little more than a pendant to that of the Theatre, with which it is generally coupled in the Puritan attacks and in the occasional interferences of authority. From 1585 to 1592, indeed, it was used as an ' easer ' to the Theatre, and the profits of the two houses were pooled under an arrangement between Henry Lanman and the Burbadges.[2] The companies who occupied the Curtain can for the most part only be guessed at.[3] At the time of the inhibition of 14 June 1584 it was probably occupied by Lord Arundel's men. Tarlton appeared at it, but not necessarily after the formation of the Queen's company.[4] Prizes of the School of Defence were occasionally played at it from 1579 to 1583.[5] Unlike the Theatre, the Curtain was certainly reopened after the inhibition of 1597. It is likely that the Chamberlain's men repaired to it in October of that year, and remained at it until the Globe was ready in 1599. The same satirist, who tells us that the Theatre was closed in 1598, tells us that the Rose, which was continuously occupied by the Admiral's men, and the Curtain were open; [6] and

---

[1] Reproduced in Baker, 36, 135, with a photographic enlargement of the building, wrongly identified with the *Theatre*. It is shown as a round or hexagonal structure, with a large flag, standing in the middle of a square paled plot ; but too much stress must not be laid on what is probably only a cartographic symbol. Immediately south of it is Bedlam. Kiechel tells us that the house had three galleries, and de Witt that it was an ' amphitheatrum ' (cf. pp. 358, 362). In the epilogue to *Three English Brothers* (1607) it is a ' round circumference '.   [2] Cf. p. 393.

[3] Fleay, 40, 88, 145, 201, 300, assigns it as follows : Sussex's (1576–83) Arundel's and Oxford's (1584), Howard's and Hunsdon's (1585), Oxford's (1586–8), Pembroke's (1589–97), Chamberlain's (1597–9), Derby's (1599–1600), uncertain company (1601), Queen Anne's (1604–9), Duke of York's (1610–23). But, of course, this *is* guessing.

[4] Tarlton, 16. If *Tarlton's Jig of a Horse Load of Fools*, taken from a manuscript of Collier's (Tarlton, xx), is genuine, that also was given at the Curtain.

[5] *Sloane MS.* 2530, ff. 4, 12, 43, 44, 46.

[6] Guilpin, *Skialetheia* (S. R. 8 Sept. 1598), Sat. v :
                              if my dispose
          Perswade me to a play, I'le to the Rose,
          Or Curtaine, one of Plautus comedies,
          Or the patheticke Spaniards tragedies ;
and in the *Preludium*, of a ' Cittizen . . . comming from the Curtaine '.

a clue to the actors at it is given by Marston's reference to
' Curtain plaudities ' in the closest connexion with *Romeo
and Juliet*.[1] In 1600 Robert Armin, of the Chamberlain's
men, published his *Fool upon Fool*, in which he called himself
' Clonnico de Curtanio Snuffe '. In the 1605 edition he changed
the name to ' Clonnico del Mondo Snuffe '. The direct connexion of the Chamberlain's men with the Curtain probably
ended on the opening of the Globe. But a share in it belonged
to Thomas Pope, when he made his will on 22 July 1603,
and another to John Underwood, when he made his on
4 October 1624. Both were of the Chamberlain's men,
although Underwood cannot have joined them until about
1608.

The Curtain did not go entirely out of use when the Chamberlain's left it. It must have been the theatre near Bishopsgate
at which Thomas Platter saw a play in September or
October 1599.[2] It is possible that Kempe (q.v.) was then
playing there. In March 1600 one William Hawkins, barber,
of St. Giles's without Cripplegate was charged at the Middlesex
Sessions with taking a purse and £1 6s. 6d. at the Curtain, and
Richard Fletcher, pewterer, of Norwich, was bound over
to give evidence.[3]

On 22 June 1600, when the Privy Council gave authority
for the opening of the Fortune, they were given to understand
by the Master of the Revels that it would replace the Curtain,
which was therefore to be ' ruinated or applied to some other
good use '. This arrangement seems to suggest that the
Curtain was in some way under the control of Alleyn or Henslowe. It was, however, departed from, and apparently with
the tacit consent of the Council, as although they had occasion
on 10 May 1601 to instruct the Middlesex justices to suppress
a libellous play produced at ' the Curtaine in Moorefeilds ',
they did not take, as they might have done, the point that
no play ought to have been produced there at all. On
31 December they were again insisting on the limitation of
the theatres in use to two ; and on 31 March 1602 they again

---

[1] *Scourge of Villainy* (1598), xi. 37 (*Works*, iii. 372) :

> Luscus, what 's play'd to-day ? Faith now I know
> I set thy lips abroach, from whence doth flow
> Naught but pure Juliet and Romeo.
> Say who acts best ? Drusus or Roscio ?
> Now I have him, that ne'er of ought did speak
> But when of plays or players he did treat—
> Hath made a common-place book out of plays,
> And speaks in print : at least what e'er he says
> Is warranted by Curtain plaudities.

[2] Cf. p. 365.   [3] Jeaffreson, i. 259.

departed from their own principles by licensing Oxford's and Worcester's men to play at the Boar's Head. Henceforward three companies of men players were regularly tolerated, and when a draft licence was prepared for Worcester's, or as they had then become Queen Anne's, men early in the following year the Curtain and the Boar's Head were named as ' there now usuall howsen '. The Curtain is also specified for them in the Council's warrant for the resumption of plays on 9 April 1604. About 1606 they also took into use the Red Bull, and thereafter but little is heard of the Curtain. The Queen's men, however, played Day, Wilkins, and Rowley's *The Travels of Three English Brothers* there at some time before its entry on 29 June 1607. It was still theirs in April 1609, but may perhaps soon have passed to the Duke of York's men. It is mentioned, with the Globe and Fortune, in Heath's *Epigrams* of 1610, and plays heard ' at *Curtaine,* or at Bull ' and ' a Curtaine Iigge ' are objects of ridicule in Wither's *Abuses Stript and Whipt* of 1613.[1] It was used by an amateur company for a performance of Wentworth Smith's *Hector of Germany* in 1615, and it is obscurely referred to in I. H.'s *This World's Folly* of the same year.[2] Malone gathered from Sir Henry Herbert's office-book that it was used by Prince Charles's men in 1622, and soon thereafter only by prize-fighters. It was still in use in 1624, and still standing in 1627.[3]

viii. NEWINGTON BUTTS

A theatre, of which the history is very obscure, but which may have been built soon after the Theatre and Curtain, stood at Newington, a village one mile from London Bridge, divided from the Bankside by St. George's Fields, and reachable by the road which continued Southwark High Street.[4] Here there were butts for the practice of archery. Plays at Newington Butts, outside the City jurisdiction, are first mentioned in a Privy Council letter of 13 May 1580 to the Surrey justices. A similar letter of 11 May 1586 speaks more precisely of 'the theater or anie other places about Newington '. A third letter, undated, but probably belonging to 1591 or 1592, recites an order of the Council restraining

---

[1] Heath, Epigram 39 ; Wither, *Abuses*, i. 1 ; ii. 3.

[2] Cf. App. C, No. lix.

[3] *Variorum*, iii. 54, 59 ; Ordish, 106, from *Vox Graculi* (1623) and Jeaffreson, iii. 164.

[4] A writer in the *Daily News* for 9 April 1898 identifies the site of the theatre, without giving any evidence, as ' between Clock Passage, Newington Butts, Swan Place, and Hampton Street ' ; cf. *9 N. Q.* i. 386.

Strange's men from playing at the Rose, and enjoining them
to play three days a week at Newington Butts, and rescinds
it, 'by reason of the tediousness of the way, and that of
long time plays have not there been used on working days'.[1]
Possibly the theatre had come into Henslowe's hands, for
his diary records that it was at Newington that the combined
companies of the Admiral's and Chamberlain's men began
their first season after the plague of 1592–4, apparently
playing there from 5 to 15 June 1594, and then going their
separate ways to the Rose and the Theatre respectively.
The theatre is mentioned in the list given by Howes in 1631.[2]
It is said to have been 'only a memory' by 1599.[3] A bad
pun is called a 'Newington conceit' in 1612.[4]

ix. THE ROSE

[*Bibliographical Note.*—All the more important documents are printed
or calendared from the *Dulwich MSS.* with a valuable commentary in
Greg, *Henslowe's Diary* and *Henslowe Papers*, and in Collier, *Memoirs of
Alleyn* and *Henslowe's Diary.*]

The Rose owed its name to the fact that it stood in what
had been, as recently as 1547–8, a rose garden.[5] On 3 December 1552 Thomasyn, widow of Ralph Symonds, fishmonger,
granted to trustees, for her own use during life and thereafter
to the charitable uses of the parish of St. Mildred, Bread
Street, her 'messuage or tennement then called the little
rose with twoe gardens' formerly in St. Margaret's and then
in St. Saviour's, Southwark. St. Mildred's still has a plan
of the estate, which extended to about three roods.[6] A 'tenement called the Rose' is referred to in a recital of a lease
of Henry VIII's reign as the eastern boundary of other tenements, by name the Barge, the Bell, and the Cock, which
lay 'vppon the banke called Stewes' in St. Margaret's,
afterwards St. Saviour's, parish, between the highway next
the Thames on the north and Maiden Lane on the south.[7]
It is located by Mr. Rendle just to the east of the still existing

---

[1] App. D, Nos. xlvi, lxxvi, xcii.   [2] Cf. p. 373.
[3] C. W. Wallace in *N. U. S.* xiii. 2, 'as shown by a contemporary record
to be published later'.
[4] *A Woman is a Weathercock*, III. iii. 25.
[5] Rendle, *Antiquarian*, viii. 60, 'Among the early Surveys, 1 Edward VI,
we see that this was not merely a name—the place was a veritable Rose
Garden, and paid £1 3s. 4d. by the year, and the messuage called the
Rose paid £4'.
[6] *Close Roll 6 Edw. VI*, p. 5, m. 13; cf. Rendle, *Bankside*, xv; *H. P.* I.
[7] *Egerton MS.* 2623, f. 13, quoted in Henslowe, ii. 25. But in ii. 43
Dr. Greg misdescribes the Rose as on the west of the Barge, Bell, and
Cock.

Rose Alley. The site therefore lay in the Liberty of the Clink midway between those afterwards occupied by the Globe on the east and the Hope on the west. On 20 November 1574 the parish let the property for thirty-one years at £7 annually to William Griffin, vintner. Griffin assigned it on 11 December 1579 to Robert Withens, vintner, and Withens on 24 March 1585 to Henslowe.[1] There was as yet no theatre. The first mention of one as in contemplation is in an agreement of 10 January 1587 between Henslowe and one John Cholmley, citizen and grocer of London, for partnership during the next eight years and three months, should both parties live so long, in a garden plot ninety-four feet square on the Bankside in the parish of St. Saviour's, Southwark, and 'a playe howse now in framinge and shortly to be ereckted and sett vppe vpone the same '. Under this Henslowe undertook to have ' the saide play house with all furniture thervnto belonginge ' set up ' with as muche expedicion as maye be ' by John Grigges, carpenter, to pay all rents due on the premisses, and to repair the bridges and wharves belonging to them before the following Michaelmas. Cholmley undertook to bear his share of any further cost of maintaining the premises, and also to pay Henslowe the sum of £816 in quarterly instalments. In consideration of this, he was to take half of all such profits as ' shall arysse grow be colectted gathered or become due for the saide parcell of grounde and playe howse when and after yt shalbe ereckted and sett vpe by reason of any playe or playes, that shalbe showen or played there or otherwysse howsoever '. The partners are jointly to appoint ' players to vse exersyse & playe in the saide playe howse ', and collect sums themselves or by deputy of all persons coming to the performances ' excepte yt please any of the saide partyes to suffer theire frendes to go in for nothinge '. Cholmley is also to have the sole right of selling food or drink on the premises and a small house already in his tenure on the south of the plot close to Maiden Lane, ' to keepe victualinge in ' or for any other purpose, and with a right of ingress from Thames side by Rose Alley.[2] The deed does not name the property, but it cannot be doubted that it refers to a part of the Little Rose. Presumably the theatre was to be built on a garden at the back of the holding, and the existing tenement on Bankside was not to be interfered with. Henslowe had ' Rosse rentes ' of a residential character in 1602 or 1603.[3] Norden's map (1593) puts the Rose farther from the river than the Bear Garden. The Delaram and Merian drawings,

---

[1] *Henslowe Papers*, 1.   [2] Ibid. 2.   [3] Henslowe, i. 209.

on the other hand, put it very near the river, and these, although of less authority than Norden, are followed in Mr. Rendle's plan. Probably Norden's Bear Garden was an older one than that which afterwards became the Hope.[1] The provision as to the wharfs and bridges seems to indicate an intention to open the Rose at Michaelmas 1587, and I see no reason to doubt that it was in fact ready for occupation by about that date. On 29 October the Privy Council called the attention of the Surrey justices to complaints from Southwark of breaches of the rule against plays on Sunday, 'especiallie within the Libertie of the Clincke and in the parish of St. Saviour's in Southwarke'. There may, of course, have been plays at inns in the Clink, but it is more natural to take the protest as one against the newly opened Rose. No other regular theatre existed in the Clink at this time. That the Rose was built by 1588 appears from a record of the Sewer Commission for Surrey.[2] It is not in Smith's plan of 1588, but this may easily not have been quite up to date.

The next that is heard of the Rose is probably in 1592.[3] In March and April of that year Henslowe, who had recently taken his famous 'diary' into use as a financial memorandum book, noted in it some building expenditure, and a little later set out 'a note of suche carges as I haue layd owt a bowte my playe howsse in the yeare of our lord 1592'.[4] Henslowe is not known to have owned Newington Butts, or any other theatre except the Rose, and it is reasonable to assume that this is what he meant by 'my playe howsse'. The work probably began in or before January, as an entry half-way through the list is dated on 6 February. It entailed the purchase of a barge and a certain amount of breaking up and paling and wharfing. Henslowe appears to have done the

[1] Cf. Dekker, *Satiromastix*, 1247, 'th'ast a breath as sweet as the Rose, that growes by the Beare-garden'.

[2] G. L. Gomme, *The Story of London Maps* (*Geographical Journal*, xxxi. 628), '1588. Henchley.—Item, we present Phillip Henchley to pull upp all the pylles that stand in the common sewer against the play-house to the stopping of the water course, the which to be done by midsomer next uppon paine of x^s yf it be undone. x^s (done)'. Wallace, in *The Times* (1914), says that these records mention the theatre as 'new' in April 1588, and show other amercements during the next eighteen years.

[3] Dr. Greg, in Henslowe, ii. 46, is, I think, successful in showing that all the dated building entries belong to 1592 and not to 1591 or 1593. I suppose the scattered entries with the date '1591' to have been written in first, and the continuous account under the date '1592' added later, probably after Henslowe had changed the year-date in his play-entries, which seems to have been on 6 May.

[4] Henslowe, i. 7.

work himself and not by contract. He bought a mast, turned balusters, boards and laths, in part from the carpenter Grigges who is named in the agreement with Cholmley, and in part from a ' timber man ' called Lee. He bought bolts, hinges, and nails from the ironmonger at the Fryingpan in Southwark and from one Brader. He bought lime, sand, chalk, and bricks. He paid wages to carpenters, workmen, and labourers, and employed painters and a thatcher. The exact nature and extent of the work are not specified, but it included the painting of the stage, the ceiling of ' my lords rome ', and ' the rome ouer the tyerhowsse ', and the ' make-inge the penthowsse shed at the tyeringe howsse doore '. It has sometimes been supposed that the Rose never got built in 1587, and that these are the accounts, or part of them, for the original construction. This seems to me most unlikely. The total expense, with the exception of a small number of items lost by the mutilation of a page, only amounted to about £108. This could not cover more than repairs. On the other hand, these were clearly substantial repairs, and the fact that they were needed suggests that the building cannot have been a very new one. The lapse of five years since 1587 would, however, be consistent with the necessity for them. Almost simultaneously with the earliest dated entries in the building account, begins on 19 February 1592 the record of performances by Lord Strange's men, which continues to the following 22 June. If these were at the Rose, the paint on the stage can hardly have been dry in time for them, unless, as Dr. Greg suggests, the payments made in March and April were for work done a little earlier. That it was at the Rose that Strange's men played seems indicated by the Privy Council order, reciting the restraint of this company ' from playinge at the Rose on the Banckside ', which it is difficult to assign to any year but 1591 or 1592.[1] It is a little curious that nothing more is heard of John Cholmley, and I think the natural inference is that he was dead and that the partner-ship had thereby, in accordance with the terms of the agree-ment, been automatically dissolved.[2]

The assumption, in the absence of evidence to the contrary, that until he acquired a share in the Fortune Henslowe had no proprietary interest in any other theatre must explain the assignment to the Rose of all the playing recorded in the diary between 1592 and the autumn of 1600, with the exception of the few performances definitely stated to have been at

[1] App. D, No. xcii.
[2] The words ' Chomley when ' appear with other scribbles by Henslowe on the first page of the diary (Henslowe, i. 217).

Newington Butts. The further conjecture must, I think, be accepted that the season begun by the Admiral's and Chamberlain's men at Newington Butts in the summer of 1594 was transferred, so far as the Admiral's men were concerned, to the Rose after 15 June. If so, the Rose housed Strange's men again from 29 December 1592 to 1 February 1593, Sussex's from 26 December 1593 to 6 February 1594, the Queen's and Sussex's together from 1 to 9 April 1594, and the Admiral's from 14 to 16 May 1594, and then regularly from the following June until their transference to the Fortune in 1600. The only actual mentions of the theatre by name in the diary during this period are in the agreements of 1597 between Henslowe and the players Jones and Borne, in which Henslowe specifies ' the Rosse ' as ' my howsse ' in which they are to play. It was no doubt in use when Guilpin's *Skialetheia* (S. R. 8 September 1598) was written.[1] In the Lenten interval of 1595 Henslowe made ' A nott of what I haue layd owt abowt my playhowsse ffor payntynge & doinge it abowt with ealme bordes & other repracyones '. The expenditure reached a total of £108 19s., which was much about the same as that of 1592, and was supplemented in the following June by a further £7 2s. for carpenters' work, including ' mackinge the throne in the heuenes '.[2] The accounts of 1592 and 1595 suggest that the building was of wood and plaster on a brick foundation, and this is consistent with Hentzner's statement of 1598. Part of it, at least, was thatched. If the maps can be trusted, it was octagonal. In 1600 Henslowe had to find new occupants for the Rose. He records that Pembroke's men began to play there on 28 October, but only enters two unprofitable performances. Possibly the Privy Council, who had decreed in the previous July a limitation of houses to one on each side of the river, interfered. But this limitation was certainly not permanent. There is a receipt for a play bought for Worcester's men ' at the Rose ', and they probably used the house during the term of their account with Henslowe between August 1602 and May 1603. Subsequently they moved to the Curtain and Boar's Head. Henslowe's lease of the site was due to expire at the end of 1605, and this explains to some extent the following entry in the diary :

' The 25 of June 1603 I talked with Mr. Pope at the scryveners shope wher he lisse consernynge the tackynge of the leace a new of the littell Roosse & he showed me a wrytynge betwext the pareshe & hime seallfe which was to paye twenty pownd a yeare rent & to bestowe a hundred marckes vpon billdinge which I sayd I wold rather pulle

[1] Cf. p. 402.　　　　　　　　　　[2] Henslowe, i. 4.

downe the playehowse then I wold do so & he beade me do & sayd he gaue me leaue & wold beare me owt for yt wasse in him to do yt.'[1]

It is impossible to say whether 'Mr. Pope' was Thomas Pope of the King's men at the neighbouring Globe, or Morgan Pope, who was formerly interested in the Bear House, or some other Pope ; nor is it clear how he was in a position to authorize Henslowe to pull down the theatre. Dr. Greg draws the natural inference from the wording that he may have given his consent as a prospective lessee of the property.[2] In any case the Rose was not pulled down until two or three years later. The Sewers records show that in January 1604 not Philip but Francis Henslowe was amerced 6s. 8d. for it, which may mean that Lennox's men were playing there ; that on 4 October 1605 Philip Henslowe was amerced, but return was made that it was ' out of his hands ' ; that on 14 February 1606 Edward Box, of Bread Street, London, was amerced for it ; and that on 25 April 1606 Box was amerced for the site of 'the late playhouse in Maid lane '.[3]

There is no record of plays at the Rose after 1603.[4] It is in the Delaram engravings, but not in any later views except those of the Merian group, where it appears, flagged but unnamed, on the river edge.[5] Nor is it mentioned with the Hope, Globe, and Swan in Holland's Leaguer (1632). The explanation may perhaps be that the Merian engraver followed some out-of-date authority, such as Delaram, which had got the house farther north than Norden puts it, and as it had long ceased to exist, did not know its name. On the other hand, it is also just conceivable that for a short period the Rose, or some other building at the north end of the Rose site, had a renewed life as a place of public entertainment. Alleyn was paying ' tithe dwe for the Rose ' in 1622.[6] And Malone cites Herbert's ' office-book ' for a statement that after 1620 the Swan and the Rose were ' used occasionally for the exhibition of prize-fighters '.[7]

[1] Henslowe, i. 178. [2] Ibid. ii. 55.
[3] Wallace, in The Times (1914).
[4] Rendle, Bankside, xv, quotes
> In the last great fire
> The Rose did expire

and adds ' but when that was, I am not clear '. It reads like Collier.

[5] I cannot endorse the suggestion of Dr. Martin (cf. p. 378) that the ' Globe ' of Visscher (1616) was really the Rose. Baker, 165, reproducing a cut from Hollar (1640), also misnames the Globe as the Rose.

[6] Young, ii. 241.

[7] Variorum, iii. 56. I should have been happier if Malone had quoted verbatim, but I do not see that Adams, 160, explains away the statement by suggesting that a source for Malone's ' error ' is a note on p. 66, where he again cites Herbert for fencing at the Red Bull in 1623.

x. THE SWAN

[*Bibliographical Note.*—John de Witt's description and plan are published in K. T. Gaedertz, *Zur Kenntnis der altenglischen Bühne* (1888), and more exactly by H. B. Wheatley in *On a Contemporary Drawing of the Swan Theatre*, 1596 (*N. S. S. Trans. 1887–92*, 215). They are discussed by H. Logemann in *Anglia*, xix. 117, by W. Archer in *The Universal Review* for June 1888, by W. Rendle in 7 *N. Q.* vi. 221, by J. Le G. Brereton, *De Witt at the Swan* (1916, *Sh.-Homage*, 204), by myself in a paper on *The Stage of the Globe* in *The Stratford Town Shakespeare*, x. 351, and in most recent treatises on Elizabethan staging ; cf. chh. xviii, xx. Earlier material is collected by W. Rendle in *The Playhouses at Bankside in the Time of Shakespeare* (*Antiquarian Magazine and Bibliographer*, 1885, vii. 207). The facts as to Langley's purchase and the pleadings and order in the suit of *Shawe et al. v. Langley* before the Court of Requests in 1597–8 (cited as *S. v. L.*) are given by C. W. Wallace, *The Swan Theatre and the Earl of Pembroke's Servants* (1911, *E. S.* xliii. 340). T. S. Graves, *A Note on the Swan Theatre* (*M. P.* ix. 431), discusses the light thrown on the internal arrangements of the Swan by the accounts of *England's Joy* in 1602.]

The Swan stood in the Liberty and Manor of Paris Garden, at the western end of the Bankside. This manor, from which the royal ' game ' of bear-baiting took its traditional appellation, had come into the hands of the Crown as part of the possessions of the dissolved monastery of Bermondsey. It was granted in 1578 to nominees of Henry, Lord Hunsdon, conveyed by them to the Cure family, and sold for £850 on 24 May 1589 by Thomas Cure the younger to Francis Langley, a citizen and goldsmith of London. Langley, who was brother-in-law to Sir Anthony Ashley, one of the clerks to the Privy Council, held the office of Alnager and Searcher of Cloth, to which he had been appointed by the Corporation on the recommendation of the Privy Council and Sir Francis Walsingham in December 1582.[1] The site of the theatre can be precisely identified from a plan of the manor dated in 1627, but based on a survey of 1 November 1624.[2] It was in the north-east corner of the demesne, east of the manor-house, twenty-six poles due south of Paris Garden stairs, and immediately west of a lane leading to a house called Copt Hall. The outline shown is that of a double circle, or perhaps dodecahedron, divided into twelve compartments, with a small porch or tiring-house towards the road. The exact date of building is unknown. On 3 November 1594 the Lord Mayor wrote to

---

[1] *E. S.* xliii. 341 ; *Index to Remembrancia*, 277. It appears from *Hatfield MSS.* vi. 182, 184, that in May 1596 Langley was concerned in some negotiations about a missing diamond claimed by the Crown ; cf. p. 396.

[2] Printed from a contemporary copy in the Guildhall by W. Rendle in Appendix to Part II of *Harrison's Description of England* (*N. S. S.*, 1878) and Adams, 162. The original is held by the steward of the manor.

Burghley that Langley 'intendeth to erect a niew stage or
Theater (as they call it) for thexercising of playes vpon the
Banck side', and detailed the usual civic objections to the
stage as arguments in favour of the suppression of the project.[1] It is probable that Burghley refused to intervene and
that Langley proceeded at once with the erection of the
Swan, which may then have been ready for use in 1595.
It is impossible, without the Swan, to make up the tale of
four 'spielhäuser' seen by the Prince of Anhalt in 1596
(360). To 1596 again is assigned, although with probability
rather than certainty, the visit of John de Witt, who not only
names but also describes and delineates the Swan.[2] In any
case the Swan had already been in use by players before
February 1597, when Langley entered into an arrangement
for its occupation by Lord Pembroke's men.[3] The terms
of the lease provided that he should make the house ready
and furnish apparel, which he alleged cost him £300, and
should get his return for this expenditure out of the company's
moiety of the gallery takings, in addition of course to the other
moiety which in accordance with theatrical custom went to
him as rent.[4] The enterprise was rudely interrupted by the
production of *The Isle of Dogs* at the Swan itself, and the
restraint of 28 July 1597 which was the result. The leading
members of Pembroke's company joined or rejoined the
Admiral's at the Rose, and became involved in litigation with
Langley on account of their breach of covenant.[5] For a time
Langley succeeded in keeping a company together, and the
Swan remained open.[6] It was perhaps the intention of the
Privy Council order of 19 February 1598, against an intrusive
'third company' which was competing with the Chamberlain's and the Admiral's, to close it.[7] If so, Langley may
still for a time have found means of evasion, since on the

---

[1] App. D, No. cii.

[2] Cf. p. 361, and for the reliability and value of the record as evidence
for the structure and staging of theatres, chh. xviii, xx.

[3] S. v. L. 352, 'the said howse was then lately afore vsed to have playes
in hit '.

[4] Ibid., 'the Defendant should be allowed for the true value thereof
out of the Complainantes moytie of the gains for the seuerall stand-
inges in the galleries of the said howse which belonged to them '. As
'which' may follow on 'moytie', I see no reason for Wallace's inference
(360) that the galleries were structurally divided between the two parties,
instead of the takings being shared.

[5] Cf. ch. xiv (Pembroke's) and ch. xxii (Nashe).

[6] S. v. L. 353 (6 Feb. 1598), 'the said Defendant hath euer synce had
his said howse contynually from tyme to tyme exercysed with other
players to his great gaines '.

[7] App. D, No. cxiv.

following 1 May the vestry of St. Saviour's were viewing new buildings of his, and at the same time negotiating with Henslowe and Meade for money for the poor ' in regarde of theire playe-houses '.[1] During the next few years, however, such notices as we get of the Swan, while showing that it was still in existence and available for occasional entertainments, carry no evidence of any use by a regular company. Francis Meres, in his *Palladis Tamia* of 1598, tells us that it was the scene of a challenge in ' extemporall ' versifying by Robert Wilson.[2] It was one of the wooden theatres which were seen by Hentzner in the same year, and no doubt the one near which he describes the royal barge as lying.[3] On 15 May 1600 the Council sanctioned its use for feats of activity by Peter Bromvill.[4] On 7 February 1602 it was occupied by fencers, and while two of these, by names Turner and Dun, were playing their prizes upon its stage, Dun was unfortunate enough to receive a mortal wound in the eye.[5] On 6 November 1602 it was chosen by Richard Vennar for his impudent mystification of *England's Joy*. The accounts of this trans-action show that it was fitted with ' hangings, curtains, chairs, and stools ', and capable of scenic effects, such as the appear-ance of a throne of blessed souls in heaven and of black and damned souls with fireworks from beneath the stage.[6] Meanwhile Langley had died in 1601 and in January 1602 the Paris Garden estate was sold to Hugh Browker, a proto-notary of the Court of Common Pleas, in whose family it remained to 1655.[7] About 1611 it was once more taken into use for plays. *The Roaring Girl* (1611), itself a Fortune play, has an allusion to a knight who ' lost his purse at the last new play i' the Swan ',[8] and the accounts of the overseers of Paris Garden contain entries of receipts from ' the play house ' or ' the Swan ' in each April from 1611 to 1615.[9] The last entry is of so small an amount that it probably only covered a fraction of a year, and I think the inference is that the Swan was disused on the opening of the Hope in 1614.[10] If so, it had probably been taken over by Henslowe for the use of the Lady Elizabeth's men, who came into existence in

---

[1] App. D, No. cxv.   [2] App. C, No. lii.   [3] Cf. p. 362.
[4] App. D, No. cxxiii.   [5] Manningham, 130 ; Gawdy, 93.
[6] Ch. xxiii (Vennar).   [7] *E. S.* xliii. 342.   [8] Act v, sc. i.
[9] P. Norman, *The Accounts of the Overseers of the Poor of Paris Garden, 1608–71* (1901, *Surrey Arch. Colls.* xvi. 55), from *Addl. MS.* 34,110, and again by C. W. Wallace as a new discovery in *E. S.* xliii. 390. The amounts are £4 6s. 8d. in 1611, £5 3s. 4d. in 1612, £5 5s. in 1613, £3 0s. 10d. in 1614, 19s. 2d. in 1615, and £3 19s. 4d. in 1621.
[10] It can hardly have been open at the time of the Watermen's petition early in 1614 (cf. p. 370).

1611, and whose *Chaste Maid in Cheapside* was published in 1630 as 'often acted at the Swan on the Banke-side'. The Hope itself was modelled structurally upon the Swan. Its measurements were the same, and it had similar partitions between the rooms and external staircases. Its heavens, however, were to be supported without the help of posts from the stage, since this had to be removable on days of bear-baiting. It is obviously illegitimate to infer from this specification that the stage of the Swan, which was not used for bear-baiting, was also removable. The accounts of the overseers show one more payment from the 'players' in 1621, which perhaps supports the statement contained in one of Malone's notes from Sir Henry Herbert's office-book, that after 1620 the Swan was 'used occasionally for the exhibition of prize-fighters'.[1] The theatre is marked 'Old Playhouse' in the manor map of 1627. The last notice of it is in *Holland's Leaguer* (1632) as a famous amphitheatre, which was 'now fallen to decay, and like a dying swanne hanging downe her head seemed to sing her own dierge'.[2]

Many of the maps of the Bankside do not extend far enough west to take in the Swan. It is named and shown as an octagonal or decagonal building by Visscher (1616) and in maps of the Merian group (1638), but not by Hollar (1647).

xi. THE GLOBE

[*Bibliographical Note.*—The devolution of the Globe shares can be traced in the documents of three lawsuits : (*a*) Ostler v. Heminges, in the Court of King's Bench in 1616 (*Coram Rege Roll* 1454, 13 Jac. I, Hilary Term, m. 692), described by C. W. Wallace in *The Times* of 2 and 4 Oct. 1909, and in part privately printed by him in *Advance Sheets from Shakespeare, the Globe, and Blackfriars* (1909), here cited as *O. v. H.* ; (*b*) *Witter v. Heminges and Condell*, in the Court of Requests (1619-20), described by C. W. Wallace in *The Century* of Aug. 1910, and printed by him in *Nebraska University Studies*, x (1910), 261, here cited as *W. v. H.* ; and (*c*) the proceedings before the Lord Chamberlain in 1635 known as the *Sharers Papers*, and printed by Halliwell-Phillipps in *Outlines*, i. 312. Professor Wallace's descriptive articles require some corrections from the texts of his documents. Much evidence bearing upon the site of the theatre was collected by W. Rᴇndle in *The Bankside, Southwark, and the Globe Playhouse* (1877), printed by the N. S. S. as an appendix to Harrison, pt. ii (cited as Rendle, *Bankside*), in *Walford's Antiquarian*, viii (1885), 209, and in *The Anchor Brewery* (1888, *Inns of Old Southwark*, 56), by G. Hubbard in *Journal of the Royal Institute of British Architects*, 3rd series, xvii. 26, and *London and Middlesex Arch. Soc. Trans.* n. s. ii (1912), pt. iii,

---

[1] Herbert, 63 ; *Variorum*, iii. 56. Rendle, in *Antiquarian Magazine*, vii. 211, notes a 'licence for T. B. and three assistants to make shows of Italian motion, at the Prince's Arms, or the Swan' in 1623; cf. Herbert, 47.

[2] Cf. p. 376.

and most fully by W. Martin in *Surrey Archaeological Collections,* xxiii (1910), 149. Some additional facts, from records of the Sewers Commission for Kent and Surrey in the possession of the London County Council, and from deeds concerning the Brend estate, were published by Dr. Wallace in *The Times* of 30 April and 1 May 1914, and led to discussion by Dr. Martin, Mr. Hubbard, and others in *11 N. Q.* x. 209, 290, 335 ; xi. 447 ; xii. 10, 50, 70, 121, 143, 161, 201, 224, 264, 289, 347, and by W. W. Braines in *The Site of the Globe Playhouse* (1921). A paper by the present writer on *The Stage of the Globe* is in the *Stratford Town Shakespeare,* x. 351.]

In the building of the Globe use was made of the materials of the old Theatre (q.v.) which, according to *Allen v. Burbadge* (1602), the Burbadges, with Peter Street and others, pulled down on 28 December 1598, carried ' all the wood and timber therof unto the Banckside in the parishe of St. Marye Overyes, and there erected a newe playehowse with the sayd timber and woode '.[1] An earlier account gives the date of the audacious proceeding as 20 January 1599. The formal lease of the new site from the freeholder, Nicholas Brend of West Molesey, was executed on 21 February 1599. No doubt Street, who had assisted in the transfer, was the builder and had finished his job when on 8 January 1600 he contracted with Henslowe and Alleyn to put up the Fortune (q.v.) on the model, with certain modifications, of ' the late erected plaiehowse on the Banck in the saide parishe of St. Saviours called the Globe '. This contract allowed twenty-eight weeks for the work. Probably the Globe took about the same time, for it is described as ' de novo edificata ' in the inquisition on the property left by the lessor's father, Thomas Brend, which is dated on 16 May 1599.[2] It may not then have been quite finished, but it was doubtless ready for the occupation of the Chamberlain's men by the beginning of the autumn season of 1599. One of the earliest plays there produced by them was Shakespeare's *Julius Caesar* which on 21 September Thomas Platter crossed the water to see ' in dem streüwinen Dachhaus '.[3] Whether the Globe or its predecessor the Curtain was the ' wooden O ' of *Henry V,* I, prol. 13, must be more doubtful, as the prologue to Act V of the same play contemplates the triumphant return of Essex from Ireland, and in fact Essex left England on 27 March and returned, not triumphant, on 28 September 1599.[4] Jonson refers to ' this faire-fild Globe ' as the scene of

---

[1] *N. U. S.* xiii. 279 ; cf. p. 399.

[2] Wallace, in *The Times* (1914), ' Ac de et in vna domo de novo edificata cum gardino eidem pertinenti in parochia S^cl Salvatoris praedicta in comitatu Surria praedicta in occupacione Willielmi Shakespeare et aliorum '.

[3] Cf. p. 364.

[4] A rather fantastic argument of Ordish, 85, for the Curtain on the ground of the martial character of the neighbourhood is answered by Murray, i. 99.

his *Every Man Out of his Humour*, produced in the autumn of 1600.[1] The Privy Council order of the previous 22 June, which enacts that there shall be one allowed house only ' in Surrey in that place which is commonlie called the Banckside or there aboutes ', goes on to recite that the Chamberlain's men had chosen the Globe to be that one. The allowance of the house ' in Surrey called the Globe ' is confirmed by the Privy Council letter of 27 December 1601. The order of 9 April 1604 authorizes the opening after the plague of ' the Globe scituate in Maiden Lane on the Banckside in the Countie of Surrey '. This order evidently contemplates that the King's men will use the house, which was assigned to them by name as ' theire nowe vsual howse called the Globe within our County of Surrey ' by the terms of the patent of 19 May 1603. The precedent is followed in the later patents of 1619 and 1625, and there is nothing to indicate that any other company than the Chamberlain's or King's men ever performed, even temporarily, at the theatre.

The Globe was held by a syndicate, composed mainly of members of the company, on a leasehold tenure. The site, which had been garden ground, was described in the original lease with some minuteness as follows : [2]

' totam illam parcellam fundi nuper praeantea inclusam & factam in quatuor separalia gardina nuper in tenuris & occupacionibus **Thomae Burt** & **Isbrand Morris diers** & **Lactantii Roper Salter** civis Londoniae continentem in longitudine ab oriente vsque occidentem ducentos & viginti pedes assisae vel eo circiter iacentem & adiungentem viae sive venellae ibidem ex vno latere & abbuttantem super peciam terrae vocatam the Parke super bóream & super gardinum tunc vel nuper in tenura siue occupacione cuiusdam Johannis Cornishe versus occidentem & super aliud gardinum tunc vel nuper in tenura sive occupacione cuiusdam Johannis Knowles versus orientem cum omnibus domibus aedificiis structuris vijs easiamentis commoditatibus & pertinentiis adinde spectantibus vel aliquo modo pertinentibus quae dicta praemissa sunt scituata iacentia & existentia infra parochiam sancti Salvatoris in Southwarke in Comitatu Surria aceciam totam illam parcellam terrae nuper praeantea inclusam & factam in tria separalia gardina vnde duo eorundem nuper in tenura sive occupacione cuiusdam Johannis Robertes carpenter ac aliud nuper in occupacione cuiusdam Thomas Ditcher civis & mercatoris scissoris Londoniae scituatam iacentem & existentem in parochia praedicta in praedicto comitatu Surria continentem in longitudine ab oriente ad occidentem per estimacionem centum quinquaginta & sex pedes assisae vel eo circiter & in latitudine a borea ad austrum centum pedes assisae per estimacionem vel eo circiter iacentem & adiungentem super alio latere viae

---

[1] *E. M. O.* 4368.   [2] *O. v. H.* l. 110.

sive venellae praedictae & abbuttantem super gardinum ibidem tunc vel nuper praeantea in occupacione Willelmi Sellers versus orientem & super vnum aliud gardinum ibidem tunc vel nuper praeantea in tenura Johannis Burgram sadler versus occidentem & super venellam ibidem vocatam Mayden lane versus austrum cum omnibus domibus aedificijs structuris vijs easiamentis commoditatibus & pertinentiis ultimis recitatis praemissis seu alicui parti vel parcellae inde spectantibus seu aliquo modo pertinentibus simul cum libero ingressu egressu & regressu & passagio . . . per & trans praedictam viam sive venellam iacentem & existentem inter praemissa praedicta.'

The lease was granted for a term of thirty-one years from Christmas 1598 to Christmas 1629, and conveyed the property in two equal moieties, the one to Cuthbert and Richard Burbadge and the other to William Shakespeare, Augustine Phillips, Thomas Pope, John Heminges, and William Kempe.[1] With the exception of Cuthbert Burbadge these were all members of the Chamberlain's company. Each moiety was charged with a ground-rent of £7 5s. There is nothing to show how the funds for building were found. ' Wee ', said the Burbadges in 1635, ' at like expence built the Globe, with more summes of money taken up at interest, which lay heavy on us many yeeres ; and to ourselves wee joyned those deserveing men, Shakspere, Hemings, Condall, Philips, and others, partners in the profittes of that they call the House, but makeing the leases for twenty-one yeeres hath beene the destruction of ourselves and others, for they dyeing at the expiration of three or four yeeres of their lease, the subsequent yeeres became dissolved to strangers, as by marrying with their widdowes and the like by their children.' [2] This is, however, not a strictly accurate account of what took place in 1599, for Condell was not one of the original ' housekeepers ', and the original lease was for thirty-one, not twenty-one, years. In any case, the Burbadges contributed the woodwork of the Theatre.

Between the execution of the lease and the completion of the play-house, Shakespeare and his four fellows assigned their moiety to William Levison and Thomas Savage, who ' reassigned to euerye of them seuerally a fift parte of the said moitie ', so that after the building each of the five had a ' ioynt tenancie ' with the other four in a moiety of the ground and galleries, and was also ' tenant in common ' during the term of the lease.[3] Professor Wallace explains that ' the purpose of a joint-tenancy was to prevent the breaking up and scattering of an estate into fractions by keeping

---

[1] O. v. H. l. 99 ; W. v. H. 313.   [2] Halliwell-Phillipps, i. 317.
[3] W. v. H. 314.

the property always in the hands of the members, or the longest survivors, or survivor, of them all, thus not allowing it to descend to heirs'. The legal distinction is no doubt sound, but we shall find that, whatever the intention of the assignment and reassignment may have been, the Globe shares did in fact descend to heirs, and that a good deal of trouble and litigation was thereby caused.[1]

Shortly after the house was built Kempe, no doubt on his withdrawal from the company, assigned his interest to Shakespeare, Heminges, and Phillips, who by further assign-ments to and from one Thomas Cressey brought in Pope, with the result that each of the four now held a fourth part of the moiety.[2] Pope died before 13 February 1604 and left his interest to Mary Clark, *alias* Wood, and Thomas Bromley. Mary Clark must have married John Edmonds, another legatee under the will, for in 1612 an interest corre-sponding to Pope's was held by John and Mary Edmonds and Basil Nicoll.[3] Nicoll, who was Pope's executor, was presumably acting as trustee for Thomas Bromley. Edmonds, though an actor, belonged not to the King's men, but was a Queen's man by 1618. One-eighth of the house, therefore, was alienated from the company in 1604. A further alienation, which proved particularly troublesome in its results, took place on the death of Phillips in May 1605. The exact facts became a matter of legal dispute. But it appears that Phillips' interest passed first to his widow Anne as executrix, and, when her marriage in the course of 1606 to the spendthrift John Witter became known, to Heminges, who succeeded her as executor under the terms of the will. In this capacity Heminges leased an interest to the Witters on 14 February 1611 for a term of eighteen years from Christmas 1610.[4] This interest was not a fourth, but only a sixth of the moiety, since at some date between the death of Phillips and that of Sly on 16 August 1608 the moiety had been redivided to allow of the introduction of Henry Condell and William Sly into the syndicate of housekeepers.[5] A similar transac-tion took place on 20 February 1612, when Basil Nicoll and John and Mary Edmonds, then holding one-sixth of the moiety, Shakespeare and Witter, each also holding one-sixth, and Heminges and Condell, holding three-sixths, joined to convey one-seventh of the moiety to William Ostler.[6] It must,

---

[1] *Century* (Aug. 1910), 508 ; cf. p. 424.
[2] *W. v. H.* 314.   [3] *O. v. H.* l. 194.   [4] *W. v. H.* 319.
[5] Ibid. 317. Wallace dates the admission of Condell in 1610, but this seems to be an error.
[6] *O. v. H.* l. 97 ; *W. v. H.* 321.

I think, be assumed that Heminges and Condell had together purchased the share left by Sly to his son Robert.

The acquisition of the Blackfriars by the King's men in 1608 did not, at first at least, detract from the importance of the Globe as the leading London theatre. It is so accepted by foreign visitors in 1610 and again in 1611.[1]

On 29 June 1613 the house was ' casually burnt downe and consumed with fier '.[2] The event was important enough to find a record in Howes' continuation of Stowe's *Annales* : [3]

' Upon S. Peters day last, the play-house or Theater, called the Globe, upon the Banck-side near London, by negligent discharging of a peal of ordinance, close to the south-side thereof, the thatch took fire, and the wind sodainly disperst the flame round about, and in a very short space the whole building was quite consumed, and no man hurt ; the house being filled with people to behold the play, viz. of Henry the Eighth. And the next spring it was new builded in far fairer manner than before.'

Many other contemporary accounts exist. Thus Thomas Lorkin wrote to Sir Thomas Puckering on 30 June : [4]

' No longer since than yesterday, while Burbage's company were acting at the Globe the play of Henry VIII, and there shooting off certain chambers in way of triumph, the fire catched and fastened upon the thatch of the house, and there burned so furiously, as it consumed the whole house, all in less than two hours, the people having enough to do to save themselves.'

On 2 July Sir Henry Wotton wrote to his nephew Sir Edmund Bacon : [5]

' Now, to let matters of state sleep, I will entertain you at the present with what has happened this week at the Bank's side. The King's players had a new play, called *All is True*, representing some principal pieces of the reign of Henry VIII, which was set forth with many extraordinary circumstances of pomp and majesty, even to the matting of the stage ; the Knights of the Order with their Georges and garters, the Guards with their embroidered coats, and the like : sufficient in truth within a while to make greatness very familiar, if not ridiculous. Now, King Henry making a masque at the Cardinal Wolsey's house, and certain chambers being shot off at his entry, some

---

[1] Rye, 61, from *Relation* of Hans Jacob Wurmsser von Vendenheym, ' Lundi 30 [April 1610] S. E. [Prince Lewis Frederick of Württemberg] alla au Globe, lieu.ordinaire ou l'on joue les Commedies, y fut representé l'histoire du More de Venise ' ; cf. p. 369 on visit of Prince of Hesse-Cassel in 1611.　　　　　　　　　　　　　　　　　　　　　[2] W. v. H. 320.

[3] Stowe, 926. Jonas, 104, cites another record of the date from A. Hopten, *A Concordancy of Yeares* (1615).

[4] Birch, *James*, i. 253.

[5] L. Pearsall Smith, *Letters of Wotton*, ii. 32.

of the paper, or other stuff, wherewith one of them was stopped, did light on the thatch, where being thought at first but an idle smoke, and their eyes more attentive to the show, it kindled inwardly, and ran round like a train, consuming within less than an hour the whole house to the very grounds. This was the fatal period of that virtuous fabric, wherein yet nothing did perish but wood and straw, and a few forsaken cloaks ; only one man had his breeches set on fire, that would perhaps have broiled him, if he had not by the benefit of a provident wit put it out with bottle ale.'

On 8 July John Chamberlain wrote to Sir Ralph Winwood : [1]

'The burning of the Globe, or play-house, on the Bankside, on St. Peter's day, cannot escape you ; which fell out by a peal of chambers (that I know not upon what occasion were to be used in the play), the tamplin or stopple of one of them lighting in the thatch that covered the house, burn'd it down to the ground in less than two hours, with a dwelling-house adjoining, and it was a great marvaile and fair grace of God, that the people had so little harm, having but two narrow doors to get out.'

Nor was poetic chronicles of the disaster lacking. On the day after the fire took place, two ballads about it were entered in the Stationers' Register.[2] Neither is known in print, but the use of the word ' doleful ' suggests that one of them, of which the author was William Parrat, is probably identical with the following set of verses, preserved in manuscript :[3]

A Sonnett upon the pittiful burneing of the Globe playhowse in London.

Now sitt the downe, Melpomene,
  Wrapt in a sea-cole robe,
And tell the dolefull tragedie,
  That late was playd at Globe ;
For noe man that can singe and saye
[But ?] was scard on St. Peters daye.
    Oh sorrow, pittifull sorrow, and yett all this is true.

---

[1] Winwood, iii. 469.

[2] Arber, iii. 528, ' Simon Stafford . . . a ballad called the sodayne Burninge of the Globe on the Bankside in the Play tyme on Saint Peters day last 1613 '; ' Edward White . . . a doleful ballad of the general ouerthrowe of the famous theater on the Banksyde called the Globe &c by William Parrat '.

[3] Halliwell-Phillipps, *Outlines*, i. 310, ' from a manuscript of the early part of the seventeenth century, of unquestionable authenticity, preserved in the library of Sir Mathew Wilson, Bart., of Eshton Hall, co. York '. The Eshton Hall collection, originally formed by John Hopkinson in 1660, has recently been sold, with the verses, to Mr. G. D. Smith of New York. The ' Sonnett ' was first printed [by Joseph Haslewood] in *The Gentleman's Magazine* (1816), lxxxvi. 114, ' from an old manuscript volume of poems ', and therefrom by Collier, i. 371, and Hazlitt, *E. D. S.* 225.

All yow that please to understand,
    Come listen to my storye,
To see Death with his rakeing brand
    Mongst such an auditorye ;
Regarding neither Cardinalls might,
Nor yett the rugged face of Henry the Eight.
    Oh sorrow, &c.

This fearfull fire beganne above,
    A wonder strange and true,
And to the stage-howse did remove,
    As round as taylors clewe ;
And burnt downe both beame and snagg,
And did not spare the silken flagg.
    Oh sorrow, &c.

Out runne the knightes, out runne the lordes,
    And there was great adoe ;
Some lost their hattes, and some their swordes ;
    Then out runne Burbidge too ;
The reprobates, though druncke on Munday,
Prayd for the Foole and Henry Condye.
    Oh sorrow, &c.

The perrywigges and drumme-heades frye,
    Like to a butter firkin ;
A wofull burneing did betide
    To many a good buffe jerkin.
Then with swolne eyes, like druncken Flemminges,
Distressed stood old stuttering Heminges.
    Oh sorrow, &c.

No shower his raine did there downe force
    In all that Sunn-shine weather,
To save that great renowned howse ;
    Nor thou, O ale-howse, neither.
Had itt begunne belowe, sans doubte,
Their wives for feare had pissed itt out.
    Oh sorrow, &c.

Bee warned, yow stage-strutters all,
    Least yow againe be catched,
And such a burneing doe befall,
    As to them whose howse was thatched ;
Forbeare your whoreing, breeding biles,
And laye up that expence for tiles.
    Oh sorrow, &c.

E e

Goe drawe yow a petition,
 And doe yow not abhorr itt,
And gett, with low submission,
 A licence to begg for itt
In churches, sans churchwardens checkes,
In Surrey and in Midlesex.
  Oh sorrow, pittifull sorrow, and yett all this is true.

John Taylor, the water-poet, has his epigram on the theme:[1]

As gold is better that's in fier try'd,
 So is the Bank-side *Globe*, that late was burn'd ;
For where before it had a thatched hide,
 Now to a stately theator 'tis turn'd :
Which is an emblem, that great things are won
By those that dare through greatest dangers run.

Ben Jonson, in his *Execration upon Vulcan*, writes as if he had been an eye-witness:[2]

Well fare the wise men yet, on the Bank side,
My friends the watermen ! they could provide
Against thy fury, when to serve their needs,
They made a Vulcan of a sheaf of reeds,
Whom they durst handle in their holiday coats,
And safely trust to dress, not burn their boats.
But O those reeds ! thy mere disdain of them
Made thee beget that cruel stratagem,
Which some are pleased to style but thy mad prank,
Against the Globe, the glory of the Bank :
Which, though it were the fort of the whole parish,
Flanked with a ditch, and forced out of a marish,
I saw with two poor chambers taken in,
And razed ; ere thought could urge this might have been !
See the World's ruins ! nothing but the piles
Left, and wit since to cover it with tiles.
The Brethren they straight nosed it out for news,
'Twas verily some relict of the Stews ;
And this a sparkle of that fire let loose,
That was raked up in the Winchestrian goose,
Bred on the Bank in time of Popery,
When Venus there maintained the mystery.
But others fell with that conceit by the ears,
And cried it was a threatning to the bears,
And that accursed ground, the Paris-garden :
' Nay,' sighed a sister, ' Venus' nun, Kate Arden,

---

[1] *Taylors Water-Works* (1614), reprinted as *The Sculler* (1630, *Works*, 515), ep. 22 of 3rd series.
[2] *Underwoods*, lxii, written later than the Fortune fire of 9 Dec. 1621.

Kindled the fire ! ' But then, did one return,
No fool would his own harvest spoil or burn !
If that were so, thou rather wouldst advance
The place that was thy wife's inheritance.
' Oh no,' cried all, ' Fortune, for being a whore,
Scaped not his justice any jot the more :
He burnt that idol of the Revels too.
Nay, let Whitehall with revels have to do,
Though but in dances, it shall know his power ;
There was a judgement shewn too in an hour.'

The Puritans did in fact draw such morals as Jonson satirized.
Prynne, for example, finds the hand of God in ' the sudden
fearful burning, even to the ground, both of the Globe and
Fortune playhouses, no man perceiving how these fires
came '.[1]

The Globe was at once rebuilt. It was open again by
30 June 1614, when John Chamberlain wrote to Alice Carleton
that he had called upon her sister Williams, and found her
' gone to the new Globe, to a play. Indeed ', he says, ' I hear
much speech of this new playhouse, which is said to be the
fairest that ever was in England, so that if I live but seven
years longer, I may chance to take a journey to see it '.[2]
The manuscript continuator of Stowe, describing the end of
the theatre, says that the rebuilding was ' at the great charge
of King Iames, and many Noble men and others '.[3] The law-
suit documents contain no indication that any part of the
burden fell upon any one but the ' housekeepers ', who being
bound under their lease to ' mainteyne and repaire ' the
house, resolved to ' reedifie the same '. The first estimate
of cost seems to have been about £700 to £800, for a levy of
' 50li or 60li ' was called upon each seventh share of the
moiety.[4] Witter was unable to meet this demand, and as he
was also behindhand with his share of the ground-rent and
other payments, Heminges resumed possession of the seventh
and gave half of it ' gratis ' to Henry Condell. By this time
it had been ascertained that the re-edifying would be ' a verie
greate charge ', and Heminges claims that the re-edifying
of Witter's ' parte ' had in fact cost himself and Condell
' about the somme of cxxli '.[5] This would mean a total cost
of about £1,680.[6] Heminges appears to have taken a sub-

[1] *Histriomastix*, 556.   [2] Birch, *James I*, i. 329.
[3] Cf. p. 374.   [4] *W. v. H.* 320.   [5] Ibid. 321.
[6] A later statement by Shank in the *Sharers Papers* puts it at £1,400.
Heminges describes Witter's ' parte ' by a slip as one-sixth instead of one-
seventh of the moiety. If the £120 was one-twelfth of the total cost, his
figure (£1,440) would agree with that of Shank. Professor Wallace says in

lease at 20s. a year from his partners of two small parcels of
the land in 1615, and to have built on them a house, probably
a taphouse, as a private enterprise.[1]

Ostler died in December 1614, and Heminges took possession of his interest and drew the profits until October 1615,
when his daughter Thomasina, Ostler's widow, brought an
action against him for them, the result of which is unknown.[2]
Shakespeare died in April 1616, and his interest, if not
previously alienated, would have passed under his will, with
other ' leases ' to John and Susanna Hall.[3] At some time
earlier than April 1619, probably when he joined the company
about 1616, Field was admitted to be a housekeeper, and the
moiety was then divided into eighths instead of sevenths.[4]
In April 1619 Witter brought an action against Heminges and
Condell in the Court of Requests, to recover the interest
which he had forfeited at the time of the rebuilding. He
estimated the present annual value of the seventh, which he
had held, at £30 to £40, and in the course of the proceedings
expressed his willingness either to pay a rent of £13 6s. 8d.
for the half of that seventh which Heminges had not passed
over to Condell, or, alternatively, to take the profits of the
houses on the site, other than the theatre, and in return for
those to become responsible for the whole of the ground-rents
due under the principal leases. The defence consisted in a denial
of Witter's claim to benefit under the will of Augustine Phillips,
and an assertion that, after Heminges had allowed him to draw
considerable sums in respect of the share, he had deserted
his wife, at whose death Heminges ' out of charitie was at
the charges of the buryeing of her '. The depositions of the
witnesses, who included Thomas Woodford and one James
Knasborough, are unfortunately missing. Ultimately Witter
failed to proceed with his case, and on 29 November 1620 the
Court gave judgement for the defendants.

In October 1624 died John Underwood and left a share
in the Globe in trust for his children to Condell and others
as his executors. It must be supposed that he had succeeded
to Field's eighth, when the latter left the King's men in 1619.
Condell himself died in December 1627 and left his interest
to his son William until he should have made £300 out of it,
and thereafter to his widow. Heminges died in October
1630, and his interest passed to his son William as his executor.

The Times of 2 Oct. 1909, ' This amount is in fact excessive. . . . I have
other contemporary documents showing the cost was far less than £1,400.'
  [1] *W. v. H.* 323 ; Wallace in *The Times* (1914).
  [2] *O. v. H.* ll. 245 sqq.
  [3] Lambert, *Shakespeare Documents*, 87.   [4] *W. v. H.* 323.

During the last years of their lives Heminges and Condell, following out the policy of absorption which has already been illustrated, appear to have acquired in one way or another the whole of the shares formerly held by Shakespeare, by Basil Nicoll and John Edmonds as successors of Sly, and by Underwood. This fact emerges from the records known as the *Sharers Papers*, which start with a petition from Robert Benfield, Eliard Swanston, and Thomas Pollard, then important members of the King's company, to the Lord Chamberlain in 1635, to be admitted to shares as 'housekeepers' in the profits of the Globe and the Blackfriars.[1] The allegations show that the Globe had been 'formerly' divided into sixteen shares, of which eight were held by Cuthbert Burbadge and Richard Burbadge's widow Winifred, now Mrs. Robinson, in her own right and that of her son William, four by Mrs. Condell, and four by William Heminges. Afterwards Joseph Taylor and John Lowin were allowed to acquire shares, and later still the remaining Heminges interest was 'surreptitiously' purchased by John Shank. At the date of the petition, therefore, the Burbadges held seven shares, Mrs. Condell two, Shank three, and Taylor and Lowin two each. The case furnishes valuable information as to the organization of the theatre, and as to the division of outgoing and profits between the housekeepers and the actors as such. It is pretty evident that by 1635 the Globe took a secondary place to the Blackfriars in the economy of the King's men.[2] Shank admitted that he had bought a two years' term of one Globe share in 1633 and a one year's term of two more in 1634, together with interests in the Blackfriars, and seems to have thought that the £506 which he gave was full value for the purchases.[3] The Burbadges protested against being called upon to part with any part of their property to 'men soe soone shott up' and not having the 'antiquity and desert', which had customarily been looked for in housekeepers. In support of their plea they recalled the early services of their father in the building of theatres and the claims of their family to profit by 'the great desert of Richard Burbadge for his quality of playing'. They suggested that 'makeing the leases for twenty-one yeeres' to their fellows, whose widows

---

[1] Halliwell-Phillipps, i. 312.

[2] Cf. ch. xi. There was a much rougher type of audience at the Globe ; cf. Shirley, *Prologue at the Globe, to his Comedy called 'The Doubtful Heir'*, *which should have been presented at the Blackfriars*, quoted in *Variorum*, iii. 69.

[3] Cf. ch. xvii (Blackfriars).

or children subsequently alienated the profits from the company, had been their ' destruction '. The Lord Chamberlain, however, directed that the Burbadges should transfer two shares and Shank one to the three petitioners, ' at the usual and accustomed rates, and according to the proportion of the time and benefit they are to injoy '. This the order states, in the case of the Globe, as five years. Probably there is an error here. The terms bought by Shank were to expire in 1635, but at the time of the petition a suit was pending in the Court of Requests for the confirmation of a ' lease paroll ' from Sir Matthew Brend for a further nine years from 25 March 1635. The original lease of 1599 from Nicholas Brend was for thirty-one years and would have expired in 1629. But on 26 October 1613, when the rebuilding of the theatre was in hand, a fresh lease extending the term to 1635 had been granted by Sir John Bodley as trustee for Nicholas's son Matthew, who was then a minor. Not content with this, the syndicate had procured a promise of a further extension to 1644 from young Matthew himself, which he now repudiated.[1] I think that Bodley must have taken the opportunity in 1613 to raise the ground-rent from £14 10s. to £20. A draft for a return of new and divided houses, made for the Earl Marshal in 1634, has the following entry :

' The Globe playhouse nere Maid lane built by the company of players, with the dwelling house thereto adjoyninge, built with timber, about 20 yeares past, upon an old foundation, worth 14ˡˡ to 20ˡˡ per ann., and one house there adjoyning built about the same tyme with timber, in the possession of Wᵐ Millet, gent., worth per ann. 4ˡˡ [In margin, Playhouse & house, Sʳ Mathew Brend's inheritance].'

A corrected return of 1637 runs :

' The Globe playhouse nere Maide lane built by the Company of Players with timber about 20 yeares past uppon an old foundacion, worth 20ˡˡ per ann. beinge the inheritance of Sʳ Mathew Brand, Kⁿᵗ.'[2]

The petitioners in the *Sharers Papers* declare that up to Lady Day 1635 the rent for the Globe and Blackfriars together was not above £65. The original rent of the Blackfriars was £40, but this also may have been put up on the expiration of the first lease in 1629. The Court of Requests finally confirmed the extension of the lease to 1644, apparently at a still further

---

[1] Wallace in *The Times* (1914). Bodley seems to have acquired a dubious title to hold the land in his own right in 1608, raised a fine of £20 for recognizing the players' lease in 1609, and a fine of £2 on Heminges for leave to build his tap-house in 1615. Matthew Brend recovered the property through the Court of Wards, after the end of his minority, in 1622.

[2] Rendle, *Bankside*, xvii, from *Southwark Vestry Papers*. Brend was knighted in 1622.

increased rent of £55, as Shank states the combined rent of the two houses as £100. The Globe was 'pulled downe to the ground, by Sir Matthew Brand, on Munday the 15 of April 1644, to make tenements in the room of it'; that is to say, immediately upon the expiration of the nine years' term from Lady Day 1635 contemplated in the *Sharers Papers*.[1]

The precise locality of the Globe has been matter of controversy. The various contemporary documents already quoted place it beyond doubt in Surrey, and 'on the Bankside', a term which must certainly be taken to cover, not merely the row of houses looking directly upon the river, but also the whole of the western part of Southwark lying behind and south of these. With somewhat greater minuteness, the parish of St. Mary Overies is specified in the lawsuit of *Allen v. Burbadge*, and the parish of St. Saviour's in the Fortune contract. There is no inconsistency here. The two ancient parishes of St. Mary Magdalen and St. Margaret on the Hill were amalgamated under the name of St. Saviour's at the Reformation.[2] I do not know that the ancient boundaries are upon record. The Rose stood in what had been St. Margaret's, and one would therefore expect to find the Globe nearer than the Rose to the old priory church of St. Mary's. In the Privy Council order of 1604 the situation is described as 'in Maiden lane', and in the return to the Earl Marshal of 1637 as 'nere Maide lane'. But, apart from the difference between 'in' and 'nere', Maiden Lane is a fairly long thoroughfare, and so far as these indications are concerned, the Globe may have been either to the north or the south of it. Local tradition, as elaborated by Southwark antiquaries, has been inclined to put it to the south, within the area occupied by what was formerly Thrale's and is now Barclay and Perkins's Anchor Brewery, of which Maiden Lane, now Park Street, forms the northern boundary. The main reason for this is the inclusion within the brewery of the course of a passage known as Globe Alley, which ran west from Deadman's Place in a parallel line to Maiden Lane for about 360 feet and then turned northwards for another 100 feet until it debouched into the Lane. So far as measurements go, Globe Alley might be the *venella* of the 1599 lease. The name first appears in the St. Saviour's token book for 1614, where it is applied to houses formerly described as Brand's Rents, and from 1613 onwards as Sir John Bodley's

---

[1] Cf. p. 374. Wallace, in *The Times* (1914), makes Matthew Brend's lease end on 25 Dec. Yet he puts the destruction after the expiration of the lease.

[2] Stowe, *Survey*, ii. 58.

Rents.[1] Land south of Maiden Lane certainly formed part of the Brend estate, and a plot of it conveyed by Sir Matthew Brend to one Hilary Memprise in 1626 was bounded on the south by a sewer dividing it from the Bishop of Winchester's park, and on the north by ' the alley or way leading to the Gloabe Playhouse commonly called Gloabe Alley '.[2] A century later, property acquired for the brewery in 1732 is similarly described as ' fronting a certain alley or passage called Globe Alley, in antient times leading from Deadman's Place to the Globe Playhouse '.[3]

It was certainly a belief in the Thrale family that the site of the theatre itself had passed into their hands. Mrs. Piozzi, Johnson's friend, who married Henry Thrale in 1763, left the following autobiographical note of her residence in Southwark between that date and her husband's death in 1781 :

' For a long time, then—or I thought it such—my fate was bound up with the old Globe Theatre, upon the Bankside, Southwark ; the alley it had occupied having been purchased and thrown down by Mr Thrale to make an opening before the windows of our dwelling-house. When it lay desolate in a black heap of rubbish, my Mother, one day, in a joke, called it the Ruins of Palmyra ; and after that they laid it down in a grass-plot. Palmyra was the name it went by, I suppose, among the clerks and servants of the brewhouse. . . . But there were really curious remains of the old Globe Playhouse, which though hexagonal in form without, was round within.' [4]

Dr. Martin seems to think that the lady's recollection was confused and that the garden called Palmyra stood on the east of Deadman's Place opposite to Globe Alley. But, according to Concanen and Morgan it was ' on the opposite side of the street ' to the brewery.[5] However this may be, there are other notices which show that, however complete the demolition of 1644, the theatre or part of it was still regarded by tradition as standing a hundred years later amongst the tenements by which it was replaced.[6] In 1787 the brewery was purchased by Barclay and Perkins, and the

---

[1] Martin, 158.

[2] Stopes, *Burbage*, 196 ; Martin, 169 ; from *Close Roll, 3 Car. I*, pt. 23, m. 22.

[3] Martin, 174.   [4] A. Hayward, *Autobiography of Mrs. Piozzi*, ii. 33.

[5] *History of St. Saviour's* (1795), 231.

[6] T. Pennant, *London* (1791), 60, ' A little west of S. Mary Overies (in a place still called Globe Alley) stood the Globe. . . . I have been told that the door was very lately standing ' ; Concanen and Morgan, 224, ' Several of the neighbouring inhabitants remember these premises being wholly taken down about fifty years ago, having remained for many years in a very ruinous state : avoided by the young and superstitious as a place haunted by those imaginary beings called evil spirits '.

conveyance recites amongst other property a plot of ground between Globe Alley and a common sewer, from which had been cleared in 1767 some 'ruinous and decayed' tenements formerly occupied in 1715 by John Knowles and others.[1] This is probably the clearance referred to by Mrs. Piozzi. Under Acts of 1786 and 1812 Globe Alley was closed, and it is now covered over within the brewery precinct. Horwood's map of 1799 shows the eastern end already obliterated. The western end is called Globe Walk, and to the north of it is Globe Court, perhaps representing the space cleared in 1767.

On the assumption that the theatre stood in Globe Alley, there has been divergence of opinion as to the precise part of the Alley in which it stood. Mr. Rendle fixed on a spot on the north side, about 80 or 100 feet from the Deadman's Place end.[2] To this he was guided, partly by a further local tradition, according to which the site was occupied successively by a meeting-house and a windmill, and partly by an argument derived from the entries in the St. Saviour's token-book for 1621.[3] Here, under the heading 'Sir John Bodley's Rentes' are recorded in succession about ten names. Then

[1] Martin, 165, 177. It is probably a mere coincidence that John Knowles held a garden next the Globe site in 1599.

[2] Rendle, Bankside, xix; Antiquarian, viii. 216.

[3] Chalmers, Apology (1797), 114, 'I maintain, that the Globe was situated on the Bank, within eighty paces of the river, which has since receded from its former limits; that the Globe stood on the site of John Whatley's windmill, which is at present used for grinding colours; as I was assured by an intelligent manager of Barclay's brewhouse, which covers, in its ample range, part of Globe Alley; and that Whatley's wind mill stands due south from the western side of Queenhythe by the compass, which I set for the express purpose of ascertaining the relative bearings of the windmill to the opposite objects on the Thames'; W. Wilson, History and Antiquities of Dissenting Churches (1814), iv. 148, 175, 'In former days there stood here [in Globe Alley] a theatre called the "Globe" . . . Near to this place stood the meeting-house. . . . Its dissolution took place about the year 1752. . . . It is at present used for warehousing goods. A mill was also erected over it for the purpose of grinding bones'; R. Wilkinson, Londina Illustrata (1819), i. 135, 'Upon the disuse of the theatre, its site . . . was formed into a meeting-house. . . . Afterwards a mill was erected here to grind bones; and it is at present appropriated for the purpose of grinding stones and similar materials'. The plan, however, which accompanies Wilkinson's text, assigns the theatre to an improbable site some way west of the meeting-house. The Globe Alley meeting-house was built in 1672; it appears in a list of 1683, and is marked on Rocque's map of 1746 on Rendle's favourite site. Wilson only says the meeting-house was near the Globe; Wilkinson identifies the sites. Chalmers mentions the windmill, but not the meeting-house. I may add that a line drawn south from the west of Queenhithe would pass west of any possible site for the Globe. Malone's 'nearly opposite to Friday Street, Cheapside' (Variorum, iii. 63) can also only be approximate.

comes a new heading, differently written, 'Gloab Alley',
then two more names, then in the margin of the page the word
'Gloabe'. This Mr. Rendle took to mean that the Globe
was about twelve houses from the east end of the alley.
If this is an indication of the site of the Globe at all, which
is a mere conjecture, I should myself draw the inference
that it stood, not twelve, but two houses from the end of the
alley, and that a part, if not the whole, of Bodley's Rents
was outside the alley. And why should the enumerator be
supposed to have worked from the east, rather than from the
north end of the alley ? Dr. Martin, in fact, turns Mr. Rendle's
argument round in this way, and uses the token-book to
support a theory which places the theatre south of Globe
Alley, just at the angle where it turns to the north, and
360 feet, instead of Mr. Rendle's 80 or 100 feet, west of Deadman's Place.[1] Here it appears to be located in a borough
history of 1795 ; [2] and is certainly located in more than one
early nineteenth-century plan.[3] Dr. Martin has attempted
to obtain confirmation of this siting from an investigation of
the brewery title-deeds. From 1727 onwards the history of
the angle site is clear. In that year it was transferred, subject
to a mortgage, by Timothy Cason and his wife Elizabeth,
heiress of the Brend estate, to certain parishioners of
St. Saviour's. Upon it was built the parish workhouse
referred to by Concanen and Morgan. This stood just at the
outer south-west angle of Globe Alley, which Dr. Martin
conceives to have been occupied by the theatre. In 1774
a new workhouse was built, and the site of the old one bought
by the Thrales. It was conveyed with the rest of the brewery
to Barclay and Perkins in 1787, and was then described as
the ground ' on which lately stood all that great shop or
workhouse formerly used for a meeting-house '. Dr. Martin
thinks that this forgotten meeting-house may have been
confused in local tradition with that further to the east along

[1] Cf. facsimile from token-book in Martin, 157.
[2] Concanen and Morgan, *History of St. Saviour's* (1795), 224, ' It was
situated in what is now called Maid lane ; the north side and building
adjoining, extending from the west side of Counter-alley to the north side
of the passage leading to Mr. Brook's cooperage ; on the east side beyond
the end of Globe-alley, including the ground on which stood the late
parish workhouse, and from thence continuing to the south end of
Mr. Brook's passage. Under this building was Fountain-alley, leading
from Horseshoe-alley into Castle-lane.' This account appears to make
the site extend farther north than Dr. Martin allows for, right up, indeed,
to Maid Lane.
[3] Plan of 1810 in R. Taylor, *Londina Illustrata*, ii. (1825) 136 ; plan
of 1818 in Taylor, *Annals of St. Mary Overy* (1833), 140.

Globe Alley.[1] Dr. Martin suggests that the property transferred by the Casons in 1727 is to be identified with that
described in a deed executed by the same persons in 1706,
of which a copy is also to be found amongst the brewery
title-deeds, as consisting of tenements built ' where the late
playhouse called the Globe stood and upon the ground
thereunto belonging '. If this were so, he would of course
have proved his point. The deed of 1706 seems to have been
a family settlement covering various fragments of Brend
property in Southwark, which had only just been brought
together in the hands of Elizabeth Cason. The Globe site
had been settled by Sir Matthew Brend in 1624 upon his wife
Frances as a jointure. She died in 1673, and it then passed
as a jointure to Judith, wife of Sir Matthew's son Thomas and
mother of Elizabeth, under a deed of 1655 in which the reference to ' the late playhouse called the Globe ', repeated in
that of 1706, first occurs. Judith Brend had died in 1706.
    As a matter of fact, it is almost impossible to reconcile
the Southwark tradition that the Globe stood on the south
of Maiden Lane, either in Mr. Rendle's or in Dr. Martin's
interpretation of it, with more than one bit of evidence which
we owe to the research of Professor Wallace. The first of
these is the lease of 1599 itself, as recited in the pleadings of
Ostler v. Heminges. This states quite clearly that the leased
plot abutted on a piece of land called the Park ' super boream '
and on Maiden Lane ' versus austrum ', and it is difficult to
take very seriously either the Latinity which makes ' versus
austrum ' mean that the leased plot was on the south, or
the suggestion that the draughtsman was working carelessly
from a plan which had the south instead of the north of
the plot at the top of the sheet, and got the points of his
compass wrong.[2] I daresay that such things do sometimes
happen in conveyancer's offices, but it is hardly legitimate to
call them in aid as a canon of interpretation. No doubt it is
tempting to identify the piece of land called the Park with
the Bishop of Winchester's park, which lay at a reasonable
distance to the south and not to the north of Maiden Lane,
but after all this must once have extended nearly up to the
Bankside, since Maiden Lane itself is known to have been
cut out of it, and it is not at all improbable that some little

---

[1] Martin, 171. One cannot lay much stress upon hearsay locations of
the site by employees of the brewery (Martin, 183), or the discovery
of underground staging still farther south than Dr. Martin's site on a spot
which in 1599 must have been well within Winchester Park (Martin, 201),
or of a stone inscribed ' [T]heayter ', just south of Globe Alley (Martin, 184)
[2] Martin, 164.

strip of land retained the name.[1] It can only have been a very little one. The lease describes the Globe site as consisting of two plots lying apparently on opposite sides of a way or alley (*venella*) by which access was obtainable to them. One of these, that next the Park, had been the gardens of Thomas Burt, Isbrand Morris, and Lactantius Roper. It was 220 feet in length and lay between the garden of John Knowles on the east and John Cornish on the west. The southern plot, bounded by Maiden Lane on the south, had similarly been the gardens of John Roberts and Thomas Ditcher. This was only 156 feet long and 100 feet deep, and lay between the gardens of William Sellers to the east and John Burgram to the west. Now the whole space between Maiden Lane and the Thames is only from 200 to 350 feet at various points, so that there could not have been room for much of a ' park ' between the Globe site and the Bankside houses.

The evidence of the lease is confirmed in various ways by the records of presentments made by the Commissioners of Sewers for Kent and Surrey against negligent occupiers in this marshy neighbourhood. The most important entry is one of 14 February 1606 :

' It is ordered that Burbidge and Heminges and others, the owners of the Playhouse called the Globe in Maid-Lane shall before the xx[th] day of Aprill next pull vp and take cleane out of the Sewar the props or postes which stand vnder their bridge on the north side of Mayd-lane vpon paine to forfeit xx[s].'

This is endorsed ' done ', but another order of the same day requiring the same men to ' well and sufficientlye pyle boorde and fill vp viij poles more or lesse of theire wharfe against theire said Playhouse ' needed a repetition on 25 April before it received attention.[2] Earlier records, before the Globe came into existence, relate to some of the garden-holders named in the lease. A plot of John Bingham or Burgram abutted on a Maiden Lane sewer in 1596, and this is probably identical with the ' common sewer leading from Sellors gardin to the beare garden ', which William Sellers and others were ordered to cleanse on 5 December 1595. Certainly the bear garden was to the north and not the south of Maiden

---

[1] A Clink poor relief assessment of 1609 (Collier, *Alleyn Memoirs*, 91 ; Warner, 49) shows two names, each assessed for ' halfe the parke ' ; this would hardly be the Bishop's. The token-books also show persons resident in the park, but here the order of the entries points to a locality south of Maiden Lane, near the gate of the Bishop's Park (*11 N. Q.* xii. 143).

[2] Wallace in *The Times* (1914). Dr. Martin explains (*11 N. Q.* xii. 161) that, in order to conduct their patrons from Bankside to the playhouse south of Maiden Lane, ' the owners of the Globe had erected a bridge over the ditches and quagmire of Maid Lane '.

Lane. There was also a sewer bordering upon the park, and on this Jasper Morris and Thomas Burt had encroached in 1593.[1]

The old maps, as usual, do not give much help when it comes to a pinch, although the balance of their authority, for what it is worth, seems to me to be in favour of a northern site.[2] Mr. Hubbard, calculating from Visscher's map, would put the Globe on the site of the present Central Wharf, 15 feet south of the Bankside houses and 136 feet west of Bank End, and therefore not very near Maiden Lane at all.[3] I do not think that he sufficiently recognizes the imperfections of the maps from a surveyor's point of view. I doubt whether more is to be got out of them than that the Globe stood more to the east and probably more to the south than either the Hope or the Rose.[4]

The foregoing paragraphs show the state of the controversy when the body of this chapter was written. Since then Mr. Braines has taken up the investigation where it was left by Dr. Martin, with the help of the brewery title-deeds and many other documents bearing on the distribution of tenements in Maiden Lane and Globe Alley over more than a century. It now seems clear that, in view of the known history of properties north of Maiden Lane, there is no room for the Globe plot there, that this plot did pass from the Casons to the workhouse and ultimately the brewery, and that it did lie at Dr. Martin's angle site, being indeed precisely located on the map by Concanen and Morgan's description of 1795. We must therefore assume that the points of the compass were, as Dr. Martin conjectured, inverted in the lease of 1599, east with west and north with south, and that the Globe company maintained a bridge over the sewer on the opposite side of Maiden Lane to the theatre, for the convenience of visitors coming down Horseshoe Alley from the river. The *venella* of 1599 must have been a westward extension of Globe Alley, afterwards disused.

Some notion of the structural character of the Globe may be gleaned from the builder's contract for the Fortune in

---

[1] Dr. Wallace says that all these records were made by the Commissioners ' in dealing with the property of Brend and others on the north side ' of Maiden Lane. But there is no reference to ' the north side ' in the actual record. Bingham had, and Sellers may have had, more than one plot in the neighbourhood.

[2] Cf. p. 379.

[3] *R. I. B. A. Journal*, 3rd series, xvii. 26.

[4] Halliwell-Phillipps (*Calendar of Shakespeare Rarities*, 81) had a document of 1653 concerning a sewer ' in Maide Lane nere the place where the Globe playhouse lately stood ', which he considered as establishing the exact locality of the theatre. It is probably now in America.

1600.[1] The Globe was then the last new thing in theatres, and in entering into his agreement for the Fortune with Peter Street, the builder of both houses, Henslowe was careful to specify that the Globe should be taken as the model, alike as regards the arrangement of the galleries and stair-cases, the contrivances and fashioning of the stage, and all other minor points not particularly indicated. The only alterations of design set out in the agreement were that the scantlings or standard measurements of the timber should be rather stouter than those of the Globe, and that the main posts of the stage and auditorium should be shaped square and carved with figures of satyrs. It is probable, however, that a more important difference is passed without notice. The Fortune was rectangular; the Globe was almost certainly round. The reference to a circular house in *Henry V* and *A Warning for Fair Women*, both plays of about 1599, may indeed belong to the Curtain rather than the Globe, but there are similar references in *E. M. O.* (1599) and in *The Merry Devil of Edmonton* (1608), which are certainly Globe plays, and there seems no reason to doubt that the Globe is represented by the cylindrical buildings, windowless below, windowed and of narrower diameter above, which are shown in the maps of the Hondius group and in the background of Delaram's portrait of James I.[2] A few details are furnished by the various narratives of the fire of 1613. The roof was thatched, whence arose the accident. The walls were of timber, for nothing was burnt but wood and straw. The building was 'flanked with a ditch, and forced out of a marish'. It had a stage-house 'round as taylors clewe', and carried a silken flag. There were two narrow doors, and hard by stood an alehouse. The new Globe built after the fire was tiled for greater safety. In other respects there was probably no great change. The building is described in 1634 as of timber, upon an old foundation. The maps, if they can be trusted, figure it as polygonal, rather than strictly round. No doubt it was round inside; an 'amphytheator', it is called in *Holland's Leaguer*. The *Sharers Papers* of 1635 mention the tiring-house door, at which money was taken. James Wright tells us that it was a summer house, large and partly open to the weather, and that the acting was always by daylight. Malone conjectured that the name 'Globe' was taken from the sign, 'which was a figure of Hercules supporting the Globe, under which was written *Totus mundus agit histrionem*'.[3] I do not know where he got this information.

[1] Cf. p. 436.
[2] I ought not to have suggested in *The Stage of the Globe*, 356, that the first Globe might have been rectangular.   [3] *Variorum*, iii. 67.

xii. THE FORTUNE

[*Bibliographical Note.*—Most of the documents are at Dulwich, and are printed in full or in abstract by W. W. Greg in *Henslowe Papers*, and by J. P. Collier in *Alleyn Memoirs* and *Alleyn Papers*. The *Register* of the Privy Council adds a few of importance. Valuable summaries of the history of the theatre are given by W. W. Greg, *Henslowe's Diary*, ii. 56, and W. Young, *History of Dulwich College* (1889), ii. 257. The *Catalogue of the Manuscripts and Muniments at Dulwich* (1881–1903) by G. F. Warner and F. B. Bickley is also useful.]

The settlement of the Chamberlain's men in 1599 at the Globe, hard by the Rose, on Bankside, probably led Henslowe and Alleyn to plan during the same year a countermove, by the transference of the Admiral's men to a new theatrical locality in the rapidly growing districts on the north-west boundary of the City. The Rose, although not built fifteen years, was in decay, and the swamps of the Bankside had not, especially in bad weather, proved attractive to visitors. The new centre might be expected to serve in summer and winter alike, and, while in a place ' remote and exempt ' from the City jurisdiction, would be convenient for the well-to-do population, which was establishing itself in the western suburbs, along the main roads of Holborn and the Strand. The Fortune on the north, and the Blackfriars, opened about the same time on the south, delimited a region which has remained almost to our own day the head-quarters of the stage. The actual site selected lay just outside Cripplegate between Golding or Golden Lane and Whitecross Street, in the county of Middlesex, the lordship or liberty of Finsbury, and the parish of St. Giles without Cripplegate. The title-deeds at Dulwich make it possible to trace the history of the property or part of it back to the reign of Henry VIII, but for the present purpose it is sufficient to begin with 11 July 1584, the date of a lease by Daniel Gill, son of William Gill, gardener, to Patrick Brewe, goldsmith, of five tenements on the east side of Golding Lane and one on the west side of Whitecross Street at a rent of £12 a year. This lease Brewe assigned to Alleyn on 22 December 1599, for a sum of £240. Subsequently, in 1610, Alleyn bought up a reversionary lease for £100, and also, after troublesome negotiations with the numerous descendants of Daniel Gill, the freehold of the property for £340.[1] This purchase, however, and probably also the original lease, included a good deal more than the actual plot on which the theatre was built. The deed of sale recites six tenements on the east of Golden Lane and six on the west of Whitecross Street. It is pretty clear,

[1] *Henslowe Papers*, 14; Henslowe, ii. 56.

from the boundaries described, as compared with those in a temporary assignment by Alleyn of the lease, that the property dealt with in 1584 and in 1610 was the same, and it is natural to conclude that Alleyn had himself added to the number of tenements.[1] This is confirmed by a note of Alleyn's that, in addition to building the play-house, he spent £120 'for other priuat buildings of myn owne'. One such building adjoined the south side of the play-house in 1601.[2] Alleyn's note gives the cost of the play-house itself as £520, making up with the private buildings and the purchase of leasehold, reversion, and freehold, a total expenditure of £1,320.[3] The contract for building the framework was taken by Peter Street, carpenter, at £440, which presumably left Alleyn £80 for the painting and other decorative work excluded from the contract. The following is the text of the contract, which is preserved at Dulwich : [4]

'This Indenture made the Eighte daie of Januarye 1599, and in the Twoe and Fortyth yeare of the Reigne of our sovereigne Ladie Elizabeth, by the grace of god Queene of Englande, Fraunce and Irelande, defender of the Faythe, &c. betwene Phillipp Henslowe and Edwarde Allen of the parishe of Ste Saviours in Southwark in the Countie of Surrey, gentlemen, on thone parte, and Peeter Streete, Cittizen and Carpenter of London, on thother parte witnesseth That whereas the saide Phillipp Henslowe & Edward Allen, the daie of the date hereof, haue bargayned, compounded & agreed with the saide Peter Streete ffor the erectinge, buildinge & settinge upp of a new howse and Stadge for a Plaiehouse in and vppon a certeine plott or parcell of grounde appoynted oute for that purpose, scytuate and beinge nere Goldinge lane in the parishe of Ste Giles withoute Cripplegate of London, to be by him the saide Peeter Streete or somme other sufficyent woorkmen of his provideinge and appoyntemente and att his propper costes & chardges, for the consideracion hereafter in theis presentes expressed, made, erected, builded and sett upp in manner & forme followinge (that is to saie) ; The frame of the saide howse to be sett square and to conteine ffowerscore foote of lawfull assize everye waie square withoutt and fiftie fiue foote of like assize square everye waie within, with a good suer and stronge foundacion of pyles, brick, lyme and sand bothe without & within, to be wroughte one foote of assize att the leiste aboue the grounde ; And the saide fframe to conteine three Stories in heighth, the first or lower Storie to conteine Twelue foote of lawfull assize in heighth, the second Storie Eleauen foote of lawfull assize in heigth, and the third or vpper Storie to conteine Nyne foote of lawfull assize in height ; All which Stories shall conteine Twelue foote and a

---

[1] *Henslowe Papers*, 16.   Ibid. 25.   [3] Ibid. 108.
[4] Printed by W. W. Greg, *Henslowe Papers*, 4, from *Dulwich Muniments*, 22 ; also in *Variorum*, iii. 338, and Halliwell-Phillipps, *Illustrations*, 81 ; *Outlines*, i. 304.

halfe of lawfull assize in breadth througheoute, besides a juttey forwardes in either of the saide twoe vpper Stories of Tenne ynches of lawfull assize, with ffower convenient divisions for gentlemens roomes, and other sufficient and convenient divisions for Twoe pennie roomes, with necessarie seates to be placed and sett, aswell in those roomes as througheoute all the rest of the galleries of the saide howse, and with suchelike steares, conveyances & divisions withoute & within, as are made & contryved in and to the late erected Plaiehowse on the Banck in the saide parishe of Ste Saviours called the Globe ; With a Stadge and Tyreinge howse to be made, erected & settupp within the saide fframe, with a shadowe or cover over the saide Stadge, which Stadge shalbe placed & sett, as alsoe the stearecases of the saide fframe, in suche sorte as is prefigured in a plott thereof drawen, and which Stadge shall conteine in length Fortie and Three foote of lawfull assize and in breadth to extende to the middle of the yarde of the saide howse ; The same Stadge to be paled in belowe with good, stronge and sufficyent newe oken bourdes, and likewise the lower Storie of the saide fframe withinside, and the same lower storie to be alsoe laide over and fenced with stronge yron pykes ; And the saide Stadge to be in all other proporcions contryved and fashioned like vnto the Stadge of the saide Plaie howse called the Globe ; With convenient windowes and lightes glazed to the saide Tyreinge howse ; And the saide fframe, Stadge and Stearecases to be covered with Tyle, and to haue a sufficient gutter of lead to carrie & convey the water frome the coveringe of the saide Stadge to fall backwardes ; And also all the saide fframe and the Staircases thereof to be sufficyently enclosed withoute with lathe, lyme & haire, and the gentlemens roomes and Twoe pennie roomes to be seeled with lathe, lyme & haire, and all the fflowers of the saide Galleries, Stories and Stadge to be bourded with good & sufficyent newe deale bourdes of the whole thicknes, wheare need shalbe ; And the saide howse and other thinges beforemencioned to be made & doen to be in all other contrivitions, conveyances, fashions, thinge and thinges effected, finished and doen accordinge to the manner and fashion of the saide howse called the Globe, saveinge only that all the princypall and maine postes of the saide fframe and Stadge forwarde shalbe square and wroughte palasterwise, with carved proporcions called Satiers to be placed & sett on the topp of every of the same postes, and saveinge alsoe that the said Peeter Streete shall not be chardged with anie manner of pay[ntin]ge in or aboute the saide fframe howse or Stadge or anie parte thereof, nor rendringe the walls within, nor seeling anie more or other roomes then the gentlemens roomes, Twoe pennie roomes and Stadge before remembred. Nowe theiruppon the saide Peeter Streete dothe covenant, promise and graunte ffor himself, his executours and administratours, to and with the saide Phillipp Henslowe and Edward Allen and either of them, and thexecutours and administratours of them and either of them, by theis presentes in manner & forme followeinge (that is to saie) ; That he the saide Peeter Streete, his executours or assignes, shall & will att his or their owne propper costes & chardges well,

woorkmanlike & substancyallie make, erect, sett upp and fully finishe
in and by all thinges, accordinge to the true meaninge of theis presentes,
with good, stronge and substancyall newe tymber and other necessarie
stuff, all the saide fframe and other woorkes whatsoever in and vppon
the saide plott or parcell of grounde (beinge not by anie aucthoretie
restrayned, and haveinge ingres, egres & regres to doe the same)
before the ffyue & twentith daie of Julie next commeinge after the
date hereof ; And shall alsoe at his or theire like costes and chardges
provide and finde all manner of woorkmen, tymber, joystes, rafters,
boordes, dores, boltes, hinges, brick, tyle, lathe, lyme, haire, sande,
nailes, lade, iron, glasse, woorkmanshipp and other thinges whatsoever,
which shalbe needefull, convenyent & necessarie for the saide fframe
& woorkes & euerie parte thereof ; And shall alsoe make all the saide
fframe in every poynte for Scantlinges lardger and bigger in assize
then the Scantlinges of the timber of the saide newe erected howse
called the Globe ; And alsoe that he the saide Peeter Streete shall
furthwith, aswell by himself as by suche other and soemanie woorkmen
as shalbe convenient & necessarie, enter into and vppon the saide
buildinges and woorkes, and shall in reasonable manner proceede
therein withoute anie wilfull detraccion vntill the same shalbe fully
effected and finished. In consideracion of all which buildinges and
of all stuff & woorkemanshipp thereto belonginge, the saide Phillipp
Henslowe & Edward Allen and either of them, ffor themselues, theire,
and either of theire executours & administratours, doe joynctlie &
seuerallie covenante & graunte to & with the saide Peeter Streete, his
executours & administratours by theis presentes, that they the saide
Phillipp Henslowe & Edward Allen or one of them, or the executours
administratours or assignes of them or one of them, shall & will well
& truelie paie or cawse to be paide vnto the saide Peeter Streete, his
executours or assignes, att the place aforesaid appoynted for the
erectinge of the saide fframe, the full somme of Fower hundred &
Fortie Poundes of lawfull money of Englande in manner & forme
followeinge (that is to saie), att suche tyme and when as the Tymber-
woork of the saide fframe shalbe rayzed & sett upp by the saide Peeter
Streete his executours or assignes, or within seaven daies then next
followeinge, Twoe hundred & Twentie poundes, and att suche time
and when as the saide fframe & woorkes shalbe fullie effected &
ffynished as is aforesaide, or within seaven daies then next followeinge,
thother Twoe hundred and Twentie poundes, withoute fraude or
coven. Prouided allwaies, and it is agreed betwene the saide parties,
that whatsoever somme or sommes of money the saide Phillipp
Henslowe & Edward Allen or either of them, or thexecutours or
assignes of them or either of them, shall lend or deliver vnto the saide
Peter Streete his executours or assignes, or anie other by his appoyntemente or consent, ffor or concerninge the saide woorkes or anie parte
thereof or anie stuff thereto belonginge, before the raizeinge & settinge
upp of the saide fframe, shalbe reputed, accepted, taken & accoumpted
in parte of the firste paymente aforesaid of the saide some of Fower
hundred & Fortie poundes, and all suche somme & sommes of money,

as they or anie of them shall as aforesaid lend or deliver betwene the
razeinge of the saide fframe & finishinge thereof and of all the rest of
the saide woorkes, shalbe reputed, accepted, taken & accoumpted in
parte of the laste pamente aforesaid of the same somme of Fower
hundred & Fortie poundes, anie thinge abouesaid to the contrary
notwithstandinge.   In witnes whereof the parties abouesaid to theis
presente Indentures Interchaungeably haue sett theire handes and
seales.   Yeoven the daie and yeare ffirste abouewritten.

P S

Sealed and deliuered by the saide Peter Streete in the presence of
me William Harris Pub[lic] Scr[ivener] And me Frauncis Smyth
appr[entice] to the said Scr[ivener]

[*Endorsed* :] Peater Streat ffor The Building of the Fortune.

The constant references in the terms of the contract to the
model of the Globe, while bearing testimony to the stimulus
which the building of the Globe had given to theatrical
competition, leaves some uncertainty as to many details of
planning, and it is matter for regret that the ' plot ' of the
stage and staircases furnished to the builder has not itself
been preserved.   We learn, however, that the house was
a square one, 80 feet each way by outside and 55 feet by inside
measurement ;   that the stage was 43 feet wide and projected
into the middle of the yard ;   that the framework was of
wood, on a foundation of brick and piles, and with an outer
coating of plaster ;   that the framework and stage were
boarded within and strengthened with iron pikes ;   that there
were three galleries rising to a total height of 32 feet, and that
sections of these were partitioned off and ceiled as ' gentlemens rooms ', of which there were four, and ' twopenny
rooms ' ;   that the tiring-house had glazed windows ;   that
there was a ' shadowe or cover ' over the stage, and that this,
with the galleries and staircases, were tiled and supplied with
lead gutters to carry off the rain-water.   Two divergences
from the Globe model are specified :   the timber work is
to be stouter, and the principal posts of the frame work and
stage are to be square and carved with satyrs.   An ingenious
attempt has been made by Mr. William Archer and Mr. W. H.
Godfrey to reconstruct the plan of the theatre from these and
other indications, with a liberal allowance of conjecture.[1]

---

[1] *Quarterly Review*, ccviii. 442 ; *Architectural Review*, xxiii. 239.   Models
by Mr. Godfrey are at the Columbia and Illinois Universities (Adams,
277).   M. W. Sampson has pointed out in *M. L. N.* for June 1915 (cited
by Adams, 279) that the passage in *The Roaring Girl* (1611), i. 1, where
Sir Alexander Weargrave displays his house to his friends, is really a
description of the Fortune when ' Within one square a thousand heads
are laid '.

It will be observed that Henslowe, as well as Alleyn, was a party to the contract; but it is pretty clear from Alleyn's note already referred to that he found the money, and although Henslowe did in fact become his partner in the enterprise, this was under a lease of 4 April 1601, whereby he took over a moiety of the play-house and its profits for a term of twenty-four years from the previous 25 March at an annual rent of £8.[1] This lease did not include Alleyn's private tenements, but it did include some enclosed ' growndes' on the north and west of the house, and a passage 30 feet long by 14 feet wide running east from the south-west angle of the building ' from one doore of the said house to an other '. It is, I think, to be inferred from this that the main approach to the earlier Fortune theatre was from the Golden Lane side. The contract with Street is dated on 8 January 1600 and provides for the completion of the work by the following 25 July, and for the payment of the price in.two instalments, one when the framework was up and the other upon completion. In fact, however, the acquittances by Street and others, endorsed upon the Dulwich indenture, show that Henslowe acted as a kind of banker for the transaction, and made advances from time to time to Street, or to pay workmen or purchase materials, all of which were debited against the amounts payable under the contract. Work seems to have begun before 17 January. By 20 March Henslowe had paid £180 and by 4 May £240. It is therefore a little puzzling to find a payment ' at the eand of the fowndations ' on 8 May. About £53 more was paid before 10 June, making nearly £300 in all by that date. The last entry is one of 4s. to Street ' to pasify him ', which suggests that some dispute had taken place. Here the acquittances stop, but Henslowe's *Diary* indicates that he was frequently dining in company with Street from 13 June to August 8, and probably the work was completed about the latter date.[2] Alleyn had had to face some opposition in carrying out his project. He began by arming himself with the authority of his ' lord ', the Earl of Nottingham, who wrote in his favour to the Middlesex justices on 12 January 1600, explaining the reasons for leaving the Bankside and the general convenience of the new locality, and citing the Queen's ' special regarde of fauor ' towards the company as a reason why the justices should allow his servant to build ' w^(th)out anie yor lett or molestation '. This action did not prove sufficient to avert a local protest. Lord Willoughby and others com-

---

[1] *Henslowe Papers*, 25.   [2] Ibid. 11.

plained to the Council, who on 9 March wrote to the Middlesex justices informing them that the erection of a new play-house, ' wherof ther are to manie allreadie not farr from that place ', would greatly displease the Queen, and commanding the project to be ' staied '. Alleyn, however, was secure in the royal favour. He also, by offering a weekly contribution to the relief of the poor, succeeded in obtaining a certificate from the petty officials and other inhabitants of Finsbury of their consent to the toleration of the house ; and on 8 April the Council wrote again to the justices, withdrawing their previous inhibition and laying special stress on Elizabeth's desire that Alleyn personally should revive his services as a player, ' wheareof, of late he hath made discontynuance '. The letter also referred to the fact that another house was pulled down instead of the Fortune, and a formal Privy Council order of 22 June, laying down that there shall in future be one house in Middlesex for the Admiral's men, and one on the Bankside for the Chamberlain's, makes it clear that the condemned theatre was the Curtain.[1] Nevertheless, it is certain that neither the Curtain nor the Rose was in fact plucked down at this date.

The Fortune was opened in the autumn of 1600 by the Admiral's men, probably with Dekker's *1 Fortune's Tennis*, and its theatrical history is closely bound up with that of the same company, who occupied it continuously, as the Admiral's to 1603, then as Prince Henry's men to his death in 1612, and finally as the Palsgrave's men. It is only necessary to deal here with matters that directly concern the building. That it became something of a centre of disturbance in the peaceful suburbs of the north-west is shown by various entries in the records of the Middlesex Bench. On 26 February 1611, two butchers, Ralph Brewyn and John Lynsey, were charged with abusing gentlemen there. On 1 October 1612, the justices regarded it as the resort of cutpurses, and were thereby led to suppress the jigs at the end of plays, which especially attracted such persons. In 1613 a true bill was found against Richard Bradley for stabbing Nicholas Bedney there on 5 June.[2] The upkeep of the structure was expensive. A note in Alleyn's hand of sums laid out upon the play-house during the seven years 1602–8 shows an average amount of about £120. Only £4 2s. was spent during 1603, for the greater part of which year the theatres were closed, but £232 1s. 8d. in 1604.[3] No doubt

---

[1] App. D, Nos. cxvii, cxviii, cxxi, cxxii, cxxiv.
[2] Cf. ch. viii and App. D, No. cl. [3] *Henslowe Papers*, 110.

wooden buildings, open to the weather, perished rapidly. It is not unreasonable to suppose that the relations between the company and their landlords were much what they had been at the Rose ; that is to say that the latter took half the gallery receipts and bore repairs, while the former took the rest of the receipts and met all other outgoings. An unexecuted draft lease to Thomas Downton of 1608 indicates that Alleyn and Henslowe then had it in mind to bind the company more closely to the theatre, by dividing a quarter of their interest amongst the eight members of the company.[1] Possibly the plan was carried out. In asking a loan from Alleyn on a date apparently earlier than August 1613, Charles Massye, who was one of the eight, not only offers repayment out of his ' gallery mony ' and ' house mony ', but also the assignment of ' that lyttell moete I have in the play housses ' as a security.[2] Certainly the company took over the house after Henslowe's death on 6 January 1616. His share in the building passed to his widow, who contemplated a sale of it to Gregory Franklyn, Drew Stapley, and John Hamond.[3] But the deed remained unexecuted at her death in 1617, and the whole property was now once more in Alleyn's hands. On 31 October 1618 he leased it to the company for £200 a year, to be reduced to £120 at his death. With it went a taphouse occupied by Mark Brigham, the rent of a two-room tenement held by John Russell, and a strip of impaled ground 123 feet by 17 feet, lying next the passage on the south.[4] This is perhaps the garden in which, according to John Chamberlain, the players, ' not to be overcome with courtesy ', banqueted the Spanish ambassador when he visited the theatre on 16 July 1621.[5] John Russell is presumably the same whose appointment by Alleyn as a ' gatherer ' lead to a protest from William Bird on behalf of the company.[6] A few months after the ambassador's visit, John Chamberlain records the destruction of the Fortune on 9 December 1621 :[7]

' On Sonday night here was a great fire at the Fortune in Golden-Lane, the fayrest play-house in this towne. It was quite burnt downe in two howres, & all their apparell & play-bookes lost, wherby those poore companions are quite undone.'

Alleyn also notes the event in his diary.[8] On 20 May 1622 he formed a syndicate, and leased to it the site at a rent of

---

[1] Cf. ch. xi.   [2] *Henslowe Papers*, 64.   [3] Ibid. 25.
[4] Ibid. 27.   [5] Birch, *James I*, ii. 270.   [6] Cf. ch. xi.
[7] Birch, *James I*, ii. 280.   [8] Young, ii. 225.

£128 6s., under an obligation to build a new theatre at a cost of £1,000.[1] This, 'a large round brick building', was erected in the following year.[2] The site conveyed covered a space of almost exactly 130 feet square, and on it had stood, besides the buildings named in the lease of 1618, other tenements, in one of which William Bird himself lived. Mr. Lawrence has suggested that the new Fortune may have been a roofed-in house, but his evidence is hardly sufficient to outweigh the explicit statement of Wright that it 'lay partly open to the weather, and there they always acted by daylight'.[3] This can hardly refer only to the earlier building. The Fortune was dismantled in 1649 and 'totally demolished' by 1662, and the façade still extant in 1819 cannot therefore have belonged to it, although it may have belonged to a Restoration 'nursery' for young actors, possibly upon the same site.[4] No acting seems to have taken place at the Fortune after 1649.[5]

xiii. THE BOAR'S HEAD

There appear to have been at least six city inns under this sign.[6] The most famous was that on the south side of Great Eastcheap, in St. Michael's, which seems to have been regarded in the middle of the seventeenth century as the traditional locality of the tavern scenes in *Henry IV*.[7] This inn was in the occupation of Joan Broke, widow, in 1537, and in that of Thomas Wright, vintner, about 1588.[8] Another Boar's Head stood 'without' Aldgate, in the extra-mural Portsoken ward, which lay between that gate and the bars with which the liberties of the City terminated at Hog Lane.

[1] *Henslowe Papers*, 28.
[2] Cf. App. I. It is this second house that is represented as a small angular flagged building in the 'Ryther' maps.
[3] *Fortnightly Review* (May 1916).
[4] W. J. Lawrence in *Archiv* (1914), 301 ; cf. p. 520.
[5] Adams, 284, gives the history of the Fortune during 1621–49.
[6] A Boar's Head on the Bankside, which belonged to Henslowe in 1604 and previously to Alleyn (Henslowe, ii. 30), was apparently not an inn.
[7] E. Gayton, *Pleasant Notes upon Don Quixot* (1654), 277, 'Sir John of famous memory ; not he of the Boares-Head in Eastcheap'. Neither the text nor the stage-directions of *Henry IV* name the Boar's Head ; but the references to Eastcheap (*1 Hen. IV*, I. ii. 145, 176 ; II. iv. 16, 485 ; *2 Hen. IV*, II. i. 76 ; II. ii. 161) are sufficient, and when Prince Hal asks (*2 Hen. IV*, II. ii. 159) 'Doth the old boar feed in the old frank ? ', Bardolph answers, 'At the old place, my lord, in Eastcheap'. Doll Tearsheet (II. iv. 250) calls Falstaff a 'whoreson little tidy Bartholomew boar-pig '.
[8] Halliwell-Phillipps, ii. 258. Harben, 88, however, suggests that the name was transferred to this house from another on the north side of Great Eastcheap in St. Clement's.

Here, according to Stowe, there were 'certaine faire Innes for receipt of trauellers repayring to the Citie'.[1] At the Aldgate inn had been produced in 1557 a 'lewd' play called *The Sackful of Newes*, which provoked the interference of Mary's Privy Council.[2] But it seems to me exceedingly improbable that either this or the Eastcheap inn was converted into the play-house, of which we have brief and tantalizing records in the seventeenth century. Both were within the City jurisdiction, where the licensing of play-houses seems to have definitely terminated in 1596. It is true that a Privy Council letter of 31 March 1602, which directs that the combined company of Oxford's and Worcester's men shall be allowed to play at the Boar's Head, is addressed to the Lord Mayor.[3] But so are other letters of the same type, the object of which is to limit plays to a small number of houses outside the liberties, and to restrain them elsewhere over the whole area of the City and the suburbs.[4] And when, a year or two later, Worcester's men became Queen Anne's, and a draft patent was drawn up to confirm their right to play in the Curtain and the Boar's Head, both houses are described, not as in the City, but as 'within our County of Middlesex'.[5] Presumably Anne's men left the Boar's Head when the Red Bull became available for their use in 1606, and Mr. Adams has explained a mention, which had long puzzled me, of the Duke of York's men as 'the Prince's Players of Whitechapel' in 1608 by the suggestion that they succeeded to the vacant theatre.[6] If this is so, I think it affords further evidence for the theory that the Boar's Head, although it may have taken its name from the Aldgate inn, was not itself that inn, and probably not a converted inn at all, but lay just outside and not just inside the City bars. For, although part of the street between Aldgate and Whitechapel is sometimes called, as in Ogilby's map of 1677 and Rocque's of 1746, 'Whitechapel Street', yet Whitechapel proper lay outside the liberties, farther to the east

---

[1] Stowe, *Survey*, i. 126 ; ii. 72. I suppose the inn is identical with the 'Blue Bore Inne' marked by Ogilby (1677). The site is at No. 30 on the north of Aldgate High Street (Harben, 87).

[2] Dasent, vi. 168.

[3] App. D, No. cxxx. The description of this letter in the *Index to Remembrancia*, 355, as referring to 'the Boar's Head in Eastcheap' has proved misleading.

[4] App. D, Nos. cxxv, cxxix, cxxxv.   [5] Cf. ch. xiii (Anne's).

[6] Adams, 17 ; cf. ch. xiii (Duke of York's). The further suggestion of Adams, 8, that Rawlidge in 1628 (cf. p. 360) wrote 'Whitefriars' for 'Whitechapel' is less plausible. Rawlidge is only dealing with playhouses within the City.

along the Mile End Road.[1] The only other contemporary record of the Boar's Head is a letter to Edward Alleyn from his wife Joan on 21 October 1603, in which she says, 'All the companyes be come hoame & well for ought we knowe, but that Browne of the Boares head is dead & dyed very pore, he went not into the countrye at all '.[2] This Browne cannot be identified, and it is perhaps idle to conjecture that he may have been related to Robert Browne, and that it may have been at the Boar's Head that the latter played with Derby's men in 1599–1601. The Boar's Head seems to have been generally forgotten by the Restoration, but is recalled by the Marquis of Newcastle c. 1660.[3]

xiv. THE RED BULL

[*Bibliographical Note.*—The records of the suit of *Woodford v. Holland* (1613) were printed by J. Greenstreet in the *Athenaeum* for 28 Nov. 1885 from *Court of Requests Books*, xxvi, ff. 780, 890, and cxxviii, and there-from by Fleay, 194 ; and more fully with those of the later suit of 1619 (misdated 1620) by C. W. Wallace in *Nebraska University Studies*, ix. 291 (cited as *W. v. H.*). Collier, i. 374, mentions evidence on the same trans-actions as ' in the Audit Office ', and misnames the complainant John Woodward.]

Our chief knowledge of the early history of the Red Bull is derived from disputes before the Court of Requests in 1613 and 1619 between Thomas Woodford and Aaron Holland. It appears that Holland held a lease of the site, which was at the upper end of St. John Street in the parish of St. James, Clerken-well, from Anne, widow and executrix of Christopher Beding-field, and had there built a play-house. The indication of a Red Bull Yard in Ogilby and Morgan's map of 1677 to the west of St. John Street, and just north of the angle which it forms with Clerkenwell Green, no doubt defines the locality with some precision.[4] In *3 Jac. I*, that is, at some date between 24 March 1605 and 23 March 1606, he assigned one-seventh of the house to Thomas Swynnerton, ' with a gatherers place thereto belonging '. This Swynnerton transferred for £50 to Philip Stone.[5] It was subject to a rent of £2 10s., and Holland gave

[1] Adams, 17, identifies the site with Boar's Head Yard, between Middle-sex Street and Goulston Street, Whitechapel. But this is the house of 1557 (v. *supra*) within the liberties. Rocque (1746) shows an oval site, just east of Church Lane and south of the church of St. Mary, White-chapel, which .rather suggests an amphitheatre, but may be merely a churchyard.

[2] *Henslowe Papers*, 59.   [3] Cf. p. 374.

[4] The section is reproduced in Adams, 294.

[5] Not the mercer Stone who sold stuffs to the Admiral's in 1601 and 1602 (Henslowe, ii. 313); he was doubtless William Stone (Knt. in 1604).

Stone an indenture in February 1609, which was alleged not to constitute a proper lease. In 1612–13 Stone sold his seventh for £50 to Woodford, who took profits for a quarter, and then entrusted his interest to Holland, instructing his servant Anthony Payne to pay the rent. He alleged that Holland persuaded Payne to be behindhand with the rent, and withheld the profits, estimated at £30 a year. He therefore brought his action a little before May 1613. The Court called upon Holland to show cause why he should not account for the arrears of profits, and for 1s. 6d. a week due to the gatherer's place.[1] Holland replied, and the issues were referred to the arbitration of counsel, including Woodford's ' demaund of the eighteenth penny and the eighteenth part of such moneys & other comodities as should be collected or receaued . . . for the profittes of the galleries or other places in or belonging to the play howse '.[2] Counsel made an arrangement, but did not agree in their reports of its terms, and the Court ordered Holland to give Woodford an indenture similar to that given to Stone.[3] Holland got a writ of prohibition from the King's Bench, always jealous of the jurisdiction of the Court of Requests, on 6 November 1613, and Woodford began a suit against Holland in Stone's name for not making a proper indenture in 1609. This, he says, Stone conspired with Holland to withdraw. In 1619 he brought another action for his profits before the Court of Requests, in which Holland describes him as ' Woodford, *alias* Simball ', but the result is unknown.

The Red Bull, then, was built not later and probably not much earlier than 1606, a little before the first recorded mention of it in the following passage from *The Knight of the Burning Pestle*, which was almost certainly produced in the winter of 1607:

' *Citizen*. Why so sir, go and fetch me him then, and let the Sophy of Persia come and christen him a childe.

' *Boy*. Beleeue me sir, that will not doe so well, 'tis stale, it has beene had before at the red Bull.' [4]

The allusion is to an incident in the last scene of Day, Rowley, and Wilkins' *Travels of the Three Brothers*.[5] This, according

[1] *W. v. H.* 296. Professor Wallace has confused this 1s. 6d. with the profits of Woodford's seventh, and thinks that a gatherer got one-eighteenth of the receipts.

[2] I think the inference is that the gallery profits were divided in the proportion of seven-eighteenths to the house-keepers and eleven-eighteenths to the players.

[3] No order seems to have been made as to the gatherer's place.

[4] *Knight of the Burning Pestle*, IV. i. 43.

[5] *Travels of the Three Brothers* (ed. Bullen, p. 88).

to the entry in the Stationers' Register on 29 June 1607, was played at the Curtain, and according to its title-page of 1607 by the Queen's men. But there is no reason why it should not also have been played at the Red Bull, since both houses are specified as occupied by the Queen's men in their patent of 15 April 1609. In their earlier draft patent of about 1603–4, the Boar's Head and Curtain are named, and in a Privy Council letter of 9 April 1604 the Curtain only. Presumably, therefore, the Red Bull was taken into use by the Queen's men, of whom Swynnerton was one, as soon as it was built at some date between 1604 and 1606. The Red Bull is one of the three houses whose contention is predicted in Dekker's *Raven's Almanack* of 1608, and Dekker refers to it again in his *Work for Armourers*, written during the plague of 1609, when the bear garden was open and the theatres closed. He says, ' The pide *Bul* heere keepes a tossing and a roaring, when the *Red Bull* dares not stir '.[1] Its existence caused trouble from time to time to the Middlesex justices. At the end of May 1610, William Tedcastle, yeoman, and John Fryne, Edward Brian, Edward Purfett, and Thomas Williams, felt-makers, were called upon to give recognisances to answer for a ' notable outrage at the playhouse called the Red Bull '; and on 3 March 1614 Alexander Fulsis was bailed out on a charge of picking Robert Sweet's pocket of a purse and £3 at this theatre.[2] Further references to it are to be found in Wither's *Abuses Stript and Whipt* (1613), in Tomkis's *Albumazar* (1615), and in Gayton's *Pleasant Notes on Don Quixot* (1654).[3]

An entry in Alleyn's *Diary* for 1617 has been supposed to indicate that he had an interest in the Red Bull. To me it only suggests that he sold the actors there a play.[4]

[1] Dekker, *Works*, iv. 97 ; cf. p. 367. [2] Jeaffreson, ii. 64, 86.

[3] Wither, *Abuses Stript and Whipt* (1613), i. 1,

' His poetry is such as he can cull
From plays he heard at Curtain or at Bull ' ;

Albumazar, II. i. 16, ' Then will I confound her with compliments drawn from the plays I see at the Fortune and Red Bull, where I learn all the words I speak and understand not ' ; Gayton, 24, ' I have heard that the poets of the Fortune and Red Bull had always a mouth-measure for their actors (who were terrible tear-throats) and made their lines proportionable to their compass, which were sesquipedales, a foot and a half '.

[4] Collier, *Memoirs of Alleyn*, 107 ; *D. N. B.* s.v. Alleyn. The *Diary* (Young, ii. 51) runs :

' Oct. 1, 1617. I came to London in the coach and went to the red Bull. 2ᵈ.

Oct. 3. I went to the red bull and ℞ for the younger brother but 3. 6. 4. water 4ᵈ.'

The Younger Brother was entered in the Stationers' Register in 1653, but is not extant.

The Queen's men most likely occupied the Red Bull at least until 1617 when, as shown by the lawsuit of 1623, they were on the point of moving to the Cockpit in Drury Lane. Plays of theirs were printed as acted there in 1608, 1611, 1612, and 1615. *Swetnam the Woman Hater Arraigned by Women*, printed in 1620, was also played there, before Anne's death in 1619. In 1637 Thomas Heywood, formerly one of the Queen's men, included in his *Pleasant Dialogues and Dramas*, a Prologue and Epilogue, to which he prefixed the note ' A young witty lad playing the part of Richard the third : at the Red Bull : the Author because hee was interessed in the play to incourage him, wrot him this Prologue and Epilogue '.[1] This was probably, and certainly if the play was Shakespeare's, some quite exceptional performance. Similarly the ' companie of young men of this citie ', who are stated on the title-page of Wentworth Smith's *Hector of Germany* (1615) to have acted it at the Red Bull and Curtain, must be supposed to have used these theatres by some arrangement with the Queen's men.

The Red Bull afterwards passed to other companies, continued in use up to, and even occasionally during, the Commonwealth, and had a revived life after the Restoration to 1663.[2] Before 1633, and probably before 1625, it had been re-edified and enlarged.[3] Mr. Lawrence suggests that at this time it became a roofed house, which it seems certainly to have been after the Restoration.[4] But it is difficult to get away from Wright's explicit statement that it ' lay partly open to the weather, and there they always acted by daylight '.[5] Nor need the quite modern identification of it with the roofed interior depicted in *The Wits* rest upon anything but an incidental reference to the house in the text of the pamphlet.[6] Nothing is known as to the shape or galleries of the Red Bull.

xv. THE HOPE

[*Bibliographical Note.*—The Dulwich papers relating to the connexion of Henslowe and Alleyn with the bear-baiting and the Hope are to be found with a commentary in Greg, *Henslowe's Diary* and *Henslowe Papers*. Valuable material on the Bankside localities is in W. Rendle, *The Bankside, Southwark, and the Globe*, 1877 (Appendix I to Furnivall, *Harrison's Description of England*, Part II, with a reconstructed map of the Bankside and a 1627 plan of Paris Garden), *Old Southwark and its People* (1878),

---

[1] Heywood, *Pleasant Dialogues and Dramas*, 247.
[2] Adams, 300.
[3] Prynne, *Epistle* to *Histriomastix* (1633) ; W. C., *London's Lamentation for her Sins* (1625), ' Yet even then, Oh Lord, were the theatres magnified and enlarged '.   [4] *Fortnightly Review* (May 1916).
[5] Cf. App. I.   [6] Cf. ch. xviii, *Bibl. Note*.

The Playhouses at Bankside in the Time of Shakespeare (1885, *Walford's Antiquarian*, vii. 207, 274; viii. 55), *Paris Garden and Blackfriars* (1887, 7 N. Q. iii. 241, 343, 442). Some notes of Eu. Hood [Joseph Haslewood] in 1813 and A. J. K[empe] in 1833 are reprinted in *The Gentleman's Magazine Library*, xv (1904), 74, 117. Other writings on Paris Garden are by W. H. Overall (1869) in *Proc. Soc. Antiq.* 2nd series, iv. 195, J. Meymott, *The Manor of Old Paris Garden* (1881), P. Norman, *The Accounts of the Overseers of the Poor of Paris Garden, Southwark, 1608–1671* (1901) in *Surrey Arch. Colls.* xvi. 55. Since I wrote this chapter, C. L. Kingsford (1920, *Arch.* lxx. 155) has added valuable material.]

It is convenient, in connexion with the Hope, to deal with the whole rather troublesome question of the Bankside Bear Gardens. The *ursarius* or bearward was a recognized type of mediaeval *mimus*, and the rewards in which his welcome found expression are a recurring item in many a series of municipal or domestic accounts. Thus, to take one example only, the corporation of Shrewsbury entertained between 1483 and 1542 the *ursinarii, ursuarii,* or *ursiatores* of the King, the Dukes of Norfolk and Suffolk, the Marquises of Dorset and Exeter, the Earl of Derby, and the town of Norwich.[1] On more than one occasion the payment is said to be *pro agitacione bestiarum suarum.* The phrase is perhaps not free from ambiguity. The dancing bear was, until quite recently, a familiar sight in provincial England, and I have seen one even on the sophisticated slopes of Notting Hill. And illuminations dating back as far as the tenth century bear evidence to the antiquity of his somewhat grotesque *tripudium.*[2] But in the robust days of our forefathers there was an even more attractive way of agitating bears. The traditional victim of an English baiting was no doubt the bull. A Southwark map of 1542 shows a 'Bolrynge' in the middle of the High Street and a neighbouring alley still bore the name in 1561.[3] The maps of Höfnagel (*c.* 1560) and Agas (*c.* 1570) show another ring, marked 'The bolle bayting' and with a very palpable bull inside it, upon the Bankside, not far from where the Hope must afterwards have stood.[4] But the bear was also baited in London, at least from the twelfth century.[5] Erasmus is often cited as declaring that

---

[1] *Mediaeval Stage*, ii. 250 ; cf. i. 53, 68, 72 ; ii. 244 (Durham Priory), 246 (Thetford Priory), 247 (Winchester College), 248 (Magdalen, Oxford).
[2] Strutt, *Sports and Pastimes* (ed. Cox), 195.
[3] Rendle, *Old Southwark*, f. p., 31.
[4] It is also, although unnamed, in Smith's drawing of 1588, but that s probably based on Agas.
[5] William Fitzstephen (*c.* 1170–82) in J. C. Robertson, *Materials for the History of Becket* (R. S.), iii. 11, ' In hieme singulis fere festis ante prandium . . . pingues tauri cornipetae, seu ursi immanes, cum objectis depugnant canibus '

in the reign of Henry VIII ' herds ' of the animal were kept
for the purpose. This is an error. Erasmus wrote of dancing
bears; but I am afraid it must be assumed that the chief
function of the bearward attached to the Tudor Royal Household was to provide exhibitions of the more brutal, noisy,
and occasionally dangerous sport.[1] A regular office is traceable back to 1484, when Richard III in the first year of his
reign appointed his bearward John Browne to be ' Maister,
Guyder and Ruler of all our Beres and Apes '.[2] It was still
a part of the establishment of the Royal Household under
Elizabeth. A patent of 2 June 1573 to Ralph Bowes describes
it as ' the room or office of Cheif Master Overseer and Ruler
of all and singular our game pastymes and sportes, that is to
saie of all and everie our beares bulles and mastyve dogges ',
and names as Bowes's predecessors Cuthbert Vaughan and
Sir Richard Long.[3] The grant was of the nature of a commission, authorizing the holder, personally or by deputy, to
' take up ' or press animals for the royal service, and giving
him the sole right of baiting the Queen's bears, to the exclusion of any other officer or under officer appertaining to the
bears, not specially licensed or appointed by him. The
Master was presumably expected to make his profit out of the
privileges granted, for the patent did not assign him any
fee, such as the under officers, known as the Keepers of Bears
and Mastiffs, enjoyed at the hands of the Treasurer of the
Chamber.[4] But he received a reward, similar to those given
to players, of £5 through the Treasurer on the Council's
warrant, when the baiting was shown before the Queen.
These rewards are generally expressed as ' for the Game of
Paris Garden ' or ' to the Master of her Majesty's Game at
Paris Garden '; and Bowes must have joined sons or other

---

[1] Erasmus, *Adagia*, 3354, ' Sed intolerabilius est quod apud Britannos
complures alunt greges ursorum ad saltationem, animal vorax et male-
ficum '. I owe the correct reference to Mr. P. S. Allen. Presumably
' greges ' is no more than ' numbers '.

[2] Collier, i. 42, from *Harl. MS.* 433.

[3] *Egerton MS.* 2623, f. 11. Collier, who owned this document, or some
other modern, has substituted the name of John Dorrington. A copy,
exemplified for Morgan Pope on 18 Nov. 1585, is at Dulwich ; cf. *Henslowe
Papers*, 1. Long became steward of Paris Garden in 1536 (Kingsford, 159).

[4] Collier, i. 194, from list of fees payable by the Treasurer of the Chamber
in 1571 (*Cotton MS.* Vesp. C. xiv), ' keapers of Beares and Mastives, iij.
Item to Mathew Becke, Sergeaunte of the beares, for his wages per ann.
12^l 10^s 7$\frac{1}{2}^d$. Item to Symon Powlter, yoman, per ann. 14^l 6^s 3^d. Item
to Richard Darryngton M^r and kepar of the bandogges and mastives,
per ann. 21^l 5^s 10^d '. Similarly, the Treasurer's *Declared Account* for
1594–5 (*Pipe Roll*, 542) shows a total payment to keepers of Bears and
Mastiffs of £48 12s. 8$\frac{1}{2}d$. There is an error in one or other entry of 10s.

relatives with him as deputies, since Edward Bowes and Thomas Bowes were often payees instead of Ralph Bowes during his term of office.[1] Towards the end of Bowes's life it would seem that Henslowe and Alleyn, who had been baiting bears on the Bankside as licensees since 1594, were in negotiation to obtain the Mastership.[2] Probably the first idea was to buy a surrender of the office from Bowes, since the Dulwich manuscripts contain an unexecuted draft of a patent to Henslowe, following the terms of that to Bowes himself and reciting such a surrender.[3] I should suppose this negotiation to be that in connexion with which Henslowe spent £2 15s. 6d. during 1597 upon visits to Sir Julius Caesar, Master of Requests, and other Court officials, and in a fee to the Clerk of the Signet. The expenditure is entered in the diary as incurred 'a bowt the changinge of ower comysion'.[4] But before a surrender was effected it would seem that Henslowe had had to turn his thoughts to a succession. In this he was disappointed. On 4 June 1598 he wrote to Alleyn that Bowes was very sick and expected to die, and that he much feared he should lose all. Neither Caesar nor the Lord Admiral had done anything for him, and although he had received help from Lady Edmondes and Mr. Langworth, he now learnt that the reversion of the Mastership was already promised by the Queen to one Mr. Dorrington, a pensioner.[5] Bowes did in effect die very shortly after, and on 11 August 1598 John Dorrington received his patent for the Mastership.[6] To this was joined the office of Keeper of the Bandogs and Mastiffs, with a fee of 10d. a day for exercising this office and keeping twenty mastiff bitches, and a further fee of 4d. for a deputy.[7] It is not unlikely that John Dorrington

[1] The Privy Council Acts record warrants *inter alia* to Ralph in 1574 (Dasent, viii. 257), Thomas in 1576, 1577, 1578, 1579, and 1580 (ix. 121, 153, 335; x. 148; xi. 70, 392), Ralph in 1581 (xii. 321), and Edward in 1581 and 1582 (xiii. 115, 311). Edward Bowes seems to have held the Keepership of Dogs, but disclaimed having a fee of £15 17s. 4d. at the subsidy of 1588 (*M. S. C.* i. 355).

[2] Earlier licensees were William Payne and Simon Powlter (> 1574). Wistow (c. 1575), John Napton, Morgan Pope (c. 1585-7), Thomas Burnaby (c. 1590-4), and perhaps others; cf. p. 464; Wallace in *The Times* (1914); Kingsford, 171-8.   [3] *Alleyn Memoirs*, 213; cf. *Henslowe Papers*, 4.

[4] Henslowe, i. 71. Some payments of June 1597 on account of a privy seal and a patent for Alleyn (Henslowe, i. 200) may relate to this.

[5] *Henslowe Papers*, 98. Possibly an undated letter from Arthur Langworth to Alleyn (*Henslowe Papers*, 99), in which he refers to Bowes's illness and protests against a charge of not giving Alleyn sufficient help in procuring some 'place', relates to this. But it is allusive and obscure.

[6] *S. P. D. Eliz.* cclxviii. 18; cf. *Henslowe Papers*, 12.

[7] Probably Bowes had also held this keepership with his Mastership, as he was drawing a fee from the Chamber in 1596 (Henslowe, i. 128).

was related to the Richard Darrington who had held this keepership with the same fees, amounting to £21 5s. 10d. a year, in 1571. Another keepership, that of the Bears, was held in 1599 by Jacob Meade, who was closely associated with Henslowe and Alleyn in the management of the Bear garden.[1] Dorrington's grant was confirmed by James I on 14 July 1603, and on 23 July he was knighted.[2] About this time Henslowe and Alleyn, who were paying Dorrington £40 a year for licence to bait,[3] must have contemplated fresh negotiations for a transfer of the patent, for the draft in the Dulwich manuscripts, originally drawn up about 1597, has been altered by Henslowe so as to adapt it to the new reign and to a surrender by Dorrington.[4] But once again they were unsuccessful, for Dorrington died, and on 20 July 1604 the Mastership was granted to one of the invading Scots, Sir William Stuart.[5] From him, however, Henslowe and Alleyn did succeed in obtaining an assignment, and a draft patent as joint Masters and Keepers, with the fees of 10d. and 4d., is dated 24 November 1604. They had, indeed, been rather in Stuart's hands, for he had refused either to give them a licence or to take over their house and bears, and they had to pay for the surrender at what they considered the high rate of £450.[6] This we learn from a petition of about 1607, in which they appealed to the King for an increase in the daily fee by 2s. 8d., in view of their losses through restraints and the deaths of bears, and of their heavy expenses, amounting to £200 a month, whereby their privilege, which

---

[1] Muniment 19 in the *Dulwich MSS.* is a warrant of 24 Nov. 1599 by Meade to a deputy ; cf. Henslowe, ii. 38. A list of fees *c.* 1600 in *Henslowe Papers*, 108, shows, under the general heading ' Parris garden ', only two keeperships, instead of the three of 1571, that of Bears at £12 8s. 1½d., and that of Mastiffs at £21 5s. 10½d.

[2] *Henslowe Papers*, 12 ; cf. Henslowe, ii. 37.

[3] Receipts by or on behalf of Dorrington dated Jan. and April 1602 are in *Henslowe Papers*, 101 ; Henslowe, i. 212. Each is for a quarter's ' rent ' of £10, and the earlier is specified as ' for the commissyon for the Bear-garden '. A letter of May 1600 from Dorrington to Henslowe asking him and Meade to have the ' games ' ready for Court is in *Henslowe Papers*, 100. In 1603 Henslowe spent 16s. 4d. ' for sewinge at the cort ', on petitions to Dorrington, the Lord Chamberlain, and the Council, the drawing of two licences, and ' our warent for baytynge ' (*Henslowe Papers*, 109). I think that from 1603, if not earlier, he had a regular appointment as deputy to Dorrington. On 18 April 1604 he received the Treasurer of the Chamber's reward as ' Deputy Master of the Game '.

[4] *Alleyn Memoirs*, 213 ; cf. *Henslowe Papers*, 4.

[5] *S. P. D. Jac. I, 1603–10*, p. 134.

[6] *Henslowe Papers*, 101 ; *S. P. D. Jac. I*, x, p. 167. It appears from a memorandum of Alleyn's in *Henslowe Papers*, 107, that he paid £250 for his share.

was once worth £100 a year, could now not be let at all.[1]
It is doubtful whether they got any relief. They had a new
patent on 24 November 1608;[2] but about 1612 they sent up
another petition in very similar terms. A grant of £42 10s.
and 12d. a day had, indeed, been made them in March 1611
for keeping a lion and two white bears. But this was probably
menagerie work and quite apart from the baiting. They
continued as joint Masters until Henslowe's death in 1616,
when the whole office passed to Alleyn in survivorship.[3]

When baiting seemed desirable to the soul of the sovereign,
the 'game' was generally brought to the Court, wherever
the Court might happen to be.[4] The rewards of the Treasurer
of the Chamber were most often for attendances in the
Christmas holidays or at Whitsuntide. But the game might
be called for at any time to add lustre to the entertainment
of an ambassador or other distinguished visitor to Court.
Thus on 25 May 1559 French ambassadors dined with Elizabeth, 'and after dener to bear and bull baytyng, and the
Quens grace and the embassadurs stod in the galere lokyng
of the pastym tyll vj at nyght'.[5] Later French embassies
of 1561, 1572, 1581, and 1599, and a Danish embassy of 1586
were similarly honoured.[6] The custom continued during the
next reign. On 19 August 1604 there was a grand banquet
at Whitehall for Juan Fernandez de Velasco, Constable of
Castile, on the completion of peace between England and
Spain, and thereafter a ball, and after the ball 'all then took

---

[1] Henslowe Papers, 104.

[2] This is recited in a warrant to one of their deputies in Henslowe
Papers, 18.

[3] Henslowe, ii. 38. Dr. Greg gives many interesting details of the
business, and of the relations of the Masters with their agents, for which
I have not space. Others, of Bowes's time, are in Dasent, ix. 9; xiii. 101.

[4] Sydney Papers, ii. 194 (12 May 1600), 'This day she appointes to see
a Frenchman doe feates upon a rope, in the Conduit court. To morrow
she hath commanded the beares, the bull and the ape to be baited in the
tiltyard. Upon Wednesday she will have solemn dawncing'; cf. Epicoene,
iii. 1, 'Were you ever so much as look'd upon by a lord or a lady, before
I married you, but on the Easter or Whitsun-holidays? and then out
at the banqueting-house window, when Ned Whiting or George Stone
were at the stake?' George Stone was killed during the visit of Christian
of Denmark in 1606 (H. P. 105). The Court practice was followed by
the Lord Mayor and Aldermen. Payments to the bearward of Paris
Garden for pastime showed at the Conduit Heads are in Harrison, iv. 322.

[5] Machyn, 198.

[6] Ibid. 270; Nichols, Eliz. i. 305; ii. 469; Walsingham, Journal, 42;
Boississe, i. 345. There is a spirited description of a baiting before
Elizabeth at Kenilworth on 14 July 1575 in Laneham's Letter (Furnivall,
Captain Cox, 17); but I do not suppose that these were the London
bears. Leicester, whose cognizance was the bear and ragged staff, doubt-
less kept his own ursine establishment.

their places at the windows of the room which looked out upon a square, where a platform was raised, and a vast crowd had assembled to see the King's bears fight with greyhounds. This afforded great amusement. Presently a bull, tied to the end of a rope, was fiercely baited by dogs.'[1] James had introduced a new and dangerous element into the sport by using the lions which were kept in the Tower, and this also became the scene of baitings. On 5 March 1607 the Treasurer of the Chamber paid Henslowe and Alleyn no less than £30, partly for attendances with the game at Greenwich during the visit of the King of Denmark and at Whitehall during that of the Prince de Joinville, and partly for baiting of the lions in the Tower on three several occasions.[2] Stowe gives detailed descriptions of lion-baitings in 1604, 1605, 1609, and 1610, of which the first is interesting, because it was under the personal superintendence of Edward Alleyn, ' now sworne the Princes man and Maister of the Beare Garden '.[3]

But the profit of the thing, from the point of view of the Master of the Game, was not so much in the attendances at Court, as in the public baitings, which he and those holding licences from him were privileged to give with the bears and dogs, ' taken up ' by virtue of the commission or bought at their own expense, during such times as these were not required for the royal service. These public spectacles were held at what was known as the Bear Garden, under conditions much resembling those of a theatre. They played a considerable part in the life of London ; literature is full of allusions to them ; and they are described with more or less detail in the narratives of many travellers from abroad. An early account is that from the Spanish of a secretary to the Duke of Najera, who visited Henry VIII in 1544.[4] He describes the bears as baited daily, with three or four dogs to each bear, in an enclosure where they were tied with ropes, and adds :

' Into the same place they brought a pony with an ape fastened on its back, and to see the animal kicking amongst the dogs, with the screams of the ape, beholding the curs hanging from the ears and neck of the pony, is very laughable.'

In 1559 the same French ambassadors, who saw the baiting at Whitehall, were taken on the following day to Paris Garden, and ' ther was boyth bare and bull baytyng, and the capten with a c. of the gard to kepe rowme for them to see the baytyng '.[5] The next notice of any value is that of

[1] Rye, 123.   [2] *Pipe Office Declared Account*, 543, m. 194.
[3] Stowe, *Annales* (1615), 835, 865, 895.
[4] Translated by F. Madden in *Archaeologia*, xxiii. 354.
[5] Machyn, 198.

Lupold von Wedel, who was at Southwark on 23 August 1584.[1]

'There is a round building three stories high, in which are kept about a hundred large English dogs, with separate wooden kennels for each of them. These dogs were made to fight singly with three bears, the second bear being larger than the first and the third larger than the second. After this a horse was brought in and chased by the dogs, and at last a bull, who defended himself bravely. The next was that a number of men and women came forward from a separate compartment, dancing, conversing and fighting with each other: also a man who threw some white bread among the crowd, that scrambled for it. Right over the middle of the place a rose was fixed, this rose being set on fire by a rocket: suddenly lots of apples and pears fell out of it down upon the people standing below. Whilst the people were scrambling for the apples, some rockets were made to fall down upon them out of the rose, which caused a great fright but amused the spectators. After this, rockets and other fireworks came flying out of all corners, and that was the end of the play.'

It is interesting to observe that the baiting proper was supplemented with fireworks and an entertainment, which must have been of the nature of a jig.[2] The visit of Frederick, Duke of Württemberg, on 1 September 1592, is also recorded by his secretary, who says:[3]

'His Highness was shown in London the English dogs, of which there were about 120, all kept in the same enclosure, but each in a separate kennel. In order to gratify his Highness, and at his desire, two bears and a bull were baited; at such times you can perceive the breed and mettle of the dogs, for although they receive serious injuries from the bears, are caught by the horns of the bull, and tossed into the air so as frequently to fall down again upon the horns, they do not give in, so that one is obliged to pull them back by their tails, and force open their jaws. Four dogs at once were set on the bull; they, however, could not gain any advantage over him, for he so artfully contrived to ward off their attacks that they could not well get at him; on the contrary, the bull served them very scurvily by striking and butting at them.'

[1] Translated by G. von Bülow in 2 *Transactions of Royal Hist. Soc.* ix. 230, from a manuscript in the possession of Graf von der Osten at Plathe, Pomerania. I add for the sake of completeness the following lines from the *Hodoeporica* (1568, ed. 2, 1575), 224, of N. Chytraeus, whose visit was probably *c.* 1565-7:

> Opposita in Tamesis ripa, longa area paruis
> Distincta aspicitur tectis, vbi magna canum vis
> Vrsorumque alitur diuersarumque ferarum,
> Quae canibus commissae Anglis spectacula praebent,
> Hospitibusque nouis, vincti dum praelia miscent,
> Luctantes aut ungue fero, vel dentibus uncis.

[2] Cf. ch. xviii.   [3] Translated in Rye, 45.

De Witt briefly notices the 'amphitheatrum' of the Bear Garden in 1596. He says : [1]

'Est etiam quintum sed dispari [vsu ?] et structura, bestiarum concertationi destinatum, in quo multi vrsi, tauri, et stupendae magnitudinis canes discretis caueis et septis aluntur, qui ad pugnam adseruantur, iocundissimum hominibus spectaculum praebentes.'

Hentzner, who visited London in the autumn of 1598, says : [2]

'Est et alius postea locus Theatri quoque formam habens, Ursorum & Taurorum venationibus destinatus, qui à postica parte alligati à magnis illis canibus & molossis Anglicis, quos lingua vernacula Docken appellant, mire exagitantur, ita tamen, ut saepe canes isti ab Ursis vel Tauris, dentibus arrepti, vel cornibus impetiti, de vita periclitari, aliquando etiam animam exhalare soleant, quibus sic vel sauciis vel lassis statim substituuntur alii recentes & magis alacres. Accedit aliquando in fine hujus spectaculi Ursi plane excaecati flagellatio, ubi quinque, vel sex, in circulo constituti, Ursum flagellis misere excipiunt, qui licet alligatus auffugere nequeat, alacriter tamen se defendit, circumstantes, & nimium appropinquantes, nisi recte & provide sibi caveant, prosternit, ac flagella e manibus cadentium eripit atque confringit.'

To 1599 belongs the account of Thomas Platter of Basle : [3]

'The London bearbaitings usually take place every Sunday and Wednesday, across the water. The play house is built in circular form; above are a number of seated galleries ; the ground space under the open sky is unoccupied. In the midst of this a great bear is fastened to a stake by a long rope. When we came down the stairs, we went behind the play house, and saw the English dogs, of which there were about 120 chained up, each in his separate kennel, in a yard.'

Platter also describes the actual baiting of the bull and bear and of the blind bear, much as did his predecessors. On 7 September 1601 the Duc de Biron was taken to the Bear Garden, as one of the sights of London, by no less a cicerone than Sir Walter Raleigh.[4] A visit of 16 September 1602 is described in the diary of Philip Julius, Duke of Stettin in Pomerania.[5] The vogue of the Bear Garden amongst foreigners

[1] Cf. p. 362.　　　　　　　　　　[2] Hentzner, 196 ; cf. p. 363.
[3] G. Binz in *Anglia*, xxii. 460, ' Man pfleget auch alle Sontag vnndt mittwochen zu Londen, yenseits desz wassers den Berenhatz zu halten. . . . Der Schauplatz ist in die Ründe gebauwen, sind oben herumb viel geng, darauf man zusicht, vnden am boden vnder dem heitern Himmel ist es nicht besetzet. Da bande man in mitten desz platzes einen grossen Beeren an ein stock am langen seil an. . . . Wie wir die stegen hinunter kamen, gungen wir hinder den schauwplatz, besahen die Englischen docken, deren bey 120 in einem bezirk beysamen, yedoch yetwederer in einem sonderbahren ställin an einer kettin angeheftet wahren.'
[4] *Hatfield MSS.* xi. 382.
[5] G. von Bülow in 2 *Transactions of the Royal Hist. Soc.* vi. 16, ' 16 Sept. Auf den Nachmittag haben wir den Bär u. Stierhetze zugesehen . . . wohl mehr as 200 Hünde an selbigem Ort in einem besonderen Häuslein unterhalten '.

evidently lasted into James's reign, but the notices are briefer. Lewis Frederick of Württemberg, saw on 26 April 1610 the baiting both of bears and bulls ' and monkeys that ride on horseback ';[1] and Justus Zingerling of Thuringia, who was in London about the same year, mentions the ' *theatra comoedorum*, in which bears and bulls fight with dogs '.[2] Even more summary is the reference in an itinerary of Prince Otto von Hesse-Cassel in 1611.[3] But the extracts given sufficiently describe the nature of the sport, and show that bulls continued to be baited up to a late date, as well as bears, and that the serious business of the spectacle was diversified by regular humorous episodes, such as the monkey on horseback and the whipping of the blind bear. He, by the way, was called Harry Hunks, and is named by Sir John Davies in his *Epigrams*[4] of *c.* 1594, in company with the Sackerson who gave rise to a boast on the part of Master Slender,[5] and at a later date by Dekker[6] and Henry Peacham.[7] Two other famous bears were Ned Whiting and George Stone. Both are alluded to in Ben Jonson's *Epicoene* (1609),[8] and the latter also in *The Puritan* (1607).[9] The death of the ' goodly

[1] Rye, 61.   [2] Rye, 133.   [3] *Englische Studien*, xiv. 440.
[4] *Epigram* xliii :

> Publius, student at the common law,
> Oft leaves his books, and for his recreation,
> To Paris Garden doth himself withdraw,
> Where he is ravished with such delectation,
> As down among the bears and dogs he goes ;
> Where, whilst he skipping cries, ' To head ! to head ! '
> His satin doublet and his velvet hose
> Are all with spittle from above bespread :
> When he is like his father's country hall,
> Stinking with dogs and muted all with hawks ;
> And rightly on him too this filth doth fall,
> Which for such filthy sports his books forsakes,
> Leaving old Ployden, Dyer, Brooke alone,
> To see old Harry Hunks, and Sacarson.

[5] *Merry Wives*, I. i. 306.
[6] Dekker, *Work for Armourers* (1609, *Works*, iv. 98), ' At length a blind bear was tied to the stake, and instead of baiting him with dogs, a company of creatures that had the shapes of men and faces of Christians (being either colliers, carters, or watermen) took the office of beadles upon them, and whipped Monsieur Hunkes till the blood ran down his old shoulders '.
[7] *Coryats Crudities* (1611), i. 114, ' Hunks of the Beare-garden to be feared if he be nigh on '.
[8] Cf. p. 453. Nashe, *Strange News* (1592, *Works*, i. 281, also names ' great Ned ' and adds ' Harry of Tame '. In 1590 Burnaby had at the Bear Garden ' Tom Hunckes ', ' Whitinge ', ' Harry of Tame ', three other bears, three bulls, a horse, an ape. A ' great ' bear was worth £8 or £10, a bull £4 or £5 (Kingsford, 175).
[9] *Puritan*, iii. 5, ' How many dogs do you think I had upon me ? . . . almost as many as George Stone, the bear ; three at once '.

beare ' George Stone at a baiting before the King of Denmark in 1606 is lamented in the petition of Henslowe and Alleyn to the King for increased fees already described. One other interesting notice of the sport may be added from the Dulwich collection, and that is an advertisement or ' bill ' of the enter-tainment, which runs as follows :

' Tomorrowe beinge Thursdaie shalbe seen at the Beargardin on the banckside a greate mach plaid by the gamstirs of Essex who hath chalenged all comers what soeuer to plaie v dogges at the single beare for v pounds and also to wearie a bull dead at the stake and for your better content shall haue plasant sport with the horse and ape and whiping of the blind beare. Viuat Rex.' [1]

Where then was the Bear Garden ? This is a point upon which the foreign visitors are not very explicit. From them we could infer little more than that it was transpontine. It has already been pointed out that in official documents, at any rate those of a less formal character than a patent under the great seal, the Mastership is described as the Mastership of the Game of, or at, Paris Garden. With this common parlance agrees.[2] In the allusions of the pamphleteers and poets, from the middle of the sixteenth to the middle of the seventeenth century, Paris or Parish Garden is regularly the place of baiting.[3] ' The Beare-garden, commonly called Paris Garden ', says Stowe, speaking of 1583.[4] At Paris Garden, or as it is sometimes corruptly spelt, ' Pallas Garden ', Henslowe and Alleyn have their office as Masters [5] in 1607, and near it Alleyn

---

[1] Henslowe Papers, 106.

[2] Copley Accounts, s. a. 1575, in Collectanea Genealogica et Topographica, viii. 253, ' Gyven to the master of Paryshe Garden his man for goynge with Thos. Sharples into Barmensy Street to see certen mastyve dogges '.

[3] R. Crowley, One and thyrtye Epigrammes (1550, ed. E. E. T. S.), 381 :

And yet me thynke those men be mooste foles of all,
Whose store of money is but verye smale,
And yet euerye Sondaye they will surely spende
One peny or two, the bearwardes lyuyng to mende.
At Paryse garden, eche Sundaye, a man shall not fayle
To fynde two or thre hundredes for the bearwardes vaile.
One halpenye a piece they vse for to giue,
When some haue no more in their purse, I belieue ;

Jonson, Execration upon Vulcan (Works, iii. 322) :

a threatning to the bears,
And that accursed ground, the Paris-garden ;

Taylor, Bull, Bear and Horse (1638) :

And that we have obtained again the game,
Our Paris Garden flag proclaims the same.

Cf. Sir John Davies' lines already quoted ; also Dekker, ii. 125 (News from Hell), iv. 109 (Work for Armourers), &c., &c..

[4] Stowe, Annales, 695.

[5] Henslowe Papers, 15, 104. Miss Dormer Harris kindly tells me that

is living in 1609. Now the Liberty and Manor of Paris Garden is a quite well defined part of the Bankside. It lay at the extreme west end, bordering upon Lambeth Marsh, with the Clink upon its east. In it stood from about 1595 the most westerly of the theatres, the Swan.[1] Historians of Southwark are fond of suggesting that it had been the abode of the bears from an almost immemorial antiquity, and follow a late edition of Blount's seventeenth-century *Glossographia* in connecting it with the *domus* of a certain Robert de Parys, near which the butchers of London were ordered to throw their garbage in 1393.[2] I think the idea is that the garbage was found useful for feeding the bears. This theory I believe to be as much a myth as Taylor the water-poet's derivation of the name from Paris, son of Priam. Parish, rather than Paris Garden, seems, in fact, to be the earlier form, although there is nothing in the history of the place that very particularly explains it.[3] Many residents in London were of course ' de Parys ' in the fourteenth century, and the *domus* of the Robert in question, who lived some time after the first mention of ' Parish ' Garden, was pretty clearly on the City and not the Surrey side of the river.[4] It is, however, the case that before the Civil War the Butchers' Company had been

the Coventry Corporation rewarded the ' Bearward of palace Garden ' in 1576-7.

[1] Cf. p. 411.

[2] Malone, *Variorum*, xix. 483 ; Rendle, *Bankside*, iii ; *Antiquarian*, vii. 277 ; Ordish, 128.

[3] *Annales Monasterii de Bermundseia*, s. a. 1113 (Luard, *Annales Monastici*, iii. 432), ' Hoc anno Robertus Marmion dedit hidam de Wideflete cum molendino et aliis pertinentibus suis monachis de Bermundeseye ' ; *Register of Hospital of St. John*, s. a. 1420 (*Monasticon Anglicanum*, vi. 819), ' Haec sunt statuta et ordinationes concernentia locum privilegiatum vocatum Parishgardyn, alias dictum Wideflete, sive Wiles, cum pertinentiis, facta per Johannem nuper Ducem Bedfordiae, firmarium ibidem, anno Domini mccc[c]xx ' [Rules for a sanctuary, with a dominus, senescallus, ballivus, constabularius, and societas, follow] ; *Liber Fundatorum of St. John* (ibid. vi. 832), ' Molendina de Wideflete cum gardino vocato Parish-gardin . . . tenentur de Abbate de Barmondesey ' (1434). Kingsford, 157, traces the manor through Bermondsey priory, the Templars, and St. John's Hospital to the Crown in 1536.

[4] Blount, *Glossographia* (ed. 4, 1674), 469, quotes *Close Roll, 16 Rich. II*, dorso ii. Kingsford, 156, translates the writ, which is abstracted (Sharpe, *Letter Book H*, 392), ' Writ to the Mayor and Sheriffs to proclaim ordinances made in the last Parliament at Winchester to the effect that the laystall or latrine (fimarium sive sterquilinium) on the bank of the Thames near the house of Robert de Parys be removed, and a house be built on its site for the use of butchers, where they may cut up their offal and take it in boats to mid-stream and cast it into the water at ebb-tide. . . . Witness the King at Westminster 21 Feb. 16 Rich. II '. The ordinance is recorded in *Rot. Parl.* iii. 306.

accustomed to send their offal by a beadle to 'two barrow houses, conveniently placed on the river side, for the provision and feeding of the King's Game of Bears', and were directed to resume the practice after the Restoration; and possibly this is what misled Blount.[1] Obviously, however, what the butchers did in the seventeenth century is no proof of what they did in the fourteenth. And, in fact, the ordinance of 1393 is explicit in its direction that the offal is ultimately to be, not devoured by bears, but cast into mid-stream.

There is in fact nothing, so far as I know, to locate the royal Game on the Bankside at all until the middle of the sixteenth century, when it was already hard by the stews in the Liberty of the Clink, and still less, except the persistence of the name, to locate it definitely in the Liberty of Paris Garden.[2] The notice which brings Paris Garden nearest is in Foxe's *Book of Martyrs*, which contains an account of an adventure of one Ralph Morice, secretary to Cranmer, who was foolish enough to take a book of his master's, containing criticisms of the Six Articles, in a wherry from Westminster Bridge to Paul's Wharf. It chanced that Henry VIII 'was then in his barge with a great number of barges and boats about him, then baiting of bears in the water, over against the Bank'. The waterman stopped to see the fun, and the bear broke loose, and climbed into the wherry, which upset. The dangerous book fell into the Thames and was picked up by the bearward, who was the Lady Elizabeth's bearward and 'an arrant Papist'. It was only through the good offices of Cromwell that Morice escaped serious trouble. This was about July 1539.[3] Certainly it was the custom from an early date to moor the King's barge off Paris Garden.[4]

---

[1] *Index to Remembrancia*, 478.

[2] Brewer, xxi. 2. 88, 'a licence for Thomas Fluddie, yeoman of your Majesty's bears, to bait and make pastime with your Graces bears at the accustomed place at London, called the Stewes, notwithstanding the proclamation' (Sept. 1546); Machyn, 78, 'The sam day [9 Dec. 1554] at after-non was a bere-beytyn on the Banke syde, and ther the grett blynd bere broke losse, and in ronnyng away he chakt a servyng man by the calff of the lege, and bytt a gret pesse away, and after by the hokyll-bone, that within iij days after he ded '.

[3] Foxe, *Acts and Monuments* (ed. 1846), v. 388. Collier, iii. 94, cites 'a book of the expenses of the Northumberland family ' to the effect that the earl went to Paris Garden to behold the bear-baiting in 1525–6. Ordish, 129, criticizes this on the ground that the statement is not in the *Northumberland Household Book* printed by Percy. It was in fact a different book, from which Collier, i. 86, gives entries, of which one is of boat-hire from and to ' Parys gardyn '. But there is nothing about bear-baiting.

[4] *Account of Treasurer of Chamber*, s. a. 1515 (Brewer, ii. 1466), ' Hen. Anesley, conveying the King's barge from Greenwich to Parys Garden, 16ᵈ '.

The spot was marked later by the Old Barge Stairs, which stood at the west end of that part of the Bank lying in front of the Garden, just as Paris Garden Stairs stood at its east end. But the barge was not necessarily at its moorings when Henry was baiting from it. Mr. Ordish suggests that it was the common use of Paris Garden Stairs by visitors to the baiting, which led to the name being transferred to the Bear Garden itself, without any one troubling to inquire very minutely whether it stood a little to the east or a little to the west of the landing.[1] On the whole, however, I regard it as reasonably probable that there was at one time a Bear Garden in the Liberty, which fixed the traditional name for the sport, even after it had been transferred farther along the Bank.[2] It may, perhaps, be a slight confirmation of this view that the 1627 survey of Paris Garden shows a space, apparently laid out as a garden and arranged as a circle within a square, which may represent the site. It stands nearly opposite Paris Garden Stairs in a triangular bit of ground between Holland Street and the lane leading to Copt Hall. This seems to have been rather a desolate region in Elizabeth's reign, at any rate when you got beyond the row of houses which lined the bank.[3] If there was a Bear Garden there, it had clearly been abandoned some little time before 1546, as the Stews were then ' the accustomed place '. Somewhat later, the maps of Höfnagel (*c.* 1560) and Agas (*c.* 1570) show, in addition to the Bull ring already mentioned, another ring marked ' The Beare bayting ', standing immediately west of it, and like it in the Clink.[4] The animals at the stake are discernible in the rings, and to the south of each stretches a yard with a pond in the middle and kennelled dogs along the sides. It is in the Clink, too, that Norden in 1593 shows

[1] Ordish, 127.

[2] In *Shaw v. Langley* (1597) the Swan is described as ' in the oulde Parrisgardin ', although there is no specific mention of baiting (*E. S.* xliii. 345, 355).

[3] Fleetwood, writing to Burghley on 13 July 1578 (Rendle, *Antiquarian*, vii. 274, from *S. P. D. Eliz.* cxxv. 21), describes intrigues of the French ambassador ' on the Thames side behind Paris Garden toward Lambeth, in the fields . . . I got a skuller to Paris Garden, but the place was dark and shadowed with trees, that one man cannot see another unless they have *lynceos oculos* or els cattes eys, shewing how admirable a place it was for such doings. The place is that boowre of conspiracies, it is the college of male cownsell. . . . There be certain *virgulta* or eightes of willows set by the Thames near that place ; they grow now exceeding thick, and a notable covert for confederates to shrowd in ; a milkmade lately did see the French ambassador land in that *virgulta* '.

[4] The ring, without a name, is also shown in Smith's drawing (1588), but this is probably based on one of the maps.

'The Beare howse', a little west and north of 'The play howse', which is the Rose.   This evidence is consistent with what little is upon written record about the locality of the Bear Gardens.   The most important document is a deposition of John Taylor, not the water-poet, in a suit of 1620 : [1]

'He saith that he remembreth that the game of bear-bayting hath been kept in fower severall places (vizt.) at Mason Steares on the bankside ; neere Maid-lane by the corner of the Pyke Garden ; at the beare garden which was parcell of the possession of William Payne ; and the place where they are now kept.'

Taylor was then an old man of seventy-seven and his memory would easily go back to the time of the early maps.   To his testimony may be added that of Stowe, who says in his *Survey of London* (1598) : [2]

'Now to returne to the West banke, there be two Beare gardens, the olde and new places, wherein be kept Beares, Buls and other beastes to be bayted.   As also Mastiues in severall kenels, nourished to baite them.   These Beares and other Beasts are there bayted in plottes of ground, scaffolded about for the Beholders to stand safe.   Next on this banke was sometime the Bordello or stewes.'

In his *Annales* Stowe records the fall of ' the old and under propped scaffolds round about the Beare-garden, commonly called Paris garden', and the consequent death of eight persons, at 4 p.m. on Sunday, 13 January 1583.   It was, he says, ' a friendly warning to such as more delight themselves in the cruelty of beasts, than in the works of mercy, the fruits of a true professed faith, which ought to be the Sabbath day's exercise '.[3]   Dr. Dee also noted the accident in his diary, and it was reported to Burghley on the next day by the Lord Mayor and on 19 January by Recorder Fleetwood.[4]   Both of these adopt the view expressed by Stowe that it must be regarded as divine punishment for the violation of the Sabbath, and Fleetwood refers to ' a booke sett downe vpon the same matter ', which may be John Field's *Godly Exhortation by Occasion of the late Judgment of God showed at Paris Garden.* The shrewd irony of Sir Thomas More, upon a similar event,

---

[1] Rendle, *Antiquarian*, viii. 57, from *Exchequer Depositions, 18 Jac. I.* The depositions also mention a bull-house built in a dog-yard, a bear-house, a hay-house, a pond for the bears to wash in, and a pond for dead dogs.   Kingsford, 175, gives fuller extracts.

[2] Stowe, *Survey*, ii. 54.   A short passage in i. 95 adds nothing.

[3] Stowe (1615), 695.

[4] Halliwell, *Dr. Dee's Diary* (C. S.), 18 ; App. C, No. xxxi ; App. D, No. lxiv.   The ballad of which four stanzas are given by Collier, i. 244, is presumably a forgery.

when it was the church that fell, many years before at
Beverley, found little echo in the mind of the Elizabethan
Puritan.[1] A further letter from the Lord Mayor to the Privy
Council on 3 July 1583 states that by then the Paris Garden
scaffolds were ' new builded '.[2]

I find it very difficult to say which of the numerous bear
gardens mentioned by Taylor and Stowe was in use at any
given time. Mr. Rendle thought that Taylor's first two,
that at Mason Stairs and that at the corner of the Pike
Garden, were the two shown as ' The bolle bayting ' and ' The
Bearebayting ' by Agas.[3] If so, they are quite out of scale.
This is likely, since they are drawn large enough to show the
animals. They are shown east and west of each other.
Rendle puts the Pike Garden due south of Mason Stairs,
but it clearly extended more to the east in 1587. In any case
both these earlier sites were farther to the west of the Clink
than the Hope. Where then was the place on William Payne's
ground ? Mr. Rendle, after a careful comparison of Rocque's
map of 1746 and other later maps, puts it at ' the north
courtelage in the lane known as the Bear Garden ' and the
Hope at the south courtelage in the same lane.[4] I take him
to mean that the Bear Garden on Payne's ground was that
in use until 1613, and that the Hope was built a little to the
south of it. The terms of the contract with Katherens,
however, suggest that the same or practically the same site
was used. Mr. Rendle adds that ' William Payne's place next
the Thames can be traced back into the possession of John
Allen, until it came down to Edward Alleyn, and was sold by
him at a large profit to Henslowe ; the same for which
Morgan Pope in 1586 paid to the Vestry of St. Saviour's
" 6s. 8d. by the year for tithes ".'[5] This I cannot quite follow.
There seem to have been two properties standing respectively
next and next but one on the west to the ' little Rose '. Next
the Rose stood messuages called The Barge, Bell and Cock.

---

[1] More, *Works* (ed. 1557), 208, ' This is much like as at Beuerlay late,
whan much of the people beyng at a bere baytyng, the church fell sodeinly
down at euensonge tyme, and ouer whelmed some that than were in it : a
good felow, that after herde the tale tolde, " lo ", quod he, " now maie you
see what it is to be at euensong whan ye should be at the bere baytynge ".
How be it, the hurt was not ther in beinge at euensonge, but in that the
churche was falsely wrought '.

[2] App. D, No. lxx.   [3] Rendle, *Antiquarian*, viii. 57.

[4] Rendle, *Antiquarian*, viii. 57 ; *Bankside*, xxx, with map.

[5] The tithes were for ' the bear garden and for the ground adjoining
to the same where the dogs are ' (Rendle, *Bankside*, v). It was for Morgan
Pope that Bowes's patent as Master of the Game was exemplified in
1585 ; cf. p. 450.

They were leased by the Bishop of Winchester to William Payne in 1540. His widow Joan Payne assigned them to John White and John Malthouse on 1 August 1582, and White's moiety was assigned to Malthouse on 5 February 1589.[1] From him Henslowe bought the lease in 1593–4.[2] The tenements upon it were in his hands as 'Mr. Malthowes rentes' in 1603 and Alleyn was living in one of them.[3] And the lease of the Barge, Bell and Cock passed to Alleyn and was assigned by his will towards the settlement of his second or third wife, Constance, daughter of Dean Donne.'[4] To the west of this property in 1540 was a tenement once held by the prioress of Stratford. This passed to the Crown, and then to Thomas and Isabella Keyes under a Crown lease which was in Henslowe's hands by 1597. Some notes of deeds—leases, deputations, bonds—concerning the Bear Garden were left by Alleyn. Four of the deeds have since been found by Mr. Kingsford in the Record Office. It appears that, before Henslowe, both Pope and Burnaby had some of the Keyes land on a sub-lease, and that Burnaby probably had the Keyes lease itself. Payne carried on baiting in a ring just south of the Barge. The site was called Orchard Court in 1620, and stood north of the Hope. This agrees with the relation suggested by Mr. Rendle between the two 'courte-lages'. The object of the suit of 1620 was to determine whether the Hope also stood upon episcopal, or upon Crown land. Taylor's testimony was ambiguous. But it follows that the transfer southwards must have been due to a tenant who held under both leases. It was suggested in 1620 that Pope rebuilt the scaffold standings round the ring as galleries with a larger circuit. This was doubtless after the ruin of 1583. Nothing is said of a change of site at this time. Moreover, both Pope and Burnaby seem to have used the site of the Hope and its bull-house as a dog-yard. Probably, therefore, the change was made by Henslowe and Alleyn.

---

[1] Henslowe, ii. 25, from *Egerton MS.* 2623, f. 13, and *Dulwich MS.* iv. 21.

[2] Henslowe, i. 71, 'Ano do 1595 the xxviij^th of Novembere Reseved of Mr Henslow the day and yeare abov written the som of syx poundes of curant mony of England and is in part of a mor som [yf he the sayd] by twyxt the sayd Phillyp Henslow and me consaning a bargen of the beargarden I say Reseved vj^ll. By me John Mavlthouse. Wittnes I E Alley.' I take the words in square brackets, which are cancelled in the diary, to represent 'if he proceed'. In Henslowe, i. 43, are further receipts for 40s. 'in part of the bargen for the tenymentes on the bankes syd' in Dec. 1595, and sums of £10, £20, and £4 for unspecified purposes in Jan. and Feb. 1596. Kingsford, 177, gives the date of Henslowe's purchase.

[3] Henslowe, i. 209 ; cf. *Henslowe Papers*, 109.   [4] Henslowe, ii. 25.

Alleyn left a record of 'what the Bear garden cost me for my owne part in December 1594'. He paid £200 to Burnaby, perhaps only for a joint interest with Henslowe or Jacob Meade, and £250 for the 'patten', that is, I suppose, the Mastership bought from Sir William Stuart in 1604. He held his interest for sixteen years and received £60 a year, and then sold it to ' my father Hinchloe ' for £580 in February 1611.[1] There must have been considerable outgoings on the structure during this period. Another memorandum in Alleyn's hand shows an expenditure of £486 4s. 10d. during 1602–5, and a further expenditure during 1606–8 of £360 ' p^d. for ye building of the howses '.[2] This last doubtless refers in part, not to the baiting ring itself, but to a tavern and office built on ' the foreside of the messuage or tenemente called the Beare garden, next the river of Thames in the parish of St. Saviors ', for which there exists a contract of 2 June 1606 between Henslowe and Alleyn and Peter Street the carpenter.[3] But this only cost £65, and it seems to me most likely that the Bear Garden was rebuilt on the southern site at the same time. Further light is thrown on the profits of the Bear Garden by a note in Henslowe's diary that the receipts at it for the three days next after Christmas 1608 were £4, £6, and £3 14s., which may be compared with the average of £1 18s. 3d. received from the Fortune during the same three days.[4] It may be added that Crowley notes the ' bearwardes vaile ' somewhat ambiguously as ½d., 1d., or 2d.,[5] and that Lambarde in 1596 includes Paris Garden with the Theatre and Bel Savage as a place where you must pay ' one pennie at the gate, another at the entrie of the scaffolde, and the thirde for a quiet standinge '.[6]

Yet another building enterprise was undertaken in 1613, by which time an interest in the property had certainly been leased to Jacob Meade. On 29 August a contract was entered into between Henslowe and Meade and Gilbert Katherens, carpenter, for the pulling down of the Bear Garden and the erection before the following 30 November

---

[1] *Henslowe Papers*, 107. I agree with Dr. Greg (Henslowe, ii. 30, 39) that it is difficult to see what a lease from Thomas Garland to Henslowe and Alleyn in 1608 of a close called Long Slip or Long Meadow in Lambeth can have had to do with the baiting. But Alleyn added the word ' Beargarden ' to the original endorsement ' Mr Garlands lece ' (*Henslowe Papers*, 12). Perhaps the land was used for some subsidiary purpose in connexion with the Garden.

[2] *Henslowe Papers*, 110; *Architectural Review*, xlvii. 152.

[3] Full text in *Alleyn Memoirs*, 78 ; abstract in *Henslowe Papers*, 102.

[4] Henslowe, i. 214 ; cf. p. 189 (*supra*).

[5] Cf. p. 458.   [6] Cf. ch. xviii.

on or near the same site of a play-house on the model of the Swan, but with a movable stage, so as to enable the building to be used also for baitings. I reproduce the document here from Dr. Greg's text : [1]

Articles, Covenauntes, grauntes, and agreementes, Concluded and agreed vppon this Nyne and Twenteithe daie of Auguste, Anno Domini 1613, Betwene Phillipe Henslowe of the parishe of S[t] Saviour in Sowthworke within the countye of Surrey, Esquire, and Jacobe Maide of the parishe of S[t] Olaves in Sowthworke aforesaide, waterman, of thone partie, And Gilbert Katherens of the saide parishe of S[t] Saviour in Sowthworke, Carpenter, on thother partie, As followeth, That is to saie—

Inprimis the saide Gilbert Katherens for him, his executours, administratours, and assignes, dothe convenaunt, promise, and graunt to and with the saide Phillipe Henslowe and Jacobe Maide and either of them, thexecutors, administratours, & assigns of them and either of them, by theise presentes in manner and forme following : That he the saied Gilbert Katherens, his executours, administratours, or assignes shall and will, at his or theire owne proper costes and charges, vppon or before the last daie of November next ensuinge the daie of the date of theise presentes above written, not onlie take downe or pull downe all that same place or house wherin Beares and Bulls haue been heretofore vsuallie bayted, and also one other house or staple wherin Bulls and horsses did vsuallie stande, sett, lyinge, and beinge vppon or neere the Banksyde in the saide parishe of S[t] Saviour in Sowthworke, comonlie called or knowne by the name of the Beare garden, but shall also at his or theire owne proper costes and charges vppon or before the saide laste daie of November newly erect, builde, and sett vpp one other same place or Plaiehouse fitt & convenient in all thinges, bothe for players to playe in, and for the game of Beares and Bulls to be bayted in the same, and also a fitt and convenient Tyre house and a stage to be carryed or taken awaie, and to stande vppon tressells good, substanciall, and sufficient for the carryinge and bearinge of suche a stage ; And shall new builde, erect, and sett vp againe the saide plaie house or game place neere or vppon the saide place, where the saide game place did heretofore stande ; And to builde the same of suche large compasse, fforme, widenes, and height as the Plaie house called the Swan in the libertie of Parris garden in the saide parishe of S[t] Saviour now is ; And shall also builde two stearecasses without and adioyninge to the saide Playe house in suche convenient places, as shalbe moste fitt and convenient for the same to stande vppon, and of such largnes and height as the stearecasses of the saide playehouse called the Swan nowe are or bee ; And shall also builde the Heavens all over the saide stage, to be borne or carryed without any postes or

[1] *Henslowe Papers*, 19, from Dulwich Muniment 49 ; also printed in *Variorum*, iii. 343. Muniment 50 is Katherens' bond, and Muniment 51 a sub-contract of 8 Sept. 1613 with John Browne, bricklayer, to do the brickwork for £80.

supporters to be fixed or sett vppon the saide stage, and all gutters of leade needfull for the carryage of all suche raine water as shall fall vppon the same ; And shall also make two Boxes in the lowermost storie fitt and decent for gentlemen to sitt in ; And shall make the particions betwne the Rommes as they are at the saide Plaie house called the Swan ; And to make turned cullumes vppon and over the stage ; And shall make the principalls and fore fronte of the saide Plaie house of good and sufficient oken tymber, and no furr tymber to be putt or vsed in the lower most, or midell stories, except the vpright postes on the backparte of the saide stories (all the byndinge joystes to be of oken tymber) ; The inner principall postes of the first storie to be twelve footes in height and tenn ynches square, the inner principall postes in the midell storie to be eight ynches square, the inner most postes in the vpper storie to be seaven ynches square ; The prick postes in the first storie to be eight ynches square, in the seconde storie seaven ynches square, and in the vpper most storie six ynches square ; Also the brest sommers in the lower moste storie to be nyne ynches depe, and seaven ynches in thicknes, and in the midell storie to be eight ynches depe and six ynches in thicknes ; The byndinge jostes of the firste storie to be nyne and eight ynches in depthe and thicknes, and in the midell storie to be viij and vij ynches in depthe and thicknes. Item to make a good, sure, and sufficient foundacion of brickes for the saide Play house or game place, and to make it xiij^teene ynches at the leaste aboove the grounde. Item to new builde, erect, and sett vpp the saide Bull house and stable with good and sufficient scantlinge tymber, plankes, and bordes, and particions of that largnes and fittnes as shalbe sufficient to kepe and holde six bulls and three horsses or geldinges, with rackes and mangers to the same, and also a lofte or storie over the saide house as nowe it is. And shall also at his & theire owne proper costes and charges new tyle with Englishe tyles all the vpper rooffe of the saide Plaie house, game place, and Bull house or stable, and shall fynde and paie for at his like proper costes and charges for all the lyme, heare, sande, brickes, tyles, lathes, nayles, workemanshipe and all other thinges needfull and necessarie for the full finishinge of the saide Plaie house, Bull house, and stable ; And the saide Plaiehouse or game place to be made in althinges and in suche forme and fashion, as the saide plaie house called the Swan (the scantling of the tymbers, tyles, and foundacion as ys aforesaide without fraude or coven). And the saide Phillipe Henslow and Jacobe Maide and either of them for them, thexecutors, administratours, and assignes of them and either of them, doe covenant and graunt to and with the saide Gilbert Katherens, his executours, administratours, and assignes in manner and forme followinge (That is to saie) That he the saide Gilbert or his assignes shall or maie haue, and take to his or theire vse and behoofe, not onlie all the tymber, benches, seates, slates, tyles, brickes, and all other thinges belonginge to the saide Game place & Bull house or stable, and also all suche olde tymber whiche the saide Phillipe Henslow hathe latelie bought, beinge of an old house in Thames street, London, whereof moste parte is now

lyinge in the yarde or backsyde of the saide Bearegarden ; And also
to satisfie and paie vnto the saide Gilbert Katherens, his executors,
administratours, or assignes for the doinge and finishinges of the
workes and buildinges aforesaid the somme of Three Hundered and
three score poundes of good and lawffull monie of England, in manner
and forme followinge (That is to saie) In hande at thensealinge and
deliuery hereof, Three score pounds which the saide Gilbert acknow-
legeth him selfe by theise presentes to haue receaued ; And more over
to paie every weeke weeklie, duringe the firste six weekes, vnto the
saide Gilbert or his assignes, when he shall sett workemen to worke
vppon or about the buildinge of the premisses the somme of Tenne
poundes of lawffull monie of Englande to paie them there wages (yf
theire wages dothe amount vnto somuche monie) ; And when the
saide plaie house, Bull house, and stable are reared, then to make vpp
the saide wages one hundered poundes of lawffull monie of England,
and to be paide to the saide Gilbert or his assignes ; And when the
saide Plaie house, Bull house, and stable are Reared, tyled, walled, then
to paie vnto the saide Gilbert Katherens or his assignes one other
hundered poundes of lawffull monie of England ; And when the saide
Plaie house, Bull house, and stable are fullie finished, builded, and
done in manner and forme aforesaide, then to paie vnto the saide
Gilbert Katherens or his assignes one other hundred Poundes of lawffull
monie of England in full satisfacion and payment of the saide somme
of CCClx^{ll}.   And to all and singuler the covenantes, grauntes, articles,
and agreementes above in theise presentes contayned, whiche on the
parte and behalfe of the saide Gilbert Katherens, his executours,
administratours, or assignes are ought to be observed, performed,
fulfilled, and done, the saide Gilbert Katherens byndeth himselfe, his
executours, administratours, and assignes vnto the saide Phillipe
Henslowe and Jacob Maide and to either of them, thexecutours,
administratours, and assignes of them or either of them, by theise
presentes.   In witnes whereof the saide Gilbert Katherens hath here-
vnto sett his hande and seale, the daie and yere firste above written

The mark G K of Gilbert Katherens

Sealed and Deliuered in the presence of
witnes Moyses Bowler
          Edwarde Griffin

The execution of the contract must have been delayed, for the
rebuilt Bear Garden is fairly to be identified with the Hope,
of which no mention is made in the petition of the spring
of 1614 described by Taylor in *The True Cause of the Watermen's Suit*, although it had certainly come into use by the
following autumn.[1]   Here was arranged for 7 October a trial
of wit between this same Taylor and the shifty rhymer William

[1] Cf. p. 370.

Fennor.[1] The latter failed to turn up, and Taylor, who, according to his own account, had advertised 'this Bear Garden banquet of dainty conceits' and collected a great audience, was left 'in a greater puzzell then the blinde beare in the midst of all her whip-broth'. After acting part of what he had intended, he resigned the stage to the regular company :

> Then came the players, and they play'd an act,
> Which greatly from my action did detract,
> For 'tis not possible for any one
> To play against a company alone,
> And such a company (I'll boldly say)
> That better (nor the like) e'r played a play.

This company was no doubt the Lady Elizabeth's, as recon-stituted in the previous March under an agreement with Nathaniel Field on their behalf, of which a mutilated copy exists. To it Meade was a party, and there is nothing to establish a connexion between Meade and any other theatre than the Hope.[2] Jonson names the Lady Elizabeth's men as the actors of *Bartholomew Fair*, and in the Induction thereto, after a dialogue between the Stage-keeper, who is taunted with 'gathering up the broken apples for the beares within', and the Book-holder, a Scrivener reads 'Articles of Agreement, indented, between the Spectators or Hearers, at the Hope on the Bankeside, in the County of Surrey on the one party; and the Author of Bartholmew Fayre in the said place, and County on the other party : the one and thirtieth day of Octob. 1614'. According to Jonson the locality was suitable for a play on Bartholomew Fair, for it was 'as durty as *Smithfield*, and as stinking euery whit'.[3] There were disputes between Henslowe and the company, partly arising out of an arrangement that they should 'lie still' one day a fortnight for the baiting, and the combination broke up. Some of its members, apparently then Prince Charles's men, are found after Henslowe's death signing an agreement with Alleyn and Meade to play at the Hope, and to set aside a fourth of the gallery takings towards a sum of £200 to be accepted in discharge of their debt to Henslowe.

---

[1] Taylor, *Works* (1630), 304, with a reply by Fennor and rejoinder by Taylor. Incidentally Taylor mentions the arras of the theatre and the tiles with which it was covered.

[2] The Southwark vestry order of 1 May 1598 (App. D, No. cxv) seems to connect him with 'play-houses', but I doubt whether anything but the bear garden is meant.

[3] Cf. *Satiromastix*, 1247, 'Th'ast a breath as sweet as the Rose that growes by the Beare-Garden'.

Alleyn had of course resumed his part proprietorship of the house as executor and ultimate heir to Henslowe. Meade probably took actual charge of the theatre, and there is an undated letter from Prince Charles's men to Alleyn, written possibly in 1617, in which they explain their removal from the Bankside as due to the intemperate action of his partner in taking from them the day which by course was theirs. I suppose that this dispute also was due to the competition of baiting with the plays. In 1619 some disputes between Alleyn and Meade had to be settled by arbitration, and from Alleyn's memoranda in connexion with these it appears that Meade was his deputy under his patent as Master of the Game, and had also a lease from him of the house at £100 a year.[1] The Hope is mentioned from time to time, chiefly as a place of baiting, up to the civil wars.[2] It is one of the three Bankside theatres alluded to in *Holland's Leaguer* (1632), where it is described as 'a building of excellent hope' for players, wild beasts, and gladiators. Bear-baiting was suppressed by the House of Commons in 1642,[3] and the house was dismantled in 1656. The manuscript continuation of Stowe's *Annales* describes its end and the slaughter of the bears, but gives the date of its erection erroneously as 1610 instead of 1613.[4]

After the Restoration the Bear Garden was restored, and a lane called Bear Gardens, running from Bankside to New Park Street, and a sign therein of The White Bear still mark its name.[5] Its site is pretty well defined in the seventeenth-century maps as to the west of the Globe and, where that is shown, the Rose, and generally as a little nearer Maid Lane than the latter. This is consistent with a notice in the Sewers records for 5 December 1595 of a sewer which ran to the Bear Garden from a garden known to have lain a little farther east along Maid Lane than the Globe.[6]

---

[1] *Alleyn Memoirs*, 159.

[2] Ordish, 235. No date can be assigned to *A North Countrey Song* in *Wit and Drollery* (1656) :

> When I'se come there [to Paris Garden], I was in a rage,
> I rayl'd on him that kept the Beares,
> Instead of a Stake was suffered a Stage,
> And in Hunkes his house a crue of Players.

[3] Collier, iii. 102.   [4] Cf. p. 375.

[5] Ordish, 244. A Bearsfoot Alley shown farther to the east by Rocque (1746) may derive from one of the earlier baiting-places.

[6] C. W. Wallace in *The Times* (30 April 1914), 'We present John Wardner William Sellors and all the land holders or their tenantes that holde anie landes gardeines ground or tenementes abbutting vpon the common sewer leadinge from Sellors gardin to the beare garden to cast clense and scoure their and euerie one of their seuerall partes of the

The traditional day for baiting was Sunday. Crowley in 1550 describes it as taking place on 'euerye Sondaye'.[1] Naturally this did not pass without Puritan comment, to which point was given by the fall of Paris Garden on a Sunday in 1583.[2] A general prohibition of shows on Sunday seems to have followed, from which it is not likely that bear-baiting was excepted. It may be inferred that Thursday was substituted, for a Privy Council order of 25 July 1591 called attention, not only to a neglect of the rule as to Sunday, but also to the fact that every day 'the players do use to recite their plays to the great hurt and destruction of the game of bear-baiting and like pastimes, which are maintained for Her Majesty's pleasure if occasion require', and forbade plays both on Sunday and on Thursday, on which day 'those other games usually have been always accustomed and practised'.[3] Henslowe's diary seems to show that up to 1597 he kept the Sunday prohibition and disregarded the Thursday one, which is a little odd, as he was interested in the Bear Garden. But a proclamation of 7 May 1603 on the accession of James repeats the warning that there was neglect of the Sabbath, and renews the prohibition both for baiting and for plays.[4] Henslowe and Alleyn in their petition of about 1607 for increased fees lay stress on this restraint as a main factor in their alleged loss.[5] It seems from the notes of Stowe's manuscript *continuator* that during the first half of the seventeenth century Tuesday and Thursday became the regular baiting days.[6] But the agreements made by Henslowe and Meade with the Lady Elizabeth's men in 1614 profess only to reserve one day in fourteen for this purpose, of which apparently notice was to be given on the previous Monday.[7]

common sewer by Candlemas nexte vpon paine of euerie pole then vndone . . . ijˢ '.

[1] Cf. p. 458.

[2] E. Hake, *Newes out of Poules Churchyarde* (1579), Sat. v :

> What else but gaine and money gote
> Maintaines each Saboth day
> The bayting of the Beare and Bull ?
> What brings this brutish play ?

Many of the attacks on plays (App. C) also refer to baiting.

[3] App. D, No. lxxxiv.   [4] App. D, No. cxxxii.

[5] ' In the late quenes tyme fre libertie was permited with owt restrainte to bayght them which now is tacken a way frome vs especiallye one the Sondayes in the after none after devine service which was the cheffest meanes and benefit to the place ' ; cf. p. 452.

[6] Cf. p. 375.

[7] *Henslowe Papers*, 88, 125.

xvi. PORTER'S HALL

Authority was given for the erection of a new theatre by the following patent of 3 June 1615 : [1]

De concessione regard Phillippo Rosseter et aliis.   Iames by the grace of God &c. To all Maiors, Sheriffes, Iustices of peace, Bayliffes, Constables, headboroughes, and to all other our Officers, Ministers, and loving Subiectes, to whome these presentes shall come, greeting. Whereas wee by our letteres Patentes sealed with our great seale of England bearing date the ffourth day of Ianuary in the seaventh yeare of our Raigne of England Fraunce and Ireland and of Scotland the three and ffortieth for the consideracions in the same letteres patentes expressed did appoint and authorise Phillipp Rosseter and certaine others from tyme to tyme to provide, keepe, and bring vppe a convenient nomber of children, and them to practise and exercise in the quallitie of playing by the name of the children of the Revelles to the Queene, within the white ffryers in the Suburbs of our Cittie of London, or in any other convenient place where they the said Phillipp Rosseter and the rest of his partners should thinke fitting for that purpose, As in and by the said letteres patentes more at large appeareth, And whereas the said Phillipp Rosseter and the rest of his said partners have ever since trayned vppe and practised a convenient number of children of the Revelles for the purpose aforesaid in a Messuage or mansion house being parcell of the late dissolved Monastery called the white ffryers neere Fleetestreete in London, which the said Phillipp Rosseter did lately hold for terme of certaine yeres expired, And whereas the said Phillipp Roseter, together with Phillipp Kingman, Robert Iones, and Raphe Reeve, to continue the said service for the keeping and bringing vppe of the children for the solace and pleasure of our said most deere wife, and the better to practise and exercise them in the quallitie of playing by the name of children of the Revelles to the Queene, have latelie taken in lease and farme divers buildinges, Cellers, sollars, chambers, and yardes for the building of a Playhouse therevpon for the better practising and exercise of the said children of the Revelles, All which premisses are scituate and being within the Precinct of the Blacke ffryers neere Puddlewharfe in the Suburbs of London, called by the name of the lady Saunders house, or otherwise Porters hall, and now in the occupation of the said Robert Iones. Nowe knowe yee that wee of our especiall grace, certaine knowledge, and meere mocion have given and graunted, And by theise presentes for vs, our heires, and successors, doe give and graunte lycense and authoritie vnto the said Phillipp Rosseter, Phillipp Kingman, Robert Iones, and Raphe Reeve, at their proper costes and charges to erect, build, and sett vppe in and vppon the said premisses before mencioned one convenient

---

[1] Printed in M. S. C. i. 277, from P. R. 13 Jac. I, pt. 20 ; also by Collier, i. 381, and Hazlitt, E. D. S. 46, from the Signet Bill, misdescribed as the Privy Seal, of 31 May.

Playhouse for the said children of the Revelles, the same Playhouse
to be vsed by the Children of the Revelles for the tyme being of the
Queenes Maiestie, and for the Princes Players, and for the ladie Elizabeths Players, soe tollerated or lawfully lycensed to play exercise and
practise them therein, Any lawe, Statute, Act of Parliament, restraint,
or other matter or thing whatsoever to the contrary notwithstanding.
Willing and commaunding you and every of you our said Maiors,
Sheriffes, Iustices of peace, Bayliffes, Constables, headboroughes and
all other our officers and ministers for the tyme being, as yee tender
our pleasure, to permitt and suffer them therein, without any your
lettes, hinderance, molestacion, or disturbance whatsoever. In witnes
whereof, &c. Witnes our selfe at Westminster the third day of Iune.

per breve de priuato sigillo &c.

The statements made in the patent as to the objects of the
promoters can be confirmed from other sources. We know
that the lease of the Whitefriars expired at the end of 1614,
that there had been an amalgamation of the Queen's Revels
and the Lady Elizabeth's men in 1613, and that in all probability this arrangement was extended to bring in Prince
Charles's men during 1615. Unfortunately for Rosseter and
his associates, the patent had hardly been granted before
it was called in question. Presumably the inhabitants of the
Blackfriars, who had already one theatre in their midst,
thought that that one was enough. At any rate the Corporation approached the Privy Council, and alleged divers inconveniences, in particular the fact that the theatre, which was
described as 'in Puddle Wharfe', would 'adjoine so neere
vnto' the church of St. Anne's as to disturb the congregation.[1]
The Council referred the patent to the Lord Chief Justice,
Sir Edward Coke, no friend of players, or of the royal prerogative which expressed itself in patents; and when he
found a technical flaw, in that the Blackfriars, having been
brought within the City jurisdiction by the charter of 1608,
was not strictly within 'the suburbs', ordered on 26 September 1615 that the building, which had already been begun,
should be discontinued. Nevertheless, the work must have
gone so far as to permit of the production of plays, for the title-
page of Field's *Amends for Ladies* (1618) testifies that it was
acted 'at the Blacke-Fryers both by the Princes Servants
and the Lady Elizabeths'. Moreover, on 27 January 1617
the Privy Council wrote again to the Lord Mayor, enjoining
him to see to the suppression of a play-house in the Blackfriars 'neere vnto his Majestyes Wardrobe', which is said to
be 'allmost if not fully finished'.[2]

[1] Cf. App. D, No. clvii.
[2] Cf. App. D, No. clx. Collier, i. 384, without giving his authority,

It does not appear possible to say exactly where in the Blackfriars' precinct the Porter's Hall once occupied by Lady Saunders stood. It was certainly not the porter's lodge at the north-west corner of the great cloister, for this was still in 1615, as it had been since 1554, part of the Cobham house. One Ninian Sawnders, a vintner, took a lease of the chancel of the old conventual church from Sir Thomas Cawarden in 1553, and this would have been close to St. Anne's, which stood at the north-east corner of the great cloister. But Ninian died in 1553 and never got knighted. On the other hand, the rooms on the south side of the great cloister, generally described as Lygon's lodgings, had been in the tenure of one Nicholas Saunders shortly before their sale by Sir George More to John Freeman and others in 1609. Nicholas Saunders is said to have been knighted in 1603.[1] These lodgings adjoined More's own mansion house, and might at some time have served as a lodge for his porter.[2] But I do not feel that they would very naturally be described either as ' near ' or ' in ' Puddle Wharf, or as ' near ' the Wardrobe. These indications suggest some building approached either from Puddle Wharf proper or from the hill, afterwards known as St. Andrew's Hill, which ran up from it to the Wardrobe, outside the eastern wall of the Priory precinct. The Cawarden estate did not extend to this wall, and the Saunders family may quite well, in addition to Lygon's lodgings, have had a house, either on the site of the old convent gardens, or higher up the hill on the Blackwell estate, near where Shakespeare's house stood, and near also to St. Anne's. Perhaps there had been a porter's lodge on the east of the old prior's house.

says that the Corporation reported the carrying out of this mandate ' before three days had elapsed '.

[1] Shaw, ii. 107. Sir Thomas Saunders had the same lodgings c. 1551 (cf. p. 478, n. 4 ; *M. S. C.* ii. 120).

[2] Cf. ch. xvii (Blackfriars) ; *M. S. C.* ii. 93, 110, 120.

XVII

THE PRIVATE THEATRES

i. THE BLACKFRIARS

[*Bibliographical Note.*—Many documents bearing upon the history of the theatre are preserved at Loseley, and the most important are collected by Professor A. Feuillerat in vol. ii of the *Malone Society's Collections* (1913). A few had been already printed or described by A. J. Kempe in *The Loseley Manuscripts* (1835), by J. O. Halliwell-Phillipps in *Outlines*, i. 299, by J. C. Jeaffreson in the 7th *Report of the Hist. MSS. Commission* (1879), by Professor Feuillerat himself in *Shakespeare-Jahrbuch*, xlviii (1912), 81, and by C. W. Wallace, with extracts from others, in *The Evolution of the English Drama up to Shakespeare* (1912, cited as Wallace, i). In the same book and in *The Children of the Chapel at Blackfriars* (1908, cited as Wallace, ii), Professor Wallace prints or extracts documents from other sources, chiefly lawsuits in the Court of Requests and elsewhere, which supplement those discovered by J. Greenstreet and printed in F. G. Fleay, *Chronicle History of the London Stage* (1890). The references to the theatre in J. P. Collier, *History of English Dramatic Poetry* (1837 and 1879), are seriously contaminated by forgeries. Some material for the general history of the precinct is furnished in the various editions of John Stowe, *Survey of London* (1598, 1603, ed. Munday, 1618, ed. Strype, 1720, ed. Kingsford, 1908), in W. Dugdale, *Monasticon* (1817–30), by M. Reddan in the *Victoria History of London*, i. 498, and in the *Athenaeum* (1886), ii. 91. A. W. Clapham, *On the Topography of the Dominican Priory of London* (*Archaeologia*, lxiii. 57), gives a valuable account of the history and church of the convent, but had not the advantage of knowing the Loseley documents, and completely distorts the plan of the domestic buildings and the theatre. An account by J. Q. Adams is in *S. P.* xiv (1917), 64. The status of the liberty is discussed by V. C. Gildersleeve, *Government Regulation of the Elizabethan Drama*, 143.]

THE Dominicans, also called the ' preaching ' or ' black ' friars, came to England in 1221. Their first house was in Holborn.[1] In 1275 they acquired a site on the sloping ground between St. Paul's and the river, just to the east of Fleet ditch, and obtained leave to divert the walls of the City so as to furnish a north and north-west boundary to their precinct. Here grew up a very famous convent, the mother-house of all the Dominican settlements in the country. It received favours from several sovereigns, notably from Edward I and his Queen Eleanor, who were regarded as its founders ; and in return held its great buildings available for national purposes. In 1322–3 it furnished a depository for state records. It housed divers parliaments, at first in

[1] W. P. Baildon, *Black Books of Lincoln's Inn*, iv. 263 ; C. F. R. Palmer, *The Friar-Preachers of Holborn*, London (*Reliquary*, xvii. 33, 75).

its church and later in a great chamber which will be of singular interest to us, and from as early as 1311 was often found a convenient meeting-place for the Privy Council. In 1522 it was the lodging of the Emperor Charles V, and a wooden bridge and gallery were carried over the Fleet, to facilitate communications with his train in Bridewell palace. In 1529 its parliament chamber was the scene of the legatine sittings which tried the case of divorce between the same Emperor's niece Katharine and the conscience-stricken Henry VIII.[1]

By this time the friars had ceased to be a power in the land. Those of the convent had numbered seventy in 1315; there were no more than sixteen or seventeen in 1538.[2] Parts of the buildings, now all too spacious, were let out as residences. It was, perhaps, the neighbourhood of the Wardrobe, whose Master had an official residence contiguous to the east wall of the precinct, which made the Blackfriars a favourite locality for those about the Court. A list of ' them that hath lodgings within the Blak Freers ', which was drawn up in 1522, probably in connexion with the imperial visit, contains the names of Lord Zouch of Harringworth, Lord Cobham, Sir William Kingston, then carver and afterwards comptroller of the household, Sir Henry Wyatt, afterwards treasurer of the chamber, Sir William Parr, Sir Thomas Cheyne, afterwards warden of the Cinque ports and treasurer of the household, Jane, widow of Sir Richard Guildford, formerly master of the horse, and Christopher More, a clerk of the exchequer.[3] It is to be feared that some of these tenants cast a covetous eye upon the fee-simple of their dwellings, and that it was not all zeal for church reform which made Lord Cobham, for example, write to Sir Thomas Wyatt, the poet and son of Sir Henry, on 7 October 1538, ' No news, but I trust there shall not be a friar left in England before you return '.[4] Cobham and his friends had not long to wait. The deed by which the friars surrendered their property into the hands of the King is dated 12 November 1538. The annual income, derived from the rented premises, was reckoned as £104 15s. 5d., but of course this in no way represents the capital value of the site and buildings.[5] The partition of spoils, under the supervision of the Court of

---

[1] Stowe, *Survey*, i. 9, 27, 40, 64, 339; ii. 14, 44, 89; (1720) i. 3. 177; Halle, ii. 150; Nicolas, *Acts of Privy Council, passim*; *Rot. Parl.* v. 171; Clapham, 58; *V. H.* i. 498; Brewer, iv. 2483; Riley, *Memorials of London*, 90; Baldwin, 154, 261, 355, 358, 499; Gairdner, *Paston Letters*, i. 426, ' for the ease of resorting of the Lordys that are withinne the toun '.
[2] *V. H.* i. 498. [3] Brewer, iii. 2. 1053.
[4] Ibid. xiii. 2. 215. [5] Rymer, xiv. 609; Brewer, xiii. 2. 320.

Augmentations, followed in due course. Cobham got his house, although not immediately, at nine years' purchase; and between 1540 and 1550 some sixteen other parcels of the estate, many of them very substantial, were similarly alienated.[1] Finally, on 12 March 1550, during the liberal distribution of crown lands for which the authority of Henry VIII was alleged by his executors in the Privy Council, a comprehensive grant was made of all that still remained unalienated in the precinct to Sir Thomas Cawarden, the Master of the Revels, whose office had for some years past been established within its walls. Apparently Cawarden paid nothing for it, but on the other hand the King owed him a good deal for moneys spent in the service of the Revels.[2]

The Blackfriars long remained an anomaly in the local government of London. Like all monastic establishments, the friars had maintained extensive privileges within their own precinct. Nightly their porter had shut their four gates upon the city. They had done their own paving. The Lord Mayor had claimed a jurisdiction, but if this was admitted, it was only in cases of felony. The ordinary functions of civil magistracy had been exercised, when called for, by Sir William Kingston and other important tenants.[3] Naturally there had been friction from time to time with the Corporation, and on the surrender the latter, like the tenants, hoped that their opportunity was come. They addressed a petition to Henry, in which they expressed their gratification that he had ' extirped and extinct the orders of Freers to the great exaltacion of Crystes doctryne and the abolucion of Antecriste theyr first founder and begynner ', and asked for a grant of the church and the whole precinct of the Blackfriars, together with those of the three other London friaries, to be used for the special benefit of non-parishioners and of those infected by pestilence.[4] Henry, however, had not gone to the trouble of obtaining a surrender merely to inflate the powers and the revenues of a municipality. He is reported to have replied that ' he was as well hable to keep the liberties as the Friers were ', and to have handed the keys to Sir John Portinari, one of his gentlemen pensioners, who dwelt in the precinct.[5] The Blackfriars, therefore,

[1] *M. S. C.* ii. 3.

[2] Ibid. ii. 4, 6, 8, 109, 114. Cawarden had had a lease of part of the property on 4 April 1548.   [3] Stowe (1720), i. 3. 178.

[4] Printed from *Journal*, 14, f. 129, as appendix to *Memoranda, References, and Documents relating to the Royal Hospitals of the City of London* (1836).

[5] Stowe (1720), i. 3. 178. Portinari was a pensioner *c.* 1526 (Brewer, iv. 871), and he was aged 64 in 1572 (*M. S. C.* ii. 52). He was a Florentine by birth and an engineer by profession (*Sp. P.* ii. 399 ; Winwood, i. 145).

continued to be an exempt place or 'liberty', an enclave within the walls of the City, but not part of it, and with a somewhat loose and ill-defined organization of its own. The inhabitants agreed together and appointed a porter and a scavenger. A constable was appointed for them by the justices of the verge.[1] The precinct was constituted an ecclesiastical parish, known as St. Anne's after a chapel which had once served its inhabitants; and was provided with a church.[2] Petty offences were tried, and any exceptional affairs managed, as might have been done in a rural parish, by the justices, and it was to these that any administrative orders thought necessary by the Privy Council were ordinarily addressed.[3] It perhaps goes without saying that the City were not content with a single rebuff. They attempted to interfere at the time of a riot in 1551, and were snubbed by the Privy Council.[4] Under Mary they promoted legislation with a view to annexing the liberties, but without success.[5] In 1562 a sheriff, who entered the liberty to enforce a proclamation, was shut in by the prompt action of the constable, and faced with an inhibition which one of the justices hurried to obtain from a privy councillor.[6] The city remained persistent. In 1574 the Council had again to intervene.[7] In 1578 a controversy arose as to the right of the City to dispose of the goods of felons and other escheats. It was referred to two chief justices, who made a report to the effect that, while the inhabitants of both the Blackfriars and

[1] *B. M. Lansd. MS.* 155, f. 80ᵛ.

[2] *M. S. C.* ii. 2, 5, 103, 127; Stowe (1598), i. 339 · *Athenaeum* (1886), ii. 91 ; Dasent, xxvi. 448 ; xxvii. 13.

[3] In 1585 the Lord Mayor asked that the Blackfriars might contribute to the musters (Stowe, ed. Strype, i. 3. 180). In 1588 and 1593 requisitions for a levy were sent to the chief officer, i. e. the constable, and the inhabitants (Dasent, xv. 428 ; xxiv. 30). · But in 1589 similar action was taken through the Lord Mayor (Dasent, xvii. 118). A local dispute was referred to Richard Young and another Middlesex justice in 1591, with whom the Lord Mayor was joined because a City company was involved (Dasent, xx. 245, 283). Young and others again received the Council's instructions, after they had heard the inhabitants, on a building matter in 1591 (Dasent, xxi. 337). At a time of danger in 1592 the keeping of a midsummer watch was committed to Lord Cobham (Dasent, xxii. 551).

[4] Stowe (1720), i. 3. 183 ; Dasent, iii. 235 (Letter of 14 March 1551 ' to the Maiour of London to suffer the Lorde Cobham, the Lorde Wardein, and others dwelling within the Blacke Freres t'enjoye their liberties there '). The riot was put down by Sir Thomas Saunders, Sir Henry Jerningham, and William More.

[5] Stowe (1720), i. 3. 183.

[6] Stowe, ed. Strype (1720), i. 3. 184. The Blackfriars papers added by A. Munday in 1618 appear to be all notes and examinations taken by Sir Thomas Saunders, who appealed to the Earl of Arundel for support.

[7] Dasent, viii. 240, 257.

the Whitefriars enjoyed certain immunities from civic
levies and liabilities, nevertheless the soil of the precincts
lay within the City, and the City was entitled to exercise
jurisdiction therein. It may be doubted whether effect was
given to this opinion.[1]

In 1587 the Council ordered another inquiry, in order to
ascertain the precise nature of the Queen's title in the Blackfriars.[2] There had been a petition for redress of inconveniences
from the inhabitants.[3] About the same time the chief landowner,
Sir William More, appears to have suggested that the liberty
should be converted into a manor, and manorial rights con-
ferred upon him.[4] These are signs that residence in a liberty
hard by a thronging population had disclosed a seamy side.
Undesirable persons were bound to throng to a district where
the Lord Mayor's writ did not run. An open space, for
example, filled with immemorial trees planted by the friars,
had been ruined to house alleys for bowling and other unlawful games.[5] Doubtless there were those who resented
the fact that the attempt of the City to discourage interludes
had been met by the establishment of a Blackfriars theatre
in 1576, which lasted until 1584. It appears to have been
a protest from the inhabitants which led the Privy Council
to forbid the public theatre contemplated by James Burbage
in 1596, although some years later they winked at the opening
of the building as a private house. In 1596 the church fell
down, and in appointing a commission to apportion the
responsibility for repairs, the council also instructed them
to consider the government of the liberty, ' which being
grown more populus than heretofore and without any certaine
and knowen officer to keepe good orders there, needeth to
be reformed in that behalfe '.[6] The nature of the commission's

---

[1] Dasent, x. 429 ; xii. 19. Pending a decision the Lord Mayor was
directed ' not to intermeddle in any cawse within the saide liberties, savinge
onlie for the punishment of fellons as heretofore he hath don '. The report
dated 27 Jan. 1580 is printed by Ingleby, 250, from the Bridgewater MSS.
It seems to be genuine. Collier does not print it, although he mentions
it (*New Facts*, 9) in connexion with a forged Privy Council order which
he dates 23 Dec. 1579. Wallace, ii. 22, describes an unprinted statement
of the City's case, dated 27 Jan. 1579, in *Letter Book* Z, f. 23ᵛ.

[2] Dasent, xv. 137; Stowe (1720), i. 3. 177.

[3] This may be the undated petition relating both to the Blackfriars
and the Whitefriars in *B. M. Lansd. MS.* 155, f. 79ᵛ.

[4] Wallace, i. 174, from *Loseley MSS.*, bundle 425.

[5] *M. S. C.* ii. 124 ; cf. Dasent, xiii. 76.

[6] Dasent, xxvi. 448. Lord Hunsdon and Sir John Fortescue, both
residents in or near the Blackfriars, sat on the commission with the chief
justices. Lady Russell records the want of a steward and bailiff to keep
order in 1597 (*Hatfield MSS.* vii. 298).

findings is not upon record, but that the ultimate solution lay in the incorporation of the liberty in the City could hardly be doubtful. As far back as 1589 the Council had found it convenient to use the Lord Mayor as an agent for securing a proper contribution from the Blackfriars towards a levy. From 1597 onwards they showed an increased tendency to make similar use of an administrative machinery far more completely organized than that of the justices of the peace. In that year the Lord Mayor was instructed to make a collection in aid of the Blackfriars church repairs. In 1600 it again fell to him to assess the share of the liberty in a levy of men and money. In 1601 it is he who is called upon to suppress plays in Blackfriars during Lent.[1] The final step was, however, deferred until 20 September 1608, when the new Jacobean charter formally extended the jurisdiction of the city to various liberties, including both the Blackfriars and the Whitefriars, with certain exemptions as regards assessments and the tenure of offices, but with none as regards responsibility for petty offences and the keeping of the peace.[2]

I have anticipated, in order to get the question of jurisdiction out of the way. I must now return to the topography. Sir Thomas Cawarden died on 29 August 1559. He had no son, and his executors, Lady Cawarden and Sir William More, personally took over the Blackfriars estate in survivorship, as part of the settlement of his affairs.[3] Lady Cawarden's death on 20 February 1560 left More sole owner. He retained the property until his own death in 1601, and the muniment room of his house at Loseley near Guildford contains innumerable documents relating to the business transactions in which it involved him, together with some of earlier date which he inherited from Cawarden. The researches of Professor Feuillerat in these archives render it possible to reconstruct with some minuteness the arrangement of the Blackfriars and its buildings at the time of the surrender, to trace many of the changes of the next half-century, and, as part of the process, to indicate pretty definitely the locality

---

[1] Dasent, xxvii. 13 ; xxx. 134, 149 ; cf. App. D, No. cxxvi.

[2] W. de G. Birch, *Historical Charters and Constitutional Documents of the City of London*, 142. James is said to have made the City pay for the rebuilding of the Banqueting House (cf. ch. i) in return for this extension of jurisdiction (Goodman, ii. 176). Collier, *N. F.* 20, 22, 32, although ignorant of the charter, quotes documents relating to the status of the Blackfriars in 1608, of which two at least, a note of the interest of the players in the theatre and a letter in their favour signed ' H. S.', are forgeries (Ingleby, 244, 246, 256).

[3] *M. S. C.* ii. 66, 114 ; cf. Cawarden's i. p. m. in Fry, *London Inquisitiones Post Mortem*, i. 191.

and nature of the structures which were turned to theatrical uses.

The precinct covered a space of about five acres.[1] In shape it was a rough parallelogram, wider at the north than at the south. The great gate was towards the east end of the north boundary. It was reached by a short entry on the south of Bowier Row, now Ludgate Hill, just east of Ludgate. This seems to have been called Gate Street. It is now the north end of Pilgrim Street.[2] From here the boundary was the city wall, westwards for about 450 ft. to the Fleet ditch, and then southwards for about 800 ft. along the east side of the ditch. There were towers at intervals. One of these stood about 200 ft. down from the angle, and immediately south of this was the bridge over the Fleet towards Bridewell. The south and east boundaries were also walled. Between the south wall and the river ran Castle Lane, which was not within the precinct.[3] A gate in the south wall gave access across the lane to the Blackfriars 'bridge' or 'stairs', a common landing place, originally built by the Prior of St. John's, from whom, in some way not clear to me, the Friars held their estate.[4] The south-east angle of the precinct was near Puddle Wharf, and from here the boundary ran up the west side of St. Andrew's Hill to Carter Lane, bending out eastwards near the top, where the buildings of the Wardrobe joined it by an arch over the roadway, was then driven in sharply westwards by the end of Carter Lane, which was butt up against a turngate in the friars' wall, and finally ran in an irregularly diagonal line from the junction of Creed and Carter Lanes north-west to the great gate

[1] The general lie of Blackfriars can be gathered from Stowe (1598), i. 313 ; ii. 11, with the maps described in the *Bibl. Note* to ch. xvi, and the modern ordnance maps. The earlier maps are largely picturesque, and notably place far too much of the precinct on the east of Water Lane. But they seem to preserve certain details, such as the arches over the north to south highway. The old lines of the roads appear to have been preserved at the rebuilding after the great fire of 1666. I have added some details from other sources. [2] *M. S. C.* ii. 115.

[3] The reconstructed map of London by Emery Walker in C. L. Kingsford's edition of Stowe gives this name in error to Water Lane.

[4] The 1586 documents in Stowe (1720), i. 3. 178, state that the prior held of the lord of St. John's, ' who did make the bridge at the Thames '. Feuillerat, *Eliz.* 454, however, quotes a Declared Account of 1550 for ' the ereccion and buyldynge . . . of two bridges thone at the Blackfreers and thother at the Temple '. Under Elizabeth the liberty maintained the bridge as well as that at Bridewell (*Lansd. MS.* 155, f. 80ᵛ). The tenure from St. John's is also alleged (1587) in Dasent, xv. 137. It is rather curious that in an endorsement of the survey of St. John's in 1586-7 (Feuillerat, *Eliz.* 47) that house, although in Clerkenwell, is described, perhaps by a slip, as in the Blackfriars.

again. Internally the precinct was unequally divided by an irregular highway which ran north and south, from the great gate to the Blackfriars stairs. This started out of Gate Street as High Street, and lower down became Water Lane.[1] All the conventual buildings lay on the east of the highway. Here was the larger division of the precinct, measuring about 450 ft. from east to west. The western division, measuring about 150 ft., contained only a few houses and gardens. Across it ran from Bridewell Bridge to Water Lane a strip of unoccupied land, containing nothing but a ruined gallery, probably part of the provision made for the accommodation of Charles V in 1522. One of Cawarden's first acts, when he got his property, was to make a new road, with tenements and gardens to the south of it, along this strip. It became known as Bridewell Lane, and is represented by the present Union Street.[2] It must have joined Water Lane just south of a little place or *parvis* which lay in front of the west porch of the church and the adjoining entrance to the cloister. The *parvis* contained one or two houses and shops, and formed part of the continuous thoroughfare from north to south, communicating by gateways with High Street and Water Lane.[3] The conventual church itself divided the eastern portion of the precinct from west to east, extending not quite so far east as the present Friar Street. It was 220 ft. long and 66 ft. wide, and had two aisles and a chancel, which, as usual in conventual churches, was as long as the nave. There was a square porch tower over the west end. Over the junction of nave and chancel stood a belfry, visible in Wyngaerde's drawing of *c.* 1543–50, and to the north of the chancel a chapel, probably the quasi-parochial chapel of St. Anne, and a vestry.[4] Beyond these was the churchyard.[5] This was 300 ft. long by 90 ft. deep,

---

[1] *M. S. C.* ii. 115. For the 'turngate' cf. *M. S. C.* ii. 114; Strype (1720), i. 3. 184. This, with the great gate, and the gates at the Thames and Fleet bridges, made up the four gates of conventual times. The gate, over which Shakespeare had a house, where Ireland Yard debouches into St. Andrew's Hill, was probably of later date.

[2] *M. S. C.* ii. 6, 11, 109.

[3] The upper gate is described in a lease as ' a gate of the Citie of London ' (*Loseley MS.* 1396, f. 44). It may have been a relic of the pre-1276 wall. Its site is shown on the Ordnance map. The lower gate is visible in the maps of Braun and Agas. It seems to have carried Charles V's gallery over the roadway to the guest-house.

[4] *M. S. C.* ii. 9, 107, 110; Clapham, 64.

[5] The details for the rest of this paragraph are mainly taken from Crown surveys of 1548 and 1550 (*M. S. C.* ii. 6, 8), and from a memorandum by Cawarden on the grants anterior to his own (*M. S. C.* ii. 1, 103), and Professor Feuillerat's notes of the original patents which illustrate this.

and occupied about two-thirds of the space between the High Street on the west, the church on the south, and the north-eastern boundary of the precinct. A group of houses stood between it and the great gate towards Ludgate, and three others separated it from the High Street at the south west corner.[1] One of these, built up against the church and the High Street gateway, was a recluse's cell or Ankerhouse.[2] Cawarden cut a new road across the churchyard, 20 ft. north of the site of the chancel and just north of the Ankerhouse and the High Street gate. This continued Carter Lane, the turn-gate at the end of which was converted into a gate practicable for carts, and with Bridewell Lane provided a thoroughfare across the Blackfriars from east to west in addition to that from north to south. That part of the existing Carter Lane, west of Creed Lane, which was formerly known as Shoemakers' Row, doubtless represents Cawarden's new way.[3]

On the south of the nave stood the great cloister, entered by a porter's lodge in its north-west corner. It was 110 ft. square. Its eastern alley was probably in a line with a way across the church under the belfry to a door into the church-yard, and this line, preserved by Cawarden in order to provide access to the cloister from his new way, is represented by the existing Church Entry.[4] The north side of the cloister was formed by the wall of the nave. Behind the other three sides were ranged the domestic buildings of the convent. On the east were the ample Prior's lodging, which stretched back over the space south of the chancel, and farther to the south the Convent garden, covering an acre. Over part of this lodging and over the cloister alley itself was the east dorter of the friars, communicating direct with the church by a stairway.[5] The east side of the cloister also contained the Chapter-house, which probably stood in the middle, and to the south of this a school-house.[6] Behind the south-east corner were the provincial's lodging, a store-house, the common jakes, and another garden, known as the hill garden.[7]

[1] *M. S. C.* ii. 9, 107, 114; Clapham, 62; *London Inquisitiones Post Mortem*, ii. 115.   [2] Ibid. 9, 10, 112.
[3] Ibid. 111, 113.   [4] Ibid. 110; Clapham, 63.
[5] Ibid. 10, 110, 114.   [6] Ibid. 3.
[7] Some vaulted fragments stood until 1900 at a spot which must have been just east of the school-house. Possibly they formed part of the provincial's lodging. They are shown in a plan of *c.* 1670–80 (Clapham, 71), and their condition in 1900 was carefully recorded (Clapham, 69, 70, 78). Only a fragment of wall is now *in situ*, just north of what is now the west end of Ireland Yard, but appears on the seventeenth-century plan as Cloister Court. It must, however, have run out from the south-east corner of the cloister towards the east. The name Cloister Court has now passed to a yard farther south.

Another dorter stood over the south cloister alley and over some ground-floor buildings of uncertain use, which divided this alley from an inner cloister, flanked on the east by the library, and in part on the west by the infirmary, behind which were the bakehouse, brewhouse, and stables. The western end of the south alley of the main cloister formed a lavabo, and was apparently sunk to a lower level than the rest.[1] Down the western side of both cloisters extended a continuous range of buildings, the details of which will require subsequent examination. These formed two main blocks. The northern, flanking the main cloister, contained the buttery and parts of the guest-house and porter's lodge; the southern, flanking the inner cloister, was devoted to the refectory, the lower end of which, owing to the slope of the hill, seems to have stood over the infirmary. The irregular outline of Water Lane, jutting a good deal to the west after it emerged from the *parvis* in front of the church porch, left a space of some 84 ft. at its widest between this range of buildings and the lane itself. The guest-house and porter's lodge extended back into this space; it also held the convent kitchen and other subsidiary buildings.[2]

When Cawarden got his grant in 1550, a great deal of the

---

[1] Clapham, 68 ; cf. p. 486.

[2] Clapham suggests, plausibly enough, that the description (*c.* 1394) of a Dominican house in *Pierce the Ploughmans Crede* (ed. Skeat, *E. E. T. S.* 153–215) was based upon the London Blackfriars. The following passages relate to the cloister and refectory.

> Þanne kam i to þat cloister . & gaped abouten
> Whouȝ it was pilered and peynt . & portred well clene,
> All y-hyled wiþ leed . lowe to þe stones,
> And y-paued wiþ peynt til . iche poynte after oþer ;
> With kundites of clene tyn . closed all aboute,
> Wiþ lauoures of latun . louelyche y-greithed. . . .

> . . . Þanne was þe chaptire-hous wrouȝt . as a greet chirche,
> Coruen and couered . and queyntliche entayled ;
> Wiþ semlich selure . y-set on lofte ;
> As a Parlement-hous . y-peynted aboute. . . .

> . . . Þanne ferd y into fraytour . and fond þere an oþer,
> An halle for an heyȝ king . an housholde to holden,
> Wiþ brode bordes aboute . y-benched wel clene,
> Wiþ windowes of glas . wrouȝt as a Chirche. . . .

> . . . Chambers wiþ chymneyes . & Chapells gaie ;
> And kychens for an hyȝe kinge . in castells to holden,
> And her dortour y-diȝte . wiþ dores ful stronge ;
> Fermery and fraitur . with fele mo houses,
> And all strong ston wall . sterne opon heiþe,
> Wiþ gaie garites & grete . & iche hole y-glased ;
> And oþere houses y-nowe . to herberwe þe queene.

property had already been disposed of.[1] Except for the strip where he laid out Bridewell Lane and two small garden plots, nothing was left for him in the western division of the precinct. To the north the group of houses between the churchyard and the great gate had gone. To the south, Cobham had taken the rooms over the porter's lodge, with a closet window looking into the church, and he and one Sir George Harper had divided the rest of the guest-house block—'fayer great edifices', says Cawarden—that lay behind.[2] Sir Francis Bryan had taken the Prior's lodging and the convent garden, and from him they had passed to the Bishop of Ely and then to one William Blackwell. Lady Kingston had taken the inner cloister, with part of the south dorter and the rooms beneath it, the library, the infirmary, the brew-house, bake-house, and stables. Others had taken the school-house, some more of the south dorter, the provincial's lodging, the jakes, the store-house, and the hill garden, and these ultimately passed to Lady Grey. Sir Thomas Cheyne, the Lord Warden of the Cinque Ports, had taken some of the buildings west of the frater. Everything farther south, down towards the river, had also been alienated. What was left for Cawarden consisted mainly of the church itself and the churchyard, the ankerhouse, the great cloister, the chapter-house, the east dorter, the porter's lodge and buttery block, with all the rooms over these except Cobham's, the frater, the kitchen, and such buildings standing between the frater and Water Lane, as did not belong to Cheyne.[3] Much trouble was caused to Cawarden's successors by uncertainty as to the extent of Cheyne's claim.[4] No doubt the grant constituted Cawarden the chief landowner in the district, but he complained that hardly any of his property was 'mansionable', and even at the time of his death he had only brought the annual value up to £70.[5] The survey taken for the purposes of the grant puts it at no more than £19. On the other hand, the value of the stone and timber and other material of the buildings is estimated in the same survey at £879 3s. 4d., including an item of £709 11s. 0d. for lead alone. Evidently it was from the site-value and the judicious erection of new buildings and conversion of old ones, with the aid of this material, into 'mansionable' property, that Cawarden's profit was to

---

[1] *M. S. C.* ii. 1.   [2] Ibid. 13, 115.
[3] Ibid. 6, 8, gives the texts of two surveys (a) of the property leased to Cawarden on 4 April 1548, (b) of that included in his grant of 12 March 1550.
[4] Ibid. 7, 12, 35 ; cf. p. 499.
[5] *London Inquisitiones Post Mortem*, i. 191 ; cf. *M. S. C.* ii. 4, 12.

come. A convinced Protestant, he looked upon the church as a quarry. He pulled it down, with the exception of the south wall of the nave, which was to serve him as a garden wall, and the porch which he turned into a tenement. Other tenements were built on the site, and the rest of it, with so much of the churchyard as was not required for the new road, was let off. One of the tenants appears to have made tennis-courts on the site of the chancel. The demolition included St. Anne's Chapel. This had been closed during Henry's reign and used as a storehouse for the Offices of Tents and Revels. For a while the inhabitants were allowed to worship in a room under an old gallery, presumably that which became the site of Bridewell Lane; but now this passed into Cawarden's hands and he evicted them. When they plucked up heart, under Mary, to protest, he first offered them a site in the churchyard and a roof if they would be at the expense of building, and ultimately gave them an upper room, apparently at the north end of the east dorter. This fell down in 1597, and was rebuilt by the parishioners, who finally bought it, with a piece of the site of the old conventual church as a churchyard, from Sir George More in 1607–8.[1] Cawarden effected an adjustment of boundaries on the east of the cloister with the Bishop of Ely.[2] He then proceeded to build dwelling rooms along the south and east sides of the cloister.[3] They must have been fairly shallow, for they left him a great square garden, but no doubt the recess of the chapter-house permitted increased depth towards the east. Under the west wing of the new building, adjoining the buttery, was a great vaulted room, 57 ft. by 25, which must, I think, have been the lavabo of the friars.[4] East of this was a set of rooms capable of use as a separate dwelling, which came to be known as Lygon's lodgings.[5] The rest formed the capital mansion of the property, the 'great house', and was clearly intended for Cawarden's own residence. It seems to have been sometimes let and sometimes occupied by Sir William More.[6] The great garden must have been pleasant enough, with the north and west

---

[1] Stowe (1598), i. 341; *Athenaeum* (1886), ii. 91; *M. S. C.* ii. 2, 127; Hennessy, 88; *Loseley MSS.*

[2] *M. S. C.* ii. 103.   [3] Ibid. 92, 117.

[4] Ibid. 21, 31, 92, 126.

[5] Ibid. 21, 93, 119. They were let to Henry Knowles in 1565 and had been earlier occupied by Roger Lygon, Lady Parr, and Sir Thomas Saunders. Later Nicholas Saunders had them.

[6] Ibid. 117, 124, 125, show Anthony Browne, probably, as tenant in 1560, Henry Lord Hunsdon, probably, in 1584 and 1585, and Ralph Bowes in 1596.

cloister alleys left standing, and a tinkling conduit in the west end, filled by a pipe from Clerkenwell.[1]

The important part of the Blackfriars, from the point of view of theatrical topography, is the range of buildings on the western side of the two cloisters, parallel to Water Lane. The two blocks constituting this range, or so much of them as passed to Cawarden, are referred to in the surveys of 1548 and 1550 as the 'olde butterie' and the 'vpper ffrater'.[2]

[1] Dasent, xxi. 402, gives a Privy Council letter of 18 August 1591 to the Lord Mayor requiring him to repair the supply pipe from Clerkenwell ; cf. p. 494.

[2] (1548) ' A Cuchin yarde, an owlde Cuchyn, an entre or passage Ioyninge to the same, conteyninge in lengethe 84 fote, abuttinge to the lane aforseide on the weste side, being in breddethe at that ende 68 fote, Abuttinge ageanste an owlde butery on the easte side, being in breddethe at that ende 74 foote, Abuttinge to Mr Portynarys parler nexte the lane on the Southe side, And to my lorde Cobhames brick wall and garden on the Northe syde. An owlde buttery and an entrye or passage with a greate stayre therin, with Sellers therunder, with a hall place at the vpper ende of the stayre and an entere there to the ffrater ouer the same buttery, all which conteyne in lengethe 36 foote and in breddethe 95 foote, abuttinge to the cloyster on the Este side, the Cuchin on the weste side, to the lorde Cobhams howse on the Northe syde, and on the Sowthe side to a blynd parlour that my lorde warden did clame.

A howse called the vpper frater conteyninge in lengethe 107 foote and in breddethe 52 foote, abuttinge Sowthe and easte to my ladye Kingestons howse and garden, Northe to a hall where the kinges revelles lyes at this presente, and weste towardes the seide Duchie Chamber and Mr Porty-naryes howse.

Memorandum my lorde warden clamethe the seide hall, parlour, Cutchin and Chaumber.   A hall and a parlour vnder the seide frater of the same lengethe and breddethe, A litle Cuchen conteyning in lengethe 23 foote and in breddethe 22 foote abuttinge to the aforseide lane on the weste, towardes the seide parlour on the este, to Mr Portinarys howse on the northe, and to a waye ledinge to my ladye Kingestons howse on the southe, A litle Chamber with a voyde rome therunder, conteyning in lengethe 26 fote, in breddeth 10 foote, abuttinge weste to the cuchin, este to the parlour, northe to Mr Portinarys howse, and ye seid way to my ladie Kingestons howse Sowthe, with 4 small Sellers or darke holes therunder.

A voyde rome, beinge an entre towardes the lytle cytchin and colehowse, conteyning in length 30 fote and in breddethe 17 fote.

A Chamber called the Duchie Chaumber, with a darke loginge therunder, conteyninge in lengthe 50 fote and in breddethe 16 foote, abuttinge este ageanste the north ende of the seide ffrater, abuttinge weste on Mr Porti-naryes parlour —— 66s 8d.'

(1550) ' One Kitchyn yarde, an olde Kitchyn, an Entrie or passage ioyneinge to the same, Conteineinge in lengthe 84 fote, abutinge to the Lane aforesaid on the west side, beinge in bredethe at that ende three score fowrtene fote, abutinge to Mr Portinareys parler next the Lane on the southe side and to the Lord Cobham brickewall & gardeine on the Northe side. One olde Butterie & a Entrie or passage with a great staier therein, with Cellers therevnder, with a Hawle place at the vpper ende of the staiers and a entrie there to the ffrater ouer the same butterie,

From the details given in these surveys and in the leases and other documents preserved at Loseley, it is possible to form a very fair notion of their structure and uses. The chief rooms in both blocks were upon an upper floor. The northern block was 110 ft. in length from north to south and 36 ft. in width. The upper rooms, however, were only 26 ft. wide, as 10 ft. was taken up by a high stone gallery which ran along the west of the building, and was perhaps connected with the wooden gallery leading to the Fleet.[1] These rooms were four in number. That to the north, 21 ft. long, belonged to Cobham, and had a closet window looking into the church upon the south wall of which, for 20 ft. of its width, the block abutted.[2] Then came two central rooms, a large and a small one, measuring together 52 ft. in length, and then a southern one, which with an entry measured 47 ft.[3] The surveys treat the three rooms which fell to Cawarden as a single ' hall place '. All four rooms had probably formed part of the guest-house of the convent, and had lodged Charles V. The ground floor held low rooms pierced at intervals by entries and with cellars underneath them. The chief entry or gate-house was at the southern end and served Cawarden's mansion house when that was built.[4] North of this came the

which all conteinethe in lengthe 95 fote and in bredethe 36 fote, abuttinge to the Cloyster on thest side, the kitchyn on the west side, to the Lorde Cobham howse on the northe side, and on the southe side to a blinde parler that my Lord warden did Clayme. One howse called the vpper ffrater conteynethe in Lengthe 107 fote and in bredethe 52 fote, Abuttinge southe and est to the Ladie Kingston howse and gardein, northe to a hawle where the Kinges Revelles Liethe at theis presentes, and west towardes the Duchie Chamber and Mr Portinareyes howse. A voide rome, beinge an Entrie towardes the Litle Kitchyn & Cole howse, conteininge in Lengthe 30 fote and in bredethe 17 fote. One Chamber called the Duchie chamber, with a darke Lodginge there vnder, conteininge in Lengthe 50 fote and in bredethe 16 fote, abuttinge est agaynst the northe ende of the said ffrater, and abuttinge west apon Mr Portinareys parler. All which premisses be valued to be worthe by yere —— iijli vjs viijd.'

[1] *M. S. C.* ii. 14, 24, 116, 117, 119, 120 ; cf. p. 482. The stone gallery was removed in 1564.

[2] Ibid. 13, 16, 115.   [3] Ibid. 14, 16.

[4] Ibid. 7, 11, ' an entrye or passage with a greate stayre therin ' (1548, 1550), 21 ' one entrye ledinge vnder parcell of the premysses demysed from that end of the house of William More wherin John Horleye his servaunt doth lodge ' (1560), 118, ' the entre in the west ende of the garden openyng into the same garden ' (1560), 31, ' an entrye leadynge from the sayde voyde ground into the sayd dwellynge howse or tenement of the sayd Sir William More ' (1576), 63, ' the dore entry way voide ground and passage leadinge and vsed to and from the saide great yard nexte the saide Pipe Office ' (1596), 126, ' the gatehouse with the appurtenances on the west side of the sayd monastery ' (1611), ' the great gate near the playhouse ' (1617).

buttery proper and a pantry, occupying with a small entry connecting them 29 ft. ;[1] then another stepped entry into the cloister serving afterwards as Cawarden's garden gate ;[2] then probably more rooms under the two central upper rooms ; then a staircase to Cobham's upper room ;[3] and finally rooms belonging to the porter's lodge, which were 21 ft. in length.   This lodge extended backwards towards Water Lane, and over and around it were other rooms of Cobham's and yet others forming the house of Sir George Harper.[4] Some or all of these had also probably been part of the guest-house. Together with a garden of Cobham's, they occupied rather less than half the space between the northern block and Water Lane.   South of them, and included in Cawarden's grant, were the convent kitchen with a room over it, and the kitchen yard, forming a space 84 ft. wide, and in length 74 ft. at the buttery end and 68 ft. at the lane end.

The northern block, being 110 ft. long, extended right down to the southern line of the cloister, which was 110 ft. square.   Here it abutted upon the southern block.   This was 52 ft. wide.   The length of the upper frater is given in the surveys as 107 ft., and in two of More's leases as 110 ft.[5] The latter figure is probably the right one.[6] The north end of this block contained a ' great stair ', which gave access both to the frater and to the guest-house, and was itself convenient of approach both from the gate-house entry and from the lavabo at the south-west angle of the cloister.   Probably this end was built in the form of a tower, as there were rooms on and over the staircase and over the adjoining Duchy Chamber, and garrets over those.[7]   There was a garret also over the south end of the northern block.[8]   It is doubtful whether anything stood over the main portion of the southern block.[9]   This had a flat leaded roof, whereas the northern block, as its lead is not mentioned in the survey, probably had a gabled and tiled roof.   Apart from the staircase tower,

[1] M. S. C. ii. 20.
[2] Ibid. 14 (cf. 116), ' vnius paris graduum ducentium a coquina predicta vsque magnum claustrum ' (1546), 21, ' the waye ledinge from the house and garden of William More towards the Water Lane ', ' one entrye ledinge vnder parcell of the premysses demysed from the garden of William More to the voide grounde ' (1560), 119.
[3] Ibid. 16.   [4] Ibid. 115.   [5] Ibid. 27, 29.
[6] The whole length of the Neville-Farrant holding is given in 1560 (M. S. C. ii. 20) as 157½ ft., and in 1576 (M. S. C. ii. 29) as 156¼ ft. As this included 37 ft. of the northern block, 119½ ft. or 120¼ ft. seems to be left for the staircase and frater.   The difference between inside and outside measurements often causes confusion in old surveys.
[7] M. S. C. ii. 62, 119 ; cf. p. 504.
[8] Ibid. 94.   [9] Cf. p. 513.

the upper floor of the southern block consisted of the ' upper ' frater or refectory, a spacious apartment, which had been used for Parliaments and the legatine trial of Henry VIII's divorce case, and was sometimes known as ' the Parliament chamber '.[1] The ground floor is a little more difficult. The survey of 1548 assigns to it a ' blind ', that is, I suppose, a windowless, or at any rate dark, parlour, which came next the buttery block, and a hall, to which the parlour served as an entry.[2] These are said to be ' vnder the seide frater of the same lengethe and breddethe '. This might naturally be taken to mean that they were, together, of the same size as the frater above. In fact it must, I think, mean that they were of the same size as each other, for we know from another source that the south end of the frater was over a room not belonging to Cawarden at all but to Lady Kingston, and itself standing over the infirmary, which, owing to the fall of the ground, formed at that end a lower story of the block.[3] The survey does not say what the sizes of the parlour and hall were, but a later document suggests that together they underlay over two-thirds of the frater and occupied a space of 74 ft. from north to south and 52 ft. from east to west.[4] Under Cawarden's part of the southern block were cellars. To the west lay what was known as the Duchy Chamber, probably from some official use in connexion with the Duchy of Lancaster. This was a two-story building, 50 ft. long by 16 ft. wide, jutting out at right angles to the extreme north end of the frater. South of it was a house, apparently belonging to Sir Thomas Cheyne and occupied by Sir John Portinari, which touched the frater at one end, and at the other had a parlour, interposed between the end of the Duchy Chamber and Water Lane, and bounded on the north, as the Duchy Chamber itself must have been, by the kitchen yard. South of this again were a little chamber and a kitchen, with an entry from Water Lane, probably between Portinari's parlour and another house belonging to Cheyne.[5] The little chamber and kitchen were used in conjunction with the hall under the upper frater. This hall, which was paved and stood ' handsome to ' the buttery, had also been a frater, serving as a breakfast room for the friars, and in the little

[1] *M. S. C.* ii. 105.

[2] The room is described as ' intrale seu le parlour ' in Cawarden's grant of 1550.

[3] *M. S. C.* ii. 105, 124. There was yet another room under the infirmary. One Kempe, an assign of Lady Kingston's heir, tried to claim the Parliament Chamber from Cawarden, on the strength of her grant of the infirmary.

[4] Cf. p. 504.   [5] On Cheyne's houses cf. p. 499.

chamber had lived their butler.[1] Now it is noted in the surveys that Sir Thomas Cheyne had laid claim to the paved hall, the ' blind ' parlour, the little chamber, and the kitchen, and it seems very doubtful whether they were covered by the specifications of Cawarden's grant.[2] He succeeded, however, in occupying them ; and the inevitable law-suit was left for his successor.

Cawarden had had the buttery, frater, kitchen, and Duchy chamber on lease since 4 April 1548.[3] Some of these, as well as other conventual buildings, he had occupied from a still earlier date in his capacity as Master of the Tents and Revels. For these offices the propinquity of the Wardrobe rendered the Blackfriars very convenient. Already in 1511 temporary use had been made of some room in the precinct to prepare a pageant in for a joust at Westminster.[4] Before Cawarden became Master, the regular store-house of the Revels office had been at Warwick Inn.[5] The transfer to Black-friars was not completed until February 1547, but it perhaps began earlier, since the papers of the Court of Augmentations contain receipts by John Barnard, for sums spent by the King's surveyor on 'the reparayng and amendyng of the Blacke Fryers in London store howse for the seyd tentes and revelles ' during 1545.[6] The Chapel of St. Anne had been requisitioned with other houses ' to laye in tentes, maskes and revels ' before the end of Henry VIII's reign.[7] As to the exact location of the Tents there is some interesting, although conflicting, evidence. An order of the Augmenta-tions in 1550 allowed Sir Thomas Cheyne £5 a year for the use of his great room by the Tents from 25 March 1545 onwards.[8] The room intended was undeniably the paved hall or breakfast room under the frater, but Sir William More maintained in 1572 that the payment by the Augmentations was an irregular one, and that the paved hall had never been

[1] M. S. C. ii. 42–51. This hall is doubtless the ground-floor frater referred to in a document of c. 1562 (M. S. C. ii. 105).

[2] Cf. p. 499. The ' blinde parler that my Lord warden did clayme ' and ' the litle kitchyn and cole howse ' are mentioned in the survey of 1550 to define the position of other parcels. But the hall and parlour might be held to be covered by the grant of the ' howse called the vpper frater ', and I do not know what the ' little tenement ' near that held by Kirkham from Cheyne was, if it was not the little chamber and kitchen. It is noteworthy that the disputed rooms, after being included, with a note of Cheyne's claim, in the survey of 1548, were left out of Cawarden's lease of the same year.

[3] M. S. C. ii. 109.   [4] Brewer, ii. 2. 1494.   Tudor Revels, 7.
[6] Feuillerat, Edw. and Mary, 255; Wallace, i. 140.
[7] Athenaeum (1886), ii. 91.
[8] Feuillerat, Eliz. 430 ; cf. M. S. C. ii. 120 ; Wallace, i. 192.

used for the Revels and was never in fact Cheyne's.[1] Sir John
Portinari gave evidence that for some time after the surrender
of the convent it had remained empty, and that he had himself
kept the keys until Cawarden took possession of it in 1550.
Cawarden then invited him to a supper and a play in the
hall.[2] The Revels seem to have had the use of the upper
frater or parliament chamber during Henry VIII's reign.[3]
But the surveys of 1548 and 1550 locate them to the north
of this, in the southernmost of the four halls of the old guest-
house. The two central halls, together with the convent
kitchen, had been tenanted as far back as 1539 by successive
Lords Cobham, to whose house they were adjacent.[4] In 1554,
however, Cawarden sold the two rooms to George Lord
Cobham, together with the porter's lodge, which underlay
his original holding, and received as part of his consideration
a release from any claim which Cobham may have had to
the kitchen yard and to the property granted to Cawarden
on the west side of Water Lane.[5] With the upper rooms
transferred to Cobham went ' appurtenances ', which probably
included the corresponding ground-floor rooms, as these are
not traceable in More's possession and apparently formed
part of the Cobham estate when that was disposed of in the
next century.[6] The porter's lodge was all on the ground
floor. It had a frontage of 21 ft. on the cloister and ran back
for 47 ft. towards Water Lane. At the time of Cawarden's
grant in 1550 it had been occupied by John Barnard, clerk
comptroller of the Tents and Revels, but he had died in the
same year.[7] Naturally it was convenient for the officers
of the Revels to live in the Blackfriars. John Holt, the
yeoman, had a house to the north of the churchyard. Thomas
Philipps, the clerk, had the 'little chamber' west of the
frater. The paved hall served him as a wood store, and from
time to time some of Cawarden's servants lay there. About
1552 Cawarden moved Philipps to the Ankerhouse, and put
into the little chamber the deputy clerk, Thomas Blagrave,

---

[1] *M. S. C.* ii. 35. I do not know whether More deliberately confused
the Tents and Revels.

[2] Ibid. 52.   [3] Ibid. 105.

[4] Ibid. 14, 116 ; *Hist. MSS.* vii. 603.   [5] Ibid. 15.

[6] Only an abstract of title at the date of the sale exists (Barrett,
Apothecaries, 46), but Apothecaries' Hall occupies the site of these rooms.

[7] *M. S. C.* ii. 4, 9 ; Feuillerat, *Eliz.* 440. In 1552 Jane Fremownte
had succeeded Barnard (*M. S. C.* ii. 115), but she cannot have had the
whole of the original lodge, as her 4 ft. entry on Water Lane is too small
to have been the main access to the cloister. Probably part had been
granted to her neighbour, Sir George Harper. Nor did all her holding
pass to Cobham in 1554. Some of it was probably added to the house
on the north, which occupied the site of the old church porch.

who found it too small, and rented an adjoining chamber from Cheyne.[1] The paved hall was then let, with other neighbouring rooms on more than one floor, to one Woodman, who kept an ordinary in the hall and did a good deal of damage to the property.[2] Meanwhile, the Revels had apparently been moved from this first-floor hall where they lay in 1550, for when this hall is recited as the south boundary of Cobham's purchase in 1554, it is described as a house in the tenure of Sir John Cheke or his assigns.[3] So long as the Tents and Revels continued to be housed in Crown property, the offices had of course nothing to pay for rent. But after 1550 Cawarden, as naturally, claimed an allowance for rent, and in 1555 he was permitted to charge six years' arrears from Michaelmas 1549 at the rate of £3 6s. 8d. a year each for the official residences of the comptroller, clerk, and yeoman, £6 13s. 4d. for his own, £6 13s. 4d. for the office of the tents, and £6 13s. 4d. for the ' store and woorke howses of the revelles '. In the accounts for 1555–9 similar charges recur annually, but the allowance for Cawarden's own house is raised to £10 and that for the houses of the other officers to £5 each ; and the £6 13s. 4d. for the Revels office is specified as being ' for the rente of fyve greate roomes within the Blackefryers for the woorke and store howses of the Revelles '.[4] About 1560 the store-house was certainly not the hall over the buttery, but the great vaulted room in the south-west corner of the cloister, which had been the lavabo of the friars.[5] On the other hand, Sir John Cheke's tenure of his house had ceased and the vacated rooms had become available for workhouses. This is evident from the terms of a lease of the same rooms to Sir Henry Neville, executed on 10 June 1560, just after the Revels had been removed to St. John's.[6] Cawarden had died on the previous 29 August, and the lease was one of the first dealings of William More with the property. The principal rooms leased were precisely four in number. They had been ' lately called or knowen by the name of Mr. Chekes lodginge and sythence vsed by Sir Thomas Cawarden knight deceased for the office of the Quenes Maiesties Revelles '. They were bounded on the north by Lord Cobham's house, on the east by the houses of More and of Sir Henry Jerningham, who was Lady Kingston's

---

[1] M. S. C. ii. 44, 53 ; cf. p. 502.   [2] Ibid. 51, 121.
[3] Ibid. 16.
[4] Feuillerat, Edw. and Mary, 210, 230, 242, 301 ; Eliz. 103, 107.
[5] M. S. C. ii. 118, ' one other grete rome or vawte next the ground next the entre in the west ende of the garden openyng into the same garden wherin now the robes of the revelles do lye ' (Lease of 12 Feb. 1560).
[6] M. S. C. ii. 19.

son and heir, and on the west by another house of More's in the occupation of Richard Frith, and by the way leading to More's house and garden and a piece of void ground. Under them and leased with them were the buttery and pantry; and the lease also covered a cellar and a 'greate rome in manner of a grete seller having a chimpney' which I suppose to have been the late Revels store-house. The upstairs rooms were approximately 157 ft. long, 27 ft. wide at the north end, and 22 ft. wide at the south end.[1] The length agrees approximately with the sum of the lengths of the upper frater and of the hall over the buttery not included in Cobham's purchase of 1554; and it was evidently from these that Neville's holding was taken. But the head of the staircase must have interfered with his width in the middle, and it will be observed that, while he had the full width of the northern block, he had less than half the full width (52 ft.) of the frater. Evidently Cawarden had partitioned the frater to make it 'mansionable', and in particular had divided it into two tenements by a partition from north to south. Neville's was the eastern division. The western division and the rooms at the top of the staircase tower were in the tenure of Richard Frith, who had taken a twenty-four years' lease from Cawarden in April 1555 and had obtained a renewal from More on 24 December 1559. Here, in 1561, Frith kept a dancing-school.[2] Neville's lease also gave him a share in More's water-supply, a strip of the void ground, formerly the convent kitchen yard, between the northern block and Water Lane, and a right of way to the buttery and pantry through the rest of that ground, which was reserved to More. Neville's strip lay just south of Cobham's garden wall. That reserved by More was partly taken up by ways to his garden and gate-house entries. In the space between these was erected in 1561 a public conduit, which received the water-supply after it left More's tap, and passed it on to the Earl of Pembroke's house at Baynard's Castle. Here also stood a tennis ground, tenanted with a cellar under the northern block by Frith.[3] The gate-house entry, or at least the way to it, served Frith's house, as well as More's own. Near it were certain rooms, reserved for More's use or that of his servant John Horley, which may have been constructed out of the 'blind' parlour. The great stairs in the tower between the two blocks were probably assigned to Frith. They were not included in Neville's lease, and he was specifically debarred from any right of access through More's house

---

[1] Cf. p. 489.   [2] *M. S. C.* ii. 105, 118.   [3] Ibid. 119, 120.

or garden except by More's licence. It was probably contemplated that he would build stairs to the upper floor for
himself, and this is perhaps why More exacted no fine on
the execution of the lease.[1] At any rate Neville did build
stairs on the west of the house, placing them not in his own
strip of yard but in More's, with his water-cock in a little
room at the stair foot. The pale of Frith's tennis court was
altered to allow of access between it and Neville's stairs
from More's garden entry to his gate-house entry.[2] In his
own strip Neville built a kitchen and another set of stairs
behind it which must have led into the extreme north end
of his house, as the site of the kitchen underlay, not Neville's
own rooms, but those purchased by Cobham in 1554. The
rest of the strip served as a woodyard, and had a privy in
it. Presumably the original convent kitchen acquired by
Cawarden had been pulled down. Within the house Neville
put up partitions, turning his four rooms into six, of which
it may be inferred that two lay in the northern block and
four in the southern, and adorning one of these latter with
wainscoting most of the way round, and with a great round
portal.[3] About Lady Day 1568 More bought back the lease
from Neville for £100, doubtless in consideration of the
improvements.[4] For a time it seems to have been occupied
by the Silk Dyers Company.[5] On 6 February 1571 it was let
to William Lord Cobham, the terms of whose lease closely
resemble those of Neville's, but record the changes made
during his predecessor's tenancy.[6] Cobham gave up the
house in 1576, and on 27 August of that year Neville wrote
to More to recommend a new applicant for the tenancy,
his friend Richard Farrant. With it came an application
from Farrant himself. Apparently his tenancy entailed the
removal of an Italian, who may have been one of the silk
dyers, and he desired to be allowed to take down one of the
partitions. On 17 September he wrote to ask that a small
room, 6 ft. by 4½ ft., occupied by More's man Bradshaw
might be added to his holding.[7] His lease was executed on
20 December.[8] It gives him all the rooms which Neville
had had, with the exception of the former Revels store-
house, which is now described as ' that great rome nowe
vsed for a wasshynge howse '; and it adds the little room
specially asked for, which had been contrived by throwing

[1] Wallace, i. 175.   [2] M. S. C. ii. 119.
[3] Ibid. 27; Wallace, i. 175.   [4] Wallace, i. 175.
[5] M. S. C. ii. 120.   [6] Ibid. 27.
[7] Jahrbuch, xlviii. 92; Wallace, i. 131.
[8] Ibid. 93; M. S. C. ii. 28; Wallace, i. 132.

together a privy and a coal-house. Richard Farrant was Master of the Children of Windsor Chapel, and deputy to William Hunnis as Master of the Children of the Chapel Royal, and his object in taking the house was to have a room in which the children could give public representations for profit of the plays which they were afterwards to perform at Court. He carried out his plan, and so the old frater of the friars, once the parliament chamber of the realm, became the first Blackfriars theatre.[1]

More, according to his own account, was not best pleased at the use made of his house. He complained that Farrant, after pretending that he only meant to teach the children in it, had made it a ' continuall howse for plays ' to the offence of the precinct, and to fit it for the purpose had pulled down and defaced Neville's partitions, spoiled the windows, and brought the house to great ruin. He had also sub-let certain portions, and, as he was not entitled to do this under his lease without licence, More claimed the forfeiture of the lease. At this moment, on 30 November 1580, Farrant died, leaving the house to his widow Anne. For some months there were no plays in the theatre. Then Hunnis resolved to carry on Farrant's enterprise himself, and on a recommendation from the Earl of Leicester More appears to have given at least a tacit consent to a sub-letting by Anne to Hunnis and one John Newman on 20 December 1581. They were to do repairs and pay her £6 13s. 4d. in rent more than the £14 due to More. An unfortunate slip of the scrivener's pen cut Mrs. Farrant's profit down to £6 6s. 8d. They also gave bonds of £100 each for the due fulfilment of their covenants, and according to Newman's statement to More, paid £30 down. According to Mrs. Farrant they neglected their repairs and were extremely irregular with their rent, so that she was put to great shifts in order to satisfy Sir William

---

[1] On the plays performed there, cf. chh. xii, xiii (Chapel, Paul's, Oxford's). Collier appears to have been aware, probably from the Lyly prologues and the reference in Gosson, *P. C.* 188, of the existence of the earlier Blackfriars playhouse, and to have dated it, by a singular coincidence, in 1576. He knew nothing of the real facts, but inferred (*H. E. D. P.* i. 219) that the undated petition of the Blackfriars inhabitants, which is really of 1596, was of 1576, on the strength of a reference in it to a banishment of the players from the City, which an incorrect endorsement on a *Lansdowne MS.* (cf. App. D, No. lxxv) had led him to place in 1575. This did not prevent him from also assigning the petition, with a forged reply from the players, to 1596 (cf. p. 508). He proceeded to forge (*a*) an order dated 23 Dec. 1579 for the toleration of Leicester's men at the Blackfriars (*New Facts*, 9), and (*b*) a memorial by Shakespeare and others as Queen's men and Blackfriars ' sharers ' in 1589 (*New Facts*, 11 ; cf. Ingleby, 244, 249).

More, disposing of a small reversion given her by the Queen, pawning her plate and jewels, selling a dozen of gold buttons here and a set of viols there, and borrowing of powerful friends such as Lord Cobham or Henry Sackford, the Master of the Tents.   Meanwhile Hunnis and Newman disposed of their interest to one Henry Evans, a scrivener, and More, incensed at this, took definite steps in the spring of 1583 to recover his house by executing a fresh lease to one of his men, Thomas Smallpiece, and setting Smallpiece to sue for the ejectment of Evans.   The latter tried to elude him by a further transfer of the sub-lease to the Earl of Oxford, who passed it on to John Lyly, the poet ; and thus, says More, the title was 'posted over from one to another from me' contrary to the conditions of the original lease.   Doubtless Hunnis, Lyly, and Evans were all working together under the Earl's patronage, for a company under Oxford's name was taken to Court by Lyly in the winter of 1583-4 and by Evans in the winter of 1584-5, and it seems pretty clear that in 1583-4, at any rate, it was in fact made up of boys from the Chapel and Paul's.[1]   More, however, pursued his point, and about Easter 1584 recovered legal possession of his house. Some months before, Anne Farrant, in despair, had appealed to Sir Francis Walsingham, and had also brought actions at common law against Hunnis and Newman for the forfeiture of their bonds.   They applied to the Court of Requests to take over the case, and there is no formal record of the outcome.   But in January 1587 Mrs. Farrant was again complaining to the Privy Council, and Sir John Wolley was asked to bring about a settlement between her and More, who was his father-in-law.[2]

So ends the story of the first Blackfriars theatre.   The premises which it had occupied came into the hands of Henry Lord Hunsdon, who was also about the same time tenant of More's mansion house and garden.[3]   It would seem that Lord Oxford and Lyly had passed on to Hunsdon their sub-leases from the Farrants and that, even when he recovered

---

[1] Cf. ch. xii (Chapel).

[2] *Jahrbuch*, xlviii. 99 ; Wallace, i. 152 (Will of Farrant, 30 Nov. 1580), 153 (Anne Farrant to More, 25 Dec. 1580), 154 (Leicester to More, 19 Sept. 1581), 158 (Anne Farrant to Walsingham, *c.* 1583), 159 (Court of Common Pleas, *Farrant v. Hunnis* and *Farrant v. Newman*, 1583-4), 160 (Court of Requests, *Newman and Hunnis v. Farrant*, 1584), 177 (Wolley to More, 13 Jan. 1587), 174 (Memoranda by More, *c.* 1587 ; cf. Dasent, xv. 137).

[3] *M. S. C.* ii. 123.   More's rental of 1584 includes £50 from Hunsdon for the mansion house, £20 from Oxford, £8 from Lyly ; that of 1585 the same three sums, all from Hunsdon.   But the two smaller sums represent twice Farrant's rent, which was £14.

legal possession from the court, More did not care to interfere with this arrangement. But there was evidently some friction. The sub-leases were due to expire in 1590 or 1591, and in April 1586 More refused to renew them. His excuse was that ' The howses yow had of Lyllye I determyne that assone as theye bothe shall cum into my handes to kepe them to the onelye vse of me and mye chylderne '. In acknowledging this decision, Hunsdon complained that the pipe of water belonging to one of the houses had been diverted to serve that of Lord Cobham. In 1590 he made a fresh attempt to secure a renewal. More at first drafted a letter of consent, but then changed his mind and told Hunsdon that he needed the houses for his daughter Lady Wolley and for himself on his visits to London. Hunsdon had suffered annoyance because the tenant of the next house ' having the vse of the leades, either by negligence or otherwise, suffereth the boyes to cutt upp the lead with knifes or to boore yt through with bodkyns wherby the rayne cometh throwghe '.[1] This allusion, together with that to the pipe of water, makes it clear that Hunsdon's houses included the rooms covered by Neville's lease of 1560, in which the right of dancing-master Frith to use the leads over the southern block is expressly safeguarded. I think it is probable that the two houses are merely the southern and northern sections of the Farrant holding, separately sublet to Hunsdon. It is known that Farrant himself, while in occupation of the theatre, had let off certain rooms. More's wish to retain the property for family reasons did not long outlast its immediate purpose of decently covering a refusal to the Lord Chamberlain. Frith's tenancy also came to an end, and for some period between 1590 and 1596 the rooms formerly constituting the upper frater were reunited in the occupation of William de Laune, a doctor of physic. The rooms to the north of them, after his appointment as Chamberlain of the Exchequer on 23 November 1591, were used by More for the purposes of the Pipe Office.[2] The buttery and pantry beneath were probably also relet in 1591.[3]

I must now turn to the history of the ' paved hall ' and ' blind parlour ' under the upper frater and the little chamber and kitchen to the west of these, all of which, when Cawarden

[1] Kempe, 495 ; M. S. C. ii. 123 ; Wallace, i. 186 (More to Hunsdon, 8 April 1586 ; Hunsdon to More, 27 April 1586 ; Hunsdon to More, 14 April 1590 ; More to Hunsdon, draft, 17 April 1590 ; More to Hunsdon, 18 April 1590). Did the Paul's ' boyes ' keep up connexion with the Blackfriars by learning dancing and perhaps playing in Frith's school ?

[2] M. S. C. ii. 61, 93, 94, 98.

[3] Ibid. 123 (Skinner to More, 11 Oct. 1591).

obtained possession in 1550, were under the shadow of a claim
by Sir Thomas Cheyne. Blagrave's occupation of the little
chamber terminated when the Revels Office moved to
St. John's in 1560, and on 10 December 1564 More drafted
a lease of it to one Laurence Bywater, who had in fact been
in occupation since 1560.[1] It is described as consisting of
a hall, a chamber above, a little room below, a kitchen,
a yard, ' a long entrie coming in ouer the yard bourded and
railed ', and a vault or cellar. The paved hall had been let
by 1572 to William Joyner, who used it as a fencing-school.
In this year Cheyne's claim was renewed by one Henry Pole
and his wife Margaret, who was the widow of Cheyne's eldest
son. The rooms chiefly in dispute were the paved hall and
Bywater's house, but the Poles seem also to have claimed
rooms in the tenures of Richard Frith and Thomas Hale.[2]
It may be conjectured that these were the rooms constructed
out of the blind parlour. On the other hand More made a
counter-claim, probably not very serious, to Pole tenements
in the occupation of Christopher Fenton, Thomas Austen,
and John Lewes. Incidentally, it appears that Cawarden
had not succeeded in removing all signs of papistry from the
Blackfriars, for Bywater's house is throughout described
in the interrogatories taken as the little house having chalices
and singing cakes painted in the window. The matter was
referred to arbitration.[3] Pole's case rested entirely on the
question of fact as to what the holding of Cheyne and his
predecessors actually comprised in 1540, since the grant
named no boundaries but merely gave Cheyne the houses
and lands then in his own occupation and formerly in those
of Jasper Fylole and of Thomas Ferebye and William Lylgrave.
Pole produced some witnesses who declared that before the
surrender by the friars one Purpointe had dwelt in Bywater's
house and kept a tavern in the fencing-school, and that
subsequently Ferebye and Lylgrave had occupied these
premises. They could not say that Cheyne himself had ever
had possession of them, but Pole was able to cite the order
of the Court of Augmentation in 1550 allowing Cheyne rent
for his large room as a store-house for the tents. In More's
view this rent was paid under a misunderstanding, and he

[1] Ibid. 50, 54.
[2] This may have been Thomas Hale, Groom of the Tents, who was
a witness in the case (ibid. 44), or the Thomas Hall, musician, who in
1565 was sub-tenant of Frith's garrets (ibid. 119).
[3] Ibid. 35 (memorandum by More), 36 (award by arbitrators), 40
(depositions of More's witnesses), 122 (notes of evidence by Pole's
witnesses).

seems to have suggested that the only houses occupied by
Cheyne and his predecessors were that afterwards occupied
by Portinari and one 'new built' by Cheyne, in which
apparently Lord Henry Seymour was living at the time of
the suit. Moreover, he produced a number of witnesses,
including Bywater, Blagrave, Thomas Hale, groom of the
Tents, Portinari himself, and Elizabeth Baxter, widow of
the former porter of the friars, who agreed in deposing that
the friars had never let these rooms, which were essential
as a breakfast room and a butler's lodging to their daily life,
and gave a perfectly consistent account of the various uses
of them after the surrender by Cawarden, Woodman, Phillips,
Blagrave, and Bywater, which have already been indicated
in this narrative. It does not transpire that More confided
to the arbitrators the suspicious references to Cheyne's
claim in the surveys of 1548 and 1550. However this may be,
their decision was in his favour on the substantial issue.
The Poles were required to acknowledge his right to Bywater's
house and the paved hall, as well as to the tenements of Frith
and Hale. More, on the other hand, was to abandon his
claim to the tenements of Fenton, Austen, and Lewes, and
by way of compromise was to execute a lease of Bywater's
house to the Poles at a nominal rent for fifty years or the term
of their lives. This he accordingly did. Nothing more is
heard of any of the premises involved until July 1584, just
after More had succeeded in putting an end to Lyly's theatrical
enterprise. By this date both Bywater and Joyner had gone,
and their places had been taken by another fencing-master,
an Italian, Rocco Bonetti by name.[1] Bonetti had acquired
from Margaret Pole, now a widow, her life-interest in the
butler's lodging. He had also taken over from Lyly two
leases, one of the fencing-school, the other of a house, the
property of More, immediately west of the butler's lodging.[2]
The latter he had repaired at some cost. He had even been
rash enough to put up additional buildings on More's land.
And he had not paid his workmen, to whom he owed £200.
The butler's lodging is described as being in great decay.
But this also, or its site, he appears to have enlarged, at the
expense of his neighbouring tenement on the west. He
feared the expiration of his interests, and got his friends,
of whom were Lord Willoughby, Sir John North, and Sir
Walter Raleigh, to approach More for an extension of tenure.
As regards the western house, More seems to have consented,

[1] On Bonetti's career as a fencer, cf. Wallace, i. 187 ; *M. S. C.* ii. 122 ;
Reyher, 257 ; G. Silver, *Paradoxes of Defence*, 64.

[2] *M. S. C.* ii. 56 ; Wallace, i. 188 (Willoughby to More, July 1584), 190.

after much reluctance in view of Bonetti's indebted condition, to a lease for seven years in 1586.[1] As regards the butler's lodging, he was mainly interested in the reversion after Mrs. Pole's death, and of this reversion he granted Bonetti a ten years' term by a lease of 20 March 1585.[2] The holding is described in much the same terms as those used in Bywater's lease of 1564. The measurements, however, are also given. The length from north to south was 25 ft. 2 in., and the width from east to west 22 ft. 6 in. But 4 ft. 6 in. of the length and 2 ft. of the width were not covered by Mrs. Pole's lease, and were taken, probably by an encroachment which the lease was intended to regularize, from More's tenement to the west. For the sake of greater accuracy, the measurements and boundaries of this western tenement are given. It was 33 ft. from north to south and 39 ft. 8 in. from east to west. It was bounded on the north by More's yard, on the south and west by a house of Mrs. Pole's, on the south by the way to Sir George Carey's house, and on the east by More's house in Bonetti's tenure, that is to say the house which is the subject of the lease.[3]

Sir George Carey was the eldest son of Lord Hunsdon, and himself became Lord Hunsdon on 22 July 1596.[4] He is not traceable in the Blackfriars before 1585, but continued to reside there until his death in 1603. The way to his house corresponds in position with the way to Lady Kingston's house of the 1548 survey, and he had pretty clearly acquired some or all of her property, including the infirmary under the upper frater.[5] The way must have followed a line from Water Lane, much the same as that of the present Printing House Lane. The fencing-school was accessible from it by a door next to Carey's.[6] Certain other data of the early surveys are a little difficult to reconcile with those of the later documents. The surveys indicate three parallel rows of buildings, of a comparatively insignificant character, extending over a space roughly 80 ft. square between the frater

---

[1] Wallace, i. 189 ; M. S. C. ii. 122. I do not think the lease of the fencing-school was in question between More and Bonetti. Both Raleigh's letter and the workmen's petition imply house-building, not mere internal repairs. Bonetti could have added no building to the fencing-school except perhaps the kitchen which adjoined in 1596 (ibid. 61). But the western house had been extensively rebuilt by 1584.

[2] Ibid. 55.

[3] Ibid. 56. The whole description from ' All wch six foote & a halfe ' (l. 18) to ' xxxix foote & viij inches ' (l. 29) is parenthetic, a point which the punctuation obscures.

[4] Cf. chh. ii, xiii (Chamberlain's).   [5] M. S. C. ii. 124 ; cf. p. 490.

[6] Ibid. 62 ; cf. p. 504.

block and Water Lane. The north row consisted of the two-storied Duchy Chamber, a narrow building 50 ft. by 17 ft., and the parlour of Sir John Portinari's house. These had a frontage on the kitchen yard. South of them came the rest of Portinari's house, and south of this the little chamber, 26 ft. long by 10 ft. wide, the little kitchen, 23 ft. long by 22 ft. wide, and an entry to the latter, 30 ft. long by 17 ft. wide, which I suppose to have debouched upon Water Lane. The little chamber and kitchen had their frontage on the way leading to Lady Kingston's. The house referred to as Chevne's in the 1550 survey is probably that occupied by Portinari. But Cheyne must also have had other property in the same neighbourhood, which the surveys do not mention. There was the house, probably that described as 'new built' in 1572, which he occupied himself, and which afterwards passed to Lord Henry Seymour.[1] And there were the three tenements which More claimed, but did not secure in 1572. These premises were leased as a whole by the Poles to Christopher Fenton on 31 May 1571, and appear to have been gradually cut up into smaller holdings. By 1610 there were four tenants and by 1614 five. They bounded More's property, and must have lain in the angle of Water Lane and the way to Lady Kingston's, just south of the entry to the little kitchen.[2]

The little chamber of 1548 is undoubtedly the butler's lodging leased to Bywater in 1564 and to Bonetti in 1585, which was a subject of the law-suit in 1572. But whereas it measured 26 ft. by 10 ft. in 1548, it measured 22 ft. 6 in. by 25 ft. 2 in. in 1585, and the enumeration of rooms in the two leases show that, although Bonetti may have built a small additional room upon a bit of land filched from More, there had been no substantial change since 1564. Further, while in 1548 it was bounded on the north by Portinari's holding, it was reached in 1564 by a railed and boarded entry across its yard, and documents of 1596 and 1601 make it clear that this entry terminated in a small porch opening on the kitchen yard.[3] Similarly the little kitchen, 23 ft. by 22 ft., of 1548 had been replaced in 1584 by a house 33 ft. by 39 ft. 8 in., and of this also Portinari's

[1] *M. S. C.* ii. 36, 47, 51, 122.

[2] Ibid. 36, 38, 56 ('the tenemente of Margrett Poole on the south and weste'), 70, 77, 81, 85, 125. Here must have been the chamber which Thomas Blagrave, finding the butler's lodging too small, hired of Parson Wythers, Cheyne's servant, from 1552 to 1560, and which Pole still had in 1572 (ibid. 53). But if it was strictly 'adjoininge' to his house he must have had the 'little kitchen' as well as the 'little chamber'.

[3] Ibid. 63, 71.

house had ceased to be the boundary, and a yard of More's had been substituted. Finally, More's successor, Sir George More, was in a position in 1603 to sell to one John Tice a strip of land bounded by Tice's house on the south, Water Lane on the west, and the kitchen yard on the north and east, which must have been just about where Portinari's parlour stood at the time of the 1548 survey.[1] I am now approaching the region of conjecture, but there is only one way of accounting for the facts. More must have acquired and pulled down Portinari's house, and thus not only let light and air into the somewhat congested district west of the frater, but also left room for extensions in the rear of the little houses fronting on the way to Lady Kingston's. The extension of the little chamber he had probably himself undertaken before 1564. It did not interfere with the chalices and singing cakes in the window, or prevent the house from being in decay in 1585. In 1572 it could be seen that the house had been covered with lead, but presumably was so no longer.[2] The extension of the little kitchen seems to have been an enterprise of Bonetti, of which More reaped the profits. The rest of the space gained was utilized for the fencing-school kitchen, for a staircase behind the Duchy Chamber, and for certain yards, all of which were in existence in 1596.[3] It is just possible that More also pulled down the west end of the Duchy Chamber.

By 1596 both the fencing-school and the butler's lodging had passed from the occupation of Bonetti. One Thomas Bruskett had the former and one John Favour the latter. This is the year of James Burbadge's great enterprise of the second Blackfriars theatre. Our first intimation of it is from Lord Hunsdon, in a letter to More of 9 January 1596.[4] He has heard that More has parted with part of his house for a play-house, and makes an offer for 'your other howse, which once I had also'. The deed of sale by More to James Burbadge is dated 4 February 1596.[5] The purchase money was £600. The rooms transferred are carefully described, but only a few of the measurements and boundaries are given. There were seven great upper rooms, 'sometyme being one

[1] Ibid. 125. An unfortunate hiatus in a document (ibid. 70) leaves it uncertain whether Tice occupied one of Mrs. Pole's houses or More's enlarged 'little kitchen'.

[2] Ibid. 50.   [3] Cf. p. 504.

[4] Kempe, 496; Wallace, i. 195; M. S. C. ii. 125, misdated 1595. The 'other' house was probably the mansion house, which was let to Ralph Bowes on 3 March 1596 (cf. p. 497). Hunsdon died on 22 July 1596.

[5] Halliwell-Phillipps, i. 299, from enrolment in R. O.; M. S. C. ii. 60, from counterpart executed by Burbadge in Loseley MS. 348.

greate and entire room ', enclosed with great stone walls, and reached by a great pair of winding stairs from the great yard next the Pipe Office. Other stone stairs reached leads above. These rooms had been lately in the tenure of William de Laune, doctor of physic. Beneath them, or beneath an entry between them and the Pipe Office, lay a vault, of which Burbadge was to have the use only, by a ' stoole and tonnell ' contrived in the thickness of his north wall.[1] Under some part of De Laune's seven rooms, and included in the sale, lay also rooms 52 ft. long and 37 ft. wide, known as the ' midle romes ' or ' midle stories '. These extended south to Sir George Carey's house, and were reached from a lane leading thereto, by a door next to Carey's gate. They had been in the tenure of Rocco Bonetti and were now in that of Thomas Bruskett, together with a kitchen adjoining, and two cellars reached by stairs from the kitchen, and lying under the north end of the middle rooms. Bruskett had one of these, and the other was occupied by John Favor, who dwelt in the house held for the term of her life by Mrs. Pole. This house did not go to Burbadge, but he had one of two small yards of which Favor had the other, between Mrs. Pole's house and the cellars. This yard was occupied by Peter Johnson, and Burbadge also took four rooms tenanted by Johnson, and surrounded by his yard on the south, Mrs. Pole's entry on the west, and the great yard next the Pipe Office on the north. Two of these were under De Laune's late rooms. The other two were under rooms, to the west of the north end of De Laune's, which were occupied by Charles Bradshaw, possibly the Bradshaw whose room was begged by Farrant in 1576. Bradshaw also occupied a little buttery, an entry and passage from the seven rooms, and a little room for wood and coals. This lay over the buttery, on the west side of a staircase leading to two rooms or lofts, one of which was over the east and north of Bradshaw's rooms and the other over the entry between the seven rooms and the Pipe Office. These were in the occupation of Edward Merry, who also had a room or garret over them reached by a further staircase. A staircase also led from Peter Johnson's yard to Bradshaw's rooms. Both Bradshaw's and Merry's rooms were included in Burbadge's purchase, which was completed by a small yard and privy on the north side of Pipe Office yard, east of Water Lane, south of Cobham's house, and west of a house of More's also occupied by Cobham. Burbadge was also to have the right of depositing coal and other goods

---

[1] I suppose that this was the old lavatory. If so, probably Burbadge's use terminated when this became a glass-house in 1601 ; cf. p. 506.

DIAGRAMS OF BLACKFRIARS
1596

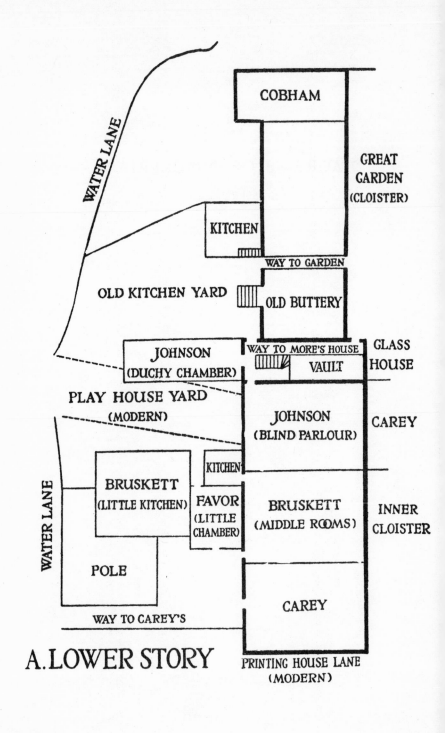

A. LOWER STORY

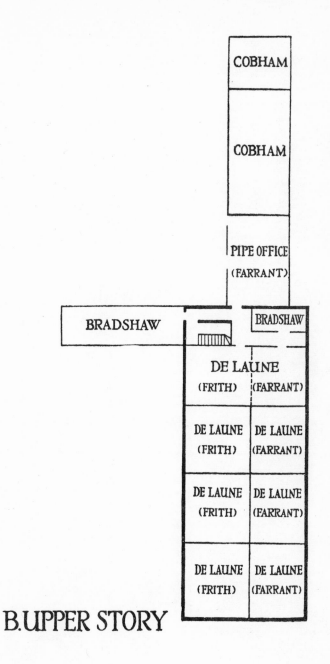

COBHAM

COBHAM

PIPE OFFICE
(FARRANT)

BRADSHAW

BRADSHAW

DE LAUNE
(FRITH)   (FARRANT)

DE LAUNE   DE LAUNE
(FRITH)   (FARRANT)

DE LAUNE   DE LAUNE
(FRITH)   (FARRANT)

DE LAUNE   DE LAUNE
(FRITH)   (FARRANT)

B. UPPER STORY

for a reasonable time in the old kitchen yard, now called 'the greate yarde next the Pipe Office', provided he did not interfere with access to the Pipe Office itself, or to More's garden or other parts of his premises. The description seems complicated, as one reads the deed, but I think that the disposition of the rooms is fairly intelligible.[1] The seven upper rooms, once a single great room, can only represent the whole of the old parliament chamber or upper frater, formerly divided into two distinct holdings. This, as we know, abutted across the staircase upon the hall in the northern block which had formed part of Farrant's holding and which More had converted into the Pipe Office in 1591.[2] The middle rooms, together with the two easternmost of Johnson's rooms, must together represent the space of the paved hall and blind parlour. There is no reason to suppose that Burbadge bought from More, or that More ever possessed, anything beyond this space on the ground floor of the frater block; and if the hall and parlour were, as I have suggested, of equal size, the total space passing to Burbadge on this floor was 74 ft. from north to south and 52 ft. from east to west. The rest of the floor had been Lady Kingston's and passed to Sir George Carey.[3] Johnson's other two rooms and Bradshaw's rooms above them, lying to the west of the north end of the seven great rooms, must be the two floors of the Duchy Chamber. The yards behind them were rendered possible by the clearance of Portinari's house. Bradshaw's two smaller rooms were on the staircase tower, and Merry's rooms and garret were partly at the top of this staircase and partly above the Duchy Chamber.

The property purchased by Burbadge was extended at various dates after his death in February 1597 by his sons Cuthbert and Richard. On 26 June 1601 they bought for £95 from Sir George More the reversion of the butler's lodging, subject to the life-interest of Mrs. Pole and to the ten years' lease after her death, which had in the interval since 1585 passed from Rocco Bonetti to Thomas Bruskett.[4] On 30 May 1610 they purchased two-thirds of the interests of the heirs of Mrs. Pole and of a mortgagee in the houses formerly held by Christopher Fenton, and on 7 July 1614 also purchased the remaining interest. These houses cost them in all £170.[5] If, as is not unlikely, they also purchased

---

[1] The account in Wallace, ii. 37, is not trustworthy; it assumes, in lieu of the Duchy Chamber and staircase tower, a 'north section' of the building 40 ft. from north to south.   [2] Cf. p. 498.
[3] Wallace, i. 196; ii. 38, is misleading here.   [4] *M. S. C.* ii. 70.
[5] Ibid. 76 (conveyance by Sir Richard Michelborne, George Pole,

at some time the house which in 1585 stood on the site of the little kitchen of 1548, and the bit of land sold to John Tice in 1603, the whole of the plot between the frater on the east, Water Lane on the west, the kitchen yard on the north, and the way to Lord Hunsdon's house on the south, will have passed into their hands. There is no indication that they ever acquired any part of Lord Hunsdon's house. This was apparently occupied by the French ambassador in 1623, when one of its upper rooms, used as a chapel, fell, and many persons were killed. Camden in his notes for Jacobean annals confused this room with the theatre.[1] About 1629 the King's printers, Robert Barker and John Bill, secured Hunsdon House for their press, and it remained the King's printing house until the Great Fire.[2] On 19 December 1612 the Burbadges obtained from the Cobham estate a piece of land for the enlargement of the yard near the Pipe Office, which was serving twenty years later to turn coaches in.[3]

To make an end for the present of topography, the fortunes of the property to the north of the Burbadge purchases may be briefly traced. Sir William More died in 1601 and his son and successor, Sir George, had no need for a Pipe Office. The rooms were therefore leased, with others, on 23 April 1601 to Sir Jerome Bowes at a rent of £14 6s. 8d. ' and certein glasses '.[4] I think that the other rooms included the old lavatory of the friars, once a Revels storehouse and thereafter a wash-house for More's mansion, and that it was in this room that Bowes established the glass-house which became an important industry of the Blackfriars.[5] On 19 June 1609 Sir George More sold this property, subject to Bowes's lease, together with the mansion house, the great garden and all that remained to him within the great cloister, to a syndicate,

and Charles Pole), 84 (conveyance by Richard and Elizabeth Mansell), 125.   [1] *Variorum*, iii. 62 ; Birch, ii. 426.

[2] H. R. Plomer, *The King's Printing House under the Stuarts* (2 *Library* ii. 353).

[3] *M. S. C.* ii. 83 (Recital of conveyance by trustees of Lady Howard) ; cf. p. 512.

[4] Ibid. 98 (Recital of lease in deed of sale of 1609).

[5] Ibid. 93, ' all that greate Vault or lowe roome adioyneing to the said greate Garden lyeing and being at the south west end of the said greate garden nowe vsed and imployed for a glassehowse ' (1609). By 26 June 1601 (*M. S. C.* ii. 70) the way south of the kitchen yard has become ' the yard or way . . . which leadeth towardes the glassehouse nowe in the tenure of Sir Ierom Bowes '. Bowes had obtained a patent for making drinking-glasses in 1592 and occupied a warehouse under the church in 1597 (*D. N. B.*). Dekker, *Newes from Hell* (1606, *Works*, ii. 97), says, ' Like the Glass-house Furnace in Blacke-friers, the bonefiers that are kept there neuer goe out '.

whose members in 1611 divided the purchase amongst themselves.[1] The former Pipe Office, now called the gatehouse, with its yard, part of the glass-house, and a strip of the garden 23 ft. 10 in. wide passed to William Banister. Banister's son Thomas sold them in 1616 to Gideon De Laune and De Laune in 1617 to Jacob Hardratt. Then Hardratt rebuilt the property and in 1619 sold back to De Laune a tenement which extended 43 ft. from north to south, and 24 ft. westwards from ' the great gate near the playhouse ' to the tenement occupied by a widow Basil. It had a small garden on the east, lying south of another garden belonging to De Laune.[2] The length of 43 ft. exceeds by 6 ft., the width of an entry, that of the Pipe Office rooms, the site of which De Laune's tenement no doubt occupied.

The big sale of 1609 did not include the kitchen and kitchen stairs built by Sir Henry Neville about 1560, or the wood yard which enclosed them. A bit of this yard had been included in Burbadge's purchase of 1596. The rest of the property, with the water supply, had been bought on 11 March 1601, by Henry Lord Cobham, whose house it underlay.[3] It had in fact been held by his father as far back as 1596.[4] In 1603 Cobham was attainted. His Blackfriars property was forfeited to the Crown, but regranted to his widow, Lady Kildare, and for some years remained in the hands of trustees for her and her daughter Lady Howard.[5] In 1612 an additional bit of the wood yard was sold, as already stated, to the Burbadges. Finally, in 1632 the estate was conveyed to the Company of Apothecaries, in whose hands it has since remained.[6] They must also have acquired the house of Gideon De Laune, who was one of their founders, and therefore their present premises, in their extent of 116 ft. from north to south, exactly replace the ' northern block ' of buildings which stood to the west of the main Blackfriars cloister, when Sir Thomas Cawarden took possession of it in 1550.

James Burbadge was not destined to see the success of

---

[1] *M. S. C.* ii. 92 (Deed of Sale).

[2] Ibid. 126. There is some confusion as to the position of Mrs. Basil's house. I think it was west of the gatehouse.

[3] Ibid. 88 (Deed of Sale, misdated 1602).

[4] Ibid. 64.

[5] Ibid. 83 ; *S. P. D. Jac. I,* viii. 18 (Grant to trustees for Lady Kildare). An *inquisitio* on Cobham's Blackfriars property (*1 Jac. I*) appears to be amongst the Special Commissions and Returns in the Exchequer (R. O. *Lists and Indexes,* xxxvii. 61).

[6] C. R. B. Barrett, *History of the Society of Apothecaries,* 42. The existing Hall dates from 1669–70. John Downes (cf. App. I, No. iii) and Pepys, i. 336, record the use of the older building by Davenant for plays at the Restoration. So Farrant's tradition survived.

his adventure. After all, he was prevented from establishing his theatre in 1596. Play-houses had just been suppressed in the City, and a number of the more important inhabitants of the Blackfriars disliked the idea of one being opened in their select residential precinct, where no common play-house had yet been seen. Farrant's theatre, nominally intended for the private practice of the Chapel boys, was presumably regarded as not falling within the category of common play-houses. A petition was sent to the Privy Council, amongst the signatories to which were Burbadge's neighbour, Sir George Carey, now Lord Hunsdon, Elizabeth Lady Russell, who lived a little farther up Water Lane, and Richard Field, the printer of Shakespeare's poems.[1] The extant copy of the petition is not dated, but later references assign it to November 1596, and inform us that as a result the Privy Council forbade the use of the house.[2] On James Burbadge's death in February 1597 the Blackfriars property passed to his son Richard.[3] It is not known what use he made of it before 1600, but in that year the resumption of plays by the Chapel children under Nathaniel Giles gave him an opportunity of following Farrant's example, and letting the theatre for what were practically public performances ' vnder the name of a private howse '.[4] With Giles were associated one James Robinson and Henry Evans, who had already been concerned in the enterprise of John Lyly and the Earl of Oxford ; and it was to Evans that, on 2 September 1600, Burbadge leased ' the great hall or roome, with the roomes over the same, scituate

[1] For text and discussion of bona fides cf. App. D, No. cvii. Collier, having already assigned the document to 1576 (cf. p. 496), uses it again for 1596 (*H. E. D. P.* i. 287). With it, in his first edition (i. 297), he printed a reply, now in *S. P. D. Eliz.* cclx. 117, by Pope, Richard Burbadge, Heminges, Phillips, Shakespeare, Kempe, Sly, and Tooley, on behalf of the players, which is palaeographically a forgery (Ingleby, 289) and could not be genuine in substance, since it refers to the Globe, which did not exist in 1596.

[2] Cf. p. 511. Wallace, ii. 53, thinks this an error or invention of the City in 1619, because the Privy Council registers ' giving all the official acts of that body, record no such order '. But the Privy Council registers notoriously do not record all the official acts of that body (cf. ch. ii). The petitioners of 1619 are not likely to have invented the ' peticion and indorsemente ' of 1596 to which they appealed.

[3] In the *Sharers Papers* of 1635 (Halliwell-Phillipps, i. 317) Cuthbert and the other Burbadges then living say ' now for the Blackfriers, that is our inheritance ; our father purchased it at extreame rates, and made it into a playhouse with great charge and troble '. Further, Cuthbert was associated with Richard in buying subsidiary property in 1601, 1610, 1612, and 1614 (cf. p. 505). But the leases of 1600 and 1608 were by Richard alone, and under one of these Cuthbert became his tenant.

[4] Cf. p. 511.

within the precinct of the black Friours ', for a term of twenty-
one years from Michaelmas 1600, at a rent of £40,[1] while
Evans and his son-in-law Alexander Hawkins gave a joint
bond in £400 as collateral security for due payment. Evans
set up a company, which under various names, and throughout
shifting financial managements, maintained a substantial
continuity of existence, and occupied the Blackfriars for
a period of eight years. Its fortunes are dealt with in detail
elsewhere.[2] Only those points directly bearing upon the
theatre as such need now be noted. In October 1601, when
Evans was negotiating a partnership with Edward Kirkham,
William Rastall, and Thomas Kendall, he apparently undertook to transfer his lease to Hawkins in trust to reassign
a moiety of the interest under it to these partners.[3] No
reassignment, however, was in fact made. Evans carried out
some repairs in December 1603, and trouble arose with his
partners because he severed the schoolhouse and chamber
over the same from the great hall and used them as private
apartments to dine and sup in.[4] When the playing companies
were hard hit by the plague of 1603–4, Evans began to treat
with Burbadge for a surrender of the lease.[5] This came to
nothing at the time, but in August 1608, when the Revels
company was in disgrace for playing Chapman's *Byron* and
Kirkham had declared a desire to make an end of the speculation, the suggestion was revived, and the surrender, probably
with the assent of Hawkins, actually took place.[6] As part of
his consideration, Evans, through a nominee, was admitted by
Burbadge into a new syndicate, of which the other members
were Burbadge himself and his brother Cuthbert, and some
of the leading players of the King's company, by whom it
was intended that the Blackfriars should now be used.[7] The

---

[1] Fleay, 211, 234, 240.   [2] Cf. ch. xii.
   [3] Fleay, 224, 230, 245, 250. Evans maintained that the assignment
to Hawkins was absolute, to cover his liability under the bond to Burbadge.
But the court appears to have held that a reassignment was intended,
but that ' the conveyance was never perfected and sealed '.
   [4] Wallace, ii. 89, from unpublished document ; *Evans v. Kirkham* in
Fleay, 214.
   [5] Ibid. 235.   [6] Ibid. 221, 231, 235, 246.
   [7] The Burbadges say in the *Sharers Papers* of 1635, ' the more to
strengthen the service, the boys daily wearing out, it was considered that
house would be as fit for ourselves, and so purchased the lease remaining
from Evans with our money, and placed men players, which were Hemings,
Condall, Shakspeare, etc.'. They also say that the players had their
shares ' of us for nothing '. Very likely they paid no fine, but they had
to pay their quota towards rent. It is reasonable to infer that Thomas
Evans was a relative and nominee of Henry Evans. Kirkham's allegation
in the 1612 litigation that Henry Evans had shared in the Blackfriars
profits during the past four years (Fleay, 225) was not seriously contested.

King's men probably entered upon their occupation of the theatre in the autumn of 1609, and thereafter used it alterna·tively with the Globe, as their winter house, up to the end of their career in 1642.[1] The new syndicate consisted of seven partners, who may be called ' housekeepers ', in accordance with the terminology found in use in 1635, in order to dis·tinguish them from the ' sharers ' in the acting profits of the company.[2] On 9 August 1608 Richard Burbadge executed six leases, each conveying a seventh part of the play-house for a term of twenty-one years from the previous midsummer, and entailing the payment of a seventh part of the rent of £40. The six lessees were his brother Cuthbert, John Heminges, William Shakespeare, Henry Condell, William Sly, and Thomas Evans. The remaining interest he no doubt retained himself. Sly, however, died five days later, and his share was sur·rendered by his executrix, and divided amongst the other partners. On 25 August 1611 it was transferred to William Ostler. After his death on 16 December 1614 it should have passed to his widow, Thomasina, but her father John Heminges retained it, and in 1629 she estimated that he had thus defrauded her of profits at the rate of £20 a year.[3] At some date later than 1611 John Underwood must have been admitted to a share, for he owned one at his death in 1624. The original leases terminated in 1629. Probably new ones were then entered into, for by 1633 we find that the rent had been increased to £50, and in 1635 that the interest of the housekeepers had still four years to run, and that it was divided not into seven, but into eight parts. Cuthbert Burbadge and the widows of Richard Burbadge and Henry Condell still represented the original holders. Two parts had been bought in 1633 and 1634 from Heminges's son by John Shank. One part was still held in the name of Under·wood, but a third of it was apparently in the hands of Eillart Swanston. John Lowin and Joseph Taylor had each a part. As a result of the dispute the Lord Chamberlain ordered a new partition under which Shank resigned one share to be divided between Swanston, Thomas Pollard, and Robert Benfield.[4]

---

[1] Cf. ch. xiii. Collier (*New Facts*, 16) printed a document professing· to set out action taken by the City against scurrilities of Kempe and Armin at Blackfriars in 1605. But this cannot be traced in the City archives (S. Lee in *D. N. B.* s.v. Kempe), and the City did not obtain control of the Blackfriars until 1608 (cf. p. 480). It is probably a forgery.

[2] Cf. vol. i, p. 357.

[3] C. W. Wallace, *Advance Sheets from Shakespeare, the Globe, and Black·friars* (p.p. 1909).

[4] *Sharers Papers* in Halliwell-Phillipps, i. 312. Collier, *Alleyn Memoirs*,

The occupation of the Blackfriars by the King's men was not wholly peaceful. The beginning of their tenure almost exactly coincided with the grant of the new charter by which the jurisdiction of the City was extended to the precinct.[1] It was not, however, until 1619 that an attempt was made to invoke this jurisdiction against them. In that year the officials of the precinct and the church of St. Anne's, backed up by a few of the inhabitants, sent a petition to the Corporation, in which they recited the inconveniences due to a play-house in their midst, recalled the action taken by the Privy Council in 1596, as well as the Star Chamber order of 1600 limiting the London play-houses to two, and begged that conformity to the wishes of the Council might be enforced. The Corporation made an order for the suppression of the Blackfriars on 21 January 1619.[2] It clearly remained inoperative, but explains why the King's men thought it desirable to obtain a fresh patent, dated on 27 March 1619, in which their right to play at 'their private house scituate in the precinctes of the Blackfriers', as well as at the Globe, was explicitly stated.[3] They had to face another attack in 1631. Their opponents on this occasion approached Laud, then Bishop of London.[4] After some delay Laud seems to have brought the matter before the Privy Council. The idea was

105, conjectures that Alleyn bought Shakespeare's interest in April 1612, and it appears from G. F. Warner, *Dulwich MSS.* 115, 172, 174, that he forged entries in documents relating to other property of Alleyn's in Blackfriars, as a support to this conjecture.

[1] Cf. p. 480.

[2] Text in Halliwell-Phillipps, i. 311, and Harrison, iv. 323, from City *Repertory*, xxxiv, f. 38ᵛ. The two petitions of the officials and inhabitants are in *M. S. C.* i. 90, from *Remembrancia*, v. 28, 29. They are undated, but can be identified from a recital in the order. The officials allege 'that whereas in November 1596 divers both honorable persons and others then inhabiting the said precinct made knowne to the Lordes and others of the privie Counsell, what inconveniencies were likelie to fall vpon them, by a common Playhouse which was then preparinge to bee erected there, wherevpon their Honours then forbadd the vse of the said howse for playes, as by the peticion and indorsemente in aunswere thereof may appeare.... Nevertheles... the owner of the said playhouse doth vnder the name of a private howse (respectinge indeed private comoditie only) convert the said howse to a publique playhouse.' They dwell on the inconvenience caused by the congested streets and the difficulty of getting to church 'the ordinary passage for a great part of the precinct aforesaid being close by the play house dore'.

[3] Text in *M. S. C.* i. 280.

[4] Text in Collier, i. 455, from *S. P. D. Car. I*, ccv. 32, where it is accompanied by copies of the Privy Council order and letter of 22 June 1600 (App. D, No. cxxiv) and the City order of 21 Jan. 1619. Probably the copy of the petition of Blackfriars inhabitants in 1596 (cf. p. 508), now in *S. P. D. Eliz.* cclx. 116, originally belonged to this set of documents.

mooted of buying the players out and on 9 October 1633 a commission of Middlesex justices was appointed to report as to the value of their interests.[1] These were estimated by the players at £21,990, and by the commissioners at £2,900. The only offer towards a compensation fund was one of £100 from the parish of St. Anne's.[2] Evidently the proposal was allowed to drop. On 20 November 1633, the Privy Council made an order forbidding coaches to stand in Ludgate or St. Paul's Churchyard while the performances were going on, but even this regulation was practically cancelled by an amending order made at a meeting presided over by the King in person on 29 December.[3]

It is rather disappointing that the numerous documents bearing upon the occupation of the Blackfriars between 1600 and 1608 should throw so little light upon the way in which James Burbadge adapted his purchase ' with great charge and troble ' to the purposes of a theatre. The lease of 1600 did not cover the whole of the property, but only a ' great hall or roome, with the roomes over the same '. Presumably this was the case also with the leases of 1608, since the rent was the same as in 1600. The rest of the premises, with those purchased later by the younger Burbadges, may be represented by the four tenements valued at £75 a year in 1633, and the ' piece of void ground to turn coaches ' valued at £6 was doubtless the fragment of the old kitchen yard north of the approach. The Kirkham law-suits tell us that one or two rooms were reserved for the residence of Evans in 1602 and that during the early part of 1604 ' a certen rome, called the Scholehouse, and a certen chamber over the same ' had been ' seuered from the said great hall, and made fitt by' Evans 'at his owne proper cost and chardges, to dyne

---

[1] *M. S. C.* i. 386.

[2] The report of the commissioners is printed by Collier, *New Facts,* 27, and *H. E. D. P.* i. 477. It is confirmed by a memorandum of Secretary Windebank in *S. P. D. Car. I,* ccli, p. 293, and I think Ingleby, 304, is wrong in suspecting a forgery (cf. *M. S. C.* i. 386). The commissioners allowed (a) £700 to Cuthbert and William Burbadge for 14 years' purchase of the rent of £50 reserved to them by lease, (b) £1,134 for 14 years' purchase of an interest in four tenements rated at £75 and a piece of void ground to turn coaches at £6, (c) £1,066 13s. 4d. for 100 marks apiece to 16 players for ' the interest that some of them haue by lease in the said Playhouse, and in respect of the shares which others haue in the benefits thereof ', and for compensation for removal. Collier, *Reply,* 39, mentions but does not print another document containing a summary of the players' claim, with notes by Buck. But Buck was long dead. A third valuation published by Collier, in which Laz. Fletcher's name occurs, is certainly a forgery (Ingleby, 246).

[3] *M. S. C.* i. 386.

and supp in '.[1] Professor Wallace has a number of additional law-suits, still unpublished.[2] But the extracts from these given by him in 1908 add only a few details to those formerly known. They seem to amount to this. The hall was 66 ft. from north to south and 46 ft. from east to west. It was paved, and had a stage, galleries, and seats of which a schedule was attached to the lease. The stage was at one end of the hall. The school-house was at the north end of the hall.[3] At this end also must have been the entrance, as one of the petitions of 1619 locates it near the way used from part of the precinct in going to church.[4] It was doubtless by the gatehouse entry to the cloister, just beyond where the coaches turned. Unfortunately one is left quite in doubt upon the critical question as to which of the rooms known to us from earlier records were used for the theatre. It might have been the upper frater with the partitions removed; it might have been constructed out of the paved hall and blind parlour beneath, which appear to be represented by the ' midle romes ' and two of the rooms in the occupation of Peter Johnson enumerated in the conveyance to Burbadge. *A priori* one would have thought the upper frater the most likely. It may very well have been paved, like the hall beneath it, and a chamber which had held parliaments and a legatine trial could amply suffice to hold a theatre. On this supposition the rooms ' above ' the hall which were conveyed by the lease of 1600, and one of which Evans converted into a dining-room can only have been the room over the staircase and the garret over that. These, indeed, may have extended over the north end of the frater proper, although in the main that building appears, down to the time when Burbadge bought it, to have had nothing over it but leads.[5] There is a serious difficulty in the way of the alternative theory, which would identify the theatre with the ' midle romes ' on the ground floor. This is that these would most likely only be low rooms, vaulted to carry the heavy floor of the parliament chamber above. On the

---

[1] Fleay, 211, 213. I suppose it was on this that Evans spent £11 0s. 2d. in Dec. 1603 (Wallace, ii. 89).

[2] In *The Times* of 12 Sept. 1906 Professor Wallace gives the number of new suits as four ; in *The Children of the Chapel at Blackfriars* (1908), 36, as twelve. Presumably the Court of Requests suit of *Keysar v. Burbadge et al.*, printed in *Nebraska University Studies*, x. 336, is one of these.

[3] Wallace, ii. 39, 40, 41, 43, 49.   [4] Cf. p. 511.

[5] *M. S. C.* ii. 31, ' all the Leds couerynge the premysses ' (1576), 61, ' the stone staires leadinge vpp vnto the Leades or roufe over the saide seaven greate vpper romes oute of the saide seaven greate vpper romes ' (1596).

whole, the balance of probability appears to be strongly in favour of the upper frater.

Professor Wallace's account of the matter is categorical. ' The south section ', he says, ' underwent a thorough transformation. The two stories were converted into the auditorium called " the great Hall or Room ". . . . The roof was changed, and rooms, probably of the usual dormer sort, were built above the Great Hall.' [1] I do not know whether there is any evidence for this theory, which disregards a good many structural difficulties, in those parts of his recently discovered documents which Professor Wallace has not published; there is certainly none in those which he has. If not, I do not think we must assume that Burbadge undertook expensive building operations, when he had all the facilities for planning an admirable auditorium without them. Professor Wallace seems to have been led into his conjecture by an assumed necessity for providing space for three tiers of galleries. There is no such necessity, and in fact no evidence for more than one tier, although I dare say that the upper frater taken by itself was high enough for two. Professor Wallace cites a reference to ' porticibus *anglice* galleryes ', and points out that ' galleryes ' is a plural. This is so, but the ' galleryes ' were not necessarily superimposed; if one ran along the east side of the hall and the other along the west, they would still constitute a plural. Professor Wallace takes the step from his plural to three with the aid of Cockledemoy's address to ' my very fine Heliconian gallants, and you, my worshipful friends in the middle region '.[2] Obviously the ' middle region ' is not bound to be the middle one of three galleries; it may just as well be the space between the stage and the galleries.

It is beyond the scope of this inquiry to trace the detailed fortunes of the Blackfriars during its later years. By Caroline times it took place of the Globe as the principal and most profitable house of the King's men.[3] In 1653, when like the rest of the theatres it was closed, Richard Flecknoe recalled its origin and wrote its epitaph.[4] It was pulled down on

[1] Wallace, ii. 40.   [2] Marston, *The Dutch Courtesan*, v. iii. 162.
[3] Cf. p. 425.
[4] R. Flecknoe, *Miscellania* (1653), 141, ' From thence passing on to the Black-fryers, and seeing never a Play-bil on the Gate, no Coaches on the place, nor Doorkeeper at the Play-house door, with his Boxe like a Churchwarden, desiring you to remember the poor Players, I cannot but say for Epilogue to all the Playes were ever acted there :

Poor House that in dayes of our Grand-sires,
Belongst unto the Mendiant Fryers :
And where so oft in our Fathers dayes
We have seen so many of Shakspears Playes,
So many of Johnsons, Beaumonts & Fletchers.'

6 August 1655.[1] This site was used for tenements, which in course of time were replaced by *The Times* office which now occupies the site.[2]

ii. THE WHITEFRIARS

[*Bibliographical Note.*—The relevant dissertations are P. Cunningham, *The Whitefriars, the Salisbury Court, and the Duke's Theatres* (1849, Sh. Soc. Papers, iv. 89), J. Greenstreet, *The Whitefriars Theatre in the Time of Shakspere* (1888, *N. S. S. Trans.* 269), with text of the Bill and Answer in the Chancery suit of *Androwes v. Slater* (1609), and A. W. Clapham, *The Topography of the Carmelite Priory of London* (1910, *Brit. Arch. Assoc. Journal*, n. s. xvi. 15), with seventeenth-century plan of the precinct, reproduced by Adams, 312.]

The only suggestion of a sixteenth-century play-house in the Whitefriars is to be found in the statement of Richard Rawlidge in 1628 that one was suppressed there at a date under Elizabeth which he does not specify, but which may most plausibly be put at 1596 (cf. p. 359). It is not improbable that Rawlidge wrote ' Whitefriars ' when he should have written ' Blackfriars ', but Malone (*Var.* iii. 46, 52) accepted the statement and assigned the suppression to 1580. I do not suppose that Collier had any other basis than this for the ' more then 30 yeares ' of the following description which he alleged to be an extract from ' an original survey of some part of the precinct, made in March 1616 ' in his possession, and printed in his *New Facts* (1835), 44 :

' The Theater is situate near vnto the Bishopps House, and was in former times a hall or refectorie belonging to the dissolved Monastery. It hath beene vsed as a place for the presentation of playes and enterludes for more then 30 yeares, last by the Children of her Majestie. It hath little or no furniture for a playhouse, saving an old tottered curten, some decayed benches, and a few worne out properties and peeces of Arras for hangings to the stage and tire house. The raine hath made its way in and if it bee not repaired, it must soone be plucked downe or it will fall.'

[1] I do not know what value to attach to a print in the Gardiner collection, reproduced by Baker, 44, 78, as representing the theatre. It shows a Renaissance façade, which can have been no part of the mediaeval building. Adams, 197, reproduces a painting of mediaeval fragments found in rebuilding *The Times* in 1872, small ground-floor rooms divided by entries. But *The Times* must cover the site of Hunsdon House as well as that of the theatre.

[2] As an epilogue to this narrative and an example of how popular history is written, I quote D. E. Oliver, *The English Stage* (1912), 9, ' Blackfriars House, a deserted monastery on the Thames side, was granted by Edward VI in 1596 to the Court Players for their use as a playhouse, but it was not until the accession of Elizabeth that it received official sanction as a recognized place of public entertainment '.

The earliest record, therefore, on which reliance can be placed is the law-suit of *Androwes v. Slater* in 1609,[1] which recites the lease by Robert Lord Buckhurst to Michael Drayton and Thomas Woodford for six years eight months and twenty days from March 1608 of ' a messuage or mansion howse parcell of the late dissolved monastery called the Whitefriars, in Fleete streete, in the subvrbs of London ', while the articles of agreement between the sharers of the King's Revels syndicate (cf. ch. xii), of the same date, assign lodgings in the house to Martin Slater, and add

' The roomes of which howse are thirteene in number, three belowe and tenne above, that is to saie, the greate hall, the kitchin by the yard, and a cellar, with all the roomes from the east ende of the howse to the Master of the revells' office, as the same are now severed and devided.' [2]

The precinct of the former priory of the Carmelites or White Friars lay between Fleet Street and the river, to the east of Serjeants' Inn and to the west of Water Lane, which divided it from Salisbury Court, the old inn of the bishops of Salisbury, which had passed to the Sackvilles in the sixteenth century, and ultimately became known as Dorset House (Stowe, *Survey*, ii. 45). The precinct was a liberty, and its history, from the point of view of local government, had been closely analogous to that of the Blackfriars. Like the Black-friars, it came under complete civic control in this very year of 1608 (cf. p. 480). The Whitefriars mansion itself the Sackvilles probably acquired from the family of Thomas Lord De La Warr, to whom a grant of priory property was made in 1544 (Dugdale, vi. 1572).

From the King's Revels the Whitefriars passed to the occupation of the Queen's Revels (cf. ch. xii) in 1609, and continued in their use both before and after their amalgama-tion with the Lady Elizabeth's in March 1613. It is named on the title-pages of *Woman a Weathercock* (1612) and *The Insatiate Countess* (1613), and a reference in the prologue to ' daughters of Whitefriars ' shows that it was also the locality of *Epicoene* (1609). In February 1613 it was ' taken up '

---

[1] Jonas, 132, however, quotes from the register of St. Dunstan's, White-friars, with the date 29 Sept. 1607, ' Gerry out of the playhouse in the Friars buried ', which suggests use of the theatre before 1608. The King's Revels may well have started by 1607. He also quotes, without date, ' We present one playhouse in the same precinct, not fitting these to be now tolerable '.

[2] I do not know why Adams, 312, identifies the play-house with a cloister shown in Clapham's plan. Surely it is more likely to have been the hall also shown at the north-west corner.

by some London apprentices for an invitation performance of Robert Tailor's *The Hog Hath Lost His Pearl* (q.v.). From March 1613 the amalgamated companies had Bankside theatres available, first the Swan and afterwards the Hope, but it is clear from the Watermen's petition (cf. p. 370) that, at any rate before the Hope was built, they mainly used the Whitefriars. Daborne in a letter to Henslowe of 5 June 1613 speaks of the company 'comming over', presumably from the Whitefriars to Bankside, and on 9 Dec. 1613 suggests that a play of his would be suitable for Henslowe's 'publique howse', from which it may perhaps be inferred that Henslowe had also an interest in a 'private' house at the time (*Henslowe Papers*, 72, 79). Apparently conversion into a public theatre was then contemplated, for on 13 July 1613 the Master of the Revels received a fee of £20 'for a license to erect a new play-house in the White-friers, &c.' (*Var.* iii. 52). But this scheme was stopped by the Privy Council.[1] On 3 June 1615 Rosseter and others obtained their patent for the Porter's Hall theatre in Blackfriars (cf. p. 472), which contemplated its use by the Revels, the Prince's, and the Lady Elizabeth's, and incidentally recited that the Revels Children had been trained and exercised in the Whitefriars 'ever since' 1610. The amalgamation was dissolved in the spring of 1616, and the Lady Elizabeth's and the Revels probably disappeared from London. If, therefore, the Whitefriars continued in use, it was probably by Prince Charles's men, who would have been left homeless by the demolition of Porter's Hall early in 1617. That it did continue in use and that a renewed lease was still held by some of the parties interested in the house in 1608 is indicated by the suit of *Trevell v. Woodford* before the Court of Requests in 1642, from which it appears, according to Peter Cunningham, that Sir Anthony Ashley, the then landlord of the house, entered the theatre in 1621, and turned out the players, on the pretence that half a year's rent was due to him. In 1629 the Whitefriars was replaced by the Salisbury Court theatre, built on the site of an old barn just on the other side of Water Lane.

---

[1] *P. C. Acts* (1613–14), 166. One Sturgis had leased a house and garden from Sir Edward Gorge, and sublet the garden to 'one Rossetoe Kynman and others, who goe aboute to erecte a p[l]aye house thereupon'.

XVIII

THE STRUCTURE AND CONDUCT OF THEATRES

[*Bibliographical Note.*—The only Restoration treatises which throw any light on the pre-Restoration theatre are R. Flecknoe, *A Short Discourse of the English Stage* (1664), and J. Wright, *Historia Histrionica* (1699), extracts from which are in Appendix I.

Archaeological material was brought together by E. Malone in *Variorum* iii. 51, and J. P. Collier in *H. E. D. P.* iii. 140.

Modern investigation may be said to begin with the discovery of the Swan drawing in 1888. The principal dissertations up to 1916 are :

K. T. Gaedertz, *Zur Kenntnis der altenglischen Bühne* (1888) ; H. B. Wheatley, *On a contemporary Drawing of the interior of the Swan Theatre, 1596* (1888, *N. S. S. Trans. 1887–92*, 215) ; W. Archer, *A Sixteenth-Century Playhouse* (1888, *Universal Review*), *The Stage of Shakespeare* (10 Aug. 1907, *Tribune*), *The Fortune Theatre, 1600* (12 Oct. 1907, *Tribune*, repr. *Jahrbuch*, xliv. 159), *The Swan Drawing* (11 Jan. 1908, *Tribune*), *The Elizabethan Stage* (1908, *Quarterly Review*, ccviii. 442), *The Playhouse* (1916, *Shakespeare's England*, ii. 283) ; R. Genée, *Ueber die scenischen Formen Shakespeare's in ihrem Verhältnisse zur Bühne seiner Zeit* (1891, *Jahrbuch*, xxvi. 131) ; E. Kilian, *Die scenischen Formen Shakespeares in ihrer Beziehung zu der Aufführung seiner Dramen auf der modernen Bühne* (1893, *Jahrbuch*, xxviii. 90), *Shakespeare auf der modernen Bühne* (1900, *Jahrbuch*, xxxvi. 228) ; H. Logeman, *Johannes de Witt's Visit to the Swan Theatre* (1897, *Anglia*, xix. 117) ; C. Grabau, *Zur englischen Bühne um 1600* (1902, *Jahrbuch*, xxxviii. 232) ; W. J. Lawrence, *Some Characteristics of the Elizabethan-Stuart Stage* (1902, *E. S.* xxxii. 36), *The Elizabethan Playhouse* (1912, 1913), *Night Performances in the Elizabethan Theatres* (1915, *E. S.* xlviii. 213), *New Light on the Elizabethan Theatre* (May 1916, *Fortnightly Review*), *A Forgotten Playhouse Custom of Shakespeare's Day* (1916, *Book of Homage*, 207), *Horses on the Elizabethan Stage* (*T. L. S.* 5 June 1919), *He 's for a Jig or* —— (*T. L. S.* 3 July 1919) ; K. Mantzius, *History of Theatrical Art* (1903–9) ; E. E. Hale, *The Influence of Theatrical Conditions on Shakespeare* (1904, *M. P.* i. 171) ; E. Koeppel, *Die unkritische Behandlung dramaturgischer Angaben in den Shakespeare-Ausgaben* (1904, *E. S.* xxxiv. 1) ; W. Bang, *Zur Bühne Shakespeares* (1904, *Jahrbuch*, xl. 223) ; W. Keller, *Nochmals zur Bühne Shakespeares* (1904, *Jahrbuch*, xl. 225) ; A. H. Tolman, *Shakespeare's Stage and Modern Adaptations* (1904, *Views about Hamlet*, 115), *Alternation in the Staging of Shakespeare's Plays* (1909, *M. P.* vi. 517) ; C. Brodmeier, *Die Shakespeare-Bühne nach den alten Bühnenanweisungen* (1904) ; R. Prölss, *Von den ältesten Drucken der Dramen Shakespeares* (1905) ; P. Monkemeyer, *Prolegomena zu einer Darstellung der englischen Volksbühne* (1905) ; G. P. Baker, *Hamlet on an Elizabethan Stage* (1905, *Jahrbuch*, xli. 296), *Elizabethan Stage Theories* (3 Nov. 1905, *The Times Literary Supplement*) ; C. H. Kaulfuss-Diesch, *Die Inszenierung des deutschen Dramas an der Wende des 16 und 17 Jahrhunderts* (1905) ; G. F. Reynolds, *Some Principles of Elizabethan Staging* (1905, *M. P.* i. 581, ii. 69), *Trees on the Stage of Shakespeare* (1907, *M. P.* v. 153), *What we know of the Elizabethan Stage* (1911, *M. P.* ix. 47), *William Percy and his Plays* (1914, *M. P.* xii. 109); J. Corbin, *Shakespeare and the Plastic Stage* (1906, *Atlantic Monthly*, xcvii. 369), *Shakespeare his Own Stage Manager* (1911, *Century*, lxxxiii. 260); R. Bridges, *On the Influence of the Audience* (1907, *Stratford Town Shakespeare*, x. 321); E. K. Chambers, *On the Stage of the Globe* (1907, *Stratford Town Shakespeare*, x. 351); C. C. Stopes, *Elizabethan Stage Scenery* (June 1907, *Fortnightly Review*); R. Wegener, *Die Bühneneinrichtung des Shakespeareschen Theaters* (1907); W. H. Godfrey, *An Elizabethan Playhouse* (1908, *Architectural Review*, xxiii. 239; cf. xxxi. 53); C. W. Wallace, *The Children of the Chapel at Blackfriars* (1908); F. Schelling, *The Elizabethan Playhouse* (1908, *Proc. of Philadelphia Num. and Antiq. Soc.*); A. A. Helmholtz-Phelan, *The Staging of Court Dramas before 1595* (1909, *M. L. A.* xxiv. 185); V. E. Albright, *The Shaksperian Stage* (1909), *Percy's Plays as Proof of the Elizabethan Stage* (1913, *M. P.* xi. 237); A. R. Skemp, *Some Characteristics of the English Stage before the Restoration* (1909, *Jahrbuch*, xlv. 101); W. Creizenach, *Bühnenwasen und Schauspielkunst* (1909, *Gesch. des neueren Dramas*, iv. 401); B. Neuendorff, *Die englische Volksbühne im Zeitalter Shakespeares nach den Bühnenanweisungen* (1910); H. H. Child, *The Elizabethan Theatre* (1910, *C. H.* vi. 241); H. Conrad, *Bemerkungen zu Lawrence' Title and Locality Boards* (1910, *Jahrbuch*, xlvi. 106); C. R. Baskervill, *The Custom of Sitting on the Elizabethan Stage* (1911, *M. P.* viii. 581); J. Q. Adams, *The Four Pictorial Representations of the Elizabethan Stage* (April 1911, *J. G. P.*); F. A. Foster, *Dumb Show in Elizabethan Drama before 1620* (1911, *E. S.* xliv. 8); A. Forestier, *The Fortune Theatre Reconstructed* (12 Aug. 1911, *Illustrated London News*); M. B. Evans, *An Early Type of Stage* (1912, *M. P.* ix. 421); T. S. Graves, *A Note on the Swan Theatre* (1912, *M. P.* ix. 431), *Night Scenes in the Elizabethan Theatres* (1913, *E. S.* xlvii. 63), *The Court and the London Theaters during the Reign of Elizabeth* (1913), *The Origin of the Custom of Sitting upon the Stage* (1914, *J. E. G. P.* xiii. 104), *The Act Time in Elizabethan Theatres* (1915, *Univ. of Carolina, Studies in Philology*, xii. 3), *The Ass as Actor* (1916, *S. Atlantic Quarterly*, xv. 175); G. H. Cowling, *Music on the Shakespearian Stage* (1913); H. Bell, *Contributions to the History of the English Playhouse* (1913, *Architectural Record*, 262, 359); W. G. Keith, *The Designs for the first Movable Scenery on the English Stage* (1914, *Burlington Magazine*, xxv. 29, 85); W. Poel, *Shakespeare in the Theatre* (1915), *Some Notes on Shakespeare's Stage and Plays* (1916); J. Le G. Brereton, *De Witt at the Swan* (1916, *Book of Homage*, 204); A. H. Thorndike, *Shakespeare's Theater* (1916); T. H. Dickinson, *Some Principles of Shakespeare Staging* (1916, *Wisconsin Shakespeare Studies*, 125). More recent papers are noted in the *Bulletin* of the English Association. R. C. Rhodes' *The Stagery of Shakespeare* (1922) deserves consideration.

It remains to give some account of the iconographical material available. Of four representations of the interiors of play-houses, the only one of early date (*c.* 1596) is (*a*) Arend van Buchell's copy of a drawing by Johannes de Witt of the Swan, published in 1888 by Gaedertz and in more accurate facsimile by Wheatley (*vide supra*). The other three are Caroline. (*b*) A small engraving in a compartment of the title-page of W. Alabaster, *Roxana* (1632), may be taken as representing a type of academic stage, as the play was at Trinity, Cambridge, *c.* 1592. (*c*) A very similar engraving in the title-page of N. Richards, *Messallina* (1640), if it represents a specific stage at all, is less likely to represent the second Fortune, as suggested by Skemp in his edition of the play, or the Red Bull, as suggested by Albright, 45, than Salisbury Court, where it is clear from Murray, i. 279, that most of the career of the Revels company, by whom it was produced, was spent. (*d*) An engraved frontispiece to Francis

Kirkman's editions (1672, 1673) of *The Wits, or Sport upon Sport* (originally published by Marsh, 1662) has been shown by Albright, 40, to have been erroneously regarded as a representation of the Red Bull, to which there is an incidental reference in the preface to Part II, and must be taken to show the type of stage on which the ' drolls ' contained in the book were given ' when the publique Theatres were shut up '.

A Court interlude, with performers and spectators, might be supposed to be represented in (*e*) a woodcut prefixed to Wilson's *Three Lords and Three Ladies of London* (1590), but the subject is not that of the play, and the cut is shown by A. W. Pollard (*English Miracle Plays*, ed. 6, 1914) to be taken from S. Batman, *The Travayled Pylgrime* (1569), and ultimately from a fifteenth-century illustration to O. de la Marche's *Chevalier Délibéré*.

Of the exteriors of theatres there are (*f*) a small engraving of *Theatrum* in a compartment of the title-page of Jonson's *Works* (1616), which may be merely a bit of classical archaeology, but appears to have the characteristic Elizabethan hut, and (*g*) a series of representations, or perhaps only cartographical symbols, in the various maps detailed in the bibliographical note to ch. xvi. Doubtfully authentic is (*h*) a façade of the Blackfriars, reproduced by Baker, 78, from a print in the collection of Mr. Henry Gardiner, with a note (44) that the owner and various antiquarians ' believe it genuine ' ; and almost certainly misnamed (*i*) a façade engraved as a relic of the second Fortune in R. Wilkinson, *Londina Illustrata* (1819), ii. 141, and elsewhere, which is plausibly assigned by W. J. Lawrence, *Restoration Stage Nurseries*, in *Archiv* (1914), 301, to a post-Restoration training-school for young actors.

A small ground-plan (*k*) of the Swan appears upon a manor map of Paris Garden in 1627, reproduced by W. Rendle in Harrison, ii, App. I.

A rough engraving (*l*) on the title-page of *Cornucopia, Pasquils Nightcap* (1612) shows a section of the orchestra of a classical play-house as seen from the stage, and throws no light on contemporary conditions ; and (*m*) the design by Inigo Jones described in ch. vii is of uncertain date, and intended for the private Cockpit theatre at Whitehall.

I know of no representation of an English provincial stage, and unfortunately E. Mentzel, who describes (*Gesch. der Schauspielkunst in Frankfurt am Main*, 38) a woodcut of a play, with signboards, by English actors, probably at Frankfort, Nuremberg, or Cassel, in 1597, does not reproduce it. Some notion of the improvised stages used by travelling companies for out-of-door performances may be obtained from the continental engravings reproduced by Bapst, 153, by Rigal in *Petit de Julleville*, iii. 264, 296, and by M. B. Evans, *An Early Type of Stage* (*M. P.* ix. 421).

An engraving of the Restoration stage of the Theatre Royal, Drury Lane (built 1663), from *Ariane, ou Le Mariage de Bacchus* (1674), and another of the same house as altered in 1696, from *Unhappy Kindness* (1697), are reproduced by Lawrence, i. 169 ; ii. 140. Of the five engravings of the Duke's Theatre, Dorset Garden (built 1671), in E. Settle, *Empress of Morocco* (1673), one is reproduced by Albright, 47, and another by Lawrence, ii. 160, and Thorndike, 110.

Graphic attempts to reconstruct the plan and elevation of a typical Elizabethan stage will be found in the dissertations cited above of Brodmeier, Wegener, Archer, Godfrey, Albright, Corbin (1911, by G. Varian and J. Hambridge), and Forestier, and in the picture reproduced in W. N. Hills, *The Shakespearian Stage* (1919).

Various revivals have also been carried out on Elizabethan stages, with more or less of archaeological purism, notably in London (W. Poel, *Shakespeare in the Theatre*), Paris (*Sh.-Jahrbuch*, xxxv. 383), Harvard (G. P. Baker in *Sh.-Jahrbuch*, xli. 296), and Munich (*Sh.-Jahrbuch*, xlii. 327).]

tectum

porticus

sedilia

orchestra

ingressus

mimorum
ædes

proscænium.

planities siue arena.

quintum sed dispari et penultica, bestiacium confectat-
oni destinatum, in quo multi ursi, tauri, et stupenda
magnitudinis canes, distinctis caueis & septis aluntur; qui
ad

A HISTORY of the theatres would not be complete without some account of their general structure and economy in the disposition of auditorium and stage. I propose to begin with the more assured or less important points, as a clearing of the way for the difficult and controverted problems of scenic setting, on some of which I am afraid that no very secure conclusion can be reached.

It is necessary, in the forefront, to appreciate the distinction between the 'common' or 'public' play-houses and the 'private' houses, which, so far as our period is concerned, were Paul's, the Blackfriars, and the Whitefriars. This distinction is in its origin somewhat a technical one, for there is no reason to suppose that in the private houses the performances were private, in the sense that access to them could not be obtained, on payment, by members of the general public. Probably it is to be explained in relation to the Elizabethan system of State control of theatres, and represents an attempt to evade the limitations on the location and the number of play-houses which had been established through the action, first of the civic authorities and later of the Privy Council itself. This view receives support from the allegations made during the campaign for the suppression of the Black-friars in 1619 that the owner 'doth vnder the name of a private howse (respectinge indeed private comoditie only) convert the said howse to a publique playhouse '.[1]

It can hardly be supposed, however, that Burbadge could have hoodwinked the Privy Council merely by calling the Blackfriars a 'private' house, without finding any other means of differentiating it from the 'public' houses, and it is quite possible that the technical distinction, for which modern analogies could be found, consisted in the fact that admission was paid for in advance and no money taken at the doors.[2] Mr. Lawrence has very appropriately quoted in this connexion the Common Council regulations of 1574, in which an exception is made for performances 'withowte publique or comen collection of money of the auditorie, or

[1] *M. S. C.* i. 91 ; cf. ch. xvii. The Blackfriars is still the 'private house' of the King's men in the patent of 1619 issued to them after this controversy.

[2] It is true that, when the prentices took up Whitefriars for *The Hog Hath Lost His Pearl* in 1613, the admission *per bullettini* is said to have been 'for a note of distinction from ordinary comedians'. But the companies had no need to continue any special system of admission after they had the protection of their patents ; Dekker (*vide* p. 523) speaks of gatherers at private houses in 1609. After the Restoration, 'ballatine, or tickets sealed for all doors and boxes' were introduced at the Duke's Theatre in 1660 (R. W. Lowe, *Thomas Betterton*, 75).

behoulders theareof '; and though I do not suggest that the extension of this principle to Paul's or the Blackfriars fell within the intention of the order, the evasion may have been allowed, within the gates of Paul's or in a liberty, and for a well-conducted house attended by a well-to-do audience, to hold.[1] If so, it is probable that Paul's from the beginning and the earlier Blackfriars were in effect private houses. But the actual terminology does not emerge before the revival of the boy companies in 1599 and 1600. For some years past the title-pages of plays had vaunted them as ' publikely acted '.[2]   A corresponding ' priuately acted ' appears for Blackfriars in Jonson's *Cynthia's Revels* (1601) and *Poetaster* (1602), and for Paul's in Middleton's *Blurt Master Constable* (1602), while the antithesis is complete in Dekker's *Satiromastix* (1602), which was presented ' publikely ' by the Chamberlain's and ' priuately ' by Paul's. Somewhat later we find Field's *Woman a Weathercock* (1612) acted ' priuately ', and Chapman's *Revenge of Bussy D'Ambois* (1613) ' at the priuate Playhouse ' in the Whitefriars.[3] But by this time the distinction may be taken for granted as well established in general use.[4]

From the point of view, however, of stage arrangements, the technical *differentia* of a private house is less important than certain subsidiary characteristics.[5] The private houses were all in closed buildings, were occupied by boys, and charged higher prices than the ordinary theatres. These facts entailed variations of structure and method, which will require attention at more than one point. They naturally became less fundamental, but did not entirely disappear, after the transfer of the Blackfriars to the King's men in

---

[1] Lawrence, i. 230 ; cf. App. D, No. xxxii.

[2] The earliest example is *The Troublesome Reign of King John* (1591).

[3] But ' priuately ' is also used of strictly private performances on the title-pages of *Caesar's Revenge* (1607) acted at Trinity College, Oxford, and, later, W. Montague's *Shepherd's Paradise* (1659) acted by amateurs at Court.

[4] T. M., *Black Book* (1604), in Bullen, *Middleton*, viii. 42, ' arch tobacco-taker of England . . . upon stages both common and private'; *Malcontent* (1604), ind., ' we may sit upon the stage at the private house '; *Sophonisba* (1606), *ad fin.*, ' it is printed only as it was represented by youths, and after the fashion of the private stage '; Dekker, *Gull's Horn Book* (cf. App. H), ' Whether therefore the gatherers of the publique or priuate Play-house stand to receiue the afternoones rent ' ; Dekker, *Seven Deadly Sins* (1606, *Works*, ii. 41), ' All the Citty lookt like a priuate Play-house, when the windowes are clapt downe '; *Roaring Girl* (1611), ii. 1, ' the private stage's audience, the twelve-penny stool gentlemen ' ; *Daborne to Henslowe* (1613, *Henslowe Papers*, 79), ' as good a play for your publique howse as ever was playd '.

[5] Cf. Wright (App. I).

1609, and probably passed still further into the background after the introduction of roofed public houses in the Caroline age.[1] The title-pages generally describe the Blackfriars, the Cockpit, and Salisbury Court as ' private ' houses right up to the closing of the theatres, but the term, in so far as it connotes anything different from ' public ', seems to have lost what little meaning it ever had.[2]

De Witt, about 1596, describes the Theatre, Curtain, Rose, and Swan as ' amphiteatra ', and Hentzner in 1598 adds that they were all ' lignea '.[3] The Globe and the Hope were built later on the same structural model. The Fortune was also of wood, but square. Of the shape and material of the Red Bull we know nothing. Prologues and epilogues often refer to the internal appearance of the auditorium as presenting a ' round ', ' ring ', ' circuit ', ' circumference ', or ' O '.[4] If we can rely upon the draughtsmanship of the London maps, the external outline was rather that of a polygon. This evidence must not be pressed too far, for there is probably an element of cartographic symbolism to be reckoned with. The same house may appear in one map as a hexagon, in another as an octagon or decagon, and the late Hollar group differs from its predecessors in using a completely circular form. But there is confirmation in the Paris Garden manor map of 1627, which shows the ground-plan of the Swan decagonal, and in the statement of Mrs. Thrale that the ruins of the Globe still visible in the eighteenth century were hexagonal without and round within. This was of course the later Globe built in 1613, and there is some reason for thinking that the earlier Globe may have been of rather

---

[1] Lawrence (*Fortnightly*, May 1916) has shown that the rebuilt Fortune of 1623 and Red Bull of *c.* 1632 were probably roofed, and Wright's description confuses the two phases of these houses.

[2] Chapman's *Byron* (1625) is said to have been acted ' at the Blacke-Friers and other publique Stages ', Heywood's *English Traveller* (1633), *A Maidenhead Well Lost* (1634), and *Love's Mistress* (1636) to have been ' publikely acted ' at the Cockpit, and Shirley's *Martyred Soldier* (1638) to have been acted ' at the Private House in Drury Lane and at other publicke Theaters '. This is exceptional terminology, but shows the obsolescence of the distinction. [3] Cf. ch. xvi, introd.

[4] *Old Fortunatus* (Rose, 1599), prol. 81, ' this small circumference '; *Warning for Fair Women* (? Curtain, 1599), prol. 83, 88, ' all this fair circuit . . . this round '; *Hen. V* (Curtain or Globe, 1599), prol. 11, ' this cockpit . . . this wooden O '; *E. M. O.* (Globe, 1599), prol. 199, epil. 4406, ' this thronged round . . . this faire-fild Globe '; *Sejanus* (Globe, 1603), comm. v, ' the Globe's fair ring '; *Three English Brothers* (Curtain or Red Bull, 1607), epil., ' this round circumference '; *Merry Devil of Edmonton* (Globe, 1608), prol. 5, ' this round '. On the other hand, *Whore of Babylon* (Fortune, 1607), prol. 1, ' The charmes of Silence through this Square be throwne '.

different design. The verses on the fire by which it was destroyed speak of the stage-house ' as round as taylers clewe ', and the early Hondius map, while it shows the Rose as polygonal, shows the Globe as circular, with the upper half of less diameter than the lower. This construction reappears in the Delaram drawings, and is so peculiar that the representation may well be realistic. There was an obvious precedent for the amphitheatrical form in the bear and bull rings which preceded the public theatres, and I do not know that we need go back with Ordish to a tradition of round mediaeval play-places, Cornish or English, or to the remains of Roman occupation. A ring is the natural form in which the maximum number of spectators can press about an object of interest.[1]

There is nothing to show that, for the main fabric, any material but timber was used, until the Fortune was rebuilt of brick in 1623. Timber is provided for in the contracts for the earlier Fortune and the Hope, and these were modelled on the Globe and Swan. Oak was to be mainly used for the Hope ; no fir in the lower or middle stories. Burbadge's lawsuits show that timber was the chief object of his expenditure on the Theatre, although some ironwork was also employed, presumably to tie the woodwork together. The dismantled fabric of the Theatre was used for the Globe. Henslowe used a good deal of timber for the repairs of the Rose in 1592–3, and did the house ' about with ealme bordes ' in 1595. There was also some brickwork, and the Fortune and Hope were to have brick foundations, a foot above the ground. The Fortune was to be covered with lath, lime, and hair without. Henslowe also used plaster, and I do not see anything inconsistent with a substantially wooden structure in De Witt's statement that the Swan was ' constructum ex coaceruato lapide pyrritide . . . ligneis suffultum columnis '. This has been regarded as an error which prejudices the reliability of De Witt's observations, but the description is too precise to be disproved by Hentzner's generalized ' lignea ', and after all the strength of the building was naturally in the columns, and the flints and mortar—a common form of walling in the chalk districts of England—may well have filled up the interstices between these. De Witt adds that the columns might deceive the shrewdest ' ob illitum marmoreum colorem'.[2]

---

[1] Ordish, 12.

[2] Before the Swan was built, Nashe wrote in *The Unfortunate Traveller* (1594), ' I sawe a banketting house belonging to a merchant that was the meruaile of the world. . . . It was builte round of green marble like a Theater without ' (*Works*, ii. 282).

De Witt has also been criticized for giving the seating capacity of the Swan as 3,000. I dare say this is merely the exaggerated round estimate of a casual visitor, but Wheatley calculates from the drawing that the galleries might hold 2,000, and it would not be surprising if our rude forefathers sat a bit closer than we care to do. Moryson speaks even more largely of theatres ' more remarkable for the number, and the capacity, than for the building ', and ' capable of many thousands ', while no less than 2,000 got into Trinity College hall for the academic plays of 1615.[1] The frame of the Fortune was 80 ft. square without and 55 ft. square within. This allows a depth of $12\frac{1}{2}$ ft. for the galleries, and Corbin calculates a seating capacity, allowing 18 in. for a seat and 18 in. square for a standing man, of 2,138 or 2,558 at a pinch.[2] We do not know that the Swan was not larger than the Fortune, and have therefore no right to assume that De Witt was seriously out. Wright tells us that the Globe, Fortune, and Red Bull were ' large ' houses ; he is comparing them with the private houses of Caroline days.[3] The allusion in *Old Fortunatus* to the ' small circumference ' of the Rose perhaps hardly indicates that it was below the average size.

The Swan drawing is our one contemporary picture of the interior of a public play-house, and it is a dangerous business to explain away its evidence by an assumption of inaccurate observation on the part of De Witt, merely because that evidence conflicts with subjective interpretations of stage-directions, arrived at in the course of the pursuit of a ' typical ' stage. Still less can it be discredited on the ground that it was merely made by Van Buchell on ' hearsay evidence ' from the instructions of De Witt.[4] It is a copy, like the accompanying description on the same piece of paper, of De Witt's original, which De Witt says he drew (' adpinxi ') in order to bring out an analogy which had struck him between the English and the Roman theatres. It was for this reason also, no doubt, that he marked certain features of the structure on the drawing with the names of what he thought to be their classical prototypes. I do not, of course, suggest that the drawing has the authority of a photographic record. De Witt is more likely to have made it as an afterthought in his inn than during the actual performance, and

---

[1] Cf. chh. iv, xvi (introd.).　　[2] *Atlantic Monthly* (1906), xcvii. 369.
[3] Kirkman also says in the preface to *The Wits* (1672), ' I have seen the Red Bull Playhouse, which was a large one ' ; but he is referring, more certainly than Wright, to the rebuilt house.
[4] Cf. Albright, 40 ; Lawrence, i. 12, and *E. S.* xxxii. 44.

he may well have omitted or misrepresented features.   Certainly he can hardly have seen the trumpeter sounding when the action had already begun.   And the draughtsmanship is bad, and may have been made worse by the copyist.[1]   The upper part is done, with an attempt at perspective, as he may have seen it from a point in the middle, or perhaps the upper, gallery somewhat to the right of the centre ; the lower part as from full face, so that the pillars stand equidistant from the edges of the stage, as they would not have appeared to him in perspective.   His doors and the compartments of his stage gallery are of uneven sizes.[2]   But, with all its faults, the drawing is the inevitable basis of any comprehensive account of the main structural features of a playhouse, and I propose, leaving aside for the present the question of the possible hangings which it does not show, to take its parts one by one and illustrate them from other sources, and in particular from Henslowe's contracts for the construction of the Fortune in 1600 and the Hope in 1614.[3]

The outline of the building is round, or slightly ovoid.[4] The floor, which shows no traces of seating, is marked ' planities siue arena '.   This is the space ordinarily known as the ' yard ', a name which it may fairly be taken to have inherited from the inn-yards, surrounded by galleries and open overhead, in which, in the days before the building of the Theatre in 1576, more or less permanent play-houses had grown up.[5]   Spectators in the yard always stood, and the more unstable psychology of a standing, as compared with a seated, crowd must always be taken into account in estimating the temperament of an Elizabethan audience.   These are the ' groundlings ', and the poets take their revenge for occasional scenes of turbulence in open or covert sneers at their ' understanding '.[6]

---

[1] There is a dot in Wheatley's facsimile over the second well-marked ' r ' of the word ' orchestra '.   Is it possible that Van Buchell misread it ' orchestia ' ?

[2] Cf. Brereton in *Homage*, 204.   [3] Cf. ch. xvi.

[4] The *Theatrum* of Jonson's 1616 Folio t.p. is oval, rather than round, but it is safer to take this, in spite of its hut, as representing Jonson's notion of a classical theatre.

[5] Cf. ch. xvi.   Graves, 32, tries to minimize the structural influence of inn-yards on the theatres, and even doubts whether the actors preferred to act in these ' rather than in the great halls '.   But I do not think that he makes much of a case.   Had the inns, indeed, ' great halls ' at all ?

[6] Gosson, *P. C.* (1582), ' it is the fashion of youthes to go first into the yarde, and to carry theire eye through every gallery ' ; *Hamlet*, III. ii. 10, ' tear a passion to tatters, to very rags, to split the ears of the groundlings, who for the most part are capable of nothing but inexplicable dumb-shows and noise ' ; Dekker, *G. H. B.* (1609), ' your *Groundling* and

Well into the yard, leaving space for the groundlings on three sides of it, projects a quadrangular stage, which is marked 'proscaenium'.[1] The breadth is perhaps rather greater than the depth.[2] This was certainly the case at the Fortune, where the stage was 43 ft. wide, and extended 'to the middle of the yarde', a distance of 27½ ft. The level of the stage may be some 3 or 4 ft. above the ground. Two solid trestles forming part of its supports are visible, but at the Fortune it was paled in with oak, and in view of the common use of the space below the stage to facilitate apparitions and other episodes requiring traps this was probably the normal arrangement.[3] It has been thought that the stage of the Swan, like that of the Hope, which was in many respects modelled upon it, may have been removable. But this is hardly consistent with the heavy pillars which, in this respect certainly unlike the Hope, it carries. Moreover,

Gallery-Commoner buyes his sport by the penny . . . neither are you to be hunted from thence, though the Scar-crows in the yard hoot at you, hisse at you, spit at you, yea, throw durt euen in your teeth '; *Bartholomew Fair* (1614), ind. 51, ' the vnderstanding Gentlemen o' the ground here, ask'd my iudgement ', 59, 79 ; *The Hog Has Lost His Pearl* (1614), prol. :
> We may be pelted off for ought we know,
> With apples, egges, or stones, from thence belowe ;

W. Fennor, *Descriptions* (1616) :
> the understanding, grounded, men for their just reward,
> Shall gape and gaze among the fools in the yard.

So later, *Vox Graculi* (1623), ' they will sit dryer in the galleries then those who are the understanding men in the yard ' ;

Shirley, *The Changes* (1632) :
> Many gentlemen
> Are not, as in the days of understanding,
> Now satisfied with a Jig ;

Shirley, *The Doubtful Heir* (1640), prol. :
> No shews, no frisk and, what you most delight in,
> Grave understanders, here's no target-fighting.

[1] *Proscenium* is the proper classical word for the space in front of the *scena* ; cf. p. 539.

[2] Albright has no justification for introducing into his reconstruction of a typical Shakespearian stage the tapering, instead of quadrangular, platform which characterizes the late engraving in *The Wits*, and to a less degree those in *Roxana* and *Messallina*.

[3] Wegener, 125, collects examples of the use of traps. They served, *inter alia*, for the representation of ' hell-mouth ', which the Elizabethan stage inherited from the miracle-plays (cf. p. 544), and the space under the stage was known as ' hell ' ; cf. Dekker, *News from Hell* (1606, *Works*, ii. 92, 139), ' Mary the question is, in which of the *Play-houses* he [the Devil] would have performed his prize. . . . Hell being vnder euerie one of their *Stages*, the Players (if they had owed him a spight) might with a false Trappe doore haue slipt him downe, and there kept him, as a laughing stocke to al their yawning spectators. . . . Tailors . . . (as well as Plaiers) haue a hell of their owne, (vnder their shop-board).'

the Hope had to be available for bear-baiting, which entailed an open arena, and there is no evidence, and very little likelihood, that baiting ever took place at the Swan. Like other theatres, it sometimes accommodated gymnasts and fencers, but these would use the stage.[1] There are no rails round the stage, such as we may infer the existence of at the Globe.[2] The only scenic apparatus visible is a large bench, on which a lady sits, while another stands behind her in an attitude of surprise, at the rapid approach from an outer corner of the stage of a man in an affected attitude, with a hat on his head and a long staff in his hand. You might take him for Malvolio cross-gartered, were there any chance that *Twelfth Night* could have been written when the drawing was made, or produced at the Swan.[3] Probably he is a returning traveller or a messenger bringing news. The floor of the stage is apparently bare. Sometimes rushes were laid down, at any rate for interior scenes.[4] The Globe produced *Henry VIII*

---

[1] Cf. Graves, 41. The register of the association of Masters of Defence (*Sloane MS.* 2530 ; cf. extracts in A. Hutton, *The Sword and the Centuries*, 259) records many ' prizes ' played at theatres and theatrical inns during the sixteenth century ; cf. App. D, Nos. lx–lxii, *Case is Altered*, II. vii. 28, ' First they [maisters of defence] are brought to the publicke *Theater* ', and for later periods Henslowe, i. 98 (the Rose, 1598), the fatal contest at the Swan in 1602, and Herbert, 47, 81. For acrobats cf. App. D, No. cxxiii, on the use of the Swan by Peter Bromvill in 1600. Henslowe, i. 98, 106, records loans in connexion with vaulting performances with a horse, perhaps at the Rose, in 1598 and 1599 by John Haslett or Hassett, who was also paid for court performances (App. B) in 1603 and 1608.

[2] T. M. *Black Book* (1604, Bullen, *Middleton*, viii. 7) opens with *Lucifer ascending, as Prologue to his own Play* :

> Now is hell landed here upon the earth,
> When Lucifer, in limbs of burning gold,
> Ascends the dusty theatre of the world, . . .
>   . . . my tortured spleen
> Melts into mirthful humour at this fate,
> That heaven is hung so high, drawn up so far,
> And made so fast, nailed up with many a star ;
> And hell the very shop-board of the earth, . . .
>   . . . And now that I have vaulted up so high
> Above the stage-rails of this earthen globe,
> I must turn actor and join companies.

Rails are shown in the late *Roxana* and *Messallina* engravings of indoor stages.

[3] Cf. H. Logeman in *Anglia*, xix. 117.

[4] Dekker, *G. H. B.* (1609), ' on the very Rushes where the Commedy is to daunce . . . must our fethered *Estridge* . . . be planted ' . . . ' Salute all your gentle acquaintance, that are spred either on the rushes, or on stooles about you . . . take vp a rush, and tickle the earnest eares of your fellow gallants ' ; *1 Hen. IV*, III. i. 214, ' She bids you on the wanton rushes lay you down '. In *The Gentleman Usher* (c. *1604*, Blackfriars),

in 1613 ' with many extraordinary circumstances of pomp and majesty, even to the matting of the stage '.

Circling the yard and raised above it are three tiers of galleries, each containing three rows of seats. Beneath the first gallery De Witt wrote ' orchestra', above its seats 'sedilia', and between the middle and upper galleries ' porticus '. In the classical theatre ' porticus ' was the name for a covered gallery, and the classical analogy also makes it clear that by ' orchestra' De Witt meant to indicate the position occupied by the spectators of highest rank, corresponding to the seats of Roman senators, to which the name of the obsolete dancing place immediately in front of them had been transferred. It was not until the Restoration that the orchestra was allocated to the music.[1] The fronts of the galleries are supported by a number of turned posts. In the Fortune all the chief supports, presumably both in the auditorium and on the stage, were to be square and made ' palasterwise, with carved proporcions called Satiers '. Internal painting was contemplated, but was not covered by the contract. Other references to painted theatres suggest that the Eliza-bethan builders were not content with bare scaffolds, but aimed at a decorative effect.[2] Three seems to have been the regular number of galleries. Kiechel bears witness to it for the Theatre and Curtain in 1585; and there were three at the Fortune and at the Hope. The lowest gallery at the Fortune was 12 ft. high, the next 11 ft., and the uppermost 9 ft., and each of the two latter jutted out 10 in. beyond that below. This gives a total height of 32 ft., about three-fifths of the interior width of the house. The maps, therefore, make the buildings rather disproportionately high.

---

ii. i. 72, ' Enter Bassiolo with Servants, with rushes and a carpet ', and Bassiolo says,

> lay me 'em thus,
> In fine smooth threaves ; look you, sir, thus, in threaves.
> Perhaps some tender lady will squat here,
> And if some standing rush should chance to prick her,
> She'd squeak, and spoil the songs that must be sung.

[1] Lawrence, i. 39, 161.

[2] G. Harvey (1579, *Letter Book*, 67), ' sum maltconceivid comedye fitt for the Theater, or sum other paintid stage whereat thou and thy liuely copesmates in London may lawghe ther mouthes and bellyes full for pence or twoepence apeece '; Spenser, *Tears of the Muses* (1591), 176, ' That wont with comick sock to beautefie The painted Theaters '; cf. Graves, 68. Coryat, i. 386, in 1608, found a Venice playhouse ' very beggarly and base in comparison of our stately Play-houses in England : neyther can their Actors compare with us for apparell, shewes and musicke '. So in *Case is Altered*, ii. vii. 30, the plays in Utopia (= England) are ' set foorth with as much state as can be imagined '.

The uppermost gallery has a roof, marked 'tectum'. This in the earlier Globe was of thatch, which caused the fire of 1613, and left the unlucky King's men with little but 'wit to cover it with tiles'. I think the Rose was also thatched ; but the Fortune and Hope were tiled. In view of the jetties, such a roof would give some protection to those in the galleries, but the groundlings had none. Both the drawing and the maps confirm the statement of Wright that the Globe, Fortune, and Red Bull were 'partly open to the weather', and this was doubtless also the case with their predecessors.[1]

De Witt does not indicate any internal gallery partitions, but the Swan had these by 1614, for they were to be the model for 'two boxes in the lowermost storie fitt and decent for gentlemen to sitt in ', which were to be constructed at the Hope. Similarly the Fortune was to have ' ffower convenient divisions for gentlemens roomes, and other sufficient and convenient divisions for twoe pennie roomes, with necessarie seates '. These were to be ceiled with lath and plaster. An earlier example of the technical use of the term ' room ' for a division of the auditorium occurs in the draft Theatre lease of 1585, which gave the landlord a right to sit or stand in ' some one of the upper romes ', if the places were not already taken up. If the clause, like the rest of the draft, merely reproduced the covenants of the 1576 lease, the term was of long standing. Probably the divisions were of varying sizes. There would not have been much point in cutting up the space available for ' twopennie roomes ' into very small sections, but there were also ' priuate roomes ', which are perhaps the same as the ' gentlemens roomes ' of the contracts.[2] If so, these were probably to the right and left of the stage in the lowest gallery. But the whole question of seating and prices is rather difficult, and it is further complicated by obscurely discerned changes of fashion, which involved the adoption of the very inconvenient custom of sitting on the stage, and the consequent abandonment by the gentry of what was called the lord's room. Prices also, no doubt, tended to grow, at any rate for the better seats ; the ' popular ' prices always remained low.[3] I do not know whether the professional actors ever contented themselves, after their establishment in London, with merely sending round the hat,

[1] App. I ; but cf. p. 524, n. 1.
[2] *Malcontent* (*1604*, Globe), ind., ' Good sir, will you leave the stage ? I'll help you to a private room ' ; cf. Sir J. Davies' epigram, *infra*.
[3] Wright, *Hist. Hist.* 407, ' The prices were small (there being no scenes) '.

or, in mediaeval phrase, making a ' gatheryng '.[1] Fixed
prices must certainly have been the rule by the time of
Kiechel's visit in 1585, for he tells us that, on the occasion
of a new play, double prices were charged. This practice
helps to explain the fluctuating receipts in Henslowe's diary,
and was still in force in the seventeenth century.[2] Spenser
and his friends could have their laugh at a play for 1d. or
2d. in 1579, and ten years later Martin Marprelate could be
seen for 2d. at the Theatre and 4d. at Paul's.[3] Higher prices
are already characteristic of the private houses. In 1596
Lambarde informs us of a regular scale, apparently applicable
to all public entertainments. None, he says, who ' goe to
Paris Gardein, the Bell Savage or Theatre, to beholde beare
baiting, enterludes or fence play, can account of any pleasant
spectacle unlesse they first pay one pennie at the gate, another
at the entrie of the scaffolde and the thirde for a quiet
standing'. Platter, in 1599, reports the same scale and adds
a distinction, not made by Lambarde, between standings
and seats. You paid 1d. to stand on the level, 1d. at an inner
door to sit, and 1d. at a third door for one of the best places
with a cushion.[4] The twopenny galleries or rooms long
continued to be the resort of the ordinary playgoer, if he was
not satisfied to stand in the yard for a penny.[5] He sat close,

---

[1] L. Wager's *Mary Magdalene* (1566) has a prologue which says that
the actors will take ' halfpence or pence ' from the audience, but this was
probably used by strolling actors and continues the miracle-play tradition. At almost the same date, a jest in *Merry Tales, Wittie Questions
and Quick Answers* (1567, Hazlitt, *Jest Books*, i. 145) tells how men stood
at the gate of a play at Northumberland Place, ' with a boxe (as the
facion is) who toke of euery persone that came in a peny or an half peny
at the least '.

[2] J. Mayne in *Jonsonus Virbius* (1638) :
　　So when thy Fox had ten times acted been,
　　Each day was first, but that 'twas cheaper seen ;
　　And so thy Alchemist played o'er and o'er,
　　Was new o' the stage, when 'twas not at the door.

[3] G. Harvey (p. 530, *supra*) ; cf. Lyly, *Pappe with an Hatchet* (*Works*,
iii. 408) ; cf. *Martin's Month's Mind* (1589, App. C, No. xl). Lodge,
Scillaes Metamorphosis (1589), will not ' tie my pen to Pennie-knaves
delight ', and S. Rowlands, *Letting of Humour's Blood in the Head Vein*
(1600), bids poets not ' To teach stage parrots speak for penny pleasure ' ;
cf. *Case is Altered*, I. i. 104, ' Tut, giue me the penny, giue me the peny,
I care not for the Gentlemen, I, let me haue a good ground '.

[4] Cf. ch. xvi, introd. Field says in 1583 (App. C, No. xxxi), ' Euery
dore hath a payment, & euery gallerie maketh a yeerely stipend '.

[5] *E. M. O.* (1599), ind. 425, ' Let me neuer liue to looke as highe as the
two-pennie roome, againe ' ; T. Garzoni, *Hospitall of Incurable Fooles*
(tr. 1600), epist., ' a Player that in speaking an Epilogue makes loue to
the two pennie roume for a plaudite ' ; *Satiromastix* (1602), epil. 2690,
' Are you pleas'd ? . . . if you be not, by'th Lord Ile see you all—heere

and the insolent poets and pamphleteers classed him with the groundlings as a ' stinkard '.[1] His domain certainly included the top gallery, but about the other galleries I am not sure. There are some puzzling allusions to penny galleries and rooms, but probably these are not distinct from the ' twopenny ' ones, and the explanation is to be found in the practice of paying the twopence in two instalments, one on entrance, the other at the gallery door.[2] It did not long remain possible to get one of the best seats for the 3d. quoted by Platter, even if there was not already in his time a higher charge for ' the priuate roomes of greater price '.[3] There were both

for your two pence a peice agen before Ile loose your company . . . Good night, my twopenny Tenants ' ; Mad World, my Masters (c. 1604–6), v. ii. 36, ' some . . . that . . . took a good conceit of their parts into th' twopenny room ' ; Woman Hater (1607), prol. 5, ' I do pronounce this, to the utter discomfort of all twopenny Gallery men, you shall have no bawdery ' ; Fleire (1607), ii. 30, ' They (like your common players) let men come in for twopence a peece ' ; Dekker, News from Hell (1606, Works, ii. 96), ' You may take him . . . in the afternoones, in the twopeny roomes of a Play-house, like a Puny, seated Cheeke by Iowle with a punke ', Seven Deadly Sins (1606, ii. 53), ' Sloth . . . will come and sit in the two-pennie galleries amongst the gentlemen, and see their knaveries and their pastimes ', The Dead Term (1608, iv. 55), ' Players . . . prostitute them-selues to the pleasures of euery two-penny drunken Plebeian ', Lanthorn and Candle-Light (1608, iii. 216), ' Pay thy twopence to a Player, in his gallerie maist thou sitte by a Harlot', Raven's Almanac (1609, iv. 184), ' As if you sat in the moste perspicuous place of the two-penny gallerie in a play-house ' ; Roaring Girl (1611), v. 1, ' One of them is a nip ; I took him once i' the two-penny gallerie at the Fortune ' ; &c., &c.

¹ Dekker, Seven Deadly Sins (1606, Works, ii. 53), ' Their houses smoakt euery after noone with Stinkards who were so glewed together in crowdes with the steames of strong breath, that when they came foorth, their faces lookt as if they had beene per boyld ', Raven's Almanac (1609, iv. 194), ' Hee shall be glad to play three houres for two pence to the basest stinkard in London, whose breth is stronger than garlicke, and able to poison all the twelve penny roomes ', Work for Armourers (1609, iv. 96), ' tearme times, when the Twopeny Clients and Peny Stinkards swarme together to heere the Stagerites ' ; vide n. 2, infra, and p. 534, n. 1.

² Satiromastix (1602), 1669, ' a Gentleman or an honest Cittizen shall not sit in your pennie-bench Theaters, with his Squirrell by his side cracking nuttes . . . but he shall be Satyr'd and Epigram'd vpon ' ; T. M. Black Book (1604), ' penny-rooms at theatres ' ; T. M. Ant and Nightingale (1604), ' stinkards sitting in the penny galleries of a theatre, and yawning upon the players ' ; Dekker, Gull's Horn Book (1609, Works, ii. 208), ' thou . . . hast vouchsafed to be acquainted with penny galleries ' ; Wit Without Money (c. 1614), iv. 1, ' break in at plays like prentices for three a groat, and crack nuts with the scholars in peny rooms again '.

³ A. Copley, Wits, Fits and Fancies (1595; ed. 1614, p. 124), tells of a man cast off by his brother, an actor, who sent him sixpence in a sheet of paper, to show that, ' though his brother had vowed not in seven years to see him, yet he for his sixpence could come and see him upon the stage at his pleasure '. If Platter's 3d. was the highest normal charge in the sixteenth century, the 6d. may represent a first night's charge.

sixpenny and twelvepenny rooms by 1604.[1] These may
have been the same private rooms at varying prices, according
as the play was old or new. I take it that you only got
a single seat, even in a ' private ' room, for your 6d. or 12d.,
and not the whole room. Overbury or another gives 12d. as
the price of the ' best room ' as late as about 1614, but in
the same year the ordinary scale of charges was greatly
exceeded throughout the house on the production of *Bartholomew Fair* at the Hope, where a speaker in the induction says,
' it shall be lawful to judge his six-penny-worth, his twelve-
penny-worth, so to his eighteen-pence, two shillings, half-a-
crown, to the value of his place, provided always his place
get not above his wit'. This must have been a quite exceptional occasion, not merely a new play, but a new play at
a new house. Similarly, when Richard Vennar brought the
gulls to his swindle of *England's Joy* in 1602, ' the price at
cumming in was two shillings or eighteenpence at least '.

A special compartment in one of the galleries was not the
only privilege offered to the more fashionable playgoer.
He might, at one time or another, sit ' over the stage ' and
on the stage. De Witt's drawing shows, at the back of the
stage, a raised gallery divided into six small boxes, in each
of which one or two spectators appear to be placed.[2] It is
reasonable to suppose that these are sitting ' over the stage '.[3]

---

[1] Most of the allusions to 6d. charges relate to private houses (cf. p. 556),
but Beaumont's grammar lecture (cf. ch. xxiii) gives this price for the
Bankside, and T. M. *Black Book* (1604, Bullen, *Middleton*, viii. 41) has
' I give and bequeath to you Benedick Bottomless, most deep cut-purse,
all the benefit of . . . the sixpenny rooms in play-places, to cut, dive and
nim '. Later, *The Actors Remonstrance* (1643) professes that the players
will not admit into their ' sixpenny rooms those unwholesome enticing
harlots that sit there merely to be taken up by prentices or lawyers'
clerks '; cf. Lawrence, i. 36, who thinks that the lord's rooms became
the sixpenny rooms. For the 1s. charge, cf. p. 533, n. 1, and *Malcontent*
(1604), ind. 63, ' I say, any man that hath wit may censure, if he sit in
the twelvepenny room '; Dekker, *G. H. B.* (1609), ' When at a new play
you take up the twelve-penny rome next the stage ; (because the Lords
and you may seeme to be haile fellow wel-met) there draw forth this
booke, read alowd, laugh alowd, and play the *Antickes*, that all the garlike
mouthed stinkards may cry out, *Away with the fool* '; *Hen. VIII* (1613),
prol., ' may see away their shilling '; Overbury, *Characters* (ed. Rimbault,
154, *The Proud Man*), ' If he have but twelvepence in 's purse he will
give it for the best room in a play-house '.

[2] They include women, and certainly look more like spectators than
actors or musicians.

[3] E. Guilpin, *Skialetheia* (1598), ep. 53 :
  See you him yonder, who sits o're the stage,
  With the Tobacco-pipe now at his mouth ?
In *E. M. O.* (1599), 1390 (Q₁), Brisk is said to speak of lords ' as familiarlie
as if hee had . . . ta'ne tabacco with them ouer the stage i' the Lords

And some or all of those ' over the stage ' again, appear to
have sat in ' the lords room ' or ' rooms '.[1] Of such a room
we first hear in 1592, when Henslowe, repairing the Rose,
paid 10s. ' for sellynge of the Rome ouer the tyerhowsse '
and 13s. ' for sellinges my lords Rome '. The entry rather
suggests that this was not so much a room for ' lords ', as
a room primarily reserved for the particular ' lord ', under
whose patronage the actors played ; but however this may
be, it was probably available by courtesy for other persons
of distinction. The practice of sitting on the stage itself
first emerges about 1596.[2] It was general by the seventeenth
century, and was apparently most encouraged at the Blackfriars, where it perhaps lent itself best to the structural
character of the building.[3] It was known at Paul's, but was

roome '. Dekker-Wilkins, *Jests to Make you Merry* (1607, *Works*, ii. 292),
has a jest of ' one that sat ouer the stage ' on a wench in the twopenny
room. *Farmer-Chetham MS.* (seventeenth-century, ed. Grosart, i. 104)
has an epigram on Spongus, who ' Plays at Primero over the stage '.

[1] *Satiromastix* (1602), 2612, ' You must forsweare to venter on the
stage when your play is ended, and to exchange curtezies and comple-
ments with gallants in the Lordes roomes '. The subject is well discussed
by Lawrence (i. 29), *The Situation of the Lords' Room*.

[2] Sir J. Davies, *Epigrams* (prob. < 1596), ep. 28, *In Sillam*, ' He that
dares take Tobacco on the stage ' ; ep. 3, *In Rufum* :

> Rufus the Courtier at the theatre
> Leauing the best and most conspicuous place,
> Doth either to the stage himselfe transfer,
> Or through a grate doth show his doubtful face,
> For that the clamorous frie of Innes of court
> Filles vp the priuate roomes of greater prise :
> And such a place where all may haue resort
> He in his singularitie doth despise.

It is not, I think, sitting on the stage that is satirized in J. Hall, *Virge-
demiarum* (1597), i. 3, but a performance by illiterate amateurs on a ' hired
Stage '.

[3] *C. Revels* (1601), ind. 138 :

' 3. Child . . . Here I enter.

1. What, vpon the stage too ?

2. Yes: and I step forth like one of the children, and ask you, Would
you have a Stool, Sir ?

3. A Stoole Boy ?

2. I Sir, if you'le giue me sixe Pence, I'le fetch you one.

3. For what I pray thee ? what shall I doe with it ?

2. O God Sir ! will you betraye your Ignorance so much ? why, throne
your selfe in state on the stage, as other Gentlemen vse Sir ' ;

All Fools (c. 1604), prol. 30 :

> if our other audience see
> You on the stage depart before we end,
> Our wits go with you all and we are fools.

Isle of Gulls (1606), ind., ' But come boy, furnish us with stools '. . . .
' He [the author] is not on the stage amongst gallants preparing a bespoke
Plaudite '.

inconvenient on so small a stage.[1] And, as it certainly originated at the public houses, so it maintained itself there, in spite of the grumbles of the ordinary spectators, with whose view of the action the throng of feathered and restless gallants necessarily interfered.[2] It may have been profitable to the actors as sharers, but as actors they resented the restriction of the space available for their movements which it entailed.[3] The prologue to Jonson's *The Devil is an Ass*

K. B. P. (*1607*), ind. 41 :

Wife below Rafe below.

Wife. Husband, shall I come vp husband ?
Citizen. I cunny. Rafe helpe your mistresse this way : pray gentlemeи. make her a little roome, I pray you sir lend me your hand to helpe vp my wife. . . . Boy, let my wife and I haue a cupple stooles. . . . Come vp Rafe.

It must not be assumed from this burlesque that women usually sat on the stage, even at the private houses.

[1] *What You Will* (1602), ind., ' Let's place ourselves within the curtains, for good faith the stage is so very little, we shall wrong the general eye else very much ' ; *Faery Pastoral* (1603), author's note, ' If so be that the Properties of any of These, that be outward, will not serue the turne by reason of concourse of the People on the Stage, Then you may omit the sayd Properties '. In *Wily Beguiled* (possibly a Paul's play), 2021, comes the s. d. ' Stands vpon a stoole ', in a wood scene.

[2] *E. M. O.* (*1599*), 585 (Q$_1$), ' Sit o' the stage and flout ; prouided, you haue a good suit ' ; 1784, ' rich apparell . . . takes possession of your stage at your new play ' ; *A Mad World, my Masters* (*c. 1604-6*), v. ii. 38, ' The actors have been found i' th' morning in a less compass than their stage, though it were ne'er so full of gentlemen ' ; *Woman Hater* (1607), i. 3, ' All the Gallants on the stage rise, vail to me, kiss their hand, offer me their places '. It is true that *Roaring Girl* (1611), ii. 1, has ' the private stages audience, the twelve-penny stool gentlemen ', but this may only point to a higher price for a stool at the private house, and in any case cannot outweigh the allusions of Davies and Jonson before the Black-friars, or probably Paul's, were reopened, or T. M. *Black Book* (1604, Bullen, *Middleton*, viii. 42), ' Barnaby Burning-glass, arch tobacco-taker of England, in ordinaries, upon stages both common and private' ; Dekker, *G. H. B.* (1609), ' Whether therefore the gatherers of the publique or priuate Play-house stand to receiue the afternoones rent, let our Gallant (hauing paid it) presently aduance himselfe vp to the Throne of the Stage ' (cf. the whole passage on the procedure and advantages of sitting on the stage, where Dekker clearly mingles traits of both types of house, in App. H). Wallace, ii. 130, argues that the custom was started at Black-friars and was confined to the private houses, but is hopelessly confuted by C. R. Baskervill in *M. P.* viii. 581.

[3] *Malcontent* (1604, Globe), ind. :
' Enter W. Sly, a Tire-man following him with a stool.
Tireman. Sir, the gentlemen will be angry if you sit here.
Sly. Why, we may sit upon the stage at the private house. Thou dost not take me for a country gentleman, dost ? dost think I fear hissing ? . . .
Lowin. Good sir, will you leave the stage ? I'll help you to a private room.
Sly. Come, coz, lets take some tobacco ' ;
M. D'Olive (1606, Blackfriars), IV. ii. 173, ' I'll take up some other fool

of 1616 contains a vigorous protest.[1] But the gallant liked
to be seen as well as to see, and liked to slip in and out of the
tiring house and hob-nob with the players.   It was not until
Caroline times that the custom became intolerable.[2] On the
stage stools were provided for those who did not care to sit
on the rushes, and for these they paid at least sixpence and
sometimes a shilling.[3]   One result of the introduction of sitting
on the stage appears to have been that the lord's room lost
its attractiveness and consequently its status.   It fell into the
background, and became the haunt of a rather disreputable
class of playgoer.   The lords were now to be found either on
the stage itself, or in the private rooms of the lower gallery.
Presumably the ' grate ' to which the courtier of Sir John
Davies' epigram relegated himself, was in the lord's room,
perhaps fitted with a casement for scenic purposes.[4]   The
change is chronicled by Dekker in the passage of *The Gull's
Horn Book*, in which the gull is instructed how to behave
himself in a play-house.   He must by all means advance
himself up to the throne of the stage.

' I meane not into the Lords roome (which is now but the Stages
Suburbs) : no, those boxes, by the iniquity of custome, conspiracy of
waiting-women and Gentlemen-Ushers, that there sweat together, and
the couetousnes of Sharers, are contemptibly thrust into the reare,

for the Duke to employ :. every ordinary affords fools enow ; and didst
not see a pair of gallants sit not far hence like a couple of bough-pots
to make the room smell ? '
   Yet, Grandee's, would you were not come to grace
   Our matter, with allowing vs no place.
   Though you presume Satan a subtill thing,
   And may haue heard hee's worne in a thumbe-ring ;
   Doe not on these presumptions, force vs act,
   In compasse of a cheese-trencher. This tract
   Will ne'er admit our vice, because of yours.
   Anone, who, worse than you, the fault endures
   That your selues make ? when you will thrust and spurne,
   And knocke vs o' the elbowes, and bid, turne ;
   As if, when wee had spoke, wee must be gone,
   Or, till wee speake, must all runne in, to one,
   Like the young adders, at the old ones mouth ?
   Would wee could stand due North ; or had no South,
   If that offend : or were Muscouy glasse,
   That you might looke our Scenes through as they passe.
   We know not how to affect you. If you'll come
   To see new Playes, pray you affoord vs roome.

[2] Wallace, ii. 142.
[3] Dekker, *G. H. B.* (1609), ' You may . . . haue a good stoole for sixpence . . . creepe from behind the Arras, with your Tripos or three-footed
stoole in one hand, and a teston mounted betweene a forefinger and
a thumbe in the other ' ; cf. pp. 535, n. 3, 536, n 2.
[4] Cf. ch. xx.

and much new Satten is there dambd, by being smothred to death in darknesse.'

I return to the guidance of De Witt. The boarding between the yard and the lower gallery, which in the Fortune was overlaid with iron pikes, presumably to prevent the ground-lings from climbing over, shows two apertures, to right and left of the stage, one of which is marked ' ingressus '. From these steps lead to the lower gallery itself, and we may infer the presence of a passage to staircases behind, by which the upper galleries were reached. The contracts show that the Fortune, like the Globe, and the Hope, like the Swan, were to have external staircases.[1] Perhaps this accounts for the greater diameter of the lower part of the Globe in the London maps. Of external doors there were only two at the Globe, which caused trouble at the time of the fire, and two also at the Fortune, when Alleyn leased a share of it to Henslowe in 1601. One of these would in each case have been a door to the tiring house, giving access to the stage and the lord's room, while the other served the body of the theatre.[2] Those bound for the galleries paid their pennies at the theatre door, passed through the yard to the ' ingressus ', and made additional payments there and in the 'rooms', according to the places selected.[3] The custom explains itself by the arrangement between the sharers of companies and the housekeepers of theatres, which gave the latter a proportion of gallery takings in lieu of rent. ' Gatherers ', appointed by the persons interested, collected the money, and although this was put into a locked box, whence the modern term ' box-office ', there were abundant opportunities for fraud. At need, the gatherers could serve as super-numeraries on the stage.[4]

At the back of the stage, and forming a chord to an arc of the circular structure of the play-house, runs a straight wall, pierced by two pairs of folding doors, on which De Witt has written ' mimorum aedes '. Above it is the gallery or lord's room already described. This wall is the ' scene ', in the primary sense ; it is also the front of the ' tire-house ',

---

[1] Godfrey (*Architectural Review*, xxiii. 239) has no authority for his internal roofed staircases and landings in the narrow spaces between the galleries and the sides of the stage.

[2] Henslowe made a ' penthowsse shed at the tyeringe howsse doore ' of the Rose in 1591. Doubtless the stage could also be reached from in front ; cf. the *K. B. P.* passage on p. 536.

[3] Gosson, *P. C.* (1582, App. C, No. xxx), tells how youths are wont ' to go first into the yarde, and to carry theire eye through euery gallery ' in search of attractive company ; cf. p. 532.

[4] Cf. p. 541, and ch. xi.

or in modern phrase 'green-room', a necessary adjunct of
every theatre. The Theatre depositions of 1592 speak of
this as ' the attyring housse or place where the players make
them readye '. The drawing indicates nothing in the way of
hangings over either wall or doors, but in some theatres
these certainly existed. Thus Peacham, in his *Thalia's
Banquet* (1620) referring to much earlier days, tells us that

> Tarlton when his head was onely seene,
> The Tire-house doore and Tapistrie betweene,
> Set all the multitude in such a laughter,
> They could not hold for scarce an hour after.[1]

The front of the tiring-house is the ' scene ' in the Renaissance sense, and its characteristics will be of great concern in
later chapters.[2]   The Fortune tire-house was to be within

---

[1] Peacham, however, may be merely versifying the story of the choleric
justice and the provincial audience which laughed when he ' first peept
out his head ' in Nashe, *Pierce Penilesse* (*Works*, i. 188), and reading in
a feature, in the process, of the stage as known to himself ; and the same
applies to Davenant, *The Unfortunate Lovers* (*c. 1638*), prol., on the playgoers of old times :

> For they, he swears, to the theatre would come,
> Ere they had din'd, to take up the best room ;
> There sit on benches, not adorn'd with mats,
> And graciously did vail their high-crown'd hats
> To every half-dress'd player, as he still
> Through the hangings peeped to see how the house did fill.

For Caroline practice, cf. T. Goffe, *Careless Shepherdess* ind. :

> I never saw Rheade peeping through the curtain,
> But ravishing joy entered into my heart ;

also Tatham's prologue for the Fortune players, when they moved to the
Red Bull in 1640 :

> Forbear
> Your wonted custom, banding tile and pear
> Against our curtains, to allure us forth ;
> I pray, take notice, these are of more worth ;
> Pure Naples silk, not worsted.

I defer a full consideration of stage hangings to the chapters on staging ;
cf. vol. iii, p. 78.

[2] For the classical sense of *Scaena*, cf. the passage from Vitruvius
quoted in vol. iii, p. 3. Florio, *Dictionary* (1598), s.v. *Scena*, ' a skaffold,
a pavillion, or forepart of a theatre where players make them readie,
being trimmed with hangings, out of which they enter upon the stage ',
points to the identity of scene and tire-house front. This structure has
therefore precisely the double function of the ' domus ' of the court plays ;
cf. ch. xix. I owe the quotation to Graves, 15, who adds, *The Englysshe
Mancyne upon the foure Cardynale Vertues* (*c.* 1520), ' a disgyser yt goeth
into a secret corner callyd a sene of the pleyinge place to chaunge his
rayment ', and Palsgrave, *Acolastus* (1540), prol., ' our scenes, that is to
saye, our places appoynted for our players to come forth of '. The English
' Mancyne ' is a translation, earlier than A. Barclay's, of Dominic Mancini's
De Quatuor Virtutibus (1516), and the original has only ' Histrio, qui in
scaenam vadit '. The notion of *scena* as not a mere wall, but a shelter

the frame of the theatre, and would not, therefore, unless it projected on to the stage, have more depth than about 12 ft. Mr. Brereton, in a careful analysis of the drawing, suggests that the Swan tire-house may not have extended the full width of the stage, but may have left room to come and go on either side of its front.[1] If so, some projection is not improbable, but one cannot rely much upon the hazardous interpretation of bad draughtsmanship. The ground-plan of the Swan seems to show an annexe at one point, and of course additional depth could easily be obtained in this way. Moreover, there were at least three stories available. The spectators in the lord's room would not take up the whole depth on the level of the middle gallery, and there must have been a corresponding space on that of the top gallery. Henslowe ceiled ' the rome ouer the tyerhowsse ' in 1592, and an inventory of the Admiral's men in 1598 includes effects ' leaft above in the tier-house in the cheast '. No doubt a fair amount of accommodation was needed. The tire-house was not merely a dressing-room and a storehouse. Here came the author, to rail at the murdering of his lines, and the gallants to gossip and patronize the players.[2] Here were the book-holder, who prompted the speeches, surveyed the entrances and exits, and saw to the readiness of the properties ; [3] the tireman,

for performers, is mediaeval, and appears to go back to an early definition from σκῆνος, a hut or tent, found, e. g., side by side with the regular mediaeval misunderstanding of the classical art of acting in Hugutius, *Liber Derivationum*, ' Scena est umbraculum siue locus obumbratus in theatro et cortinis coopertus similis tabernaculis mercenariorum, quae sunt asseribus vel cortinis opertae, et secundum hoc scena potest dici a scenos, quod est domus, quae in modum domus erat constructa. In umbraculo latebant personae larvatae, quae ad vocem recitatoris exigebantur ad gestus faciendos ' ; cf. Herrmann, 280, W. Cloetta, *Komödie und Tragödie im Mittelalter* (1890), 38 ; *Mediaeval Stage*, ii. 208. It is revised on humanist lines by Jodocus Badius Ascensius in the *Praenotamenta* to his Terence of 1502, ' Intra igitur theatrum ab una parte opposita spectatoribus erant scenae et proscenia, id est loca lusoria ante scenas facta. Scenae autem erant quaedam umbracula seu absconsoria, in quibus abscondebantur lusores, donec exire deberent. Ante autem scenas erant quaedam tabulata, in quibus personae qui exierant ludebant.'

[1] The *Roxana* engraving shows a projecting building at the back of the stage, but this can hardly be regarded as throwing light upon sixteenth-century structure.

[2] C. *Revels* (1601), ind. 160. The author is not ' in the Tiring-house, to prompt us aloud, stampe at the Booke-holder, sweare for our Properties, cursse the poore Tire-man, rayle the Musique out of tune ' ; *Bartholomew Fair* (1614), ind. 8, ' I am looking, lest the *Poet* heare me, or his man, Master Broome, behind the Arras. . . . Hee has (sirreuerence) kick'd me three, or foure times about the Tyring-house, I thanke him, for but offering to putt in, with my experience ' ; v. iii. 57, ' I would be glad drinke with the young company ; which is the Tiring-house ? '

[3] *Every Woman in her Humour*, p. 354, ' He would . . . stamp and

who fitted the dresses and the beards, furnished stools, and in the private theatres took charge of the lights ;[1] the stage-keeper ;[2] the grooms and 'necessary attendants', waiting to draw curtains, to thrust out beds, and to carry benches and banquets on and off.[3] Here, too, was the head-quarters of the music, although in the public theatres the music was largely incidental, and was often played on, or above, or even below the stage, as might seem most appropriate to any particular action.[4] Music between the acts was not

stare (God blesse us,) like a play-house book-keeper when the actors misse their entrance '; *R. J.* I. iv. 7,

> Nor no without-book prologue, faintly spoke
> After the prompter, for our entrance.

The actor's signal for entrance was already his 'cue'; cf. *M. N. D.* III. i. 77, 'And so every one according to his cue'; *Isle of Gulls*, ii. 2, 'you know your que'; ii. 3, 'She hath entred the Dutches iust at her que'.

[1] *2 Ant. Mellida*, II. i. 30, 'The tiring man hath not glued on my beard half fast enough'. A tireman appears in the inductions to *Malcontent*, 'Enter W. Sly, a Tire-man following him with a stool', and to *What You Will*, 'Enter Tireman with lights'. 'Steven the tyerman' of the Admiral's in 1596 is probably the Steven Magett of other entries by Henslowe (i. 31, 44, 45).

[2] Speakers in the induction to *Bartholomew Fair* (1614) are the Booke-Holder and the Stage-Keeper, who 'kept the *Stage* in Master *Tarletons* time', and whose work is 'sweeping the *Stage*? or gathering vp the broken apples for the beares within?'

[3] The Fortune company, *c.* 1617 (*H. P.* 85), offer to employ a dismissed 'gatherer' as 'a nessessary atendaunt on the stage' and to mend garments. On 27 Dec. 1624 the Master of Revels (*Var.* iii. 112; Herbert, 74) issued a warrant of protection for Nicholas Underhill, Robert Pallant, John Rhodes, and eighteen others 'all imployed by the kings maiesties servantes in theire quallity of playinge as musitions and other necessary attendantes'. In *Devil's Charter* (1607), 3016, is the s. d. 'Alexander vnbraced betwixt two Cardinalls in his study looking vpon a booke, whilst a groome draweth the curtaine'. Is this 'groom' a character or an 'attendant'? In any case attendants were naturally, with musicians and even 'gatherers' (on whom cf. ch. xi), used at need for supernumeraries ; cf. the gatherers in the *Frederick and Basilea* plot (1597, *H. P.* 136) and *2 If You Know Not Me* (1606), p. 297, 'Enter . . . the waits in sergeants' gowns'. The long list of men and boys in the procession at the end of *1 Tamar Cham* (1602, *H. P.* 148) must have taxed all such resources. For the use of boys as attendants, cf. *Bartholomew Fair*, v. iii. 65, 'Ha' you none of your pretty impudent boyes, now; to bring stooles, fill Tabacco, fetch Ale, and beg money, as they haue at other houses?' Seventeenth-century gossip (*Centurie of Prayse*, 417) made Shakespeare join the stage as a 'serviture'.

[4] Lawrence, i. 75, ii. 159; Wegener, 150; G. H. Cowling, *Music on the Shakespearian Stage*, 29, 70, 80. I refer to Cowling and to E. W. Naylor, *Shakespeare and Music*, for discussions of the instruments used—drums, timbrels, bells (percussion instruments), sackbuts, trumpets, horns (brass instruments), cornets, hautboys, recorders, fifes (wood instruments), viols, lutes, citterns, pandores (string instruments)—of such terms as 'flourish', 'sennet', 'tucket', 'peal', 'alarum', 'consort', and of other technical matters with which I am not qualified to deal. The Admiral's

unknown, but we learn from the induction to the *Malcontent* that it was 'not received' by the audience at the Globe in 1604.[1] There was also, of course, the final 'jig'.[2] For an overture, the public theatres seem to have employed nothing beyond three soundings of a trumpet, the last of which was the signal for the prologue to begin.[3] Probably the musical element tended to increase. A special music-room perhaps existed already at the Swan in 1611, and, if so, may have been, as it was in the later theatres, in the upper part of the tire-house.[4]

inventories of 1598 (*H. P.* 115, 116, 118) include 'iij trumpettes and a drum, and a trebel viall, a basse viall, a bandore, a sytteren . . . j chyme of bells . . . iij tymbrells . . . j sack-bute'.

[1] *Malcontent*, ind. 89. The additions for the King's are 'to entertain a little more time, and to abridge the not-received custom of music in our theatre'. But 'abridge' only means shorten, and there are s. ds. for music between the acts of *Sejanus* (Globe, *1603*) and in the plot of *Dead Man's Fortune* (Admiral's, c. 1590, *H. P.* 133); cf. Dekker, *Belman of London* (1608, *Works*, iii. 76), 'These were appointed to be my Actes, in this goodly Theater, the musicke betweene, were the Singers of the Wood'. But such evidence is rare, and Lawrence, i. 75, and Cowling, 67, do not discriminate sufficiently the practice of the public theatres from that of the private theatres on the one hand and the early neo-classic court plays on the other. Here music is an integral part of the *intermedii* or dumb-shows, which are little more than survivals in the full-blown public drama ; cf. F. A. Foster in *E. S.* xliv. 8, and *Hamlet*, III. ii. 13, 'inexplicable dumb-shows'.   [2] Cf. p. 551.

[3] *Alphonsus*, prol., 'after you haue sounded thrise, let Venus be let downe from the top of the Stage'; Heywood, *Four Prentices*, prol., 'Do you not know that I am the prologue ? Do you not see the long black velvet coat upon my back ? Have I not all the signs of the prologue about me ? Have you not sounded thrice ? '; Dekker, *Satiromastix*, epist., 'In steed of the trumpets sounding thrice, before the play begin, it shall not be amisse . . . first to beholde this short Comedy of Errors'; *G. H. B.* (cf. App. H), 'untill the quaking prologue hath (by rubbing) got cullor into his cheekes, and is ready to give the trumpets their cue that hee 's upon point to enter'; *E. M. O.* (Q₁), 107, 'Inductio, sono secundo', 402, 'Sound the third time. Enter Prologue'. Jonson has a similar arrangement (F₁) in the private house plays *Cynthia's Revels* and *Poetaster*, but probably the trumpets were here replaced by more elaborate music ; cf. *1 Ant. Mellida*, ind. 1, 'the music will sound straight for entrance'; *What You Will*, ind. 1 (s. d.), 'Before the music sounds for the Act'; *C. Revels* (Q₁), 1435, 'Like an unperfect Prologue, at third musique'. Surely this is the origin of the 'first', 'second', and 'third' (or 'curtain tune') music of the Restoration and eighteenth-century overtures, described by Lawrence, ii. 155. Exceptionally the prologue in Percy's *C. and C. Errant* is between the second and third sounding.

[4] *Chaste Maid in Cheapside*, v. iv. 1 (s. d.), 'There is a sad song in the music-room'; cf. *Thracian Wonder*, IV. i. 182, 'Pythia speaks in the musick Room behind the Curtain', 186, 'Pythia above, behind the curtains'. But these, although early plays, are in late prints, and the other examples of a music-room 'above' given by Lawrence, i. 91, are Caroline. Jasper Mayne says of Jonson (1638, *Jonsonus Virbius*), 'Thou laid'st no sieges to the music-room'. My own impression is that when the lord's

The Fortune tire-house was to have ' convenient windowes and lightes glazed '. Some of these may have looked into the auditorium, and have been used for scenic purposes. But the maps show external windows here and there in the walls, and these would be necessary to light both the tire-house and the galleries. We have a picture of Burbadge leaning out of an upper window to greet with abuse the disturbers of his peace at the Theatre in 1590. The yard and the stage itself were, of course, lit, in the absence of a roof, from above. Performances were ordinarily by daylight; before the end of the sixteenth century the time for beginning had been fixed at 2 o'clock.[1] The stage-directions point to a frequent enough use of lamps and tapers, but always to give the illusion of scenic darkness. Plays, however, lasted at least two hours, sometimes half an hour or even an hour longer, and there was the jig to follow.[2] It must therefore be doubtful whether, in the depth of winter, daylight could have served quite to the end. Webster complains that the ill-success of *The White Devil* was due to its being given ' in so dull a time of winter, and presented in so open and black a theatre '. Perhaps the shorter plays were chosen for the shorter days, or the jig was omitted. But it is also possible that some primitive illumination, in the form of cressets, or baskets of tarred and flaring rope, was introduced.[3]

room over the tire-house was disused by spectators (cf. p. 537) it became indifferently available for actors and for music, and that here, rather than, as is possible, higher still in the scenic wall, was the normal place for the seventeenth-century music, when it was not needed elsewhere, or the space needed for other purposes. The introduction of the high pro-scenium arch at the Restoration caused difficulties, and various experi-ments were tried in placing the music above (Lawrence, i. 91, 161 ; ii. 160 ; W. G. Keith, *The Designs for the First Movable Scenery on the English Public Stage* in *Burlington Magazine*, xxv. 29, 85), before the modern situation was adopted.   [1] Cf. ch. x.

[2] *R. J.*, prol. 12, ' the two hours' traffic of our stage ' ; *Alchemist*, prol. 1, ' these two short hours ' ; *Hen. VIII*, prol. 13, ' two short hours ' ; *T. N. K.*, prol. 28, ' Sceanes . . . worth two houres travell ' ; Heywood, *Apology*, 11 (Beeston's c. v.), ' two houres well spent ' ; *Barth. Fair*, ind., ' the space of two hours and a half and somewhat more '. Perhaps plays tended to grow shorter. Fenton (1574) and Northbrooke (1577–8) give ' two or three houres ', and Whetstone (1578) three hours (cf. App. C), but Dekker (cf. p. 533, n. 3) seems to regard three hours as an exception-ally long period.

[3] Cotgrave, *French-English Dict.* (1611), s.v. Falot, ' a cresset light (such as they use in playhouses) made of ropes wreathed, pitched and put into small and open cages of iron ' ; cf. Lawrence, ii. 13, who thinks the cressets were part of the lighting of private houses. But would they not smoke and smell badly, if used indoors ? There is no particular reason for translating the *lucernae* of Christ Church hall in 1566, with Schelling and Lawrence, as ' cressets '.

The actors themselves were not wholly without protection from the elements. De Witt depicts two heavy classical columns, which stand on square bases rather farther back than the middle of the stage and a little way from each side of it. These support a pent-house roof, which starts from the level of the eaves of the ' tectum ' over the top gallery, and descends in a steep slope to a level opposite to the middle of the second gallery, where it slightly projects beyond the supporting columns. Behind and above it rises a kind of hut, conspicuous above the ' tectum ' and forming a superstructure to the tire-house. Its front has less width than that of the tire-house, and its side is shown in clumsy perspective, which is apparently followed round by the pent-house below it. The pent-house is the only thing in the drawing, that can represent the ' shadow ' or ' heavens ', which several allusions point to as a regular feature in the public theatres, and which certainly existed at the Rose, the Fortune—and therefore presumably the Globe—and the Hope.[1] But it must be admitted that this sharply sloping roof, coming down low and considerably impeding the vision of the spectators at any rate in the top gallery, does not agree very well with the notion of a heavens dominating the stage, elaborately decorated, and serving for the display of spectacular effects, which were surely meant to be visible to all. It is possible that De Witt's halting draughtsmanship has failed him in

---

[1] Nashe (iii. 329), epist. to *Astrophel and Stella* (1591), ' here you shal find a paper stage streud with pearle, an artificial heau'n to ouershadow the faire frame '; *Wagnerbook* (1594, cf. ch. xx), ' Now aboue all was there the gay Clowdes vsque quaque adorned with the heavenly firmament, and often spotted with golden teares which men callen Stars. There was liuely portrayed the whole Imperiall Army of the faire heauenly inhabitauntes '; *Birth of Hercules* (1597 <), i. 1, s. d., ' Ad comoediae magnificentiam apprime conferet ut coelum Histrionium sit luna et stellis perspicue distinctum '; Heywood, *Apology* (c. *1608*), 34, of the Roman theatre, ' the covering of the stage, which we call the heavens '; Cotgrave, *Dict.* (1611), s.v. *Volerie*, ' a place over a stage, which we call the heavens '. The same word was used for the state over a throne ; cf. Cotgrave, s.v. *Dais*, ' a cloth of estate, canopie, or Heaven, that stands over the heads of Princes thrones '. Graves, 24, gives examples of heavens used in Tudor pageants. It is to be noted that the ' heavens ' and ' hell ' (cf. p. 528) of a theatre continue characteristic features of mediaeval staging (cf. *Mediaeval Stage*, ii. 86, 137, 142) ; cf. *All Fools*, prol. 1 :

> The fortune of a stage (like Fortunes selfe)
> Amazeth greatest judgments ; and none knowes
> The hidden causes of those strange effects
> That rise from this Hell, or fall from this Heaven.

The theory of J. Corbin in *Century* (1911), 267, that the heavens was a mere *velarium* or cloud of canvas thrown out from the hut, will not fit the evidence ; cf. Lawrence, ii. 6.

the attempt to tackle the architectural perspective from a difficult angle in an upper gallery. My impression is that, by giving too much height to the bottom gallery, he has got the two other galleries out of line with the stories of the tire-house to which they correspond, and that the lower gallery should really be on the level of the stage, the middle gallery on that of the gallery ' over the stage ', and the top gallery on that of the rather obscure story above. If so, the front of this story would have been visible, and may have contained some aperture of which account has not yet been taken in formulating theories of staging.[1] And I think that the columns were really higher and the roof flatter than De Witt has drawn them. It is perhaps less easy to suggest that the columns stood farther forward than De Witt has placed them, but the roof may well have projected farther over them. They are solid enough to bear a much greater weight than the drawing indicates. However these things may have been at the Swan—I am not blind to the dangers of attempting to convert what De Witt has shown into something which he has not shown—one may, perhaps, infer that more extensive roofing than the pent-house of the drawing would afford was contemplated by the Fortune contract, which provides for ' a shadowe or cover over the saide stadge ', and the Hope contract, which is even more precise in its specification of ' the Heavens all over the saide stage '. In both cases there were to be gutters to carry away rainwater. The heavens at the Hope were ' to be borne or carryed without any postes or supporters to be fixed or sett uppon the saide stage ', and it has been thought that other theatres of later date than the Swan may also have dispensed with posts. But there is little ground for this theory, other than the obvious obstruction which the posts would offer to vision.[2] Howes seems to refer to the arrangement at the Hope as an innovation, and it can hardly be unrelated to the special need for a removable stage at that house. On the other hand the posts may very likely have been slighter than De Witt has shown them. At the Fortune they were, like other ' princypall and maine postes ', square and carved ' palasterwise ' with satyrs. The posts are worked into the action of several plays, and Kempe tells us that pickpockets were pilloried by being tied to them.[3]

---

[1] Cf. vol. iii, p. 78. Is this, or the hut, the ' garret ' of R. M.'s *A Player* (cf. p. 546) ?

[2] I do not now regard as tenable my suggestion in *The Stage of the Globe* (*Stratford Town Shakespeare*, x. 351) that De Witt represented as outstanding columns what were really mere pilasters in the tire-house wall.

[3] Kempe, *Nine Days Wonder*, 6, ' I remembred one of them to be

The hut has two windows in front, and a door in the visible side. It has been suggested that it may really have stood rather more forward than De Witt indicates, jutting out from the tire-house so as to be directly over a part of the heavens.[1] An analogous superstructure is observable in most of the map-representations of theatres. That of the later Globe in Visscher's map of 1616 seems to have two bays, one behind another, instead of the one bay of the Swan drawing, and would have required more space. The ' Theatrum' of Jonson's 1616 Folio has an L-shaped superstructure. The object of a jut forward would be to facilitate the descents and ascents from and to the heavens, which formed popular features in many plays, and which must have been contrived by some kind of machinery from above.[2] From the roof of this hut floats a flag, with the figure of a swan upon it, and at the door stands a man, apparently blowing a trumpet, from which depends a smaller flag also bearing a swan. There is abundant evidence that the play-houses flew flags when they were open for performances, and took them down when Lent or a plague rendered playing impossible.[3] The

a noted Cut-purse, such a one as we tye to a poast on our stage, for all people to wonder at, when at a play they are taken pilfring ' ; cf. *Nobody and Somebody*, 1893,

Somebody

Once pickt a pocket in this Play-house yard,
Was hoysted on the stage, and shamd about it ;
also ch. xx, p. 75 ; ch. xxi, pp. 108, 141.

[1] For criticism of the drawing of the heavens and hut, cf. Graves, 22, and Brereton in *Homage*, 204.

[2] Henslowe paid in 1595 for ' mackinge the throne in the heuenes ' at the Rose ; cf. R. M., *Micrologia* (1629), in Morley, *Character Writings*, 285, *A Player*, ' If his action prefigure passion, he raves, rages, and protests much by his painted heavens, and seems in the height of this fit ready to pull Jove out of the garret where perchance he lies leaning on his elbows, or is employed to make squibs and crackers to grace the play '. Wegener, 133, gives examples of the use of machines ; for the throne, cf. vol. iii, p. 77.

[3] Field (1583, App. C, No. xxxi), ' Those flagges of defiance against God ' ; Vennar's apology (1614) for *England's Joy* (1602, cf. ch. xxiii). ' The report of gentlemen and gentlewomens actions, being indeed the flagge to our theatre, was not meerely falcification ' ; *A Mad World, my Masters* (1604–6), i. i. 38, iii. iii. 143, ' 'Tis Lent in your cheeks ; the flag's down ' . . . ' The hair about the hat is as good as a flag upo' th' pole, at a common playhouse, to waft company ' ; Dekker, *Raven's Almanac* (1609, *Works*, iv. 210), ' Another ciuill warre doe I finde will fal betweene players. . . . For it is thought that Flag will be aduanced (as it were in mortall defiance against Flag)' ; *Work for Armourers* (1609, *Works*, iv. 96), ' Play-houses stand . . . the dores locked vp, the flagges . . . taken down ' ; *Curtain-Drawer of the World* (1612), ' Each playhouse advanceth his flag in the aire, whither quickly at the waving thereof are summoned whole troops of men, women, and children '. The maps regularly show flags

trumpeter is no doubt giving one of the three ' soundings ' which preluded the appearance of the prologue in his traditional long black velvet cloak.[1] Nor did the flag and the trumpet exhaust the resources of the Elizabethan art of advertisement. The *vexillatores* of the miracle-play would perhaps have been out of keeping with London conditions.[2] But it was customary to announce after the epilogue of each performance what the next was to be.[3] And public notification was given by means of play-bills, of which we hear from as early a date as 1564, and which were set up on posts in conspicuous places up and down the city and probably also at the play-house doors.[4] Copies seem also to have been

on the theatres. The Globe fire in 1613 ' did not spare the silken flagg ' (cf. p. 421). Heywood, *Apology*, 22, mistranslates Ovid's ' Tunc neque marmoreo pendebant vela theatro ' as :
> In those days from the marble house did waive
> No sail, no silken flag, no ensign brave.

[1] Cf. p. 542 ; *Cynthia's Revels*, ind., where the boys struggle for the cloak ; *Woman Hater*, prol. 1, ' Gentlemen, Inductions are out of date, and a Prologue in Verse, is as stale as a black Velvet Cloak, and a Bay Garland ' ; *Birth of Hercules* (1597 <), prol. 5, ' Thepilogue is in fashion ; prologues no more ' ; and much later, *Coronation*, prol. 4,
> he
> That with a little Beard, a long black Cloak,
> With a starch'd face, and supple leg hath spoke
> Before the plays the twelvemonth.

The prologue appears to be a composite figure, partly representing the poet, and deriving also in part from the presenter of dumb-shows, in part from the Chorus of neo-classic tragedy, and in part from the ' exposytour in doctorys wede ', developed by miracle-plays and moralities out of the Augustine of the *Prophetae* ; cf. *Mediaeval Stage*, ii. 52, 72, 153, 417, 423, 426, 429, 448 ; F. A. Foster in *E. S.* xliv. 13 ; F. Lüders, *Prolog und Epilog bei Shakespeare* (*Sh.-Jahrbuch*, v. 274) ; Creizenach, 275. The short dramatic inductions, often introducing actors *in propria persona*, favoured by Jonson, Marston, and others about the beginning of the seventeenth century, attempt to give new life to a waning convention.

[2] Cf. *Mediaeval Stage*, ii. 141, 156. Drums and trumpets were used as advertisements in the city at any rate until 1587 (App. C, Nos. xvii, xxxi, xxxviii), and were traditional in the provinces up to the middle of the eighteenth century (Lawrence, ii. 58). Parolles tells us (*All's Well*, iv. iii. 298) that Captain Dumain ' has led the drum before the English tragedians '. Henslowe (i. 118) bought a drum and two trumpets for the Admiral's ' when to go into the contry ' in Feb. 1600. In *Histriomastix*, ii. 80, ' One of them steppes on the Crosse, and cryes, A Play '.

[3] H. Moseley, pref. verses to F_1 of Beaumont and Fletcher (1647) :
> As after th' Epilogue there comes some one
> To tell spectators what shall next be shown ;
> So here am I.

This is, of course, only Caroline evidence ; for the continuance of the practice after the Restoration, cf. Lawrence, ii. 187.

[4] *Grindal to Cecil* (1564, App. D, No. xv), ' these Histriones, common playours who now daylye, butt speciallye on holydayes, sett vp bylles ' ;

available for circulation from hand to hand.[1] On 30 October
1587 John Charlwood entered in the Stationers' Register
a licence for ' the onely ympryntinge of all manner of billes
for players '. This passed from him to James Roberts, and
was transferred by Roberts to William Jaggard on 29 October
1615.[2] No theatrical bill of the Elizabethan or Jacobean
period is preserved, although a manuscript bill for the Bear
Garden is amongst Alleyn's papers at Dulwich.[3] Four late
seventeenth-century bills are at Claydon; they are brief
announcements, which give the names of the plays, but not
those of the authors or actors.[4] There is no evidence of anything corresponding to the modern programme, with its
cast and synopsis of scenes.[5] The audience gathered early,
as there were few, if any, reserved seats.[6] The period of
waiting was spent in consuming fruit or sweetmeats and liquid
refreshment, and in expressing impatience if the actors
failed to make an appearance in good time.[7] Tobacco was

Merry Tales, &c. (1567; cf. ch. xxiii, s.v. Vennar), ' billes . . . vpon
postes about London '; Northbrooke (1577, App. C, No. xvi), ' they use
to set vp their billes vpon postes certain dayes before'; Gosson, *S.A.* (1579,
App. C, No. xxii), 44, ' If players can . . . proclame it in their billes, and
make it good in theaters '; Rankins (1587, App. C, No. xxxviii), ' sticking
of their bills in London '; Marston, *Scourge of Villainy* (Bullen, iii. 302),
' Go read each post, view what is play'd to-day '; *Histriomastix,* v. 69,
' Text-bills must now be turned to iron bills '; *Warning for Fair Women,*
(> *1599*) :
> 'Tis you have kept the Theatres so long,
> Painted in play-bills upon every post,
> That I am scorned of the multitude.
Wither, *Abuses Stript and Whipt* (1613), ii. 2 :
> But, by the way, a Bill he doth espy,
> Which showes theres acted some new Comedy.
In *Bartholomew Fair,* v. iii. 6, Cokes ' reads the Bill ' of the motion;
cf. Lawrence (ii. 55), *The Origin of the Theatre Programme.*
  [1] *Devil an Ass,* I. iv. 43, ' Hee giues him the Play-bill '.
  [2] Arber, ii. 477; iii. 575.   [3] *Henslowe Papers,* 106.
  [4] Lawrence, ii. 240.
  [5] Jonson, in printing plays, and following him the editors of the Beaumont and Fletcher F₁ often give the scene and the actors' names, and
casts appear in *Duchess of Malfi* (1623). But these are not necessarily
taken from any documents put before the audiences.
  [6] Lawrence, ii. 154; cf. the stipulation in Burbadge's lease (p. 387),
and W. Fennor, *Compter's Commonwealth* (1617), 8, ' he that first comes
in is first seated, like those that come to see playes '.
  [7] Cf. p. 540 (Tatham), and the notices of Hentzner and Platter (ch. xvi,
introd.). In *K. B. P.* the wife comes with her pockets full of sweetmeats,
which she bestows upon the actors, liquorice (i. 77), green ginger (ii. 279),
sugar-candy (ii. 366), and her husband brings beer (iii. 631). The liquorice
would open Ralph's pipes ; cf. ch. xii (Westminster) and *C. Revels,*
ind. 215, ' I would thou hadst some sugar candyed, to sweeten thy mouth ' ;

freely used, especially by the gallants on the stage.[1] Books
were also hawked up and down, and a game of cards might
beguile the tedium of waiting.[2] The galleries were full of
light women, who found them a profitable haunt, but whose
presence did not altogether prevent that of ladies of position,
probably in the private rooms, and possibly masked.[3]

If the audience liked a play, the actors expected a *Plaudite*
of hand-clapping; if otherwise, they took their chance of
hissing and ' mewing ', or of a pointed withdrawal of spectators from the stage.[4] The device of a *claque* was not

Overbury, *Characters* (ed. Rimbault, 113, *A Puny-Clarke*), ' Hee eats
ginger-bread at a play-house '.

[1] Cf. pp. 534, 536 and Hentzner (ch. xvi, introd.) ; *C. Revels*, ind. 122,
' I haue my three sorts of Tabacco, in my Pocket, my light by me ' ;
K. B. P. i. 224, ' Fie, this stinking Tobacco kils men, would there were
none in *England*, now I pray Gentlemen, what good does this stinking
Tobacco ? do you nothing, I warrant you make chimnies a your faces ' ;
Dekker, *G. H. B.*, ' By sitting on the stage, you may . . . get your match
lighted ' ; *Scornful Lady*, I. ii. 52, ' They wear swords to reach fire at
a play ' ; *Sir Giles Goosecap*, IV. ii. 87 (street-scene), ' By this fire, they
do, my lord '. Burn, 84, cites a note by Sir J. Caesar in *Lansd. MS.* 160,
p. 302, of a speech by James in a Star Chamber case of 1613, in which
he advised gentlemen of the Temple not to frequent plays, whence the
smoke of tobacco and the presence of painted ladies should deter them.

[2] W. Fennor, *Descriptions* (1616), ' I suppose this Pamphlet will hap
into your hands before a Play begin, with the importunate clamour of
" Buy a new Booke ! " by some needy companion that will be glad to
furnish you with worke for a turned teaster '. Dekker, *G. H. B.* (cf.
App. H), recommends cards.

[3] *V. P.* xiv. 593, 599, records a charge against the ambassador Foscarini
(1611–15) of pursuing a woman, and ' sometimes attending the public
comedies and standing among the people on the chance of seeing her '.
Foscarini said he only went three or four times to the play and that the
archduke's ambassador and his wife did the same. It was given in
evidence that the ambassador Giustiniani (Dec. 1605–Oct. 1608) went
with the French ambassador and his wife to see *Pericles* at a cost of
20 crowns. This must have been at the Globe. For the presence of
harlots, cf. pp. 534, 535 ; vol. i, p. 255.

[4] Dekker, *G. H. B.* (1609, *Works*, ii. 201), ' you can neither shake our
Comick Theater with your stinking breath of hisses, nor raise it with the
thunder-claps of your hands ' (cf. also App. H) ; *Isle of Gulls*, ind., ' Tis
growne into a custome at playes if anyone rise (especially of any fashionable
sort) about what serious busines soeuer, the rest thinking it in dislike of
the play, tho he neuer thinks it, cry " Mew ! by Jesus, vilde ! " and leaue
the poore hartlesse children to speake their Epilogue to the emptie seates '.
Later a Gent. says, ' See it be baudy, or by the light I and all my friends
will hisse ', and the Prologue replies, ' You shoulde not deale gentlemanlike
with us els ' ; E. Guilpin, *Skialetheia* (1598), prol. to Sat., ' It is the grand
hisse to a filthy play ' ; *Roaring Girl*, prol., ' If that he finds not here,
he mews at it ' ; *T. and C.*, epil. :

> my fear is this,
> Some galled goose of Winchester would hiss ;

Downfall of Robin Hood, ad fin. :

> if I fail in this,
> Then let my pains be bailled with a hiss ;

unknown.[1] The applause was often invited in the closing
speech or in a formal epilogue, on the same lines as the prologue, which it seems to have replaced in favour about the end
of the sixteenth century.[2] This might also lead up to or perhaps represent the prayer for the sovereign, of which there
are traces up to a late date, and which was analogous to the
modern use of ' God Save the King '.[3] The accompanying
prayer for the ' lord ' of the players, on the other hand,
cannot be shown to have been adopted into the public
theatres.[4] Finally, the epilogue might indicate a coming
dance.[5] Of this a little more needs to be said. The players
have amongst other elements in their ancestry the mediaeval
mimes, and they inherit the familiar mimic tradition of
multifarious entertainment. The ' legitimate ' drama was
not as yet on its pedestal. The companies of the 'eighties
and even the early 'nineties were composed of men ready at
need to eke out their plays by musical performances and
even the ' activities ' of acrobats. This is perhaps most
obvious in the continental companies, which had to face the
obstacles to a complete intelligence between stage and
audience introduced at the tower of Babel. Such a cosmo-
politan mingling of drama and ' activities ' as we may
suppose *The Labours of Hercules* to have been was a valuable
resource.[6] But at home also we find Strange's and the
Admiral's men showing their ' activities ' at court. and Symons

---

Devil an Ass, III. v. 41 :
          If I could but see a piece . . .
          Come but to one act, and I did not care—
          But to be seene to rise, and goe away,
          To vex the Players, and to punish their *Poet*—
          Keepe him in awe !

[1] *Isle of Gulls*, ind., ' a prepared company of gallants to aplaud his
iests and grace out his play ' ; *Histriomastix*, ii. 137, ' *Belch*. ' What 's an
Ingle ? *Posthaste*. One whose hands are hard as battle doors with clapping
at baldness '. For the special use of ' ingle ' (= ' intimate ') in the sense
of a patron of players, cf. *Poetaster*, I. ii. 18, ' What ! shall I have my
sonne a stager now ? an enghle for players ? a gull ? a rooke ? a shot-
clogge ? to make suppers, and bee laught at ? '

[2] Cf. p. 547, n. 1.

[3] *K. to K. a Knave* (1594), *ad fin.* ; *Looking-Glass*, 2282 ; *Locrine*, 2276 ;
2 Hen. IV, epil. 35, ' And so kneele down before you ; but indeed, to
pray for the Queene ' ; *Two Wise Men and All the Rest Fools* (1619),
epil., ' It resteth that we render you very humble and hearty thanks, and
that all our hearts pray for the king and his family's enduring happiness,
and our country's perpetual welfare. *Si placet, plaudite* ' ; cf. ch. xxii.

[4] Cf. ch. x.

[5] *M. N. D.* v. i. 360, ' Will it please you to see the epilogue, or to hear
a Bergomask dance between two of our company ? ' ; *Much Ado*, v. i. 130,
' Strike vp, pipers. *Dance* ' ; *A. Y. L.* v. iv. 182.

[6] Cf. ch. xiii (Leicester's).

the acrobat becoming a leader amongst the Queen's, and even so late as 1601 Henslowe fitting out the Admiral's boy Nick to tumble in the presence of royalty.   The country tours of the Queen's were for some time accompanied by a Turkish rope dancer.[1]   In the theatres themselves Italian players made their success and their scandal, with the help of tumbling women.[2]   Whether English players did the same we do not know.   But we do know that the dance by way of afterpiece was a regular and enduring custom.[3]   It was known as the jig.[4]   At first, perhaps, nothing more than such dancing, with the help of a variety of foreign costumes, as was also an element in the early masks, it developed into a farcical dialogue, with a musical and Terpsichorean accompaniment,

[1] Murray, ii. 206, 293, 304, 367, ' upon the Q. players at the dancing on the rop' (1590, Bridgnorth), ' vnto the Torkey Tumblers ' (1589–90, Ipswich), ' to certen playars, playinge uppon ropes at the Crosse Keyes ' (1590, Leicester), ' to the Quenes men when the Turke wente vpon roppes at Newhall ' (22 April 1590, Norwich) ; *Coventry Corp. MS.* A 7 (b), ' the Queens players & the turk' (1589–90, Coventry) ; cf. Nashe, *Epistle to Strange Newes* (1592, *Works*, i. 262), ' Say I am as verie a Turke as hee that three yeeres ago ranne vpon ropes '.   A Gloucester payment of 1594–5 for ' a wagon in the pageant for the Turke ' (Murray, ii. 285) may or may not refer to the acrobat of 1590.

[2] Cf. ch. xiv.

[3] Both Hentzner (1598) and Platter (1599) describe it ; cf. ch. xvi, introd.   Platter saw it at both the Globe and the Curtain, where it was ' Englisch unndt Irlendisch '.   Von Wedel also describes something very much like a well-developed jig after a baiting on the Bankside in 1584 (cf. ch. xvi, Hope).

[4] Gosson, *P. C.* (1582 ; cf. App. C, No. xxx), ' daunsing of gigges ' ; *Much Ado*, II. i. 78, ' Wooing . . . is hot and hasty, like a Scotch jig, and full as fantastical ' ; *Hamlet*, III. ii. 132, ' O God, your only jig-maker ' ; *E. M. O.* (Q₁), 1147, ' a thing studied, and rehearst as ordinarily at his comming from hawking, or hunting, as a Iigge after a play ' ; *Jack Drum*, i. 404, ' as the Iigge is cal'd for when the play is done ' ; R. Knolles, *Six Bookes of a Commonweal* (1606), 645, ' Now adayes they put at the end of euerie Tragedie (as poyson into meat) a comedie or jigge ' (translating Bodin's ' obscoena quadam fabula turpissimis ac sordidissimis narrationibus condita ') ; Cotgrave (1611), ' Farce . . . also, the Iyg at the end of an Enterlude, wherein some pretie knauerie is acted ' ; Dekker, *A Strange Horse Race* (1613, *Works*, iii. 340), ' As I haue often seene, after the finishing of some worthy Tragedy, or Catastrophe in the open Theaters, that the sceane after the Epilogue hath been more blacke (about a nasty bawdy jigge) then the most horrid sceane in the play was : The stinkards speaking all things, yet no man understanding any thing ' ; cf. the late Shirley allusion on p. 528.   The term is sometimes more loosely used. In *James IV*, 82, 88, 620, 636, 661, 666, 673, 1116, the speakers of the Induction call the main action a jig ; cf. *1 Tamburlaine*, prol. 1, ' iygging vaines of riming mother wits '.   Swaen (*Sh.-Jahrbuch*, xlvi. 122) points out that a tune known as *The Cobler's Jig* would fit the dialogue song by cobblers in *Locrine*, 569.   Naylor, 124, gives some account of jig tunes and derives the term from *giga*, an instrument of the fiddle type.

for which popular tunes, such as *Fading*, were utilized.[1]
This transformation was perhaps due to the initiative of
Tarlton, to whom several jigs are attributed.[2] But he was
followed by Kempe and others, and in the last decade of the
sixteenth century the jig may be inferred from the Stationers'
Register to have become almost a literary type.[3] Nashe
in 1596 threatens Gabriel Harvey with an interlude, and
' a Jigge at the latter end in English Hexameters of *O neighbour
Gabriell, and his wooing of Kate Cotton* '.[4] In 1597 Henslowe
bought two jigs from two young men for the Admiral's at
a cost of 6*s.* 8*d.*[5] In 1598 ' Kemps Jigge ' was being sung in
the streets.[6] The Middlesex justices made a special order
against the lewd jigs, songs, and dances at the Fortune in
1612.[7] Unfortunately few jigs have survived except from
a late date or in German adaptations.[8] Two or three, however,
appear amongst collections of ballads to which they are cognate

---

[1] Cf. the quotation from *K. B. P.* on p. 557, and ch. v.

[2] Tarlton and Kempe (cf. ch. xv) are spoken of as acting in ' merriments '. I doubt whether anything more technical is meant than a farcical episode in a play, perhaps helped out with such ' gags ' as *Hamlet*, III. ii. 42, deprecates.

[3] Arber, ii. 297, 298, 571, 600, 601, 669, 670, 671 ; iii. 49, 50, ' a newe Northerne Jigge ' (5 Jan. 1591), ' the seconde parte of the gigge betwene Rowland and the Sexton ' (16 Dec. 1591), ' the thirde and last parte of Kempes Jigge ' (28 Dec. 1591), ' a merrie newe Jigge betwene Jenkin the Collier and Nansie ' (14 Jan. 1592), ' a plesant newe Jigge of the broomeman ', ascribed in the margin to Kempe (16 Jan. 1595), ' a pleasant Jigge betwene a tincker and a Clowne ' (4 Feb. 1595), ' a ballad of Cuttinge George and his hostis beinge a Jigge ' (17 Feb. 1595), ' Master Kempes Newe Jigge of the kitchen stuffe woman ' (2 May 1595), ' Phillips his gigg of the slyppers ' (26 May 1595), ' a pretie newe Jigge betwene Ffrancis the gentleman Richard the farmer and theire wyves ' (14 Oct. 1595), and ' Kemps newe Jygge betwixt a Souldiour and a Miser and Sym the clown ' (21 Oct. 1595) ; cf. ch. xv (Tarlton). Creizenach, 312, cites a list of jig titles by Hoenig in *Anzeiger für deutsches Altertum*, xxii. 304.

[4] *Have With You to Saffron Walden* (*Works*, iii. 114).

[5] Henslowe, i. 70, 82.

[6] E. Guilpin, *Skialetheia*, Sat. v.

[7] App. D, No. cl ; cf. the quotation from Dekker, *supra* ; *Hamlet*, II. ii. 522, of Polonius, ' He 's for a jig or a tale of bawdry, or he sleeps ' ; Wither, *Abuses Stript and Whipt* (1613), ii. 3, ' a Curtaine Iigge, a Libell, or a Ballet '. Possibly the Middlesex order has a bearing on the curious variant in the Epistle to Jonson's *Alchemist* (1612), where some copies lament ' the concupiscence of jigges and daunces ', others of ' daunces and antikes '.

[8] *The Black Man* is in Kirkman's *The Wits* (1672), and *Singing Simpkin* is ascribed in undated texts to the Caroline Robert Cox, but a tune of this name was known in Basle in 1592, and a German jig of 1620 seems to be a translation ; cf. Herz, 132 ; F. Bolte, *Die Singspiele der englischen Komödianten und ihrer Nachfolger* (1893, *Theatergeschichtliche Forschungen*, vii) ; W. J. Lawrence (*T. L. S.* 3 July 1919).

in metrical form, notably one ascribed to ' Mr Attowel ', whom we should, I think, identify with the sixteenth-century George, rather than the seventeenth-century Hugh, of that name.[1] Another, *Rowland's Godson*, seems to be the surviving member of a well-known cycle.[2]

Nor was the jig the only form of afterpiece which had its savour in an Elizabethan play-house. Tarlton again, and after Tarlton Wilson, won reputation in the handling of ' themes ', which appear to have been improvisations in verse, strung together on some motive supplied by a member of the audience.[3] It has been suggested that complete plays were also sometimes given by the method of improvised dialogue on a concerted plot which was followed in the Italian *commedie dell' arte*.[4] This must remain very doubtful. The Italian practice and the stock characters, pantaloon, zany, and harlequin, of the *commedie dell' arte* were certainly known in England ; but we have the clear evidence of *The Case is Altered* that by 1597 at any rate they had not been naturalized.[5] If improvisation

---

[1] A. Clark, *Shirburn Ballads*, 244 (cf. S. R. list, *supra*, s. a. 1595), ' Mr Attowel's Jigge : betweene Francis, a Gentleman ; Richard, a farmer ; and their wives '. It is in four scenes, sung respectively to the tunes of ' Walsingham ', ' The Jewishe Dance ', ' Buggle-boe ', and ' Goe from my windo '. In *Roxburghe Ballads*, i. 201 ; ii. 101, are ' Clod's Carroll, a proper new jigg ', and ' A mery new Jigge '. Collier's ' Jigge of a Horse Loade of Fooles ' (*New Facts*, 18 ; cf. Halliwell, *Tarlton*, xx) is probably a fake.

[2] Clark, 354, from *Bodl. Rawlinson Poet. MS.* 185 (*c.* 1590), ' A proper new ballett, intituled Rowland's god-sonne '. It is to the tune of ' Loth to departe '. Nashe, *Summer's Last Will and Testament*, 76, mentions this jig. Two parts of a ' Rowlandes godson moralised ' were entered in S. R. on 18 and 29 April 1592. Rowland is not a character, and numerous German allusions to and adaptations of a jig beginning ' Oh neighbour Rowland ' (Herz, 134) have probably some other original. A ' Roland and the Sexton ' is in the S. R. list, *supra*. A verse dialogue in *Alleyn Papers*, 8, mentions ' bonny Rowland ' and is probably a jig of his cycle ; another (p. 29) does not read to me like a jig.

[3] Cf. ch. xv (Tarlton, Wilson) and Nashe, *Pierce Penilesse* (*Works*, i. 244), ' the queint Comaedians of our time, That when their Play is doone, do fal to ryme '. Armin's (q.v.) *Quips Upon Questions* (1600) are probably themes, or based upon the conception of themes. A theme is introduced in *Histriomastix*, ii. 293. The Lord sets it :
> Your poetts and your pottes
> Are knit in true-love knots,
and a sixteen-line ' song extempore ' by Posthaste follows. The verses on ' theames ' in Gascoigne's *Posies* (ed. Cunliffe, 62) are not, I think, improvisations.

[4] Smith, *Commedia dell' Arte*, 175 ; cf. M. J. Wolff, *Shakespeare und die Commedia dell' arte* (*Sh.-Jahrbuch*, xlvi. 1).

[5] *C. is A.* II. vii. 36, of the players in Utopia (England), ' *Sebastian.* And how are their plaies ? as ours are ? extemporall ? *Valentine.* O no ! all premeditated things '. The references of Whetstone, *Heptameron* (1582), *Sp. Tragedy*, IV. i. 163, Middleton, *Spanish Gypsy*, IV. ii. 38, are specifically

went beyond the gagging of a clown, it was probably only
in some exceptional experiment or *tour de force*.[1] As exceptional also we may regard Vennar's spectacular *Englands
Joy* of 1602 and the wager plays, in which actors or even
amateurs challenged each other to compete in rendering
some ' part ' of traditional repute.[2] One would like to know
more about the play, apparently a monologue, ' set out al
by one virgin ', at the Theatre in 1583.[3]

Many of the characteristics of the public theatres naturally
repeated themselves at the Blackfriars, the Whitefriars, and
Paul's. The distinctive features of these, as already indicated,
arose from the structure of the buildings, from the higher
prices charged, and in the beginning at least from the employment of singing boys as actors. Some assimilation of ' public '
and ' private ' methods was bound to follow upon the
acquisition of the Blackfriars by men actors in 1609, but
the period during which this was the principal house of
the King's company lies outside the scope of this survey.

The exact location of Paul's is obscure, but we know that
its auditorium was round and its stage small.[4] Whitefriars
and both the earlier and the later Blackfriars were in rooms
which had formed part of mediaeval conventual buildings,
rectangular, roofed, and more analogous to courtly halls
than to popular rings. No room at Farrant's disposal would
have given him a stage of a greater width than 27 ft. Burbadge's theatre was 66 ft. from north to south, and 46 ft.
from east to west. It was on the second story of his purchase that he could have best constructed it. The stage,
which stood on a paved floor, was probably towards the
south end, and as the whole space available was something

to French and Italian practice, and so too, presumably, *A. C.* v. ii. 216,
' The quick comedians Extemporally will stage us '. The interpretation
of *Hamlet*, II. ii. 420, ' For the law of writ and the liberty, these are the
only men ', is open, but Falstaff says in *1 Hen. IV*, II. iv. 309, ' Shall we
have a play extempore ? '

    [1] *Hamlet*, III. ii. 42 ; cf. *John a Kent and John a Cumber*, iii, *ad fin.*,
' One of us Johns must play beside the book '.

    [2] In *K. B. P.*, ind. 94, where Ralph ' should have playd Jeronimo with
a Shooemaker for a wager ' ; *Ratseis Ghost* (1605, Halliwell-Phillipps, i. 326),
' I durst venture all the mony in my purse on thy head to play Hamlet
with him for a wager ' ; Dekker, *Jests to Make You Merrie* (1607, *Works*,
ii. 282), ' A paire of players, growing into an emulous contention of one
anothers worth, refusde to put themselves to a day of hearing (as any
Players would haue done) but stood onely vpon their good parts ' ; cf.
ch. xvi (Fortune), ch. xv (Alleyn).

    [3] Cf. ch. xi, p. 371.

    [4] *2 Ant. Mellida*, prol., ' within this round . . . this ring ' ; cf. p. 536.
Fawn (1604–6), prol., has ' this fair-filled room ', but the play was transferred to Paul's from Blackfriars.

like 100 ft. long by 52 wide, we may guess that partitions had been put up to screen off a tiring-house behind it and a passage by which the tiring-house could be reached.[1] The entrance would be at the north end, where a great flight of stairs led up from a yard large enough for coaches to turn in. There were galleries, but not necessarily three distinct tiers of galleries, as in the public theatres, for which, indeed, there would hardly have been height enough.[2] And there was a ' middle region ' in which the spectators sat, instead of standing as they did in the public ' yards '.[3] This, which was a feature also of the later private houses, came to be known as the ' pit ', but as the derivation of this term is from ' cockpit ', it may not be of earlier origin than the building of the Cockpit or Phoenix theatre in Drury Lane about 1617.[4] A roofed theatre would not require a specially constructed ' heavens ', as descents could be worked through the ceiling from a room above. There is no clear evidence for a lord's room at any of the private houses.[5] But there were ' boxes ', at any rate at the Whitefriars.[6] Evidence for seats on the stage has already been furnished. There is much to suggest that the audience was a more select one than that of the public theatres.[7] Elizabeth cannot be shown

---

[1] For the existence of tiring-houses in private theatres, cf. inductions to *Jack Drum's Entertainment* (Paul's) and *C. Revels* (Blackfriars).

[2] Cf. ch. xvii.

[3] *Dutch Courtesan* (c. *1603*, Blackfriars), v. iii. 162, ' my very fine Heliconian gallants, and you my worshipful friends in the middle region '.

[4] Cf. Wright (App. I). For the origin of the term, cf. the c. v. of L. Digges to Shakespeare's *Poems* (1640) :

> Let but Beatrice
> And Benedicke be seene, loe in a trice
> The cock-pit, galleries, boxes, are all full,
> To hear Malvoglio that crosse-garterd gull.

[5] Dekker, *G. H. B.* (cf. App. H), with its mingling of ' public ' and ' private ' features, cannot be relied on. The *Roxana* and *Wits* engravings show spectators ' over the stage ', but cannot be treated as evidence for the private houses. The *Messallina* engraving only shows a window closed by curtains.   [6] Cf. p. 556, *infra*.

[7] *1 Ant. Mellida* (Paul's), prol., ' select and most respected auditors ' ; *What You Will* (Paul's), ind., ' the female presence, the genteletza, the women ' ; *Jack Drum's Entertainment* (Paul's), ind., ' this choise selected influence '. But it was still mixed enough ; cf. Jonson's c. v. to *Faithful Shepherdess* (Revels, c. 1608–9) :

> The wise and many-headed bench that sits
> Upon the life and death of plays and wits—
> Composed of gamester, captain, knight, knight's man,
> Lady or pusill that wears mask or fan,
> Velvet or taffata cap, rank'd in the dark
> With the shop's foreman, or some such brave spark,
> That may judge for his sixpence.

to have ever attended the Blackfriars, but Anne certainly did.[1] And the price of the seats, which ranged from 6*d.* to 2*s.* 6*d.*, was of itself sufficient to keep out persons of the ' groundling ' or ' stinkard ' type.[2] Performances did not necessarily take place every day, and they could begin rather later and go on rather longer than those out of doors, since they were not dependent on daylight.[3] Windows were certainly used, for we hear of them being clapped down to give the illusion of night scenes.[4] But candles and torches supplied an artificial lighting.[5] As both the Paul's boys and those of

[1] Cf. chh. i, x, and *M. L. R.* ii. 12.

[2] Jonson, *supra*; *Mich. Term* (*c.* 1606, Paul's), ' sixpenny fees all the year long '; Otho of Hesse-Cassel (1611, Whitefriars), ' hier kostet der eingang einen halben schilling nur, da an andern orten wohl eine halbe kron '; *Scornful Lady* (1613–16, ? Whitefriars), iv. i. 238, ' I . . . can see a play For eighteen-pence again : I can, my lady '; *Wit Without Money* (? 1614, Whitefriars), i. 1, ' And who extoled you in the half-crown boxes, where you might sit and muster all the beauties '. So later, Jonson, *Magnetic Lady* (*1632*, Blackfriars), ind., ' the faeces or grounds of your people, that sit in the oblique caves and wedges of your house, your sinful sixpenny mechanicks '. I am rather puzzled by Percy, *C. and C. Errant*, ' Poules steeple stands in the place it did before ; and twopence is the price for the going into a newe play there '. Even in 1589 (cf. p. 532) the price at Paul's was 4*d.* according to a Marprelate tract, and William Darrell in that year paid 6*d.* (Hall, *Society in Elizabethan Age*, 211).

[3] In *Isle of Gulls* (1606, Blackfriars), ind., a Gent. can only see an act or two out, for ' I lay in bed till past three a clock, slept out my dinner and my stomache will toule to supper afore fiue '. Otho of Hesse-Cassel (1611) says that the Whitefriars plays were at three, and from Michaelmas to Easter only. Percy, on the other hand (cf. ch. xii), says that the Paul's boys were not allowed to begin before four, after prayers, and the gates of Paul's shut at six. So, too, *Ram Alley* (King's Revels), epil., ' Thus two hours have brought to end '. Gerschow in 1602 (cf. ch. xii) says that the Chapel acted once a week ; cf. *Eastward Hoe* (1605, Blackfriars), epil., ' May this attract you hither once a week '.

[4] Dekker, *Seven Deadly Sins* (1606, *Works*, ii. 41), ' All the Citty lookt like a priuate Play-house, when the windowes are clapt downe, as if some *Nocturnall*, or dismal *Tragedy* were presently to be acted '.

[5] *What You Will* (1601, Paul's), ' Enter Atticus, Doricus, and Philomuse, they sit a good while on the stage before the Candles are lighted. . . . Enter Tier-man with lights '; *Mich. Term* (1607, Paul's), ' Ours [terms] haue but sixpenny fees all the year long, yet we dispatch you in two hours without demur : your suits hang not long here after candles be lighted '; *Faithful Shepherdess* (1608–9, Blackfriars), Beaumont's c. v., ' Some like, if the wax lights be new that day '. Otho of Hesse-Cassel (1611) says that the Whitefriars plays were ' nur bei lichtern '. Later we have G. Wither, *Fair Virtue* (1622), 1781 :
those lamps which at a play
Are set up to light the day ;
Lenton, *The Young Gallants Whirligig* (1629) :
spangled, rare perfumed attires,
Which once so glister'd at the torchy Friars.
Cf. Lawrence (ii. 1), *Light and Darkness in the Elizabethan Theatre* ; also *E. S.* xlviii. 213.

the Chapel were primarily choristers, it is not surprising that music played a considerable part in the entertainment provided. Musical interludes were given between the acts, and Gerschow records a preliminary concert of an hour in length before the play began at the Blackfriars in 1602.[1] Sometimes also a boy came forward and danced between the acts.[2] At Paul's there was at the back of the stage a ' musick tree ', which apparently rose out of a ' canopie ' and bore a ' musick house ' on either side of it.[3]

---

[1] Cf. ch. xii; and for evidence of inter-act music, Lawrence, i. 81; Cowling, 68. Papers on *Early Elizabethan Stage Music* in *Musical Antiquary* (Oct. 1909, Jan. 1913) show the origin of the musical tradition in the earlier boy-companies; for its seventeenth-century development, cf. Wallace, ii. 114.

[2] *Faithful Shepherdess* (1608-9, Blackfriars), Beaumont's c. v. :
  Nor wants there those who, as the boy doth dance
  Between the acts, will censure the whole play.
In *K. B. P.* (1607, Blackfriars) a boy dances after Acts i and iii, and the citizens comment, ' I will haue him dance *Fading* ; *Fading* is a fine Iigge '. After Act ii there are fiddlers. After Act iv Ralph intervenes with a May Day speech.

[3] *2 Ant. Mellida*, v. i. 50, ' Andrugio's ghost is placed betwixt the music-houses'; *Faery Pastoral*, s. ds., ' Highest aloft and on the Top of the Musick Tree the Title The Faery Pastoral. Beneath him pind on Post of the Tree The Scene Eluida Forest Lowest of all ouer the Canopie ΝΑΠΑΙΤΒΟΔΑΙΟΝ or Faery Chappell '. . . . ' Here they shutt both into the Canopie Fane or Trophey ' ; *Cuck Queenes and Cuckolds Errants*, prol. by Tarlton, ' standing at entrance of the doore and right vnder the Beame '. I think Graves, 14, rightly explains ' Trophey ' as ' arch ', on the analogy of its use for a triumphal arch in Dekker, *Coronation Pageant* (1603). The only other use of ' canopy ' for a structural part of a theatre seems to be in *Sophonisba*, iv. 1, ' Play softly within the canopy '. . . . ' Syphax hasteneth within the canopy, as to Sophonisba's bed '. This is a Blackfriars play, but it might conceivably have been written for Paul's.